ROYAL HORTICULTURAL SOCIETY

GARDEN PLANTS AND FLOWERS
THROUGH THE YEAR

ROYAL HORTICULTURAL SOCIETY

GARDEN PLANTS AND FLOWERS
THROUGH THE YEAR

IAN SPENCE

LONDON, NEW YORK,
MUNICH, MELBOURNE, DELHI

FIRST EDITION 2003

Senior Editor	Annelise Evans
Senior Art Editor	Alison Donovan
Project Art Editor	Murdo Culver
Designers	Gillian Andrews, Vanessa Hamilton, Rachael Smith
Additional Editors	Louise Abbott, Pamela Brown, Candida Frith-Macdonald, Letitia Luff
Managing Editor	Anna Kruger
Managing Art Editor	Lee Griffiths
Media Resources	Lucy Claxton, Richard Dabb
Picture Researcher	Samantha Nunn

REVISED EDITION 2007

Senior Editor	Helen Fewster
Senior Art Editor	Joanne Doran
Editors	Joanna Chisholm, Jane Simmonds
DTP Designer	Louise Waller
Production Controller	Luca Frassinetti
Managing Editor	Anna Kruger
Managing Art Editor	Alison Donovan

DORLING KINDERSLEY (DELHI)

DTP Coordinator	Pankaj Sharma
DTP Designers	Govind Mittal, Harish Aggarwal, Pushpak Tyagi
Editors	Pankhoori Sinha, Saloni Talwar
Design Lead	Kavita Dutta

First published in Great Britain in 2003 by
Dorling Kindersley Limited, London

This revised edition published in 2007,
in association with the Royal Horticultural Society, by
Dorling Kindersley Limited
80 Strand, London WC2R 0RL

A Penguin Company

2 4 6 8 10 9 7 5 3 1

A CIP catalogue record for this book is available from
The British Library

ISBN 978 1 40531 815 0

Colour reproduction by MDP, UK
Printed and bound by Hung Hing, China

see our complete catalogue at
www.dk.com

contents

Key to symbols used in the text

♀	RHS Award of Garden Merit
↕	Height of mature plant
↔	Spread of mature plant
❄❄❄	Fully hardy: plant can withstand temperatures down to -15 °C (5°F)
❄❄	Frost-hardy: plant can withstand temperatures down to -5°C (23°F)
❄	Half-hardy: plant can withstand temperatures down to 0°C (32°F)
✾	Frost-tender: plant may be damaged by temperatures below 5°C (41°F)

introduction

Gardening has never been more popular than it is today. It has become a huge industry, supplying everything from garden ornaments and gadgets to hard landscaping materials, with a proliferation of expert advice in the media on all aspects of gardening from design to topiary.

In the midst of this, we sometimes forget that the real stars of the show are the plants. There is an astonishing diversity and a huge number of garden plants available to the gardener, from tiny alpines to large trees. Plant breeders also introduce more and more new cultivated varieties, or cultivars, each year. Some of these new plants go just as quickly out of fashion, but others go on to become firm favourites.

It can therefore seem daunting and confusing, especially to those new to gardening, to have to select from this vast array of plants and mass of information. This is where I hope this book will help.

RHS Garden Plants and *Flowers* includes a selection of plants that have proved to be reliable performers in the garden. Most are robust, hardy, and not difficult to grow. Some may need a little tender loving care to see them through harsh winters, but the results are well worth the effort. There are also a few more unusual plants.

To make your choice as easy as possible, every entry is illustrated so that you can judge the plant's appeal for yourself. The entries have been divided into several chapters, dealing with different types of plant, and within chapters, are arranged alphabetically by botanical name. This is because not all plants have a common name, and some common names are shared by more than one plant; where they exist, common names are listed too.

As well as basic information on each featured plant, there is practical advice on caring for plants as well as quick-reference lists of plants for different sites and uses in the garden. Once you start growing plants, like me, you may be hooked for life.

Happy gardening!

IAN SPENCE

A–Z of GARDEN PLANTS

In this plant catalogue, more than 2,500 plants are illustrated, and information given on many more, to enable you to create your own collection of star plants for the garden. To make it easier to choose, the catalogue is divided into chapters covering different groups of plants, from trees and shrubs to climbing plants, flowering plants, bamboos and grasses, and ferns. Within each chapter, plant entries are ordered alphabetically by their botanical names, so that you can quickly look up a particular plant. Familiar common names are included in each entry.

Trees and Shrubs

woody plants through the year

Trees and shrubs are long-lived woody plants. Trees usually have a single main stem or trunk with a head of branches growing out from it, often above a length of bare trunk. Shrubs have several branches that emerge near the base of the plant, without a central trunk. However, some trees have shrubby tendencies and naturally develop more than one stem; others, such as *Amelanchier*, can be pruned and grown as shrubs with several stems.

Trees and shrubs are an essential part of any garden. They act as a backdrop to other plants and provide structure when herbaceous perennials and annuals have died away over winter. Some are beautiful enough to grow as solitary specimens, but most are grown in borders. They are versatile plants and some can be used for hedging too – hedges benefit the garden more than fences as they attract wildlife, and many birds nest in hedges. Choose the right ones, and trees and shrubs will provide interest all year round.

SIZE AND SHAPE
Before you select trees and shrubs, consider their final shape and size. There is a wide variety, and each one will affect the style and feel of the garden. If you are planning an informal scheme then trees and shrubs with a more lax or bushy growth habit will fit in well. However, if you are after a formal design then columnar shapes, like the Italian cypress (*Cupressus*), may be more suitable.

Of course you can modify the shape of some trees and shrubs by pruning, or you could try your hand at topiary. Dense evergreens like yew (*Taxus*) and box (*Buxus*) are among the plants that adapt well to this kind of treatment, and you can let your imagination run riot, as long as what you do fits in with the overall style of the garden.

Do also be aware of the ultimate height and spread of the trees and shrubs you choose. Those with a columnar habit will cast smaller shadows than those that spread out; equally, small trees create less shade than large ones. If you only have a small plot, remember that too large a tree might throw most of the garden into shade. So, select your trees and shrubs with care: they will be in the ground for a long time, and it is not so easy to move them once they are established.

PLANTING TREES AND SHRUBS
You can plant trees and shrubs at any time of year if they have been raised in containers. Water the plants thoroughly both before and after planting. However, bare-root trees and shrubs must be planted during the dormant season, from November to March. To plant them at the right depth, align the stem's dark soil "tidemark" with the top of the planting hole.

SPRING

Camellia japonica 'Adolphe Audusson' *p.32*   *Abutilon megapotamicum p.16*

SUMMER

Callistemon pallidus p.30   *Hypericum calycinum p.74*

AUTUMN

Acer palmatum 'Sango-kaku' *p.19*   *Hypericum androsaemum p.74*

WINTER

Viburnum tinus 'Variegatum' *p.127*   *Daphne bholua* 'Jacqueline Postill' *p.48*

Salix helvetica p.114   *Abies nordmanniana* 'Golden spreader' p.15   *Daphne cneorum* p.48   *Magnolia* 'Elizabeth' p.86

Lithodora oleifolia p.84   *Argyranthemum* 'Mary Wooton' p.25   *Elaeagnus* x *ebbingei* 'Gilt Edge' p.50   *Calluna vulgaris* 'Silver Knight' p.31

Acer palmatum 'Garnet' p.18   *Viburnum opulus* 'Xanthocarpum' p.127   *Sorbus sargentiana* p.118   *Ilex aquifolium* 'J.C. van Tol' p.75

Arctostaphylos x *media* 'Woods Red' p.24   *Prunus* x *subhirtella* 'Autumnalis Rosea' p.101   *Skimmia japonica* 'Rubella' p.117   *Erica carnea* 'December Red' p.53

ABELIA

summer and autumn

THESE DECIDUOUS AND EVERGREEN shrubs are grown for their profuse clusters of white, pink, or cerise flowers and glossy, rounded foliage. The flowers are borne on slender, arching stems during summer and autumn, and in some species, such as *Abelia chinensis* and *A. schumannii*, they are scented. The size of different cultivars can vary dramatically, from 1.5m (5ft) to 5m (15ft) or more in height, and between 2m (6ft) and 4m (12ft) in width. Abelias are generally trouble-free and ideal for sunny border sites. If you have room, they make attractive planting partners for lespedezas (*see p.81*) and hydrangeas (*see pp.72–73*). In areas prone to frost, plant less hardy species against a warm, south- or west-facing wall.

Hardiness Frost-hardy ✳✳ to half-hardy ✳.

Cultivation Grow in any fertile, well-drained soil in full sun and shelter from cold, drying winds. **Prune** deciduous species in late winter or early spring, removing misplaced or crossing shoots to maintain a good shape. For evergreen species, lightly trim back after flowering any flowered shoots that would spoil the symmetry. **Take** softwood cuttings in early summer, or semi-ripe cuttings in late summer (*see p.394*).

Abelia × *grandiflora* ♀
↕ 3m (10ft) ↔ 4m (12ft), semi-evergreen, fragrant flowers in midsummer to autumn ✳✳

ABELIOPHYLLUM DISTICHUM

White forsythia · *late winter to early spring*

↕↔ 1.5m (5ft)

CLUSTERS OF FLOWERS borne on the bare wood of this deciduous shrub open from late winter to perfume the garden with a delicate scent. Matt green leaves follow, and turn purple before falling in autumn. This open, spreading shrub is related to the forsythia (*see p.58*) and just as versatile. You can grow it as a freestanding shrub in a sunny border, but train it against a sheltered, south- or west-facing wall and it will reward you by bursting into flower earlier and more profusely. It makes a fine companion for other early-flowering shrubs such as mahonias (*see p.87*), forsythias, and viburnums (*see pp.126–127*).

Hardiness Fully hardy ✳✳✳, provided that the wood was well ripened by a good summer. Early flowers may be damaged by frosts.

Cultivation Grow in fertile, well-drained soil in full sun. **Prune** after flowering; if freestanding, cut back flowered shoots to strong buds or shoots close to the base. If wall-trained, cut back all flowered shoots to within 2–4 buds of a permanent framework. **Take** semi-ripe cuttings, or layer low-growing shoots, in summer (*see pp.394–395*).

Abelia schumannii ♀
↕ 2m (6ft) ↔ 3m (10ft), deciduous, lightly scented flowers in late summer to autumn ✳✳

Abelia floribunda ♀
↕ 3m (10ft) ↔ 4m (12ft), evergreen, flowers early summer, may spread further when grown against a wall ✳

Abeliophyllum distichum
Taller if grown against a wall, white flowers sometimes tinged with pink

ABIES

Silver fir

year-round

LONG, SWEEPING BRANCHES are a typical feature of these stately, evergreen conifers. They make excellent specimen trees, and can also be used to provide shelter from wind or as a screen. The needles usually range in colour from mid-green to bluish-green, with silvery undersides. In late spring and early summer, some plants produce decorative cones; erect, purplish-blue ones on the upper branches will be female, while the pendent cones lower down are male, usually green maturing to brown or purplish-blue. For small gardens there are several small and even dwarf firs, such as *Abies balsamea* 'Nana' which grows to just 1m (3ft), ideal for a rock garden. For the largest spaces, *A. grandis* attains a majestic stature of up to 45m (150ft).

Hardiness Fully hardy ✲✲✲, but frost may damage young foliage.

Cultivation Grow in any fertile, moist but well-drained, neutral to slightly acid soil in sun, sheltered from cold winds. Most tolerate a little shade. Like most conifers, they need no pruning. Sow seed (*see pp.391–392*) in containers when ripe or in winter; expose seed to cold for three weeks before sowing. Firs are prone to infestation by adelgids, black aphid-like insects covered in a fluffy white secretion. They may cause foliage to yellow, but can usually be tolerated.

Abies veitchii (Veitch fir)
‡ 15–20m (50–70ft) ↔ 4–6m (12–20ft), fast-growing, with 5–8cm (2–3in) long female cones

Abies procera ♀ (Noble fir)
‡ 25–45m (80–150ft) ↔ 6–9m (20–28ft), silvery grey bark, bears large green or brown, 15–25cm (6–10in) long female cones

Abies lasiocarpa 'Compacta' ♀
‡ 3–5m (10–15ft) ↔ 2–3m (6–10ft), small, slow-growing type of corkbark fir, with a neat conical shape

Abies koreana (Korean fir)
‡ 10m (30ft) ↔ 6m (20ft), produces decorative female cones that are 5–8cm (2–3in) long, from a young age

Abies nordmanniana 'Golden Spreader' ♀
‡ 1m (3ft) ↔ 1.5m (5ft), slow-growing, shrubby dwarf conifer with spreading branches and greenish-brown cones

ABUTILON

Flowering maple,
Indian mallow

spring to autumn

A LONG FLOWERING SEASON, often continuously from spring until autumn, is a key attraction of these rather spindly-stemmed shrubs, most of which benefit from some support. They flower in shades of red, orange, soft violet-blue, pink, and white; some even have bicoloured blooms. There are also several that have variegated leaves. Tender and half-hardy types can be planted out with summer bedding, staked with canes if necessary; hardier species can be trained against a sunny, sheltered wall, or in warmer areas are excellent for adding height to a border.

Hardiness Frost-hardy ✳✳ to frost-tender ❀.

Cultivation Grow in any fertile, well-drained soil or loam-based compost in a container. Position in full sun; in frost-prone areas grow abutilons in pots in a sheltered site and bring the plants under frost-free cover during winter. **Prune** in late winter or early spring, cutting back flowered shoots to a permanent framework of main stems (*see p.383*), and taking out any misplaced or crossing shoots.
Sow seed (*see pp.391–392*) in heat in spring; take softwood cuttings in spring, or semi-ripe cuttings in summer (*see p.394*). If whiteflies or red spider mite infest plants under cover, biological controls may be effective (*see p.397*).

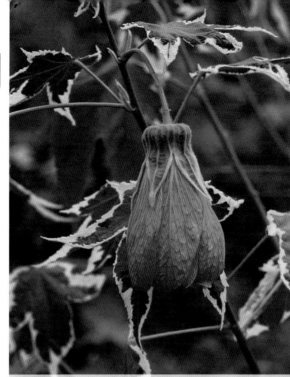

Abutilon 'Souvenir de Bonn' ♀
↕ to 3m (10ft) ↔ 2–3m (6–10ft), vigorous, erect evergreen, flowers from spring into early autumn ✳

Abutilon megapotamicum ♀ (Trailing abutilon)
↕↔ 2m (6ft), semi-evergreen or evergreen, ideal against a wall; flowers borne from summer to autumn ✳✳

Abutilon 'Boule de Neige'
↕ to 4m (12ft) ↔ to 3m (10ft), vigorous evergreen, erect to spreading habit, flowers from spring to autumn ✳

WHITEFLY ON LEAVES can be a problem, but usually only on the more tender abutilons that are grown under glass for all or part of the year.

Abutilon vitifolium 'Veronica Tennant' ♀
↕ 5m (15ft) ↔ 2.5m (8ft), fast-growing, deciduous, upright – sometimes tree-like – shrub, flowers in early summer ✳✳

Abutilon vitifolium var. *album*
‡5m (15ft) ↔ 2.5m (8ft), fast-growing, deciduous shrub, sometimes tree-like, flowering in early summer ✲✲

ACACIA
Wattle   *winter to spring*

‡to 30m (100ft)
↔to 10m (30ft)

CLUSTERS OF TINY, often sweetly fragrant, bright yellow flowers clothe these fast-growing, deciduous and evergreen trees and shrubs in winter or spring. In frost-prone climates, the hardier species that will survive outdoors need a warm, sheltered site – ideally, against a sunny wall – to flower well. Grow them with other winter-flowering evergreens, such as mahonias (*see p.87*), sarcococcas (*p.116*), and viburnums (*pp.126–127*), for an uplifting winter display.

Hardiness Half-hardy ✲ to frost-tender ❀.

Cultivation Grow in reasonably fertile, neutral to acid (lime-free) soil. Position in full sun, out of cold winds. In colder areas, grow in pots of loam-based compost and take under frost-free cover in winter. **Prune** (*see pp.382–383*) deciduous species in spring, removing any crossing or misshapen branches to maintain a good framework, and evergreens after flowering, lightly trimming shoots that spoil the shape of the tree. Cut flowered shoots on wall-trained shrubs to within two to four buds of the permanent framework in late winter or early spring. **Sow** seed (*see pp.391–393*) at 18°C (64°F) in spring after soaking in warm water until the seeds are swollen. Take semi-ripe cuttings (*see p.394*) in summer.

ACALYPHA
                                                          summer

THESE TROPICAL SHRUBS make exotic bedding plants for summer in a cool climate, where they are also often cultivated as pot plants. Some, for example *Acalypha hispida*, the chenille plant or red-hot cat's tail, are grown for their long, catkin-like clusters of usually pinky-crimson or scarlet flowers. Others, such as *A. wilkesiana*, have inconspicuous flowers but ornamental foliage, that is mottled or variegated. Given the right conditions, they can grow very quickly and make fine accent plants, although they may not reach their full height in a single season.

Hardiness Frost-tender ❀.

Cultivation Outdoors, grow in fertile, well-drained soil in full sun or partial shade. If growing them in pots, use a soilless compost and position in full light. **Keep** plants in frost-free conditions throughout the winter; they are susceptible to damage at temperatures below 10–13°C (50–55°F). **Feed** with a balanced fertilizer at monthly intervals in spring and summer, and water regularly during summer. **Lightly trim** shoots that spoil the shape of the plant. **Take** softwood cuttings in spring or semi-ripe cuttings in late summer (*see p.394*).

Abutilon pictum 'Thompsonii'
‡5m (15ft) ↔ 2–5m (6–15ft), evergreen, erect shrub or small tree, flowers from spring to autumn ✲

Acacia baileyana ❦ (Cootamundra wattle)
‡5–8m (15–25ft) ↔ 3–6m (10–20ft), small tree or large shrub, evergreen, abundant flowers from winter to spring ✲

Acalypha wilkesiana (Copperleaf)
‡to 2m (6ft) ↔ 1–2m (3–6ft), spreading shrub, green- or copper-tinted flowers often hidden by blue, pink, or coppery leaves

ACER

Maple

spring to autumn

ACERS ARE PRIZED FOR THEIR DELICATE FOLIAGE, which is particularly fine and fern-like in some cultivars of Japanese maple (*Acer palmatum*). There is enough variety in the group to provide interest at any time of the year. Some have brightly coloured leaves in spring, others have variegated grey-green, white, or pink foliage, and many give a brilliant display of intense reds, yellows, and oranges in autumn. Nearly all maples are deciduous. Several also have handsome bark, which helps to enliven the winter months; on *Acer griseum* it peels attractively, while on *A. davidii* and *A. pensylvanicum* it is striped and streaked in green and white. The inconspicuous spring flowers are followed by winged fruits. Maples include both trees and shrubs, with a type to suit most gardens. The largest trees make striking specimens if you have the space, while smaller trees and those of shrubby habit can be grown in gardens of any size. Many cultivars are excellent grown in containers; the restricted root space will keep them compact, and less hardy varieties can also be moved to a sheltered position close to the house during the coldest months.

Hardiness Most fully hardy ✱✱✱, some frost-hardy ✱✱.

Cultivation Maples prefer well-cultivated soil in sun or partial shade. **Plant** container-grown trees at any time of the year, but bare-root trees only when dormant, from late autumn to early spring. Water well before and after planting, and continue watering regularly during the first year. **Shelter** those with delicate foliage from cold winds and late frosts that can scorch the young leaves. **Stake** taller maples and those grown in exposed gardens. **Prune** young plants to form the basic framework for the tree or shrub; after this maples need minimal pruning. Remove badly placed and crossing shoots to maintain a well-balanced shape (*see p.382*), and cut out any dead or diseased wood from late autumn to midwinter, or in spring for plants in containers. **Sow** seed outside as soon as it is ripe (*see pp.391–392*) and take softwood cuttings of cultivars in early summer (*see p.394*). In some cultivars, mites may cause small growths called galls; although unsightly, these are harmless.

Looking after maples in containers

Maples grown in containers require more care than those planted in open ground, because the roots cannot grow deep down in search of water and nutrients. A thick mulch (*see p.388 and below*) will help retain moisture, but you will still need to water regularly – probably daily during dry spells. Top-dress the container annually (*see below*) in early spring to remove weeds and algal growths in the surface layer and ensure that the plant has the nutrients it requires for the growing season. Every three to five years, repot your maple, either back into the same container with fresh compost, or into a slightly larger one. Remove the plant from its pot, then gently tease out the roots and cut back any large, coarse ones. Put the tree in the new container, then fill in with fresh compost so the root ball sits at the same level as before. Water in well and mulch.

❶ Using a trowel or a small hand fork, scrape away the top 5cm (2in) of old compost and mulch, here bark chippings, and discard.

❷ Top up the container with fresh compost mixed with some slow-release fertilizer. Water well and top with a fresh mulch to suppress weeds.

① *Acer cappadocicum* ‡20m (70ft) ↔ 15m (50ft) ② *circinatum* ‡5m (15ft) ↔ 6m (20ft)
③ *davidii* ‘George Forrest’ ♀ ‡↔ 15m (50ft), interesting bark ④ *griseum* ♀ ‡↔ 10m (30ft), attractive bark ⑤ *japonicum* ‘Aconitifolium’ ♀ ‡5m (15ft) ↔ 6m (20ft) ⑥ *negundo* ‘Flamingo’ ‡15m (50ft) ↔ 10m (30ft) ⑦ *negundo* ‘Variegatum’ ‡15m (50ft) ↔ 10m (30ft) ⑧ *palmatum* f. *atropurpureum* ‡8m (25ft) ↔ 10m (30ft) ⑨ *palmatum* ‘Bloodgood’ ♀ ‡↔ 5m (15ft)

⑩ *palmatum* 'Butterfly' ↕3m (10ft) ↔1.5m (5ft) ⑪ *palmatum* 'Chito-seyama' ♀ ↕2m (6ft)
↔3m (10ft) ⑫ *palmatum* 'Corallinum' ↕1.2m (4ft) ↔1m (3ft) ⑬ *palmatum* Dissectum
Atropurpureum Group ↕2m (6ft) ↔3m (10ft) ⑭ *palmatum* 'Garnet' ♀ ↕2m (6ft) ↔3m (10ft)
⑮ *palmatum* var. *heptalobum* ↕5m (15ft) ↔6m (20ft) ⑯ *palmatum* 'Linearilobum' ↕5m (15ft)
↔4m (12ft) ⑰ *palmatum* 'Red Pygmy' ♀ ↕↔1.5m (5ft) ⑱ *palmatum* 'Sango-kaku' ♀

↕6m (20ft) ↔5m (15ft) ⑲ *platanoides* 'Crimson King' ♀ ↕25m (80ft) ↔15m (50ft)
⑳ *pseudoplatanus* 'Brilliantissimum' ♀ ↕6m (20ft) ↔8m (25ft) ㉑ *rubrum* 'October
Glory' ♀ ↕20m (70ft) ↔10m (30ft) ㉒ *rubrum* 'Schlesingeri' ↕20m (70ft) ↔10m (30ft)
㉓ *saccharinum* ↕20m (70ft) ↔12m (40ft) ㉔ *shirasawanum* 'Aureum' ♀ ↕↔6m (20ft)

AEONIUM

year-round

PRIZED FOR THEIR EXOTIC FORMS, aeoniums bear tight rosettes of fleshy leaves in shades of light green to a striking black-purple. From spring to summer, they send up clusters of small starry flowers in pale to bright yellow, white, pink, or copper-red. With some species, the flowering stem dies back once the seed is set. Aeoniums look stunning in containers, especially grouped with other succulents, or with the dark leaves of cultivars such as 'Zwartkop' contrasted with silvery-blue or grey foliage. Grow them in pots on a patio or in a well-drained border in sun or partial shade. They are tender, so will have to be brought into frost-free conditions for the winter.

Hardiness Frost-tender ✸; they can withstand short periods of frost in dry conditions.

Cultivation Grow in fertile, very well-drained soil or gritty compost, in sun or partial shade. **Keep** the plants fairly dry during their dormant period in winter. **Sow** seed (*see pp.391–392*) in heat in spring. **Take** cuttings (*see p.394*) in early summer, waiting until the cut surface of the cuttings calluses, or heals over, before inserting them in gritty compost. Place them in good light and keep warm and on the dry side until rooted. Aeoniums are prone to attack by aphids (*see p.398*).

AESCULUS

Horse chestnut, Buckeye *spring and autumn*

HORSE CHESTNUTS ARE HANDSOME trees with fingered leaves that turn golden yellow or glowing orange in autumn. In spring and early summer, they are covered in large spikes or "candles" of white or pink flowers. In autumn, their smooth- or prickly-coated, rounded fruits split to reveal shiny, brown seeds or conkers; they can cause stomach upsets if eaten. Because of their size – up to 25m (80ft) – most horse chestnuts can be grown only in large gardens. Their spreading branches and large leaves cast a deep shade under which little will grow. However, *Aesculus × mutabilis* 'Induta' and *A. parviflora* are shrubby and smaller in size and look impressive in medium-sized gardens. They are best used as large specimens in lawns.

Hardiness Most garden species are fully hardy ✳✳✳.

Cultivation Grow in any fertile soil in sun or partial shade. **Prune** young trees to remove misplaced or crossing shoots (*see p.382*) in late winter or early spring to maintain a healthy framework of branches and good symmetry. **Sow** seed (*see pp.391–393*) in a seedbed outdoors as soon as it is ripe. *A. parviflora* can be propagated by removing suckers – cut away a stem with its own roots at the base of the plant and replant it.

AUTUMN FOLIAGE

Aesculus parviflora ♥
↕ 3m (10ft) ↔ 5m (15ft), suckering shrub that will grow in all but very poorly-drained soils, smooth-skinned fruits

Aeonium 'Zwartkop' ♥
↕↔ to 1m (3ft), pyramid-shaped spikes of yellow flowers appear in late summer, superb architectural plant for summer display

Aesculus × neglecta 'Erythroblastos' ♥
↕ 10m (30ft) or more ↔ 8m (25ft), red stalks and leaves that unfold cream, then pink, yellow, and finally green by midsummer

Aesculus hippocastanum ♥
↕ 25m (80ft) ↔ 20m (70ft), vigorous tree with a rounded, spreading shape, bears the familiar, spiky-shelled conker

AGAVE

year-round

NATIVE TO DESERTS AND MOUNTAINS, these bold, structural succulents have fleshy, spiked leaves up to 2m (6ft) long, in wide-spreading rosettes. In summer, mature plants may produce funnel-shaped flowers on leafless stems that soar up to 8m (25ft). With most species, the main rosette dies after flowering and fruiting, but leaves a number of offsets – smaller rosettes that develop around it – to mature in later years. These can be split off to make new plants. In frost-prone areas, grow agaves in containers that can be moved into frost-free conditions over winter. If frost is not a problem, grow them as specimen plants in borders protected from excessive winter wet. The spiked leaves are very sharp, so avoid planting them close to seating and play areas.

Hardiness Half-hardy ❁ to frost-tender ❁.

Cultivation Grow in slightly acid, fertile, very well-drained soil or gritty compost in full sun. **Sow** seed (*see pp.391–392*) in heat in early spring. **Remove offsets** in autumn or spring. Insert unrooted offsets in pots containing equal parts peat-free compost and sharp sand. Rooted offsets can be treated like mature plants.

ALNUS

Alder

spring to summer

‡to 25m (80ft)
↔ to 10m (30ft)

FAST-GROWING AND TOLERANT of poor soils, alders are useful trees and shrubs. They are deciduous, and broadly conical in shape, with toothed leaves, and delicate catkins appearing in late winter to spring. The catkins, usually yellow, are followed by green fruits that turn brown in autumn and look like tiny pine cones. Alders, especially those with ornamental foliage such as *Alnus rubra, A. glutinosa,* and *A. incana,* make attractively light, slender specimen trees. They do not mind wet feet, so they are a sound choice for a damp site or by a stream or pond. As they are quick-growing, they make ideal screens or windbreaks.

Hardiness Fully hardy ❁❁❁.

Cultivation Grow in fertile, moist, but well-drained soil in full sun; *A. cordata* and *A. incana* will tolerate dry soils. **Pruning** is rarely necessary: remove branches that cross or spoil the shape of the tree between the time of leaf-fall and midwinter to avoid sap bleeding. **Sow** seed (*see pp.391–393*) in a seedbed as soon as it is ripe. **Take** hardwood cuttings in winter (*see p.394*).

Alnus incana (Grey alder)
‡20m (70ft) ↔ 10m (30ft), makes an excellent windbreak because it thrives in cold, exposed situations

Agave americana 'Mediopicta' ♀
‡2m (6ft) ↔ 3m (10ft), impressive specimen plant when mature, in warm regions flowers in summer on stems up to 8m (25ft) tall ❁

Alnus cordata ♀
‡25m (80ft) ↔ 6m (20ft), originates from the Mediterranean and tolerates dry soil, catkins appear in late winter before the leaves

Alnus glutinosa 'Imperialis' ♀
‡25m (80ft) ↔ 10m (30ft), mid-green, deeply cut leaves to 10cm (4in) long, sticky when young, good as lawn specimen

AMELANCHIER

Juneberry,
Snowy mespilus

spring and autumn

A TREE FOR ALL SEASONS, the amelanchier is superb value in the garden. Spring to early summer is a high point, when these broad, shrubby trees bear masses of beautiful, star- or saucer-shaped, pink to white flowers, just as the bronze-pink young leaves are opening. Add to this their richly coloured autumnal foliage, juicy fruits, and light, airy growing habit, and you have a plant that has something of interest all year round. The small, maroon to purple-black fruits are very attractive to birds. Make the most of this fine tree by growing it as a specimen. Amelanchiers also make substantial additions to shrub borders.

Hardiness Fully hardy ✳✳✳.

Cultivation Grow in acid (lime-free), fertile, well-drained soil in sun or partial shade. *A. asiatica* is lime-tolerant. **Prune out** branches that cross or spoil the shape in late winter or early spring. **Remove** suckers (shoots growing up at ground level away from the main stem) in winter. **Sow** seed (*see pp.391–393*) outdoors as soon as it is ripe. **Take** greenwood or semi-ripe cuttings (*see p.394*) in summer. **Peg** low branches into the soil in autumn to root (*see layering, p.395*). If any branch appears "scorched" or blackened, as if held in the smoke of a bonfire (the sign of a disease called fireblight), it must be removed.

ANDROMEDA

Bog rosemary

spring to early summer

↕ to 40cm (16in)
↔ to 60cm (24in)

IMAGINE A HEATHER with long, narrow, green leaves, and you have the bog rosemary, a small, wiry-stemmed, evergreen shrub that enjoys the same conditions as ericas (*see pp.52–53*) and callunas (*see p.31*), being native to peat bogs in cool regions. *Andromeda polifolia* is the most commonly grown species; its cultivars vary in size, from 5cm (2in) to 40cm (16in) tall, and in flower colour – either pink or white. Bog rosemaries only thrive in moist, acid (lime-free) soils. If your soil is not suitable, a raised bed or container filled with ericaceous (acid) soil or compost will suffice. They enjoy a woodland setting or a shady rock garden.

Hardiness Fully hardy ✳✳✳.

Cultivation Grow in moist, acid soil with plenty of well-rotted organic matter added to it, in sun or partial shade. If your soil is dry, spread a layer of leafmould or garden compost around the plants each spring, ideally after heavy rain; this will help retain moisture and keep down weeds. **Take** softwood cuttings in summer (*see p.394*), or pot up rooted layers in autumn or spring (*see p.395*).

ARALIA

spring to early autumn

↕↔ to 10m (30ft)

THESE EXOTIC-LOOKING TREES grow mainly in mountainous woodland. Their large, handsome leaves are arranged in pairs; in some, they are covered in large bristles. *Aralia elata* is the largest species. In late summer and early autumn, they produce clusters or spikes of small, white or greenish-white flowers (with no hint of pink), followed by black fruits. Aralias are suitable only for large gardens, in prominent positions where their striking leaves can be admired. They look good in shady borders, woodland plantings, and by streams.

Hardiness Fully hardy ✳✳✳ to frost-hardy ✳✳.

Cultivation Grow in fertile soil with plenty of well-rotted organic matter added, in an open or part-shaded site, sheltered from strong winds that may damage the leaves. Trees in very fertile soil can produce soft growth prone to damage by frost. **Remove** badly placed branches or frost-damaged shoots in early spring, and remove suckers growing up around the tree when seen. If variegated forms produce shoots with all-green leaves, prune them out. **Sow** seed (*see pp.391–392*) in containers as soon as ripe; place in a cold frame. **Take** root cuttings (*see p.394*) in winter. Aphids may attack the soft flower stalks.

Amelanchier lamarckii ♥
↕10m (30ft) ↔ 12m (40ft), upright-stemmed, leaves emerge as bronze, then turn dark green, white flowers appear mid-spring

① *polifolia* 'Alba' ↕15cm (6in) ↔ 20cm (8in), semi-prostrate, free-flowering ② *polifolia* 'Compacta' ♥ ↕30cm (12in) ↔ 20cm (8in), dense, twiggy habit

Aralia elata 'Variegata' ♥
↕↔ 10m (30ft) vigorous, deciduous tree, leaves grow to 1.2m (4ft) long with good autumn colour, flowers late summer to early autumn

ARAUCARIA ARAUCANA

Monkey puzzle   *year-round*

ONE OF THE MOST ANCIENT TREES, the monkey puzzle is so-called because its branches are clad in sharp, scale-like leaves that make them uncomfortable, if not impossible, to climb. Although hailing from the tropical rainforest, this araucaria is fully hardy, and has long been a garden favourite for its novelty value. Many, unfortunately, are planted in gardens that are far too small (especially since they are deceptively slow-growing when young), necessitating unsightly lopping that completely ruins their shape. They need plenty of room for their forms to develop – at first conical, then losing the lower branches to form a graceful, rounded head atop a tall, clear trunk. Male and female cones tend to be borne on different trees; female cones are more rounded than the male ones.

Hardiness Fully hardy ✳✳✳.

Cultivation Grow in any fertile, well-drained soil in an open site, but sheltered from cold winds. **Sow** seed (*see pp.391–393*) in a seedbed as soon as it is ripe. **Take** cuttings (*see p.394*) from vertical shoot tips in midsummer and root in a cold frame. Cuttings from horizontal branches never make upright trees.

ARBUTUS

Strawberry tree   *year-round*

ARBUTUS ARE BROAD, sometimes bushy trees with attractive, peeling, red-brown bark and dark, glossy leaves. Clusters of tiny white or pink flowers are produced from autumn to spring. These are followed by bright orange to red, strawberry-like fruits (hence the common name) which are edible, if rather tasteless. Although they can reach up to 15m (50ft), they are slow-growing and many will remain small shrubs for several years. Arbutus are excellent for a large shrub border or as specimens, where their handsome, coloured barks can be admired.

Hardiness Fully hardy ✳✳✳ when mature (young trees not so) to frost-hardy ✳✳.

Cultivation Grow in fertile soil, enriched with plenty of bulky, well-rotted organic matter, in a sheltered site in full sun with protection from cold winds, even when mature. Both *A.* × *andrachnoides* and *A. unedo* will tolerate alkaline (limy) soils; other species, such as *A. menziesii*, need acid soils. **Prune out** any misplaced shoots to maintain a good shape in winter or late spring when the tree is dormant, but keep pruning to a minimum. **Sow** seed (*see pp.391–392*) in containers as soon as it is ripe and place in a cold frame. **Take** semi-ripe (stem-tip) cuttings in summer (*see p.394*).

Arbutus × *andrachnoides* ♀
↕↔ 8m (25ft), white, sometimes pink-tinged, flowers in autumn to spring, grown mostly for red bark, fruits are rare ✳✳✳

Araucaria araucana
↕ 15–25m (50–80ft) ↔ 7–10m (22–30ft), has tough, dark grey-brown bark with horizontal ridges

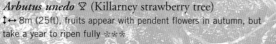

Arbutus unedo ♀ (Killarney strawberry tree)
↕↔ 8m (25ft), fruits appear with pendent flowers in autumn, but take a year to ripen fully ✳✳✳

Arbutus menziesii ♀
↕↔ 15m (50ft), spreading, sometimes shrubby habit, free-flowering, bears white flowers in 20cm (8in) spikes in early summer ✳✳✳

ARCTOSTAPHYLOS

Bearberry *winter, spring, and autumn*

THESE MOSTLY EVERGREEN, low-maintenance shrubs originate from western North America, particularly California. They range in habit from mat-forming to upright; some bearberries eventually reach 6m (20ft) tall with a similar spread, while *Arctostaphylos alpina* is just 5cm (2in) tall and 20cm (8in) across. All bear bunches of delicate, white to pink, urn-shaped flowers in winter or spring. Small berries, usually scarlet but sometimes brown, purple, or black, follow in autumn. Low-growing bearberries look excellent as ground cover in a shrub border or in a large rock garden. The larger, upright species look at home in an open, woodland garden.

Hardiness Fully hardy ✳✳✳ to half-hardy ✳.

Cultivation Grow in moist, fertile, well-drained, acid (lime-free) soil in full sun or partial shade. Less hardy species need shelter. **Sow** seed (*see pp.391–392*) in containers in a cold frame in autumn, immersing the seeds in boiling water for about 20 seconds before sowing. This softens the hard seed coats. **Take** semi-ripe cuttings (*see p.394*) in summer or layer in autumn (*see p.395*). Shoots growing along the soil surface often produce roots at the leaf joints, layering naturally. Lift, sever, and pot these up to make new young plants.

ARGYRANTHEMUM

Marguerite *summer to autumn*

ARGYRANTHEMUMS ARE HARD-WORKING shrubs that produce a succession of cheery, daisy blooms from early summer through to autumn. There are single- and double-flowered types, in hues of white, soft yellow to apricot, and pale pink to deep cerise. Formerly classed as chrysanthemums, they have similar foliage: almost fern-like, and either green or greyish-green. They are invaluable in pots, in summer bedding schemes or in mixed borders where they inject a light and breezy feel. Some make elegant specimens or are trained as standards (in a "lollipop" shape with a single, bare stem and a bushy head).

Hardiness Frost-hardy ✳✳ (in mild areas) to half-hardy ✳.

Cultivation Grow in well-drained fertile soil in full sun. Most species will tolerate salt-laden winds in coastal areas. **Pinch out** the growing tips of young plants to encourage a bushy habit. **Prune back** flowered shoots to within 2.5cm (1in) of their base after flowering or in early spring. **Apply** a deep winter mulch if the temperature in your area falls below −5°C (23°F) for long periods, taking cuttings in late summer as an insurance against losses. Alternatively, lift the plants and overwinter in frost-free conditions. **Take** softwood cuttings in spring or semi-ripe cuttings in summer (*see p.394*).

Arctostaphylos × media 'Wood's Red'
↕ to 10cm (4in) ↔ to 50cm (20in), low-growing and densely branched, suitable for a rockery or the front of a shrub border ✳✳✳

Argyranthemum gracile 'Chelsea Girl' ♀
↕↔ 60cm (24in), compact plant with relatively sparse flowers, grown for its filigree foliage, good as a specimen plant ✳

Argyranthemum 'Vancouver' ♀
↕ 90cm (36in) ↔ 80cm (32in), compact plant with double flowers and grey-green leaves, works well in a cottage garden ✳

ARTEMISIA

see also pp.188–189

Mugwort, Sagebrush, Wormwood

year-round

↕5cm–1.5m (2in–5ft)
↔15cm–1.5m (6in–5ft)

ARTEMISIAS HAVE FERNY, aromatic, grey or silver foliage that gives year-round interest and acts as a foil for flowering plants or those with bolder leaves. There are evergreen and deciduous types, all bearing tiny, unimpressive flowers – the leaves are the chief draw. Artemisias look good in herb gardens (French tarragon is a form of *Artemisia dracunculus*), rock gardens, and shrub or flower borders. They are often featured in drought-tolerant, Mediterranean-style gardens, although a few, notably *A. lactiflora*, need moist soil.

Hardiness Fully hardy ✳✳✳ to frost-hardy ✳✳.

Cultivation Grow in fertile, well-drained soil in a sunny position. *A. arborescens* needs the extra protection of a warm wall in frost-prone areas. In heavy clay soil, dig in plenty of coarse grit to improve drainage; plants can be short-lived in wet conditions. **Prune** plants that have grown over-large and leggy to the ground, in autumn or spring, to encourage a compact habit. **Sow** seed (*see pp.391–392*) in containers in a cold frame in autumn or spring. **Take** heel cuttings in early summer (*see p.394*). **Prone** to mildew (*see p.398*) in damp.

AUCUBA

year-round

AUCUBAS ARE USEFUL, evergreen shrubs grown for their bold, glossy foliage and large fruits. They hardly ever suffer from pests and diseases, and tolerate all sorts of difficult growing conditions, including full shade, dry soils, pollution, and salt-laden winds. This makes them a popular choice for town gardens. Aucubas can be used as specimen plants in lawns, in mixed and shrub borders, or for informal hedging (if trimmed, they do not fruit as well). The variegated and spotted cultivars (such as 'Sulphurea Marginata' and 'Crotonifolia') make a bright splash in a dark corner where little else will grow.

Hardiness Fully hardy ✳✳✳.

Cultivation Grow in any fertile soil except waterlogged conditions, in full sun or full shade; variegated species prefer partial shade. In areas with hot summers, grow in full shade. Use soil-based potting compost if growing it in a container. Feed plants in pots once a month with a liquid fertilizer, and water freely when in full growth, but sparingly in winter. **Trim** aucubas in spring to shape and cut back hard if they are growing too large. Prune wayward shoots by cutting them well back into the centre of the bush. **Sow** seed (*see pp.391–392*) in containers in autumn. **Take** semi-ripe cuttings (*see p.394*) in summer.

Argyranthemum 'Mary Wootton'
↕1.1m (3½ft) ↔ 1m (3ft), open habit, grey-green leaves, flowers open pale pink but fade to white with age ✳

Argyranthemum 'Jamaica Primrose' ♀
↕1.1m (3½ft) ↔ 1m (3ft), open habit with long branching stems, flowers are 6cm (2½in) across, good to train as a standard ✳

① *abrotanum* ♀ ↕↔ 1m (3ft), semi-evergreen, flowers in late summer ✳✳✳ ② *arborescens* ♀ ↕1m (3ft) ↔ 1.5m (5ft), evergreen with silky leaves ✳✳✳

Aucuba japonica
↕↔ 3m (10ft), female plants will produce bright red berries (*see inset*) if a male is grown nearby

AZARA

midwinter to midsummer

STRONGLY VANILLA-SCENTED FLOWERS are the main attraction of this group of evergreen shrubs and small trees. The flowers are produced in tight clusters or spikes carried on the undersides of the branches, with different species flowering at times ranging from midwinter to midsummer. The flowers have no petals, but showy stamens give them a decorative, fluffy appearance. Berries may follow after hot summers. These trouble-free shrubs need a sunny and sheltered position, ideally against a warm wall: they are often wall-trained. The green leaves vary in size and are sometimes in distinctive unequal pairs, with a small leaf opposite a much larger one.

Hardiness Fully hardy ✳✳✳ to half-hardy ✳.

Cultivation Grow in moist soil enriched with plenty of well-rotted organic matter. Site in sun or partial shade, sheltered from cold winds, which will scorch the leaves and cause them to drop. In colder areas, grow and train azaras against warm, sunny walls. **Prune out** shoots that spoil the shape of the shrub after flowering; if wall-trained, prune back flowered shoots to two to four buds above the permanent framework of branches.

BALLOTA

year-round

THESE EVERGREEN OR SEMI-EVERGREEN PLANTS form mounds or mats of rounded, aromatic, yellow-green to grey-green leaves. Small, funnel-shaped flowers in shades of green, purple, white, or pink are produced from late spring until late summer, but the attractive foliage is the main reason for growing ballotas. They make an excellent foil for more colourful plants, such as brightly flowered border phloxes (*see pp.306–307*) daylilies (*Hemerocallis, see p.258*), and achilleas (*see pp.166–167*). For a more subtle effect, grow them alongside plants such as lavender (*Lavandula, see pp.80–81*) for contrasting foliage textures within the same colour range.

Hardiness Fully hardy ✳✳✳ to frost-hardy ✳✳.

Cultivation Grow in poor, dry soil that is free-draining. Position in full sun. **Trim back** all flowered shoots to within 2.5cm (1in) of old growth after flowering or in mid- to late spring; alternatively, trim back in spring to keep the plants compact. A thick, dry winter mulch helps protect borderline hardy plants in cold areas. **Divide** perennials (*see p.395*) in spring. **Take** softwood cuttings of shrubs in late spring or semi-ripe cuttings in early summer (*see p.394*).

BERBERIS

Barberry   *spring, summer, and autumn*

BARBERRIES ARE GROWN FOR their ornamental foliage and their glowing, yellow to dark orange flowers. The flowers are produced in spring and summer, usually in small clusters, and are often followed by colourful fruits in autumn. There are evergreen and deciduous barberries, many of the latter showing fiery autumn colours. All have spiny stems, making an excellent choice for an impenetrable hedge, but with a wide range of species and cultivars to choose from, you can find a barberry for almost any aspect in the garden. They range from large specimens for hedging or borders to dwarf shrubs suitable for rock gardens.

Hardiness Fully hardy ✳✳✳ to frost-hardy ✳✳.

Cultivation Grow in any moist but well-drained soil. Position in full sun or partial shade: autumn colours and fruiting are best in full sun. **Prune** after flowering: lightly trim or prune shoots that spoil the shape of evergreens and cut back flowered shoots of deciduous types to strong buds or shoots. Trim hedges after flowering. **Take** semi-ripe cuttings of both types or softwood cuttings of deciduous types in summer (*see p.394*). Powdery mildew can be a problem (*see also p.398*); cut out badly affected parts and apply a fungicide.

Azara microphylla ♀ (inset: *microphylla* 'Variegata')
↕10m (30ft) ↔ 4m (12ft), hardiest of the species, will also tolerate full shade ✳✳✳

① **'All Hallows Green'** (syn. *Marrubium bourgaei* 'All Hallows Green') ↕60cm (24in) ↔ 75cm (30in) ✳✳✳
② *pseudodictamnus* ♀ ↕45cm (18in) ↔ 60cm (24in) ✳✳✳

Berberis darwinii ♀
↕↔ 3m (10ft), upright, evergreen, flowering in spring, sometimes again in autumn, with blue-black fruits in autumn ✳✳✳

Berberis thunbergii 'Rose Glow' ♀
↕ 1m (3ft) occasionally more ↔ 2.5m (8ft), rounded and deciduous, with the first leaves of the season unvariegated ✳✳✳

Berberis × *stenophylla* 'Corallina Compacta' ♀
↕↔ to 30cm (12in), evergreen, a dwarf cultivar of this normally large species, makes good edging ✳✳✳

Berberis wilsoniae
↕ 1m (3ft) ↔ 2m (6ft), mounding evergreen, with bright red-orange autumn leaf colour ✳✳✳

Berberis julianae ♀
↕↔ 3m (10ft), dense, upright evergreen, oblong blue-black fruits with a white bloom on them in autumn ✳✳✳

Berberis thunbergii 'Dart's Red Lady'
↕ 1m (3ft) occasionally more ↔ 2.5m (8ft), deciduous, deep red-purple leaves turning bright red (*see inset*) in autumn ✳✳✳

Berberis 'Goldilocks'
↕ 4m (12ft) ↔ 3m (10ft), evergreen, first upright, then spreading in shape, leaves to 5cm (2in) long ✳✳✳

BETULA

Birch

spring, autumn, and winter

THESE GRACEFUL, DECIDUOUS trees provide a display in every season: the textured bark, often peeling and silvery-white or coppery-brown, looks stunning in winter when there is little else to see; male and female flowers are borne in separate catkins on the same tree during spring, and the small, toothed, mid- to dark green leaves generally turn a soft yellow in autumn. This is a large group, with several species suitable for small gardens. The slender forms of many species look particularly attractive if room can be found for a small group of trees. The spreading *Betula medwedewii* and the popular weeping birches are among the most beautiful and elegant of specimen trees for a garden.

Hardiness Fully hardy ✳✳✳.

Cultivation Grow in reasonably fertile, well-drained soil. Site in sun or light, dappled shade; most will tolerate exposed positions. **Prune out** any misplaced or crossing branches during winter, when the trees are dormant, to maintain a healthy framework of branches. **Sow** seed (*see pp.391–392*) in a seedbed outdoors in autumn. **Take** softwood cuttings (*see p.394*) in summer. Mildew (*see p.398*) may appear, but mature trees should recover without spraying, which would in any case be impractical. Young trees could be treated if badly affected.

Betula papyrifera (Canoe birch, Paper birch)
↕ 20m (70ft) ↔ 10m (30ft), newly exposed bark is pale orange-brown, paling with age, and autumn leaves are yellow to orange

Betula medwedewii (Transcaucasian birch)
↕↔ 5m (15ft), growth is upright at first, becoming more spreading with age, male catkins to 10cm (4in) long (*see inset*)

***Betula pendula* 'Youngii'** (Young's weeping birch)
↕ 8m (25ft) ↔ 10m (30ft), a domed form of the usually upright silver birch, suitable for small gardens

Betula nigra (Black birch, River birch)
↕ 18m (60ft) ↔ 12m (40ft), conical to spreading in habit, the bark becoming fissured and grey-white or blackish on old trees

***Betula utilis* 'Silver Shadow'** ♀
↕ 18m (60ft) ↔ 10m (30ft), with larger leaves than many other birches and particularly bright white bark

BRACHYGLOTTIS

Senecio   *summer*

EVERGREEN SHRUBS WITH CLUSTERS of creamy-white to deep yellow flowers in summer, these are ideal for exposed and coastal gardens. 'Sunshine', the most widely grown, belongs to a popular group of small cultivars called the Dunedin Group. Usually about 75cm (30in) tall, these form mounds of oval, wavy-edged leaves, hairy at first, and produce clusters of bright yellow flowerheads from summer until autumn. Other choices include *Brachyglottis repanda*, a spreading shrub to 3m (10ft) tall and wide with dark-green leaves and creamy-white flowers, and the compact *B. rotundifolia*, at 1m (3ft) more suitable for small gardens. Grow them in shrub borders; the foliage makes an effective contrast to narrow-leaved shrubs such as hebes (*see pp.68–69*).

Hardiness Fully hardy ✳✳✳ to half-hardy ✳, exceptionally cold spells may damage soft stems.

Cultivation Grow in well-drained soil in full sun. **Trim back** or lightly prune shoots that spoil the shape of the shrub after flowering. **Take** semi-ripe cuttings (*see p.394*) in summer.

BUDDLEJA

Butterfly bush   *early to late summer*

↕ to 5m (15ft)

THE FRAGRANT FLOWERS of buddlejas are wonderful for attracting hordes of butterflies. Most widely grown is the hardy *Buddleja davidii* and its cultivars, most growing to 2.5–3m (8–10ft) tall in a single season, with pink, purple, lilac, or white flowers in conical spikes on tall, arching shoots from late summer to early autumn. *B. globosa*, the orange ball tree, is a larger, rounded shrub, also hardy, that flowers in early summer. Buddlejas may be deciduous, semi-evergreen, or evergreen. They make an effective backdrop to other summer-flowering shrubs such as St. John's wort (*Hypericum, see p.74*) or potentillas (*see p.99*).

Hardiness Fully hardy ✳✳✳ to frost-tender ✿.

Cultivation Grow in fertile, well-drained soil in full sun; poorer soils are tolerated. **Prune** *B. davidii* and its cultivars by cutting old stems back to the base, in early spring (*see p.383*). Trim other buddlejas after flowering, only to keep them neat and within bounds. **Take** semi-ripe cuttings (*see p.394*) in summer or hardwood cuttings of *B. davidii* in autumn. If caterpillars are troublesome, pick them off by hand.

BUPLEURUM FRUTICOSUM

Shrubby hare's ear,   *midsummer to*
Thorow-wax   *autumn*

EXCELLENT FOR COASTAL AREAS because it will withstand salt spray from the sea, this evergreen has a spreading habit, making it ideal for covering a wall or bank. The small, starry, yellow flowers surrounded by leafy bracts are borne in rounded clusters from midsummer until autumn. This can grow to be a large and dense shrub, so it needs positioning near the back of a shrub or mixed border. Grow with other shrubs such as hawthorns (*Crataegus, see p.46*), St. John's wort (*Hypericum, see p.74*), and buddlejas (*see left*).

Hardiness Fully hardy ✳✳✳ (borderline in cold areas).

Cultivation Will grow in any well-drained soil, preferring full sun in a warm, sheltered site. **Prune off** the fading flowers to prevent seeds forming. Trim back shoots that spoil the shape of the shrub in mid- or late spring: it will also tolerate hard pruning if it outgrows its space. **Sow seed** (*see pp.391–392*) in a container in a cold frame in spring. **Take** semi-ripe cuttings (*see p.394*) in summer.

Brachyglottis 'Sunshine' ♥
↕75cm (30in) ↔ 1m (3ft), tolerant of all but the shadiest, dampest positions, thrives in seaside gardens ✳✳✳

① *davidii* 'Royal Red' ♥ ↕3m (10ft) ✳✳✳ ② *davidii* 'White Profusion' ♥ ↕3m (10ft) ✳✳ ③ *globosa* ♥ ↕↔5m (15ft) ✳✳ ④ 'Lochinch' ♥ ↕2.5m (8ft) ↔ 3m (10ft) ✳✳✳

Bupleurum fruticosum
↕2m (6ft) ↔ 2.5m (8ft)

BUXUS

Box, Boxwood   *year-round*

EVERGREEN BOX IS ONE OF the garden's most versatile
plants. Although many varieties are naturally large
and shrubby, all respond well to regular trimming,
making them equally at home in formal and informal
settings. Tiny, yellow-green flowers appear in spring,
but it is the neat, leathery foliage that steals the show.
Used in hedges or screens, it furnishes a constant
backdrop for seasonal action in the borders. You can
clip box into ornamental topiary shapes; simple forms
need trimming only once or twice a year. Dwarf boxes
were traditionally used to create knot gardens and
parterres; they are also excellent for edging paths and
borders, and as ground cover. There are many types
of box, some of them variegated.

Hardiness Fully hardy ✳✳✳ to frost-hardy ✳✳.

Cultivation Box needs fertile, well-drained soil, ideally in partial
shade; dry soil and full sun can cause dull or scorched foliage.
Trim shrubs and hedges in summer; box tolerates hard pruning in late
spring if fed and well watered after. **Take** semi-ripe cuttings in summer
(*see p.394*). **Box suckers**, pale green, aphid-like insects that excrete
white honey dew, may impede growth from spring to summer. These
are only a problem on young plants.

CALLICARPA

Beauty berry   *autumn to winter*

↕1–3m (3–10ft)
↔1–2.5m (3–8ft)

APTLY NAMED, THE BEAUTY BERRY is
valued for its vibrantly coloured,
bead-like, autumn berries. These
remain on bare stems of deciduous
species after the leaves fall, bringing
colour to a winter garden. Berries may be violet, lilac,
white, or dusky purple and are most abundant after a
long, hot summer. If you have space, plant groups of
three or more to maximize fruiting. These shrubs are
deciduous or evergreen with deep green or bronze
leaves and varied habits. They bear clusters of small,
white, red, purple, or pink flowers in summer. Other
berrying shrubs and trees, such as cotoneasters (*see
p.45*) and sorbus (*see p.118*), make good companions.

Hardiness Fully hardy ✳✳✳ to frost-tender ❋.

Cultivation Fertile, well-drained soil in full sun or light, dappled
shade is suitable. **Cut back** the previous year's growth to the main
stems in early spring (*see p.383*). If drastic pruning is required, cut
back flowered shoots close to the base. **Sow** seed (*see pp.391–393*)
in pots in a cold frame in autumn or spring. **Take** softwood cuttings in
spring or semi-ripe cuttings in summer (*see p.394*).

CALLISTEMON

Bottlebrush   *spring to autumn*

↕1–15m (3–50ft)
↔1–8m (3–25ft)

THE DISTINCTIVE, BRISTLY flower spikes
that give these evergreen shrubs and trees
their common name emerge in spring
or summer. *Callistemon linearis* and
C. speciosus bloom into autumn. Bold
hues of crimson, purple, pink, white, or gold flowers
are set off by simple, leathery leaves. *C. citrinus*
'Firebrand' also boasts silvery-pink shoots. Habits
vary, but many have a spreading form. Tie them in
loosely to trellis for an unusual wall covering. Natives
of Australia, bottlebrushes thrive at the base of a warm
wall in a shrub border, with ceanothus (*see p.36*) and
lavenders (*see pp.80–81*). Grow tender species in
containers and overwinter them under cover.

Hardiness Fully hardy ✳✳✳(borderline) to frost-tender ❋.

Cultivation Bottlebrushes like moist but well-drained, neutral to acid
(lime-free) soil, in full sun. **Lightly trim** any shoots that spoil the shape
of the shrub, after flowering; the plants tolerate hard pruning if frost-
damaged or grown out of their allotted space. **Sow** seed (*see pp.391–
393*) on the surface of moist compost, in spring at 16–18°C (61–64°F).
Take semi-ripe cuttings in late summer (*see p.394*).

sempervirens � ✳✳✳ ① 'Elegantissima' ♀ ↕↔ 1.5m (5ft)
② 'Handsworthiensis' ↕↔ 5m (15ft) ③ 'Latifolia Maculata' ♀
↕2.5m (8ft) ↔ 2m (6ft) ④ 'Suffruticosa' ♀ ↕1m (3ft) ↔ 1.5m (5ft)

Callicarpa bodinieri **var.** *giraldii*
↕3m (10ft) ↔ 2.5m (8ft), deciduous, upright bush, clusters of
small pink flowers in midsummer ✳✳✳

Callistemon pallidus (Lemon bottlebrush)
↕↔ 2–4m (6–12ft), erect to spreading shrub, downy shoots, dark to
grey-green leaves, 10cm (4in) flowers late spring to midsummer ❋

CALLUNA VULGARIS

see also p.48 and pp.52–53

Scot's heather,
Ling

*midsummer to
late autumn*

BELOVED BY BEES, THIS EVERGREEN SHRUB and its cultivars has stems thickly encrusted with purple, red, pink, or white bell-shaped flowers from midsummer to late autumn. The flower spikes can be up to 10cm (4in) long, but become shorter as the plants age. The foliage usually is dark green, and purple-tinged in winter; the linear leaves lie flat along the stems. There are over 500 prostrate to upright cultivars to choose from; all make excellent ground cover, and some have striking foliage, like the terracotta 'Firefly'. Make space for heathers in wildlife gardens, in bold groups of three or five, or more, together with dwarf rhododendrons (*see pp.104–107*) and conifers.

Hardiness Fully hardy ✿✿✿.

Cultivation Callunas need an open site with well-drained, acid (lime-free) soil. **Cut back** flowered shoots to within 2.5cm (1in) of older growth in early spring. **Mulch** with leafmould or composted bark (*see p.388*) in spring or autumn to encourage growth, especially in young plants. **Take** semi-ripe cuttings 5cm (2in) long in midsummer (*see p.394*). **Layer** shoots in spring as for ericas (*see p.52*).

'Gold Haze' ♈
↕10–60cm (4–24in) ↔ 45cm (18in), pale yellow foliage is retained all year, white flower spikes are 5–10cm (2–4in) long

'Anthony Davis' ♈
↕45cm (18in) ↔ to 75cm (30in), grey-green leaves, white flowers over 10cm (4in) long, good for cutting

'Robert Chapman' ♈
↕25cm (10in) ↔ 65cm (26in), gold foliage turns red and orange in winter and spring, purple flower spikes are 5–10cm (2–4in) long

'Silver Knight'
↕40cm (16in) ↔ to 75cm (30in), downy grey foliage darkens to purple-grey in winter, flower spikes are 5–10cm (2–4in) long

'Beoley Gold' ♈
↕35cm (14in) ↔ to 75cm (30in), pure white flower spikes are 5–10cm (2–4in) long

CAMELLIA

spring

‡1–20m (3–70ft)
↔60cm–8m (2–25ft)

THESE ELEGANT, EVERGREEN SHRUBS suit a range of uses from borders to woodland settings. They are also excellent container plants, and this is an ideal way of growing them if your soil is alkaline (high lime content), since camellias prefer a neutral to acid soil. There are over 250 species, and the largest are very tall, but there are many smaller cultivars that are more suited to most gardens. The exquisite flowers in shades of pink, scarlet, and white appear in spring and last for several weeks. Borne singly or in clusters, they last well as cut flowers and some are slightly fragrant. Flowers may be single or double, and vary considerably in size, the largest measuring 13cm (5in) or more across, but the average bloom is about half that size. Most commonly grown camellias are hardy, although *Camellia reticulata* and its cultivars are half-hardy and need a sheltered site. Dark green, glossy foliage ensures that camellias stay handsome all year.

Hardiness Fully hardy ✳✳✳ to frost-tender ❀.

Cultivation Grow in moist but well-drained, humus-rich, acid soil (pH 5.5–5.6). **Shelter** from cold winds and position in partial shade, since early sun may damage the buds and flowers on frosty mornings. **Plant** with the top of the root ball just below the surface of the soil. Mulch in spring with 5–8cm (2–3in) leafmould or shredded bark. **Feed** with a balanced fertilizer in mid-spring and again in early summer, and keep well watered during dry spells to prevent bud drop. **Protect** roots with a thatch of bracken or straw during prolonged cold spells. **Prune** lightly to shape in late spring or early summer after flowering, and deadhead. **Take** semi-ripe cuttings from late summer until early winter (*see p.394*). Virus disease may blemish flowers, and camellias may be attacked by vine weevils (*see p.398*).

Pruning young camellias

Young camellias develop a variety of habits. Careful pruning of young plants can help produce a well-balanced shape and encourage new, bushy growth. Reduce any thin, weak growth by cutting back to two or three buds or pruning it out entirely. Established plants require very little pruning. If plants have outgrown their space they can be cut back hard in early spring.

Shorten vigorous main shoots to balance shape

Remove badly placed dual leader

Pinch out tips to encourage branching at base

Tall central stem makes plant suitable for training against wall

① *Camellia* 'Inspiration' ♥ ‡4m (12ft) ↔ 2m (6ft) ② *japonica* 'Adolphe Audusson' ♥ ‡9m (28ft) ↔ 8m (25ft) ③ *japonica* 'Alexander Hunter' ♥ ‡9m (28ft) ↔ 8m (25ft) ④ *japonica* 'Apollo' ‡9m (28ft) ↔ 8m (25ft) ⑤ *japonica* 'Ave Maria' ♥ ‡9m (28ft) ↔ 8m (25ft) ⑥ *japonica* 'Berenice Boddy' ♥ ‡9m (28ft) ↔ 8m (25ft) ⑦ *japonica* 'Betty Sheffield Supreme' ‡2–4m (6–12ft) ↔ 1.5–3m (5–10ft) ⑧ *japonica* 'Elegans' ♥ ‡9m (28ft) ↔ 8m (25ft) ⑨ *japonica* 'Gloire

de Nantes' ♀ ‡9m (28ft) ↔ 8m (25ft) ⑩ *japonica* 'Guilio Nuccio' ♀ ‡9m (28ft) ↔ 8m (25ft)
⑪ *japonica* 'Hagoromo' ♀ ‡9m (28ft) ↔ 8m (25ft) ⑫ *japonica* 'Julia Drayton' ‡9m (28ft) ↔ 8m
(25ft) ⑬ *japonica* 'Jupiter' ♀ ‡9m (28ft) ↔ 8m (25ft) ⑭ *japonica* 'Mrs D.W. Davis' ‡9m (28ft)
↔ 8m (25ft) ⑮ *japonica* 'R.L. Wheeler' ♀ ‡9m (28ft) ↔ 8m (25ft) ⑯ *japonica* 'Rubescens
Major' ‡9m (28ft) ↔ 8m (25ft) ⑰ *reticulata* 'Arch of Triumph' ‡3m (10ft) ↔ 5m (15ft)

⑱ *reticulata* 'William Hertrich' ‡15m (50ft) ↔ 5m (15ft) ⑲ *tsaii* ‡10m (30ft) ↔ 5m
(15ft) ⑳ × *williamsii* 'Anticipation' ♀ ‡4m (12ft) ↔ 2m (6ft) ㉑ × *williamsii* 'Bow
Bells' ‡4m (12ft) ↔ 1–3m (3–10ft) ㉒ × *williamsii* 'Donation' ♀ ‡5m (15ft) ↔ 2.5m (8ft)
㉓ × *williamsii* 'J.C. Williams' ♀ ‡2–5m (6–15ft) ↔ 1–3m (3–10ft) ㉔ × *williamsii*
'Saint Ewe' ♀ ‡2–5m (6–15ft) ↔ 1–3m (3–10ft)

CARAGANA

late spring

THESE DECIDUOUS SHRUBS OR SMALL TREES thrive in exposed sites with dry soils. They are found from Eastern Europe to China and their tolerance of difficult conditions makes them very garden-worthy. They have attractive leaves, and delicate, pea-like flowers in yellow, white, or pink, followed in autumn by long, slender, brown pods. Caraganas are useful as a windbreak or can be grown in a shrub or mixed border with other trees and shrubs. *Caragana arborescens* 'Pendula' is often sold grafted on top of a straight, clear stem to form a small weeping standard. The dwarf *C. arborescens* 'Nana' is slow-growing, to 75cm (30in) tall and wide, with twisted branches; it makes an unusual rock-garden plant.

Hardiness Fully hardy ✳✳✳.

Cultivation Grow in well-drained, reasonably fertile soil in full sun. Will also tolerate poor, dry soils in exposed places. **Prune** minimally, only to remove any misplaced shoots, in late winter or early spring. **Sow** seed in containers in a cold frame as soon as it is ripe (*see pp.391–392*); or sow in spring, pre-soaking the seeds before sowing to soften the seed coat. **Take** softwood cuttings in spring (*see p.394*).

CARPINUS

Hornbeam
spring to autumn

THERE ARE 35–40 SPECIES of these deciduous, woodland trees, several of which make good garden trees and can also be grown as handsome hedges. Grown as trees, they have an elegant habit, ranging from columnar and pyramid-shaped – the flame-like *Carpinus betulus* 'Fastigiata' being particularly popular – to rounded and spreading. Their beech-like foliage is mid- to dark green and often glossy; smooth, fluted grey bark is another pleasing feature. In spring, they produce yellow-green catkins, followed by drooping, hop-like, green fruits, maturing to brown or yellow. Autumn foliage colour is striking, too, the leaves turning to gold and amber.

Hardiness Fully hardy ✳✳✳.

Cultivation Grow in reasonably fertile, well-drained soil in sun or partial shade. **Prune** young trees to remove any misplaced or crossing branches in late winter or early spring; trim hedges in mid- to late summer. Hornbeams can withstand severe pruning if they outgrow their space. **Sow** seed in a seedbed outdoors in autumn (*see pp.391–393*). **Take** greenwood cuttings in early summer (*see p.394*).

CARYOPTERIS

late summer to autumn

SMALL, DAINTY SHRUBS with a mound-forming habit, caryopteris bear masses of small, fluffy flowers in shades of blue. The group includes both these deciduous shrubs and some perennials, found in a variety of habitats from dry, hot slopes to woodland. They flower from late summer until autumn; most have grey- or silvery-green foliage, giving a cool look, although 'Worcester Gold' has warm yellow foliage. Caryopteris are elegant front-of-border shrubs, especially planted in groups; they make a striking contrast with yellow-flowered potentillas (*see p.99*) or St. John's wort (*Hypericum, p.74*).

Hardiness Fully hardy ✳✳✳ to frost-hardy ✳✳.

Cultivation Grow in light but moderately fertile soil, in full sun. Plant against a warm wall in very cold areas, especially if summers are also cool. **Prune** the previous year's flowered shoots in early spring, cutting them back to only three or four good buds, so that a permanent stubby framework of shoots develops. If necessary, caryopteris can be cut down almost to soil level. **Sow** seed in autumn in a cold frame (*see pp.391–392*). **Take** softwood cuttings in late spring, or semi-ripe cuttings in early summer (*see p.394*).

Caragana arborescens (Pea tree)
↕6m (20ft) ↔ 4m (12ft), thorny shrub, light green leaves made up of 12 leaflets, pale lemon flowers in late spring

Carpinus betulus ♀
↕25m (80ft) ↔ 20m (70ft), as a tree pyramid-shaped, rounded when mature; as hedge (*see above*) retains brown leaves over winter

Caryopteris × *clandonensis* 'Kew Blue'
↕1m (3ft) ↔ 1.5m (5ft), excellent on chalky soils, leaves silver-grey underneath, attractive seedheads ✳✳✳

CASSIOPE

late spring to early summer

ORIGINATING FROM WINDSWEPT ARCTIC and alpine regions, this is a small group of dwarf, evergreen shrubs with a ground-hugging habit. They have tiny, overlapping, almost scale-like leaves that clasp the short, slender stems. In late spring and early summer, they produce tiny, nodding, bell-shaped flowers that hang singly or in pairs. The flowers are white, sometimes tinged red. Cassiope do best in acid (lime-free) soil and need plenty of moisture. They are so small that they are really only suitable for the rock garden or alpine trough, or perhaps planted in drifts in open woodland. 'Edinburgh' is the easiest to grow, and looks good with dwarf rhododendrons and conifers in an open position.

Hardiness Fully hardy ✳✳✳. Late frosts may damage the flowers.
Cultivation Best grown in a sheltered site in moist, acid (lime-free) soil in partial shade or an open sunny site. *C. tetragona* tolerates some lime. **Sow** seed in a container in a cold frame in autumn (*see pp.391–392*). **Take** semi-ripe cuttings in summer (*see p.394*), and layer shoots in autumn or early spring (*see p.395*).

CATALPA

spring to late autumn

CATALPAS ARE DECIDUOUS TREES with year-round appeal, with their showy, often beautifully coloured foliage, large flowers, and distinctive seed pods. The bell-shaped flowers are borne in upright clusters in mid- and late summer. They are followed in autumn by bean-like seed pods, usually more than 30cm (1ft) long. Catalpas have a wide, spreading habit and are best admired when grown as specimen trees in a lawn. Several varieties can be pollarded (cutting the trunk to a metre, then cutting stems back to this stubby head each year) to produce lollipop-shaped, foliage shrubs with very large, ornamental leaves. They will thrive in sheltered town gardens.

Hardiness Fully hardy ✳✳✳, although soft, young shoots can be prone to frost damage.
Cultivation Grow in fertile, moist but well-drained soil in full sun, with shelter from strong winds. In cold gardens, protect young plants from severe frosts with fleece. **Prune** in late winter or early spring, either to pollard (*see above*), or in trees, only to maintain a healthy branch framework. **Sow** seed in pots in autumn (*see pp.391–392*). **Take** softwood cuttings in late spring or summer (*p.394*).

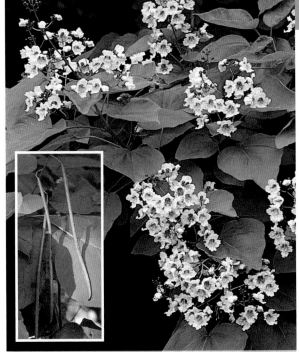

Catalpa bignonioides ♀ (Indian bean tree)
↕↔ 15m (50ft), broad heart-shaped leaves, fragrant flowers, pencil-thin seed pods to 40cm (16in) long (*see inset*)

Cassiope 'Edinburgh' ♀
↕↔ to 25m (10in), low-growing but with upright shoots, flowers produced at stem tips in late spring

Catalpa bignonioides 'Aurea' ♀
↕↔ 10m (30ft), slow-growing, leaves bronze when young and unfold in early summer, good pollarded to form a shrub (*see inset*)

Catalpa speciosa
↕↔ 15m (50ft), spreading habit, flowers larger and showier than most other catalpas, seed pods to 50cm (20in) long

CEANOTHUS

California lilac   *spring and autumn*

VIGOROUS, SPREADING SHRUBS, California lilacs are
grown for their masses of usually blue, but sometimes
white or pink flowers. They flower abundantly, in
small fluffy clusters at the tips of stems or on small
sideshoots. Most of the evergreen ceanothus are best
suited to growing against a wall or fence or in a
sheltered spot. Prostrate or low-growing species make
superb ground-cover plants and are ideal for sloping
banks. The deciduous types, generally hardier than
the evergreens, make more compact plants, especially
if pruned annually back to a stubby framework of
stems, and are ideal in a border. California lilacs are
not very long-lived, and dislike being transplanted.

Hardiness Fully hardy ✳✳✳ to frost-hardy ✳✳.

Cultivation Grow in any reasonably fertile soil in full sun, sheltered
from strong, cold winds. Tolerant of limy soils, but may develop yellow
leaves (chlorosis) on shallow, chalky soils. **Prune** in early spring, lightly
trimming evergreens to maintain a good shape, and cutting deciduous
types back to a permanent framework; treat all wall-trained plants as
for deciduous species. **Take** greenwood cuttings of deciduous types in
summer or semi-ripe cuttings of all types in late summer (*see p.394*).

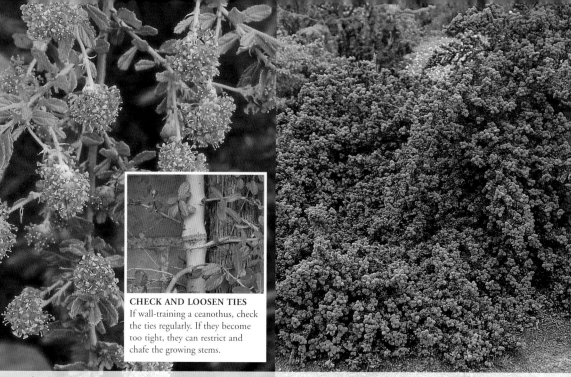

CHECK AND LOOSEN TIES
If wall-training a ceanothus, check
the ties regularly. If they become
too tight, they can restrict and
chafe the growing stems.

Ceanothus 'Cascade' ♥
↕↔ 4m (12ft), vigorous, arching evergreen, flowering from spring to
early summer ✳✳

Ceanothus 'Blue Mound' ♥
↕ 1.5m (5ft) ↔ 2m (6ft), prostrate, mound-forming evergreen,
flowering in late spring ✳✳

Ceanothus 'Blue Cushion'
↕ 45–75cm (18–30in) ↔ 1–2m (3–6ft), spreading but dense and tidy evergreen, ideal as a ground-cover
plant, flowering profusely in summer ✳✳

Ceanothus × *pallidus* 'Perle Rose'
↕↔ 1.5m (5ft), bushy, deciduous type, flowering from midsummer to
autumn ✳✳✳

CEDRUS
Cedar   *year-round*

THESE LARGE, EVERGREEN conifers make impressive specimen trees, needing plenty of space if their stature is to be fully appreciated (although there are some dwarf cultivars). Conical when young, they later develop spreading, horizontal branches. Cedars are best grown on their own, or with other large trees where space allows; they are very long-lived. Their needles are arranged in clusters on short shoots; there are cedars with either bright golden or glaucous blue foliage, as well as plain green. Male cones are cylindrical and light brown; female cones are oblong or barrel-shaped, and green when they first appear, ripening and turning brown over two years.

‡to 40m (130ft)
↔to 10m (30ft)

Hardiness Fully hardy ✲✲✲.

Cultivation Grow in any reasonably fertile soil in an open, sunny position. **Prune** only if the trees happen to produce two leading shoots, cutting out the weaker shoot in autumn. **Sow** seed (*see pp.391–393*) in spring after keeping them moist and in a refrigerator at 0–5°C (32–41°F) for three weeks.

CERATOSTIGMA
Chinese plumbago   *late summer to autumn*

TRUE BLUE, LATE-SUMMER FLOWERS, from pale Wedgwood to deep indigo, distinguish these small shrubs, all growing to about 1m (3ft) tall. The group also includes the woody-based perennial *Ceratostigma plumbaginoides*, which is half the height and perfect for the front of a border. There are deciduous, evergreen, or semi-evergreen species, the leaves of all turning red in autumn to provide a brilliant foil for late flowers. Their colouring is particularly dramatic in a mixed or shrub border next to yellow daylilies (*Hemerocallis, see p.258*) or St. John's wort (*Hypericum, see p.74*). Growth often dies back in very cold winters, but usually regrows in spring.

Hardiness Fully hardy ✲✲✲.

Cultivation Grow in light, reasonably fertile soil, in full sun. **Prune back** to within 2.5cm (1in) of a permanent framework after flowering or in early spring. Remove any growth that has been damaged during winter in spring; new shoots will appear from the base. **Take** softwood cuttings in spring or semi-ripe cuttings in summer (*see p.394*). Shoots can be layered (*see p.395*) in autumn. Susceptible to powdery mildew (*see also* Mildew, *p.398*); treat badly affected plants with fungicide.

CERCIDIPHYLLUM
Katsura tree   *autumn*

FIERY AUTUMN DISPLAYS OF yellow, orange, and red leaves that smell of burnt sugar when crushed are the chief attraction of this tree. The mid-green, oval to rounded leaves are also bronze when young. The best autumn colour is produced on acid (lime-free) soils. All katsuras belong to one species, *Cercidiphyllum japonicum*. There is a weeping form, and also a variety that is a smaller tree, despite being called *magnificum*. Planted as a specimen tree, the katsura can show off its form, pyramidal when young and becoming more rounded with age. Open woodland settings are also attractive if space allows.

Hardiness Fully hardy ✲✲✲, although the young leaves may be damaged by late frosts. New foliage should grow again.

Cultivation Grow in good, fertile soil enriched with plenty of well-rotted organic matter in sun or partial shade, sheltered from cold, drying winds. **Prune out** any crossing branches or those that spoil the shape of the tree in late winter or early spring. Plants often develop several main stems, but these can be reduced to one if desired, provided that the tree is still young. **Take** semi-ripe cuttings in midsummer (*see p.394*).

Cedrus deodara 'Aurea' ♀
‡5m (15ft), a slow-growing cultivar with golden-yellow spring foliage that becomes greener in summer

Ceratostigma willmottianum ♀
‡1m (3ft) ↔ 1.5m (5ft), bushy deciduous shrub with purple-edged leaves, turning red in autumn

Cercidiphyllum japonicum ♀ (Katsura tree)
‡20m (70ft) ↔ 15m (50ft), eventual size is affected by climate, and the tree tends to remain smaller in cooler areas

CERCIS

Redbud

spring and autumn

‡↔ to 10m (30ft)

DECIDUOUS TREES from woodland edges, these make excellent specimen plants in a lawn or in a large shrub border. They are grown for their foliage and their clusters of pink or purple flowers, borne in profusion in spring before the leaves. The flowers of the Judas tree, *Cercis siliquastrum*, appear directly on the branches and even the trunk. This is the largest species; choose *C. chinensis* or *C. canadensis* for a smaller garden; the latter can also be kept small by pollarding (cut the trunk to a metre, then cut the shoots that emerge back to this head each year). The leaves of all species are heart-shaped, and turn yellow in autumn.

Hardiness Fully hardy ✳✳✳; frosts may damage young growth.

Cultivation Grow in fertile, moist but well-drained soil in full sun or partial shade. Plant while the trees are young; older plants resent root disturbance. **Prune out** crossing branches in late winter or early spring to maintain a healthy, well-shaped framework. *C. canadensis* 'Forest Pansy' can be pollarded in early spring for larger, showier foliage.

Sow seed (*see pp.391–392*) in containers in a cold frame in autumn. **Take** semi-ripe cuttings (*see p.394*) in summer.

CHAENOMELES

Flowering quince,
Japanese quince, Japonica

winter, spring, and autumn

‡ to 2.5m (8ft)
↔ to 5cm (15ft)

THESE VERSATILE SHRUBS, among the first to flower, are usually grown in shrub borders or trained against a wall or fence, but also make useful ground cover or an informal hedge, even in shade. Deciduous and spiny-branched, they flower in shades of red and pink. The flowers, single or double, are borne all along the stems, appearing before and with the leaves. They are followed in autumn by apple-like, yellow to green fruits, which are edible after being cooked, although the true edible quince is a different tree, *Cydonia*.

Hardiness Fully hardy ✳✳✳.

Cultivation Grow in reasonably fertile soil: they are best not planted in very limy (alkaline) soil, where the leaves may yellow (chlorotic). Position in full sun or partial shade. **Cut back** flowered shoots after flowering: cut to strong buds lower down, or if wall-trained cut back to the permanent framework. **Sow** seed (*see pp.391–393*) in containers in a cold frame or outdoors in a seedbed. **Take** semi-ripe cuttings (*see p.394*) in summer or layer shoots (*see p.395*) in autumn.

Chaenomeles × superba 'Crimson and Gold' ✿
‡ 1m (3ft) ↔ 2m (6ft), later flowering than others, into late spring, green fruit ripening to yellow in autumn

Cercis canadensis 'Forest Pansy' ✿ (Eastern redbud)
‡↔ 5m (15ft), may not flower in all locations, but the purple foliage gives a reliable display

Chaenomeles speciosa 'Moerloosei' ✿
‡ 2.5m (8ft) ↔ 5m (15ft), particularly early-flowering, with fragrant fruits (*see inset*) in autumn

Chaenomeles × californica 'Enchantress'
‡ 2.5m (8ft) ↔ 2m (6ft), the autumn fruits are large and golden yellow

CHAMAECYPARIS
False cypress   *year-round*

IDEAL FOR HEDGING, these evergreen, coniferous trees are not overly vigorous and tolerate some clipping; their attractive growth habit also makes many of them handsome specimen plants. Grow them with other conifers such as *Cupressus* (*see p.47*), or with large rhododendrons (*see pp.104–107*). There are also many dwarf or slow-growing cultivars, and these can be used in smaller borders or even in large rock gardens. The leaves are scale-like and flattened; contact with the foliage may aggravate some skin allergies. False cypresses bear round or oval male cones in spring, which are followed in summer by round or angular female cones that ripen in autumn.

Hardiness Fully hardy ✳✳✳.

Cultivation Grow in moist but well-drained, preferably neutral to acid (lime-free) soil, although they will tolerate deep, chalky soils. Position in full sun. **Trim** trees used for hedging from late spring to autumn, but do not cut into older wood. **Sow** seed (*see pp.391–393*) in a seedbed outdoors in spring or take semi-ripe cuttings (*see p.394*) in late summer. If heavy infestations of conifer aphids cause browning of foliage, use insecticide in spring.

CHIMONANTHUS PRAECOX
Wintersweet   *winter*

POWERFULLY FRAGRANT, WAXY flowers hang from the bare shoots of *Chimonanthus praecox* throughout winter. This deciduous shrub has flowers that are pale sulphur-yellow, stained brown or purple inside. Young plants take a few years to reach flowering age. Although the shrub is not unattractive in leaf, winter is its real season of interest, so plant it near a doorway or where you will come across it and its extraordinary scent on winter walks. It can also be trained against a sunny wall, and this may be advisable in cooler areas, because good, sunny summers are needed to ripen the wood in an open position.

Hardiness Fully hardy ✳✳✳; frosts may damage unripened wood.

Cultivation Grow in any fertile, well-drained soil in full sun. **Prune** only mature shrubs that flower regularly in late winter, when dormant, or in early spring. Cut out any crossing or misshapen branches to maintain a healthy framework and good shape; cut back the shoots of wall-trained plants to 2–4 buds above the permanent framework of branches. **Sow** seed (*see pp.391–392*) in containers in a cold frame as soon as it is ripe. **Take** softwood cuttings (*see p.394*) in summer.

CHIONANTHUS
Fringe tree   *summer*

LARGE, ATTRACTIVE SHRUBS, fringe trees are grown for their long, narrow leaves and their fragrant, white flowers, which are borne in clusters during summer. Two spreading, deciduous shrubs from this large and varied genus are grown in gardens: *Chionanthus retusus* has upright flower clusters and peeling bark, while *C. virginicus* has hanging flower clusters and larger leaves that have bright, golden-yellow autumn colour. In autumn, the flowers of both are followed by blue-black fruits. Fringe trees make excellent specimen plants; they also work well grown in a shrub border along with plants such as abelias (*see p.14*), choisyas (*see p.40*), or camellias (*see pp.32–33*).

Hardiness Fully hardy ✳✳✳.

Cultivation Grow in reasonably fertile soil in full sun: *C. retusus* tolerates limy (alkaline) soil, but *C. virginicus* needs an acid soil. Flowering and fruiting are best in climates with hot summers. **Prune out** crossing or badly placed branches in winter or early spring, to prevent growth becoming unhealthily crowded. **Sow** seed (*see pp.391–392*) in containers in a cold frame in autumn; germination may take as long as 18 months.

TREES AND SHRUBS

39

① *lawsoniana* 'Pembury Blue' ♀ ↕15m (50ft) ② *noot-katensis* 'Pendula' ♀ ↕30m (100ft) ③ *obtusa* 'Nana Aurea' ♀ ↕2m (6ft) ④ *pisifera* 'Filifera Aurea' ♀ ↕12m (40ft)

Chimonanthus praecox 'Grandiflorus' ♀
↕4m (12ft) ↔ 3m (10ft), flowers that are both larger and a deeper yellow than the species

Chionanthus virginicus
↕3m (10ft) ↔ 3m (10ft) or more, the lower branches can be pruned back to the trunk to encourage a more tree-like form

CHOISYA

Mexican orange blossom *year-round*

THE GLOSSY, AROMATIC FOLIAGE of these evergreen shrubs ensures that they have year-round appeal in any garden, quite apart from the fact that most give a superb, late summer and autumn show of abundant, starry, sweetly fragrant flowers. Of the commonly available Mexican orange blossoms, 'Aztec Pearl' and *Choisya ternata* are particularly good value, since they also produce an early flush of blooms in late spring before the main flowering towards the end of summer. Although *C. ternata* SUNDANCE rarely flowers, this is more than made up for by its spring foliage, which can light up the dullest border with a ray of sunshine.

Hardiness Fully hardy ✳✳✳ to frost-hardy ✳✳.

Cultivation Choisyas prefer a fertile, well-drained soil in full sun, but tolerate partial shade. The frost-hardy varieties benefit from the extra warmth of a south-facing wall, and a winter mulch. **Trim** any shoots that spoil the shape of the shrub after flowering. **Take** semi-ripe cuttings in summer (*see p.394*). Snails and slugs have a liking for these shrubs; while the plant is small and vulnerable, it is well worth discouraging them (*see p.260*).

CISTUS

Rock rose, Sun rose *early to late summer*

↕↔ most to 1m (3ft), some to 2m (6ft)

ROCK ROSES ARE EVERGREENS, grown for their profuse, saucer-shaped flowers in white to purplish-pink. They appear from early to late summer; each bloom lasts only one day but is quickly replaced to keep the display going. Rock roses thrive in sunny spots in a shrub border, at the base of a wall, around a patio, or spilling over the side of a raised bed. Usefully, they appreciate dry conditions and poor soil, and so grow very well as low-maintenance container plants and alongside demanding plants such as shrub roses that take a lot out of the soil. They can be short-lived; it is worth taking cuttings to make replacement plants.

Hardiness Frost-hardy ✳✳.

Cultivation Grow rock roses in full sun, in poor to reasonably fertile, well-drained soil, including chalky soil. **Pinch out** the growing tips of young plants to encourage a bushy habit; lightly trim shoots that spoil the shape of the shrub in spring, or after flowering. Old, woody plants are best replaced. **Sow** seed (*see pp.391–392*) in a cold frame when it is ripe, or in spring. **Take** softwood cuttings in summer (*see p.394*).

CLERODENDRUM

late summer to autumn

THIS IS A LARGE GROUP OF TROPICAL and subtropical plants, although some of the elegant, shrubby species are robust enough to be grown outdoors in cooler, temperate climates. The hardy, deciduous shrubs include *Clerodendrum trichotomum*, a large shrub for a large garden or woodland glade, and the glory flower (*C. bungei*), smaller but still up to 2m (6ft) tall. This species is only frost-hardy and will be happiest in a warm, sheltered border. Both are valued for their large clusters of often fragrant flowers, usually produced from late summer to autumn.

Hardiness Fully hardy ✳✳✳ to frost-tender ❋.

Cultivation Grow in soil enriched with well-rotted organic matter to make sure it is fertile and moist but well-drained, in full sun.
Pruning is rarely needed by *C. trichotomum;* wayward branches can be removed, or shoots trimmed, in late winter or early spring. *C. bungei* should be cut back to a low, permanent framework in early spring.
Sow seed (*see pp.391–392*) at 13–18°C (55–64°F) in spring. **Take** semi-ripe cuttings in summer (*see p.394*), rooting them in a heated propagator. *C. bungei* tends to produce suckers (a new shoot growing from below ground) that can make new plants: scrape back the soil to find one that has developed some roots in autumn or spring; carefully cut it away from the parent plant; and pot it up.

Choisya ternata SUNDANCE ♀ ('Lich')
↕↔ 2.5m (8ft), the buttery young foliage of this cultivar is best in bright sun, achieving only a greenish-yellow in shade ✳✳

① × *argenteus* 'Peggy Sammons' ♀ ↕↔ to 1m (3ft)
② × *dansereaui* 'Decumbens' ♀ ↕↔ 1m (3ft) ③ × *hybridus*
↕↔ to 1.5m (5ft) ④ × *skanbergii* ♀ ↕↔ to 90cm (36in)

Clerodendrum trichotomum var. *fargesii* ♀
↕↔ 5–6m (15–20ft), dark clusters of fruits that follow the pinky-white flowers in midsummer to late autumn ✳✳✳

CLETHRA

Summer-sweet, Sweet
pepper bush, White alder

*mid- to
late summer*

THESE EVERGREEN AND DECIDUOUS SHRUBS and trees
are grown for their handsome foliage and spikes of
white flowers. The blooms are very fragrant and are
borne from mid- to late summer; sited beneath the
canopy of a woodland garden, they will perfume the
still air wonderfully. Summer-sweets can also be
grown in a shady corner of a shrubbery, or close to
a seating area where their scent can be enjoyed. The
lily-of-the-valley tree (*Clethra arborea*) is tender, and
in temperate climates is best grown in a large tub so
that it can be moved under cover to a conservatory
or greenhouse for the winter.

Hardiness Fully hardy ❋❋❋ to half-hardy ❋.

Cultivation Grow in dappled shade in acid (lime-free), fertile, moist,
well-drained soil. In containers, use an ericaceous compost. **Prune out**
wayward branches in late winter, and for *C. alnifolia,* once mature, cut
back a few of the old stems to the base; this stimulates strong new
growth. *C. arborea* need only be deadheaded, although it can be
pruned to fit the available space. **Sow** seed (*see pp.391–392*) at
6–12°C (43–54°F) in spring or autumn. **Take** semi-ripe cuttings of
deciduous species in mid- or late summer (*see p.394*).

COLUTEA

Bladder senna

summer

↕↔ 2–3m (6–10ft)

DECORATIVE, GREENISH-BROWN,
inflated seed pods give these deciduous
shrubs their common name. They are
good all-round plants with soft, pale
or blue-green foliage and, in summer,
large, yellow or brown, pea-like flowers that are
followed by the fat pods. Bladder sennas are very
resilient plants, and can be used in problematic sites
such as exposed and coastal areas, sloping, free-
draining banks, gardens affected by urban pollution,
and sites with poor, dry soils.

Hardiness Fully hardy ❋❋❋ to frost-hardy ❋❋.

Cultivation Bladder sennas will tolerate most conditions although
they prefer reasonably fertile, well-drained soil in full sun. **Prune** them
according to the available space; either removing only wayward, dead
or damaged branches, or keeping the shrub small by cutting it down
to a low, permanent framework in late winter or early spring.
C. arborescens can also be trained as a standard. **Sow** seed (*see
pp.391–392*) in autumn or early spring and germinate with the
protection of a cold frame.

CORDYLINE

Cabbage palm,
Cabbage tree

year-round

THE PALM-LIKE CORDYLINES are architectural shrubs
that can bring a touch of the exotic to a temperate
garden. In frost-free areas, use them as focal points;
given the time and space most species will become
tree-like in stature. In colder areas, grow them in pots
and move them under frost-free cover in winter;
cordylines make handsome plants in a conservatory or
greenhouse. These plants are mainly valued for their
spiky, leathery leaves, often variegated or brightly
coloured. An occasional bonus in summer are tall,
heavy stems of white, perfumed flowers, followed by
bead-like berries in white, red, purple, or blue.

Hardiness Half-hardy ❋❋ to frost-tender ❋; some cultivars can
withstand freezing, but the top-growth may be damaged.

Cultivation Grow in fertile, well-drained soil in full sun or semi-
shade; the cultivars with coloured foliage prefer some shade. In
containers, use any good potting compost with some added grit and
top-dress annually in spring (*see p.386*). **Sow** seed (*see pp.391–392*)
in spring at 16°C (61°F), or for an instant result cut well-rooted suckers
(small plantlets growing up around the central crown) away from the
parent plant in spring and pot them up individually.

Clethra arborea (Lily-of-the-valley tree)
↕8m (25ft) ↔ 6m (20ft), young shoots are red, the spikes of flowers
may be up to 15cm (6in) long ❋

Colutea arborescens (Bladder senna)
↕↔ 3m (10ft), flowers over a very long period in summer, often still
in bloom as the first pods are developing ❋❋❋

Cordyline australis 'Torbay Red' ♀
↕3–10m (10–30ft) ↔ 1–4m (3–12ft), the eventual size is largely
dependent on the prevailing climate ❋❋

CORNUS

Dogwood

year-round

BEAUTIFUL FLOWERHEADS, DECORATIVE BARK, and vibrant autumn leaves make these outstanding garden plants. Dogwoods include deciduous shrubs, small trees, and woody-based perennials. Some, such as *Cornus alternifolia*, have an airy, tiered shape, and make graceful specimen trees. Many of the shrubby types, such as *C. alba*, *C. sanguinea*, and *C. sericea* and their cultivars, are grown principally for their bright red, yellow, or green bark. These dogwoods are especially welcome in winter, when the thickets of stems seem to glow with colour, at its most intense if the plants are regularly coppiced. Creeping *C. canadensis* can be used in woodland or as ground cover in a shrub border. The small, starry flowers are borne in clusters at the tips of the shoots, and in dogwoods grown for their flowering displays, for example *C. capitata*, *C. florida*, *C. kousa*, *C. nuttallii*, and many hybrids, they are surrounded by prominent petal-like bracts (modified leaves), which may be cream, white, or pink. In some plants, the berries or strawberry-like fruits that follow the flowers in autumn could cause mild stomach upset if eaten.

Hardiness Fully hardy ❀❀❀ to frost-hardy ❀❀.

Cultivation Dogwoods can be grown in sun or partial shade. **Plant** flowering dogwoods (those with large bracts) in fertile, neutral to acid soil with plenty of well-rotted organic matter added to it. All other types tolerate a wide range of conditions. Those that are grown for their winter stem colour are best positioned in full sun. **Prune** those grown for stem colour hard (coppice) every spring to produce young shoots, which have the brightest colour (*see below*). Other dogwoods require little pruning except to keep them within bounds or to maintain the shape of the shrub; cutting out one in four of the older shoots in late winter or early spring every year will restrict the spread of the shrub. **Renovate** neglected plants by cutting out old wood at the centre of the shrub. **Sow** seed in a seedbed in autumn, or expose it to a period of cold weather and sow in spring (*see pp.391–393*). Take hardwood cuttings (*see p.394*) of dogwoods grown for stem colour in autumn.

How to coppice dogwoods

Allow a full year after planting for the shrub to develop, then cut back hard before growth starts in spring. Afterwards apply a general organic fertilizer around the shrub to encourage strong new growth and mulch with a thick layer of well-rotted organic matter.

▷ **Pruning for coloured stems** *In the first year after planting, cut back all the stems to 5–8cm (2–3in) from the base. After this the stems can be cut back each spring to just above two buds of the previous year's growth; this allows the plant to develop into a larger shrub.*

Hardest pruned shrub remains smallest

Old wood will be hidden by shrubs in front

◁ **Staggered pruning** *Where shrubby dogwoods are planted in a group, coppicing to varying levels creates a sloping effect rather than a dense mass of stems of uniform height. This is particularly useful for breaking up a border and making it look more interesting.*

① *Cornus alba* 'Elegantissima' ♀ ‡↔ 3m (10ft), stems, leaves ② *alba* 'Kesselringii' ‡↔ 3m (10ft), stems, leaves ③ *alba* 'Sibirica' ♀ ‡↔ 3m (10ft), stems ④ *alba* 'Spaethii' ♀ ‡↔ 3m (10ft), stems, leaves ⑤ *alternifolia* 'Argentea' ♀ ‡ 3m (10ft) ↔ 2.5m (8ft), leaves ⑥ *capitata* ‡↔ 12m (40ft), flowers, fruits ⑦ *controversa* 'Variegata' ♀ ‡↔ 8m (25ft), flowers, leaves ⑧ 'Eddie's White Wonder' ‡ 6m (20ft) ↔ 5m (15ft), flowers, autumn leaves ⑨ *florida* 'Cherokee Chief' ♀ ‡ 6m

(20ft) ↔ 8m (25ft), flowers, autumn leaves ⑩ *florida* 'Spring Song' ‡6m (20ft) ↔ 8m (25ft), flowers, autumn leaves ⑪ *florida* 'Welchii' ‡6m (20ft) ↔ 8m (25ft), flowers, autumn leaves ⑫ *kousa* var. *chinensis* ♀ ‡7m (22ft) ↔ 5m (15ft), bark, flowers, autumn leaves ⑬ *kousa* 'China Girl' ‡7m (22ft) ↔ 5m (15ft), bark, flowers, autumn leaves ⑭ *kousa* 'Satomi' ♀ ‡7m (22ft) ↔ 5m (15ft), bark, flowers, autumn leaves ⑮ *macrophylla* ‡12m (40ft) ↔ 8m (25ft), flowers ⑯ *mas* ‡↔ 5m (15ft),

flowers, fruits, autumn leaves ⑰ 'Norman Hadden' ♀ ‡↔ 8m (25ft), flowers, fruits ⑱ *nuttallii* ‡12m (40ft) ↔ 8m (25ft), flowers, fruits ⑲ *nuttallii* 'Colrigo Giant' ‡12m (40ft) ↔ 8m (25ft), flowers, fruits ⑳ 'Porlock' ♀ ‡10m (30ft) ↔ 5m (15ft), flowers ㉑ *sanguinea* 'Winter Beauty' ‡3m (10ft) ↔ 2.5m (8ft), stems ㉒ *sericea* 'Flaviramea' ♀ ‡2m (6ft) ↔ 4m (12ft), stems ㉓ *sericea* 'Kelseyi' ‡75cm (30in) ↔ 1.5m (5ft), stems

CORYLOPSIS

spring

THE SLENDER, BARE SHOOTS of these small trees and shrubs bear fragile, pendent clusters of bell-shaped flowers in spring before the leaves emerge. The flower clusters are fragrant and are up to 15cm (6in) long. The leaves are broadly oval, and pale to dark green. These are graceful shrubs with open, spreading habits, and look handsome in partly shaded sites, such as in a woodland setting. Combine these trouble-free plants with other early flowering trees and shrubs, such as *Corylus avellana* 'Contorta' (*see right*), magnolias (*see p.86*), and small willows (*Salix, see pp.114–115*).

Hardiness Fully hardy ✱✱✱, although late frosts may damage the flowers.

Cultivation Corylopsis prefer reasonably fertile, acid (lime-free) soil that is reliably moist but well-drained and in partial shade. **Prune out** misplaced or crossing shoots if necessary, to maintain a good shape and healthy framework of shoots, immediately after flowering. **Take** greenwood cuttings – from slightly more mature shoots than softwood – in summer (*see p.394*). Layer shoots in autumn (*see p.395*).

CORYLUS

Hazel   *late winter, spring, and autumn*

LONG CATKINS AND ATTRACTIVE FOLIAGE and habits make hazels worthy garden plants. These small to medium-sized, deciduous shrubs and trees begin the season in late winter or spring by producing yellow, occasionally purple, male catkins. Broadly heart-shaped, toothed leaves follow that may be coloured. Some foliage displays autumnal tints. *Corylus avellana* 'Contorta', also called Harry Lauder's walking stick, has strikingly twisted stems that enhance the winter garden and are favourites with flower arrangers. Edible hazelnuts and filberts are produced by *C. avellana* and *C. maxima* in autumn. Larger hazels look good as specimens; use smaller species in a border with shrubs such as hamamelis (*see p.68*) or mahonias (*see p.87*).

Hardiness Fully hardy ✱✱✱.

Cultivation Hazels grow well in fertile, well-drained, preferably chalky (limy) soil, in sun or partial shade. **Remove** suckers (strong, straight growths from the base of the plant) as soon as you see them. **Layer** shoots (*see p.395*) in autumn. **Prune** if needed only to keep them in shape, in winter or early spring (*see p.383*).

COTINUS

Smoke bush   *summer and autumn*

‡5–10m (15–30ft)
↔ 5–8m (15–25ft)

THIS SMALL GROUP OF deciduous shrubs and small, bushy trees is prized for its ornamental, colourful foliage and unusual flowers. These are tiny, but mass in great plumes above the foliage in summer. They resemble puffs of smoke from a distance – hence the common name. The flowers are followed by tiny fruits lasting into autumn, when the foliage usually changes colour. That of *Cotinus coggygria* 'Royal Purple' turns from dark red-purple to red; that of *C.* 'Grace' from purple to a bright, translucent scarlet. They look particularly good in autumn as specimens or planted in groups.

Hardiness Fully hardy ✱✱✱.

Cultivation Cotinus prefer reasonably fertile, well-drained soil, in sun or partial shade. Purple-leaved types have the best-coloured foliage in full sun. **Cut out** misplaced or crossing shoots to maintain a well-shaped flowering shrub, in late winter or early spring (*see p.382*). For the best foliage display, keep 3–5 main stems to 60–90cm (24–36in) long and in early spring cut all shoots to 2–3 buds above the main stems. **Take** softwood cuttings (*see p.394*) in summer or layer shoots (*see p.395*) in spring.

Corylopsis glabrescens
‡↔ 5m (15ft), upright shrub, dark green leaves with blue-green undersides, flowers in mid-spring

Corylus avellana 'Contorta' (Corkscrew hazel)
‡↔ 5m (15ft), upright shrub with mid-green leaves, 6cm (2½in) catkins in late winter and early spring (*see inset*)

① *coggygria* 'Royal Purple' ‡↔ 5m (15ft), flowers green, turning grey in autumn ② 'Grace' ‡ 6m (20ft) ↔ 5m (15ft), vigorous, flowers purple-pink

COTONEASTER

summer and autumn

DENSE BUT DAINTY FOLIAGE, a variety of ornamental forms, and autumn berries ensure this plant a place in many gardens. There are many deciduous, semi-evergreen, and evergreen shrubs to choose from. Tiny, pink or white flowers in summer are followed by masses of berries in vivid reds and yellows – all much appreciated by birds. The wide range of growth habits makes cotoneasters suitable for many sites. They can be grown as freestanding shrubs, weeping trees, hedging, trained against walls, or as ground cover. You can also use dwarf species in a rock garden.

Hardiness Fully hardy ✳✳✳.

Cultivation Reasonably fertile, well-drained soil in sun or partial shade is best, but most cotoneasters tolerate dry conditions. Larger shrubs need protection from cold, drying winds. Dwarf evergreens fruit better if they are sheltered. Most cotoneasters require little pruning, but will tolerate hard renovation pruning (*see p.384*) if required. **Trim** formal hedges in mid- or late summer. **Take** greenwood cuttings of deciduous species in early summer and semi-ripe cuttings of evergreens in late summer (*see p.394*).

Cotoneaster divaricatus
↕ 2.5m (8ft) ↔ 3m (10ft), erect, deciduous shrub, dense leaves turn red in autumn (*see inset*), pink-tinged white flowers in summer

Cotoneaster atropurpureus 'Variegatus' ♥
↕ 45cm (18in) ↔ 90cm (35in), deciduous, compact, prostrate or wall shrub, leaf edges pink and red in autumn, orange-red berries

Cotoneaster horizontalis ♥ (Fishbone cotoneaster)
↕ 1m (3ft) ↔ 5m (15ft), deciduous shrub, spreads in herringbone pattern, red autumn leaves (*inset*), pinky-white flowers in late spring

Cotoneaster × watereri 'John Waterer' ♥
↕ ↔ 5m (15ft), vigorous, evergreen or semi-evergreen shrub or tree, clusters of white flowers in summer

CRATAEGUS

Hawthorn   *late spring and autumn*

THESE EXTREMELY HARDY TREES and shrubs are particularly valuable in exposed or coastal gardens. They are usually spiny, deciduous, and medium-sized, with a rounded or spreading habit. Their mid- to dark green foliage often has attractive tints in autumn. Hawthorns produce flat clusters of white or pink blossoms at the ends of the branches. Birds enjoy the berries that follow in autumn, which are mostly scarlet, but sometimes are coloured black, orange, yellow, or blue-green. *Crataegus laevigata* and *C. monogyna* make good hedging plants. The berries may cause stomach upsets if eaten.

Hardiness Fully hardy ✸✸✸.

Cultivation Hawthorns will grow in any soil, except waterlogged ground, in full sun or partial shade. **Prune out** any crossing or misshapen branches in winter or early spring, to maintain a good shape and healthy framework of branches. Trim hedges after flowering or in autumn. **Remove** seed from the berries as soon as they are ripe and sow in a seedbed or in containers (*see pp.391–393*). Germination may take up to 18 months.

CRYPTOMERIA JAPONICA

Japanese cedar   *year-round*

THIS CONIFEROUS TREE FROM THE FORESTS of China and Japan is grown for its neat, conical or columnar habit and evergreen foliage. This is produced in cloud-like clumps of soft, glossy, dark green needles. Large, round, female cones are borne singly and the smaller, male cones cluster at the shoot tips. The red-brown bark is rugged and fibrous. This is a large tree, reaching up to 25m (80ft), but there are also several smaller cultivars that have pleasingly tinted foliage. Japanese cedars make handsome specimen trees, and the smaller types also blend well in a border with rhododendrons and azaleas (*see pp.104–107*). Try dwarf forms in a large rock garden with heaths (*Erica, see pp.52–53*) and heathers (*Calluna, see p.31*).

Hardiness Fully hardy ✸✸✸.

Cultivation The Japanese cedar tolerates most well-drained soils, including chalky (limy) soils, in full sun or partial shade. It grows best in deep, fertile, moist but well-drained soil that has been enriched with organic matter. **Provide** shelter from cold, drying winds. This shrub requires no formal pruning. **Cut back** stems to within 60–90cm (24–36in) of ground level in spring, to reshape untidy specimens.

x CUPRESSOCYPARIS LEYLANDII

Leyland cypress   *year-round*

‡35m (120ft)
↔5m (15ft)

THIS WIDELY GROWN CONIFEROUS TREE is most often used as a hedging or screening plant. It has a tapering habit and smooth bark that becomes stringy as it ages. The dense sprays of scale-like foliage are dark green with grey tints. Its dark brown female cones are larger than its yellow male cones. Cultivars with tinted foliage are available, in tones of gold, grey-green, blue-grey, bronze, and lime-green. The Leyland cypress is a very fast-growing tree – if well maintained from a young plant, it forms a fine hedge or specimen tree, but if neglected, it can become a monster. If it grows too big, it is better to take it out and start again: you cannot cut it back into old wood because it will not regrow.

Hardiness Fully hardy ✸✸✸.

Cultivation Any deep, fertile, well-drained soil in full sun or partial shade will suit this vigorous tree. When grown as a specimen, it needs no formal pruning. **Trim** hedging plants two to three times a year (without cutting into the old wood), finishing in early autumn (*see p.384*). **Take** semi-ripe cuttings (*see p.394*) in late summer.

Craetaegus laevigata 'Paul's Scarlet' ♥
‡↔ to 8m (25ft), thorny, deciduous tree, lobed leaves, abundant flower clusters in late spring are occasionally followed by red berries

Cryptomeria japonica 'Elegans Compacta' ♥
‡2–4m (6–12ft) ↔ 6m (20ft), conical shrub, leaves are dark green when new, turning bronze in autumn, as shown here

x *Cupressocyparis leylandii* ♥
Often grown as a hedge which must be trimmed several times a year to keep it under control

CUPRESSUS

Cypress   *year-round*

FROM THE SLENDER SILHOUETTE of the Italian cypress (*Cupressus sempervirens*) to the more stately Monterey cypress (*C. macrocarpa*), these evergreen, coniferous trees have attractive columnar or conical habits. There are also a few weeping cypresses. Cypresses have scale-like, sometimes glaucous foliage in dark, grey- or blue-green. The bark sometimes peels; the smooth cypress (*C. arizonica* var. *glabra*) has reddish-purple bark. Female cones are small and round and remain for several years; male cones are green and found on the shoot tips. Large cypresses are excellent specimen trees; smaller ones can be grouped with other conifers or shrubs. *C. macrocarpa* is good as a hedging plant, especially in coastal areas.

Hardiness Fully hardy ✳✳✳ to half-hardy ✳.

Cultivation Since they come from dry, hillside forests, cypresses tolerate dry soils and grow in any well-drained soil in full sun. Provide shelter from cold, drying winds. **Trim** hedges in late spring (*see p.384*), but do not cut back into old wood because it will not regrow. **Take** semi-ripe cuttings (*see p.394*) in late summer. **Canker** may cause bark to recede, killing twigs and then the tree; cut affected branches back to healthy wood to stop it spreading.

CYTISUS

Broom   *spring and summer*

ABUNDANT, PEA-LIKE FLOWERS are produced by these deciduous to evergreen shrubs in spring and summer. The flowers are often fragrant and are borne singly or in clusters, in a variety of shades from white and crimson to yellow. Long, flat, often downy seed pods follow. The usually small, palm-like leaves are mostly mid-green, but the shrubs often become leafless as they mature. Brooms vary in habit from prostrate or spreading to upright, arching or bushy. Smaller species and cultivars suit a rock garden and larger species a shrub or mixed border. The splendid, tree-like *Cytisus battandieri* (*see below*) can be trained against a south-facing wall or fence, where it benefits from the shelter and its silvery leaves reflect the sun.

Hardiness Fully hardy ✳✳✳ to frost-tender ❄.

Cultivation Grow brooms in reasonably fertile soil in full sun. Less hardy species need protection from cold, drying winds. Brooms thrive in poor, acid soils, but some may become chlorotic (show yellowing leaves) on shallow, chalky soils. **Plant** young container-grown shrubs because older plants resent root disturbance. **Prune** flowered shoots to 2–3 buds above the main stems, after flowering. Do not cut into old wood because they do not regrow readily.

Cytisus × praecox 'Warminster' ♀ (Warminster broom)
↕ 1.2m (4ft) ↔ 1.5m (5ft), deciduous, compact shrub with arching stems, flowers in mid- to late summer ✳✳✳

Cupressus macrocarpa 'Goldcrest' ♀
↕ to 5m (15ft) ↔ 2.5m (8ft), narrowly conical, shallowly ridged bark, dense foliage ✳✳✳

Cytisus battandieri ♀ (Pineapple broom)
↕↔ 5m (15ft), deciduous, upright shrub, silvery leaves, pineapple scented flowers from mid- to late summer ✳✳

Cytisus scoparius (Common broom)
↕↔ 1.5m (5ft), deciduous, upright shrub with arching stems, abundant flowers in late spring ✳✳✳

DABOECIA CANTABRICA

Cantabrican heath,
St. Dabeoc's heath

early summer to mid-autumn

THIS EVERGREEN, HEATHER-LIKE SHRUB has given rise to a large number of garden plants. They are grown for their spikes of urn-shaped flowers, appearing from early summer to mid-autumn, in white and purple-crimson, and are typically larger than those of other heaths and heathers. The leaves are small, thin, and dark green. The species has a height of 25–40cm (10–16in) and spreads to 65cm (26in), but the cultivars vary in size. These shrubs make useful ground-cover plants, around taller heathers or other acid-loving shrubs such as rhododendrons (*see pp.104–107*). If your soil is alkaline, grow them in large pots or a raised bed, in ericaceous compost.

Hardiness Fully hardy ❋❋❋ to half-hardy ❋.

Cultivation These shrubs need well-drained, acid (lime-free) soil in full sun; they will tolerate neutral soil in partial shade. Daboecias are susceptible to root rot, particularly on heavy, wet soils, so on clay soil dig in some coarse grit to improve drainage. **Prune back** flowered growth in early or mid-spring each year to keep the plant shapely; the easiest way to do this is by clipping it over with shears. **Take** semi-ripe cuttings (*see p.394*) in midsummer.

DAPHNE

winter to spring

DELICIOUSLY FRAGRANT FLOWERS are borne very early, or sometimes very late, in the year on these shrubs, so plant them where the wonderful scent can be fully appreciated. The flowers, in shades of red-purple, pink, white, and yellow, may be followed by round, white, pink, red, orange, or purple fruits. Mostly slow-growing, daphnes are generally compact enough for even small gardens. They may be upright, bushy, or prostrate in habit, and there are deciduous, semi-evergreen, and evergreen species, all with neat, usually dark but sometimes variegated leaves. All parts of these plants are toxic, and the sap may irritate skin.

Hardiness Fully hardy ❋❋❋ to frost-hardy ❋❋.

Cultivation Grow in reasonably fertile soil that is well-drained but does not dry out, and is preferably neutral (neither acid nor alkaline). Position in sun or partial shade; all resent root disturbance, so choose the site carefully. **Mulch** annually with organic matter around the base (*see p.388*) to keep the roots cool and moist. **Prune** only if absolutely necessary, in late winter or early spring. **Sow** seed in a cold frame as soon as it is ripe (*see pp.391–392*). **Take** softwood cuttings in early and midsummer, and semi-ripe cuttings in late summer (*see p.394*).

Daphne cneorum (Garland flower)
↕ 15cm (6in) or more ↔ to 2m (6ft), trailing evergreen with pink or occasionally white, very fragrant flowers in late spring ❋❋❋

Daboecia cantabrica 'William Buchanan' ♥
↕ 35cm (14in) ↔ 55cm (22in) ❋❋

Daphne bholua 'Jacqueline Postill' ♥
↕ 2–4m (6–12ft) ↔ 1.5m (5ft), upright evergreen, fragrant flowers in winter or early spring, black-purple fruits ❋❋❋ (borderline)

Daphne mezereum 'Bowles' Variety'
↕ to 2m (6ft) ↔ 1m (3ft), vigorous, upright, deciduous shrub, flowers in late winter or early spring, followed by yellow fruits ❋❋❋

Daphne laureola subsp. *philippi*
‡45cm (18in) ↔ 60cm (24in), low, spreading evergreen, lightly
scented flowers in late winter and early spring, black fruits ✳✳✳

DAVIDIA INVOLUCRATA

Dove tree, Ghost tree,
Handkerchief tree

spring

THIS EXTRAORDINARILY BEAUTIFUL tree is festooned
with pure white bracts (modified leaves) along the
branches in spring. Its unique appearance is reflected
in the variety of common names. The leaves are up
to 15cm (6in) long, oval in shape with heart-shaped
bases and sharply pointed tips. Mid-green and
strongly veined, they have reddish stalks and soft hairs
underneath. The bracts surround small flowerheads,
which are followed by greenish-brown fruits in
autumn. Davidia is a large tree; it is related to the
dogwoods (*Cornus, see pp.42–43*), which include
more compact, but less dramatic, species suited
to smaller gardens.

Hardiness Fully hardy ✳✳✳.

Cultivation Grow in fertile, well-drained but moisture-retentive soil,
in sun or partial shade. Position where there is shelter from strong,
cold winds. **Trim out** any crossing or misplaced branches on young
trees in late winter or early spring. **Sow** whole fruits in a container as
soon as ripe (*see pp.391–392*): germination will take at least two
winters outdoors. Seed-raised trees may take up to ten years to reach
flowering size. **Take** hardwood cuttings in winter (*see p.394*).

DEUTZIA

spring to summer

‡↔ to 3m (10ft)

CLUSTERS OF STARRY, white or pink
flowers, fragrant on *Deutzia gracilis*
and *D. scabra*, almost smother these
deciduous shrubs from mid-spring to
midsummer. Most have oval leaves,
although some are prettily willow-
like. All are are easy to grow. The larger ones make
good specimen plants, often developing attractively
peeling bark as they mature, although in colder
regions it is best to grow the less hardy types among
other trees and shrubs, or in the shelter of a warm
wall. Try them alongside shrubs such as mock orange
(*Philadelphus, see p.93*) and weigelas (*see p.128*) for
a harmonious early-summer show.

Hardiness Fully hardy ✳✳✳ to frost-hardy ✳✳.

Cultivation Grow in fertile soil that is not too dry, ideally in full sun;
some tolerate partial shade. **Cut back** flowered stems to strong buds or
young shoots lower down. Encourage new growth on mature plants by
cutting one in three or four of the old branches to the base. **Sow** seed
in containers in a cold frame in autumn (*see pp.391–392*). **Take** softwood cuttings in summer or hardwood cuttings in autumn (*see p.394*).

Daphne mezereum (Mezereon)
‡1.2m (4ft) ↔ 1m (3ft), upright, deciduous cottage-garden classic,
flowers in late winter or early spring, fleshy red fruits ✳✳✳

Davidia involucrata ♀
‡15m (50ft) ↔ 10m (30ft), this tree needs plenty of space to
develop its shape and be seen at its best

① *gracilis* ‡↔ 1m (3ft) ✳✳✳ ② × *hybrida* 'Mont Rose' ♀
‡↔ 1–2m (3–6ft) ✳✳✳ ③ *ningpoensis* ♀ ‡↔ 2m (6ft) ✳✳✳
④ *scabra* ‡3m (10ft) ↔ 2m (6ft) ✳✳✳

DIPELTA

late spring to early summer

THESE UPRIGHT OR ARCHING, deciduous shrubs bloom in late spring to early summer, bearing clusters of tubular flowers at the tips of the branches and where the leaf stems join the shoots. The white or pink flowers are fragrant and backed by two papery bracts (modified leaves) that stay on the plant as the fruits develop. Narrow, pointed, pale to mid-green leaves and pale brown, peeling bark add to the attraction. Suitable for a shrub border or as specimen plants, these Chinese natives complement lilacs (*Syringa, see p.121*) and flowering currants (*Ribes, p.109*). Dipeltas can be tricky to propagate and may take a little finding, but once off to a good start they are easy to grow, so the search is worthwhile.

Hardiness Fully hardy ✳✳✳.

Cultivation Grow in fertile, well-drained, and preferably alkaline (limy) soil, in sun or partial shade. **Prune back** flowered shoots to strong buds lower down after flowering. Once mature, encourage new growth by cutting about one in three or four of the old stems back to the base of the shrub. **Sow** seed (*see pp.391–393*) in a seedbed in autumn or spring. **Take** softwood cuttings (*see p.394*) in summer.

DISANTHUS CERCIDIFOLIUS

autumn

BRILLIANT AUTUMN HUES of yellow, orange, red, and purple, often all on display at the same time, are the main attraction of this rounded shrub. The round leaves are similar to those of cercis (*see p.38*), as the name suggests, but the two have very different flowers. In mid-autumn, disanthus produces small, slightly fragrant, spidery, bright rose-red flowers. This shrub is native to mountain and forest habitats, and is ideal as a specimen in a woodland setting. For a superb show of leaf colour in contrasting shapes in autumn, combine it with acers (*see pp.18–19*).

Hardiness Fully hardy ✳✳✳, but late frosts may damage the young growth.

Cultivation Grow in preferably well-drained, lime-free soil that has been enriched with well-rotted organic matter. Position in sun or partial shade where it will be sheltered from strong, cold winds. **Prune** minimally after flowering, cutting out only any crossing stems and those that spoil the shape of the shrub (*see p.382*). **Sow** seed in a seedbed in autumn or spring (*see pp.391–393*). **Layer** low-growing shoots (*see p.395*) in autumn.

ELAEAGNUS

year-round

TOUGH, FAST-GROWING, and resistant to coastal winds, these are immensely useful shrubs. Evergreen or deciduous, they have ornamental, lance-shaped to oval leaves. These may be plain green or silvery, and there are also many with silver or gold variegation. Evergreen elaeagnus make good hedging plants, and the variegated types are great for brightening up a dull border when used as specimen plants. As a bonus, small clusters of bell-shaped, sometimes very fragrant flowers are borne in summer or autumn, and these are occasionally followed by small berries.

Hardiness Fully hardy ✳✳✳.

Cultivation Grow in fertile, well-drained soil; dry soils are tolerated, but the leaves may become yellow on shallow, chalky soils. Position ideally in full sun; evergreens tolerate partial shade. **Prune** deciduous plants in late winter or early spring, evergreens in mid- or late spring, removing any crossing branches and those that spoil the shape (*see p.382*). Trim hedges in late summer. **Cut out** any shoots that revert to plain green leaves on variegated types. **Take** greenwood cuttings in late spring or early summer, or semi-ripe cuttings of deciduous species in late summer (*see p.394*).

Dipelta floribunda ♥
↕↔ 4m (12ft), upright shrub, flowers in late spring and early summer, tolerates quite poor soils

Disanthus cercidifolius ♥
↕↔ 3m (10ft); the leaves are a cloudy blue-green before they take on these vibrant autumn colours

Elaeagnus × *ebbingei* 'Gilt Edge' ♥
↕↔ 4m (12ft), dense, rounded to spreading evergreen, leaves silver-scaly beneath, creamy white flowers in autumn

Elaeagnus pungens 'Maculata'
‡4m (12ft) ↔ 5m (15ft), dense, slightly spiny evergreen, pendent silvery-white flowers in autumn, brown berries ripening to red

EMBOTHRIUM COCCINEUM

Chilean fire bush,
Flame flower

late spring and early summer

SPECTACULAR WHEN IN FLOWER, this evergreen tree or shrub and its cultivars have an upright, but freely branching or suckering habit, and are capable of very rapid growth in mild conditions. The glowing scarlet flowers are carried in dense clusters in late spring and early summer. The narrowly lance-shaped leaves are up to 13cm (5in) long. In cool climates, the plant is happiest against a warm wall or in a sheltered spot, such as a woodland garden in a sunny glade; in areas where there are few frosts, it will tolerate a more open aspect and make a good specimen tree, especially if the slightly hardier 'Norquinco' is chosen.

Hardiness Fully hardy ✳✳✳ (borderline) to frost-hardy ✳✳.

Cultivation Grow in fertile, neutral to acid (lime-free) soil enriched with well-rotted organic matter, in full sun or partial shade. **Trim off** any crossing shoots and those that spoil the shape in late winter or early spring. **Sow** seed (*see pp.391–392*) at 13–16°C (55–61°F) in spring. **Take** greenwood cuttings in early summer, or semi-ripe cuttings in mid- or late summer (*see p.394*). Take root cuttings, or dig up rooted shoots (suckers) growing up around the main plant, in winter.

ENKIANTHUS

spr[...]

PENDENT FLOWER CLUSTERS and rich autumn foliage tints give these plants two seasons of inter[...]. A small group, they are for the most part deciduous shrubs, sometimes trees. The small, delicate flowers are borne at the branch tips from mid-spring to early summer. They are urn- to bell-shaped, in shades from cream or pure white to pink and deep purple-red, with contrasting veins. The autumn display is if anything more distinctive and varies according to the species. *Enkianthus campanulatus* passes through every shade from yellow to red; *E. perulatus* turns brilliant scarlet; and *E. cernuus* f. *rubens* is flushed reddish-purple. They make ideal specimens in a woodland garden.

Hardiness Fully hardy ✳✳✳.

Cultivation Grow in acid (lime-free), moist but well-drained soil enriched with well-rotted organic matter. Position in an open site in full sun or partial shade. **Prune** in late winter or early spring, only to remove misplaced or crossing branches. **Sow** seed at 18–21°C (64–70°F) in late winter or early spring (*see pp.391–393*). **Take** semi-ripe cuttings in summer (*see p.394*) or layer in autumn (*see p.395*).

Elaeagnus 'Quicksilver' ♀
‡↔4m (12ft), fast-growing, deciduous, clump-forming shrub, flowers in summer and bears yellow fruits in autumn

Embothrium coccineum
‡10m (30ft) ↔ 5m (15ft) or more, ✳✳

① *campanulatus* ♀ ‡↔ 4–5m (12–15ft) ② *cernuus* f. *rubens* ♀ ‡↔ 2.5m (8ft) ③ *deflexus* ‡2.5–4m (8–12ft) ↔ 3m (10ft) ④ *perulatus* ♀ ‡↔ to 2m (6ft)

…TH MASSES of tiny, usually bell-shaped flowers
… and pink to white, with some bicolours. In some
…urled leaves are tinted with red or gold, or colour
… choice of cultivars can ensure interest all through
… species make colourful ground cover, while the taller,
…*a arborea*, can make excellent specimen plants in
…re related to heathers (*Calluna, see p.31*), are mainly
found in … but will grow in a variety of conditions.

Hardiness Fully hardy ✳✳✳ to frost-hardy ✳✳.

Cultivation Grow in well-drained, acid soil in an open site in full sun. A few winter- and spring-flowering types such as *E. carnea* and *E. × darleyensis*, will tolerate a slightly alkaline (limy) soil, as will summer-flowering *E. manipuliflora*, *E. terminalis*, and *E. vagans*. **Cut back** flowered shoots to within 2.5cm (1in) of the old growth after flowering. For taller, tree-like cultivars cut back the stems to within two or three buds of the base, or to a permanent framework of shoots in early spring. **Layer** (*see below*) or take semi-ripe cuttings in mid- or late summer (*see p.394*). Heaths may be susceptible to fungal root rot in warm and wet conditions: improve drainage to avoid this.

Using heaths in the garden

Heaths are valuable *plants because they can provide colour and interest throughout the year. They require very little attention beyond clipping over once a year after flowering, making them ideal for a low-maintenance garden. Different colours can be grouped en masse in their own bed, but they are also effective growing with dwarf conifers such as junipers (see pp.76–77) and with rhododendrons (see pp.104–107). If you have alkaline soil, lime-hating heaths can be grown in a raised bed filled with ericaceous (lime-free) compost or in large pots on the patio.*

Easy ways to increase your plants

Layering *Heaths and heathers root readily from the stems, so propagating them by layering is much easier than taking cuttings. From early to mid-autumn or in spring, make a shallow trench around the plant and refill with soil mixed with a little sharp sand and peat substitute, for example leafmould, to provide a good rooting medium. Bend down healthy shoots and cover with some of the prepared soil. Peg down the shoots with wire staples or weigh down with a stone. The stems need not be cut. The next year, cut off the rooted stems; replant where they can grow into new plants.*

Each shoot will become new plant

Original plant roots

New roots form on stems

Dropping *Lift a mature plant in spring. Dig a hole big enough to take not only the roots but two-thirds of the top-growth. Drop the plant into the hole and fill in around the roots with soil and a mixture of equal parts grit and lime-free compost between the shoots. Arranging the shoots in rows or around the edge of the hole will make it easier to weed between them. Firm in gently and label. Keep well watered during dry spells. By autumn, the buried stems should have developed roots. Lift the plant and cut the rooted shoots from the parent. Pot up the young plants and grow on, or plant them in a sheltered spot.*

① *Erica arborea* var. *alpina* ♀ ‡2m (6ft) ↔ 85cm (34in) ② *carnea* 'Ann Sparkes' ♀ ‡15cm (6in) ↔ 25cm (10in) ③ *carnea* 'December Red' ‡15cm (10in) ↔ 45cm (18in) ④ *carnea* 'Eileen Porter' ‡↔ 20cm (8in) ⑤ *carnea* 'Foxhollow' ♀ ‡15cm (6in) ↔ 40cm (16in) ⑥ *carnea* 'Springwood White' ♀ ‡15cm (6in) ↔ 45cm (18in) ⑦ *carnea* 'Vivellii' ♀ ‡15cm (6in) ↔ 35cm (14in) ⑧ *ciliaris* 'David McClintock' ‡40cm (16in) ↔ 45cm (18in) ⑨ *ciliaris* 'White Wings'

‡15cm (6in) ↔ 45cm (18in) ⑩ *cinerea* 'C.D. Eason' ♀ ‡25cm (10in) ↔ 50cm (20in) ⑪ *cinerea* 'Eden Valley' ♀ ‡20cm (8in) ↔ 50cm (20in) ⑫ *cinerea* 'Fiddler's Gold' ♀ ‡25cm (10in) ↔ 45cm (18in) ⑬ *cinerea* 'Hookstone White' ♀ ‡35cm (14in) ↔ 65cm (26in) ⑭ *cinerea* 'Purple Beauty' ‡30cm (1ft) ↔ 55cm (22in) ⑮ *cinerea* 'Windlebrooke' ♀ ‡15cm (6in) ↔ 45cm (18in) ⑯ × *darleyensis* 'Jenny Porter' ♀ ‡30cm (1ft) ↔ 60cm (2ft) ⑰ × *darleyensis* 'White Glow'

‡25cm (10in) ↔ 50cm (20in) ⑱ *erigena* 'Golden Lady' ♀ ‡30cm (1ft) ↔ 40cm (16in) ⑲ *tetralix* 'Alba Mollis' ♀ ‡20cm (8in) ↔ 30cm (1ft) ⑳ *vagans* 'Birch Glow' ♀ ‡30cm (1ft) ↔ 50cm (20in) ㉑ *vagans* 'Lyonesse' ♀ ‡25cm (10in) ↔ 50cm (20in) ㉒ *vagans* 'Mrs D.F. Maxwell' ♀ ‡30cm (1ft) ↔ 45cm (18in) ㉓ *vagans* 'Valerie Proudley' ♀ ‡15cm (6in) ↔ 30cm (1ft) ㉔ × *williamsii* 'P.D. Williams' ♀ ‡30cm (1ft) ↔ 45cm (18in)

TREES AND SHRUBS

summer

GLOSSY, EVERGREEN FOLIAGE and a profusion of flowers are the attractions of these excellent shrubs. Borne over a long period, mainly in summer, the flowers are tubular or saucer-shaped, in shades of white, pink, or red. Escallonias are undemanding plants, being fairly fast-growing and drought-tolerant. Widely grown as tough, wind-resistant hedging, they also make fine freestanding shrubs in a shrub or mixed border. They are particularly good in coastal areas, where the tough leaves stand up to salt-laden winds. Try them with other robust shrubs, such as cotinus (*see p.44*), lilacs (*Syringa, see p.121*), St John's wort (*Hypericum, see p.74*), and potentillas (*see p.99*).

Hardiness Fully hardy ✳✳✳ to half-hardy ✳.

Cultivation Grow in fertile, well-drained soil. Position in full sun, with shelter from cold, drying winds. Half-hardy types grow best with the protection of a sheltered wall. **Trim** back shoots that spoil the shape of the shrub lightly in mid- or late spring. **Clip** hedges after flowering. **Take** softwood cuttings in early summer or semi-ripe cuttings in late summer; or try hardwood cuttings from late autumn to winter (*see p.394*).

Escallonia 'Apple Blossom' ♥
↕↔ 2.5m (8ft), compact bush, slow-growing, flowers in early and midsummer, suitable for hedging ✳✳

Escallonia 'Langleyensis' ♥
↕ 2m (6ft) ↔ 3m (10ft), arching, evergreen to semi-evergreen shrub, flowers in early and midsummer ✳✳✳

Escallonia 'Pride of Donard' ♥
↕ 1.5m (5ft) ↔ 2.5m (8ft), compact, erect shrub (*see inset*), flowers are larger than most and borne in early to midsummer, suitable for hedging ✳✳

Escallonia rubra 'Woodside'
↕ 75cm (30in) ↔ 1.5m (5ft), dwarf form, flowers from summer to early autumn, cut out any overly vigorous shoots promptly ✳✳✳

EUCALYPTUS

Gum, Ironbark

year-round

THESE DISTINCTIVE TREES and shrubs are grown for their handsome, often aromatic, evergreen foliage, and their ornamental bark. The foliage is usually mid- or grey-green and leathery. The young, or juvenile, leaves are most attractive, and look rather like silvery-blue pennies on *Eucalyptus gunnii*. They grow longer and droop as the plants mature. Small clusters of petalless flowers open in summer, and may be white, creamy yellow, or red. The bark is smooth and white in some species, flaking or striped in shades of green or tawny brown in others. As specimen trees they grow quickly and need quite a bit of space. However, with hard pruning (coppicing) each year, they may be grown as shrubs, which retain the appealing juvenile foliage.

Hardiness Fully hardy ✳✳✳ to frost-tender ✿.

Cultivation Grow in fertile, neutral to slightly acid soil that does not easily dry out, in full sun, preferably with shelter from cold winds. **Prune** crossing or misplaced branches in late winter or early spring; to form a shrub, cut back stems to within two or three buds of the base, forming a stubby framework (*see below, left*). **Sow** seed at 13–18°C (55–64°F) in spring or summer (*see pp.391–392*).

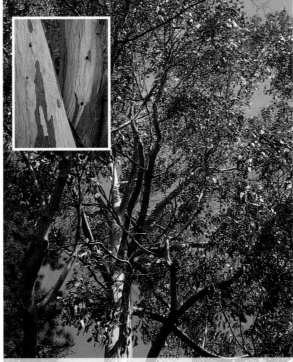

Eucalyptus dalrympleana ♀ (Mountain gum)
‡20m (70ft) ↔ 8m (25ft), vigorous tree, blue-green new leaves, flowers late summer to autumn, tolerates chalk soil ✳✳✳ (borderline)

EUCRYPHIA

summer to autumn

‡to 15m (50ft)
↔ to 8m (25ft)

VALUED FOR THEIR late flowering, this a small group comprises mostly evergreen, columnar trees and shrubs. Their beautiful, often fragrant flowers are white, occasionally pink or with pink edges to the petals, and have a fluffy mass of stamens at the centre. They are borne from summer to early autumn, once the plants are a few years old. The leaves are leathery, usually oval but sometimes made up of narrow leaflets along a central stalk. Eucryphias make glorious specimen plants or flowering hedges in a sheltered spot.

Hardiness Fully hardy ✳✳✳ to frost-hardy ✳✳

Cultivation Grow in fertile, moist but well-drained soil that is neutral to acid (lime-free). *E. × nymansensis* tolerates alkaline soil. Position with the roots in shade and the crown in full sun. Needs shelter from cold, drying winds in all but mild areas. **Remove** fading flowers if the plant is small enough to make this practical. **Prune out** any crossing or dead wood in late winter or early spring, or lightly trim shoots that spoil the shape in mid- or late spring (or for *E. lucida*, after flowering). Do not overprune, or you will lose the flowers. **Take** semi-ripe cuttings (*see p.394*) in summer, and overwinter new plants in frost-free conditions.

COPPICING a gum tree, especially the snow and cider gums, is done by cutting back all stems to 2–3 buds every spring.

Eucalyptus gunnii ♀ (Cider gum)
‡10–25m (30–80ft) ↔ 6–15m (20–50ft), flowers in summer or autumn (*see inset*), bark shed in late summer ✳✳✳ (borderline)

Eucalyptus pauciflora subsp. *niphophila* ♀ (Snow gum)
‡6m (20ft) ↔ 6–15m (20–50ft), slow-growing, flowers late spring to summer, bark shed late summer to autumn ✳✳✳

Eucryphia glutinosa ♀
‡10m (30ft) ↔ 6m (20ft), deciduous or semi-evergreen tree or shrub, flowers in mid- to late summer, tolerates exposed sites ✳✳✳

EUONYMUS

Spindle tree

year-round

COLOURFUL FOLIAGE IS the main feature of this large group of shrubs and trees. Deciduous types have fiery autumn foliage and decorative, lobed fruits, while most of the evergreens have bright variegation that brings colour to the garden all year. The leaves are variable, but usually broadly oval, and small clusters of purple-red or red-brown flowers appear in late spring or summer. The evergreens can be used as specimen shrubs in borders, or as hedging or ground cover. Some *Euonymus fortunei* types will climb if planted by a wall. Young plants are useful in winter windowboxes and containers. All parts may cause mild stomach upset if eaten.

Hardiness Fully hardy ✽✽✽ to frost-hardy ✽✽.

Cultivation Grow in any well-drained soil; deciduous species are more drought-tolerant. Site in full sun (especially variegated types) or partial shade; in full sun they need moist soil. Shelter evergreens from cold, drying winds. **Prune** deciduous types in late winter or early spring if needed and evergreens if necessary after flowering (*see p.383*). **Sow** seed (*see pp.391–392*) in a container in a cold frame as soon as it is ripe. **Take** softwood cuttings of deciduous species, and semi-ripe cuttings of evergreens in summer (*see p.394*).

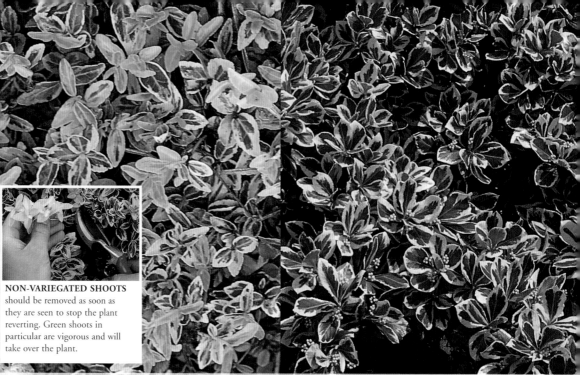

NON-VARIEGATED SHOOTS should be removed as soon as they are seen to stop the plant reverting. Green shoots in particular are vigorous and will take over the plant.

Euonymus fortunei 'Emerald 'n' Gold' ♥
‡60cm (24in) ↔ 90cm (36in), dense, bushy, evergreen shrub, gold leaf edges turn pink in winter, white fruits and orange seeds ✽✽✽

Euonymus fortunei 'Silver Queen'
‡2.5m (8ft) ↔ 1.5m (5ft), upright, evergreen bush, occasional, pale green flowers and pink fruits, climbs if given support ✽✽✽

Euonymus alatus ♥ (Winged spindle)
‡2m (6ft) ↔ 3m (10ft), dense, deciduous shrub, red-purple fruits with orange seeds, dark green leaves until autumn ✽✽✽

Euonymus japonicus 'Ovatus Aureus' ♥
‡4m (12ft) ↔ 2m (6ft), slow-growing, evergreen bush or tree, good for hedging, rarely fruits, tends to revert to all-green shoots ✽✽

Euonymus oxyphyllus
‡2.5m (8ft) or more ↔ 2.5m (8ft), upright, slow-growing deciduous species, dull-green leaves before autumn ✽✽✽

EUPHORBIA

Milkweed, Spurge

see also pp.242–243

spring and summer

IN THIS LARGE AND WIDELY VARIED group of plants, there are a few evergreen shrubs and trees. They are grown for their impressive foliage and distinctive flowerheads. The leaves are mostly narrow and lance-shaped – in *Euphorbia characias* they are blue-green and very architectural. *E. × martini* has leaves that are flushed purple when young, on red-tinged stems; its flowerheads are long-lasting and borne in spring and summer. The flowers are brown and honey-scented in *E. mellifera*, the honey spurge, and yellow-green with dark-red nectar glands in *E. × martini*. Spurges are suitable for coastal gardens. All parts of euphorbias can cause severe discomfort if eaten, and contact with the milky sap may irritate skin.

Hardiness Fully hardy ✽✽✽ to frost-hardy ✽✽.

Cultivation Grow in well-drained soil in full sun. Dig in plenty of coarse grit on heavy clay soils to improve drainage. **Take** softwood cuttings (*see p.394*) in spring or early summer, wearing gloves, and dipping the ends in lukewarm water to stem the bleeding of sap.

EXOCHORDA

Pearl bush

spring to summer

↔ 2–4m
(6–12ft)

SHOWY, PURE WHITE blooms wreath the branches of these shrubs in spring to summer; not for nothing is the most popular variety named 'The Bride'. All are deciduous, with an attractive, arching habit, and are equally impressive grown with other shrubs in a border or as isolated specimen plants. They flower at around the same time or a little later than the spring-flowering magnolias (*see pp.86–87*) and their flowers are more resistant to frost, which makes them an excellent alternative for a blossom display in frost-prone areas where magnolia flowers might be spoiled.

Hardiness Fully hardy ✽✽✽.

Cultivation Grow in fertile, moist, but well-drained soil; these shrubs will tolerate all but the shallowest, chalky soils, where the leaves may become yellow (chlorotic). Position in full sun or partial shade. **Cut back** flowered shoots to strong buds or young lower growths after flowering. Encourage fresh growth on mature plants by cutting one in three or four older branches back to the base every few years. **Take** softwood cuttings (*see p.394*) in summer.

FAGUS

Beech

summer to autumn

THESE STATELY, DECIDUOUS TREES are grown for their fine forms and handsome foliage. They are large and spreading, with wavy edged or toothed, oval leaves. In most, these are pale green when they first open in spring, maturing to dark green and then taking on soft yellow or russet-brown tones in autumn, but there are several beeches with dramatic, dark, purple or coppery foliage. All make fine specimen trees in a large garden; the common beech, *Fagus sylvatica*, is also popular as a hedge; when clipped, it retains its brown leaves all winter. For smaller gardens, look for narrow or compact forms, such as 'Purpurea Pendula', with branches that often trail to the ground.

Hardiness Fully hardy ✽✽✽; the North American beech *F. grandiflora* needs long, warm summers to thrive.

Cultivation Grow in any well-drained soil; even chalk is tolerated. Position in sun or partial shade; purple-leaved types have the best foliage colour in full sun. **Prune out** crossing branches and any that spoil the shape of the tree in late winter or early spring. **Trim** hedges of *F. sylvatica* in mid- to late summer. Sow seed in a seedbed in autumn or spring (*see pp.391–393*). Beeches are favourites of grey squirrels, which although entertaining can cause some damage.

Euphorbia characias 'John Tomlinson' ♥
↕↔ 1.2m (4ft), upright shrub, huge and heavy flowerheads from early spring to early summer, becoming almost round ✽✽

Exochorda × macrantha 'The Bride' ♥
↕ 2m (6ft) ↔ 3m (10ft), forms a compact, arching mound with fragrant flowers in late spring and early summer

Fagus sylvatica 'Dawyck Purple' ♥
↕ 20m (70ft) ↔ 5m (15ft), particularly good purple-leaved type, also one of the narrowest columnar forms

FATSIA JAPONICA

Japanese aralia,
Japanese fatsia

year-round

THE LARGE, GLOSSY GREEN LEAVES of these evergreen, spreading shrubs are ideal for creating a jungly garden, and make a dramatic contrast to feathery foliage plants such as ferns (*see pp.356–365*). An excellent architectural plant for a shady border, it tolerates pollution and thrives in city gardens, but is also a good choice for coastal areas, where the tough leaves will withstand salt-laden winds and sea spray. Broad, upright clusters of rounded, creamy white flowerheads are produced in autumn, followed by small, round, black berries that are inedible. There are also some variegated cultivars, but they tend to be less hardy.

Hardiness Fully hardy ✳✳✳ (species) to frost-hardy ✳✳ (cultivars).

Cultivation This shrub will thrive in any fertile, moist but well-drained soil in full sun or partial shade, but needs shelter from cold, drying winds. **Trim** lightly or prune shoots that spoil the shape in mid- or late spring. **Remove** the fading flowers unless seed is wanted. **Sow** seed (*see pp.391–393*) at 15–21°C (59–70°F) in autumn or spring. **Take** greenwood cuttings (*see p.394*) in early or midsummer. Cold winds may cause blackening and die-back of shoots and leaves.

FICUS CARICA

Common fig

summer

‡3m (10ft)
↔4m (12ft)

UNLIKE MOST FIGS, *Ficus carica* is hardy. It can be grown as a free-standing tree, but will quickly spread to cover a large area if trained against a wall. The handsome, deciduous foliage is its main attraction; it does produce edible figs, but these do not always mature in cooler climates. The fruits are green when young and mature after a second, long, hot summer into dark green, purple, or dark brown figs. The leaves can cause skin rashes in sunlight (photodermatitis).

Hardiness Fully hardy ✳✳✳.

Cultivation Figs prefer moist but well-drained soil, enriched with plenty of well-rotted organic matter, in full sun or partial shade, with shelter from cold, drying winds. **Restrict** the roots in a large pot or by a barrier in the soil for better fruiting. **Tie in** regularly new shoots of wall-trained plants. **Prune out** misplaced or crossing shoots that spoil the shape in late winter or early spring; prune wall-trained plants to fit available space. **For best fruits**, pick off larger, green fruitlets on the main stems in autumn to leave smaller ones to ripen next year; protect them with fleece from cold winds and frosts. Wasps attack ripe fruits.

FORSYTHIA

late winter to spring

THESE SUPERBLY RELIABLE, deciduous shrubs will be covered in flowers every spring and sometimes in late winter, no matter what the weather throws at them. The bright yellow blooms appear in profusion all along the length of the stems, singly or in small clusters, before the leaves open. Most forsythias are medium-sized, bushy or upright shrubs; a few are semi-evergreen. These versatile shrubs can be grown either freestanding or trained against a wall or a fence, and *Forsythia × intermedia* also makes a good hedging plant. A classic spring planting combination involves forsythias along with red-flowering currants (*Ribes, see p.109*).

Hardiness Fully hardy ✳✳✳.

Cultivation Reasonably fertile, moist but well-drained soil is needed. **Position** in full sun or partial shade. **Prune back** flowered shoots to strong shoots lower down after flowering. Cut about one-third to a quarter of old stems on mature plants to the base every 4–5 years: cut back hard neglected, leggy plants over two years to rejuvenate (*see p.384*). **Trim** hedges in summer. **Take** greenwood cuttings in early summer or semi-ripe cuttings in late summer (*see p.394*). **Birds** may eat some of the flower buds.

Fatsia japonica ♀
‡↔ 1.5–4m (5–12ft), leaves are 15–40cm (6–16in) across ✳✳✳

Ficus carica
The leathery leaves can reach 24cm (10in) across and are fairly tolerant of salty air

Forsythia suspensa (Golden bell)
‡↔ 3m (10ft), upright or arching, leaves mid- to dark green, flowers in early and mid-spring, tolerates north- or east-facing wall

FOTHERGILLA

spring and autumn

THERE ARE JUST TWO SPECIES of these deciduous, low-growing shrubs from woodlands and swamps. They are grown for their bottlebrush-like clusters of scented flowers which are produced before the leaves unfold. Fothergillas also have attractive, dark green foliage, which has toothed edges and turns brilliant shades of red, orange, and golden yellow in autumn. The witch alder (*Fothergilla gardenii*) is the smaller of the two, forming a dense bush with a height and spread of 1m (3ft); it flowers in spring. The slow-growing *F. major* is an upright shrub and has more glossy leaves; its flowers are occasionally tinged with pink.

Hardiness Fully hardy ✳✳✳.

Cultivation Grow fothergillas in moist but well-drained, acid (lime-free) soil that has been enriched with well-rotted organic matter. **Position** in full sun or partial shade; full sun encourages more flowers and better autumn colour. **Prune off** crossing or misshapen shoots that spoil the shape of the shrub in late winter or early spring, only if necessary (*see p.382*). **Sow** seed (*see pp.391–393*) in a container in autumn or winter; it will take two years to germinate. **Take** softwood cuttings (*see p.394*).

FRAXINUS

Ash

spring to autumn

THESE DECIDUOUS TREES ARE TOUGH as well as decorative. They tolerate pollution, wind, and coastal conditions, and have fine foliage and sometimes coloured winter bark. The leaves are made up of small leaflets along central stalks up to 50cm (20in) long. Fast-growing, ash trees have attractive habits, ranging from narrow or columnar to round or spreading. Ash trees have tiny flowers, but those of *Fraxinus ornus* and *F. sieboldiana* are decorative. Most are suitable only for large gardens, being 15–30m (50–100ft) tall: the weeping *F. excelsior* 'Pendula' is smaller than many. Ashes seed themselves about quite prolifically, so be vigilant in rooting out any seedlings. They look good with trees such as birches (*Betula, see p.28*), beeches (*Fagus, see p.57*), and oaks (*Quercus, see p.103*).

Hardiness Fully hardy ✳✳✳ to frost-hardy ✳✳.

Cultivation Ash trees need fertile, moist soil that is well-drained and neutral to acid (lime-free); *F. angustifolius* and *F. ornus* tolerate fairly dry soils from acid to alkaline (limy). **Position** in full sun. **Sow** seed (*see pp.391–393*) in autumn or spring in an open cold frame; the seed requires 2–3 months of cold before it will germinate.

Forsythia × *intermedia* 'Lynwood Variety' ♀
↕↔ 3m (10ft), bushy habit, sharply toothed leaves, flowers are 2.5–3.5 (1¼–1½in) across and borne in early and mid-spring

Fothergilla major ♀
↕ 2.5m (8ft) ↔ 2m (6ft), flowers in late spring and early summer, found naturally in dry woods and rocky riverbanks

Fraxinus excelsior 'Jaspidea' ♀
↕ 30m (100ft) ↔ 20m (70ft), yellow shoots and leaves in winter and spring, leaves dark green in summer, distinct black buds in winter

summer to late autumn

THE BRIGHTLY COLOURED, PENDULOUS FLOWERS of fuchsias are unmistakeable. They vary from elegant, single and semi-double forms to frilly, fully double blooms, and appear from summer until late autumn. Deciduous or evergreen shrubs, fuchsias are very versatile. They can be planted in mixed borders and as hedging, some can be trained against walls or grown as standards or pillars (*see below*), and cultivars with a trailing habit are ideal in raised containers, where the flowers spill over the edges to great effect. Fuchsias can be divided into two groups, hardy to frost-hardy and half-hardy to tender. The former may lose all their leaves in harsh winters, but will reshoot in the spring if they have been well planted and mulched. The latter, with a wide range of extravagant flowers, can be grown outdoors in the summer, making showy plants either in borders or in containers underplanted with annuals, but need some protection during severe winters: keep half-hardy types in a frost-free greenhouse, shed, or garage, and tender plants in a slightly warmer place.

Hardiness Hardy ✳✳✳ to frost-tender ✸.

Cultivation Grow in fertile, moist but well-drained soil in full sun or partial shade, with shelter from cold, drying winds. **Plant** hardy fuchsias with the base of the stem 5cm (2in) below the soil surface, and protect them with a deep winter mulch of bark chippings or similar material. Plant out tender cultivars in early summer, when the threat of frost has passed. **Water** well in summer and feed with a balanced liquid fertilizer every two weeks. **Cut** the old stems of hardy fuchsias to the ground in spring. **Lift** tender cultivars in autumn, keeping them in a frost-free place during winter and spring, watering sufficiently to keep them just moist. **Take** softwood cuttings in spring (*see pp.394*). Vine weevils sometimes cause damage, especially in pots where larvae may eat large areas of root (*see p.398*). Treat grey mould (botrytis) with fungicide, and rust (tiny orange pustules) by removing affected leaves.

Pruning and training

Pinching out produces dense growth

Rounded bushy head formed by regular pinching out

Tips of main stems pinched out at required height

Lower shoots are tied to horizontal canes to achieve neat outline

Bush When each shoot has made about three pairs of leaves, pinch out the tip. This encourages the plant to produce sideshoots. Continue to do this three or four times and then allow the plant to flower.

Standard This shape is achieved by training a shoot up a cane, removing sideshoots. When the main stem reaches the required height, pinch out the tip and treat the top as for a bush. Training takes 2–3 years.

Pyramid Allow the main stem to grow to 23cm (9in). Pinch out the tip, keeping one shoot to continue as a new leader. Pinch out all sideshoots at three pairs of leaves. Repeat until the right height and shape is reached.

Column Allow two shoots to develop as central stems, and stop them at the desired height. Pinch the sideshoots regularly to create dense, bushy growth. As with a standard, this takes 2–3 years.

① *Fuchsia* 'Alice Hoffman' ♀ ↕↔45–60cm (18–24in) ✳✳ ② 'Andrew Hadfield' ↕20–45cm (8–18in) ↔20–30cm (8–12in) ✸ ③ 'Annabel' ♀ ↕↔30–60cm (12–24in) ✳ ④ *arborescens* ↕2m (6ft) ↔1.7m (5½ft) ✸ ⑤ 'Auntie Jinks' ↕15–20cm (6–8in) ↔20–40cm (8–16in) ✳ ⑥ 'Autumnale' ♀ ↕15–30cm (6–12in) ↔30–60cm (1–2ft) ✳ ⑦ × *bacillaris* ↕↔60–120cm (2–4ft) ✳✳ ⑧ 'Ballet Girl' ♀ ↕30–45cm (12–18in) ↔45–75cm (18–30in) ✳ ⑨ 'Bicentennial' ↕30–45cm (12–18in)

㊶ 'Mrs Lovell Swisher' ♀ ‡45–60cm (18–24in) ↔ 30–60cm (12–24in) ❋ ㊷ 'Mrs Popple' ♀
‡↔ 1–1.1m (3–3½ft) ❋❋❋ ㊸ 'Nellie Nuttall' ♀ ‡15–45cm (6–18in) ↔ 30–45cm (12–18in) ❋
㊹ 'Other Fellow' ‡↔ 30–45cm (12–18in) ❋ ㊺ *paniculata* ♀ ‡↔ to 2m (6ft) ❋❋ ㊻ 'Peppermint
Stick' ‡↔ 45–75cm (18–30in) ❋ ㊼ 'Phyllis' ♀ ‡1–1.5m (3–5ft) ↔ 75–90cm (30–36in) ❋❋
㊽ *procumbens* ‡10–15cm (4–6in) ↔ 1–1.2m (3–4ft) ❋❋ ㊾ 'Red Spider' ‡15–30cm (6–12in)

↔ 30–60cm (12–24in) ❋ ㊿ 'Riccartonii' ♀ ‡2–3m (6–10ft) ↔ 1–2m (3–6ft) ❋❋❋
�51 'Royal Velvet' ♀ ‡45–75cm (18–30in) ↔ 30–60cm (12–24in) ❋ 52 'Rufus' ♀ ‡45–75cm
(18–30in) ↔ 30–60cm (12–24in) ❋❋ 53 'Swingtime' ♀ ‡30–60cm (12–24in) ↔ 45–75cm
(18–30in) ❋ 54 'Thalia' ‡↔ 45–90cm (18–36in) ❀ 55 'Tom Thumb' ♀ ‡↔ 15–30cm
(6–12in) ❋❋ 56 'Winston Churchill' ♀ ‡↔ 45–75cm (18–30in) ❋

GARRYA

winter

LONG CATKINS ADORN these tough, large, evergreen shrubs from mid- to late winter. Male and female flowers are borne on separate plants, the male catkins being more dramatic. Most widely grown is the silk-tassel bush, *Garrya elliptica*. *G.* × *issaquahensis* 'Pat Ballard' has red-purple shoots, glossy leaves, and purple-tinged catkins. Garryas are versatile: they can be grown in a border, trained against a wall, or even used as hedging. They tolerate urban pollution, and the leathery, wavy-edged leaves stand up to salt-laden winds and sea spray in coastal areas. Grow with other winter-flowering shrubs like *Jasminum nudiflorum* (*see p.76*) trained against a wall, mahonias (*see p.87*), and Christmas box (*Sarcococca, see p.116*).

Hardiness Fully hardy ✳✳✳ (borderline) to half-hardy ✳.
Cultivation Grow in reasonably fertile, well-drained soil, in full sun or partial shade; shelter from cold winds in areas with severe frosts. **Prune** lightly after flowering, cutting out shoots that spoil the shape. Garryas tolerate hard renovation pruning (*see p.384*). **Take** semi-ripe cuttings (*see p.394*) in summer.

GAULTHERIA

Pernettya

autumn

COLOURFUL AUTUMN FRUITS are the main attraction of these trouble-free, evergreen shrubs. They bear small flowers just 7mm (¼in) long, usually in small clusters, in spring or summer. These are followed in autumn by berries in dusky shades of red, purple, and pink to white. These are edible; all other parts cause stomach upsets if eaten. Small to medium-sized, these shrubs have neat, dark green, leathery leaves and varied habits. Gaultherias can be grown in shrub borders, rock gardens, or woodland settings, and they make excellent companions for rhododendrons (*see pp.104–107*). Some have been subject to name changes, and they are often sold simply as pernettyas.

Hardiness Fully hardy ✳✳✳ to half-hardy ✳.
Cultivation Gaultherias need acid (lime-free), moist soil, ideally in partial shade, although they will tolerate full sun where the soil is permanently moist. **Prune** lightly after flowering, cutting back shoots that spoil the shape of the shrub. Restrict the spread of plants by removing suckering growths. **Sow** seed (*see pp.391–393*) in containers outdoors in a cold frame in autumn. **Take** semi-ripe cuttings (*see p.394*) in summer or remove rooted suckers in spring and replant.

Gaultheria tasmanica
↕8cm (3in) ↔ to 25cm (10in), mat-forming, flowers in spring, sometimes white or yellow fruits borne freely even in shade ✳✳✳

Garrya elliptica 'James Roof' ♀
↕↔4m (12ft), vigorous shrub, male plants noted for particularly long catkins up to 20cm (8in) ✳✳✳

Gaultheria mucronata 'Mulberry Wine' ♀
↕↔1.2m (4ft), female, suckering shrub, berries if a male, for example *G. mucronata*, is planted nearby ✳✳✳

Gaultheria × *wisleyensis* 'Pink Pixie'
↕to 30cm (12in) ↔45cm (18in), vigorous, upright, spreads by suckers, pink-tinged flowers in late spring and early summer ✳✳✳

GENISTA

Broom

spring to summer

THESE ELEGANT SHRUBS are grown for their pretty, pea-like yellow flowers, borne in small clusters from spring to summer. They are related to the other brooms, cytisus (*see p.47*) and spartiums (*see p.118*). The leaves are small. Although some species are almost leafless and almost all are deciduous, the green stems give some colour to a garden even in winter. Habits vary from upright to arching, tree-like forms. Brooms contrast well with broader-leaved plants such as ceanothus (*see p.36*) and fatsias (*see p.58*). The Mount Etna broom makes a graceful specimen in a lawn or shrub border, while dwarfer species, like the dense, spiny *Genista hispanca*, suit rock gardens. Some have sharp spines: take care when siting them.

Hardiness Fully hardy ✳✳✳ to half-hardy ✳.

Cultivation Genistas like light, poor to reasonably fertile, well-drained soil, in full sun. Little pruning is required apart from removing misplaced or crossing shoots that spoil the shape, in late winter or early spring. Avoid cutting into old wood, because it will not produce new shoots. **Sow** seed (*see pp.391–393*) in a cold frame in autumn or take semi-ripe cuttings (*see p.394*) in summer.

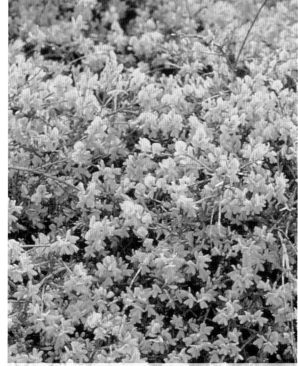

Genista lydia ♀

↕ to 60cm (24in) ↔ to 1m (3ft), domed shrub with spine-tipped, blue-green shoots, flowers in early summer ✳✳✳

GINKGO BILOBA

Maidenhair tree

summer and autumn

PERHAPS THE MOST ANCIENT of all living trees, the ginkgo is an upright or columnar tree when young and becomes spreading as it ages. The deciduous foliage, which is similar to that of maidenhair ferns (*Adiantum, see p.360*) and gives the tree its common name, turns a soft, golden yellow in autumn. Catkin-like, yellow male flowers and tiny female flowers are produced on separate trees. Given warm summers, female flowers produce plum-like, yellow-green fruits in autumn that smell unpleasant but contain large, edible nuts that are traditionally roasted. Trouble-free and easy to grow, ginkgos will tolerate atmospheric pollution and are excellent as landscape trees, as specimens, in borders, or even in containers.

Hardiness Fully hardy ✳✳✳.

Cultivation Any fertile, well-drained soil, in full sun will suit ginkgos. **Cut out** any crossing or misshapen branches that spoil the shape of the tree, in late winter or early spring, to maintain a healthy framework (*see p.382*). **Sow** seed (*see pp.391–393*) in a cold frame as soon as it is ripe. **Take** semi-ripe cuttings (*see p.394*) in summer.

Genista aetnensis ♀ (Mount Etna broom)

↕↔ 8m (25ft), weeping shrub or small tree, leaves produced only on the younger shoots, fragrant flowers borne in profusion at ends of shoots in mid- to late summer ✳✳

Gingko biloba ♀

↕ to 30m (100ft) ↔ to 8m (25ft), extinct in the wild, the ginkgo has long been grown in temples and as a street tree in China and Japan

GLEDITSIA

spring to autumn

DECORATIVE FOLIAGE AND SEED PODS, and an elegant, spreading habit, make these deciduous trees beautiful specimen plants. The glossy, ferny leaves are divided into as many as 24 smaller, pale to dark green leaflets. In autumn, long, curved and twisted, pendent seed pods and foliage in yellow tints give further interest. The widely grown honey locust, *Gleditsia triacanthos*, usually has spiny trunks and shoots. 'Elegantissima' is a much smaller and thornless form of this tree, while 'Rubylace' has dark bronze-red young leaves that turn to dark bronze-green by midsummer. To highlight the autumn foliage of these trees, grow them alongside dark-leaved shrubs like cotinus (*see p.44*).

Hardiness Fully hardy ✼✼✼, although they are susceptible to frost damage when young.
Cultivation Grow gleditsias in any fertile, well-drained soil, in sun. **Pruning** is rarely necessary **Sow** seed (*see pp.391–393*) in an open frame in autumn. Prepare the seed by chipping each seed coat with a knife or rubbing it with sandpaper to allow moisture in. **Gall midges** may cause swellings on the leaves.

GRISELINIA LITTORALIS

Broadleaf

year-round

‡ to 8m (25ft)
↔ to 5m (15ft)

THIS VIGOROUS, DENSE, EVERGREEN, upright shrub or small tree can make a superb windbreak hedge in an exposed garden. It is grown for its tough and handsome foliage. Tiny flowers are borne in late spring, with male and female blossoms on separate plants. They are followed by purple fruits in autumn if plants of both sexes are grown together. Although most often used as hedging, griselinias also make handsome specimen plants in a border. They are particularly good in coastal areas, where the leathery leaves can withstand salt-laden winds and sea spray.

Hardiness Fully hardy ✼✼✼ (borderline).
Cultivation Light, fertile, well-drained soil in full sun, with shelter from cold, drying winds, is required. **Prune lightly** in mid- or late spring, cutting back shoots that spoil that shape of the shrub. **Trim** hedges once or twice a year. **Sow** seed (*see pp.391–393*) in spring at 13–18°C (55–64°F) or take semi-ripe cuttings (*see p.394*) in summer.

HALESIA

Silver bell,
Snowdrop tree

*spring and
autumn*

BEAUTIFUL IN SPRING, this small group of deciduous, trouble-free shrubs and trees is grown for its pendent, bell-shaped, pure white flowers. These are generally borne in late spring, sometimes in early summer, and are followed in autumn by winged green fruits and golden foliage. The forms can vary from conical, as in *Halesia monticola*, to spreading, as in *H. carolina* or *H. diptera*. The more spreading types can be grown as trees or as shrubs in gardens of any size. Found naturally in woodland and woodland margins and near riverbanks, halesias make pleasing specimens as shrubs for the back of a border or as trees in a woodland setting.

Hardiness Fully hardy ✼✼✼.
Cultivation These plants prefer fertile, moist but well-drained, preferably neutral to acid (lime-free) soil that is enriched with well-rotted organic matter. Position in sun or partial shade with shelter from cold winds. **Remove** misplaced or crossing shoots, in winter or late spring, to maintain a good shape. **Sow** seed (*see pp.391–393*) at 14–25°C (57–77°F) in autumn. **Take** softwood cuttings (*see p.394*) in summer, or layer low-growing shoots (*see p.395*) in spring.

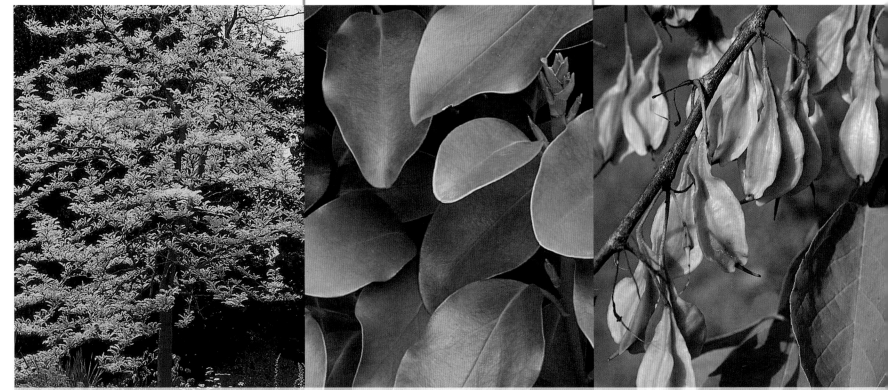

Gleditsia triacanthos 'Sunburst' ♀
‡ 12m (40ft) ↔ 10m (30ft), fast-growing and thornless, light canopy can be underplanted so particularly suited to gardens

Griselinia littoralis ♀
There are variegated forms, but the plain green is best for hedging

Halesia monticola
‡ 12m (40ft) ↔ 8m (25ft), usually conical, vigorous tree, flowers in late spring before or just as leaves unfold, fruits heavily (*as shown*)

× HALIMIOCISTUS

late spring to late summer

CHARMING, FRAGILE FLOWERS are the main attraction of these small, evergreen shrubs. They are crosses between cistus (*see p.40*) and halimiums (*see right*). The flowers resemble rock roses (*Helianthemum, see p.70*) and are usually pure white or blotched with deep red at the bases of the petals. Several of these trouble-free, often spreading hybrids are grown in gardens, with flowering periods from late spring to late summer. Found where their parent species grow together in hot, dry, Mediterranean areas, they are happy in a rock garden or dry, sunny border alongside roses (*see pp.110–113*) and shrubs such as cistus and lavenders (*Lavandula, see p.80*).

Hardiness Fully hardy ✳✳✳ to frost-hardy ✳✳; less hardy if grown in shade or in very fertile soil.

Cultivation Plant these shrubs in very well-drained soil in full sun. **Provide** shelter from cold, drying winds. **Pruning** is rarely needed, but if necessary in mid- or late spring, lightly trim shoots that spoil the shape of the shrub. **Take** semi-ripe cuttings (*see p.394*) in late summer.

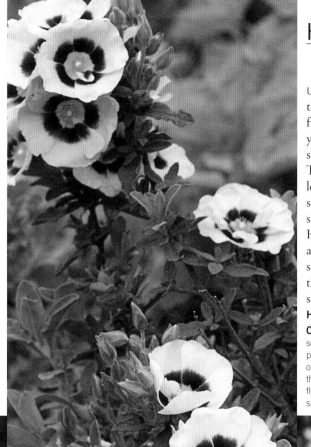

HALIMIUM

late spring to early summer

UPRIGHT TO SPREADING, but almost all compact, these small, evergreen shrubs bear sprays of flowers from late spring to early summer. These are golden yellow, occasionally white, and their petals are sometimes blotched at the bases with maroon-purple. They will flower best in long, hot summers. Their leaves are generally small, light to grey-green, and sometimes silver-scaly or hairy. These trouble-free shrubs usually have an upright or spreading habit. Halimiums are naturally found in dry, rocky places and they thrive in rock gardens or at the front of a sunny border. You can also display them in pots on the patio, placed in the sunniest corner for the best show of flowers.

Hardiness Frost-hardy ✳✳.

Cultivation Halimiums like moderately fertile, well-drained, sandy soil, in full sun, with shelter from cold, drying winds. Choose the planting site carefully, since plants resent disturbance or transplanting once they are established. **Trim lightly** or prune back shoots that spoil the shape after flowering; deadheading plants will help to prolong flowering. **Sow** seed (*see pp.391–393*) at 19–24°C (66–75°F) in spring. **Take** semi-ripe cuttings (*see p.394*) in late summer.

× *Halimiocistus sahucii* ♀
‡45cm (18in) ↔ 90cm (36in), compact, mounding or spreading, narrow-leaved, flowers in summer, one of most reliably hardy ✳✳✳

× *Halimiocistus wintonensis* 'Merrist Wood Cream' ♀
‡60cm (24in) ↔ 90cm (36in), spreading shrub, white woolly leaves, flowers from late spring to early summer ✳✳✳ (borderline)

Halimium 'Susan' ♀
‡45cm (18in) ↔ 60cm (24in), spreading shrub, flowers appear in summer and are often semi-double

HAMAMELIS

Witch hazel

autumn and winter

FRAGRANT, SPIDERY BLOOMS and autumn colour make these medium-sized to large, deciduous shrubs essential in the winter garden. The striking flowers, with four narrow, twisting, ribbon-like petals, cluster thickly on bare stems from autumn to early spring. Frost does not damage them. The broad, oval leaves turn yellow in autumn. Try witch hazels as specimen plants in borders, or grow them in groups. Evergreen Christmas box (*Sarcococca confusa, see p.116*), which is also scented and winter-flowering, will show off the upright, open forms of witch hazels and fill the garden with delicious scent on the coldest of days.

Hardiness Fully hardy ❊❊❊.

Cultivation Witch hazels prefer reasonably fertile, moist but well-drained, ideally neutral to acid (lime-free) soil. They will stand chalk if in deep, humus-rich soil. Position them in sun or partial shade, in an open but not exposed spot. **Prune** any crossing shoots, in late winter or early spring, to maintain a good shape. **Named** witch hazels are grafted and are best bought from a nursery or garden centre.

SUCKERS should be removed, otherwise they will spoil the shrub. Pull them off, or cut them off, at the base. Watch for buds sprouting and rub off.

Hamamelis 'Brevipetala'
↕↔ 4m (12ft), upright shrub, soft, hairy, blue-green leaves turn rich yellow in autumn, very fragrant flowers in mid- and late winter

HEBE

year-round

VARIED AND ATTRACTIVE, EVERGREEN FOLIAGE and pretty flowers, in a huge range of shrubs from low, sprawling plants to large domed bushes, means that there is a hebe for almost any situation. Hebes have neat, matt or glossy foliage in tones of grey-, blue- or true green, sometimes with coloured edges. Spikes up to 30cm (12in) long or clusters of small flowers are usually borne from early to midsummer. They vary in hue from white to pinks, blues, purples, or red. Hebes provide year-round interest in mixed or shrub borders, rock gardens, gravel gardens, or even in pots on the patio. In mild areas, particularly coastal ones, they can be used as hedging or as ground cover.

Hardiness Fully hardy ❊❊❊ to half-hardy ❊.

Cultivation Hebes grow in poor to reasonably fertile, moist but well-drained, preferably neutral to slightly alkaline (limy) soil. Sun or partial shade, with shelter from cold, drying winds, is best. **Remove** any misplaced growths that spoil the shape, in late winter or early spring, but little pruning is needed. **Take** semi-ripe cuttings (*see p.394*) in summer or autumn. **Downy mildew** may infect leaves in damp conditions: avoid watering from above and pick off spoiled leaves.

Hamamelis × intermedia 'Pallida' ♆
↕↔ 4m (12ft), vase-shaped habit, bright green leaves turn gold in autumn, large flowers in mid- to late winter

Hamamelis × intermedia 'Diane' ♆
↕↔ 4m (12ft), vase-shaped habit, bright green leaves turn orange, yellow, or red in autumn (*see inset*), flowers in mid- to late winter

Hebe albicans ♆
↕ 60cm (24in) ↔ 90cm (36in), dense, mound-forming or spreading shrub, flowers from early to midsummer ❊❊❊

Hebe ochracea 'James Stirling' ♥
‡45cm (18in) ↔ 60cm (24in), dense, upright, then arching shrub with stiff shoots; foliage is golden yellow all year round, flowers are borne in late spring and early summer ✳✳✳

HEDERA

see also pp.142–143

Ivy   *year-round*

ALTHOUGH IT IS KNOWN AS A CLIMBING plant, there are a few named cultivars of the common ivy, *Hedera helix*, available that have an unusual, shrubby habit. Like the climbing ivies, they are evergreen and famously tough plants. *Hedera helix* 'Congesta' forms a neat, dense bush with erect, spire-like shoots. It is compact and would make a striking addition to a rock garden. *Hedera helix* 'Erecta' is more vigorous, with stiffly upright stems, and slow-growing. It is better suited to a shrub or mixed border, perhaps where its small leaves contrast with, for example, ferns (*see pp.358–365*) or broad-leaved plants such as bergenias (*see p.198*). The stems are quite brittle, so are best grown in a sheltered spot, or with the support of other shrubs or a wall.

Hardiness Fully hardy ✳✳✳.

Cultivation Ivies grow in a variety of soils, but do best in fertile, moist but well-drained, preferably alkaline (limy) soil, in sun or partial shade, sheltered from wind. **Trim** to shape the shrubs at any time of the year. **Take** semi-ripe cuttings (*see p.394*) in summer.

CLIPPING HEBES with shears in mid- to late spring removes any frost-damaged growth, keeps a neat shape, and encourages new growth. You can also do this to deadhead hebes in late summer.

① *helix* 'Congesta' ♥ ‡↔ 45cm (18in)
② *helix* 'Erecta' ♥ ‡↔ 1m (3ft)

Hebe 'Great Orme' ♥
‡↔ 1.2m (4ft), open, rounded bush, flowers from midsummer right through to mid-autumn, fading to white as they age ✳✳

Hebe pinguifolia 'Pagei' ♥
‡30cm (12in) ↔ 90cm (36in), erect, then semi-prostrate habit, purple stems, flowers from late spring to early summer ✳✳✳

HELIANTHEMUM

Rock rose, Sun rose

late spring to midsummer

‡to 45cm (18in) ↔ 60cm (24in)

THE PRETTY, PAPERY, saucer-shaped flowers of these little evergreen shrubs have ensured that they remain a firm favourite of gardeners. Most grow to only 15–30cm (6–12in) tall. A profusion of blooms, in a wide range of vivid and pale colours, are borne over a long period from late spring to midsummer against a background of silver to grey- or mid-green foliage. They love to bask in sunshine and, with their compact habit, thrive in dry conditions, such as a rock garden or a raised bed, or at the front of a border. A gravel mulch suits them very well, both looking good and giving them a dry, warm, free-draining surface over which to spread.

Hardiness Fully hardy ✳✳✳ to frost-hardy ✳✳.

Cultivation Rock roses enjoy well-drained, neutral to alkaline (limy) soil, in full sun. **Pruning** is very easy; after flowering use garden shears to trim the flowered shoots back to the old growth. **Take** softwood cuttings (*see p.394*) in late spring or early summer.

Helianthemum 'Rhodanthe Carneum' ♀
‡30cm (12in) ↔ 45cm (18in), sometimes sold as 'Wisley Pink', with an especially long flowering season ✳✳✳

HELIOTROPIUM

Heliotrope, Cherry pie

summer

‡↔ 60cm (24in)

HELIOTROPE IS A TREASURED cottage-garden plant, loved for its dense, sweetly-scented flowerheads. Most heliotropes on sale are related to *Heliotropium arborescens*, the only commonly grown species, which although it is a woody shrub is quite tender – hence heliotropes are most often used in frost-prone climates as bedding or container plants, for summer display. They can be overwintered under cover, but new plants grown over winter from cuttings taken from the parent often make more successful, bushier plants to set out the following year. The wrinkled leaves are sometimes tinged purple, complementing the tiny blue or purple flowers borne in large clusters throughout summer.

Hardiness Half-hardy ✳.

Cultivation Grow heliotropes in any fertile, moist but well-drained soil, in full sun. In containers such as pots, tubs, and windowboxes, use any good-quality potting compost. **Sow** seed (*see pp.391–393*) at 16–18°C (61–64°F) in spring. **Take** softwood or semi-ripe cuttings (*see p.394*) in summer.

Helianthemum 'Fire Dragon' ♀
‡20–30cm (8–12in) ↔ 30cm (12in), a very low and compact plant sometimes sold as 'Mrs Clay' ✳✳✳

Helianthemum lunulatum
‡15cm (6in) ↔ 25cm (10in), small-flowered with a cascading habit, good for a sunny bank ✳✳✳

Heliotropium arborescens 'Marine'
‡45cm (18in) ↔ 30–45cm (12–18in), flowerheads to 15cm (6in) across

HIBISCUS

spring to autumn

FAMOUS FOR THEIR SPECTACULAR FLOWERS from spring until autumn, hibiscus are available in a rainbow of bright hues. The blooms are carried against glossy-green, occasionally variegated foliage. Although the group includes many annuals and perennials, as well as shrubs, the woody, deciduous *Hibiscus syriacus* and its cultivars are the most commonly grown in cool climates because they are fully hardy. Hibiscus are a welcome addition to a border, and thrive in large pots. This is particularly useful if you want to grow the Hawaiian hibiscus (*H. rosa-sinensis*) or other tender species, since the container can be moved under cover over winter.

Hardiness Fully hardy ✿✿✿ to frost-tender ✿.

Cultivation Grow in moist, well-drained, preferably slightly alkaline (limy) soil, in full sun. The longer and hotter the summer, the more flowers are produced, so give hibiscus a warm, sheltered position in cooler areas, and apply a winter mulch (*see p.388*). Little pruning is needed other than to remove wayward branches and any dead or damaged wood. **Sow** seed (*see pp.391–392*) at 13–18°C (55–64°F) in spring. **Take** semi-ripe cuttings in summer (*see p.394*), or layer shoots (*see p.395*) in late spring.

Hibiscus syriacus 'Oiseau Bleu' ♀
↕3m (10ft) ↔ 2m (6ft), very popular for its novel colour, and frequently sold under the name 'Blue Bird' ✿✿✿

HIPPOPHAE

Sea buckthorn   *autumn*

THESE TOUGH, DECIDUOUS shrubs or small trees are popular low-maintenance plants with a handsome, upright habit and narrow, silvery leaves. In autumn, abundant orange berries are borne if a male and a female are grown together; those of the willow-leaved sea buckthorn (*Hippophae salicifolia*) are said to be the most nutritious fruits that can be grown in temperate climates. They have a sharp taste like lemon and can be used in juice and preserves. The common sea buckthorn (*H. rhamnoides*) has spiny stems and is invaluable in areas buffeted by salt-laden winds and sea spray, where it can be used for hedges, windbreaks, and stabilizing sandy banks.

Hardiness Fully hardy ✿✿✿.

Cultivation Ideal conditions are full sun in moist but well-drained, slightly alkaline (limy) soil; in practice, these resilient plants will survive most well-drained and sandy soils and periods of drought, strong winds, and heavy rain. **Prune out** only those stems that are crossing or spoiling the shape of the shrub. **Sow** seed (*see pp.391–392*) in a cold frame as soon as it is ripe or in spring. **Take** semi-ripe cuttings in summer or hardwood cuttings in autumn (*see p.394*), or layer shoots (*see p.395*) in autumn.

Hibiscus syriacus 'Diana' ♀
↕3m (10ft) ↔ 2m (6ft), bears some of the largest flowers for this species, to 13cm (5in) across ✿✿✿

Hibiscus syriacus 'Woodbridge' ♀
↕3m (10ft) ↔ 2m (6ft), with flatter, more mallow-like, but intensely coloured blooms ✿✿✿

Hippophae rhamnoides ♀
↕↔ 6m (20ft), bushy shrub or small tree, the berries persist on female plants through to winter

HYDRANGEA

see also p.143

summer and autumn

‡↔ 1m (3ft) to 7m (22ft)

THESE SHRUBS HAVE LONG BEEN GARDEN favourites for their large, stately flowerheads. These may be flat or domed and are made up of clusters of tiny, fertile flowers and larger, sterile flowers with petal-like sepals. The many cultivars of the most common species, *Hydrangea macrophylla*, include two types: hortensias have round "mopheads" of sterile flowers, whereas lacecaps have flat flowerheads of fertile flowers edged with sterile ones. Flower colour is affected by the acidity or alkalinity of the soil. Hydrangea blooms are blue on acid soils and pink on alkaline (limy) soils; on neutral soils, the hues can be mixed, often being bluish-pink. The white-flowered cultivars are not affected. Most garden hydrangeas are deciduous. Some hydrangeas also have flaky, peeling bark and handsome foliage, which has good autumn colour. These excellent plants can be used in many sites, especially as specimen plants or in borders. The flowers dry to parchment shades and are useful in arrangements.

Hardiness Fully hardy ✳✳✳ to frost-hardy ✳✳.

Cultivation Hydrangeas thrive in moist, well-drained, fertile soil in sun or partial shade, if sheltered from cold, drying winds. **Pruning,** for most cultivars except those mentioned below, consists of cutting out misplaced or crossing shoots in late winter or early spring. **Sow** seed (*see pp.391–393*) in containers in spring. **Root** soft stem-tip cuttings in early summer or take hardwood cuttings in winter (*see p.394*). Hydrangea blooms may be spoiled by grey mould (botrytis) in very wet summers.

How to prune hydrangeas

Hard pruning (see left) of H. paniculata *in early spring – before it produces its flowering shoots – results in a much better show of flower. If not pruned, the plants, which normally put on a lot of growth, become very tall and the flowers appear only at the tips where they are difficult to see.*

Hard pruning involves cutting off all the previous year's flowering wood to leave a base of woody stems, as low as 25cm (10in) in exposed gardens or 60cm (24in) at the back of a border. Cut each stem back to a pair of healthy buds at the required height. Neglected plants also respond well to this type of hard pruning.

Light pruning is advisable for hortensias (*also called mophead hydrangeas), all other* H. macrophylla *cultivars,* H. serrata *and its cultivars, and 'Preziosa'. These hydrangeas all flower on stems formed in the previous year. On the whole, they manage this without much attention, but a little annual pruning enhances flowering and keeps the shrubs healthy.*

Leave old flowerheads over winter to protect the new buds. Then, in late winter or early spring, prune the previous year's flowered shoots by up to 30cm (12in) to just above two strong buds (see inset). Cut out weak and thin shoots and prune one or two of the oldest stems to the base.

① *Hydrangea arborescens* 'Annabelle' ♀ ‡↔ 2.5m (8ft) ✳✳✳ ② *arborescens* 'Grandiflora' ♀ ‡↔ 2.5m (8ft) ✳✳✳ ③ *aspera* Villosa Group ♀ ‡↔ 1–4m (4–12ft) ✳✳✳ ④ *involucrata* 'Hortensis' ♀ ‡1m (3ft) ↔ 2m (6ft) ✳✳ ⑤ *macrophylla* 'Ayesha' (hortensia) ‡1.5m (5ft) ↔ 2m (6ft) ✳✳✳ ⑥ *macrophylla* 'Blue Bonnet' (hortensia) ‡2m (6ft) ↔ 2.5m (8ft) ✳✳✳ ⑦ *macrophylla* 'Bouquet Rose' (hortensia) ‡2m (6ft) ↔ 2.5m (8ft) ✳✳✳ ⑧ *macrophylla*

'Hamburg' (hortensia) ‡2m (6ft) ↔ 2.5m (8ft) ✽✽✽ ⑨ *macrophylla* 'Lanarth White' ♀ (lacecap) DIAMOND ('Interhydia') ♀ ‡3–7m (10–22ft) ↔ 2.5m (8ft) ✽✽✽ ⑯ *paniculata* 'Praecox' ‡3–
‡↔ 1.5m (5ft) ✽✽✽ ⑩ *macrophylla* 'Mariesii Perfecta' ♀ (lacecap) ‡2m (6ft) ↔ 2.5m (8ft) ✽✽✽ 7m (10–22ft) ↔ 2.5m (8ft) ✽✽✽ ⑰ *paniculata* 'Unique' ♀ ‡3–7m (10–22ft) ↔ 2.5m (8ft) ✽✽✽
⑪ *macrophylla* 'Veitchii' ♀ (lacecap) ‡2m (6ft) ↔ 2.5m (8ft) ✽✽✽ ⑫ *paniculata* 'Brussels Lace' ⑱ 'Preziosa' ♀ ‡↔ 1.5m (5ft) ✽✽ ⑲ *quercifolia* ♀ ‡2m (6ft) ↔ 2.5m (8ft) ✽✽✽ ⑳ *quercifolia*
‡3–7m (10–22ft) ↔ 2.5m (8ft) ✽✽✽ ⑬ *paniculata* 'Floribunda' ‡3–7m (10–22ft) ↔ 2.5m (8ft) SNOW QUEEN ('Flemygea') ‡2m (6ft) ↔2.5m (8ft) ✽✽✽ ㉑ *serrata* ‡↔1.2m (4ft) ✽✽ ㉒ *serrata*
✽✽✽ ⑭ *paniculata* 'Grandiflora' ♀ ‡3–7m (10–22ft) ↔ 2.5m (8ft) ✽✽✽ ⑮ *paniculata* PINK 'Bluebird' ♀ (lacecap) ‡↔1.2m (4ft) ✽✽ ㉓ *serrata* 'Rosalba' ♀ (lacecap) ‡↔1.2m (4ft) ✽✽

HYPERICUM

St. John's wort

summer to autumn

THIS DIVERSE GROUP ranges from large shrubs to small annuals and perennials, but in summer all bear similar, distinctive, bright yellow flowers with a central boss of golden stamens. Some are decorated with berries through autumn. The shrubs are most commonly cultivated; both evergreen and deciduous species provide lovely autumn colour. There is a hypericum for most situations: the larger species are good for a border, smaller ones for a rock garden. The spreading Rose of Sharon (*Hypericum calycinum*) makes ideal ground cover, although it can become invasive so is not recommended for borders.

↔ 1–2m (3–6ft)

Hardiness Fully hardy ✳✳✳ to half-hardy ✳✳.

Cultivation Larger shrubs prefer moist but well-drained soil in sun or partial shade, the small rock-garden types full sun and good drainage. *H. androsaemum* and *H. calycinum* tolerate even deep shade. **Trim** in spring to keep them neat; larger deciduous species can be cut back hard to a permanent framework in early spring to keep them smaller. **Take** semi-ripe cuttings in summer (*see p.394*).

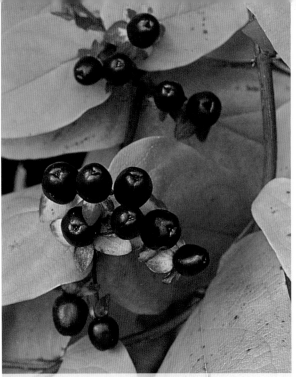

Hypericum androsaemum (Tutsan)
‡75cm (30in) ↔ 90m (36in), bushy, deciduous shrub, flowers in midsummer, red berries ripen to black in autumn ✳✳✳

ILEX

Holly

year-round

HOLLIES ARE BEST KNOWN for winter berries and stiff, prickly, evergreen foliage, but not all are spiny. Their glossy leaves may be plain dark or mid-green, or may be edged, splashed, or striped with silver or gold. The flowers are tiny, the berries usually red or black; they can cause a stomach upset if eaten. Female plants berry only if a male is nearby; hollies are often sold by sex so you can be sure of fruiting. Grow hollies in woodland, with winter-flowering shrubs like sarcococcas (*see p.116*) or mahonias (*see p.87*), or as specimens, so their dense, shapely forms and pale grey bark can be appreciated. *Ilex × altaclerensis* and *I. aquifolium* cultivars can be used as formal hedging, but frequent trimming can mean fewer berries.

Hardiness Fully hardy ✳✳✳ to half-hardy ✳✳.

Cultivation Best planted in late winter or early spring. Full sun encourages bright colour in variegated hollies, but otherwise site in sun or shade in moist, well-drained soil. **Prune** free-standing specimens only if needed to maintain a well-balanced shape; trim hedges in late summer. Topiary may need an extra trim in spring. **Take** semi-ripe cuttings in late summer or autumn (*see p.394*).

PRUNING GROUND COVER
Encourage fresh growth by cutting *H. calycinum* back to the ground in spring, either with shears or a nylon-line trimmer.

Hypericum calycinum (Aaron's beard, Rose of Sharon)
‡60cm (24in) ↔ indefinite, evergreen or semi-evergreen with creeping, rooting stems, flowers from summer to autumn ✳✳✳

Hypericum olympicum* f. *uniflorum
‡25cm (10in) ↔ 30m (12in), deciduous shrub, flowers throughout summer, good for a rock garden ✳✳✳

Ilex × altaclerensis 'Golden King' ♀
‡6m (20ft) ↔ 4m (12ft), compact, female shrub, good conical form (see inset) but berries can be sparse in some years ✳✳

INDIGOFERA

early su...

↔ 2–3m (6–10ft)

THE EVERGREEN AND D[...] shrubby indigoferas are the [...] commonly cultivated in this larg[...] and varied group. They need space to grow and show off their elegant habits, for example in a shrub border, perhaps with euonymus (*see p.56*) and escallonias (*see p.54*), or trained against a sunny wall. Indigoferas bear masses of pea-like flowers from early summer until early autumn, against a background of soft-green leaves. *Indigofera amblyantha* and *I. heterantha* are the hardiest species, and thus the best choice in temperate climates, unless you can provide a sheltered, south-facing wall. They respond well to annual pruning.

Hardiness Fully hardy ✳✳✳ to frost-hardy ✳✳.

Cultivation Grow in moist but well-drained soil, in full sun. **Prune** hard in frost-prone climates only; in early spring, cut all stems down to within a few buds of their bases, leaving a low stubby framework (*see p.383*). For wall-trained shrubs, in late winter or early spring, remove or tie in branches growing too far outwards, and trim sideshoots to within three or four buds of the main branches. **Take** semi-ripe cuttings in early or midsummer (*see p.394*).

Ilex aquifolium 'J.C. van Tol' ♀
↕ 6m (20ft) ↔ 4m (12ft), broadly shaped female tree, self-fertile so berries are guaranteed every year without a male nearby ✳✳

Ilex aquifolium 'Ferox Argentea' ♀ (Hedgehog holly)
↕ 8m (25ft) ↔ 4m (12ft), slow-growing, upright, densely prickly male with spines both over and on the leaves ✳✳

Ilex aquifolium 'Amber' ♀
↕ 6m (20ft) ↔ 2.5m (8ft), compact, pyramid-shaped, female tree, reliably bears abundant fruit when a male holly is close by ✳✳

Ilex × altaclerensis 'Camelliifolia' ♀
↕ 14m (46ft) ↔ 12–15m (40–50ft), large, conical, female shrub with no spines, leaves up to 13cm (5in) long ✳✳

Indigofera amblyantha ♀
↕ 2m (6ft) ↔ 2.5m (8ft), deciduous shrub, particularly free-flowering ✳✳✳

...y species of itea
...e are very widely
...for their tiny white
...e in catkin-like clusters
..., and also for their
...milar to that of holly. The
... *ilicifolia* are valuable for
prov... ...enery; those of the deciduous
I. virginica g... ...cular autumn display of reds
and purples before th...y fall.

Hardiness Fully hardy ✳✳✳ to frost-hardy ✳✳.

Cultivation The less hardy evergreen iteas like fertile, moist, well-drained soil in a sunny, sheltered position; they thrive against a sunny, south-facing wall and with a thick winter mulch (*see p.388*), especially while young. Deciduous species prefer the shady, damp, slightly acid conditions of a woodland garden or dense shrub border. **Trim** evergreens only as necessary to keep them neat. Deciduous iteas can be kept shapely by cutting the flowered shoots back to strong, non-flowering sideshoots; once plants are mature, cut back one stem in four to the base each year to prevent congestion (*see p.383*). If wall-trained, cut back flowered shoots to a few buds from the framework branches. **Sow** seed when ripe (*see pp.391–393*). **Take** soft stem-tip cuttings in spring, or semi-ripe cuttings in summer (*see p.394*).

JASMINUM NUDIFLORUM

see also p.144

Winter jasmine   *winter*

↔ 3m (10ft)

MOST COMMONLY GROWN jasmines are climbers, but this one is a shrub, albeit a rather lanky one. The winter jasmine (*Jasminum nudiflorum*) may not be quite as intensely perfumed as its summer-flowering cousins, but is highly valued nevertheless for its golden flowers through the barest months of the year. This slender-stemmed, arching, often quite untidy plant is best wall-trained, perhaps with other winter favourites such as garryas (*see p.64*). Cut sprigs and bring them indoors while the buds are still closed; the warmth of a room should force them into flower early for a touch of winter cheer and delicate scent.

Hardiness Fully hardy ✳✳✳.

Cultivation Grow in fertile, well-drained soil in full sun or partial shade. **Prune** flowered shoots back to strong buds, and once plants are older, after flowering, remove up to one in four of the main stems at the base to encourage fresh growth (*see p.383*). **Take** semi-ripe cuttings in summer or autumn (*see p.394*); alternatively shoots can be layered (*see p.395*) in autumn.

JUNIPERUS

Juniper   *year-round*

THESE EVERGREEN, CONIFEROUS TREES and shrubs are grown for their sculptural habits and colourful foliage. They come in all shapes and sizes; large trees, dwarf cultivars, and spreading shrubs, and their leaves, or needles, can be dark green, golden yellow or even blue. A fantastic tapestry of shapes, colours and of textures can be built up by growing a collection of junipers together, or with other conifers. The females bear round, fleshy cones, rather like berries; these are used in cooking and also as one of the flavourings of gin. Junipers will tolerate a wide range of conditions: larger trees can be used as specimens, small shrubs in a rock garden with alpines, and prostrate cultivars as ground cover.

Hardiness Fully hardy ✳✳✳ to frost-hardy ✳✳.

Cultivation Junipers are unfussy and will grow in any well-drained soil, in sun or partial shade. **Pruning** is unnecessary, although if prostrate species spread too far you can remove selected stems carefully to keep them within bounds. Propagation is tricky, and seed may take up to five years to germinate, so new plants are probably best bought from a nursery.

① *ilicifolia* ♀ ↕ 3–5m (10–15ft), flowers from midsummer to early autumn ✳✳ ② *virginica* (Sweetspire, Tassel-white) ↕ 1.5–3m (5–10ft), flowers in summer ✳✳✳

Jasminum nudiflorum ♀ (Winter jasmine)
↕↔ 3m (10ft), deciduous shrub with fragrant flowers in winter, leaves are dark green and appear after flowering

Juniperus squamata 'Blue Star' ♀
↕ 40cm (16in) ↔ to 1m (3ft), a compact, spreading bush forming wave-like, cascading shapes ✳✳✳

KALMIA

mid-spring to early summer

KALMIAS ARE ACID-LOVING, evergreen shrubs with clusters of pretty, pink, bowl-shaped flowers in mid-spring and early summer. Throughout the year, the branches are clothed with the glossy, leathery leaves. The larger kalmias, such as *Kalmia latifolia* and its cultivars, are spectacular in borders or among groves of trees. Small species, for example *K. microphylla*, can be used in a rock or woodland garden with heathers and dwarf rhododendrons, which require similar soil conditions.

Hardiness Fully hardy ❋❋❋.

Cultivation Grow in moist, acid (lime-free) soil, preferably in partial shade unless the ground remains continually damp; a layer of leafmould, pine needles, or compost around the plants in spring will help retain moisture. If you live in an area with limy soil, grow kalmias in pots filled with ericaceous (lime-free) compost. **Prune** after flowering only if necessary to trim shoots that spoil the shape of the shrub. If you have a leggy specimen, then renovate it over several seasons (*see p.384*) – except *K. angustifolia*, which can be cut back hard in a single year, and will regrow well. **Take** semi-ripe cuttings in midsummer (*see p.394*), or layer low-growing shoots in late summer (*see p.395*).

Juniperus scopulorum 'Skyrocket'
↕6m (20ft) ↔ 50–60cm (20–24in), pencil- thin, columnar tree that provides a spectacular focal point ❋❋❋

Juniperus × *pfitzeriana* 'Pfitzeriana Aurea'
↕90cm (36in) ↔ 2m (6ft), spreading shrub, the golden yellow needles become greenish-yellow over winter ❋❋❋

Juniperus chinensis 'Pyramidalis' ♀
↕2m (6ft) ↔ 60cm (24in), small cultivar with a neat, compact shape ❋❋❋

Juniperus communis 'Compressa' ♀
↕80cm (32in) ↔ 45m (18in), dwarf and very slow-growing, suitable for combining with alpine plants in a trough or rock garden ❋❋❋

Kalmia angustifolia ♀ (Sheep laurel)
↕60cm (24in) ↔ 1.5m (5ft), mound-forming shrub, flowers are occasionally white

KERRIA JAPONICA

Jew's mantle

spring and year-round

↔ to 3m (9ft)

KERRIA AND ITS CULTIVARS are vigorous, suckering shrubs that are good value all year-round. In mid and late spring, they bear single or double, golden yellow flowers. The deciduous foliage is bright green, grey-green, or variegated with creamy white. When the leaves fall, winter interest is then provided by the dense clumps of arching, light green stems. Grow kerrias in a border where they have room to spread out among other shrubs, or as part of a display of winter stems together with dogwoods (*Cornus, see pp.42–43*).

Hardiness Fully hardy ✳✳✳.

Cultivation Grow kerrias in fertile, well-drained soil in full sun or partial shade. **Prune** the stems when they have flowered to sideshoots or strong buds lower down on the shrub (*see p.383*). **Divide** the bush in autumn (*see p.395*), or propagate from suckers (stems growing up from the roots) in spring. Find a sucker and dig down to check it has developed some roots of its own. Cut it away from its parent, cut back its stem by a half, and replant it.

KOELREUTERIA

spring to autumn

↔ 10m (30ft)

THESE MAKE FINE SPECIMEN trees throughout the year. They have a spreading shape, elegant, deciduous leaves, large clusters of yellow flowers in summer, and unusual, bladder-like fruits in the autumn. The golden rain tree (*Koelreuteria paniculata*) is the most widely available, and also perhaps the most impressive, of the three species. Its leaves emerge reddish-pink in spring, mature to mid-green, and give a lovely show of butter-yellow tints in autumn. In mid- and late summer, it bears sprays of small, golden flowers, up to 30cm (12in) long, followed by pink- or red-flushed fruit capsules. The flowers are more abundant in areas with long, hot summers.

Hardiness Fully hardy ✳✳✳ to frost-hardy ✳✳.

Cultivation Grow in fertile, well-drained soil in full sun. **Prune** out any damaged or dead wood (*see p.382*) when dormant in winter, but no further pruning is necessary. **Sow** seed (*see pp.391–392*) in autumn, in a container, and place in a cold frame.

FRUIT CAPSULES

Kerria japonica 'Picta'
‡ 1.5m (5ft) ↔ 2m (6ft)

Kerria japonica 'Golden Guinea' ♀
‡ 2m (6ft) ↔ 2.5m (8ft), very large single flowers up to 6cm (2½in) across

Koelreuteria paniculata ♀ (Golden rain tree, Pride of India)
‡ ↔ 10m (30ft), leaves to 45cm (18in) long ✳✳✳

KOLKWITZIA AMABILIS

Beauty bush *late spring to early summer*

‡ 3m (10ft)
↔ 4m (12ft)

IN FULL FLOWER, the beauty bush is an amazing sight. From late spring to early summer, the pale- to deep-pink blooms are borne in such numbers that they almost completely obscure the tapered, dark green leaves. This is a deciduous, suckering shrub with an elegant, arching habit. It makes an excellent border plant and is also wonderful grown as a specimen, so that its charms can be enjoyed to the full. Cultivars with brighter pink flowers or orange-yellow young foliage are available.

Hardiness Fully hardy ✻✻✻; foliage may be damaged by late frost.

Cultivation This shrub prefers well-drained soil, preferably in full sun, although it will tolerate some shade. **Prune** shoots after they have flowered, to strong buds or shoots lower down on the plant. On mature plants, cut out about one-third to a quarter of old branches to the ground to encourage new growth (*see p.383*). **Propagate** the shrub from suckers (stems growing up from the roots) in spring. Find a sucker and dig down to check that it has developed some roots of its own. Cut it away from its parent, cut back its stems by half, and then replant it. Water well.

LABURNUM

Golden rain *late spring to early summer*

‡↔ to 8m (25ft)

AS THE COMMON NAME SUGGESTS, these spreading trees are grown for their bright-yellow, pea-like flowers, which are produced in long pendent clusters in late spring and early summer. Any of this small group of compact trees is an excellent choice for a specimen tree in a small garden. Create a lovely arch, tunnel, or pergola of golden rain – simply tie in the branches to a frame while they are young and supple. In this way, the pendent flowers can be enjoyed at their best. Plant purple flowers, such as alliums (*see pp.174–175*), beneath them for a pleasing contrast. Weeping cultivars are available.

Hardiness Fully hardy ✻✻✻.

Cultivation Site laburnums in well-drained soil in full sun. **Train** them by tying in shoots as they grow. In late summer, trim the sideshoots to two or three buds from the main stems to encourage branching, and more flowers. Remove any wayward shoots when they are still young, in late winter (*see p.382*). **Sow** seed of species (*see pp.392–392*) in a cold frame in autumn; plant out the seedlings quickly because they resent root disturbance.

LAURUS NOBILIS

Sweet bay, Bay laurel *year-round*

THE SWEET BAY FORMS a large shrub or small, conical tree with evergreen, aromatic foliage that is used as a culinary flavouring. Cultivars with golden leaves are also available. Both male and female flowers are greenish-yellow, but are borne on separate plants in spring; if grown together, then black berries may follow on the female. Bay is often clipped and looks elegant with other formal topiary, such as box (*Buxus, see p.30*), or in a pot as a handsome patio plant. Neat bushes or standards in containers have the bonus of being easily moved under cover in winter, if needed. Bay can also be grown in its natural form as a specimen, in borders, or against a wall.

Hardiness Frost-hardy ✻✻; foliage may be damaged by cold winds.

Cultivation Grow in moist, well-drained soil, in sun or partial shade, with some shelter. Remove wayward or crossing shoots of naturally shaped bay (*see p.382*). **Clip** topiary once or twice in summer to keep it neat. **Sow** seed (*see pp.392–392*) in pots in a cold frame in autumn; take semi-ripe cuttings (*see p.394*) in summer. Round, brown scale insects may be a problem on plants growing under cover; remove any shoots with mildew (*see p.398*).

Kolkwitzia amabilis 'Pink Cloud' ♀
Widely available

Laburnum × *watereri* 'Vossii' ♀
‡↔ 8m (25ft), flower clusters up to 60cm (2ft) long

Laurus nobilis ♀
‡ 12m (40ft) ↔ 10m (30ft), widely available, contact with foliage may inflame skin allergies

LAVANDULA

Lavender   *mid- to late summer*

LAVENDERS ARE DESERVEDLY POPULAR PLANTS, grown for their evergreen, aromatic foliage, and scented flowers in mid- to late summer. There are many types, some more strongly perfumed than others, most with silvery foliage and nectar-rich blooms that are irresistible to pollinating bees. To dry the flowers so you can enjoy their summery aroma in winter, cut them before they are fully open and hang them upside down in bunches in a dry place. Lavenders can be used in borders and are classic partners for roses; they are wonderful grown as low edging for a bed, sending up great wafts of scent as you brush past. Some species are not fully hardy but can be easily grown in pots and taken into a conservatory over winter.

Hardiness Fully hardy ✳✳✳ to half-hardy ✳.

Cultivation Lavenders are undemanding, provided that they have well-drained soil in full sun. **Trim** in early or mid spring: use shears to create a neat, rounded mound, taking off shoot tips but never cutting into old, bare wood. Trim lightly again to remove faded flower stalks (*see right*). **Sow** seed in a container in a cold frame in spring (*see pp.391–392*). **Take** semi-ripe cuttings in summer (*see p.394*) for quicker results.

DEADHEADING LAVENDER
Neaten up lavender bushes when the flowers have faded, by trimming them over with a pair of garden shears, back to within 2.5cm (1in) of the old growth.

Lavandula pedunculata subsp. *pedunculata* ♥
↕↔ 60cm (24in), attractive relative of the vigorous French lavender, *L. stoechas* ✳✳✳ (borderline)

Lavandula angustifolia 'Munstead'
↕ 45cm (18in) ↔ 60cm (24in), more compact than the species so better for border edging ✳✳✳

Lavandula angustifolia 'Hidcote' ♥
↕ 60cm (24in) ↔ 75cm (30in), compact lavender whose vivid flowers contrast spectacularly with the grey leaves ✳✳✳

Lavandula angustifolia 'Nana Alba' ♥
↕↔ 30cm (12in), forms a very compact, neat bush, good for containers and edging, widely available ✳✳✳

Lavandula 'Marshwood'
↕↔ 60cm (24in), bushy plant with similar flowers to the French lavenders ✳✳✳ (borderline)

LAVATERA
see also p.270

Mallow   ***summer to autumn***

:→ 2m (6ft)

THERE ARE LOTS OF MALLOWS; the shrubby ones need space to grow as they get quite large, but they respond well to hard pruning. They are valued for their profusion of ice-cream-coloured flowers in summer and autumn. The foliage of both deciduous and evergreen types is soft green, with downy hairs, rather coarse in appearance, so these shrubs are best used to provide a substantial backdrop for smaller ornamental plants; put them near the back of the border, preferably against a wall in areas with very cold winters. Mallows are ideal for coastal gardens, enjoying the sandy soil and often mild, frost-free conditions.

Hardiness Fully hardy ✳✳✳ to frost-hardy ✳✳.

Cultivation Mallows prefer light, sandy soil in full sun, but tolerate heavier ground. In cold regions, the frost-hardy species may need shelter from cold, drying winds, for example a south-facing wall. **Prune** in early spring to keep the shrub compact, cutting stems back almost to the base. **Take** softwood cuttings (*see p.394*) in early summer; lavateras can be short-lived and it is wise to grow replacements.

LESPEDEZA

Bush clover   ***late summer to autumn***

‡ 2m (6ft)
↔ 3m (10ft)

THE BUSH CLOVERS are named for their blue-green leaves, borne in groups of three and looking like those of the common clover. There are annual and perennial species, but the most commonly available are the deciduous shrubs, which are mainly grown for their pea-like flowers. They hang in long, dense clusters from the arching branches towards the end of summer and into autumn. This late flowering time makes lespedezas invaluable plants to team with rudbeckias (*see p.317*) and Michaelmas daisies (*Aster, see pp.192–193*) for a fabulous display of warm, glowing colours late in the season. Very cold winters may cut these plants down, but they will regrow.

Hardiness Fully hardy ✳✳✳.

Cultivation Grow in light, well-drained soil in full sun. **Prune** in early spring by cutting back all the stems to a low framework; if severe winters cause the top-growth to die back, then cut stems right down to the base of the plant. **Sow** seed in containers outdoors in spring (*see pp.391–392*). *L. thunbergii* can be divided (*see p.395*), also in spring.

Lavandula angustifolia '**Loddon Pink**' ⚥
‡45cm (18in) ↔ 60cm (24in), more compact than the species and thus better for border edging ✳✳✳

① × *clementii* '**Burgundy Wine**' ⚥ ‡↔ 2m (6ft) vigorous, semi-evergreen ✳✳✳ ② × *clementii* '**Barnsley**' ‡↔ 2m (6ft) vigorous, semi-evergreen, white flowers age to pink ✳✳✳

Lespedeza thunbergii ⚥
‡ 2m (6ft) ↔ 3m (10ft), flowers in early autumn, may only achieve full height in warmer areas where the top-growth survives winter

LEUCOTHOE

spring and autumn

THESE DECIDUOUS, EVERGREEN and semi-evergreen shrubs resemble pieris (*see pp.96–97*) in many ways, with an upright habit, arching branches, and attractive, bell-like, white flowers that appear in spring. The leaves of all are handsome, but novel foliage colour is an added attraction in cultivars of *Leucothoe fontanesiana* such as 'Rainbow' and 'Scarletta', which has dark red-purple young foliage that turns dark green in summer and then bronze in winter. Leucothoes grow best in a shady position, accompanying shrubs such as rhododendrons (*see pp.104–107*), ericas (*see pp.52–53*) and pieris, which all like similar soil conditions. Most are good choices for a woodland garden; the small *L. keiskei* is suitable for a rock garden.

Hardiness Fully hardy ✳✳✳ to frost-hardy ✳✳.

Cultivation Grow in partial or deep shade, in soil that is acid (lime-free) and reliably moist; add plenty of well-rotted organic matter. **Prune** in late winter or early spring, only to take out any crossing or badly placed branches. **Sow** seed in containers in a cold frame in spring (*see pp.391–392*). **Take** semi-ripe cuttings (*see p.394*) in summer.

LEYCESTERIA FORMOSA

Himalayan honeysuckle   *summer to autumn*

A FAST-GROWING SHRUB with hollow, bamboo-like stems, this has unusual flowers appearing in summer, followed by small, round berries. The white flowers are covered by distinctive bracts (leaves growing at the flower base), forming drooping, pagoda-like clusters that made the plant a popular choice in Victorian shrubberies. These bracts persist to enclose purple-red berries. It is less widely grown today, which is a pity as it provides a long season of interest, from blue-green shoots in spring to good autumn colour. The stems remain attractive during winter and look effective among other shrubs with colourful winter stems, such as the dogwoods (*Cornus, see pp.42–43*).

Hardiness Fully hardy ✳✳✳ (borderline).

Cultivation Grow in reasonably fertile, well-drained soil, in full sun or partial shade. **Protect** from cold, drying winds and protect with a thick layer (mulch) of organic matter around the base of the plant in winter if severe frosts are forecast (*see p.388*). **Prune** after flowering by cutting back flowered shoots to young sideshoots or strong buds lower down – or, in spring, cut all the stems back hard (*see p.383*). **Sow** seed in containers in a cold frame in autumn (*see pp.391–392*). **Take** softwood cuttings in summer (*see p.394*).

LIGUSTRUM

Privet   *year-round*

MOST COMMONLY USED AS HEDGING, privets are evergreen or semi-evergreen shrubs found in many an urban garden, since they happily withstand shade and pollution. Easy to grow, they thrive in most garden soils and situations. White flowers with a musty scent appear in spring or summer, followed by black fruits, but the dense, neat foliage is the main feature. The habit can be upright or conical, rounded or spreading. Some species, such as *Ligustrum japonicum*, with large, glossy leaves, can be used as specimen shrubs or in a border. Others, such as the golden privet (*L. ovalifolium* 'Aureum'), make the best hedges.

Hardiness Fully hardy ✳✳✳ to frost-hardy ✳✳.

Cultivation Grow in any well-drained soil in full sun or partial shade; variegated cultivars produce the best-coloured foliage in full sun. **Prune** shrubs in late winter or early spring, cutting out any overcrowded or crossing branches. **Clip** hedges at least twice a year. **Sow** seed in containers in a cold frame in autumn or spring (*see pp.391–392*). **Take** semi-ripe cuttings in summer, or hardwood cuttings in winter (*see p.394*). **Leaf miners** may attack privet, making characteristic ribbon-like markings, but they do no lasting damage.

Leucothoe fontanesiana 'Rainbow'
↕1.5m (5ft) ↔ 2m (6ft), clump-forming variety that makes good underplanting for a woodland garden, flowers in late spring ✳✳✳

Leycesteria formosa ♥
↕↔ 2m (6ft), upright, thicket-forming habit, suited to a woodland garden or shrub border, flowers from late summer to early autumn

Ligustrum lucidum 'Excelsum Superbum' ♥
↕↔ 10m (30ft), conical-shaped tree or shrub, evergreen leaves, flowers in late summer ✳✳✳

LINUM ARBOREUM
see also p.278

Flax
late spring to summer

↕↔ 30cm (12in)

THIS TOUGH LITTLE SHRUB has flowers of deep yellow. Individual blooms are short-lived, but there are always plenty to take their place, following on from late spring through summer. As with many other types of flax, the flowers usually close in the afternoon. A dwarf evergreen, this flax originates in scrubby regions of Greece and western Turkey, and is very suitable for sloping, free-draining banks, rock gardens, or the front of a sunny border. Create a Mediterranean feel by growing it with other sun-loving, green and gold plants such as golden marjoram (*Origanum*, *see p.91*), helianthemum (*see p.70*), or gold-variegated elaeagnus (*see pp.50–51*).

Hardiness Frost-hardy ✳✳.

Cultivation Grow in light, reasonably fertile soil with added organic matter; dig in coarse grit on heavy clay soils to improve drainage (*see p.377*). The plant must have a warm, sunny spot. Protect it from winter wet, if possible, by placing a cloche over it. **Sow** seed in spring or autumn in containers in a cold frame (*see pp.391–392*). **Take** semi-ripe cuttings (*see p.394*) in summer.

LIQUIDAMBAR
autumn

↕ to 25m (80ft)
↔ to 12m (40ft)

THESE DECIDUOUS TREES BEAR maple-like leaves that turn to stunning shades of purple, crimson, orange, and gold in autumn. In late spring tiny, yellow-green flowers are produced, followed by spiky, round fruit clusters. Liquidambars have an upright, open habit and look attractive either in a woodland setting or as specimens, isolated from other trees. The sweet gum (*Liquidambar styraciflua*) is really excellent value as a garden tree, pyramid-shaped with glossy, dark-green leaves and grey, deeply grooved bark. In autumn, its leaves are a blaze of fiery colour for up to six weeks.

Hardiness Fully hardy ✳✳✳ to frost-hardy ✳✳.

Cultivation Grow in reasonably fertile, preferably acid (lime-free), moist but well-drained soil. The best autumn colour is produced in full sun, but they will tolerate partial shade. **Prune** young trees to remove any crossing or misplaced branches, in late winter or early spring (*see p.382*). **Sow** seed in containers in a cold frame in autumn (*see pp.391–392*). **Take** soft stem-tip cuttings (*see p.394*) in summer.

LIRIODENDRON

Tulip tree
summer and autumn

↕ to 20m (70ft)
↔ to 12m (40ft)

EXCELLENT AS A SPECIMEN, the tulip tree has distinctive leaves that turn from dark green to butter-yellow in autumn. The trees are deciduous, with a stately, broadly columnar habit. In summer, mature trees produce curiously tulip-shaped, pale green flowers, although these are not really visible from a distance. It is only in warm summers, when the wood has been well ripened, that the tree is likely to flower well. It is well worth growing for the foliage alone, but only if you have plenty of space. For a smaller garden, choose the more compact *Liriodendron tulipifera* 'Aureomarginatum'.

Hardiness Fully hardy ✳✳✳.

Cultivation Grow in reasonably fertile soil that is moist but well-drained, and preferably slightly acid (lime-free). Will grow in full sun or partial shade. **Prune out** any crossing or misshapen branches while trees are young, in late winter or early spring, to create a healthy, well-shaped framework of branches (*see p.382*). **Sow** seed in containers in a cold frame in autumn (*see pp.391–392*). Leaf spot (*see p.399*) may affect trees, but is generally worth treating only if they are young.

Linum arboreum ♀
Thick, glaucous leaves often produced in rosettes

① *styraciflua* '**Golden Treasure**' ↕10m (30ft) ↔ 6m (20ft)
② *styraciflua* '**Worplesdon**' ♀ ↕ 25m (80ft) ↔ 12m (40ft), in autumn, leaves turn purple

Liriodendron tulipifera ♀
↕ 30m (100ft) ↔ 15m (50ft), vigorous, broadly columnar to conical tree, leaves to 15cm (6in) long, flowers 6cm (2½in) long

LITHODORA

summer

LITHODORAS ARE SMALL, spreading, evergreen shrubs grown for their profusion of funnel-shaped, blue or white flowers that appear mainly in the summer. Previously known as lithospermums, they can be upright or prostrate in habit, and have spear-shaped leaves that vary from dark green to grey-green. The leaves are hairy, which helps the plants conserve moisture. They originate from southern Europe and so enjoy free-draining hot, dry conditions. They make good ground-cover plants in a rock garden, at the front of a border, or in an alpine trough where they can cascade over the edge.

Hardiness Fully hardy ✳✳✳ to frost-hardy ✳✳.

Cultivation Grow most lithodoras in well-drained, ideally alkaline (limy) soil, in full sun; however, *L. diffusa* 'Heavenly Blue' needs acid soil with well-rotted organic matter added to it. If growing it in an alpine trough, use a compost mix of equal parts loam, leafmould, and grit. **Trim** shoots that spoil the shape after flowering, or to rejuvenate plants, shear over flowered shoots to within 2.5cm (1in) of the old growth in early spring. **Take** semi-ripe cuttings in summer (*see p.394*). Lithodoras are occasionally troubled by aphids (*see p.398*).

Lithodora oleifolia ♥
‡20cm (8in) ↔ 30m (12in), semi-upright, loosely branched, flowers change from pink-tinged buds to sky-blue when fully open ✳✳✳

LONICERA

see also p.146

Honeysuckle

winter and year-round

THESE HONEYSUCKLES ARE SHRUBS, not the climbers that are most commonly grown. There are two distinct types: deciduous species grown for their powerfully perfumed flowers (the most popular species, such as *Lonicera fragrantissima*, bearing these in the depths of winter), and small-leaved evergreens such as *L. nitida* and *L. pileata*, which have tiny flowers but a dense, neat habit, and are valuable for hedging and ground cover respectively. All tolerate a wide range of conditions and need little maintenance. Their berries can cause mild stomach upset if eaten.

Hardiness Fully hardy ✳✳✳.

Cultivation Grow in any well-drained soil in full sun or partial shade. **Trim** deciduous shrubs after flowering if needed to restrict size, cutting back flowered shoots to strong sideshoots lower down. When plants grow old and growth is crowded, take out a main branch at the base. Evergreens can be trimmed as necessary. If *L. nitida* is grown as a hedge, it will need trimming at least twice, in summer. **Sow** seed (*see pp.391–392*) in a container when ripe, placing it in a cold frame. **Take** semi-ripe cuttings of evergreens in summer, and hardwood cuttings of deciduous types in autumn (*see p.394*). Aphids (*see p.398*) can be troublesome, particularly on plants in full sun.

Lithodora diffusa 'Heavenly Blue' ♥
‡15cm (6in) ↔ 60cm (24in), fast-growing, mat-forming shrub with many branches, popular rockery plant, leaves hairy on both sides, flowers from late spring through summer ✳✳✳

Lonicera × purpusii 'Winter Beauty' ♥
‡2m (6ft) ↔ 2.5m (8ft), twiggy habit, deciduous or semi-evergreen, heavily scented winter flowers, berries rarely produced

LUMA

year-round

‡ 6–15m (15–20ft)
↔ 5–15m (15–50ft)

THESE SOUTH AMERICAN evergreen shrubs and small trees have aromatic, leathery leaves and cup-shaped, white flowers, blooming in summer and autumn. *Luma apiculata* is also prized for its striking peeling bark. The oval leaves are usually dark green, though *L. apiculata* 'Glanleam Gold' has foliage with creamy yellow margins. The flowers are followed by purple or black berries. Grow lumas in small groups, or as a specimen in a lawn. In areas with cold winters, they perform best against a warm wall. *L. apiculata* can also be used as a hedging plant.

Hardiness Frost-hardy ✳✳

Cultivation Grow in fertile soil, enriched with well-rotted organic matter, in full sun or partial shade. **Prune out** any crossing or misshapen branches (*see p.382*) in late winter or early spring to maintain a good shape and a healthy framework of branches and clip regularly to keep it neat. **Trim** hedges in spring. **Sow** seed in containers in a cold frame in spring (*see pp.391–392*); lumas may also self-seed in the garden. **Take** semi-ripe cuttings in late summer (*see p.394*).

MAACKIA

mid- to late summer

IF YOU ARE LOOKING FOR an unusual specimen tree for the garden, consider a maackia. Deciduous, it has fine leaves made up of several oval leaflets. In summer, it produces erect clusters of tiny, white, pea-like flowers, followed by long, flat seed pods. Native to woodland in East Asia, maackias are slow-growing trees. Although it may ultimately reach 15m (50ft), *Maackia amurensis* would be suitable for smaller gardens for many years. *M. chinensis* is slightly smaller, at 10m (30ft) tall, with attractive, silvery grey-blue leaves. As well as specimen trees, maackias look good alongside other slender, delicate trees such as birches (*Betula, see p.28*) and rowan (*Sorbus, see p.118*).

Hardiness Fully hardy ✳✳✳.

Cultivation Maackias like reasonably fertile, well-drained soil that is neutral to acid (lime-free), in full sun. Little pruning is needed; remove any shoots that spoil the shape of young trees to encourage a good form (*see p.382*). **Sow** seed, after soaking, in containers or in a seedbed in autumn (*see pp.391–393*). **Take** stem-tip cuttings in early or midsummer (*see p.394*).

Lonicera nitida
‡ 2m (6ft) ↔ 1.2m (4ft), evergreen, flowers in spring, purple-blue berries, excellent for hedging or topiary

Lonicera fragrantissima
‡ 2m (6ft) ↔ 3m (10ft), arching habit, deciduous or semi-evergreen, fragrant winter flowers best in full sun and shelter, dull red berries

Luma apiculata ♀
‡↔ 10–15m (30–50ft), upright, vigorous, cinnamon-brown and cream bark, flowers from midsummer to mid-autumn, purple berries

Maackia amurensis
‡ 15m (50ft) ↔ 10m (30ft), open, spreading habit, flowers in mid- and late summer

MACLURA

summer and autumn

THE MACLURAS GROWN IN GARDENS are large, deciduous shrubs or small trees, prized for their elegant foliage and unusual fruits. Both a male and a female need to be planted to obtain fruits, or you can buy a female plant with a male branch grafted on to it. They need long, hot summers to grow well and fruit. *Maclura pomifera* has a rounded habit and is thorny when young. It has tiny, cup-shaped, yellow-green flowers and dark green leaves that turn yellow in autumn, surrounding the fruits. *M. tricuspidata* is smaller and bushier, up to 6m (20ft) tall and wide, flowers in summer, and bears edible, orange-red fruits. Grow macluras among other shrubs or as specimens; *M. pomifera* can also be used for hedging.

Hardiness Fully hardy ✳✳✳. Unripened shoots on young plants may be damaged by spring frosts.

Cultivation Grow in reasonably fertile soil in full sun. **Prune** young trees in late winter or early spring to remove any misplaced or crossing shoots; cut frost-damaged growth back to a strong bud. **Sow** ripe seed in pots in a sheltered spot outside (*see pp.391–392*). **Take** semi-ripe cuttings in summer, or take root cuttings in winter (*see p.394*).

MAGNOLIA

early spring to early summer

‡ to 20m (70ft)
↔ to 15m (50ft)

SPLENDID, SOLITARY, often fragrant, cup- or saucer-shaped flowers distinguish these stately, slow-growing, deciduous and evergreen trees and shrubs. A magnolia in full flower is a sight never to be forgotten. The range of flower colours includes pure white, pink, rich purple, and shades of creamy and greenish-yellow. Most flower between early spring and early summer, many before the tough, but handsome leaves unfurl. Some produce cone-like pods studded with red-coated seeds in autumn. Magnolias make fine specimens; some can be wall-trained.

Hardiness Fully hardy ✳✳✳ to frost-tender ❄.

Cultivation Grow in moist but well-drained, fertile soil in sun or partial shade. They prefer neutral to acid (lime-free) soil, but some tolerate alkaline soil. **Prune** only if absolutely necessary, in late winter or early spring. **Take** softwood cuttings of deciduous species in early summer; take semi-ripe cuttings of evergreens in late summer or early autumn (*see p.394*). Magnolias are prone to coral spot, seen as orange pustules on dying stems; remove affected wood at once and burn it.

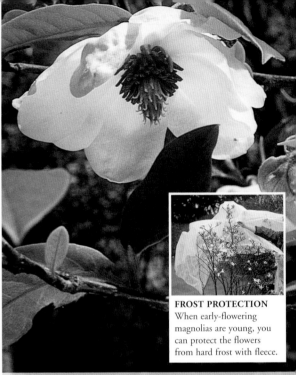

FROST PROTECTION
When early-flowering magnolias are young, you can protect the flowers from hard frost with fleece.

Magnolia wilsonii ♀
‡↔ 6m (20ft), deciduous shrub or tree, red-purple shoots, leaves felted red-brown underneath, flowers in late spring ✳✳✳

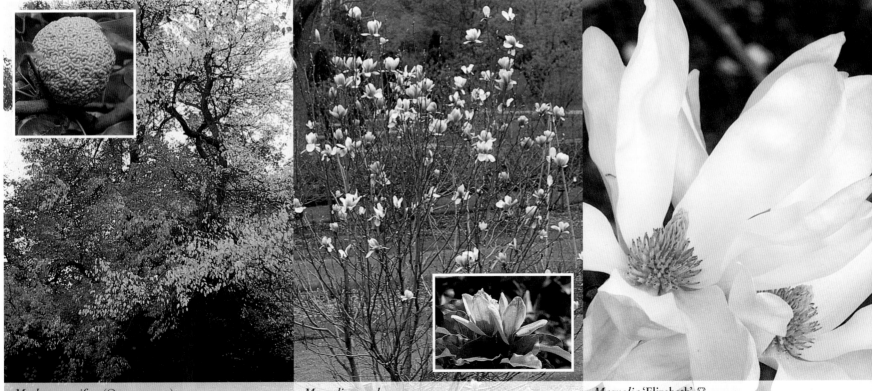

Maclura pomifera (Osage orange)
‡15m (50ft) ↔ 12m (40ft), flowers in early summer, fruits (*see inset*) up to 13cm (5in) across

Magnolia × *soulangeana*
‡↔ 6m (20ft), deciduous shrub or tree, may be wall-trained, flowers open in mid- and late spring, on bare branches ✳✳✳

Magnolia 'Elizabeth' ♀
‡10m (30ft) ↔ 6m (20ft), deciduous tree, leaves bronze when young, then dark green, flowers mid- to late spring ✳✳✳

MAHONIA

winter and spring

‡60cm–5m (2–15ft)
↔ 1–4m (3–12ft)

THESE EVERGREEN SHRUBS are valued for their honey-scented, winter (occasionally spring) flowers and attractive foliage. The large, leathery leaves are divided into spiny leaflets. Most have either rounded clusters or starburst spikes of usually yellow flowers that last for many weeks over winter, followed by purple to black berries. Although mahonias are mostly upright, some have a low-growing, spreading habit and make good ground cover. Taller ones are ideal at the back of a border or as specimen plants. Use with other winter-interest plants such as holly (*see Ilex, pp.74–75*) and *Viburnum × bodnantense* (*see pp.126–127*).

Hardiness Fully hardy ✳✳✳ to frost-hardy ✳✳.

Cultivation Mahonias prefer reasonably fertile soil enriched with well-rotted organic matter. Most prefer full or partial shade, but tolerate full sun where the soil is moist at all times. **Prune** after flowering, lightly cutting back shoots that spoil the shape. Mahonias regrow well from hard pruning if necessary (*see p.384*). **Take** semi-ripe cuttings (*see p.394*) from late summer until autumn.

Magnolia stellata ♀ (Star magnolia)
‡3m (10ft) ↔ 4m (12ft), deciduous shrub, flowers in early to mid-spring before the leaves unfurl ✳✳✳

Mahonia × media 'Charity'
‡to 5m (15ft) ↔ to 4m (12ft), vigorous hybrid with prominent flower clusters from late autumn to late winter ✳✳✳

Magnolia 'Susan' ♀
‡4m (12ft) ↔ 3m (10ft), deciduous shrub, dark red-purple buds open in mid-spring (see inset), petals often twisted ✳✳✳

Mahonia × wagneri 'Pinnacle' ♀
‡↔ 1.5m (5ft), leaves bronze when young, maturing to bright green, flowers in spring ✳✳✳

Mahonia aquifolium 'Apollo' ♀
‡60cm (24in) ↔ 1m (3ft), low-growing, with bright yellow flowers in spring, foliage turns rich purple (*as above*) in autumn ✳✳✳

MALUS

Crab apple

spring and autumn

AMONG THE MOST POPULAR flowering trees, especially since so many are ideally sized for the smaller garden, crab apples are renowned for their pink or white spring blossom. Golden or scarlet fruits follow in the autumn; inedible raw, they can be made into wine and jellies. The fruits attract birds, and the autumn foliage colour of these trees is often brilliant too, making them a real focus of interest late in the year. All crab apples are deciduous; some form a rounded crown, while others (such as *Malus floribunda*) have long, arching branches that are particularly graceful. They look equally good as specimens or with other small trees, such as hawthorns (*Crataegus, see p.46*), birches (*Betula, p.28*), and rowans (*Sorbus, p.118*).

Hardiness Fully hardy ✳✳✳.

Cultivation Grow in reasonably fertile soil that is moist but well-drained, in full sun; most tolerate partial shade. **Prune** young trees to remove any shoots that spoil a good branch framework in late winter or early spring (*see p.382*). **Sow** cleaned seed of *M. baccata* and *M. hupehensis* in autumn, in a seed bed (*see pp.391–393*); most others are grafted by nurserymen to control their size.

Malus hupehensis ♀
↕↔ 12m (40ft), vigorous, spreading habit, large flower clusters in mid- to late spring (*see inset*), good autumn leaf colour

MESPILUS GERMANICA

Medlar

spring, summer, and autumn

↕ 6m (20ft)
↔ 8m (25ft)

THE MEDLAR IS A DECIDUOUS tree or large shrub that originates in mountainous regions of southern Europe and Asia. It makes an interesting specimen tree, with a pleasing, spreading habit, bowl-shaped, white (occasionally pink-tinged) flowers that appear from late spring to early summer, and round, fleshy fruits that follow in autumn. The fruits can be made into jelly. Raw fruits are an acquired taste; they are edible, but only when well ripened or partly rotted ("bletted"). The medlar is lovely in autumn with other fruiting trees, such as hawthorns (*Crataegus, see p.46*) or crab apples (*Malus, see left*).

Hardiness Fully hardy ✳✳✳.

Cultivation Grow in reasonably fertile, moist but well-drained soil in full sun or partial shade. **Pruning** is unnecessary except to remove any shoots that are crossing, dead or misshapen in late winter or early spring (*see p.382*). **Sow** seed in a seedbed in autumn (*see pp.391–393*).

Malus 'John Downie' ♀
↕ 10m (30ft) ↔ 6m (20ft), narrow habit, conical when mature, reliable and heavy cropper, fruit to 3cm (1¼in) long, good for jelly

Malus floribunda ♀ (Japanese crab apple)
↕↔ 10m (30ft), dense, spreading habit, flowers in mid- and late spring, small, yellow fruits in autumn

Mespilus germanica
The foliage turns yellow-brown in autumn

METASEQUOIA GLYPTOSTROBOIDES
Dawn redwood **spring to autumn**

THIS PREHISTORIC TREE was once known only from
fossils, and following its rediscovery in the wild was
introduced to British gardens only in 1948. It makes
an outstanding specimen tree standing alone in grass
or on the edge of woodland. Native to the valley
forests of central China, it is one of the few conifers
that are deciduous, and has a narrow, conical shape,
fibrous bark, and graceful branches. The soft, feathery
leaves are a bright, fresh green; in autumn, they turn
gold and then russet-brown. The female cones are
light brown, on stalks; male cones are pendent. The
dawn redwood should only be considered for very
large gardens because it can reach a considerable
height very quickly.

Hardiness Fully hardy ✳✳✳.

Cultivation Grow in moist but well-drained soil enriched with well-
rotted organic matter, in full sun. In early years, growth is fast but will
slow down once the tree starts to reach around 10m (30ft) tall. **Sow**
seed in a seedbed (see pp.391–393) in autumn. **Take** hardwood
cuttings in autumn or root semi-ripe cuttings in midsummer with
bottom heat in a propagator (see p.394).

MORUS
Mulberry **summer to autumn**

THE BLACK, WHITE, AND RED MULBERRIES, native
to China, South-western Asia, and the Americas
respectively, were first cultivated to provide leaves for
the silkworm industry. All have raspberry-shaped,
edible fruits, first white or green, then ripening to
dark purple, yellow, or red among attractive, rounded
or heart-shaped leaves that turn yellow in autumn.
Orange, scaly bark provides winter interest.
Mulberries become beautifully shaped trees with age,
so grow them as specimens – the small, weeping,
white mulberry (*Morus alba* 'Pendula') is an excellent
choice for small gardens. Do not site mulberries
overhanging paving, or the fruits will stain it badly.

Hardiness Fully hardy ✳✳✳.

Cultivation Grow in reasonably fertile soil enriched with well-rotted
organic matter, in full sun, with shelter from cold, drying winds. **Prune**
only in late autumn or early winter, if necessary. If pruned at any other
time, the cuts will "bleed" sap badly. Sow seed in containers in a cold
frame in autumn (see pp.391–392). **Take** semi-ripe cuttings in
summer, or hardwood cuttings in autumn (see p.394). Susceptible to
powdery mildew (see p.398), which can be treated with a fungicide.

MYRTUS COMMUNIS
Common myrtle **spring to autumn**

‡↔ to 3m (10ft)

GROWN FOR ITS RICH, delicate
scent, myrtle is a bushy, upright,
evergreen shrub or tree with
glossy, dark-green, aromatic
leaves. It produces white, sweet-
smelling, bowl-shaped flowers in abundance from
spring to autumn. Both the flowers and the purple-
black berries that follow in autumn are dependent on
long, hot summers. Myrtles only thrive in a warm,
sheltered position. They look well in shrub and mixed
borders, or as an informal hedge. They can also be
trained against a wall, or grown in containers for a
patio where their scent can be best appreciated.

Hardiness Frost-hardy ✳✳.

Cultivation Grow in reasonably fertile, moist but well-drained soil
or loam-based compost, in full sun with shelter. **Lightly trim** or prune
shoots that spoil the shape in mid- or late spring. If wall-trained, after
flowering or in late winter or early spring, cut back flowered shoots
to within 2–4 buds of the main stems. Trim hedges in spring (see
p.384). **Sow** seed in containers in a cold frame in autumn (see
pp.391–392). **Take** semi-ripe cuttings in late summer (see p.394).

Metasequoia glyptostroboides ♀
‡ 20–40m (70–130ft) ↔ 5m (15ft) or more, tolerates waterlogged
sites, growth is slower on dry sites

Morus nigra ♀ (Black mulberry)
‡ 12m (40ft) ↔ 15m (50ft), fruits pleasant if a little dull eaten raw,
but good for jam and wine

Myrtus communis ♀
Branches arching with age, thrives in town and seaside gardens

NANDINA DOMESTICA

Heavenly bamboo

spring, summer, and autumn

‡ to 2m (6ft)
↔ to 1.5m (5ft)

GROWING WILD in the mountain valleys of India, China and Japan, heavenly bamboo is an elegant, upright shrub, grown for its flowers, fruits, and handsome foliage. The leaves are red to reddish-purple when young, mature to green, and then turn vivid crimson again in late autumn. In midsummer, small clusters of star-shaped, white flowers with yellow centres are produced, followed, in warmer climates or after hot summers, by bright red fruits. Nandinas are evergreen or semi-evergreen, but may not survive very cold winters. Grow it with other shrubs that have good autumn leaf colour. The low-growing *Nandina domestica* 'Firepower' makes an excellent ground cover.

Hardiness Frost-hardy ✲✲.

Cultivation Grow in moist but well-drained soil in full sun. **Prune back** hard after planting, then prune in mid-spring to keep the plant tidy and maintain a good shape (*see p.383*). **Sow** seed in containers in a cold frame as soon as it is ripe (*see pp.391–392*). **Take** semi-ripe cuttings in summer (*see p.394*).

NEILLIA

late spring to early summer

‡↔ 2m (6ft)

UNUSUAL SHRUBS with handsome foliage and flowers, neillias provide plenty of year-round interest. They are deciduous, originating from the Himalayas and East Asia, and are characterized by graceful, arching stems and dark, glossy leaves and, in late spring to early summer, masses of handsome, bell-shaped, pinkish-white or rose-pink flowers. Neillias have a thicket-forming habit, ideal for the back of a shrub or mixed border, or as a screen. If you have room for a single-season show, they look fantastic with other shrubs that flower at the same time, such as weigelas (*see p.128*) or mock oranges (*Philadelphus, see p.93*).

Hardiness Fully hardy ✲✲✲.

Cultivation Grow in fertile, well-drained soil in full sun or partial shade. **Prune back** flowered shoots after flowering to strong buds or shoots lower down on the stem. On mature plants, cut out an entire old branch every three or four years to encourage new growth from the base of the shrub (*see pp.382–383*). **Take** greenwood cuttings in early summer (*see p.394*), or dig up well-rooted, naturally layered stems from the edges of the plant (*see p.395*).

NYSSA

Tupelo

autumn

THE TUPELO IS A DECIDUOUS TREE prized for its outstanding foliage, which is bronze when young, matures to dark green, then turns to brilliant hues of amber, ruby, and gold in autumn. It does produce tiny green flowers, followed by small, blue fruits, which are enjoyed many by birds. However, the autumn foliage tints are the main attraction. Tupelo makes an ideal specimen tree, and looks effective planted near water (it thrives in wet, swampy areas). Try *Nyssa sinensis* with birches (*Betula, see p.28*) as the golden autumn foliage of the birch will contrast brilliantly with the tupelo's scarlet leaves.

Hardiness Fully hardy ✲✲✲, but best in areas with hot summers.

Cultivation Grow in fertile, moist but well-drained, neutral to acid soil, in sun or partial shade with shelter from cold, drying winds. **Choose** young, container-grown specimens, since they resent root disturbance more and more as they get older. **Trim** shoots that are crossing or misplaced in late winter or early spring to maintain a good shape and healthy framework (*see p.382*). **Sow** seed in a seedbed in autumn (*see pp.391–393*). **Take** greenwood cuttings in early summer, or semi-ripe cuttings in midsummer (*see p.394*).

Nandina domestica ♀
Can be invasive and "weedy" in hot climates, but behaves well in temperate gardens

Neillia thibetica
‡↔ 2m (6ft), suckering shrub with an upright then arching habit, tolerates most soils, blooms best in sun

Nyssa sinensis ♀
‡↔ 10m (30ft), broadly conical, often multi-stemmed habit, usually with sweeping lower branches, green leaves turn fiery in autumn

OLEARIA

Daisy bush   *spring to autumn*

THIS GROUP OF EVERGREEN SHRUBS is grown for its leathery leaves and and daisy-like flowers borne singly or in clusters from spring to autumn. Flower colours are predominantly white, but include blue, mauve, pink, and yellow. *Olearia × haastii* is a dense, bushy shrub with fragrant flowers. It is tolerant of salt-laden winds and can be grown as an informal hedge or windbreak. *O. macrodonta* is an upright shrub with holly-like, sharp-toothed foliage, white underneath. Its flowers are highly fragrant. *O. nummulariifolia* is a rounded, slow-growing shrub that does best planted against a warm, sunny wall where it is protected from drying winds. The dark green leaves look effective next to plants with bright leaves, such as elaeagnus (*see pp.50–51*). *O. solandri* is a dense, heather-like shrub with strongly scented flowers over a long period.

Hardiness Fully hardy ✱✱✱ to frost-tender ❀.

Cultivation Grow in fertile, well-drained soil in full sun, with shelter from cold, drying winds. **Prune** lightly in early spring, removing shoots that spoil the shape of the shrub. **Trim** hedges after flowering. They all tolerate hard pruning. **Take** semi-ripe cuttings in summer (*see p.394*).

ORIGANUM   *see also p.295*

Marjoram, Oregano   *summer*

AROMATIC PLANTS FROM the Mediterranean, marjorams may be shrubs, subshrubs (shrubs that are woody only at the base), or herbaceous perennials. All are very similar: small, with an upright to spreading habit and tiny, pink to mauve flowers borne through summer amid more conspicuous, often brightly coloured bracts (modified leaves). The flowers are magnets for bees and other pollinating insects. Larger species are suited to a herb bed, raised bed, or in containers near the house, where the fragrant leaves can be rubbed to release their scent. They also look good as edging plants for borders or paths, where they will sprawl contentedly. Grow the tiniest species, such as *Origanum amanum*, in a rock garden or alpine trough, so they are not swamped by larger plants.

Hardiness Fully hardy ✱✱✱ to frost-hardy ✱✱.

Cultivation Grow in full sun in poor to reasonably fertile soil. Very rich soil encourages leafy growth at the expense of flowers. Marjorams prefer a free-draining, alkaline (limy) soil. **Cut back** old flowered stems in early spring (*see p.383*). **Take** cuttings of new shoots growing from the base in late spring and treat as softwood cuttings (*see p.394*).

OSMANTHUS

                                    early to mid-spring

USEFUL FOR A SHRUB BORDER or woodland garden, this group of evergreen shrubs is grown for its glossy, dark green foliage, and white, occasionally yellow or orange flowers, scented like jasmine. These are produced in early and mid-spring and are followed by round, blue-black fruits. *Osmanthus heterophyllus* and *O. × fortunei* have spiky, holly-like foliage. Osmanthus has a dense, neat habit, and is an effective foil to showier shrubs in the border. *O. delavayi* and *O. burkwoodii* are good for hedging, while *O. heterophyllus* 'Aureomarginatus' will liven up a dull corner with its yellow-margined leaves.

Hardiness Fully hardy ✱✱✱ to frost-tender ❀.

Cultivation Grow in fertile, well-drained soil in sun or partial shade and shelter from cold, drying winds. **Trim** lightly or prune back shoots after flowering, taking out any that spoil the shape of the shrub (*see p.382*). Trim hedges in summer. All species tolerate hard pruning if necessary (*see p.384*). **Sow** seed in a container in a cold frame as soon as it is ripe (*see pp.391–392*). **Take** semi-ripe cuttings (*see p.394*) in summer and put in a propagator with bottom heat, or layer low-growing shoots in autumn or spring (*see p.395*).

① × **haastii** ‡ 2m (6ft) ↔ 3m (10ft) ✱✱✱ ② **macrodonta** ♀ ‡ 6m (20ft) ↔ 5m (15ft) ✱✱✱ ③ **nummulariifolia** ‡↔ 2m (6ft) ✱✱✱ ④ **solandri** ‡↔ 2m (6ft), scented ✱✱

Origanum 'Kent Beauty'
‡ 10cm (4in) ↔ 20cm (8in), prostrate, with trailing stems, semi-evergreen, named for its hop-like flowers ✱✱✱

① × **burkwoodii** ♀ ‡↔ 3m (10ft), rounded habit, good for topiary ✱✱✱ ② **delavayi** ♀ ‡ 2–6m (6–20ft) ↔ 4m (12ft), rounded habit, can be wall-trained ✱✱✱

OXYDENDRUM ARBOREUM

Sorrel tree, Sourwood *summer and autumn*

‡15m (50ft)
↔ 8m (25ft)

THE SORREL TREE IS A deciduous tree or large shrub with a conical or columnar habit. It is a dual-season tree for interest, with white flowers in the summer and boldly coloured foliage in the autumn. Its flowers, produced in late summer and early autumn, are tiny, about 6mm (¼in) long, but gain impact by being borne in large, airy plumes, up to 25cm (10in) long, at the ends of the shoots. The leaves are glossy, toothed, and dark green through summer, turning brilliant shades of red, yellow, and purple in autumn. Grow it as a specimen tree or in a woodland setting.

Hardiness Fully hardy ✿✿✿.

Cultivation Grow a sorrel tree in fertile, moist but well-drained soil, preferably acid (lime-free), avoiding exposed sites. **Prune** young trees in late winter or early spring to remove any crossing or misplaced branches. **Sow** seed in a container in a cold frame in autumn (*see pp.391–392*). **Take** semi-ripe cuttings in summer (*see p.394*).

PAEONIA

see also p.298

Tree peony *late spring to early summer*

‡↔ to 2.2m
(7ft)

SHRUBBY PEONIES, as opposed to the herbaceous kinds that die down each year, are commonly known as tree peonies. These peonies also have the characteristically voluptuous flowers in a wide range of colour, occasionally scented, borne from late spring to early summer, with the bonus of permanent stature in a mixed planting. Flowers can be single or double, cup- or saucer-shaped, and up to 30cm (12in) across. The stamens in the centre are often in a contrasting colour. Leaves are usually mid- to dark green, often feathery. Grow these peonies in a shrub, mixed, or herbaceous border.

Hardiness Fully hardy ✿✿✿ to frost-hardy ✿✿. Late frosts may damage young growths and flower buds.

Cultivation Grow in deep, fertile soil enriched with well-rotted organic matter, in full sun or partial shade. Peonies prefer shelter from cold, drying winds. **Prune out** flowered shoots and, from time to time, old wood to encourage bushy growth (*see p.382*). **Take** semi-ripe cuttings in summer (*see p.394*).

Paeonia suffruticosa 'Cardinal Vaughan' (Moutan)
‡↔ to 2.2m (7ft), flowers 15–30cm (6–12in) across in late spring and early summer, dark green leaves blue-green beneath ✿✿✿

Oxydendrum arboreum

PRUNING SPENT WOOD
Once shoots have flowered and set seed, they die back to new growth. Prune spent shoots back to a new leaf in autumn.

Paeonia delavayi ♀
‡2m (6ft) ↔ 1.2m (4ft), flowers up to 10cm (4in) across in early summer, leaves dark green and blue-green underneath ✿✿✿

Paeonia delavayi var. *ludlowii* ♀
‡↔ 2.5m (8ft), flowers up to 13cm (5in) across in late spring, new leaves deep maroon (*see inset*), then bright green ✿✿✿

PAULOWNIA

late spring and summer

‡ to 12m (40ft)
↔ to 10m (30ft)

THESE VIGOROUS, DECIDUOUS trees make striking additions to the garden. They grow and flower best in areas with long, hot summers. The fast-growing foxglove tree (*Paulownia tomentosa*) is tolerant of air pollution. *P. fortunei* is smaller, to 8m (25ft) tall. Both bear their fragrant flowers in late spring, often on near-bare branches. Although they can make fine specimen trees in a lawn, they are best coppiced (*see Cornus, pp.42–43*) for bold, "tropical" foliage, a good way to get the best from them in areas where they do not flower reliably, or in small gardens.

Hardiness Fully hardy ✼✼✼. Young trees may be damaged by frosts unless protected in their early years.

Cultivation Grow in fertile, well-drained soil in full sun. In frost-prone areas, shelter from cold, drying winds. **Prune** paulownias grown as trees only if necessary. To obtain big leaves, cut back stems to within 2–3 buds of the main framework of shoots in early spring. **Sow** seed in containers in a cold frame in spring or autumn (*see pp.391–392*). **Take** root cuttings in winter (*see p.394*). Young plants benefit from being grown on in pots and overwintered under glass.

PEROVSKIA

late summer to early autumn

A GRACEFUL SHRUB, perovskia has tall, wand-like stems of tiny, violet-blue flowers in late summer or early autumn. Both stems and leaves are usually grey-white or grey-green, and the foliage is aromatic, with a pleasantly sharp, lemony scent. The stems can reach a height of up to 1.2m (4ft) in a single season, bearing their small flowers along about half their length. Perovskias add height and a cloud of hazy blue in a massed herbaceous planting, and like perennials, are best cut back hard each spring, or they will become leggy and bare. They also look striking against a grey or white-painted wall.

Hardiness Fully hardy ✼✼✼.

Cultivation Grow in well-drained soil that is poor or reasonably fertile in full sun. Perovskias will grow in dry, chalky soils and in coastal areas. **Prune hard** in spring, cutting back the previous season's growth to within 5–10cm (2–4in); gradually, a permanent, stubby, woody framework will develop (*see inset, below*). **Take** softwood cuttings in late spring, or semi-ripe cuttings in summer (*see p.394*).

PHILADELPHUS

Mock orange *early to midsummer*

DELICIOUSLY FRAGRANT FLOWERS are a feature of this group of mainly deciduous shrubs. The flowers are cup or bowl-shaped, single, semi double, and double, and usually white, often with yellowish stamens. They are produced either singly or in clusters. The leaves are mid-green; *P. coronarius* has white-variegated and golden-leaved forms. There is no missing a mock orange in flower, since the scent drifts in the air for a considerable distance. Grow them in a shrub border, with other early and midsummer-flowering shrubs like weigelas (*see p.128*), or as specimen plants.

Hardiness Fully hardy ✼✼✼ to half-hardy ✼.

Cultivation Grow in any reasonably fertile, well-drained soil, in full sun or partial shade. *P. microphyllus* needs full sun, while the golden-leaved *P. coronarius* 'Aureus' must have some shade. **Prune** after flowering, cutting back flowered stems to strong buds or new shoots lower down. On mature plants, cut one or two old branches to the base each year to encourage new growth. **Take** softwood cuttings in summer, or hardwood cuttings in autumn or winter (*see p.394*). Aphids may be troublesome, as may powdery mildew (*see pp.398–399*), pick off mildew-affected leaves and avoid overhead watering.

PRUNING PEROVSKIAS
Before new growth starts, cut away old stubby parts of the plant that did not shoot the previous year.

Paulownia tomentosa ♀ (Foxglove tree, Empress tree)
‡ 12m (40ft) ↔ 10m (30ft), flowers well (inset) the year after a hot summer; coppice plants for velvety leaves up to 50cm (20in) across

Perovskia 'Blue Spire' ♀
‡ 1.2m (4ft) ↔ 1m (3ft), leaves slender and silver-grey, hugging the stems, the flowers resemble those of lavender

① 'Belle Etoile' ♀ ‡ 1.2m (4ft) ↔ 2.5m (8ft) ② *coronarius* 'Aureus' ♀ ‡ 2.5m (8ft) ↔ 1.5m (5ft) ③ *microphyllus* ‡↔ 1m (3ft) ④ 'Virginal' ‡ 3m (10ft) or more ↔ 2.5m (8ft)

PHLOMIS

see also p.306

early to midsummer

THESE ATTRACTIVE AND UNDEMANDING, evergreen shrubs are grown for their sage-like foliage and their unusual, often hooded, flowers. The leaves are variable in shape: narrow and lance-shaped to more oval. In colour, they range from light green to grey-green, and are often hairy. The flowers are produced in early and midsummer in shades of golden yellow, lilac-pink, purple to pink, and occasionally white and are borne in dense tiers, or clusters, on tall, erect stems. Then, ornamental seedheads extend the interest into winter. These small to medium-sized shrubs have an upright or rounded habit. Phlomis look particularly at home among herbs such as sage and lavender (*see p.80*), but they can also be grown in mixed or shrub borders. There are also some herbaceous phlomis.

Hardiness Fully hardy ✻✻✻ to frost-hardy ✻✻.

Cultivation Grow these shrubs in any fertile, well-drained soil in full sun. **Deadhead** for a longer flowering display and lightly trim any shoots that spoil the overall shape of the shrubs when flowering has finished. **Sow** seed (*see pp.391–393*) in spring, or take softwood cuttings (*see p.394*) in summer.

PHORMIUM

New Zealand flax

year-round

WITH STRIKING, SWORD-LIKE FOLIAGE and exotic-looking flowers, these architectural plants develop into large, handsome clumps that can act as focal points in a border or gravel, by a building, or even as specimen plants in a lawn. Their versatility is enhanced by the range of leaf colours available, from bronze-green with rose-pink margins to dark green with red, orange, or pink stripes. In summer, in milder areas, they produce tall, leafless spikes bearing abundant tubular flowers in erect clusters. These may not flower in colder areas. With their thick, tough leaves they are also ideal for coastal gardens where they often flower well. Plant a phormium in a large pot to add a touch of drama to a patio or terrace.

Hardiness Frost-hardy ✻✻ to half-hardy ✻.

Cultivation Grow phormiums in fertile, moist but free-draining soil where they receive full sun. Although these plants are not completely hardy, in frost-prone areas they may survive winter temperatures as low as -12°C (10°F) if they are given a deep mulch (*see p.388*) around their roots. **Sow** seed (*see pp.391–393*) in spring. **Divide** the woody crowns of large, established clumps, also in spring, to increase stocks (*see p.395*); you may need a large knife to cut through the crown.

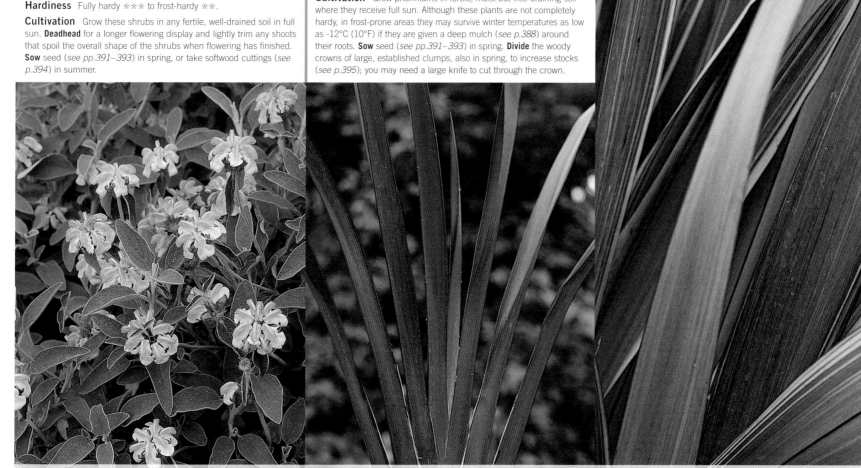

Phlomis fruticosa ♀ (Jerusalem sage)
↕1m (3ft) ↔ 1.5m (5ft), mound-forming ✻✻✻ (borderline)

Phormium 'Bronze Baby'
↕↔ 60–80cm (24–32in), dull red flower spikes are up to 4m (12ft) tall ✻✻

Phormium 'Sundowner' ♀
↕↔ 2m (6ft), yellow-green flower spikes to 2m (6ft) tall ✻✻

PHOTINIA

spring and year-round

THESE EVERGREEN OR DECIDUOUS SHRUBS and trees are grown for their attractive foliage and varied habits. Some are spreading trees, but many are upright or rounded shrubs, ranging in height from 3m (10ft) to 12m (40ft). They produce small clusters of tiny, white flowers in summer, although the deciduous species are mainly prized for their autumn leaf colours and fruits. Evergreen types often have striking, reddish new leaves in spring before they turn glossy dark or mid-green. Photinias look good in a shrub border or as specimen plants. They can also be used as hedging plants, where regular trimming encourages new, coloured foliage, or as standard plants in large pots.

Hardiness Fully hardy ✳✳✳ to frost-hardy ✳✳; young growth may be damaged by late spring frosts.

Cultivation Grow in fertile, moist but well-drained soil, in full sun or partial shade with protection from cold winds. **Trim** any crossing or misshapen shoots in winter or early spring, to maintain a good shape and a healthy framework of shoots. Trim hedges in summer when the colour of the young growth has faded. **Propagate** all types by semi-ripe cuttings in summer; sow seed of deciduous types in autumn (*see pp.391–393*). **Powdery mildew** may spoil the leaves (*see p.399*).

PHYGELIUS

summer to autumn

‡ 1–1.2m (3–4ft)
↔ 1–1.5m (3–5ft)

HANGING CLUSTERS OF FLOWERS produced over a long period in summer, and often into autumn, are the main reason for growing these evergreen or semi-evergreen shrubs. They have oval- to lance-shaped leaves, and flowers in several shades of yellow, orange-red, creamy yellow, and orange. Phygelius will thrive in a shrub border or at the base of a warm wall and spreads by means of suckers. Where temperatures often fall below freezing, treat them as herbaceous perennials – although the top-growth may be killed off, they should grow away again in spring.

Hardiness Frost-hardy ✳✳.

Cultivation Phygelius like fertile, moist, well-drained soil in full sun. **Deadhead** to encourage more flowers. **Protect** the roots, in frost-prone areas, with a dry winter mulch of straw or bracken. Overwinter young plants in frost-free conditions. **Cut back** the stems in spring of plants being treated as herbaceous perennials; otherwise lightly trim any shoots that spoil the shape. **Take** softwood cuttings (*see p.394*) in late spring or remove rooted suckers for replanting in spring.

Phormium 'Dazzler'
‡ 1m (3ft) ↔ 1.2m (4ft), flowers (*see inset*) are 5cm (2in) long ✳✳

Phormium tenax ♀
‡ 4m (12ft) ↔ 2m (6ft), dull red flower spikes are up to 4m (12ft) tall ✳✳

Photinia × fraseri 'Red Robin' ♀
‡ ↔ 5m (15ft) upright evergreen shrub or small tree, bronze to scarlet young foliage, flowers in mid- to late spring ✳✳

① *aequalis* 'Yellow Trumpet' ♀ ‡ 1m (3ft) ② × *rectus* 'African Queen' ♀ ‡ 1m (3ft) ③ × *rectus* 'Moonraker' ‡ to 1.5m (5ft) ④ × *rectus* 'Salmon Leap' ♀ ‡ 1.2m (4ft)

PICEA

Spruce
year-round

SPRUCES ARE EVERGREEN, coniferous trees grown mainly for their dense foliage and attractive shapes. The most familiar is the Norwegian spruce or "Christmas tree", *Picea abies*. The needles, which vary in colour from dark green to the silvery blue of *P. pungens* 'Koster', make a good textural contrast to plants with bolder leaves. In summer and autumn, older trees produce cones, which emerge green or red then mature to purple or brown. The larger spruces are useful on their own, to show off their handsome forms, or in groups, especially to create shelter. Like all evergreen conifers, they provide a year-round backdrop and add structure to the garden. The dwarf or slow-growing spruces are suitable for small spaces and rock gardens.

Hardiness Fully hardy ✳✳✳ to frost-hardy ✳✳.

Cultivation Grow in any deep, moist, but well-drained soil, ideally neutral to acid (lime-free), in full sun. No pruning required. **Sow** seed in containers in a cold frame in spring (*see pp.391–392*). **Take** stem-tip cuttings (*see p.394*) of dwarf forms in late summer. May attract aphids (*see pp.398–399*); treat only badly affected young or dwarf plants.

PICRASMA QUASSIOIDES

Quassia
autumn

THIS ELEGANT, UPRIGHT TREE is grown mainly for its attractive foliage, which fades to lovely shades of yellow, orange, and scarlet before the leaves drop in autumn. Oriental in origin, *Picrasma quassioides* bears a passing resemblance to the tree of heaven, *Ailanthus altissima*, to which it is related. Each glossy, mid-green leaf is divided into several leaflets. In early summer, minute, bowl-shaped green flowers are borne in clusters, but they have little ornamental value. Site this fine tree in an open position in a shrub border, or on the edge of a woodland setting with other trees and shrubs that also have good autumn colour, such as *Disanthus cercidifolius* (*see p.50*) and *Nyssa sinensis* (*see p.90*).

Hardiness Fully hardy ✳✳✳.

Cultivation Grow in fertile, well-drained soil in full sun or partial shade. In frost-prone areas, choose a site that is not exposed to cold, drying winds. **Prune out** any crossing branches and those that spoil the shape of the tree in late winter or early spring. **Sow** seed in containers in a cold frame in autumn (*see pp.391–392*).

PIERIS

late winter and spring

↕ to 5m (15ft)
↔ to 4m (12ft)

THESE COLOURFUL EVERGREEN shrubs are valued for their glossy, leathery foliage and delightful flowers. They are best placed in a shrub border or woodland garden, or in a container. Not all are large; 'Little Heath' and 'Purity' are popular for small gardens or pots. The young leaves are often brilliantly coloured, and, in spring, clusters of small, white, or pink flowers almost cover the shrub. Rhododendrons and azaleas (*see pp.104–107*) and ericas (*see pp.52–53*) make good companions, as all require similar soil.

Hardiness Fully hardy ✳✳✳ to frost-hardy ✳✳; the young growth may be damaged by late frosts in spring.

Cultivation Grow in reasonably fertile, moist but well-drained, acid (lime-free) soil, or ericaceous compost, in full sun or partial shade. In frost-prone areas, shelter from cold, drying winds and early morning sun (which can damage frosty leaves). **Trim back** any shoots that spoil the shape after flowering, and remove faded flowers if the shrubs are not too large. **Sow** seed in containers in a cold frame in spring or autumn (*see pp.391–392*). **Take** softwood cuttings in early summer, or semi-ripe cuttings from mid- to late summer (*see p.394*).

① *abies* ↕ to 40m (130ft) ↔ 6m (20ft) ② *glauca* 'Conica' ↕ 2–6m (6–20ft) ↔ 1–2.5m (3–8ft) ③ *mariana* 'Nana' ♡ ↕↔ to 50cm (20in) ④ *pungens* 'Koster' ♡ ↕ 15m (50ft) ↔ to 5m (15ft)

Picrasma quassioides
↔ 8m (25ft), autumn foliage shown here

Pieris japonica 'Blush' ♡
↕ 4m (12ft) ↔ 3m (10ft), compact and rounded shrub, pink-flushed, later all-white flowers in late winter and spring ✳✳✳

Pieris japonica 'Flamingo'
‡4m (12ft) ↔ 3m (10ft), compact, rounded shrub, dark red buds, dark pink flowers in late winter and spring ✳✳✳

PINUS

Pine   *year-round*

THE PINES COMPRISE A LARGE and varied group of evergreens, both trees and shrubs, with distinctive, needles, ornamental cones, and attractive, scaly bark. The larger species are very tall trees with striking, sparsely branched silhouettes compared with other conifers. Habits vary, from slender giants such as the Scots pine (*Pinus sylvestris*) to the umbrella-shaped stone pine (*P. pinea*). Where a spacious garden allows, they make grand specimen trees, either individually or in groups, and also excellent windbreaks; *P. radiata* and *P. nigra* tolerate coastal exposure. There are medium-sized and dwarf pines, often very slow-growing, for the smaller garden and for rock gardens; look especially among the cultivars of *P. sylvestris*, *P. densiflora*, and *P. mugo*.

Hardiness Fully hardy ✳✳✳ to frost-hardy ✳✳.

Cultivation Grow in any well-drained soil in full sun. Some species may be short-lived in shallow, chalky soils; *P. nigra* and *P. mugo* both tolerate chalk. No pruning required. **Sow** seed in a cold frame in spring (*see pp.391–393*). Pines may attract aphids (*see pp.398–399*) but rarely need treatment.

Pinus mugo 'Mops' ♀ (Dwarf mountain pine)
‡to 3.5m (11ft) ↔ to 5m (15ft), often much smaller; dense, near-spherical bush, very resinous, scaly grey bark ✳✳✳

Pieris formosa var. forrestii 'Wakehurst' ♀
‡to 5m (15ft) ↔ 4m (12ft), upright, suckering shrub, excellent new foliage, large white flower clusters in late winter and spring ✳✳

Pinus patula ♀ (Mexican weeping pine)
‡15–20m (50–70ft) ↔ 6–10m (20–30ft), spreading or rounded tree, reddish-brown bark, thrives in mild areas ✳✳

Pinus nigra ♀ (Austrian pine, European black pine)
‡to 30m (100ft) ↔ 6–8m (20–25ft), domed tree, brown or black bark that becomes deeply fissured with age (*see inset*) ✳✳✳

PITTOSPORUM

year-round

‡ to 20m (70ft)
↔ to 6m (20ft)

GLOSSY, LEATHERY LEAVES, often with wavy edges and sometimes variegated, are the main attraction of these evergreen shrubs. They have a naturally dense, neat habit but also respond well to pruning. The lower branches may be removed to produce a more tree-like shape, allowing for some underplanting. In mild areas, they make handsome specimen plants or windbreak hedges for coastal gardens. Dark-leaved forms form an excellent contrast to bright-leaved or variegated shrubs such as elaeagnus (*see pp.50–51*) and euonymus (*see p.56*). In spring and early summer, they bear small, five-petalled flowers.

Hardiness Frost-hardy ✲✲ to frost-tender ❅.

Cultivation Grow in fertile, moist but well-drained soil, in full sun or partial shade; site those with variegated or purple foliage in sun for the best colour. Must be sheltered from cold, drying winds in frost-prone areas. **Prune** out any crossing or misplaced shoots in late winter or early spring; trim hedges in spring and late summer. **Sow** seed (*see pp.391–392*) as soon as it is ripe, or in spring in containers in a cold frame. **Take** semi-ripe cuttings (*see p.394*) in summer.

PONCIRUS TRIFOLIATA

Japanese bitter orange

spring, summer, and autumn

‡↔ 5m (15ft)

THIS ROUNDED, BUSHY, deciduous shrub deserves to be more widely grown for its beautiful and fragrant flowers and orange-like fruits; although *Poncirus* is related to citrus trees, these are inedible. White flowers, again similar to orange blossom, appear in late spring and early summer, to be followed by the fruits; as these ripen, they may be accompanied by a second, smaller flush of blossom. The dark green leaves gradually turn yellow in autumn. Grow in a shrub border, or against a sunny wall in colder areas. Sharp spines on the stems also make it a good choice for a thick hedge.

Hardiness Fully hardy ✲✲✲.

Cultivation Grow in fertile, well-drained soil in full sun and provide shelter from cold, drying winds. **Prune off** any crossing or misshapen shoots that spoil the shape of the shrub in late winter or early spring. **Trim** hedges once or twice in summer. **Sow** seed (*see pp.391–392*) in a container in a cold frame in autumn. **Take** semi-ripe cuttings (*see p.394*) in summer and root in a propagator with bottom heat.

POPULUS

Aspen, Cottonwood, Poplar

summer and autumn

THE LEAVES OF THESE VIGOROUS, deciduous trees are perhaps their prettiest feature, usually showing silvery undersides when ruffled by the wind. Some are also balsam-scented. In a large garden, these make fine specimen trees or windbreaks, and look good with birches (*Betula, see p.28*), beeches (*Fagus, see p.57*), or oaks (*Quercus, see p.103*), but plant them well away from buildings and drains; they have invasive roots. Shapes vary, from the spreading common aspen (*Populus tremula*), with rounded leaves, to the conical Canadian poplar (*P. × canadensis*) and the classic columnar Lombardy poplar (*P. nigra* var. *italica*). Poplars bear catkins in early spring, usually with male and female flowers on separate trees.

Hardiness Fully hardy ✲✲✲.

Cultivation Poplars tolerate all but waterlogged soils, but grow best in fertile, moist but well-drained soil. Position in full sun. **Prune out** any crossing, dead or misplaced branches that spoil the shape of young trees in late winter or early spring. Remove any suckers growing up from the ground around the tree in autumn or winter. **Take** hardwood cuttings (*see p.394*) in winter.

POPULUS TREMULA ♀
The leaves of this broad tree tremble in any breeze; bronze when young, they turn yellow in autumn.

① *tenuifolium* ♀ ‡ to 10m (30ft) ✲✲ ② *tenuifolium* 'Irene Paterson' ♀ ‡1.2m (4ft) ✲✲ ③ *tenuifolium* 'Tom Thumb' ♀ ‡1m (3ft) ✲✲ ④ *tobira* ♀ ‡2–10m (6–30ft) ✲

Poncirus trifoliata
The fruits are green at first and then ripen to yellow-orange; they resemble miniature oranges but are inedible

Populus × jackii 'Aurora'
‡15m (50ft) ↔ 6m (20ft), has leaves marked with both cream and pink splashes

POTENTILLA

Cinquefoil

see also p.311

summer to autumn

‡1m (3ft)
↔1.5m (5ft)

BEARING BRIGHT FLOWERS for many weeks over summer and autumn, these reliable shrubs are excellent value for a border. There are also many non-woody potentillas, with very similar flowers – most shrubby types are cultivars of *Potentilla fruticosa*. Their flowers are cup- to saucer-shaped, borne singly or in small clusters, and produced in colours from purest white to shades of pink, red, orange, and yellow. Because they flower over such a long period, they make good foils for other plants with a briefer flowering display. Wider than they are tall, they also make good low hedging.

Hardiness Fully hardy ✳✳✳.

Cultivation Grow in poor to reasonably fertile soil that is well drained. Position most in full sun, red-flowered types in light shade. **Cut back** flowered shoots to within 2.5cm (1in) of old growth after flowering or in early spring; the easiest way to do this is with shears. **Sow** seed (*see pp.391–392*) in containers in a cold frame in autumn or spring. **Take** softwood cuttings (*see p.394*) in early summer.

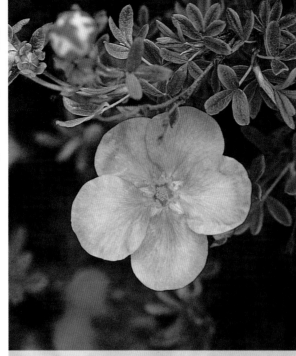

***Potentilla fruticosa* 'Daydawn'**
‡1m (3ft) ↔ 1.2m (4ft), a compact plant with flowers flushed with both yellow and pink shades

Mint bush

late spring to summer

THESE EVERGREEN SHRUBS are grown for their aromatic leaves and clusters of bell-shaped flowers. Bushy or spreading, they have mid- to dark green or grey-green leaves that smell of mint, and flower from late spring until summer. In frost-prone areas, the purple- to pink-flowered *Prostanthera ovalifolia* and *P. rotundifolia* need protection in winter. In milder areas, they thrive in the shelter of a warm wall; the hardier, white-flowered *P. cuneata* may be grown in sheltered borders. Position it towards the back or centre of a grouping with lower plants in front, because it often becomes bare at the base, and hard pruning to correct this is not possible.

Hardiness Frost-hardy ✳✳ to half-hardy ✳.

Cultivation Grow in reasonably fertile, well-drained soil, and site in full sun. If growing them in pots, use a loam-based compost and grow in full light. **Trim** or lightly prune back shoots that spoil the shape of the shrub after flowering. Avoid hard pruning, which can be detrimental. **Sow** seed (*see pp.391–392*) indoors in spring. **Take** semi-ripe cuttings (*see p.394*) in summer.

***Potentilla fruticosa* 'Primrose Beauty'** ♀
‡1m (3ft) ↔ 1.5m (5ft), a tidy, densely growing cultivar with larger flowers than many, to 3.5cm (1½in) across

***Potentilla fruticosa* 'Red Ace'**
‡1m (3ft) ↔ 1.5m (5ft), the flowers have yellow backs and their colour tends to fade if the plant is sited in full sun

***Prostanthera cuneata* ♀ (Alpine mint bush)**
‡↔ 30–90cm (1–3ft), has small, very aromatic, glossy leaves and flowers profusely in late spring ✳✳

TREES AND SHRUBS

PRUNUS

Ornamental cherry

spring, autumn, and winter

THIS GROUP CONTAINS TWO VERY DIFFERENT types of plant: ornamental or flowering cherries that are deciduous, and evergreen laurels. In spring, ornamental cherries billow with blossom in shades of pink, white, and sometimes red. *Prunus × subhirtella* produces its delicate flurries of flowers in mild spells from autumn to spring. Some, such as *P. maackii* and *P. serrula*, are also grown for their rich cinnamon-coloured bark, and others, like *P. sargentii*, have leaves that colour well in autumn. Laurels, on the other hand, are dense, bushy evergreens, such as *P. laurocerasus* and *P. lusitanica*, with much less showy flowers but handsome, glossy leaves. Prunus also includes many trees grown especially for fruit, including plum, peach, and cherry, but the fruits of laurels and most ornamental cherries can cause severe discomfort if eaten and should be left for the birds. Ornamental cherries are upright, rounded or spreading trees or shrubs; many are suitable for smaller gardens, and make excellent specimen plants. Laurels are classic and reliable hedging plants.

Hardiness   Fully hardy ✳✳✳ to frost-hardy ✳✳.

Cultivation   Grow in any moist, well-drained soil in full sun or partial shade. **Water** young trees well until they are properly established. **Prune** each of the types slightly differently. For most deciduous shrubs and trees, simply remove any misplaced shoots to maintain a good shape. This is best done in summer to avoid the fungal disease silver leaf, to which cherries are susceptible. For *P. glandulosa* and *P. triloba*, prune hard after flowering. **Trim** deciduous hedges after flowering and use secateurs to cut back evergreens in early to mid-spring. **Sow** seed of species in containers outside in autumn (*see pp.391–392*), or propagate deciduous cultivars by greenwood cuttings, which are taken slightly later than softwood cuttings when the stem is a little firmer and darker (*see p.394*). Ornamental cherries are sometimes attacked by caterpillars, and birds occasionally strip the flower buds.

Using ornamental cherries in the garden

Wall of blossom   Ornamental cherries can be trained against a wall to provide a generous display in even the smallest garden. Once the shrub has formed a framework, all that is needed is some routine tying in and pruning. Cut out older shoots that produce little growth and tie in younger shoots as replacements; new growth should be tied in while still young and pliable. Shorten weak shoots to encourage stronger growth, and prune back flowered shoots, while the plant is growing in late spring or summer. Check all ties when pruning, and replace any that are broken or restricting the stems.

Ornamental hedging   Several ornamental cherries are suitable for growing as hedging. Evergreen shrubs such as P. laurocerasus and P. lusitanica make dense screens, whereas deciduous species, such as P. spinosa, P. cerasifera, and its cultivars like 'Nigra', will be more open. When planting, prepare the soil by adding plenty of well-rotted organic matter. Make sure the top of the root ball is just below soil level and firm in gently. The usual planting distance for hedging is 60–75cm (24–30in). Water well after planting and, in exposed situations, erect a wind barrier until the plants become established.

① *Prunus* 'Accolade' ♥ ↕↔ 8m (25ft), early spring ② *avium* 'Plena' ♥ ↕↔ 12m (40ft), mid-spring ③ *cerasifera* 'Nigra' ♥ ↕↔ 10m (30ft), early spring, followed by plum-like, edible fruit ④ × *cistena* ♥ ↕↔ 1.5m (5ft), late spring ⑤ *glandulosa* 'Alba Plena' ↕↔ 1.5m (5ft), late spring ⑥ 'Kanzan' ♥ ↕↔ 10m (30ft), mid- and late spring ⑦ 'Kiku-shidare-zakura' ♥ ↕↔ 3m (10ft), mid- and late spring ⑧ *laurocerasus* 'Otto Luyken' ♥ ↕ 1m (3ft) ↔ 1.5m (5ft), evergreen, spring and autumn ⑨ *lusitanica* subsp. *azorica* ↕↔ 20m (70ft), evergreen, early summer ⑩ *maackii* ↕10m (30ft) ↔ 8m (25ft), mid-spring ⑪ 'Okame' ♀ ↕10m (30ft) ↔ 8m (25ft), early spring ⑫ *padus* 'Watereri' ♀ ↕15m (50ft) ↔ 10m (30ft), late spring ⑬ 'Pandora' ♀ ↕10m (30ft) ↔ 8m (25ft), early spring ⑭ 'Pink Perfection' ♀ ↕↔ 8m (25ft), late spring ⑮ *sargentii* ♀ ↕ 20m (70ft) ↔ 15m (50ft), mid-spring ⑯ *serrula* ♀ ↕↔ 10m (30ft), late spring ⑰ 'Shirofugen' ♀ ↕ 8m (25ft) ↔ 10m (30ft), late spring ⑱ 'Shogetsu' ♀ ↕5m (15ft) ↔ 8m (25ft), late spring ⑲ *spinosa* ↕5m (15ft) ↔ 4m (12ft), early to mid-spring, followed by blue-black fruit (sloes) used to flavour alcohol ⑳ 'Spire' ♀ ↕10m (30ft) ↔ 6m (20ft), mid-spring ㉑ × *subhirtella* 'Autumnalis Rosea' ♀ ↕↔ 8m (25ft), autumn to spring ㉒ 'Taihaku' ♀ ↕ 8m (25ft) ↔ 10m (30ft), mid-spring ㉓ *triloba* ↕↔ 3m (10ft), early and mid-spring ㉔ 'Ukon' ♀ ↕ 8m (25ft) ↔ 10m (30ft), mid-spring

PYRACANTHA

Firethorn

spring and autumn

EVERGREEN FOLIAGE, DAINTY WHITE FLOWERS, and bright autumn berries make these spiny shrubs both popular and useful. From late spring to midsummer, flat clusters of small, 5-petalled, open flowers, like those of the hawthorn, appear. Berries in vivid shades of orange, scarlet, and golden yellow follow and often persist through the winter – unless the birds eat them. Firethorns are spreading or upright in habit, and can be grown as freestanding shrubs, as hedging, or, more commonly, trained against a wall or fence in a fan or espalier (several horizontal tiers) shape.

Hardiness Fully hardy ✷✷✷ to frost-hardy ✷✷.

Cultivation Firethorns like fertile, well-drained soil in full sun or partial shade and tolerate north-facing walls. In frost-prone areas, give shelter from cold winds. **Prune** freestanding shrubs in late winter or early spring by removing shoots that spoil the shape. In midsummer, prune each sideshoot of wall-trained shrubs to two or three buds from the base; tie in shoots regularly. Trim hedges in midsummer. **Sow** seed in containers in a cold frame in autumn (*see pp.391–393*) or root semi-ripe cuttings with bottom heat in summer (*see p.394*). **Scab**, a fungus which causes dark, scabby patches in damp weather, may affect berries and leaves; cut out affected shoots to healthy wood.

Pyracantha 'Soleil d'Or'
↕ 3m (10ft) ↔ 2.5m (8ft), upright habit, flowers in early summer ✷✷✷

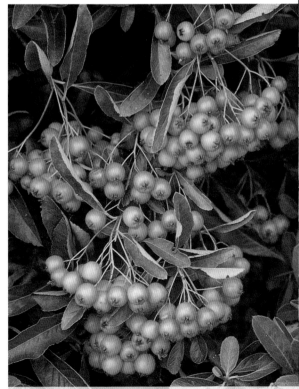

Pyracantha 'Orange Glow' ♀
↕↔ 3m (10ft), upright, then spreading habit, flowers in late spring followed by dark orange to orange-red berries ✷✷✷

Pyracantha 'Mohave'
↕ 4m (12ft) ↔ 5m (15ft), vigorous, bushy habit, flowers in early summer followed by long-lasting berries ✷✷

Pyracantha 'Golden Charmer' ♀
↕↔ 3m (10ft), vigorous, bushy habit with arching branches, flowers in early summer ✷✷✷

PYRUS

Pear   *spring, summer, and autumn*

PEARS ARE VALUED NOT ONLY for their sometimes edible fruits, but also for their flowers, and in some cases, their attractive habits exemplified by the silvery weeping pear (*see below*). The trees are usually deciduous, and some have good autumn colour. The flowers, which appear in spring, are white or pink. Fruit shapes vary from the typical pear shape to round; many varieties have been developed over the centuries for their fine-flavoured fruits. Ornamental varieties include *Pyrus calleryana*, which is thorny and develops red foliage and round, brown fruits in autumn, and the snow pear (*P. nivalis*), which has silvery grey leaves – both have conical habits and flower in spring. The more compact ornamental pears are ideal for a small garden as specimens in a lawn.

Hardiness Fully hardy ✳✳✳.

Cultivation Grow pears in fertile, well-drained soil in full sun. **Prune out** any shoots that spoil the shape of the tree in late winter or early spring. **Fruiting pears** in particular may suffer from canker, areas of sunken, split bark, which can kill branches as it spreads: cut back stems to healthy wood. Aphids and caterpillars may also attack foliage.

QUERCUS

Oak   *summer and autumn*

OAKS ARE LARGE, STATELY TREES, known for their longevity, with attractive foliage and fissured bark. They form a large group of deciduous and evergreen trees with a great range of leaf shapes and colours and growth habits. Acorns 1–3cm (½–1¼in) long are borne in autumn. Many deciduous oaks are excellent for autumn colour, with foliage in a variety of brilliant shades. The classic common or English oak (*Quercus robur*) with the typical oak leaf is a huge, spreading tree so is suited only to parks or woods, but if you have a large garden, there are smaller – although still large – oaks that are well worth growing as specimen trees. Plant the sapling in its permanent position because it may not survive later transplanting.

Hardiness Fully hardy ✳✳✳ to frost-hardy ✳✳.

Cultivation Oaks need deep, fertile, well-drained soil in partial shade. Evergreens prefer full sun and frost-hardy species shelter from cold, drying winds. **Prune out** shoots that spoil the shape of the tree on planting; mature oaks need little pruning except the removal of dead wood (*see p.382*). **Sow** acorns in a seedbed or cold frame as soon as they fall (*see p.393*).

Quercus ilex ♀ (Holm oak)
↕25m (80ft) ↔ 20m (70ft), evergreen with smooth, dark grey bark, variable leaves silvery grey when young, thrives in coastal sites ✳✳

Pyrus salicifolia 'Pendula' ♀
↕5m (15ft) ↔ 4m (12ft), ideal for smaller gardens, willowy, silvery felted leaves, pear-shaped green fruits 3cm (1¼in) long

Quercus coccinea (Scarlet oak)
↕20m (70ft) ↔ 15m (50ft), rounded canopy, pale grey-brown bark, dark green leaves turn red in autumn, needs lime-free soil ✳✳✳

Quercus laurifolia
↕↔ 20m (70ft), rounded habit with grey-black bark, leaves bronze when young and lasting well into winter, needs lime-free soil ✳✳✳

Rhododendron, Azalea   *late autumn to early summer*

DRAMATIC, SOMETIMES STRONGLY SCENTED flowers are borne on these shrubs from late autumn through until summer. The flowers vary in size and shape, but they are mainly bell-shaped, often with attractive, contrasting markings on the petals, and are carried singly or in large clusters known as trusses. This is a large and highly variable group containing thousands of hybrids and species, deciduous and evergreen, with flowers of every colour. Their natural habitats include both dense forest and high alpine slopes, and they range in habit from huge trees up to 25m (80ft) tall to dwarf shrubs no more than 15cm (6in) high. All require acid (lime-free) soil. The leaves also vary hugely in size, from 4mm (⅛in) to 75cm (30in) long. In some species, the undersides of the leaves and young stems are covered in a dense, woolly covering of hairs or scales (called indumentum). The young growth of some can be attractive, with colours of red to bronze-brown or metallic blue-green, and many deciduous rhododendrons have strong autumn leaf colours. Rhododendrons have a variety of uses in the garden: dwarf alpine species are at home in a rock garden, and larger woodland types are excellent for brightening shady spots. More compact varieties are good for growing in containers on the patio, and this is useful if you do not have acid (lime-free) soil.

Hardiness Fully hardy ✳✳✳ to frost-tender ❀.

Cultivation Grow in moist but well-drained, acid (lime-free) soil, ideally pH 4.5–5.5. Site in dappled shade if possible, but most dwarf alpine species will tolerate full sun. Shallow planting is essential; the top of the root ball should be level with the surface of the soil. **Mulch** annually with leafmould or lime-free compost. **Snap off** the old flowerheads when the flowers have faded, using your forefinger and thumb to twist them to one side. Be careful not to damage the developing new buds just below, which contain the flowers for the following year. **Propagate** by layering (*see p.395*). If leaves are affected by powdery mildew or rusts, cut out all affected growth. Ensure good drainage to avoid root rot.

Tree rhododendrons

Tree rhododendrons are very large plants, most often seen in public parks and too large to be suitable for many gardens. Hardy evergreens, they are spectacular when in flower because they tend to produce the largest flower clusters of all the types of rhododendron. Some tree rhododendrons also have attractive peeling bark.

Deciduous azaleas

Azaleas have generally small to medium-sized leaves and small flowers. Most are deciduous, and often colour wonderfully in autumn. In spring and early summer, they are an almost solid mass of flowers in colours ranging from salmon-pink to red and various shades of yellow, typically with a delicious scent. Some can grow quite tall, but they are easily controlled with occasional, but not hard, pruning.

Shrub rhododendrons

The most common and well-known type of rhododendron, these are rounded and range in size from less than 1m (3ft) to 4m (12ft). The flower clusters vary from quite small to large trusses in a wide range of bold colours. The added bonus with the small shrub rhododendrons is that most of them are evergreen, and their attractive leaves will therefore continue to act as a background to other plants throughout the year.

① *Rhododendron arboreum* ‡12m (40ft) ↔ 4m (12ft), tree ✳✳ ② *argyrophyllum* ‡6m (20ft) ↔ 2.5m (8ft), evergreen shrub ✳✳✳ ③ *arizelum* ‡↔ 8m (25ft), tree ✳✳✳ ④ *augustinii* ‡↔ 2.2m (7ft), tree ✳✳✳ ⑤ *austrinum* ‡↔ 3m (10ft), deciduous azalea ✳✳✳ ⑥ *'Azuma-kagami'* ‡↔ 1.2m (4ft), evergreen azalea ✳✳✳ ⑦ *'Beauty of Littleworth'* ‡↔ 4m (12ft), evergreen shrub ✳✳✳ ⑧ *'Beethoven'* ♀ ‡↔ 1.3m (4½ft), evergreen azalea ✳✳✳ ⑨ *'Blue Diamond'* ‡↔ 1.5m (5ft), evergreen shrub ❀❀❀ ⑩ 'Blue Peter' ♀ ↕↔3m (10ft), evergreen shrub ❀❀❀ ⑪ 'Cilpinense' ♀ ↕↔1.1m (3½ft), evergreen shrub ❀❀❀ ⑫ *cinnabarinum* ↕6m (20ft) ↔2m (6ft), evergreen shrub ❀❀❀ ⑬ 'Corneille' ♀ ↕↔1.5–2.5m (5–8ft), deciduous azalea ❀❀❀ ⑭ 'Crest' ♀ ↕↔3.5m (11ft), evergreen shrub ❀❀❀ ⑮ 'Cunningham's White' ↕↔6m (20ft), evergreen shrub ❀❀❀ ⑯ 'Cynthia' ♀ ↕↔6m (20ft), evergreen shrub ❀❀❀ ⑰ *davidsonianum* ♀ ↕4m (12ft) ↔3m (10ft),

evergreen shrub ❀❀❀ ⑱ *falconeri* ♀ ↕12m (40ft) ↔5m (15ft), tree ❀❀❀ ⑲ *fortunei* subsp. *discolor* ♀ ↕6m (20ft) ↔3m (10ft), tree ❀❀❀ ⑳ 'Fragrantissimum' ♀ ↕↔2m (6ft), evergreen shrub ❀ ㉑ *fulvum* ↕5m (15ft) ↔3m (10ft), tree ❀❀❀ ㉒ 'George Reynolds' ♀ ↕↔2m (6ft), deciduous azalea ❀❀❀ ㉓ 'Glory of Littleworth' ↕↔1–1.5m (3–4ft), deciduous azalea ❀❀❀ ㉔ 'Glowing Embers' ↕↔2m (6ft), deciduous azalea ❀❀❀

㉕ *Rhododendron* 'Golden Torch' ♀ ↕↔ 1.5m (5ft), evergreen shrub ✳✳✳ ㉖ 'Hatsugiri' ↕↔ 60cm (24in), dwarf evergreen azalea ✳✳✳ ㉗ 'Hinode-giri' ↕↔ 60cm (24in), dwarf evergreen azalea ✳✳✳ ㉘ 'Hinomayo' ♀ ↕↔ 60cm (24in), dwarf evergreen azalea ✳✳✳ ㉙ 'Homebush' ♀ ↕↔ 1.5m (5ft), deciduous azalea ✳✳✳ ㉚ 'Hydon Dawn' ♀ ↕↔ 1.5m (5ft), evergreen shrub ✳✳✳ ㉛ 'Irohayama' ♀ ↕↔ 60cm (24in), dwarf evergreen azalea

✳✳✳ ㉜ 'John Cairns' ♀ ↕↔ 1.5m (5ft), evergreen azalea ✳✳✳ ㉝ 'Kirin' ↕↔ 1.5m (5ft), evergreen azalea ✳✳✳ ㉞ 'Kure-no-yuki' ↕↔ 1m (3ft), evergreen azalea ✳✳✳ ㉟ 'Lavender Girl' ♀ ↕↔ 2.5m (8ft), evergreen shrub ✳✳✳ ㊱ 'Linda' ♀ ↕↔ 1m (3ft), evergreen shrub ✳✳✳ ㊲ × *mucronatum* ↕↔ 1.2–1.5m (4–5ft), semi-evergreen shrub ✳✳✳ ㊳ Nobleanum Group ↕↔ 5m (15ft), tree ✳✳✳ ㊴ *occidentale* ♀ ↕↔ 3m (10ft), deciduous shrub ✳✳✳ ㊵ 'Pink Pearl' ↕↔ 4m (12ft), evergreen shrub ❋❋❋ ㊶ 'Polar Bear' ♀ ↕5m (15ft) ↔ 4m (12ft), tree ❋❋❋ ㊷ 'President Roosevelt' ↔ 2m (6ft), evergreen shrub ❋❋❋ ㊸ 'Ptarmigan' ♀ ↕↔ 90cm (36in), dwarf evergreen shrub ❋❋❋ ㊹ 'Purple Splendour' ♀ ↕↔ 3m (10ft), evergreen shrub ❋❋❋ ㊺ *rex* subsp. *fictolacteum* ♀ ↕↔ 12m (40ft), tree ❋❋❋ ㊻ 'Saint Valentine' ↕1.5m (5ft) ↔ 2m (6ft), evergreen shrub ❋ ㊼ 'Strawberry Ice' ♀ ↕↔ 2m (6ft), deciduous azalea ❋❋❋ ㊽ 'Susan' ♀ ↕↔ 3m (10ft), evergreen

shrub ❋❋❋ ㊾ 'Temple Belle' ↕↔ 2m (6ft), evergreen shrub ❋❋❋ ㊿ *thomsonii* ↕↔ 6m (20ft), tree ❋❋❋ � *veitchianum* Cubittii Group ↕1.5m (5ft) ↔ 1m (3ft), evergreen shrub ❋ ㉒ 'Vuyk's Rosyred' ♀ ↕75cm (30in) ↔ 1.2m (4ft), evergreen azalea ❋❋❋ ㉓ 'Vuyk's Scarlet' ♀ ↕75cm (30in) ↔ 1.2m (4ft), evergreen azalea ❋❋❋ ㉔ *yakushimanum* ↕↔ 2m (6ft), evergreen shrub ❋❋❋ ㉕ *yunnanense* ↕6m (20ft) ↔ 4m (12ft), tree ❋❋❋

RHAMNUS

autumn

CULTIVATED FOR THEIR FOLIAGE, which in deciduous species usually colours well in autumn, rhamnus are mostly thorny shrubs, native to a range of habitats, from woodland, heath and scrub, to fen and bog. They bear small, cup-shaped flowers, often fragrant and attractive to bees (particularly those of *Rhamnus frangula*, syn. *Frangula alnus*), followed by decorative red fruits that usually ripen to purple or black. These make a very striking contrast with the leaves of white-variegated *R. alaternus* 'Argenteovariegata', a popular evergreen, but one that needs some shelter in cold areas. Grow rhamnus in a shrub border, or a wild or woodland garden. They also make good informal hedges.

Hardiness Fully hardy ✵✵✵ to frost-hardy ✵✵.

Cultivation Grow in reasonably fertile, reliably moist soil, in full sun or partial shade. **Prune out** any crossing or misplaced shoots that spoil the shape in late winter or early spring. Trim hedges in early spring. **Sow** seed in containers in a cold frame as soon as it is ripe (*see pp.391–392*). **Take** softwood cuttings in early summer (*see p.394*).

RHAPHIOLEPIS

early summer and autumn

THESE ARE EVERGREEN SHRUBS with glossy, dark-green foliage and fragrant flowers that look similar to apple-blossom. The white or pink flowers appear among the leaves in small clusters in spring or summer, making an eye-catching display. They are good companions to small flowering trees such as crab apples (*Malus, see p.88*) and hawthorns (*Crataegus, p.46*). Rhaphiolepis generally grow into dense, compact shapes, around 2m (6ft) tall and wide, although there are one or two much smaller varieties. However, they are not fully hardy, so need the protection of a warm, sunny wall. Alternatively, grow the smaller types in containers, and take them under frost-free cover for the winter.

Hardiness Frost-hardy ✵✵ to half-hardy ✵.

Cultivation Grow outdoors in moist but well-drained soil in full sun, with shelter from cold, drying winds. If growing them in pots, use a loam-based compost and water moderately in summer, giving monthly feeds of a balanced fertilizer. **Trim** lightly after flowering, removing stems that spoil the shape of the shrub. **Take** semi-ripe cuttings in late summer (*see p.394*), or layer shoots in autumn (*see p.395*).

RHUS

Sumach

summer and autumn

THE SHRUBS AND TREES in this group are grown for their bold, dissected leaves, which turn to vivid hues of ruby, gold, and amber as the temperature falls in autumn. The tiny flowers are borne in candle-like clusters in spring or summer; more impressive are the spikes of usually crimson fruits that then develop, although these appear only when male and female plants are grown together. Sumachs look best at the back of a shrub border or in a woodland garden, teamed with other good autumn foliage plants. Some, such as *Rhus typhina* with its craggy form, also make architectural specimens. Sumachs can be invasive; cut out suckers whenever they appear.

Hardiness Fully hardy ✵✵✵ to frost-tender ❀.

Cultivation Grow in reasonably fertile, moist, but well-drained soil, in full sun for best autumn colour. **Prune out** shoots that are crossing or spoil the shape of the shrub in late winter or early spring. Or in early spring cut back stems to within 2–3 buds from the base or the main shoots. **Sow** seed in a seedbed in autumn (*see pp.391–393*). **Take** semi-ripe cuttings in summer, or root cuttings in winter (*see p.394*). Prone to coral spot, which appears as orange pustules on branches that begin to die. Cut affected growth right out and burn it.

Rhamnus frangula **syn.** *Frangula alnus* (Alder buckthorn)
↕↔ 5m (15ft), bushy, spreading habit, deciduous, tiny greenish-white flowers, leaves turn red in autumn ✵✵✵

Rhaphiolepis umbellata ♀
↕↔ 1.5m (5ft), slow-growing, bushy, rounded habit, flowers in early summer, berries only after long, hot summers ✵✵

Rhus typhina ♀ (Stag's horn sumach, Velvet sumach)
↕ 5m (15ft) ↔ 6m (20ft), deciduous, arching, suckering shrub or tree, dense velvety coating on stems, brilliant autumn colour ✵✵✵

RIBES
Flowering currant

mid- to late spring

CLOSELY RELATED TO EDIBLE CURRANT BUSHES, most ornamental ribes have a blackcurrant- or even cat-like scent, both in flower and when the leaves are crushed. These are old-fashioned, cottage-garden-style, mainly deciduous shrubs, grown for their cheering spring flowers; pink-flowered *Ribes sanguineum* is a traditional partner for yellow forsythias (*see p.58–59*). It is also often seen as a flowering hedge. There are ribes that flower in cerise, pale pink, white, or greenish-yellow. They do bear fruits, although these are usually inedible. Most make quite large shrubs, but they can be wall-trained, and there are compact varieties, including one or two with golden foliage.

Hardiness Fully hardy ✲✲✲ to frost-hardy ✲✲.

Cultivation Grow in reasonably fertile, well-drained soil, in full sun. *R. laurifolium* tolerates partial shade. **Prune** after flowering, cutting back flowered shoots to strong buds or shoots lower down the stem. Prune out one or two old main branches on mature plants every three or four years. If wall-trained, after flowering or in late winter, cut back flowered shoots to within 2–4 buds of the permanent framework. Trim hedges after flowering. **Take** hardwood cuttings of deciduous ribes in winter and semi-ripe cuttings of evergreens in summer (*see p.394*).

Ribes sanguineum **'Pulborough Scarlet'** ♀
‡3m (10ft) ↔ 2.5m (8ft), upright, vigorous habit, flowers with white centres in spring, blue-black fruits ✲✲✲

ROBINIA

spring, summer, and autumn

ROBINIAS ARE TREES AND SHRUBS found in woodland and thickets in North America. They are usually thorny and have bright, graceful, long leaves, and, in late spring and early summer, sprays of white or pink, pea-like flowers. These are followed by large, dark brown seedpods. Grow the trees as specimens in a lawn, and the shrubby species in a large shrub border, especially among darker-leaved trees or shrubs. *Robinia pseudoacacia* 'Frisia', which may be coppiced (*see p.42*) and grown as a foliage shrub, and *Acer palmatum* 'Rubrum', with dark red-purple leaves (*see pp.18–19*), make striking companions.

Hardiness Fully hardy ✲✲✲.

Cultivation Robinias like full sun in reasonably fertile soil, ideally moist but well-drained, but will tolerate dry, poor soils. Shelter from strong winds; the branches are rather brittle and break easily. **Prune out** any misplaced or crossing branches that spoil the shape of young trees in late summer or early autumn (*see p.382*). Remove any suckers (shoots growing up from the ground around the tree). **Sow** seed in a container in a cold frame in autumn (*see pp.391–392*). **Take** root cuttings (*see p.394*) in autumn.

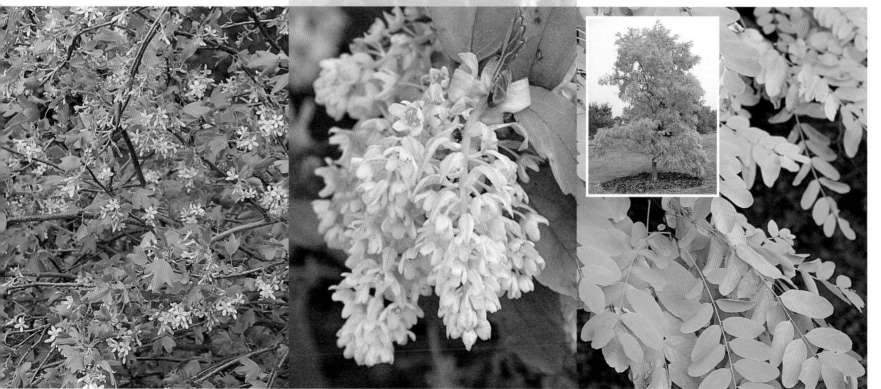

Ribes odoratum (Buffalo currant)
‡↔ 2m (6ft), upright, deciduous shrub, aromatic flowers in mid- to late spring, black fruits, leaves turn red and purple in autumn ✲✲✲

Ribes laurifolium
‡1m (3ft) ↔ 1.5m (5ft), spreading, evergreen, leathery leaves, flowers in late winter and early spring, tolerates semi-shade ✲✲✲

Robinia pseudoacacia **'Frisia'** ♀ (False acacia, Black locust)
‡15m (50ft) ↔ 8m (25ft), fast-growing, suckering tree, fragrant flowers, foliage turns orange-yellow (*see inset*) in autumn

TREES AND SHRUBS

Rose

early summer to autumn

SUPERB, OFTEN HIGHLY SCENTED FLOWERS in summer and autumn make roses enduring garden favourites. They are mostly deciduous shrubs, and with hundreds of colourful varieties to choose from, there is one suitable for almost any situation. Shrub roses look best mixed with other plants in borders; the miniature varieties can be grown in rock gardens and in large pots. The flowers, borne in clusters at the tips of upright, sometimes arching or trailing, thorny stems, are excellent for cutting. They vary enormously in form and size, from small single or double blooms to immense, rounded doubles. Colours range from purest white through yellows and pinks to deep blackish-crimson. The red autumn fruits (hips) of some roses also make a striking display.

Hardiness Fully hardy ✳✳✳.

Cultivation Grow in an open, sunny position, in fertile soil with plenty of well-rotted organic matter. **Plant** bare-root roses when dormant, from late autumn to early spring, container-grown plants at any time. **Feed** with a balanced fertilizer in spring and mulch with organic matter. **Prune** in late winter or early spring; deadhead to encourage more flowers. **Take** hardwood cuttings (*see p.394*) in autumn. Blackspot, powdery mildew, or rust may affect roses. Choose disease-resistant cultivars if possible.

Modern bush roses

‡ to 1m (3ft)
↔ to 1m (3ft)

These upright shrubs are useful in borders and beds, being compact and repeat-flowering with single or double flowers. They bear large flowers singly or in small clusters (*hybrid tea*) or small flowers in large clusters (*floribunda*). Prune hard, cutting the main stems of hybrid tea roses to 20–25cm (8–10in) and those of cluster-flowered roses to 25–45cm (10–18in) above the ground, and reducing sideshoots to two or three buds.

Dwarf patio roses

‡ 60cm (24in)
↔ 60cm (24in)

Compact shrubs with a bushy habit, these roses are ideal for growing at the front of borders, in containers or even in a rock garden. They produce abundant clusters of single to double, sometimes scented flowers in a wide range of colours throughout summer. Grow them in fertile soil in full sun. Only light pruning is needed: cut down the main stems and sideshoots by no more than one-third to half their length.

Ground-cover roses

‡ to 60cm (24in)
↔ to 1m (3ft)

Spreading in habit, these roses have numerous stems bearing clusters of small flowers, usually double or semi-double and lightly scented. They are ideal for ground cover and also for edging paths or growing in large pots. Prune to keep plants to the desired size, cutting to an outward-facing bud. If sideshoots are overcrowded, prune to two to four buds. Every three or four years cut out the oldest wood to encourage new growth; if neglected, they can be cut back hard.

Standard roses

‡ to 2m (6ft)
↔ to 1.5m (5ft)

Ideal for pots, formal schemes, or to add height in borders, these are modern bush roses top-grafted onto clear stems of rootstocks; ramblers (see pp.150–151) can be used to make weeping or trailing standards. There are two types of standards; half-standards have a stem of 75cm (2½ft) and full-standards a stem of 1.1m (3½ft). Both need permanent staking. Prune the head according to the rose type used.

Modern shrub roses

‡ 1.2–2m (4–6ft)
↔ to 2m (6ft)

A diverse group of roses, varying in size, habit, and flower type. Most are upright with flowers similar to modern bush roses, and make impressive specimen plants. Some have only one flush of blooms while others repeat-flower through the summer. Heavy pruning can spoil their character: remove dead or diseased wood and shorten main stems by up to one-third, sideshoots by half. Cut one in three old stems to the base each year.

Old garden roses

‡ 1.2–2m (4–6ft)
↔ to 2m (6ft)

A varied group, upright or arching, most flowering once (these are pruned after flowering) but some repeat-flowering, most with semi-double or double flowers, often fragrant. Position arching types so they do not crowd plants, and give only a light annual pruning, removing some older wood to encourage new shoots from the base of the shrub. Upright types require only occasional removal of thin, weak, or dead shoots.

① *Rosa* AMBER QUEEN ('Harroony') ♥ ‡↔ 60cm (24in), floribunda ② ANGELA RIPPON ('Ocaru') ‡ 45cm (18in) ↔ 30cm (12in), miniature modern bush ③ ANNA FORD ('Harpiccolo') ♥ ‡↔ 45cm (18in), patio ④ 'Ballerina' ♥ ‡ 1.5m (5ft) ↔ 1.2m (4ft), modern shrub ⑤ 'Belle de Crécy' ♥ ‡ 1.2m (4ft) ↔ 1m (3ft), old rose ⑥ 'Boule de Neige' ‡ 1.5m (5ft) ↔ 1.2m (4ft), old rose ⑦ 'Bourbon Queen' ‡ 2.5m (8ft) ↔ 1.5m (5ft), old rose ⑧ 'Buff Beauty' ♥ ‡↔ 1.2m (4ft), modern shrub ⑨ **'Cécile Brünner'** ♀ ‡75cm (30in) ↔ 60cm (24in), old rose ⑩ **'Charles de Mills'** ♀ ‡↔ 1.2m (4ft), old rose ⑪ **'Chinatown'** ♀ ‡1.2m (4ft) ↔ 1m (3ft), modern shrub ⑫ CONSERVATION ('Cocdimple') ‡↔ 45cm (18in), patio ⑬ **'Cornelia'** ♀ ‡↔ 1.5m (5ft), modern shrub ⑭ **'Crimson Glory'** ‡↔ 60cm (24in), hybrid tea ⑮ **'Doris Tysterman'** ‡1.2m (4ft) ↔ 75cm (30in), hybrid tea ⑯ **'Elizabeth Harkness'** ‡80cm (32in) ↔ 60cm (24in), hybrid tea ⑰ ENGLISH GARDEN ('Ausbuff') ‡1m (3ft) ↔ 75cm (30in), modern shrub ⑱ **'English Miss'** ♀ ‡75cm (30in) ↔ 60cm (24in), floribunda ⑲ ESCAPADE ('Harpade') ♀ ‡75cm (30in) ↔ 60cm (24in), floribunda ⑳ **'Fantin-Latour'** ♀ ‡1.5m (5ft) ↔ 1.2m (4ft), old rose ㉑ **'Felicia'** ♀ ‡1.5m (5ft) ↔ 2.2m (7ft), modern shrub ㉒ FRAGRANT CLOUD ('Tanellis') ‡75cm (30in) ↔ 60cm (24in), hybrid tea ㉓ **'Fru Dagmar Hastrup'** ♀ ‡1m (3ft) ↔ 1.2m (4ft), old rose

㉔ *Rosa* 'Frühlingsmorgen' ‡2m (6ft) ↔ 1.5m (5ft), modern shrub ㉕ *gallica* 'Versicolor' ♀ ‡80cm (32in) ↔ 1m (3ft), old rose ㉖ 'Geranium' ♀ ‡2.5m (8ft) ↔ 1.5m (5ft), old rose ㉗ 'Glenfiddich' ‡80cm (32in) ↔ 60cm (24in), floribunda ㉘ GRAHAM THOMAS ('Ausmas') ♀ ‡↔ 1.2–1.5m (4–5ft), modern shrub ㉙ 'Great Maiden's Blush' ‡2m (6ft) ↔ 1.35m (4½ft), old rose ㉚ HANNAH GORDON ('Korweiso') ‡80cm (32in) ↔ 60cm (24in), floribunda

㉛ Iceberg ('Korbin') ♀ ‡80cm (32in) ↔ 65cm (26in), floribunda ㉜ 'Ispahan' ♀ ‡1.5m (5ft) ↔ 1.2m (4ft), old rose ㉝ 'Julia's Rose' ‡75cm (30in) ↔ 45cm (18in), hybrid tea ㉞ 'Just Joey' ♀ ‡↔ 75cm (30in), hybrid tea ㉟ LAURA ASHLEY ('Chewharla') ‡60cm (24in) ↔ 1.2m (4ft), ground cover ㊱ 'Madame Isaac Pereire' ♀ ‡2.2m (7ft) ↔ 2m (6ft), old rose ㊲ 'Maiden's Blush' ♀ ‡1.2m (4ft) ↔ 90cm (36in), old rose ㊳ MARGARET MERRIL ('Harkuly') ♀ ‡80cm (32in) ↔ 60cm (24in), floribunda ㊴ MOUNTBATTEN ('Harmantelle') ♈ ↕1.2m (4ft) ↔ 75cm (30in), floribunda ㊵ 'National Trust' ↕↔ 60cm (24in) hybrid tea ㊶ 'Nevada' ♈ ↕↔ 2.2m (7ft), modern shrub ㊷ PEACE ('Madame A. Meilland') ♈ ↕1.2m (4ft) ↔ 1m (3ft), hybrid tea ㊸ 'Perle d'Or' ♈ ↕1.2m (4ft) ↔ 1m (3ft), old rose ㊹ 'Pink Favorite' ↕↔ 75cm (30in), hybrid tea ㊺ POLAR STAR ('Tanlarpost') ↕1m (3ft) ↔ 70cm (28in), hybrid tea ㊻ PRETTY POLLY ('Meitonje') ♈ ↕↔ 45cm (18in), patio ㊼ ROBIN REDBREAST ('Interrob') ↕↔ 45–60cm (18–24in), ground cover ㊽ ROSEMARY HARKNESS ('Harrowbond') ↕↔ 80cm (32in), hybrid tea ㊾ *rugosa* ↕↔ 1–2.5m (3–8ft), species ㊿ 'Silver Jubilee' ♈ ↕1.1m (3½ft) ↔ 60cm (24in), hybrid tea � 'Souvenir de la Malmaison' ↕↔ 1.5m (5ft), old rose ㉒ 'The Fairy' ♈ ↕↔ 60–90cm (24–36in), floribunda ㉓ 'The Queen Elizabeth' ↕2.2m (7ft) ↔ 1m (3ft), modern bush ㉔ TRUMPETER ('Mactru') ♈ ↕↔ 60cm (24in), floribunda

ROSMARINUS

Rosemary   *year-round*

AROMATIC AND EVERGREEN, these rather angular shrubs add height and structure to a herb garden, and also grow well in pots. Native to Mediterranean regions, they can, although hardy, suffer badly in cold wet winters. The upright types benefit from the shelter of a sunny wall, while the less hardy, prostrate forms much prefer spreading over a gravel mulch or even a stony bank or retaining wall, rather than sitting on chilly wet soil. The leaves of rosemary are dark green, while the stems often have a greyish bloom. From mid-spring to early summer, and now and again in late summer, they bear clusters of blue, mauve, or white, tubular flowers towards the shoot tips.

Hardiness Frost-hardy ✳✳; *Rosmarinus officinalis* and cultivars withstand -10°C (14°F) if well-drained.

Cultivation Grow in well-drained to dry, relatively poor soil, in full sun. **Trim** lightly but regularly to keep plants bushy and to encourage the soft, succulent young shoots that are best for cooking. **Sow** seed (*see pp.391–392*) in a container in a cold frame in spring. **Take** semi-ripe cuttings (*see p.394*) in summer.

RUBUS

↔ 3m (10ft)

see also *p.152*

early summer, autumn, and winter

THESE ARCHING SHRUBS, related to brambles, bear simple, rose-like flowers in early summer, in white, red, purple, or pink. In some, such as the thornless 'Benenden' and the spectacularly bright *Rubus spectabilis* 'Olympic Double', the flowering period is the main season of interest; these suit a wild or woodland garden. *R. biflorus*, *R. cockburnianus*, and *R. thibetanus* are also grown for winter interest, with a white bloom on their prickly stems that makes them stand out. They look good with willows (*Salix, see right*) and dogwoods (*Cornus, see pp.42–43*) grown for colourful winter stems, and like them are best pruned hard annually.

Hardiness Fully hardy ✳✳✳.

Cultivation Grow in well-drained, reasonably fertile soil. Position in full sun for the brightest winter stems. **Prune** rubus grown for their flowers lightly, cutting back flowered shoots to strong buds or shoots lower down. Prune those grown for winter stems hard, in early spring, cutting stems to within three buds of the base, then feed and mulch. **Take** hardwood cuttings in early winter (*see p.394*).

SALIX

Willow   *spring, summer, and winter*

THIS IS A LARGE AND VARIED group of deciduous trees and shrubs. Spring catkins are one of the striking features, but they also have attractive habits, and in some cases decorative stems. Willows seen growing in the wild are often massive trees, but there are many small and medium-sized ones – the weeping *Salix caprea* 'Kilmarnock' is a favourite centrepiece for a small lawn or border. Some of the larger species, generally too vigorous for most gardens, can be grown as shrubs, cut back annually to make them compact and encourage brightly coloured stems. *S. alba* 'Britzensis', for example, makes a fine winter display with mahonias (*see p.87*), Christmas box (*Sarcococca, see p.116*), and dogwoods (*Cornus, see pp.42–43*).

Hardiness Fully hardy ✳✳✳.

Cultivation Grow in any deep, moist but well-drained soil, except chalky soils, in full sun. **Pruning** is rarely necessary except for those grown for winter stems; in early spring, cut these stems back to within three or four buds of the base or to a permanent stubby framework (*see right, and p.383*). **Take** greenwood cuttings in early summer, or hardwood cuttings in winter (*see p.394*). Willow cuttings root easily.

① *officinalis* ↕↔ 1.5m (5ft) ② *officinalis* 'McConnell's Blue'
♀ ↕↔ 1.5m (5ft) ③ *officinalis* **Prostratus Group** ↕ 15cm
(6in) ↔ 1.5m (5ft) ④ *officinalis* '**Roseus**' ↕↔ 1.5m (5ft)

Rubus cockburnianus
↕↔ 2.5m (8ft), thicket-forming, small, purple flowers in summer, black fruits, attractive although unpalatable

Salix helvetica ♀ (Swiss willow)
↕ 60cm (2ft) ↔ 40cm (16in), an upright, bushy shrub, leaves grey-green above and silvery white beneath, catkins in early spring

Salix gracilistyla 'Melanostachys'
‡3m (10ft) ↔ 4m (12ft), upright shrub, silky-hairy grey-green leaves turn glossy green, dramatic black catkins in early to mid-spring

SAMBUCUS

Elder
mid-spring to autumn

THESE DECIDUOUS SHRUBS AND TREES are grown for their flowers and ornamental foliage. From spring to early summer, they produce dense, flat clusters of white or creamy yellow flowers followed by black or glossy red fruits. The leaves may be blackish-purple, dark green, or golden yellow, and are made up of small leaflets, deeply fringed in some cultivars. Elders are suitable for shrub and mixed borders or as specimens. Planted together, dark and yellow-leaved types contrast well. *Photinia × fraseri* 'Red Robin' (*see p.95*) with its red young foliage is also a good companion.

Hardiness Fully hardy ✳✳✳.

Cultivation Grow in reasonably fertile soil that is moist but well-drained. Position in full sun or partial shade: leaves colour most strongly in full sun, but retain colour better in dappled shade. **Prune** only to remove crossing or misplaced shoots, in winter or early spring; or, for the best leaf colour, cut back stems to within two or three buds of the base or to a permanent framework in early spring. Prune hard to restrict size if necessary. **Sow** seed (*see pp.391–392*) in a container in a cold frame in autumn. **Take** hardwood cuttings in winter, or softwood cuttings in early summer (*see p.394*). Blackfly (*see Aphids, pp.398–399*) may infest young growth, but can be treated.

COPPICING WILLOWS
Several species of willow can be cut back to the base in spring; this will produce the most brightly coloured winter stems.

Salix caprea 'Kilmarnock' (Kilmarnock willow)
‡1.5–2m (5–6ft) ↔ 2m (6ft), weeping stems are grafted on to upright rootstock, catkins in mid-and late spring, dark green leaves

Salix alba 'Britzensis' ♥
‡25m (80ft) ↔ 10m (30ft), naturally a large tree, annual coppicing will keep it in bounds, dull-green leaves, catkins in spring

Sambucus racemosa 'Plumosa Aurea' (Red-berried elder)
‡↔ 3m (10ft), bushy shrub, leaves are bronze when new (*see inset*) and can scorch in full sun, flowers in mid-spring

SANTOLINA

Cotton lavender   *summer*

‡ 15–75cm (6–30in)
↔ 20cm–1m (8–36in)

COMPACT, ROUNDED, evergreen – or rather, "evergrey" – shrubs, these can be used as low hedges or to edge borders, and are ideal for rock gardens, being naturally found in dry sites. They are grown principally for their fine, aromatic foliage. The long-stemmed flowerheads are button-like, yellow or creamy-yellow, surrounded by broad rings of similarly coloured bracts (modified leaves) that make them more conspicuous. The plants spread to cover the ground, and effectively suppress weeds. For a heady mix of scents, grow with other aromatic herbs, such as lavender (*Lavandula, see pp.80–81*) and rosemary (*Rosmarinus, see p.114*).

Hardiness Frost-hardy ✳✳.

Cultivation Grow in poor to reasonably fertile soil that is well-drained and in full sun. **Cut back** flowered shoots to within 2.5cm (1in) of old growth in spring. **Sow** seed (*see pp.391–392*) in containers in a cold frame in autumn or spring. **Take** semi-ripe cuttings (*see p.394*) in late summer and root in a propagator with bottom heat.

PRUNING SANTOLINAS
Never cut santolinas back beyond the point where you can see fresh growth shooting from old wood.

SARCOCOCCA

Christmas box,   *winter and*
Sweet box   *year-round*

A SMALL GROUP OF TOUGH EVERGREEN shrubs, sarcococcas are invaluable in the garden in winter. Their dense forms, clothed in glossy, dark green leaves, add visual interest by blooming in winter, bearing clusters of white flowers followed by round, glossy berries. Their greatest attraction, however, is scent: the flowers are not showy, but this is more than made up for by the fragrance, sweet and powerful over a surprising distance even on the coldest winter's day. A few cut stems will scent a whole room. Grow them with other winter-flowering plants, such as *Viburnum* × *bodnantense* 'Dawn' (*see pp.126–127*) and *Helleborus niger* (*see p.257*), or as an informal hedge.

Hardiness Fully hardy ✳✳✳.

Cultivation Grow in reasonably fertile, moist but well-drained soil, enriched with well-rotted organic matter. Position in deep or partial shade: they tolerate full sun if the soil is reliably moist. **Trim** or prune back any stems that spoil the shape of the shrub after flowering, but not too much; trimming shoots too closely may result in fewer flowers. **Sow** seed (*see pp.391–392*) in containers outdoors in autumn or spring. **Take** semi-ripe cuttings (*see p.394*) in late summer, or remove suckers for transplanting in late winter.

SENECIO CINERARIA   *see also p.325*

Cineraria   *spring, summer, and autumn*

‡↔ to 60cm (24in)

THESE MOUNDING evergreen shrubs are grown chiefly for their leaves, soft like felt, in a range of delicate shapes and shades of silvery green and grey. Yellow flowerheads are produced in the second year after sowing, but the plants are often discarded after one season. The flowers are not particularly attractive, and the foliage is at its pristine best only when plants are young. They can be grown in shrub borders, but are mainly used as dot plants or edging in bedding schemes, where their foliage can act as a foil for flowering plants. A classic combination is cinerarias with red salvias (*see pp.318–319*); for a more subdued effect, pair it with purple heliotropes (*see p.70*).

Hardiness Frost-hardy ✳✳.

Cultivation Grow in reasonably fertile soil in full sun. **Trim** plants if necessary to improve the shape. **Sow** seed (*see pp.391–393*) in spring at 19–24°C (66–75°F). **Take** semi-ripe cuttings (*see p.394*) in mid- or late summer. Prone to rust; in bedding schemes, affected plants are best removed to prevent it from spreading.

Santolina pinnata 'Sulphurea'
‡ 75cm (30in) ↔ 1m (3ft), feathery, finely divided, grey-green leaves, flowers in midsummer

Sarcococca confusa ♀
‡ 2m (6ft) ↔ 1m (3ft), dense and rounded, slow-growing shrub that is very useful for fairly dry, shady areas

① *cineraria* 'Silver Dust' ♀ ‡↔ 30cm (12in), particularly bright foliage ② *cineraria* 'White Diamond' ‡ 30–40cm (12–16in) ↔ 30cm (12in), usually grown as perennial

SKIMMIA

late winter to summer

‡↔ to 6m (20ft)

SKIMMIAS ARE HANDSOME evergreens, all with similar looks but varying widely in size, with many compact varieties for the smaller garden. Clusters of starry flowers, sometimes scented, open in spring, but are prominent in bud through the winter in several forms. The flowers are followed by fleshy, round, black, red, or white berries; some skimmias have male and female plants, so both are needed for fruit. The pointed leaves are dark, glossy, and aromatic. Skimmias are reliable players in winter-interest schemes, adding structure and colour next to deciduous shrubs like hamamelis (*see p.68*), and height to groupings of winter- and spring-flowering heathers (*Calluna, see p.31*).

Hardiness Fully hardy ✳✳✳.

Cultivation Grow in reasonably fertile, moist but well-drained soil, with well-rotted organic matter added. Position in light or dappled shade; *S. × confusa* 'Kew Green' will tolerate full sun. **Prune** only if necessary. **Sow** seed (*see pp.391–392*) in containers in a cold frame in autumn. **Take** semi-ripe cuttings (*see p.394*) in late summer.

Skimmia japonica 'Rubella' ♀
‡↔ to 6m (20ft), this male bears no fruit, but has fine red buds in autumn and winter, flowers in mid- and late spring

SOPHORA

spring to late summer

GROWN FOR THEIR FINE FOLIAGE and their clusters of bright flowers, these trees and shrubs need long, hot spells to flower well, but are worth growing for the leaves alone. These are composed of small leaflets arranged along a central leaf stalk, and have a very elegant appearance. There are both decidous and evergreen sophoras. The pea-like flowers are carried in clusters at the end of the branches, in colours that include purple-blue to white and golden-yellow. Sophoras look good in a shrub border, or near a sheltered wall in cooler regions to encourage flowering. In cold areas, grow the less hardy types in pots, and take under frost-free cover for the winter.

Hardiness Fully hardy ✳✳✳ to frost-hardy ✳✳.

Cultivation Grow in reasonably fertile, well-drained soil, in full sun. Use a loam-based compost in pots, water freely in summer and feed at monthly intervals with a balanced fertilizer. **Prune** out any misplaced or crossing shoots that spoil the shape of young trees in late winter or early spring, to create a healthy framework of branches. **Sow** seed (*see pp.391–392*) in a container in a cold frame as soon as they are ripe.

Skimmia japonica
‡↔ to 6m (20ft), variable in shape, fragrant white flowers in mid- and late spring, male and female forms

Skimmia × confusa 'Kew Green' ♀
‡ 0.5–3m (1½–10ft) ↔ 1.5m (5ft), a male cultivar with aromatic leaves and fragrant white flowers in spring but no fruit

Sophora davidii
‡ 2.5m (8ft) ↔ 3m (10ft), bushy or spreading, deciduous shrub or tree, flowering in late summer or early autumn when mature

SORBUS

Mountain ash, Rowan, Whitebeam

spring to autumn

UPRIGHT, COLUMNAR, OR SPREADING trees and shrubs, sorbus have an attractive branch structure and flowers in spring or summer. Their foliage is ornamental, with leaves in a range of shapes, often colouring well in autumn, and the bark is textured when mature, but the main highlight is the autumn show of berries, which are attractive to birds. These are mostly in shades of red, orange, and yellow, but some have white berries, often tinted pink, as in the tree *Sorbus cashmiriana* (syn. *S. rosea*). The thicket-forming shrub *S. reducta* has crimson berries that become white as the leaves turn red and purple in autumn. Use sorbus as specimens or grow in a border with hawthorns (*Crataegus, see p.46*) or amelanchiers (*see p.22*) for a richly coloured autumn display.

Hardiness Fully hardy ✱✱✱.

Cultivation Grow in any reasonably fertile, moist but well-drained soil, in full sun or dappled shade. **Prune** out crossing or misplaced shoots in late winter or early spring, but only if necessary. **Sow** seed (*see pp.391–392*) in a container in a cold frame in autumn.

SPARTIUM JUNCEUM

Broom, Spanish broom

early summer to early autumn

✦ to 3m (10ft)

THIS PLANT IS CLOSELY related to cytisus (*see p.47*) and genistas (*see p.65*), both also commonly called broom. Spanish broom is a wonderful plant for coastal gardens, suitable for a shrub border or training against a warm, sunny wall. It is an upright shrub, with slender, dark green shoots and few leaves. From early summer until early autumn, it produces masses of fragrant, pea-like flowers, followed by flattened, dark brown seed pods. The intense yellow of the flowers would make a lively contrast to the similarly shaped, rich blue flowers of *Sophora davidii* (*see p.117*).

Hardiness Frost-hardy ✱✱.

Cultivation This plant likes reasonably fertile, well-drained soil; thrives in coastal areas and on chalky soils. Needs full sun. **Trim** or prune shoots that spoil the shape of the shrub, lightly in mid- or late spring. Older specimens may be renovated by cutting back fairly hard in spring. **Sow** seed (*see pp.391–392*) in containers in a cold frame in spring or autumn. It is a plant that will often self-seed.

SPIRAEA

spring to summer

THERE IS A SPIRAEA FOR ALMOST any position in the garden. This varied group of semi-evergreen and deciduous shrubs contains many elegant and easily cultivated plants, in various sizes. They are grown mainly for their dense clusters of small, saucer-shaped or bowl-shaped flowers, carried at the branch tips in spring and summer. These range from white, pink, and yellow, to purple. Some spiraeas have coloured leaves, like *Spiraea japonica* 'Goldflame', which has bronze-red young leaves that turn to bright yellow, then to mid-green; its flowers are dark pink.

Hardiness Fully hardy ✱✱✱, although new growth may be damaged by frosts.

Cultivation Grow in fertile, moist but well-drained soil in full sun. **Prune** most spiraeas, which flower on older wood, after flowering, cutting back the flowered shoots to strong buds or shoots lower down the shrub. Encourage new growth from the base of mature plants by cutting out about one in every three or four old stems each year. Prune *S. japonica* and its cultivars, which flower on the current year's growth, differently, cutting them back to a permanent low framework of shoots in early spring. **Take** greenwood cuttings in summer (*see p.394*).

A LOW HEDGE
'Snowmound' is, as its name suggests, dense in habit, so makes a good compact hedge. Prune immediately after flowering.

① *aria* 'Lutescens' ♈ ‡10m (30ft), brown-speckled red berries
② *aucuparia* ‡15m (50ft) ③ 'Joseph Rock' ‡10m (30ft)
④ *sargentiana* ♈ ‡↔10m (30ft)

Spartium junceum ♈
Plants in sheltered positions may become tall and leggy; in an exposed seaside garden, winds will keep the growth dense

Spiraea nipponica 'Snowmound' ♈
‡↔ 1.2–2.5m (4–8ft), fast-growing, deciduous, smothered with white flowers in early summer

STACHYURUS

late winter to early spring

A SMALL GROUP OF SPREADING, deciduous and semi-evergreen shrubs, these are grown for their late winter and early spring flowers, which are small, bell-shaped, and pale yellow. The yellow buds are produced in clusters along the bare stems in autumn, opening in spring before the leaves appear. Only *Stachyurus chinensis* and *S. praecox* are reliably and widely grown; *S. chinensis* is the smaller of the two. Both have pointed, dark green leaves on arching, slender, glossy shoots, which are red-brown in *S. praecox* and purplish in *S. chinensis*. 'Magpie' is a popular variegated cultivar. Grow them in a shrub or mixed border, or against a wall.

Hardiness Fully hardy ✳✳✳.

Cultivation Grow in light, moist, but well-drained, acid (lime-free) soil in full sun or partial shade. Position in a spot sheltered from cold, drying winds. **Prune out** any crossing or misplaced shoots after flowering. Mature plants may be rejuvenated, when necessary, by cutting them to the base after flowering. **Sow** seed (*see pp.391–392*) in a cold frame in autumn. **Take** semi-ripe cuttings (*see p.394*) consisting of a sideshoot with a sliver of older stem (a "heel") attached in summer.

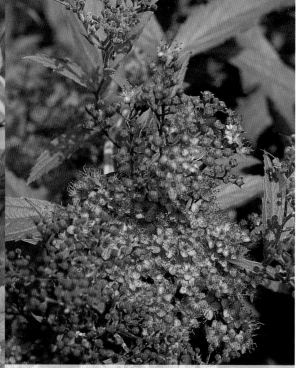

Spiraea japonica 'Anthony Waterer'
↕ to 1.5m (5ft) ↔ 1.5m (5ft), deciduous, leaves are bronze when young and often edged pink or white, flowers in mid- and late summer

FORMAL SHAPES
Vigorous spiraeas such as this may seem too large for a small garden, but can be confined by regular clipping into tight, formal shapes.

Spiraea japonica GOLDEN PRINCESS ('Lisp') ♥
↕ 2m (6ft) ↔ 1.5m (5ft), deciduous, foliage is bronze-red when young then bright yellow and red in autumn, purple-pink flowers

Spiraea × vanhouttei
↕ 2m (6ft) ↔ 1.5m (5ft), a graceful, arching, deciduous shrub, profuse flowers almost obscure the leaves in early summer

Stachyurus praecox ♥
↕ 1–4m (3–12ft) ↔ to 3m (10ft), deciduous shrub, one of the first to flower in late winter and early spring

STEWARTIA

mid- to late summer and autumn

‡6–25m (20–80ft)
↔3–8m (10–25ft)

A SUCCESSION OF FLOWERS in the summer, fine autumn colour, and beautifully textured bark on older specimens all make these large, evergreen or deciduous trees and shrubs worth growing. The rose-like, white flowers have creamy yellow stamens in the centre and are produced singly or in pairs. Stewartias are related to camellias (*see pp.32–33*) and prefer broadly similar conditions, making excellent specimen trees in a woodland setting or shady border. Try them with eucryphias (*see p.55*) which bear similar open, white flowers at different times of the year depending on the species.

Hardiness Fully hardy ✳✳✳ to frost-hardy ✳✳.

Cultivation Grow in moist but well-drained, reasonably fertile, neutral to acid (lime-free) soil. Position in full sun or partial shade, with shelter from strong, cold winds. Buy container-grown plants and choose the right spot first time; they resent root disturbance. **Sow** seed (*see pp.391–392*) in a cold frame in autumn. **Take** greenwood cuttings in early summer or semi-ripe cuttings from mid- to late summer (*see p.394*), or layer low-growing shoots in autumn (*see p.395*).

STYRAX

Snowbell
early to midsummer

BELL-SHAPED, PURE WHITE or pink-tinged flowers give these graceful plants their common name. A large group of deciduous or evergreen shrubs and small trees, most are compact enough to be included in almost any garden. The dainty, fragrant flowers are produced in summer on short branches formed in the previous year. The leaves are variable in shape, and some colour well in autumn. Shrubby snowbells are ideal for a border with mock oranges (*Philadelphus, see p.93*), weigelas (*see p.128*), and potentillas (*see p.99*); plant trees where the flowers can be seen from below.

Hardiness Fully hardy ✳✳✳.

Cultivation Grow in moist but well-drained soil that has been enriched with well-rotted organic matter, and is preferably neutral to acid (lime-free). Position in full sun or partial shade, with protection from cold, drying winds. **Prune out** any misplaced or crossing shoots that spoil the shape of shrubs or young trees in late winter or early spring. **Sow** seed (*see pp.391–392*) as soon as ripe: this needs some care, maintaining 15°C (59°F) for three months and then keeping the seedlings frost-free until they are established. **Take** greenwood cuttings (*see p.394*) in summer.

SYMPHORICARPOS

Snowberry
autumn and winter

THESE DECIDUOUS SHRUBS are grown for their autumn and winter show of berries, which are usually white or rose-tinted, but are dark blue or purple in some species. In summer, they bear clusters of small, bell-shaped flowers which, although too small to have impact, are rich in nectar and attract bees and other beneficial insects into the garden. The berries last well into winter as they are not eaten by wildlife; they may irritate the skin. Often forming thickets, these are very hardy plants and tolerant of a wide range of conditions including poor soil and pollution. They are best grown in a wild garden along a boundery with other shrubs, such as hawthorn (*Crataegus, see p.46*), to form a screen or mixed informal hedge.

Hardiness Fully hardy ✳✳✳.

Cultivation Grow in any reasonably fertile, well-drained soil, and position in full sun or partial shade. **Prune out** misplaced or crossing shoots that spoil the shape of the shrub in late winter or early spring (*see p.382*); reduce size by cutting back flowered stems to strong shoots lower down, after flowering. **Divide** large, clumping plants in autumn (*see p.395*). **Take** greenwood cuttings in summer, or hardwood cuttings in autumn (*see p.394*).

Stewartia pseudocamellia ♀
‡20m (70ft) ↔ 8m (25ft), peeling bark (*see inset*), leaves turn yellow and then orange and red, flowers in midsummer ✳✳✳

Styrax obassia ♀ (Fragrant snowbell)
‡12m (40ft) ↔ 7m (22ft), broadly columnar tree, downy leaves that turn yellow and red in autumn, flowers in early and midsummer

Symphoricarpos × *doorenbosii* 'White Hedge'
‡1.5m (5ft) ↔ indefinite, an upright, thicket-forming shrub, flowers in mid- and late summer, densely clustered fruits

...

SYRINGA

Lilac

early summer

...

RENOWNED FOR THEIR BEAUTIFUL and exquisitely scented flowers in early summer, these deciduous shrubs, traditionally mauve-flowered, are also available in white, cream, pale yellow, pink, magenta, and wine red. Most lilacs in gardens are the familiar cultivars of *Syringa vulgaris*, with a relatively short but always eagerly anticipated season in bloom, their flowers borne in distinctive conical clusters. These can grow quite large, and suit the back of a border or a wild garden area well, or can be pruned to a more shapely form. However there are others, such as *S. meyeri* 'Palibin', that fit into any small garden and can even be trained as standards.

Hardiness Fully hardy ❋❋❋; late frosts may damage new growth.
Cultivation Grow in fertile soil enriched with well-rotted organic matter, preferably neutral to alkaline. Site in full sun. **Deadhead** young lilacs to prevent the plant's energy going into setting seed. **Prune out** any crossing or misshapen branches in late winter or early spring (*see p.382*). *S. vulgaris* and its cultivars can be renovated by pruning hard. **Sow** seed (*see pp.391–392*) in a cold frame, as soon as ripe or in spring. **Layer** low-growing shoots (*see p.395*) in early summer.

RENOVATING LILACS
When cut back hard, old *S. vulgaris* cultivars make vigorous new growth that will need thinning. They should flower again by the third year.

Syringa meyeri 'Palibin' ♀
↕ 1.5–2m (5–6ft) ↔ 1.2m (4ft), slow-growing, rounded shrub, smaller but profuse flower clusters in late spring and early summer

Syringa vulgaris var. *alba*
↔ 7m (22ft), white-flowered form of this highly fragrant, spreading shrub or small tree, which usually has lilac-blue flowers

Syringa × *josiflexa* 'Bellicent' ♀
↕ 4m (12ft) ↔ 5m (15ft), upright shrub, flower clusters are larger than many, up to 20cm (8in) long, in late spring and early summer

Syringa vulgaris 'Primrose'
↔ 7m (22ft), spreading shrub or small tree, small clusters of flowers in unusual colour for lilacs, flowers in late spring to early summer

Syringa pubescens 'Superba' ♀
↕ to 6m (20ft) ↔ 6m (20ft), erect, bushy shrub, small clusters of flowers in early summer and then intermittently until autumn

...

TAMARIX

Tamarisk   *mid spring and late summer*

INVALUABLE IN SEASIDE GARDENS, these are graceful deciduous shrubs or small trees with red-brown, arching stems. Their flowers are pink and carried in dense, plume-like sprays. Naturally found in coastal sites, tamarisks happily withstand salt-laden winds and sea spray. They have tiny, tough, feathery leaves from which little water evaporates; this makes them ideal for a windbreak hedge or screen where winds are not cold. In a sheltered site, they do grow leggy if not checked by regular pruning. Most widely seen are *Tamarix tetrandra*, flowering in mid- to late spring, and *T. ramosissima*, which flowers from late summer.

Hardiness Fully hardy ✳✳✳.

Cultivation Grow in full sun, in well-drained soil in coastal areas or in moist soil with shelter from cold, drying winds in inland gardens. **Prune** young plants almost to ground level after planting and trim regularly to stop plants becoming top-heavy (*see p.383*). Cut flowered stems of spring-flowering types back to strong new shoots; prune autumn-flowering types slightly harder, in early spring; all tolerate renovation pruning, almost to the base. **Sow** seed (*see pp.391–392*) as soon as it is ripe in containers in a cold frame. **Take** hardwood cuttings in winter or semi-ripe cuttings in summer (*see p.394*).

TAXUS

Yew   *year-round*

VERSATILE AND ADAPTABLE CONIFERS, yews are grown for their handsome evergreen foliage and sculptural forms. They have reddish-brown, often peeling bark and narrow, very dark green leaves (there are also golden forms). Female plants bear red berries in autumn. Yews can be grown as freestanding trees or clipped into topiary shapes, and make possibly the best formal hedges; prostrate ones make good ground cover. Yews grow faster than many people think, and will make a dense hedge in under ten years. Unlike most conifers, they can be pruned hard into old wood, so are easy to renovate if overgrown or damaged. All parts except the red fruits' flesh are poisonous.

Hardiness Fully hardy ✳✳✳.

Cultivation Grow in any except wet soil, and in any site, from full sun to full shade. **Trim** hedges and clipped shapes in summer and early autumn. Renovate in autumn to early winter. **Sow** seed (*see pp.391–393*) as soon as ripe in a cold frame or seedbed; they may take two years or more to germinate. **Take** semi-ripe cuttings (*see p.394*) in late summer, choosing upright shoots (except for prostrate forms), otherwise they may not form a central upright stem.

Taxus baccata 'Fastigiata' ♀ (Irish yew)
↕ 10m (30ft) ↔ 6m (20ft), female, particularly narrow as a young plant, forms striking, smoke-like column (*see inset*) when mature

Tamarix ramosissima 'Pink Cascade'
↕↔ 5m (15ft), flowers in dense clusters in late summer and early autumn, on the new year's shoots

Taxus baccata 'Fastigiata Aureomarginata' ♀
↕ 3–5m (10–15ft) ↔ 1–2.5m (3–8ft), broadly conical tree, female, gold-variegated cultivar that will suit even the smallest garden

Taxus baccata 'Dovastonii Aurea'
↕ 3–5m (10–15ft) ↔ 2m (6ft), female tree with a spreading, tiered form on distinctively drooping shoots

TEUCRIUM
Germander   *summer*

GROWN FOR THEIR AROMATIC FOLIAGE and attractive summer flowers, these small evergreen and deciduous shrubs are part of a large group that also includes non-woody plants. The leaves are often grey-green with silvery undersides, and the flowers are tubular or bell-shaped, in shades of pink, yellow, or blue, and are borne in clusters in summer. A sheltered border or a sunny wall will be necessary in colder areas, but wall germanders (*Teucrium chamaedrys*) make good hedging and edging plants in milder regions. Grow with other summer-flowering shrubs that enjoy the same conditions, such as lavenders (*Lavandula, see pp.80–81*), artemisias (*see p.25*), and rosemary (*Rosmarinus, see p.114*) for an aromatic mix.

Hardiness Fully hardy ✳✳✳ to frost-hardy ✳✳.

Cultivation Grow in well-drained soil that is slightly alkaline (limy); the smaller species require very sharply drained soil. Position in full sun. **Trim back** growth to maintain a good shape in spring or late summer, after flowering. **Take** softwood cuttings in early summer, or semi-ripe cuttings in late summer, rooting both in a heated propagator (*see p.394*). Overwinter young plants in frost-free conditions.

THUJA
Arborvitae   *year-round*

THESE CONIFERS, BOTH LARGE AND SMALL, make handsome specimen trees, and also hedges because they stand up well to clipping. They have flattened sprays of scaly foliage, usually aromatic. The white cedar, *Thuja occidentalis,* is a rounded tree that can reach 20m (70ft), with billowing branches, peeling, orange-brown bark, and apple-scented leaves. It has many different forms, and widely varying colours and sizes. 'Caespitosa', for example, is cushion-like and slow-growing, reaching only 30cm (12in) high, suitable for a rock garden. *T. plicata* is a popular hedge, but otherwise only suitable for large gardens. It also has a range of smaller forms, like blue-green 'Hillieri', growing to just 2m (6ft).

Hardiness Fully hardy ✳✳✳.

Cultivation Grow in deep, moist but well-drained soil. Position in full sun, with shelter from cold, drying winds. **Trim** hedging in spring and late summer. **Sow** seed (*see pp.391–392*) in late winter in containers in a cold frame or take semi-ripe cuttings (*see p.394*) in late summer. Prone to aphids (*see pp.398–399*) and small, limpet-like pests known as scale insects: if these become a problem, control with insecticide.

THYMUS
Thyme   *summer*

‡ to 30cm (1ft)
↔ to 60cm (2ft)

LOW-GROWING EVERGREEN shrubs with small, aromatic leaves and pretty flowers, thymes will attract bees and other beneficial insects into the garden. During summer, they produce clusters of tiny flowers, usually in pink, purple, or white. Provided that they do not sit in the wet, thymes can be grown in a range of situations, with border plants or with other decorative herbs such as lavenders (*Lavandula, see pp.80–81*) and with chives. They are ideal for the front or edges of a bed, and mat-forming types can be planted in crevices between paving, where stepping on them will release the scent from the foliage. In containers, perhaps with other herbs, they will trail over the edges attractively.

Hardiness Fully hardy ✳✳✳ to frost-hardy ✳✳.

Cultivation Grow in neutral to alkaline (limy) soil that is well-drained. Position in full sun. **Trim back** after flowering to keep the plants compact. **Sow** seed (*see pp.391–392*) in a container in a cold frame in spring or divide plants (*see p.395*) in spring. **Take** softwood cuttings (*see p.394*) in mid- to late summer.

Teucrium polium
‡↔ 30cm (12in), mound-forming and deciduous, this flowers abundantly in summer ✳✳✳

① *occidentalis* 'Rheingold' ♀ ‡1–2m (3–6ft) ↔ to 1–1.2m (3–4ft), yellow leaves are tinted pink when young ② *plicata* (Western red cedar) ‡20–35m (70–120ft) ↔ 6–9m (20–30ft)

① *doerfleri* 'Bressingham' ‡10cm (4in) ② 'Doone Valley' ‡13cm (5in) ③ 'Peter Davis' ‡15cm (6in) ④ *pulegioides* 'Bertram Anderson' ♀ ‡to 30cm (12in) – all ✳✳✳

TILIA

Lime, Linden

spring, summer, and autumn

LARGE, STATELY, DECIDUOUS trees, limes are grown for their habit, foliage, and scented flowers. All have broadly oval to rounded, bright or dark green leaves that turn yellow in autumn. From midsummer, they produce hanging clusters of creamy-white or pale yellow flowers. These attract pollinating insects, bees in particular, into the garden. They are followed by dry fruits that are nut-like in appearance, but not edible. As the trees age, the silver-grey bark becomes fissured. Limes can be used as specimen trees, but you must have a spacious garden to accommodate one.

Hardiness Fully hardy ✳✳✳.

Cultivation Grow in moist, but well-drained soil; limes prefer alkaline (limy) or neutral soil, but will tolerate acid soils. Avoid wet sites or very dry conditions, and sites exposed to strong, cold winds. Position in full sun or partial shade. **Prune** in late winter or early spring, cutting out any crossing or misplaced shoots that spoil the shape of young trees. **Keep** seed in cold conditions for 3–5 months before sowing in containers in a cold frame in spring (*see pp.391–392*). **Aphids** attack, but cannot harm, limes; however, the sticky honeydew they excrete can be a nuisance as it rains from the tree in summer: do not plant limes where they will overhang paths or parked cars.

Tilia henryana
↕↔ to 25m (80ft), a spreading tree, leaves red-tinged when young, flowering in late summer to early autumn

TRACHYCARPUS

Fan palm

year-round

THESE EVERGREEN PALMS have dark green leaves made up of many pointed segments joined in a fan shape. They usually form a strong single main stem, as in the Chusan palm *Trachycarpus fortunei*, which is the most widely seen in gardens. Small yellow flowers are borne in summer in large, hanging clusters, which emerge from close to the bases of the leaves. Male and female flowers are borne on separate plants in early summer: if they are grown together, female plants produce round, blue-black fruits. Superb feature plants, Chusan palms can be grown in large pots in cold areas and brought into frost-free conditions for the winter. Grow among bamboos and ornamental grasses (*see pp.340–355*) or with ferns (*see pp.356–365*) for a jungle look in a sheltered courtyard.

Hardiness Frost-hardy ✳✳.

Cultivation Grow in well-drained, fertile soil. Position in full sun or partial shade with shelter from cold, drying winds. **Pruning** is unnecessary, but trim off dead leaves (do not cut close to the trunk). **Sow** seed (*see pp.391–393*) in spring or autumn at 24°C (75°F).

Tilia oliveri
↕15m (50ft) ↔ 10m (30ft), flowering in midsummer, this species is less troubled by aphids than many limes

Tilia platyphyllos (Large-leaved lime)
↕30m (100ft) ↔ 20m (70ft), a broad column of a tree, with leaves up to 15cm (6in) long, flowers in midsummer

Trachycarpus fortunei ♀ (Chusan palm)
↕to 20m (70ft) ↔ 2.5m (8ft), seldom reaches anything like this height in temperate gardens, generally remaining a small tree

TSUGA

Hemlock

year-round

A GRACEFUL FORM, USUALLY BROADLY conical and made up of tiers of sweeping branches, is the main attraction of these evergreen conifers. They come in almost every size you can imagine, from 30cm (12in) to 30m (150ft) tall, with needle-like leaves that vary in colour from bright green to blue-grey to silvery-grey (often flashing pure white underneath), so there should be one to suit almost every garden. In addition, *Tsuga heterophylla*, the western hemlock, makes a fine hedge. All hemlocks grow very well in shade. Male and female flowers appear in separate clusters on the same tree, and the small, hanging cones ripen in the same year as they are produced.

Hardiness Fully hardy ✳✳✳.

Cultivation Grow in moist but well-drained, preferably neutral to slightly acid soil, enriched with well-rotted organic matter on planting. Position in sun or partial shade with shelter from cold, drying winds. **Pruning** is unnecessary, as for most conifers, unless damaged growth needs to be removed. Trim hedges from early to late summer. **Sow** seed (*see pp.391–392*) in containers in a cold frame in spring or take semi-ripe cuttings (*see p.394*) in late summer or early autumn.

ULEX

Furze, Gorse

spring

EVERGREEN AND PRICKLY, gorse is ideal for a tough barrier hedge. *Ulex europaeus* is an upright, rounded to bushy shrub with spine-tipped green shoots, and even the leaves are reduced to rigid spines, making it almost impossible to penetrate. Although the main flowering period is in spring, flowers are borne singly or in clusters almost all year round in mild climates. The pea-like, bright yellow blooms have a coconut-like scent, bringing a surprisingly exotic element to the spring garden. The equally spiny dwarf gorse, *U. gallii,* is more spreading in shape, reaching only 2m (6ft), and flowers from late summer. Both will suit a hot border or a sunny, sloping site, where little else will grow apart from other robust, drought-tolerant shrubs.

Hardiness Fully hardy ✳✳✳.

Cultivation Grow in poor, sandy, acid to neutral, well-drained soil; plants may become very leggy on rich, fertile soils. Position in full sun. **Cut back** flowered shoots to within 2.5cm (1in) of old growth after flowering or in mid-spring every two or three years. **Take** semi-ripe cuttings in summer (*see p.394*).

ULMUS

Elm

summer and autumn

IN SPITE OF POPULAR BELIEF, there are several elms that can be grown in countries that have suffered the ravages of Dutch elm disease. These deciduous trees have appealing foliage, which turns golden-yellow in autumn, and an attractive habit. They also produce clusters of tiny, red-tinted, bell-shaped flowers, usually in spring but sometimes in autumn, followed by winged green fruits. Larger elms such as *Ulmus pumila* are suitable as specimen trees in larger gardens; they also make classic "punctuation marks" for stretches of informal hedgerow. *U.* × *hollandica* 'Jacqueline Hillier' is a shrubby elm reaching only 2.5m (8ft), and is also suitable for use as hedging.

Hardiness Fully hardy ✳✳✳.

Cultivation Grow in any well-drained soil in full sun or partial shade. **Prune out** any crossing or misplaced branches that spoil the shape of the tree in late winter or early spring. **Sow** seed (*see pp.391–392*) in containers outdoors in spring or autumn, or take softwood cuttings (*see p.394*) in summer. While Dutch elm disease is a fatal and incurable problem, the elms suggested here are partially resistant, as are Asian elms such as the Chinese elm *U. parvifolia* and its cultivars.

Tsuga canadensis
↕ to 25m (80ft) ↔ to 10m (30ft), the best choice if your soil tends to be alkaline (limy), this tree has many smaller cultivars

Ulex europaeus 'Flore Pleno' ♡
↕ to 2.5m (8ft) ↔ 2m (6ft), has double flowers and does not produce seed

Ulmus pumila
↕ 20–30m (70–100ft) ↔ 12m (40ft), bears tiny, red flowers in early spring and has lance-shaped leaves

year-round

FLOWERS, FRUITS, AND FOLIAGE are all valued in this large and widely varying group of evergreen, semi-evergreen, and deciduous shrubs. The flowers are pink, or pink-flushed white or cream, and in some plants intensely fragrant. They are borne in winter, spring, or summer, often in rounded clusters at the ends of the branches. The red or black berries that follow may also be ornamental; if space allows, grow several plants of the same species together to ensure good pollination and a more generous show of berries. On a species such as *Viburnum opulus* these help to attract wildlife into the garden. The foliage also provides interest. On some viburnums, the leaves are rough-textured, on others smooth and glossy, while many have striking, prominent veins. Most deciduous types colour brilliantly in autumn. Viburnums are usually grown in shrub borders or mixed borders or in woodland settings, but *V. macrocephalum* is less hardy and best grown against a wall.

Hardiness Fully hardy ✳✳✳ to frost-hardy ✳✳.

Cultivation Grow in any good soil that is moist but well-drained. Position in full sun or partial shade, and in areas prone to heavy frosts shelter evergreen species from cold, drying winds. **Prune** deciduous species after flowering, lightly trimming shoots that spoil the shape of the shrub. Most deciduous types and *V. tinus* will tolerate hard pruning. Remove misplaced branches or crossing shoots from evergreens in late winter or early spring to maintain a good framework. **Sow** seed in containers in a cold frame in autumn (*see pp.391–392*), or propagate deciduous species by greenwood cuttings, which are taken slightly later than softwood cuttings when the stem is a little firmer and darker (*see p.394*). Sooty moulds may form on the foliage of *V. tinus* if colonized by whiteflies: control with a suitable insecticide if necessary. Remove the affected leaves of plants suffering from leaf spot.

Using viburnums in the garden

In the border Viburnums are ideal shrubs for hedging or for a mixed border, since many, such as V. opulus, have an attractive, naturally rounded habit that requires little or no pruning; 'Compactum' is especially neat. Others are more architectural, for instance the tiered V. plicatum 'Mariesii'. V. davidii is a useful evergreen for shade.

Pinch out tips to keep head compact

As a standard The evergreen V. tinus is suitable for training as a standard; underplanting will add interest beyond the viburnum's own flowering period. Training takes three or four years. Train the main stem to the desired height and pinch out the tip to encourage lots of new sideshoots to form the head. Keep pinching out sideshoots to keep it dense and rounded.

Any shoots appearing on stem must be rubbed out

① *Viburnum acerifolium* ‡1–2m (3–6ft) ↔ 1.2m (4ft), deciduous ② × *bodnantense* 'Charles Lamont' ♀ ‡3m (10ft) ↔ 2m (6ft), deciduous ③ × *bodnantense* 'Dawn' ♀ ‡3m (10ft) ↔ 2m (6ft), deciduous ④ × *burkwoodii* ‡↔ 2.5m (8ft), evergreen ⑤ × *burkwoodii* 'Anne Russell' ♀ ‡2m (6ft) ↔ 1.5m (5ft), evergreen ⑥ × *carlcephalum* ♀ ‡↔ 3m (10ft), deciduous ⑦ *carlesii* 'Aurora' ♀ ‡↔ 2m (6ft), deciduous ⑧ 'Chesapeake' ‡2m (6ft) ↔ 3m (10ft), semi-evergreen ⑨ *davidii* ♀

‡↔ 1–1.5m (3–5ft), evergreen ⑩ *dentatum* ‡↔ 3m (10ft), deciduous ⑪ *farreri* ♀ ‡ 3m (10ft) ↔ 2.5m (8ft), deciduous ⑫ × *globosum* 'Jermyns Globe' ‡ 2.5m (8ft) ↔ 3m (10ft), evergreen ⑬ × *juddii* ♀ ‡ 1.2m (4ft) ↔ 1.5m (5ft), deciduous ⑭ *macrocephalum* ‡↔ 5m (15ft), evergreen ⑮ *opulus* 'Compactum' ♀ ‡↔ 1.5m (5ft), deciduous ⑯ *opulus* 'Xanthocarpum' ♀ ‡ 5m (15ft) ↔ 4m (12ft), deciduous ⑰ *plicatum* 'Mariesii' ♀ ‡ 3m (10ft) ↔ 4m (12ft), deciduous

⑱ *plicatum* 'Pink Beauty' ♀ ‡ 3m (10ft) ↔ 4m (12ft), deciduous ⑲ 'Pragense' ♀ ‡↔ 3m (10ft), evergreen ⑳ *rhytidophyllum* ‡ 5m (15ft) ↔ 4m (12ft), semi-evergreen ㉑ *sargentii* ‡↔ 3m (10ft), deciduous ㉒ *sieboldii* ‡ 4m (12ft) ↔ 6m (20ft), deciduous ㉓ *tinus* 'Eve Price' ♀ ‡↔ 3m (10ft), evergreen ㉔ *tinus* 'Variegatum' ‡↔ 3m (10ft), evergreen

WEIGELA

late spring to early summer

FOR A SHOWY DISPLAY OF FLOWERS in spring or summer, few shrubs are more reliable than weigelas. The flowers, bell- or funnel-shaped, come in shades of ice-cream pink to ruby red and occasionally pure white or yellow. Weigelas are deciduous, and most grow to around 1.5m (5ft), making them suitable for even small backyards. They do well in almost any reasonable garden soil and can withstand neglect. If space allows, plant them with other shrubs that flower around the same time, such as potentillas (*see p.99*) or mock oranges (*Philadelphus, see p.93*). Just make sure they have room to show off their arching stems.

Hardiness Fully hardy ✳✳✳.

Cultivation Grow in any fertile, well-drained soil in full sun or partial shade. Variegated types produce the best coloured foliage in full sun, golden-leaved forms in partial shade. **Cut back** flowered stems after flowering to strong buds or shoots lower down the shrub. Once plants are mature and growth is crowded, cut out an entire old branch or two, to encourage new growth from the base. **Take** greenwood cuttings in early summer or semi-ripe cuttings in midsummer, or try hardwood cuttings from autumn until winter (*see p.394*).

Weigela 'Eva Rathke'
↕↔ 1.5m (5ft), compact, upright then cascading shrub, flowers open from ruby buds to pink in late spring and early summer

Weigela florida 'Foliis Purpureis' ♥
↕ 1m (3ft) ↔ 1.5m (5ft), low, spreading habit, tolerant of pollution, likes a warm, sunny site, flowers in late spring and early summer

Weigela 'Looymansii Aurea'
↕↔ 1.5m (5ft), slow-growing, spreading, arching habit, leaf colour is best in partial shade, flowers in late spring and early summer

Weigela 'Florida Variegata' ♥
↕↔ 2–2.5m (6–8ft), large but dense and bushy, tolerant of urban pollution, flowers profusely in late spring and early summer

YUCCA

year-round

PERHAPS BEST KNOWN AS A HOUSE PLANT, the yucca makes a spectacular architectural plant for the garden. Yuccas include around 40 evergreen shrubs and trees, all of which come from hot, dry deserts and plains. They usually have a stout, upright stem, and with maturity, some spread and become branched. Their sword-like leaves are produced in shades of mid- to dark green or blue-green. A few have cream or yellow edges. Towering spikes of bell-shaped, usually white flowers rise above the leaves in sumer and autumn. Use yuccas as dramatic focal points in a border, or in pots on the patio. They grow and flower particularly well in mild coastal areas. In cold, frost-prone areas, yuccas must be taken under frost-free cover for winter.

Hardiness Fully hardy ✳✳✳ (in mild areas) to frost-tender ✲.

Cultivation Grow in any well-drained soil in full sun. If growing them in pots, use a loam-based compost; water freely during summer and feed with a balanced fertilizer at monthly intervals. **Sow** seed in spring at 13–18°C (55–64°F) (*see pp.391–392*). **Take** root cuttings in winter (*see p.394*), or remove rooted suckers (plantlets around the main crown) in spring and replant.

ZAUSCHNERIA

Californian fuchsia   *late summer to autumn*

THIS EXOTIC-LOOKING SHRUB offers spectacular colour late in the season when most other plants are past their peak. Evergreen in its native California, it may die back in temperate regions, but should recover. It bears show-stopping, narrow trumpets on the tips of shoots, which appear over a long period in late summer and autumn. Californian fuchsias thrive in hot, sunny sites with sharp drainage. Rock gardens or dry stone walls are perfect. They can also be planted in a mixed or herbaceous border alongside other late-flowering shrubs and perennials, such as hardy fuchsias (*see pp.60–63*), rudbeckias (*see p.317*), asters (*see pp.192–193*), and sedums (*see p.324*).

Hardiness Fully hardy ✳✳✳ to frost-hardy ✳✳.

Cultivation Grow in reasonably fertile, well-drained soil in full sun, with shelter from cold, drying winds. **Protect** in winter in cold areas by spreading a layer of organic matter around the crown of the plant to shield from severe frosts. **Sow** seed in a container in a cold frame in spring (*see pp.391–392*). **Take** cuttings of strong young shoots from the base in spring, treat as softwood cuttings (*see p.394*), and root in a propagator.

ZELKOVA

autumn

THESE STATELY TREES COMBINE a distinctive, upright, then spreading habit with dark green leaves that turn to fiery shades of yellow, orange, and red in autumn. There are about six species in the group; all are deciduous and are often confused with their close relatives, the elms (*Ulmus, see p.125*). They have tiny, green flowers in spring followed by small, green fruits. Zelkovas make handsome specimens for large gardens or open spaces, or to flank wide avenues. Good companions include limes (*Tilia, see p.124*) and birches (*Betula, see p.28*). For smaller gardens, choose a dwarf cultivar of *Z. serrata*, such as 'Goblin', which makes a 1m (3ft) tall, bushy shrub.

Hardiness Fully hardy ✳✳✳.

Cultivation Grow in deep, fertile soil that is moist but well-drained, in full sun or partial shade. Protect from cold, drying winds in frost-prone areas. **Prune** young trees in late winter or early spring, removing any branches that are crossing or misplaced and that spoil the shape of the tree (*see p.382*). **Sow** seed in containers outdoors in autumn (*see pp.391–392*). **Take** softwood cuttings in summer (*see p.394*).

Yucca gloriosa ♀ (Spanish dagger)
↕↔ 2m (6ft), long, blue-green leaves mature to dark green, mature plants flower in late summer ✳✳

Zauschneria californica
↕ to 30cm (12in) ↔ 50cm (20in), evergreen or semi-evergreen, clump-forming ✳✳✳ (borderline)

Zelkova serrata ♀
↕ to 30m (100ft) ↔ 18m (60ft), spreading habit, smooth grey bark peels to show orange patches beneath, rich autumn colour (*above*)

Climbing Plants

climbers through the year

In the wild, climbing plants work their way up their hosts naturally by different means. Some, like ivy (*Hedera*), have aerial roots that attach themselves to their support. Sweet peas (*Lathyrus*) and passion flowers (*Passiflora*) send out tendrils, which quickly coil around anything they touch, while others, such as clematis, have twining leaf stalks that spiral around their host.

Most climbers are perennial, but a few are annual, grown from seed each year. Their upward mobility makes them extremely versatile for covering unsightly walls and fences, creating scented archways or pergolas, building living screens over trellis, or training up an obelisk to add height to beds and borders – the possibilities are endless. Climbers are also superb in small spaces where the only way to go is up, and you can achieve stunning effects and prolong the season of interest by simply planting two together.

PLANTING CLIMBERS
Before planting climbers, take into consideration the soil and site. Bear in mind that soil at the base of a wall can be very dry so dig your planting hole at least 45cm (18in) away from the wall, incorporate plenty of organic matter to help your climber establish, and angle the plant back towards the wall. You may need to supply some initial encouragement to get tendril

and twining types to travel up their supports. Usually inserting a cane next to the plant and attaching it to the support is sufficient in the early stages, tying the plant to the cane regularly until it reaches the permanent support.

CLIMBERS IN CONTAINERS
Most climbing plants can be grown in containers, which is particularly useful if you have only a small garden: train them against walls or fences from the pot, just as you would if they were growing in the open ground. You could also try growing them up obelisks or wigwams to create features that can be enjoyed from every angle. Containers are also ideal for less hardy climbers like some jasmines; move the pot to a sheltered spot or greenhouse for the winter months.

Like all plants in pots, climbers need more attention if they are to thrive. Choose the largest you can handle: the more compost in the pot, the slower it will be to dry out. Use a loam-based compost as it holds nutrients and water longer than a soilless compost. If you use a pot with only a single drainage hole, place crocks over the hole to prevent it getting blocked by compost. Insert the support system right at the start, so that plants can be trained to it. And keep the pots well watered, especially during dry spells; a decorative grit or pebble mulch may help conserve moisture.

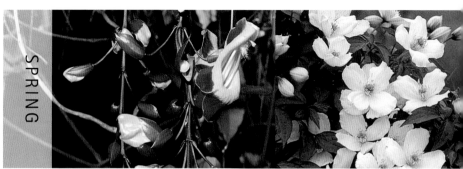

SPRING

Thunbergia mysorensis p.153

Clematis montana var. *grandiflora p.139*

SUMMER

Lathyrus odoratus 'Mars' *p.145*

Clematis 'Vyvyan Pennell' *p.139*

AUTUMN

Vitis coignetiae p.155

Solanum rantonnetii 'Royal Robe' *p.153*

WINTER

Akebia quinata p.134

Hedera helix 'Buttercup' *p.142*

SPRING

Clematis montana 'Tetrarose' *p.139*   *Wisteria floribunda* 'Multijuga' *p.155*   *Gelsemium sempervirens p.141*   *Hydrangea anomala* subsp. *petiolaris p.143*

SUMMER

Thunbergia alata p.153   *Rosa* 'Zéphirine Drouhin' *p.151*   *Trachelospermum jasminoides p.154*   *Lonicera* x *brownii* 'Dropmore Scarlet' *p.146*

AUTUMN

Actinidia kolomikta p.134   *Solanum crispum* 'Glasnevin' *p.153*   *Parthenocissus tricuspidata p.148*   *Plumbago auriculata p.149*

WINTER

Hedera helix 'Pedata' *p.142*   *Clematis tibetana p.138*   *Hedera colchica* 'Dentata Variegata' *p.143*   *Hedera helix* 'Little Diamond' *p.143*

ACTINIDIA

spring and summer

THE ATTRACTIONS OF these large, clambering plants are their deciduous foliage, and in warm climates their flowers and fruits. They will twine through mesh, or taut wires, on a sunny wall. The large, simple leaves of variegated actinidias look like they have been splashed with white, and sometimes pink, paint. The effect is that of huge petals, and is as pretty but much longer-lasting than a floral display. White, often scented flowers appear in early summer. These are followed by edible fruits provided that you have a self-fertile cultivar or have planted a male and a female close to each other. The crop needs plenty of sun to set and ripen. *Actinidia deliciosa*, the kiwi fruit or Chinese gooseberry, is the only species grown commercially.

Hardiness Fully hardy ✳✳✳ to frost-hardy ✳✳.

Cultivation Choose a spot with fertile, well-drained soil in a sunny, sheltered position; full sun will encourage fruiting. **Prune** in late winter to keep within the available space (*see p.384*). **Sow** seed (*see pp.391–392*) in containers in a cold frame in spring or autumn, or take semi-ripe cuttings (*see p.394*) in late summer.

AKEBIA

Chocolate vine

early spring

THE COCOA-COLOURED FLOWERS of this small group of twining, woody climbers give them their common name. They hang from the branches in long clusters through early spring and, if the summer is long and hot, are followed by impressive, sausage-shaped fruits that ripen from green to purple. In milder areas, the dark green leaves of the semi-evergreen *Akebia quinata* do not fall in winter and become tinged purple in the cool weather. Spring interest is provided by the new leaves of the deciduous *A. trifoliata*, which are a striking bronze. Chocolate vines are splendid plants for a pergola or archway, where the spicy fragrance of the flowers can be enjoyed fully. They can grow quite large, so provide a sturdy support.

Hardiness Fully hardy ✳✳✳, but late frosts may damage flowers.

Cultivation Chocolate vines are not very demanding and can be grown in any moist but well-drained soil, in sun or partial shade. **Pruning** is minimal – simply trim back after flowering to keep it under control (*see p.384*). **Sow** seed (*see pp.391–392*) in containers in a cold frame, or on the windowsill, as soon as it is ripe, or take semi-ripe cuttings (*see p.394*) in summer.

AMPELOPSIS

summer and autumn

↕ 5–12m (15–40ft)

USING TWISTING TENDRILS, these handsome, deciduous climbers can cling to walls or fences or can be trained over pergolas or old trees. They are grown for their large leaves, which give a fiery display of colour in autumn. Variegated cultivars, such as *Ampelopsis brevipedunculata* 'Elegans' are less vigorous than the species, so suit smaller spaces, and the white and pink mottling is a welcome splash of colour on a dull wall. In warm areas, following the tiny, late-summer flowers, you may get masses of ornamental pink, blue, black, or orange berries.

Hardiness Fully hardy ✳✳✳, although *A. brevipedunculata* 'Elegans' benefits from the shelter of a warm wall.

Cultivation Grow in any moist but well-drained soil in sun or partial shade. Fruits are more abundant in sun or if the roots are restricted in a container. **Trim** vigorous plants in spring (*see p.384*), making sure that tendrils are kept clear of roof tiles and gutters. **Sow** seed (*see p.391–392*) in a cold frame in autumn, or take softwood cuttings (*see p.394*) in summer.

Actinidia kolomikta ♥
↕ 5m (15ft) or more, leaves emerge purple and become striped with broad bands of pink and white as they mature ✳✳✳

Akebia quinata
↕ 10m (30ft), the undersides of the leaves are blue-green and are evergreen in milder climates ✳✳✳

Ampelopsis brevipedunculata
↕ 5m (15ft), the pink or purple berries change colour to a clear sky-blue as they ripen ✳✳✳

BERBERIDOPSIS CORALLINA
Coral plant *summer to early autumn*

THIS IS A TWINING, WOODY perennial. It has long, heart-shaped leaves with tiny spines around the edges, but it is mainly grown for its fuchsia-like flowers that hang from the shoots like baubles through summer to early autumn. It is excellent scrambling through a tree, which will provide it with the ideal conditions of some shelter and partial shade. The snowy mespilus (*Amelanchier, see p.22*) or rowan (*Sorbus, see p.118*) make good supports since the red flowers of the coral plant bridge the gap between the spring flowers and autumn colour of the tree. Alternatively, train it against a shaded, sheltered wall.

Hardiness Frost-hardy ❋❋.

Cultivation Plant in neutral or acid (lime-free) soil and dig in plenty of well-rotted organic matter. Choose a shady area with shelter from cold winds and protect roots in winter with a thick mulch (*see p.388*). **Tie in** young shoots to their support (*see p.380*). **Trim** in late winter or early spring if it becomes too big (*see p.384*). **Sow** seed (*see pp.391–392*) in a cold frame in spring; root semi-ripe cuttings (*see p.394*) in late summer; or layer shoots (*see p.395*) in autumn.

CAMPSIS
Trumpet creeper, Trumpet vine *late summer to autumn*

‡10m (30ft)

THE ONLY TWO CAMPSIS, *Campsis radicans* and *C. grandiflora*, have been crossed to produce the popular hybrid *C.* × *tagliabuana*. From late summer until autumn, they produce exotic flowers, usually in shades of yellow, orange, or red, in small clusters amongst dark green leaves. These woody-stemmed climbers cling with aerial roots, although they will need some extra support. They are impressive growing up a wall, fence, or pergola, or through a large tree.

Hardiness Fully hardy ❋❋❋ to frost-hardy ❋❋.

Cultivation Grow in moist but well-drained soil. In areas with sharp frosts, they are best grown against a warm, sunny wall. **Fan out** the young stems to provide good coverage of the support and cut away misplaced shoots; it may take 2–3 years to establish a main framework of branches. You will need to tie in young shoots until the aerial roots take firm hold (*see p.380*). Once the framework is in place, prune sideshoots back to two or three buds every year, after flowering. Keep clear of roofs and gutters. **Sow** seed (*see pp.391–392*) in containers in autumn or root semi-ripe cuttings in summer (*see p.394*).

CELASTRUS
Bittersweet, Staff vine *autumn*

BITTERSWEET COMES INTO ITS OWN in autumn. When many other plants are starting to die down, it is beaded with yellow berries that split open when they are ripe to reveal pink or red seeds within, rather like tiny pomegranates. They follow discreet clusters of green flowers, but the males and females are on separate vines so you need more than one plant for fruit unless you choose a self-fertile cultivar. The most commonly cultivated are the woody, deciduous climbers: American bittersweet (*Celastrus scandens*) and Oriental bittersweet (*C. orbiculatus*) and its cultivars. Train them against a wall, fence, or pergola, or encourage one to scramble up through a large tree.

Hardiness Fully hardy ❋❋❋ to frost-tender ❋❋.

Cultivation Bittersweet prefers full sun, but will tolerate partial shade, in any well-drained soil. It needs a strong support, so if you want to grow it through a tree choose one at least 10m (30ft) tall. **Prune** in late winter or early spring to keep it within its space (*see p.384*). **Sow** seed (*see pp.391–392*) as soon as it is ripe or in spring, or take semi-ripe cuttings in summer (*see p.394*).

Berberidopsis corallina
‡5m (15ft), widely available climber

Campsis × *tagliabuana* 'Madame Galen' ♀
‡10m (30ft), by far the most widely available and popular of this group of climbers ❋❋

Celastrus scandens
‡10m (30ft), bears yellow-orange fruits with red seeds ❋❋❋

CLIMBING PLANTS

Old man's beard, Traveller's
joy, Virgin's bower

*late winter to
late summer*

OFTEN KNOWN AS THE QUEEN OF CLIMBERS, the climbing clematis have been favourites of gardeners for many years because of their beautiful blooms. There are hundreds to choose from with varied habits, from clump-forming herbaceous plants to evergreen scramblers up to 15m (30ft) or more that will clothe large trees. Many more are less vigorous and perfectly suited to growing on fences or through shrubs. The flowers vary widely in size, shape, and hue – from large, flat blooms to small nodding bells in soft and bold shades of white, gold, orange, and blue to pinks and scarlets, often with a contrasting boss of anthers. The foliage also varies, but is delicately shaped. Some, such as *Clematis tangutica,* have attractive, silky seedheads.

Hardiness Hardy ✳✳✳ to half-hardy ✳✳.

Cultivation Clematis are divided into groups for pruning (*see below*), but other cultivation needs are similar for all types. **Grow** clematis in well cultivated soil with plenty of organic matter, in sun or partial shade. Climbers should be planted deeply, with the top of the rootball 8cm (3in) below the soil surface to help overcome clematis wilt, a disease which causes the plant to die back suddenly to soil level. If this happens, the stems may shoot again from buds below the surface. **Tie in** a newly planted clematis to a cane and angle it towards the permanent support to encourage the plant to cling. **Sow** seed of species when they are ripe in autumn (*see pp.391–393*) and place in a cold frame. **Take** softwood cuttings in spring or semi-ripe cuttings in summer (*see p.395*).

Pruning group 1

This group produces flowers in spring from the previous year's growth. The flowers are usually bell-shaped or single and 2–5cm (¾–2in) long or saucer-shaped and 4–5cm (1½–2in) across. Prune after flowering to remove dead or damaged shoots; shorten others to the allotted space. This encourages new growth in summer that will bear flowers in the following spring. Once established, vigorous montana types need regular pruning only to stop them outgrowing their space. Cut back overgrown plants hard, then leave for at least three years.

Pruning group 2

These large-flowered hybrids flower in late spring and early summer on sideshoots produced in the previous year. They are deciduous. The flowers are held upright and may be single, semi-double, or fully double, 10–20cm (4–8in) across, and are mostly saucer-shaped. In late winter or early spring, prune out any weak or damaged shoots back to their point of growth or cut out entire shoots if they are damaged. It may be easier on a large plant to cut the sideshoots back by going over the plant with a pair of garden shears, but make sure that all the dead wood has been removed.

Pruning group 3

All the clematis in this group bear flowers on the current year's wood. The large-flowered hybrids are deciduous with single, saucer-shaped flowers, 8–15cm (3–6in) across, in summer and early autumn. Species and small-flowered hybrids flower from summer to late autumn. Their blooms may be single or double, star- or bell-shaped, or tubular and 1–10cm (½–4in) across. Prune this group in late winter or early spring by cutting all the stems back to about 30cm (12in) above the ground, just above a pair of healthy buds. Make sure that any dead growth is completely cut out.

① *Clematis* 'Abundance' ♀ ‡3m (10ft) ↔ 1m (3ft), group 3 ② 'Alba Luxurians' ♀ ‡1.5m (5ft) ↔ 1m (3ft), group 3 ③ *alpina* ♀ ‡2–3m (6–10ft) ↔ 1.5m (5ft), group 1, fluffy seedheads ④ *alpina* 'Frances Rivis' ♀ ‡2–3m (6–10ft) ↔ 1.5m (5ft), group 1, fluffy seedheads ⑤ *armandii* ‡3–5m (10–15ft) ↔ 2–3m (6–10ft), group 1, evergreen ✳✳ ⑥ 'Ascotiensis' ‡3–4m (10–12ft) ↔ 1m (3ft), group 3 ⑦ 'Beauty of Worcester' ‡2.5m (8ft) ↔ 1m (3ft), group 2 ✳✳ ⑧ 'Bees' Jubilee' ‡2.5m

(8ft) ↔ 1m (3ft), group 2, partial shade ⑨ 'Bill MacKenzie' ♀ ‡ 7m (22ft) ↔ 2–3m (6–10ft), group 3, fluffy seedheads ⑩ *cirrhosa* ‡ 2.5–3m (8–10ft) ↔ 1.5m (5ft), group 1, evergreen, silky seedheads ✻✻ ⑪ 'Comtesse de Bouchaud' ♀ ‡ 2–3m (6–10ft) ↔ 1m (3ft), group 3 ⑫ 'Doctor Ruppel' ‡ 2.5m (8ft) ↔ 1m (3ft), group 2 ⑬ 'Duchess of Albany' ‡ 2.5m (8ft) ↔ 1m (3ft), group 3 ⑭ 'Elsa Späth' ‡ 2–3m (6–10ft) ↔ 1m (3ft), group 2 ⑮ 'Etoile Rose' ‡ 2.5m (8ft) ↔ 1m (3ft), group 3 ⑯ 'Etoile Violette' ♀

‡ 3–5m (10–15ft) ↔ 1.5m (5ft), group 3 ⑰ *flammula* ‡ 6m (20ft) ↔ 1m (3ft), group 3, prefers sheltered sun ✻✻ ⑱ *florida* var. *sieboldiana* ‡ 2.5m (8ft) ↔ good for containers, group 2 ⑲ 'Gravetye Beauty' ‡ 2.5m (8ft) ↔ 1m (3ft), group 3 ⑳ 'Hagley Hybrid' ‡ 2m (6ft) ↔ 1m (3ft), group 3, fades in sun ㉑ 'Henryi' ♀ ‡ 3m (10ft) ↔ 1m (3ft), group 2 ㉒ 'H.F. Young' ‡ 2.5m (8ft) ↔ 1m (3ft), group 2 ㉓ 'Huldine' ♀ ‡ 5m (15ft) ↔ 2m (6ft), group 3

㉔ *Clematis* 'Hybrida Sieboldii' ↕3m (10ft), group 2, prefers full sun ㉕ 'Jackmanii' ♀
↕3m (10ft), group 3 ㉖ 'John Warren' ↕3m (10ft), group 2 ㉗ 'Kathleen Dunford'
↕2.5m (8ft), group 2 ㉘ 'Lasurstern' ♀ ↕2.5m (8ft), group 2 ㉙ 'Lincoln Star' ↕2.5m (8ft),
group 2, flowers fade in full sun ㉚ *macropetala* ↕3m (10ft), group 1, decorative seedheads
㉛ *macropetala* 'Markham's Pink' ♀ ↕3m (10ft), group 1, decorative seedheads

㉜ 'Madame Edouard André' ↕2.5m (8ft), group 2 ㉝ 'Madame Julia Correvon' ♀
↕3m (10ft), group 3 ㉞ 'Minuet' ♀ ↕3m (10ft), group 3 ㉟ *montana* ↕5–14m (15–46ft), group 1
㊱ *montana* var. *grandiflora* ♀ ↕10m (30ft), group 1 ㊲ *montana* var. *rubens* ↕10m (30ft),
group 1 ㊳ *montana* 'Tetrarose' ♀ ↕5m (15ft), group 1 ㊴ 'Mrs George Jackman' ♀ ↕2.5m
(8ft), group 2 ㊵ 'Nelly Moser' ♀ ↕3m (10ft), group 2, fades in full sun ㊶ 'Niobe' ♀ ↕2–3m

(6–10ft), group 2, fades in full sun ㊷ 'Paul Farges' ♀ ‡9m (28ft), group 3 ㊸ 'Perle d'Azur' ‡3m (10ft), group 3 ㊹ 'Proteus' ‡3m (10ft), group 2 ㊺ 'Pruinina' (syn. 'Plum Beauty') ‡2–3m (6–10ft), group 1, decorative seedheads ㊻ *rehderiana* ♀ ‡7m (22ft), group 3 ㊼ 'Richard Pennell' ♀ ‡3m (10ft), group 2 ㊽ 'Rouge Cardinal' ‡3m (10ft), group 3, prefers full sun ㊾ *tangutica* ‡6m (20ft), group 3, decorative seedheads ㊿ 'The President' ♀ ‡3m (10ft), group 2

� *tibetana* ‡2–3m (6–10ft), group 3, bright yellow, bell-shaped flowers, prefers sun ㊼ 'Venosa Violacea' ♀ ‡3m (10ft), group 3 ㊾ 'Ville de Lyon' ‡3m (10ft), group 3, best grown through an evergreen shrub, because lower foliage may become scorched ㊾ *viticella* 'Purpurea Plena Elegans' ♀ ‡3m (10ft), group 3 ㊾ 'Vyvyan Pennell' ‡3m (10ft), group 2

CLIANTHUS

Glory pea   *summer*

GROWN FOR THEIR SUMMER FLOWERS, these trailing plants are easily encouraged to climb if they are tied in regularly to their supports. Sturt's desert pea (*Clianthus formosus*) is a perennial in warm climates, but is tender and so best grown as an annual in temperate gardens. It is a good plant for hanging baskets. Lobster claw (*C. puniceus*) is hardy enough to survive a light frost, especially if given the added protection of a warm, south-facing wall, and will bring a tropical feel to the garden. There are some stunning cultivars available with crimson, rose-pink, or pure white flowers.

Hardiness Frost-hardy ✳✳ to frost-tender ❀.

Cultivation Grow in a container of gritty, loam-based compost and move under cover in winter, or outdoors in well-drained, fertile soil. Glory peas need full sun, shelter from cold winds, and a deep, dry, winter mulch (*see p.388*). Even with these precautions, *C. puniceus* may be knocked back by frost, but will often resprout from the base. **Little pruning** is needed: trim shoots by no more than one-third, after flowering, only if it becomes necessary. **Sow** seed (*see pp.391–392*) at 18ºC (64ºF) in spring.

COBAEA

                        summer to autumn

ONLY THE CUP AND SAUCER VINE (*Cobaea scandens*) is commonly cultivated. Although a perennial climber, it is tender and so in frost-prone climates it is best used as an annual. It has rich green leaves and creamy-white, fragrant blooms that become purple as they age. Cultivars that remain white are also available. Grow this lovely plant over an arbour or an archway, where the perfume of the flowers can easily be enjoyed, or train it on a sunny wall. In colder areas, a good option is to grow a cobaea through a tree or shrub so that there is no ugly, bare support left at the end of the season. Alternatively, use it in containers and hanging baskets and let the shoots trail over the rim.

Hardiness Frost-tender ❀, although *C. scandens* can survive cold snaps close to 0ºC (32ºF).

Cultivation Grow in well-drained soil, in a sheltered spot with full sun. **Sow** seed (*see pp.391–392*) at 18ºC (64ºF) in spring, and plant out when the threat of frost has passed, or root softwood cuttings (*see p.394*) in summer.

DICENTRA

                        see also pp.228–229

                        summer to autumn

‡ 1m (3ft)

THESE CLIMBING PERENNIALS have unusual flowers that appear on the scrambling, slender stems throughout summer. In common with the non-climbing, spreading or clump-forming dicentras, the flowers look as if they have been gently inflated. There are two commonly available climbing species: *Dicentra macrocapnos*, which has ferny foliage and yellow flowers into late autumn, and *D. scandens*, which has deeply lobed, mid-green leaves. They are excellent plants for walls or fences at the back of a border, or for training through a shrub or a hedge.

Hardiness Fully hardy ✳✳✳, but frost may damage early growth.

Cultivation Dicentras prefer moist, slightly alkaline (limy), humus-rich soil and partial shade. They are perfect for a woodland garden or other shady spot, but will tolerate more sun in reliably damp soil. **Sow** seed (*see pp.391–392*) in containers in a cold frame as soon as it is ripe, or wait until spring. **Slugs** (*see p.398*) may leave large holes in the leaves, so it is worth protecting young plants against them.

Clianthus formosus (Sturt's desert pea)
‡ 20cm (8in) ↔ 1m (3ft) ❀

Cobaea scandens ♥ (Cathedral bells, Cup and saucer vine)
‡ 10–20m (30–70ft), less if grown as an annual

Dicentra scandens
‡ 1m (3ft), flowers may also be white or tipped with pink ✳✳✳

ECCREMOCARPUS SCABER

Chilean glory flower   *late spring to autumn*

THIS FAST-GROWING, EVERGREEN climber has several cultivars. From late spring until autumn, spectacular clusters of exotic, brightly-coloured flowers appear. They are eye-catching clambering up a fence or wall, through a large shrub, or over an arch. The effect is especially striking when combined with other climbing plants such as morning glories (*Ipomoea, see p.144*). The light-green, or grey-tinted foliage is composed of neat leaflets. In colder areas, Chilean glory flowers are best used as annuals or as container plants, but in warm climates they can be grown as short-lived perennials.

Hardiness   Frost-hardy ✳✳✳ to frost-tender ❀.

Cultivation   Grow in fertile, well-drained soil in a sunny position, or in a container of loam-based potting compost to be moved under cover in winter. **Tie in** to its support regularly (*see p.380*) until the tendrils get a firm grip. **Trim** plants grown as a perennials in early spring to fit the available space (*see p.384*). **Sow** seed (*see pp.391–392*) at 13-16°C (55-61°F) in late winter or early spring or root softwood cuttings (*see p.394*) in spring or summer in a propagator.

FALLOPIA

late summer to autumn

THESE ENTHUSIASTIC VINES CAN GROW very fast, so if you have a vast expanse of bare wall, or an ugly structure such as a shed, that needs cover quickly, they are a good choice. Before you buy, however, check that you have room to grow this rampant climber; in too small an area it will need constant pruning just to keep it under control. If you do have the space, these deciduous, woody plants have attractive leaves and, from late summer until autumn, bear large clusters of tiny, white flowers followed by pinkish-white fruits. All fallopias are vigorous but *Fallopia japonica*, also known as Japanese knotweed, is a pernicious weed. Its underground roots can spread very quickly to take over your own, and your neighbour's, garden.

Hardiness   Fully hardy ✳✳✳.

Cultivation   Grow in almost any soil, in full sun or partial shade, with a strong, long-lasting support. **Trim** in early spring if it gets too big (*see p.384*). **Sow** seed (*see pp.391–392*) in containers in a cold frame in spring, or as soon as it is ripe. **Root** semi-ripe cuttings in summer or hardwood cuttings in autumn (*see p.394*).

GELSEMIUM SEMPERVIRENS

Carolina jasmine, Evening trumpet, False yellow jasmine   *spring to late summer*

‡3–6m (10–20ft)

OF THESE TWINING PERENNIALS, *Gelsemium sempervirens* is the only common ornamental. It has handsome, glossy leaves and from spring to late summer clear-yellow, perfumed flowers. In places prone to frost, it needs the protection of a warm wall, or it can be grown in a container and brought under cover in winter. In warmer areas, it is lovely climbing over a pergola or arch, beneath which you can linger to enjoy the sweet fragrance of the flowers. All parts of the plant are toxic and have been used historically as a poison.

Hardiness   Frost-tender ❀; will survive a short spell at 0°C (32°F).

Cultivation   Grow in well-drained soil, in full sun or semi-shade, with shelter from cold, drying winds. **Plant** in containers in frost-prone areas so it is easy to move under cover in winter. Use a loam-based potting compost and repot or top-dress annually. **Thin out** the flowered stems when they have faded. **Sow** seed (*see pp.391–392*) at 13–18°C (55–64°F) in spring, or take semi-ripe cuttings (*see p.394*) in summer.

Eccremocarpus scaber **Anglia Hybrids**
‡3–5m (10–15ft), these cultivars are a mixed selection with red, pink, orange, or yellow flowers ✳✳

Fallopia baldschuanica (Mile-a-minute plant, Russian vine)
‡12m (40ft), often confused with the equally popular *F. aubertii*

Gelsemium sempervirens ♛

HEDERA

CLIMBING PLANTS

Ivy

year-round

IVY LEAVES COME IN MANY SHAPES and shades of green, some with bright gold or silver variegation that will cheer up a dull corner. Young ivies creep flat against surfaces using aerial roots, but at maturity they become tree-like, with large, bushy growths high in the air that provide a refuge for wildlife. In summer, mature ivies bear tiny flowers, followed by attractive, globe-shaped heads of black, orange, or yellow berries. These woody, evergreen climbers vary hugely in size, hardiness, and shade tolerance, so there is bound to be one suited to your garden. Grow them up a wall or tree, or let them scramble as ground cover. Contrary to popular belief, ivies do not damage walls unless there are already cracks in the mortar.

Hardiness Fully hardy ✳✳✳ to half-hardy ✳✳.

Cultivation Ivies tolerate most soils, especially alkaline (limy), and most positions, but all grow best in fertile soil enriched with well-rotted organic matter. Green-leaved types thrive in shade; variegated cultivars prefer more light and some shelter from cold winds. **Prune** to fit the available space at any time of year (*see p.384*); keep clear of roofs and gutters. **Root** semi-ripe cuttings in summer (*see p.394*).

Hedera helix 'Anna Marie'
↕ 1.2m (4ft), a small cultivar best used on a sheltered wall, leaves are 4–6cm (1½–2½in) across ✳✳

Hedera hibernica ♀ (Irish ivy)
↕ 10m (30ft), this vigorous climber can provide fast ground cover or clothe a wall, leaves are 5–8cm (2–3in) across ✳✳✳

Hedera helix 'Buttercup'
↕ 2m (6ft), compact ivy, butter-yellow in sun – a good contrast for coppery bark (see inset), leaves 6cm (2½in) or more across ✳✳✳

Hedera helix 'Pedata' (Bird's foot ivy)
↕ 4m (12ft), excellent wall-cover ivy, leaves are 4–6cm (1½–2½in) across ✳✳✳

Hedera colchica 'Dentata Variegata' ♀
‡5m (15ft), use as ground cover or train up a wall, leaves are 15cm (6in) across ✳✳✳

HUMULUS

Hop **spring to autumn**

HOPS ARE TWINING, PERENNIAL climbers, with soft, hairy shoots that die down in winter. They are admired for their large, ornamental leaves, which are often patterned with white or yellow. In summer, male and female flowers are borne on separate plants; males in clusters and females in unusual spikes that resemble papery, green pine-cones. The female hop flowers are used in brewing beer, and also in fresh or dried flower arrangements. Hops are vigorous but not rampant, perfect for any area if provided with trellis, wires, or mesh to wind around, or for growing through a large shrub or small tree.

Hardiness Fully hardy ✳✳✳.

Cultivation Grow in moist, well-drained soil in sun or partial shade. **Root** softwood cuttings in spring (*see p.394*). **Cut back** dead stems in winter, or in spring in cold areas. **If your hop looks floppy,** and after watering and feeding it fails to perk up, remove a little of the outer bark at the base of one of the stems. If you see brown stripes in the tissue beneath remove the entire plant, and the soil around its roots, because it is likely to have verticillium wilt: this action will prevent the disease from spreading. If the stem seems healthy, cut it off cleanly below the wound and stay on the look-out for a possible cause.

HYDRANGEA

Climbing hydrangea *see also pp.72–73* **early to midsummer**

‡15m (50ft)

THE CLIMBING HYDRANGEAS are popular for their abundance of huge, frothy white flowers in summer. Evergreen species such as *Hydrangea seemannii* and *H. serratifolia* are only frost-hardy, but are great year-round plants, with large, leathery leaves. The deciduous *H. anomala* subsp. *petiolaris* is commonly grown in cooler areas and has the bonus of leaves that turn golden-yellow in autumn. These sturdy plants will cling, using aerial roots, to large areas of wall, fence, or even old tree stumps. Once established, they grow quickly to provide invaluable cover, particularly on a shady, north- or east-facing wall where little else can thrive.

Hardiness Fully hardy ✳✳✳ to frost-hardy ✳✳.

Cultivation Grow in any moist, well-drained soil in sun or shade. **Prune** to fit space after flowering (*see p.384*). **Root** softwood cuttings in early summer or hardwood cuttings in autumn (*see p.394*) or layer in spring (*see p.395*). **Mildew** (*see p.398*) and grey mould (botrytis) can be troublesome: cut back affected parts to healthy-looking wood and dispose of the trimmings, but not onto the compost heap.

143

CLIMBING PLANTS

Hedera helix 'Little Diamond'
‡30cm (12in), a tiny, slow-growing ivy, perfect for a rock garden, leaves are 4–6cm (1½–2½in) across ✳✳

Humulus lupulus 'Aureus' ♀ (Golden hop)
‡6m (20ft), the golden leaves are brightest in full sun, fragrant flowers

LAYERING SHOOTS
Peg a shoot to the ground, aerial roots downwards, and lightly cover 15cm (6in) of the stem with soil. When rooted, cut from the parent and plant in its new position.

Hydrangea anomala subsp. *petiolaris* ♀
‡15m (50ft), flowerheads may reach an impressive 25cm (10in) across ✳✳✳

CLIMBING PLANTS

IPOMOEA

Morning glory

summer to autumn

THESE ANNUALS AND PERENNIALS can flower through the year in warm climates. In cooler areas, they can all be used very successfully as annuals during summer, or the perennials can be grown in containers and brought under cover in winter. They are mostly fast-growing, twining climbers or trailing plants, with abundant trumpet- or tube-shaped flowers in jewel-like reds and purples, and pretty whites and pinks. The mid- to deep-green leaves vary in shape. Train it through trellis in a sunny site, or up an obelisk with other climbers such as sweet peas (*Lathyrus, see facing page*) for a fine floral show. They can also be used to liven up shrubs that do not flower in summer.

Hardiness Frost-tender ❋.

Cultivation Grow in well-drained soil in full sun with shelter from cold, drying winds. **Tie** stems into their supports in the early stages of growth (*see p.380*). **Trim** perennials in spring only if they are getting too big (*see p.384*). **Sow** seed (*see pp.391–392*) singly in pots at 18°C (64°F) in spring. Chip each seed coat or soak in water for 24 hours before sowing to ensure germination.

JASMINUM

Jasmine, Jessamine

see also p.76

summer

‡2–12m (6–40ft)

MANY OF THE TWINING, climbing jasmines are tender, but are worth growing because of their honeyed, fragrant, usually yellow or white flowers. They are lovely in any situation, although in frost-prone areas even the hardier species need the shelter of a sunny wall. In cool climates it is worth taking cuttings in case of a harsh winter; in very cold areas, grow in pots and move under cover in winter. The common jasmine (*Jasminum officinale*), *J. beesianum* and *J. × stephanense*, are quite hardy and bear heavily perfumed flowers in summer. Common jasmine is vigorous and may smother a small arch or trellis.

Hardiness Frost-hardy ❋❋ to frost-tender ❋.

Cultivation Grow jasmines in fertile, well-drained soil in full sun, or in containers using a loam-based potting compost. **Prune** *J. mesnyi* after flowering: cut back flowered shoots to two or three buds from the old wood. **Thin out** the old and flowered shoots from *J. officinale*; thin other jasmines after flowering (*see p.384*). **Root** semi-ripe cuttings in summer (*see p.394*).

LAPAGERIA ROSEA

Chilean bellflower

summer to late autumn

‡5m (15ft)

THE CHILEAN BELLFLOWER is a woody, twining climber, with leathery, dark green leaves. It is prized for its exotic, fleshy, raspberry-red flowers, borne in summer and late autumn. There are also luscious white and pink cultivars available. It is native to dense forest and in cultivation prefers a similarly still, shady environment. A sheltered site, close to the house for extra warmth, but away from full sun, is perfect. In cold areas, the Chilean bellflower is best grown in a container and moved under cover in winter.

Hardiness Frost-hardy ❋❋ (borderline).

Cultivation Grow in well-drained, slightly acid soil improved with plenty of well-rotted organic matter. In containers, use an ericaceous potting compost. **Mulch** thickly over the rooting area through the winter (*see p.388*), especially in cool climates. **Trim** over-long stems to fit the available space (*see p.384*) if needed, but leave unpruned if at all possible. **Sow** seed (*see pp.391–392*) at 13–18°C (55–64°F) in spring, or root semi-ripe cuttings (*see p.394*) in summer.

① *lobata* ‡2–5m (6–15ft), perennial ② *purpurea* ‡3m (10ft), annual ③ *tricolor* 'Heavenly Blue' ‡4m (12ft), annual ④ *tricolor* 'Milky Way' ‡4m (12ft), annual

Jasminum mesnyi ♀ (Primrose jasmine)
‡3m (10ft) ↔ 1–2m (3–6ft), habit is naturally that of an open shrub, but it is usually trained as a climber ❋

Lapageria rosea ♀

LATHYRUS ODORATUS

Sweet pea

see also p.269

summer to late autumn

‡2–2.5m (6–8ft)

Sweet peas are the most familiar climbers in this group, prized for their showy, usually fragrant flowers in opulent shades of red, pink, mauve, blue, and white. If they are regularly deadheaded, and have the nutrients from rich soil or regular feeding, they will bloom from summer until late autumn. The climbers of this group are very versatile: they cling with tendrils that corkscrew tightly around almost any support. Train them on trellis, netting, wires, obelisks, through shrubs, or over an arch. There are other perennial peas, also with richly-coloured, sweet-smelling flowers, such as *Lathyrus latifolius*.

Hardiness Fully hardy ✳✳✳ to frost-hardy ✳✳.

Cultivation Grow in fertile soil in full sun or dappled shade. Dig lots of well-rotted organic matter into the ground. Feed plants fortnightly (*see p.386*). **Sow** seed (*see pp.391–393*) in a deep, preferably bottomless pots or sweet peas tubes in a cold frame, or in situ under cloches, in early spring. For earlier flowers, sow in a cold frame in autumn. **Deadhead** regularly (*see p.390*) or flowering will cease. **Slugs**, snails, and aphids (*see p.398*) are common.

Lathyrus odoratus '**Bridget**'
‡ 2m (6ft) or more, sweetly scented ✳✳

Lathyrus odoratus '**Nimbus**'
‡ 2m (6ft) or more, delicately scented ✳✳

SOWING SEED in tube pots avoids root disturbance; sow singly and cover with 1cm (½in) of compost almost to the rim; plant out the whole pot.

Lathyrus odoratus '**Mars**'
‡ 2m (6ft) or more, sweetly scented ✳✳

Lathyrus odoratus '**Anniversary**'
‡ 2m (6ft) or more, gently scented ✳✳

Lathyrus odoratus '**Midnight**'
‡ 2m (6ft) or more, lightly scented ✳✳

LONICERA

see also p.84

Honeysuckle   *late spring to autumn*

A CLASSIC COTTAGE-GARDEN FAVOURITE, honeysuckles are valued for their delicate flowers that are often fragrant enough to perfume the entire garden. The twining climbers are especially popular. They are very adaptable and can be trained on walls, through large shrubs or trees, or used as spreading ground cover. They are particularly lovely around a seating area where the scent can be enjoyed while you relax. There are many available that produce flowers in many shades. Snowy white and double-cream are traditional, but there are exotic, rich scarlet, coral, and gold honeysuckles available. The red or black berries can cause a slight stomach upset if they are eaten. There are also shrubby species.

Hardiness Fully hardy ✳✳✳ to half-hardy ✳.

Cultivation Grow in any moist but well-drained soil, in full sun or preferably partial shade, ideally with the roots in shade. **Prune** to fit the available space in early spring or after flowering. The easiest way to tidy up larger specimens is to cut them with a hedgetrimmer (*see p.384*). **Sow** seed (*see pp.391–392*) in a cold frame as soon as it is ripe. **Aphids** (*see p.398*) are fond of climbing honeysuckles.

Lonicera japonica 'Halliana' ♀
↕10m (30ft), vigorous evergreen or semi-evergreen, very fragrant flowers from late spring to late summer, red berries in autumn ✳✳✳

Lonicera × *americana*
↕7m (22ft), deciduous, very fragrant flowers in summer and early autumn, red berries in autumn ✳✳✳

TRAINING HONEYSUCKLE
Encourage the soft new shoots to climb by winding them around their support, here wires stretched up a wooden pergola post.

Lonicera × *brownii* 'Dropmore Scarlet'
↕4m (12ft), compact, deciduous or semi-evergreen, slightly fragrant flowers for a long period in summer, red berries in autumn, best grown in partial shade ✳✳✳

Lonicera × *tellmanniana*
↕5m (15ft), deciduous, flowers from late spring to midsummer, leaves are blue-white beneath ✳✳✳

Lonicera periclymenum 'Serotina' ♀
‡7m (22ft), deciduous, very fragrant flowers in mid- and late summer, red berries ✷✷✷

LOPHOSPERMUM

summer to autumn

THIS SMALL GROUP OF PERENNIAL CLIMBERS includes evergreen and deciduous plants. Their trumpet-shaped flowers are produced for a long period through the summer and autumn. The rose-pink, or occasionally white or purple, blooms are shown off beautifully by the velvety, fresh-green leaves. They cling to their support using twining leaf-stalks, and in warm areas are wonderful for training through shrubs and trees, or up an obelisk or trellis. They will also scramble without support as ground cover. In temperate climates, the tender species are best grown as annuals, or planted in containers and then moved under cover during the winter.

Hardiness Half-hardy ✲ to frost-tender ❊.

Cultivation Plant in a spot in full sun. The soil should be moist but quite well drained: dig some grit into the planting area to improve drainage on heavy soils (*see p.377*). In a container, it is a good idea to use standard loam-based compost with added sharp sand or grit. **Propagate** with seed (*see pp.391–393*) sown at 19–24°C (66–75°F) in spring, or root semi-ripe cuttings (*see p.394*) in summer.

MAURANDELLA ANTIRRHINIFLORA

Violet twining snapdragon

summer to autumn

‡1–2m (3–6ft)

DELICATE AND SLENDER-STEMMED, this twining climber is a herbaceous perennial with lush, bright green leaves that provide a splendid backdrop for the main attraction: the flowers. They are borne in abundance throughout the summer and autumn and are usually violet, but sometimes purple or white. Plant it so it can wind its way through trellis, taut wires, or netting attached to any vertical surface. It is grown as an annual in cool climates, but the shorter season means it does not grow to full size; combine it with other climbers to cover a larger area and prolong the display.

Hardiness Half-hardy ✲.

Cultivation Grow in moist but well-drained soil in light shade, or in sun with some shade at midday. Protect from cold, drying winds. **Deadhead** regularly (*see p.390*), and if growing it as a perennial, remove the dead top-growth at the end of the season. **Sow** seed (*see pp.391–393*) at 13–18°C (55–64°F) in spring. Take softwood cuttings (*see p.394*) in spring and root in a propagator.

Lonicera periclymenum 'Graham Thomas' ♀
‡7m (22ft), deciduous, very fragrant flowers in mid- and late summer, red berries ✷✷✷

Lophospermum erubescens ♀ (Creeping gloxinia, Climbing foxglove)
‡1.2–3m (4–10ft), evergreen, widely available ❊

Maurandella antirrhiniflora
Flowers have violet, purple, or sometimes pink lobes

PARTHENOCISSUS

Virginia creeper · *autumn*

VIRGINIA CREEPERS CAN CLING strongly to almost any surface using tiny suckers at the end of their tendrils. These deciduous, woody climbers are grown for their attractive leaves that give an amazing, bonfire-like show of colour in autumn. The dense foliage has the added bonus of providing a home for a variety of beneficial wildlife. Tiny, summer flowers may be followed by toxic black berries. These are vigorous vines that can be trained to cover walls, fences, and any ugly garden structures, or can be used to scramble through a large tree. Virginia creepers are easily controlled, but take care where they climb because the suckers can leave unsightly marks on walls and fences.

Hardiness Fully hardy ❄❄❄; *Parthenocissus henryana* is frost-hardy ❄❄ unless grown against a wall.

Cultivation Grow in fertile, well-drained soil in sun or shade; grow *P. henryana* in partial shade. **Support** young plants until they firmly attach themselves (*see p.380*). **Trim** in winter and summer to keep within bounds (*see p.384*) and clear of gutters and roofs. **Sow** seed (*see pp.391–392*) in pots in a cold frame in autumn, or take softwood cuttings in summer or hardwood cuttings in winter (*see p.394*).

PASSIFLORA

Passion flower, Granadilla · *summer to autumn*

DESPITE THEIR TROPICAL APPEARANCE, some of these mostly evergreen climbers, notably the blue passion flower (*Passiflora caerulea*), can be grown outdoors in cool climates. They climb using tendrils, so need the support of stretched wires, netting, trellis, or a large shrub. They are good all-round plants, with pleasing foliage, and unusual and exotic flowers through summer and autumn that are followed by edible, but not always tasty, fruits. In warm climates, they can be used in almost any situation, but in cold areas the tender species are best grown in containers and moved under cover in autumn, well before the first frosts.

Hardiness Frost-hardy ❄❄ to frost-tender ❅; *P.* 'Amethyst', *P. manicata*, and *P.* 'Star of Bristol' may survive a frost if well-ripened.

Cultivation Grow in soil that is moist but well-drained, in full sun or partial shade, or in tubs of loam-based potting compost. Give shelter from cold winds and apply a winter mulch (*see p.388*) if grown outside in cold areas. **Root** semi-ripe cuttings (*see p.394*) in summer or layer (*see p.395*) in spring or autumn.

Passiflora caerulea ♀ (Blue passion flower)
‡ to 10m (30ft), flowers from summer to autumn, orange-yellow fruits ❄❄

① *henryana* ♀ ‡ 10m (30ft) ② *tricuspidata* ♀ (Boston ivy) ‡ 20m (70ft) ③ *tricuspidata* 'Lowii' ‡ 20m (70ft) ④ *tricuspidata* 'Veitchii' ‡ 20m (70ft)

Passiflora 'Star of Bristol' ♀
‡ to 4m (12ft), flowers from summer to autumn, bright-orange fruits ❅

Passiflora caerulea 'Constance Elliott'
‡ to 10m (30ft), fragrant flowers from summer to autumn, orange-yellow fruits ❄❄

Passiflora × exoniensis ♀
‡ to 6m (20ft), downy, rich-green leaves, flowers in summer followed by yellow, banana-shaped fruits ✿

PILEOSTEGIA VIBURNOIDES

late summer to autumn

THIS WOODY CLIMBER is valued for its sprays of starry, creamy-white flowers that are borne from late summer to autumn, and its leathery, evergreen leaves that are up to 15cm (6in) long. This vigorous plant can cling to almost any surface with aerial roots, and will make short work of covering a large tree trunk, fence, or wall. It can also be grown over a sturdy pergola or arch. Use its rich-green foliage as a background for showy spring- and summer-flowering annuals such as morning glories (*Ipomoea, see p.144*) and sweet peas (*Lathyrus, see p.145*). It is also a good plant to combine with deciduous climbers such as clematis (*see pp.136–139*), as well as being invaluable for shady north- and east-facing walls.

Hardiness Frost-hardy ✳✳✳.

Cultivation Grow in any soil in sun or shade. **Trim** in early spring to keep it under control (*see p.384*). **Root** semi-ripe cuttings (*see p.394*) in summer or layer shoots (*see p.395*) in spring.

PLUMBAGO

Leadwort *summer to late autumn*

PLUMBAGO IS GROWN for its large clusters of simple, flat flowers. There are annuals, perennials, and shrubs in the group, but the evergeen climbers are most commonly cultivated. Their bright, matt-green leaves provide the perfect foil for the sky-blue, pure white, or deep rose-pink flowers. In mild climates, grow plumbago over a pergola or arch, or against a wall. In cool areas, where temperatures fall below 7ºC (45ºF), it is best grown in a container placed in a sheltered, sunny spot, and moved under cover during the cold winter months.

Hardiness Half-hardy ✳ to frost-tender ✿.

Cultivation Grow in fertile, well-drained soil in full sun, or in containers of loam-based potting compost, and top-dress or repot in spring. **Tie** shoots of young plants (*see p.380*) into the support as they grow to create a permanant framework of well-spaced stems. **Prune** in early spring once fully established; cut back sideshoots to within two or three buds of the main branches. **Sow** seed (*see pp.391–392*) at 13–18ºC (55–64ºF) in spring or take semi-ripe cuttings (*see p.394*) in midsummer. **Whitefly** may attack if the plant is grown under glass or moved under cover through winter.

Passiflora 'Amethyst' ♀
‡ to 4m (12ft), flowers from late summer to autumn, orange fruits ✿

Pileostegia viburnoides ♀
‡ 6m (20ft), flower clusters are up to 15cm (6in) across

Plumbago auriculata ♀ (Cape leadwort)
‡ 3–6m (10–20ft) ↔ 1–3m (3–10ft), flower clusters from summer to late autumn are up to 15cm (6in) across ✳

Rose

early summer to late autumn

THE GLORIOUS DISPLAYS PRODUCED by climbing and rambling roses are one of the delights of the summer garden, but the thorny, arching stems will need some form of support and, in most cases, regular tying in. Climbers tend to have stiff stems, with the flowers, often scented, carried singly or in clusters. Some have one main show of blooms on wood produced the previous year, while others flower in succession on the current season's growth. Ramblers are generally more rampant and have more flexible stems. The sometimes scented flowers are usually borne in clusters in one main flush on the previous year's growth. Both types can be trained against walls and fences or over pergolas and other ornamental structures (*see below*).

Hardiness Fully hardy ✳✳✳ to frost-hardy ✳✳.

Cultivation Roses tolerate a wide range of conditions, but prefer fertile soil in a sunny site. Plant bare-root roses while dormant, from late autumn to early spring. Container-grown roses can be planted at any time. **Water** well after planting and keep watered until established. **Prune** sideshoots of climbers back to two or three buds in autumn or spring once the basic framework is established; cut one or two old stems to the base every three or four years to encourage new growth. Ramblers produce shoots from the base, so cut out one in three main stems after flowering each year. **Take** hardwood cuttings (*see p.394*) in autumn. Plants may be affected by mildew, blackspot, or rust. If possible choose a disease-resistant variety, improve air circulation around the plant, or spray with a suitable fungicide.

Covering an arch with a rose

Climbing or rambling roses look particularly good when trained over an arch, an arrangement that also makes it easy to enjoy the scent of the flowers. The arch must be strong enough to bear the weight of the numerous shoots and flowers in summer. Check, too, that it is securely anchored into the ground. Tie in the stems as they grow, spreading them evenly over the frame. This is much easier done while the shoots are still young and flexible, especially on climbers. Deadhead faded blooms regularly to encourage more flowers on those varieties that produce a succession.

Training a rambler into a tree

Ramblers with pliant, far-reaching stems will scramble into trees to provide a spectacular display. Check first that the tree can support the mass of growth, especially if choosing a vigorous rose. Plant the rose at least 1–1.2m (3–4ft) away from the trunk, and add plenty of organic matter to the planting hole to aid moisture retention. Site the rose on the windward side so that shoots are blown towards the tree, and train it into the tree up a length of rope leading from a stake at the rose's roots to a low branch. Protect the bark with a piece of rubber hose. No further training should be needed.

Growing a climber up a pillar or tripod

Roses trained up structures such as pillars, tripods, or obelisks add useful height to a bed or border. Choose one of the less vigorous climbers to reduce the need for pruning. Keeping stems close to the horizontal encourages the development of flowering sideshoots so, where possible, train stems in a spiral fashion around the pillar or tripod. Tie in stems regularly as they grow, while they are still young and flexible. Once they start to stiffen up, they are liable to break rather easily. Prune out any unwanted or over-long stems as necessary.

① *Rosa* 'Albertine' ♛ ‡5m (15ft) ↔ 4m (12ft), rambler ② 'Aloha' ♛ ‡3m (10ft) ↔ 2.5m (8ft), climber ③ 'American Pillar' ‡5m (15ft) ↔ 4m (12ft), rambler ④ *banksiae* 'Lutea' ♛ ‡↔ 6m (20ft), rambler ✳✳ ⑤ BREATH OF LIFE ('Harquanne') ‡2.5m (8ft) ↔ 2.2m (7ft), climber ⑥ 'Chaplin's Pink Climber' ‡5m (15ft) ↔ 2.5m (8ft), climber ⑦ 'Climbing Iceberg' ♛ ‡↔ 3m (10ft), climber ⑧ 'Compassion' ♛ ‡3m (10ft) ↔ 2.5m (8ft), climber ⑨ 'Danse du Feu'

↔ 2.5m (8ft), climber ⑩ 'Dortmund' ♀ ↕3m (10ft) ↔ 2m (6ft), climber ⑪ DUBLIN BAY ('Macdub') ♀ ↔ 2.2m (7ft), climber ⑫ 'Félicité Perpétue' ♀ ↕5m (15ft) ↔ 4m (12ft), rambler ⑬ *filipes* 'Kiftsgate' ♀ ↕10m (30ft) ↔ 6m (20ft), rambler ⑭ 'Gloire de Dijon' ↕5m (15ft) ↔ 4m (12ft), climber ⑮ 'Golden Showers' ♀ ↕3m (10ft) ↔ 2m (6ft), climber ⑯ HANDEL ('Macha') ♀ ↕3m (10ft) ↔ 2.2m (7ft), climber ⑰ 'Madame Grégoire Staechelin' ♀ ↕6m (20ft) ↔ 4m (12ft),

climber ⑱ 'New Dawn' ♀ ↕3m (10ft) ↔ 2.5m (8ft), climber ⑲ 'Paul's Lemon Pillar' ↕4m (12ft) ↔ 3m (10ft), climber ⑳ 'Pink Perpétue' ↕3m (10ft) ↔ 2.5m (8ft), climber ㉑ 'Rosy Mantle' ↕2.5m (8ft) ↔ 2m (6ft), climber ㉒ 'Sander's White Rambler' ♀ ↔ 4m (12ft), rambler ㉓ 'Zéphirine Drouhin' ↕3m (10ft) ↔ 2m (6ft), thornless climber

RUBUS

see also p.114

summer to autumn

‡6m (20ft)

RUBUS IS A LARGE GROUP of climbers and shrubs that includes blackberries and raspberries. The ornamental climbers are mainly slender, prickly, or bristly evergreens. The handsome, dark green foliage is felted white on the undersides. The clusters of flat, usually pink, summer flowers are similar to those of wild roses, and are followed by glossy fruits. Some species are very vigorous, and are best reserved for wild and woodland gardens. Others are well-behaved and splendid grown with other climbers such as jasmine (*Jasminum, see p.144*).

Hardiness Fully hardy ✳✳✳ to frost-hardy ✳.

Cultivation Grow in well-drained soil in sun or partial shade. The young stems need tying into their support regularly to keep them neat (*see p.380*). **Trim** large species only if necessary keep them in check, after flowering (*see p.384*). **Root** semi-ripe cuttings of evergreens in summer or hardwood cuttings of deciduous species in early winter (*see p.394*). **Grey mould** can result in fuzzy, fungal growth on any part of the plant; remove affected areas promptly to prevent it spreading.

SCHISANDRA

spring to summer

‡3–10m (10–30ft)

IF YOU HAVE A LARGE AREA to cover, then schisandras are good all-rounders with attractive flowers, foliage, and fruits. These twining, woody, usually deciduous climbers have glossy, mid-green leaves and pretty, white, or red flowers. They are borne in spring and summer, and are followed by bright bunches of pink or red berries if a male and female plant are grown together. Train them through trees, or over trellis attached to walls or fences. They can be grown with plants such as golden hops (*Humulus lupulus* 'Aureus', *see p.143*) for a spectacular colour contrast.

Hardiness Fully hardy ✳✳✳.

Cultivation Grow in fertile, moist, well-drained soil in sun or partial shade. **Tie in** the shoots of young plants until they begin to twine (*see p.380*), encouraging them to form a regularly spaced framework. Once this is accomplished, maintain it by cutting back sideshoots to within three or four buds of the main stems in early spring. **Sow** seed (*see pp.391–392*) in pots in a cold frame when ripe, or root semi-ripe cuttings (*see p.394*) in summer.

SCHIZOPHRAGMA

midsummer

THESE WOODY, DECIDUOUS climbers are in the same family as hydrangeas (*see p.143*). The resemblance can be clearly seen in their huge, flat clusters of creamy-white, subtly fragrant flowers. They are borne in abundance in midsummer, against a background of dark green leaves. The foliage of some cultivars is mottled silver or edged with pink. These variegated plants provide unusual ground cover when grown without support in the dappled shade beneath deciduous trees and shrubs. Train schizophragmas up walls or large tree trunks, to which they cling strongly using aerial roots. These large climbers are very heavy when mature, so choose a suitably robust support that will not collapse under the weight.

Hardiness Fully hardy ✳✳✳ to frost-hardy ✳✳.

Cultivation Grow in moist, well-drained, humus-rich soil in sun or partial shade. **Tie in** the shoots of young plants to their support until the aerial roots take hold (*see p.380*). **Trim** them in spring if they outgrow their space (*see p.384*). **Root** semi-ripe cuttings (*see p.394*) in late summer.

Rubus henryi* var. *bambusarum
‡6m (10ft), evergreen, white hairy shoots have sharp spines, bears black fruits in autumn ✳✳✳

Schisandra rubriflora
‡10m (30ft), vigorous species, young shoots are red, flowers in late spring and summer, fleshy fruits in autumn (*see inset*)

Schizophragma integrifolium ♀
‡12m (40ft) ✳✳

Solanum

spring to autumn

THIS HUGE GROUP OF PLANTS contains varieties that are annuals, perennials, shrubs, and trees, but the climbing solanums are especially popular. They are grown for their bell- or trumpet-shaped flowers in regal blues and purples, or pure white, from spring right through to autumn. In some years, shiny, round berries may follow. Although solanums count potatoes and aubergines among their number, most of the ornamental species are toxic if eaten, and can cause severe discomfort. Some care should be taken as the fruits can be very appealing to children. Solanums need a warm, sunny wall to thrive in temperate climates. Grow them with other sun-worshippers such as jasmines (*see p.144*) and roses (*see pp.150–151*).

Hardiness Frost-hardy ✳✳ to frost-tender ❀.

Cultivation Grow in well-drained soil in full sun. **Mulch** (*see p.388*) over winter, particularly young plants. In cold areas, use containers of loam-based compost and move under cover in winter. **Tie in** shoots regularly (*see p.380*). **Prune** back sideshoots to within two or three buds of main branches in late winter. **Sow** seed (*see pp.391–392*) at 18–20ºC (64–68ºF) in spring or root semi-ripe cuttings (*see p.394*) in summer in a propagator.

Thunbergia

summer to autumn

VALUED FOR THEIR ABUNDANCE of exotic, brightly coloured flowers, the tropical, perennial climbers are usually grown as annuals in cool areas, or in pots and taken under cover in winter. The blooms come in shades of gold, orange, or blue, and are borne against a background of soft green leaves. Their slender, twining stems can wind round a freestanding arch or obelisk, or through a shrub. Otherwise attach trellis, wires, or netting to a fence or wall to provide a support that they can scramble up. Create a fabulous, jewel-like display through summer by growing thunbergias with other annual climbers, such as sweet peas (*Lathyrus, see p.145*), on a single support.

Hardiness Half-hardy ✳ to frost-tender ❀.

Cultivation Grow in a reasonably sheltered site in moist, well-drained soil and full sun. In containers, use a loam-based potting compost. **Train** the young plants towards their support (*see p.380*). **Trim** thunbergias grown as perennials in early spring if they are taking up too much room (*see p.384*). **Sow** seed (*see pp.391–392*) at 16–18ºC (61–64ºF) or take semi-ripe cuttings (*see p.394*) in summer.

Thunbergia mysorensis ♀
↕ 6m (20ft), flowers in spring ❀

① *crispum* 'Glasnevin' ♀ ↕ 6m (20ft) ✳✳ ② *rantonnetii* 'Royal Robe' ↕ 1–2m (3–6ft) ✳✳ – both flower from summer to autumn

Thunbergia alata (Black-eyed Susan)
↕ 1.5–2m (5–6ft) as an annual, 2.5m (8ft) as a perennial, flowers from summer to autumn, often raised from seed ❀

Thunbergia grandiflora ♀ (Bengal clock vine, Blue trumpet vine)
↕ 5–10m (15–30ft), flowers are occasionally white ❀

TRACHELOSPERMUM

mid- to late summer

‡6–9m (20–28ft)

THESE WOODY, EVERGREEN climbers are widely available. They are grown for their glossy, dark green leaves and immaculate white, perfumed flowers in mid- and late summer, which, on *Trachelospermum asiaticum,* age to yellow. Train them against a warm wall in frost-prone areas: trellis or taut, horizontal wires, fixed 5cm (2in) away from the wall, provide perfect support for twining stems. In very cold areas, grow in a container and move under cover in winter. The mature plants can be used to support spring- and summer-flowering annuals, such as tropaeolums (*see right*), to create a stunning mass of colour.

Hardiness Frost-hardy ✳✳.

Cultivation Choose a spot with fertile, well-drained soil, in sun or partial shade, with shelter from cold, drying winds. **Mulch** (*see p.388*) over winter, particularly young plants. For containers use a loam-based potting compost. **Trim** back long shoots in spring if you find the plant is outgrowing its support (*see p.384*). **Root** semi-ripe cuttings in summer (*see p.394*).

TROPAEOLUM

see also p.333

summer to autumn

CLIMBING TROPAEOLUMS use long, twining leaf-stalks to scale fences, trellises, or pergolas. They can also scramble through shrubs, or without support grow as ground cover. In summer, they are decorated with masses of flamboyant flowers, often in glowing shades of red and yellow. Some cultivars have the bonus of variegated foliage. Many species are tender, but even the perennials can be grown successfully as annuals in cold climates. The climbing nasturtiums (*Tropaeolum majus* and some cultivars) flower best on poor soil and are a useful stop-gap in neglected plots. The leaves and flowers of annual species are edible and can be used as a peppery addition to salads.

Hardiness Frost-hardy ✳✳ to frost-tender ❋.

Cultivation Grow these plants in moist but well-drained soil in full sun. **Tie in** young stems to their support (*see p.380*) to encourage them in the right direction. **Sow** seed of perennials in containers in a cold frame when ripe. Annual seed needs temperatures of 13–16°C (55–61°F) in early spring, or can be sown in situ in mid-spring (*see pp.391–393*). **Blackfly** can smother shoots; pick or wash them off, or use a suitable insecticide.

Tropaeolum speciosum ♀ (Flame nasturtium)
‡3m (10ft), perennial, prefers acid (lime-free) soil, flowers are followed by blue berries in red, papery jackets, mulch in winter ✳✳

Trachelospermum jasminoides ♀ (Confederate jasmine, Star jasmine)
‡9m (28ft), aging flowers remain pure white, bronze winter foliage

Tropaeolum peregrinum (Canary creeper)
‡2.5–4m (8–12ft), annual, the flowers are said to resemble flying canaries ❋

Tropaeolum tuberosum 'Ken Aslet' ♀
‡2–4m (6–12ft), perennial, lift tubers and store in frost-free conditions over winter (as for dahlias, *see pp.222–223*) ✳

VITIS

Vine

summer to autumn

‡7m (22ft) to 15m (50ft)

THE ORNAMENTAL VINES in this group, unlike those grown for grapes or to make wine, are valued for their large leaves, which turn brilliant shades of bright red or plum-purple in autumn. They do bear small, blue-black fruits, but these are usually unpalatable. Strong tendrils fasten these vigorous, woody, deciduous climbers to the nearest support. Train against a wall or fence, or through a large shrub or tree. A vine makes a handsome cover for an arbour or pergola, especially over an eating area, because the leafy growth provides cool shade.

Hardiness Fully hardy ✳✳✳.

Cultivation Grow vines in well-drained, neutral or slightly alkaline (limy) soil, in full sun or semi-shade. **Prune** in winter and again in summer if growth needs to be restrained (*see p.384*). If your vine is more formally trained against a wall, prune sideshoots to two or three buds from the main framework in winter. **Sow** seed (*see pp.391–392*) in a cold frame in autumn or spring or take hardwood cuttings (*see p.394*) in winter. **Mildew** (*see p.398*) can be troublesome.

WISTERIA

Wistaria

spring to early summer

THE ORIENTAL ELEGANCE of wisterias ensures that they remain very popular. Before you buy, always check the stem for a healthy graft union: seedling plants (those growing on their own roots) take years to bloom and then only bear few, or no, flowers. They are very fragrant and borne in long clusters in spring or early summer and are followed by green, bean-like pods. These woody, deciduous, twining climbers can be trained over a sturdy arch or pergola so you can enjoy the perfume as you walk beneath, or against a wall. Wisterias are long-lived and can grow very large if they are on too rich a soil. Prune plants twice a year to keep them within bounds and maximize flowering. A low-maintenance option is to scramble wisteria through a large tree where it will need no pruning.

Hardiness Fully hardy ✳✳✳; buds may be damaged by late frost.

Cultivation Grow in moist but well-drained soil, in sun or semi-shade. **Tie in** shoots (*see p.380*) to form a permanent framework. Keep the main stems horizontal. **Trim** sideshoots in late summer to 4–6 leaves, or about 15cm (6in), from the main branches. Shorten again in winter, to 2–3 buds. **Leaf spot** (*see p.399*) can be a problem.

Wisteria floribunda 'Alba' ♀
‡9m (28ft) or more, flower clusters up to 60cm (24in) long open from base to tip, followed by velvety, green pods

Vitis coignetiae ♀
‡15m (50ft), widely available, dark green leaves are up to 30cm (12in) long (shown here with autumn colour)

Wisteria floribunda 'Multijuga' ♀
‡9m (28ft) or more, flower clusters up to 30cm (12in) long open from base to tip, followed by velvety, green pods

Wisteria brachybotrys 'Shiro-kapitan'
‡9m (28ft) or more, foliage is softly hairy, flowers clusters to 15cm (6in) long, occasionally produces double flowers

Flowering Plants

flowering plants through the year

Flowering plants are the mainstay of the garden display, providing the "understorey" of planting to complement your trees and shrubs. They include annuals, biennials, perennials, and bulbs, and although many are at their peak in summer, plenty flower happily at other times of year. Most of these plants will tolerate a wide range of soil types and differing conditions, in sun or shade, but some, like *Meconopsis*, require an acid (lime-free) soil.

DESIGNING PLANTING SCHEMES
Before you visit the garden centre or nursery, take the time to decide which plants you want and the theme or atmosphere you aim to create. It will save a lot of time and heartache if you do this beforehand! The plants you choose may be used to evoke different moods. Colour is important – more of that later – but so, too, are the texture and shape of plant leaves and stems. For instance, lots of brightly coloured small-leaved plants will help you achieve a cottage-garden effect, whereas a few plants with large leaves in cooler colours will give the garden a more contemporary feel.

To determine how many plants you'll need, it helps to find out their ultimate height and spread. You can work out how much space to leave between two plants by adding together their spreads, then dividing by two. Logically, tall plants go at the back of the border

and small ones at the front, but don't be afraid to bring some tall plants forward, towards the centre; the undulating effect will break up what might otherwise have been too flat a scheme. It also introduces an element of mystery, by partly obscuring other plants.

You can prolong your display by including a few spring-flowering bulbs, like snowdrops (*Galanthus*) and daffodils (*Narcissus*), and late-flowering perennials, such as asters and rudbeckias, in your design.

COLOUR IN THE GARDEN
The subject of colour in the garden can cause heated debate, but the choice is entirely personal and you can never be dogmatic about it. It's fun to experiment with different combinations, and if you change your mind, after the first season or two most plants can be moved without much difficulty. You can create harmonious effects using different shades of similar colours or liven things up by opting for a more contrasting scheme.

Reds, yellows, and oranges are hot colours and pack a punch, while shades of white, blue, and purple provide a cool, reflective atmosphere. The size of the border can also apparently change just through the use of colour. Hot reds and oranges draw the eye and make it seem shorter, while cool colours recede into the distance, creating the impression of a larger space.

SPRING

Scilla siberica 'Spring Beauty' *p.323*

Aquilegia vulgaris 'Nora Barlow' *p.185*

SUMMER

Inula hookeri p.263

Scabiosa 'Butterfly Blue' *p.322*

AUTUMN

Schizostylis coccinea 'Major' *p.323*

Chrysanthemum 'Pavilion' *p.213*

WINTER

Eranthis hyemalis p.236

Iris 'Austrian Sky' *p.265*

Narcissus 'Grand Soleil d'Or' *p.289*   *Tulipa* 'Queen of Night' *p.335*   *Hesperis matronalis* var. *albiflora* *p.259*   *Bellis perennis* Tasso Series *p.197*

Paeonia lactiflora 'Festiva Maxima' *p.298*   *Nymphaea* 'René Gérard' *p.292*   *Erigeron aureus* 'Canary Bird' *p.237*   *Gladiolus* 'Elvira' *p.252*

Tricyrtis ohsumiensis *p.331*   *Aster* x *frikartii* 'Mönch' *p.193*   *Colchicum speciosum* 'Album' *p.215*   *Sedum spectabile* 'Brilliant' *p.324*

Primula allionii *p.312*   *Galanthus* 'Atkinsii' *p.247*   *Hacquetia epipactis* *p.255*   *Iris unguicularis* 'Mary Barnard' *p.267*

choosing perennial plants

Herbaceous perennials are non-woody plants that grow and flower over several years. Some perennials are evergreen, but with most the top-growth dies down in winter while the roots remain alive; in spring new growth sprouts up from the base or crown of the plant. Most perennials are long-lived and perform for several years, but some such as common flax (*Linum*) have shorter lives, lasting only two or three years. Short-lived perennials do tend to seed themselves quite freely however, so it is unlikely that you will need to buy replacements.

CHOICE OF PERENNIALS

Perennial plants have astonishing variety in foliage shapes, colour, flower forms, textures, and growth habits. They range from hardy geraniums no more than 15cm (6in) tall, to stately plants like *Cephalaria gigantea*, which grows up to 2m (6ft) in height. With so much choice available it is possible to find a perennial for almost every conceivable situation, whether you prefer complementary planting, or aim for drama by contrasting colours, forms, and textures. For instance, the broad leaves of hostas make a perfect foil to the delicate fronds of some ferns, or try them with strap-shaped iris foliage.

PERENNIALS IN THE BORDER

The way perennials are used in the garden has changed a lot over the years, just as with other trends in gardening. Traditionally they were grown in herbaceous borders usually backed by a hedge or wall. This is fine if you have a large garden, but with modern gardens becoming smaller, more often than not we grow perennials in mixed borders with trees, shrubs, and annuals – and achieve some very pleasing effects.

Island beds, which are usually cut out of the lawn and may be viewed from all angles, also suit perennials. The plants benefit from being in the open with good light all round, making for sturdier growth that requires less staking. Position taller plants in the middle and gradually grade down towards the edges.

EXTENDING THE INTEREST

While most perennials are at their best in summer, there are plenty to choose from at other times of year. Spring perennials include bergenias, hellebores, pulmonarias, and primulas. Other perennials flower well into autumn and are valuable for extending the period of interest. The classic autumn flowers are chrysanthemums and michaelmas daisies (*Aster*). Choose the right ones, and in good weather you could have them in flower right through to November. Other good autumn flowerers include rudbeckias with their large daisy-like flowers, and sedums, which are excellent for attracting butterflies.

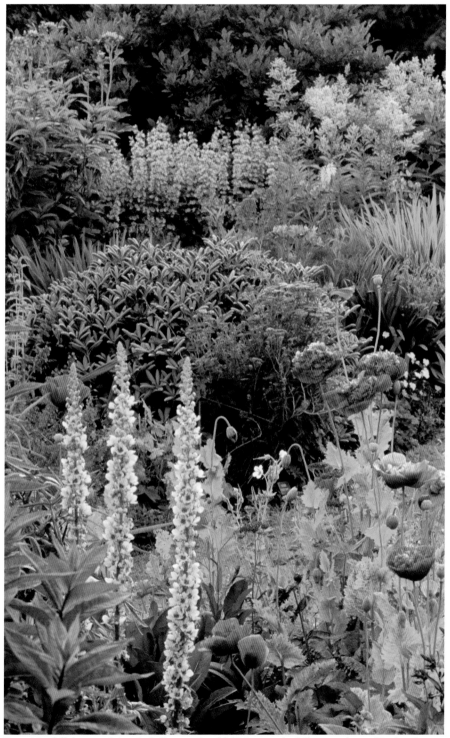

Perennials of all shapes and sizes, including poppies, delphiniums, and achilleas, may be combined against a backdrop of trees and shrubs to create a vibrant summer display.

Actaea rubra p.169   *Osteospermum* 'Whirlygig' *p.297*   *Hosta* 'Shade Fanfare' *p.261*   *Helleborus* x *hybridus* p.257

Chrysanthemum 'Pennine Oriel' *p.213*   *Anagallis tenella* 'Studland' *p.178*   *Dianthus* 'Golden Cross' *p.227*   *Sempervivum arachnoideum* p.325

Cynara cardunculus p.221   *Zantedeschia elliottiana* p.339   *Eryngium* x *oliverianum* p.238   *Physalis alkekengi* p.308

Rudbeckia laciniata 'Herbstsonne' *p.317*   *Dodecatheon dentatum* p.231   *Dianthus* 'Dainty Dame' *p.226*   *Phlox* 'Kelly's Eye' *p.307*

choosing annuals and biennials

Annual plants complete their life cycle – germination, flowering, seed production, and death – within one year. Biennials take two growing seasons: they produce leafy growth in the first year and flower in the next. Biennials and many annuals withstand frost. Annuals that are killed by cold temperatures are described as "half hardy": wait until all danger of frost has passed before planting them out in spring. If you don't want to worry about protecting tender perennials like pelargoniums over winter, you can treat them just like annuals.

SPEEDY SERVICE

Growing so quickly, this group of plants can make a cheerful splash while you wait for trees and shrubs to mature. They are a boon for new home-owners: sow a few annuals to fill the garden with colour until you have the time and money to make more permanent changes – this will keep the weeds down too. Try designing an elaborate scheme with annuals and biennials first: the fact that they are short-lived gives you freedom to experiment without spending a fortune. And if you are keen to encourage your children to cultivate an interest in gardening, give them some hardy annual seeds: they won't need special equipment and should see some rapid results.

CONTAINED ENTHUSIASM

If you don't have a garden, many annuals and biennials are eminently suitable for growing in containers. Any pot will do, so long as it has drainage holes. Ornate containers can form a focal point in a garden, but you can also place pots into borders to conceal gaps when other plants have finished flowering.

Hanging baskets and window boxes are very popular and both are ideal for annual trailing plants. Plant them correctly, and by summer you should not be able to see the framework of your basket at all. Although they are often associated with spring and summer, you can also find plants to suit autumn and winter displays too.

Do remember that all types of container need regular watering, perhaps twice a day in very hot weather. Hanging baskets are particularly prone to drying out – being high up they are more exposed to the sun and wind. But so long as you water, feed, and deadhead the plants they will give you a stunning display all summer.

For those keen on indoor flower arrangements, most annuals are suitable for cutting. If you have a vegetable plot or space in an out-of-the-way spot, sow a few annuals there so you can cut flowers for the house as and when you please.

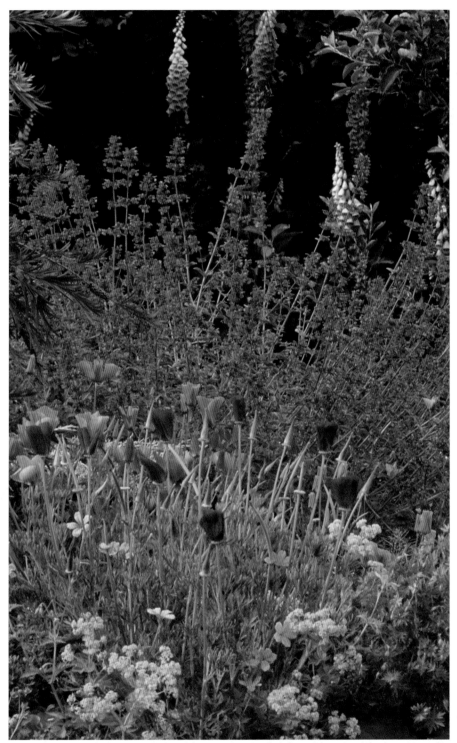

Surrounding perennial catmint (*Nepeta*), California poppies (*Eschscholzia californica*) and foxgloves (*Digitalis*) are among the annuals and biennials you can rely on to grow up fast, providing colour where you need it.

Dahlia 'Fascination' *p.222*

Moluccella laevis p.286

Lavatera trimestris 'Pink Beauty' *p.270*

Salpiglossis Casino Series *p.318*

Brachyscome iberidifolia p.200

Argemone mexicana p.187

Centaurea cyanus p.209

Dahlia 'Preston Park' *p.223*

Silybum marianum p.326

Echium vulgare 'Blue Bedder' *p.234*

Helianthus 'Monarch' *p.256*

Nicotiana 'Lime Green' *p.291*

Limnanthes douglasii p.278

Impatiens balsamina Tom Thumb Series *p.263*

Anethum graveolens p.181

Felicia amelloides 'Santa Anita' *p.244*

choosing bulbous plants

Bulbous plants are perennials equipped with a food storage organ (a swollen part of the stem or root). This enables them to stay dormant until conditions are favourable for growth. There are several distinct types: "true bulbs" consist of tightly packed leaves and a papery skin; "corms" are enlarged underground stems; "tubers" are formed from swollen roots or underground stems; "rhizomes" are underground creeping stems that grow horizontally.

GROWING BULBS

Bulbs are generally not too fussy about soil conditions, so long as they have good drainage, and most are very hardy. They tolerate almost any aspect except deep shade, with many preferring hot, sunny sites, but woodland bulbs prefer light, dappled shade. Bulbs are not only for spring displays; if you choose correctly you can have bulbs in flower for most months of the year – snowdrops in winter, tulips in spring, alliums in summer, and colchicums in autumn.

For maximum impact plant bulbs in large groups. If they are grown in formal beds, you can lift and store bulbs after flowering to make way for other plants. But if possible leave the bulbs in position to die down naturally: try interplanting with herbaceous perennials so that the dying bulb foliage is concealed by the new young growth of the perennial plants.

THE NATURALIZED WAY

Nothing heralds the arrival of spring more than a drift of daffodils flowering in grass. Most bulbs can be naturalized in grass: to get the natural effect, scatter the bulbs and plant them where they fall. As with most bulbs, plant them to at least twice their own depth, and leave the grass uncut until the bulb foliage has died down.

CONTAINER DISPLAYS

Bulbs are also easily accommodated in containers. Choose a pot to suit the size of bulbs, and ensure the container has adequate drainage holes. Once the flowers are over, move the containers to a less prominent position, or replace the bulbs with other plants.

FORCING BULBS

One of the best ways of bringing colour into the house during the dark days of winter is by forcing bulbs. Hyacinths are particularly good as they will fill your home with the most delicious scent. To get them flowering for Christmas, look for specially prepared bulbs and plant them by mid-September. If growing in containers without drainage holes use bulb fibre, and plant so the tips of the bulbs remain above compost level. Keep them in a cool dark place for a few weeks until about 2.5cm (1in) of growth has emerged and gradually bring them into warmer conditions.

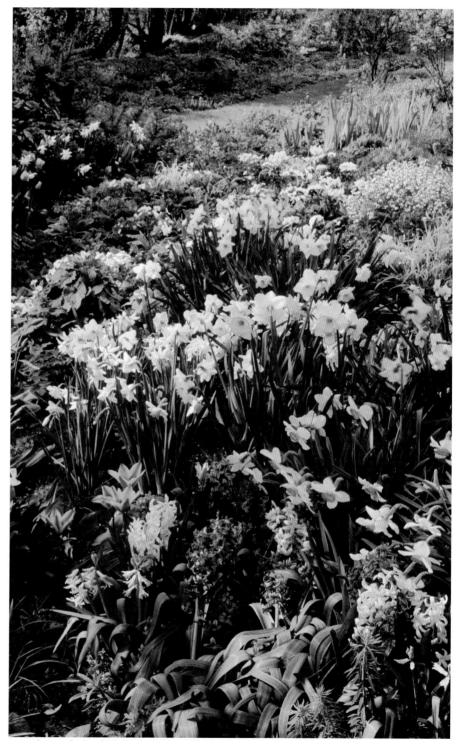

An explosion of colourful bulbs, including daffodils (*Narcissus*), tulips, and hyacinths, is an unmistakable indication that spring has arrived in the garden.

Lilium 'Enchantment' *p.274*　　*Tulipa biflora p.335*　　*Fritillaria imperialis p.246*　　*Allium unifolium p.175*

Iris confusa p.265　　*Dahlia* 'Candy Cane' *p.222*　　*Gladiolus tristis p.253*　　*Iris foetidissima p.265*

Tulipa clusiana var. *chrysantha p.334*　　*Cyclamen cilicium p.221*　　*Dahlia* 'Hillcrest Royal' *p.223*　　*Hyacinthus orientalis* 'City of Haarlem' *p.262*

Muscari armeniacum 'Blue Spike' *p.287*　　*Iris* 'Eyebright' *p.265*　　*Anenome blanda* 'White Splendour' *p.181*　　*Lilium tsingtauense p.277*

ACAENA

New Zealand burr   *summer*

THESE LOW, CREEPING herbaceous perennials form
dense mats of evergreen foliage by virtue of their
rooting stems. This makes for good ground cover in
a rock garden or at the front of a flower border, but
plants can be invasive. In summer, the plant is covered
with round flowerheads, which later develop into the
characteristic, spiny, red burrs for which these plants
are known. New Zealand burrs are valued for their
colourful leaves: *Acaena caesiiglauca* has glaucous blue
foliage, and *A. microphylla* 'Kupferteppich' has bronze
leaves and bright red burrs. Other mat-forming plants
that combine well with them include *Sedum rupestre*
and *S. obtusatum*.

Hardiness Fully hardy ✳✳✳.

Cultivation Grow in reasonably fertile soil in full sun or part shade.
If necessary, curb a spreading plant by pulling out unwanted rooted
stems. **Sow** seed (*see pp.391–392*) in containers in a cold frame
in autumn. **Make** new plants by digging up rooted stems and
transplanting them to a new position, in autumn or early spring.

ACANTHUS

Bear's breeches   *late spring to midsummer*

WITH THEIR TALL SPIKES of unusual flowers above
the striking spiny, dark green foliage, acanthus make
valuable architectural plants for the herbaceous or
mixed border. The individual tubular flowers, each
up to 5cm (2in) long, come in combinations of white,
green, yellow, pink, or purple, and are borne on spikes
up to 1.2m (4ft) tall. These are produced from late
spring to midsummer, and can be cut and dried for
indoor display. Leave a few spikes on the plant over
winter, however, since they look good when covered
in frost. Acanthus are vigorous herbaceous perennials
and associate well with other perennials such as hardy
geraniums (*see pp.250–251*) and phloxes (*see p.306*).

Hardiness Fully hardy ✳✳✳ to frost-tender ✳✳.

Cultivation Grow in any reasonably fertile soil in sun or partial
shade, although they do best in deep, fertile, well-drained loam.
Remove dead foliage and old flower spikes in late winter or early
spring. **Sow** seed in pots in a cold frame (*see pp.391–392*) in spring,
or divide clumps in spring or autumn (*see p.395*). **Take** root cuttings
in winter (*see p.394*). **Powdery mildew** may mar leaves, but only
in very dry conditions.

ACHILLEA

Yarrow   *summer to autumn*

THE FERNY, GREY-GREEN FOLIAGE and flat-topped
flowerheads of yarrows are mainstays of the cottage
garden or herbaceous border. Low-growing types are
ideal for rock gardens. Herbaceous perennials, yarrows
quickly form spreading, drought-resistant clumps that
are suited to most soil types, including chalky and
gravelly soils. Their summer flowerheads, in a wide
range of colours, attract bees, butterflies, and other
beneficial insects, making them a good choice for
wildflower borders. The flowerheads can be dried
for indoor decoration. Grow with other herbaceous
perennials such as lythrums (*see p.283*), phloxes
(*see p.306*), and sidalceas (*see p.325*). Contact with
the foliage may aggravate some skin allergies.

Hardiness Fully hardy ✳✳✳.

Cultivation Grow in moist, but well-drained soil in an open site
in full sun, although most yarrows tolerate a wide range of soils
and conditions. **Remove** faded flowers to encourage more to follow.
Sow seed outdoors (*see pp.391–393*) in situ, or divide clumps every
2–3 years in spring (*see p.395*) to increase stock and maintain vigour.
In dry, overcrowded conditions, powdery mildew may spoil foliage.

Acaena saccaticupula 'Blue Haze'
↕10–15cm (4–6in) ↔ 1m (3ft), the steely grey-blue foliage lasts
throughout the year and sets off the dark red burrs in summer

① *hirsutus* ↕15–35cm (6–14in) ✳✳✳ ② *hungaricus* ↕60–
120cm (2–4ft) ✳✳✳ ③ *mollis* ↕1.5m (5ft) ✳✳✳
④ *spinosus* ♖ ↕1.5m (5ft) ✳✳✳

Achillea 'Moonshine' ♖
↕↔ 60cm (24in), once the bright yellow flowers start to open in
summer, 'Moonshine' puts on a fine display well into autumn

Achillea × lewisii 'King Edward' ♀
↕ 8–13cm (3–5in) ↔ 23cm (9in) or more, a short yarrow with pale yellow flowerheads from early summer, ideal for a rock garden

Achillea filipendulina 'Gold Plate' ♀
↕ 1.2m (4ft) ↔ 45cm (18in), this classic variety, with golden yellow flowerheads throughout summer, is also one of the tallest

Achillea 'Forncett Candy'
↕ 85cm (34in) ↔ 45cm (18in), the pale pink flowerheads fade to almost white as they age

Achillea 'Fanal'
↕ 75cm (30in) ↔ 60cm (24in), the bold crimson flowerheads are ideal cutting material; a good contrast to grey or silvery plants

Achillea nobilis subsp. **neilreichii**
↕ 30–45cm (12–18in) ↔ 45cm (18in) or more if allowed to spread, long-lasting ivory flowerheads above aromatic grey foliage

ACONITUM

Aconite, Monkshood

early summer to autumn

MONKSHOODS ARE NAMED for their hooded flowers, which come in shades of lilac, blue, and pale yellow. These are arranged on tall spires held well above the clumps of divided green foliage. The flowers, which appear from early summer to autumn depending on variety, attract bees and butterflies into the garden. Monkshoods are spreading herbaceous perennials, at their best in reasonably moist beds and borders where they associate well with other perennials such as achilleas (*see p.167*), hemerocallis (*see p.258*), phloxes (*see p.306*), and delphiniums (*see p.224*). The flowers are good for cutting, but take care when handling this plant because all parts are toxic if eaten and contact with the foliage may aggravate some skin allergies.

Hardiness Fully hardy ✼✼✼.

Cultivation Monkshoods prefer cool, moist, fertile soil in partial shade, but most soils are tolerated, as is sun if the site is damp enough. **Stake** taller monkshoods to prevent them keeling over. **Cut down** the previous year's growth in late winter or early spring. **Sow** seed (*see pp.391–392*) in pots in a cold frame in spring. Divide clumps every three years in autumn or late winter to maintain vigour (*see p.395*).

Aconitum × cammarum 'Bicolor' ♛
‡ to 1.2m (4ft) ↔ 30cm (12in), an unusual monkshood, flowers in mid- and late summer

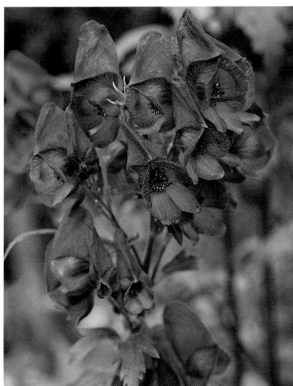

Aconitum carmichaelii 'Arendsii' ♛
‡ to 1.2m (4ft) ↔ 30cm (12in), flowers in early and mid-autumn

Aconitum 'Ivorine'
‡ 90cm (36in) ↔ 45cm (18in), a choice variety for a cool, moist site, flowers in early summer

Aconitum 'Bressingham Spire' ♛
‡ 90–100cm (36–39in) ↔ 30cm (12in), a long-flowering plant, from midsummer to autumn, and a little shorter than many monkshoods

ACTAEA

Baneberry, Bugbane · *mid-spring to autumn*

THIS GROUP OF PLANTS, which now includes those formerly known as cimicifugas, comprises a range of clump-forming perennials for woodland gardens, shady borders, or streamsides. All have attractive foliage and flowers, and in some cases fruits. Plumes or spires of small, white or pink-tinged flowers appear above the foliage from mid-spring to late summer and autumn. Varieties such as *Actaea rubra*, and *A. spicata* also develop clusters of shiny white, red, or black berries, which are highly poisonous. The divided leaves are usually green, although some of the bugbanes, for instance *Actaea simplex* 'Brunette', are prized for their bronze or purple foliage. Bugbanes combine well with other perennials such as sidalceas (*see p.325*), goldenrods (*see Solidago, p.327*), and rudbeckias (*see p.317*).

Hardiness Fully hardy ✽✽✽.

Cultivation Grow in moist, fertile soil, enriched with well-rotted organic matter, in partial shade. Keep well watered in dry spells. **Sow** seed in containers in a cold frame in autumn (*see pp.391–393*); divide plants in spring (*see p.395*).

Actaea rubra ♀
‡45cm (18in) ↔ 30cm (12in), the white flowers, as well as the red berries that follow, will enliven areas of light shade in woodland

ADONIS

Pheasant's eye · *late winter to spring*

THE SOLITARY FLOWERS of these relatively obscure, clump-forming perennials and annuals have a delicate anemone-like appeal. Some, such as *Adonis amurensis*, appear from late winter to spring, before the fine ferny foliage has had time to develop. *Adonis brevistyla* and *A. vernalis* also bloom in spring and, like many flowers at this time of year, come in shades of white and yellow. These three are all perennial. Good early-flowering companions include cyclamens (*see p.221*), doronicums (*see p.231*), and snowdrops (*see p.247*). *A. aestivalis* is a charming annual that opens its red flowers in midsummer. Adonis vary in their cultivation requirements, suiting either cool, shady, woodland conditions or sunny, open sites. Check before you buy.

Hardiness Fully hardy ✽✽✽.

Cultivation Grow *A. amurensis* and *A. brevistyla* in cool, humus-rich soil that is acidic (lime-free) in shade; *A. aestivalis* needs well-drained, alkaline (limy) soil in sun. **Sow** seed (*see pp.391–393*) in a cold frame as soon as ripe; germination is slow. Perennial adonis do not respond well to being divided.

Actaea simplex (syn. *Cimicifuga simplex*)
‡1–1.2m (3–4ft) ↔ 60cm (24in), feathery spires of flowers appear in late summer and autumn

Actaea (*Cimicifuga*) *simplex* 'Brunette' ♀
‡1–1.2m (3–4ft) ↔ 60cm (24in), fine foliage plant, has flower plumes like those of *A. simplex* (*see left*) but tinged with pink

Adonis brevistyla
‡20–40cm (8–16in) ↔ 20cm (8in), a faint flush of blue on the outside of the petals adds to the charm of this adonis

AEGOPODIUM PODAGRARIA

Ground elder **summer**

OF THE FIVE OR SO SPECIES of ground elder, most are invasive weeds that spread by underground stems, but the variegated cultivars of *Aegopodium podagraria* are worthy of the garden. *A. podagraria* 'Variegatum' makes a decorative ground cover, spreading over those moist, shady areas of the garden where little else will grow. The leaves are up to 10cm (4in) across. In early summer, it produces clusters of white flowers, but its main value lies in its foliage. Confining this perennial to poor soil, where other plants will not thrive, prevents it from becoming troublesome. Alternatively, grow it in an island bed on its own. Other plants that enjoy similar conditions include bergenias (*see p.198*) and hardy geraniums (*see pp.250–251*).

Hardiness Fully hardy ✳✳✳.

Cultivation Ground elder can be grown in any soil, even very poor ground, in full or partial shade. **Removing** fading flowers before they set seed and slicing off unwanted growth with a spade help to confine its spread. **Divide** rhizomes in autumn or spring (*see p.395*).

AETHIONEMA

Stone cress **spring to early summer**

CLUSTERS OF DAINTY FLOWERS, in cheerful shades of red, pink, creamy-white, and pure white, are the main reason for growing these annuals and evergreen or semi-evergreen, woody-based perennials. The flowers are produced on short stems from spring to early summer. The leaves are small, usually stalkless, and rather fleshy. They tend to be short-lived plants and it is best to increase them from cuttings every two or three years to make sure they perform well. As petite plants, they are obvious candidates for the front of an herbaceous border or as part of a rock garden. Try growing them with dicentras (*see p.228*), *Euphorbia polychroma* (*see p.242*), and doronicums (*see p.231*).

Hardiness Fully hardy ✳✳✳ (given good drainage).

Cultivation These plants grow best in fertile, well-drained, alkaline (limy) soil in full sun, but they also tolerate poor, acid (lime-free) soils. **Sow** seed (*see pp.391–393*) in containers in a cold frame in spring; sow seed of annuals in autumn directly where they are to grow. **Take** softwood cuttings (*see p.394*) in late spring or early summer.

AGAPANTHUS

African blue lily **midsummer to early autumn**

VIGOROUS AND CLUMP-FORMING, these large perennials bear round or pendent heads of bell-shaped flowers in deep shades of blue and violet-blue, or in white, from midsummer to early autumn. They generally have handsome, long, strappy leaves. The majority of hybrids are deciduous, while some species are evergreen. The blooms make excellent cut-flower displays, although if they are left on the plant attractive seedheads will follow. These late-flowering perennials also look particularly good in containers.

Hardiness Fully hardy ✳✳✳ to half-hardy ✳.

Cultivation Agapanthus prefer fertile, moist but well-drained soil, in full sun. Mulch them in late autumn, in cold areas, with a layer of well-rotted organic matter. **Container-grown** plants are best in loam-based compost. Water them freely during summer; sparingly in winter. During summer, feed the plants with a balanced liquid fertilizer until flowering commences. *A. campanulatus* 'Albovittatus' does better under cover if winters are very cold. **Sow** seed (*see pp.391–393*) when they are ripe or in spring. Keep the seedlings in a frost-free cold frame for their first winter. Most seedlings do not come true to type. **Divide** large clumps (*see below and p.395*) in spring.

DIVIDING A ROOTSTOCK
Use a clean, sharp knife to trim off damaged root tissue and old stems. Dust the cuts with fungicide to avoid rot.

Aegopodium podagraria 'Variegatum'
↕ 30–60cm (12–24in) ↔ indefinite

① *armenum* ↕ 15–20cm (6–8in), perennial, flowers in late spring ② *grandiflorum* ♀ ↕ 20–30cm (8–12in), perennial, flowers in late spring and early summer

Agapanthus campanulatus
↕ 60–120cm (24–48in) ↔ 45cm (18in), deciduous, grey-green leaves, flowers – sometimes white – in mid- and late summer ✳✳✳

AGASTACHE

midsummer to autumn

THESE PERENNIALS ARE GROWN for their long-lasting, loose spikes of small, tubular flowers, which are up to 30cm (12in) long and borne from midsummer until autumn. These are erect, bushy plants, with lance-shaped to oval, aromatic leaves. *Agastache* 'Tutti-frutti' has strongly aromatic foliage and pinkish-red flowers and can be grown as an annual where winters are harsh, as can the rosy-flowered *A. mexicana*. Suitable for herbaceous and mixed borders, agastaches associate well with perennials such as yarrows (*see p.166*) and phloxes (*see p.306*).

Hardiness Fully hardy ✳✳✳ to half-hardy ✳.

Cultivation Grow these plants in fertile, well-drained soil in full sun. In warm areas, the less hardy species will survive winter conditions outside if they are planted in a sheltered site. In cold areas, overwinter young plants in frost-free conditions. **Sow** seed (*see pp.391–393*) in early spring. **Take** semi-ripe cuttings (*see p.394*) in late summer. **Powdery mildew** may be a problem on the leaves in dry summers; keep the soil thoroughly watered, but avoid splashing the foliage.

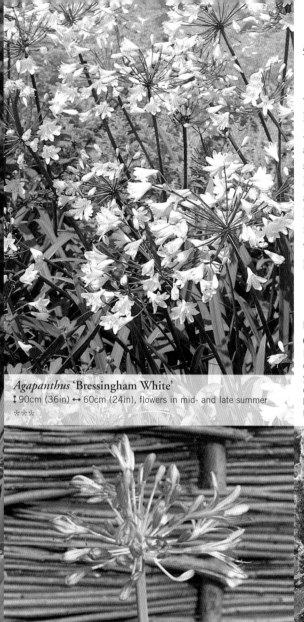

Agapanthus 'Bressingham White'
↕90cm (36in) ↔ 60cm (24in), flowers in mid- and late summer ✳✳✳

Agapanthus 'Blue Giant'
↕1.2m (4ft) ↔ 60cm (24in), flowers in mid- to late summer ✳✳✳

Agapanthus campanulatus 'Albovittatus'
↕60–120cm (24–48in) ↔ 45cm (18in), broad leaves with bold white stripes, flowers in mid- and late summer ✳✳

Agastache foeniculum (Anise hyssop)
↕90–150cm (3–5ft) ↔ 30cm (12in), flowers from midsummer to early autumn ✳✳

AGROSTEMMA

Corn cockle *summer*

‡60–90cm (2–3ft)
↔30cm (1ft)

AT ONE TIME, THE CORN COCKLE was a weed in cornfields, but these days this delightful annual is used to bring summer colour to the garden. The purple to plum-pink or white flowers are borne on slender, downy stems, and are set off by the thin, grey-green leaves. The corn cockle's delicate, lax appearance works best in a cottage garden, wildflower meadow, or annual border – or try it in containers. Growing it with other types of hardy annual allows you to create a bright tapestry of colour. The flowers are suitable for cutting and attract bees.

Hardiness Fully hardy ✳✳✳.

Cultivation Grow in poor, well-drained soil in full sun. Too fertile a soil results in leaf growth at the expense of flowers. **Sow** seed in the soil where it is to grow (*see pp.391–393*) in early spring or autumn, and thin seedlings to 23–30cm (9–12in) apart. The rather lax growth often needs staking with twiggy sticks (*see p.390*). **Remove** fading flowers to prolong flowering, or leave on to allow plants to self-seed.

AJUGA

Bugle *late spring to summer*

BUGLES MAKE EXCELLENT GROUND COVER in shade or partial shade, particularly in moist ground. They have a dense, spreading habit and can carpet large areas quickly, yet are easy to pull up if they start to grow into other plants. A few are annuals but, for the most part, those grown in gardens are evergreen or semi-evergreen perennials. The leaves of some bugles have a metallic sheen, but for added colour, choose those that are tinted bronze or purple-red, or splashed with cream and pink. From late spring until early summer, the mats of foliage are studded with short spikes of usually blue or mauve flowers. Undemanding and easy to grow, bugles are a good choice for the edge of a shady border or for growing under shrubs.

Hardiness Fully hardy ✳✳✳.

Cultivation Grow in any moist but well-drained soil in partial shade or, for good leaf colour, sun. *Ajuga reptans* and its cultivars tolerate poor soils and full shade. **Separate** rooted stems to make new plants, or take softwood cuttings in early summer (*see p.394*). In overcrowded, dry conditions, powdery mildew may spoil leaves. After flowering, remove old flower stems and excess growth to avoid it.

Ajuga reptans 'Multicolor'
‡15cm (6in) ↔ 60–90cm (24–36in), evergreen, will tolerate full shade but needs sun to bring out the lovely colours in its leaves

Agrostemma githago 'Milas'
‡60–90cm (24–36in) ↔ 30m (12in), one of several varieties grown from seed, the flowers measure up to 5cm (2in) across

Ajuga reptans 'Catlin's Giant' ♀
‡15cm (6in) ↔ 60–90cm (24–36in), the dark blue flowerheads are up to 20cm (8in) tall on this large-leaved, evergreen

Ajuga reptans 'Atropurpurea'
‡15cm (6in) ↔ 60–90cm (24–36in), the lustrous evergreen leaves look particularly effective with shade-loving primroses (*Primula*)

ALCEA

Hollyhock *summer*

AN OLD-FASHIONED, COTTAGE GARDEN FAVOURITE, hollyhocks are short-lived perennials or biennials. The tall, showy spires of flowers, up to 2.5m (8ft) tall, come in a variety of shades including shell pink, apricot, lemon, cerise, white, and purplish-black. The flowers, especially if single, are attractive to butterflies and bees. At their most impressive when grown at the back of a border or along a wall or fence, hollyhocks associate well with cottage garden favourites with soft colours and billowing outlines, such as rambling roses (*see pp.150–151*) and lilacs (*see Syringa, p.121*). Mix the brightest types with delphiniums (*see p.224*).

Hardiness Fully hardy ✳✳✳.

Cultivation Grow in reasonably fertile, well-drained soil in full sun. In exposed places, stems may require staking. **Treat** as annuals or biennials (sow one year to flower the next year) to limit the spread of hollyhock rust, the most common disease, which causes orange-brown pustules on the leaves. Rust-resistant varieties are available. **Sow** seed (*see pp.391–393*) of annuals at 13ºC (55ºF) in late winter or where it is to grow in spring. For biennials, sow in midsummer where plants are to flower and thin out or transplant small seedlings, as necessary, in autumn.

ALCHEMILLA

Lady's mantle *early summer to early autumn*

‡ 5–60cm (2–24in)
↔ 20–75cm (8–30in)

THE MOST WIDELY GROWN plant in this group of perennials, all with greyish-green leaves and frothy, luminous yellow flowers, is *Alchemilla mollis*. Drought tolerant and clump-forming, it makes excellent ground cover. The flowers appear for long periods from early summer and are good for cutting, and for drying. Most other alchemillas, such as *A. erythropoda*, are smaller. Lady's mantle self-seeds prolifically unless fading flowers are removed before they set seed. Grow it in beds and borders or along paths to soften hard lines. It associates well with shrub roses (*see pp.110–113*) and penstemons (*see p.304*), and contrasts beautifully with blue flowers.

Hardiness Fully hardy ✳✳✳ to frost-hardy ✳✳.

Cultivation Grow in any reasonably fertile soil in sun or partial shade. **Deadhead** *A. mollis* and cut back foliage after flowering for fresh leaves. **Sow** seed (*see pp.391–393*) in pots in a cold frame in spring, or divide plants (*see p.395*) in early spring or autumn.

CRYSTAL DROPS The downy leaves retain beads of sparkling dew and raindrops.

① *rosea* **Chater's Double Group** ‡ 2–2.5m (6–8ft)
↔ to 60cm (24in), vigorous, flowers in many bright or pale shades
② *rosea* **'Nigra'** ‡ to 2m (6ft) ↔ to 60cm (24in)

Alchemilla alpina (Alpine lady's mantle)
‡ 8–13cm (3–5in) ↔ to 50cm (20in), mat-forming, leaves with silvery undersides, flowers in summer, good for a rock garden ✳✳✳

Alchemilla mollis ♡
‡ 60cm (24in) ↔ 75cm (30in), velvety grey-green leaves and yellow-green flowers from early summer to early autumn ✳✳✳

ALLIUM

Ornamental onion

spring to summer

THESE DISTINCTIVE, BULBOUS perennials bear dramatic, round, or pendent clusters of bell- or star-shaped flowers in spring and summer. Some of these are up to 30cm (12in) across; some dry well for use in winter flower arrangements. Alliums range in size from small, rock-garden species to 2m (6ft) giants, but most plants are 30–90cm (1–3ft) tall. Show off their bold flowerheads in borders, among other flowering perennials, or punching through a drift of grasses. Chives (*Allium schoenoprasum*) and *A. cernuum* are good edging plants. Alliums include the edible onions, and so the strappy or cylindrical foliage has a pungent onion aroma when crushed; it often withers before the flowerheads open.

Hardiness Fully hardy ✽✽✽ to frost-hardy ✽✽.

Cultivation Grow in fertile, well-drained soil in full sun. **Plant** bulbs to two or three times their own depth in autumn. **Remove** offsets of bulbs in autumn and divide clumps (*see p.395*) in spring. **Downy mildew**, an off-white fungus, may cause leaves to wither and rot into the bulbs in damp conditions; space plants farther apart and use fungicide. Dig up and destroy bulbs attacked by onion fly maggots.

Allium cristophii ♀
‡30–60cm (12–24in) ↔ 15–19cm (6–7in), flowerheads to 20cm (8in) across in early summer, grey-green basal leaves ✽✽

Allium karataviense ♀
‡10–25cm (4–10in) ↔ 10cm (4in), broad, flat leaves, purple- or grey-green with red edges, medium flowerheads in summer ✽✽✽

Allium moly (Golden garlic)
‡15–25cm (6–10in) ↔ 5cm (2in), grey-green flat leaves, medium-sized flowerheads in summer, naturalizes rapidly into drifts ✽✽✽

DEADHEADING ALLIUMS
Seedheads may be left on for winter interest, or cut close to the ground for drying. Cutting faded flowerheads before they produce seed helps to conserve energy in the bulb for next year.

Allium 'Globemaster' ♀
‡80cm (32in) ↔ 20cm (8in), grey-green basal leaves, dramatic flowerheads to 15–20cm (6–8in) across in summer ✽✽✽

Allium cernuum (Nodding onion, Wild onion)
‡30–60cm (12–24in) ↔ 5cm (2in), vigorous, narrow dark green
leaves and stiff stems, mid- to deep pink flowers in summer ✻✻✻

Allium caeruleum ♀
‡60cm (24in) ↔ 2.5cm (1in), mid-green leaves that clasp the stem
die before small flowerheads appear in early summer ✻✻

ALSTROEMERIA

Peruvian lily   *summer*

WIDELY GROWN FOR CUT FLOWERS, these vigorous,
tuberous perennials are stalwarts of many a mixed and
herbaceous border. The flowers appear in summer,
usually in small clusters at the ends of the stems;
they are available in such a wide range of shades that
there is bound to be one to suit virtually any colour
scheme. The long, strappy leaves are mid- to grey-
green. Try growing alstroemerias combined with shrub
roses (*see pp.110–113*), sunflowers (*see Helianthus,
p.256*), and border phloxes (*see pp.306–307*).

Hardiness Hardy to -10°C (14°F) ✻✻: *Alstroemeria aurea* and
A. ligtu hybrids withstand brief periods as low as -15°C (5°F).

Cultivation Alstroemerias like moist but well-drained soil, in sun or
partial shade. **Plant** the long tubers 20cm (8in) deep in late summer
or early autumn, and handle them carefully, because they break easily.
The plants resent being disturbed, so leave them to form large clumps.
Protect them with a dry mulch of organic matter in winter (*see p.388*).
Sow seed (*see pp.391–392*) in a container in a cold frame when it is
ripe; transplant seedlings to small pots; and plant out from the pots to
avoid root disturbance. **Divide** large, established clumps (*see p.395*)
in autumn or early spring, if needed. Slugs can attack (*see p.398*);
remove and destroy plants infected by viruses (*see p.399*).

Allium flavum ♀
‡10–35cm (4–14in) ↔ 5cm (2in), glaucous leaves clasp the stems,
small heads of tiny flowers droop as they open in summer ✻✻✻

Allium unifolium ♀
‡30cm (12in) ↔ 5cm (2in), short, grey-green basal leaves that die
before small flowerheads appear in spring ✻✻

① *aurea* ‡1m (3ft) ↔ 45cm (18in) ② *ligtu* hybrids
‡50cm (20in) ↔ 75cm (20in) ③ *pelegrina* ‡↔ to 60cm (24in)
④ *psittacina* ‡1m (3ft) ↔ 45cm (18in)

ALTHAEA

midsummer to early autumn

‡1.5m (5ft)
↔45cm (18in)

THESE WOODY-BASED PERENNIALS and annuals are similar to hollyhocks (*see Alcea, p.173*), but they have smaller flowers which, unlike hollyhocks, are on stalks. The blooms appear from midsummer until early autumn in shades of lilac, deep pink, or rose-pink, sometimes with darker eyes. Althaeas have dark green leaves with lobed or toothed edges and pale undersides. The stems are strong and wiry and rarely need supporting. These are pretty plants for a mixed or herbaceous border as well as a wildflower garden. Grow them with other summer-flowering perennials, like daylilies (*see Hemerocallis, p.258*) and loosestrife (*see Lysimachia, p.283*).

Hardiness Fully hardy ✳✳✳.

Cultivation These plants tolerate a range of conditions, but do best in fertile, moist but well-drained soil. **Sow** seed of perennials in rows outdoors (*see pp.391–393*) in midsummer and transplant seedlings in early autumn; for annuals, sow seed in pots in late winter, or directly in the ground in mid-spring. **Rust**, orange-brown pustules, may afflict the leaves; pick them off and destroy them.

ALYSSUM

early summer

LOW MASSES OF BRIGHTLY COLOURFUL FLOWERS make this large group of tufted or mat-forming, evergreen perennials, and sometimes erect annuals, prized in the garden. The flowers open in early summer, in shades of pale and golden-yellow, pale to deep rose-pink, or white, and are occasionally honey-scented. The small leaves form rosettes and are coloured grey to silvery-grey, sometimes with white hairs. Alyssums are spreading, although never invasive, so can be put to many uses. Try them at the front of a border, in a rock garden, or even in soil-filled crevices in a wall. They look very effective when planted with other carpeting plants, for example *Arabis* × *arendsii* 'Rosabella' which has rose-pink flowers.

Hardiness Fully hardy ✳✳✳.

Cultivation Grow the plants in well-drained, reasonably fertile soil with added grit, in full sun. A light trim after flowering maintains a compact shape. **Sow** seed (*see pp.391–393*) in a container in autumn or spring. **Root** greenwood cuttings – new shoots that are beginning to firm up – as for soft stem-tip cuttings, in early summer (*see p.394*).

AMARANTHUS

summer to autumn

‡30cm–1.5m (1–5ft)
↔30–75cm (12–30in)

THESE ERECT OR PROSTRATE, bushy annuals or short-lived perennials have red, purple, or green stems and large, shapely leaves – some, especially in cultivars of *Amaranthus tricolor*, in bright hues of purple, maroon, bronze, gold, and red. From summer until early autumn, they produce hanging clusters up to 60cm (24in) long of crimson-purple, red, maroon, gold, rose-pink, or cream flowers that look like woolly tassels. In autumn, coloured seedheads follow. They are commonly grown as annuals in summer bedding schemes and, for truly dramatic effects, try them next to plants with large leaves or flowers of strongly contrasting colours. Some can be grown in containers and hanging baskets.

Hardiness Half-hardy ✳.

Cultivation Grow them in moist, reasonably fertile, well-drained soil, in full sun. **Keep** well watered in dry spells during summer to prolong flowering. **Sow** seed (*see pp.391–393*) in mid-spring in containers or, in milder areas, directly in the garden where plants are to grow. Thin the seedlings to 60cm (24in) apart.

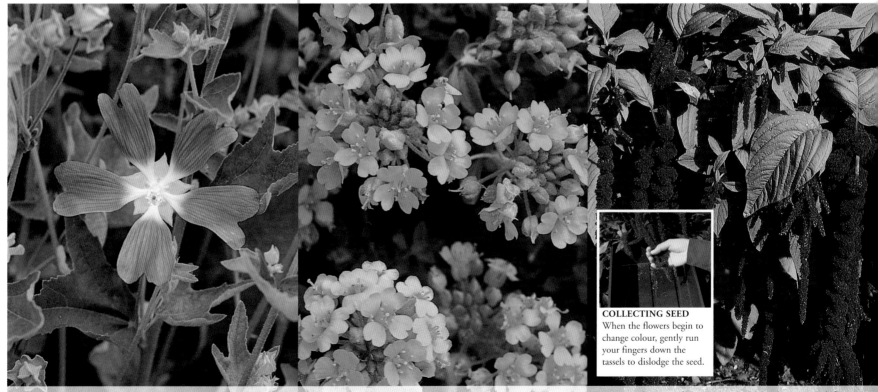

COLLECTING SEED
When the flowers begin to change colour, gently run your fingers down the tassels to dislodge the seed.

Althaea cannabina
‡2m (6ft) ↔ 60cm (24in), perennial

Alyssum wulfenianum
‡10–15cm (4–6in) ↔ to 50cm (20in), erect or prostrate evergreen

Amaranthus caudatus (Love-lies-bleeding, Tassel flower)
‡1–1.5m (3–5ft) ↔ 45–75cm (18–30in), annual or perennial, leaves up to 15cm (6in), tolerates poor soil

X AMARYGIA PARKERI

summer

‡90cm (3ft)
↔30cm (12in)

THE PARENTS OF THIS HYBRID are *Amaryllis belladonna* (*see right*) and *Brunsvigia*. Opening on bare, stout stems before the leaves appear, its large, pink or white flowers make an eye-catching addition to the summer garden. The leaves, which are up to an impressive 45cm (18in) long and grow from the base of the plant, are semi-erect and strappy. In colder areas, the plant benefits from the shelter at the foot of a warm wall, or in an herbaceous or mixed border. Grow it with other bulbous perennials, such as crinums (*see p.218*), and perennials such as achilleas (*see p.166*).

Hardiness Frost-hardy ✳✳

Cultivation Plant bulbs from early to late summer with the necks just above soil level, in full sun in sandy soil that has been enriched with well-rotted organic matter. **Water** freely during summer and feed monthly with a well-balanced fertilizer. **Remove** offsets to replant (*see p.395*) from congested plants just before they come into growth in summer. The leaves are prone to scorch. If flowers fail, eelworms and bulb flies may have eaten the bulb; dig up and discard affected plants.

AMARYLLIS BELLADONNA

autumn

STATELY, SCENTED, AND SHOWY, the clusters of flowers of this bulbous perennial open on stout stems in the autumn. It has strappy, fleshy leaves, up to 40cm (16in) long, which are produced after the flowers open. In warmer areas where frosts are rare, grow it at the base of a sunny, sheltered wall. Where winter temperatures regularly fall below –5°C (23°F), this plant is best grown in a cool greenhouse or in a conservatory. It looks attractive partnered with other autumn-flowering plants, such as coneflowers (*see Rudbeckia, p.317*), and autumn-flowering bulbs, for example autumn crocuses (*see Colchicum, p.215*).

Hardiness Frost-hardy ✳✳.

Cultivation Plant the bulbs just below soil or compost level when they are dormant, in late summer or in spring. **Outdoors**, grow them in reasonably fertile, well-drained soil in full sun and protect the foliage from frost. **Indoors**, they need a loam-based compost with additional sharp sand or grit, and full light. In the growing season, water well and feed at monthly intervals with a balanced fertilizer. **Remove** offsets (*see p.395*) in spring and grow them indoors for 1–2 seasons before planting them out. Amaryllis are prone to slug damage (*see p.398*).

Amaranthus caudatus 'Viridis'
‡1–1.5m (3–5ft) ↔ 45–75cm (18–30in), green flowers fade to cream as they age

X *Amarygia parkeri* 'Alba'

Amaryllis belladonna ♀
‡60cm (24in) ↔ 10cm (4in), each flower is up to 10cm across

ANACYCLUS

summer

‡↔ 30cm (12in)

APPEALING, DAISY FLOWERS and feathery foliage are the attractions of these creeping, low-growing annuals and herbaceous perennials. The flowers, which are usually white with yellow centres, are borne on short stems in summer, held just above a low mound of foliage; the leaves are finely cut and attractive in their own right. Anacyclus hate cold, wet conditions, and are most suited to growing in a rock garden, raised bed, or alpine trough; a top-dressing of grit over the soil will help keep their stems dry, and also enhances their sun-loving, Mediterranean look.

Hardiness Frost-hardy ❋❋, but can withstand to –5°C (23°F) if protected from winter wet.

Cultivation Grow in gritty, sharply drained soil in full sun, with shelter from the worst winter rains if possible. If growing in containers, use a mix of equal parts loam-based compost, leafmould, and sharp sand or grit. **Sow** seed in an open frame in autumn (*see pp.391–393*). **Take** softwood cuttings in spring or early summer (*see p.394*).

ANAGALLIS

Pimpernel

late spring to summer

‡to 20cm (8in)
↔ to 40cm (16in)

THE DEEP BLUE OR DEEP PINK flowers of these annuals and evergreen perennials are produced in late spring and summer, and are borne in such profusion that they almost completely hide the leaves. The flowers are open and saucer-shaped. Pimpernels are low-growing or mat-forming, with branching stems and mid-green leaves. The largest grow to only around 25cm (10in) tall, and look good in a rock garden or at the front of a border. Tiny varieties like *Anagallis tenella* 'Studland' are ideal plants for shallow pots and bowls.

Hardiness Fully hardy ❋❋❋ to frost-hardy ❋❋.

Cultivation Grow pimpernels in fertile, moist, but well-drained soil or gritty compost, in full sun. Pimpernels are short-lived so it is best to propagate them every three or four years. **Divide** in spring (*see p.395*). **Sow** seed in a container in a cold frame in spring (*see pp.391–392*). **Take** stem-tip cuttings of named varieties in spring or early summer (*see p.394*). Overwinter young plants in a frost-free greenhouse or conservatory and plant out only when any danger of frost has passed.

Anagallis monellii ♀ (Blue pimpernel)
‡10–20cm (4–8in) ↔ to 40cm (16in), perennial, red- and pink-flowered forms are available ❋❋

Anacyclus pyrethrum var. *depressus*
‡2.5–5cm (1–2in) or more ↔ 10cm (4in), perennial, leaves grey-green, solitary flowers on short, slender stems, petals red on reverse

Anagallis tenella 'Studland'
‡5–10cm (2–4in) ↔ to 40cm (16in), perennial, bright green leaves tend to be obscured by the scented flowers ❋❋❋

ANAPHALIS

Pearl everlasting — *midsummer to autumn*

THESE MEDIUM-HEIGHT, SPREADING or upright perennials have woolly, grey foliage, and clusters of papery, "everlasting" white flowers, produced from midsummer until autumn and very popular for cutting and drying. The smaller varieties suit a rock garden; grow the more upright varieties in a herbaceous or mixed border. They are ideal plants for a white-themed scheme, since the flowers and silvery foliage provide several months of colour. Pearl everlasting is also especially useful in locations that are too moist for growing other grey- or silver-leaved foliage plants that prefer better-drained soils. To dry the flowers, cut them soon after they are open and hang upside down in bunches in a light, airy place.

Hardiness Fully hardy ✳✳✳.

Cultivation Grow in reasonably fertile soil that is fairly well-drained, but does not dry out during hot spells in summer. They prefer full sun, but will tolerate partial shade. **Divide** plants in early spring (*see p.395*). **Sow** seed in a container in a cold frame in spring (*see pp.391–392*). **Take** stem-tip cuttings in early summer (*see p.394*).

ANCHUSA

Alkanet — *spring to early summer*

ALKANET FLOWERS HAVE A DEPTH OF BLUE that is not often seen in other plants. The small, but numerous flowers are produced in spring and early summer on branching stems, that are upright in taller cultivars or prostrate in the dwarf, mound-forming types, in shades of indigo, clear gentian blue, or ultramarine, some with a white centre. Bees love them. The leaves are long and thin, coarse, and often bristly. Alkanets may be annual, biennial, or perennial. The taller ones give a vivid accent to a herbaceous or mixed border. Dwarfer types, such as *Anchusa cespitosa*, bring jewel-like brilliance to a rock garden or alpine trough.

Hardiness Fully hardy ✳✳✳ to frost-hardy ✳✳.

Cultivation Grow in any moist but well-drained soil that is moderately fertile, in full sun. Most alkanets resent excessive winter wet. Dwarf types in particular must have free-draining soil, or gritty compost. **Stake** taller anchusas if necessary as they grow (*see p.390*). **Deadhead** after the first flush of flowers to encourage more later on. **Cut back** top-growth after flowering to encourage new growth that will overwinter. **Sow** seed in a container in a cold frame in spring (*pp.391–392*). **Take** basal cuttings in spring, or root cuttings in winter (*see p.394*). May suffer from mildew (*see pp.398–399*).

Anchusa capensis 'Blue Angel'
↕20cm (8in) ↔ 15cm (6in), biennial often grown as an annual, leaves bristly, flowers in summer ✳✳

① *margaritacea* ↕↔ 60cm (24in), flowers midsummer to early autumn ② *triplinervis* ♀ ↕80–90cm (32–36in) ↔ 45–60cm (18–24in), flowers in mid- and late summer

Anchusa azurea 'Loddon Royalist' ♀
↕90cm (36in) ↔ 60cm (24in), perennial, forms compact, densely flowering clumps, rarely needs staking, flowers in early summer ✳✳✳

Anchusa cespitosa
↕5–10cm (2–4in) ↔ 15–20cm (6–8in), perennial, ground-hugging, flowers in spring ✳✳✳

ANDROSACE

Rock jasmine · *late spring to late summer*

↕25cm (10in)
↔30cm (12in)

THESE PRETTY PERENNIALS make dense cushions or mats of evergreen foliage that is smothered in small pink or white flowers. The flowers are tubular and appear singly or in clusters from late spring to late summer. The cushion-forming species from high mountainous regions are ideal for an alpine house (an unheated, well-ventilated greenhouse) where they are easily protected from winter wet. The rest, however, are suitable for rock gardens, dry-stone walls, and alpine troughs, and look good with other cushion-forming plants such as saxifrages (*see pp.320–321*).

Hardiness Fully hardy ✼✼✼.

Cultivation Grow in vertical crevices in walls in moist, well-drained soil in full sun. In containers, use a loam-based compost with extra grit, and add grit at the base of planting holes to improve drainage. **Top-dress** the soil surface with grit (*see p.386*) to protect plants from wet, which causes fungal disease. **Sow** seed in a cold frame when ripe or in autumn (*see pp.391–393*). Take single rosettes as cuttings in early to midsummer; water from below to avoid wetting the rosettes.

ANEMONE

Windflower · *spring and late summer*

THIS LARGE AND VERSATILE GROUP of perennials has delightful flowers from spring to autumn, and displays a wide range of habits, sizes, and tolerance for different situations. The flowers vary from pink, blue, and violet to red and yellow. They are usually saucer- to cup-shaped with a central boss of stamens and are either solitary or in clusters. Leaves are mid- to dark green with toothed edges. Anemones are divided into three main groups: spring-flowering types, growing in woodland and pastures, some with tubers or rhizomes; tuberous Mediterranean species, flowering in spring or early summer; and larger, tall herbaceous perennials, flowering in late summer and autumn.

Hardiness Fully hardy ✼✼✼ to half-hardy ✼.

Cultivation Grow in moist, well-drained soil in sun or partial shade. Plant in autumn or spring and mulch with well-rotted organic matter (*see p.388*) for winter protection. **Sow** seed (*see pp.391–393*) in containers in a cold frame when ripe; germination may be slow and erratic. **Divide** (*see p.395*) autumn-flowering anemones in autumn or spring. Separate tubers of tuberous species in summer when they are dormant. Foliage may be disfigured by powdery mildew (*see p.398*).

Anemone × *hybrida* 'Max Vogel' (Japanese anemone)
↕1.2–1.5m (4–5ft) ↔ indefinite, prefers moist, humus-rich soil, in sun or light shade, and will flower from late summer to mid-autumn

① *carnea* subsp. *laggeri* ♀ ↕5cm (2in) ② *lanuginosa* ♀
↕to 10cm (4in) ③ *pyrenaica* ↕4–5cm (1½–2in) ④ *villosa*
var. *jacquemontii* ↕to 4cm (1½in)

Anemone pavonina
↕25cm (10in) ↔ 15cm (10in), tuberous anemone with red, pink, or purple flowers in spring; it needs sun and good drainage ✼✼✼

Anemone nemorosa ♀ (Windflower, Wood anemone)
↕8–15cm (3–6in) ↔ 30cm (12in) or more, this creeping, spring-flowering anemone is at home under hedges or deciduous trees ✼✼✼

STAKING TALL PLANTS
Tall anemones are easily blown over. Stake them early in the season, pushing the supports well into the ground and raising them as the plant grows and fills out.

Anemone vitifolia
↕1m (3ft) ↔ indefinite, the white flowers, excellent in light shade, appear in late summer and early autumn ✽✽✽ (borderline)

Anemone hupehensis 'Bressingham Glow'
↕60–90cm (24–36in) ↔ 40cm (16in), a mid- to late-summer-flowering anemone which spreads well once established ✽✽✽

Dill
summer

THE AROMATIC GREEN AND BLUE-GREEN FOLIAGE of dill is its distinctive feature, complemented in midsummer by its flattened clusters of greenish-yellow or yellow flowers. Dill is annual or biennial and has hollow, ridged stems and aniseed-scented leaves that are finely divided into thread-like leaflets. The seeds and leaves have many culinary and medicinal uses. Dill looks at its best grown with other herbs in a herb or vegetable garden, but the fine, ferny foliage also acts as a wonderful contrast to perennials with bolder leaves such as hostas *(see pp.260–261)*. The dwarf *Anethum graveolens* 'Fern Leaved' grows to only 45cm (18in) and is suitable for pots on a windowsill.

Hardiness Fully hardy ✽✽✽.

Cultivation Grow in fertile, well-drained soil in full sun with shelter from strong, cold winds. **Water** freely during dry spells in summer to prevent it running to seed. **Sow** seed *(see pp.391–393)* from spring to midsummer for a succession of fresh foliage. Young plants do not transplant well so thin seedlings to 10cm (4in) apart. If you have little space, sow a pinch of seed in a large pot and grow on the patio.

Anemone blanda 'Radar' ✿
↕↔ 15cm (6in), grows from knobbly tubers and prefers sun or partial shade and well-drained soil; it flowers in spring ✽✽✽

Anemone blanda 'White Splendour' ✿
↕↔ 15cm (6in), like 'Radar' (*see left*) in every respect, apart from its white flowers, which can be breathtaking if planted *en masse* ✽✽✽

Anethum graveolens
↕60cm (24in) or more ↔ 30cm (12in)

ANGELICA

early to late summer

‡1–2.5m (3–8ft)
↔ 1–1.2m (3–4ft)

ARCHITECTURAL ANGELICAS bring height and drama to a garden. Clump-forming perennials and biennials, their majestic stems are topped with umbrella-shaped flower clusters, followed by attractive seedheads. The flowers are lime yellow on *Angelica archangelica* and open in early summer; those of *A. gigas* appear in late summer and, like the stems, are a striking red-purple. Grow them in borders, or as specimens in a woodland setting. They also thrive in damp soil along streams or pond edges.

Hardiness Fully hardy ✳✳✳.

Cultivation Grow in deep, moist, fertile soil in full sun or partial shade. *Angelica archangelica* dies after flowering, but if the fading flowers are cut off before the seedheads form it may survive and flower for a second year. It may also self-seed freely. **Sow** seed (*see pp.391–393*) in a container in a cold frame as soon as it is ripe; do not cover with compost or grit, as it needs light to germinate. **Transplant** the seedlings while small since larger plants resent root disturbance. They will take around two years to flower from seed. Slugs and snails may be troublesome (*see p.398*).

ANOMATHECA

late spring to early summer

‡15–30cm (6–12in)
↔ 5cm (2in)

CLOSELY RELATED TO FREESIAS, this small group of perennials bears delicate flowers in shades of red, green, and pure white. These appear in late spring and early summer and are followed by brown seedheads containing scarlet seeds. Anomathecas grow from corms and, like freesias, in climates subject to winter frosts, are best grown in a container in an unheated or cool greenhouse or conservatory. In frost-free regions, plant them at the front of a sheltered border; they make splendid companions for late-flowering tulips.

Hardiness Half-hardy ✳, but will withstand occasional temperatures down to -5°C (23°F).

Cultivation Plant corms in spring 5cm (2in) deep in free-draining, sandy, reasonably fertile soil, in full sun. If growing in containers, use a loam-based compost. **Water** well and feed with a balanced fertilizer at monthly intervals during the growing season. Keep the corms completely dry while dormant. **Divide** clumps in spring, as necessary (*see p.395*). **Sow** seed (*see pp.391–393*) at 13–16°C (55–61°F) in spring, but allow up to two years for the seedlings to flower.

ANTHEMIS

late spring to late summer

AROMATIC FOLIAGE AND DAISY FLOWERS are the chief attributes of these clump-forming and mat-forming perennials. The golden-eyed, yellow or white flowers are produced in succession from late spring until late summer and are often excellent for cutting. Anthemis enjoy sunny, well-drained conditions, the smaller types such as *A. punctata* making valuable plants for the rock garden. In borders, their finely cut foliage, sometimes silver-grey, can look effective next to other filigree-leaved plants such as artemisias (*see p.25 and p.188*) and argyranthemums (*see p.24*). Alternatively, contrast anthemis with bold, sword-leaved plants such as irises (*see pp.264–267*) and yuccas (*see p.129*).

Hardiness Fully hardy ✳✳✳ to frost-hardy ✳✳.

Cultivation Grow in reasonably fertile, well-drained soil in full sun. *Anthemis sancti-johannis* and *A. tinctoria* are short-lived plants. **Cut back** hard, to the new shoots at the base, after flowering to encourage new growth and increase longevity. **Sow** seed (*see pp.391–392*) in pots in a cold frame in spring. **Divide** in spring (*see p.395*) to make new plants or take basal cuttings in spring or late summer (*see p.394*).

Angelica archangelica
‡2m (6ft) ↔ 1.2m (4ft), the leaf stalks of this aromatic herb can be candied for use in sweets and cake decoration

Anomatheca laxa ♀
‡15–30cm (6–12in) ↔ 5m (2in), each corm produces up to six flowers in early summer

Anthemis tinctoria 'E.C. Buxton'
‡45–70cm (18–28in) ↔ 60–90m (24–36in), flowers are produced in abundance all summer, if deadheaded regularly ✳✳✳

ANTHERICUM

late spring to early summer

WITH GRACEFUL, NARROW LEAVES to 40cm (16in) long, these rhizomatous perennials are ideal for naturalizing in grass. In late spring and early summer, the clumps of mid- or grey-green leaves produce delicate, lily-like, white flowers in small clusters on slender stems. The flowers are at their largest, up to 3cm (1¼in) across, in *Anthericum liliago* 'Major'. In autumn, these are followed by decorative brown seedheads. Anthericums are excellent naturalized with other wild flowers, or in a herbaceous or mixed border. They look good alongside early summer-flowering oriental poppies (*see Papaver, p.299*). The flowers are also good for cutting.

Hardiness Fully hardy ✳✳✳ to frost-hardy ✳✳.

Cultivation Grow in any fertile, well-drained soil in full sun. **Sow** seed (*see pp.391–393*) in a container in a cold frame in autumn or spring. Seedlings may take up to three years to flower. Alternatively, increase stock by dividing (*see p.395*) in spring as growth begins, although the new plants may not flower until the following year.

ANTHRISCUS

mid-spring to early summer

THE DAINTY FLOWERHEADS AND LACY FOLIAGE of *Anthriscus sylvestris*, better known as cow parsley, introduce an airy, natural charm into the garden from mid-spring until early summer. This is the most commonly grown ornamental of the various annual, biennial, and perennial types of anthriscus, although *A. cerefolium*, chervil, is an invaluable aniseed-flavoured herb. Cow parsley's tiny, white or creamy-white flowers are followed by flat seedheads. The delightful, dark-leaved *A. sylvestris* 'Ravenswing' has flowerheads with a tinge of pink. Cow parsley, usually biennial, but sometimes a short-lived perennial, is particularly at home in meadow-style plantings. In the herbaceous border, team it with spiky-flowered stachys (*see p.328*), veronicas (*p.337*), or salvias (*p.318*).

Hardiness Fully hardy ✳✳✳.

Cultivation Grow in any moist but well-drained soil, in full sun or partial shade. It self-seeds prolifically. **Sow** seed (*see pp.391–392*) in a container in a cold frame in spring or autumn. If grown well away from other cow parsleys, 'Ravenswing' produces dark-leaved seedlings.

Anthemis sancti-johannis
↕ 60–90cm (24–36in) ↔ 60m (24in), a short-lived but free-flowering plant, best supported with twiggy sticks in exposed sites ✳✳✳

Anthericum liliago (St Bernard's lily)
↕ 60–90m (24–36in) ↔ 30m (12in), this is a versatile plant for naturalistic and sophisticated schemes ✳✳✳

Anthriscus sylvestris 'Ravenswing'
↕ 1m (3ft) ↔ 30cm (12in), like all cow parsleys, this will produce self-seedlings but select only those with dark, purple-brown foliage

FLOWERING PLANTS

ANTIRRHINUM
Snapdragons   *early summer to autumn*

APPEALINGLY SHAPED FLOWERS, usually in a riot of
bright colours, make snapdragons hugely cheering.
They belong to a group of annuals and perennials
that flower from early summer until autumn. The
most popular are those grown as annuals in bedding
or cottage-garden schemes. Although technically
short-lived perennials, the best flowers are usually
obtained in their first year, so new plants should be
bought, or raised from seed, each spring. The dark
green leaves will be almost entirely hidden by the
flowers when plants are grown closely together, in
blocks or with other summer-bedding plants. There
are trailing types especially bred for hanging baskets
too. If you have a rock garden, try growing some of
the lesser-known, more delicate, shrubby snapdragons.

Hardiness Fully hardy ✳✳✳ to half-hardy ✳.

Cultivation Grow in fertile, well-drained soil in full sun. Shrubby
species require very well-drained soil and shelter from strong, cold
winds. **Remove** fading flowers to prolong flowering. **Sow** seed of
A. majus cultivars at 16–18°C (61–64°F) in early spring, and of
shrubby species in a container in autumn or spring (*see pp.391–393*).

Antirrhinum pulverulentum
↕15–20cm (6–8in) ↔ 20–30cm (8–12in), very small and creeping,
needs shelter and hates cold, wet conditions ✳✳✳ (borderline)

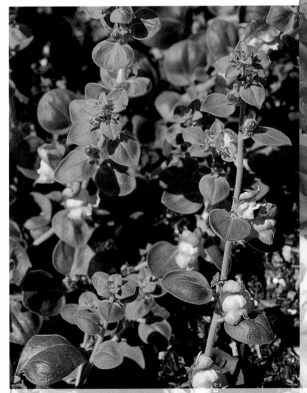

Antirrhinum hispanicum
↕20cm (8in) ↔ 45cm (18in), subshrubby, compact plant, good for
small rock gardens or an alpine trough, dislikes winter wet ✳✳✳

Antirrhinum majus **Madame Butterfly Series**
↕60–75cm (24–30in) ↔ 45cm (18in), perennial grown as annual,
good as cut flowers, long-lasting with tall stems ✳

Antirrhinum braun-blanquetii
↕↔45cm (18in), a bedding type, very densely packed flowers, ideal
for containers ✳✳✳

Aquilegia

Columbine

THE NODDING, BONNET-LIKE FLOWERS of columbines are invaluable in informal planting schemes, from a sunny cottage garden to a lightly shaded woodland area. From late spring, and in some cases until late summer, mostly bell-shaped flowers with spurred petals are borne singly or in small clusters on long stalks. Columbines are upright, vigorous perennials and the larger species, including *Aquilegia vulgaris,* are at home in dappled shade or massed in a border with upright flowering plants such as lupins (*see p.280*), delphiniums (*see p.224*) and other perennials. The alpine columbine is best grown in a rock garden in sharply drained soil.

Hardiness Fully hardy ✳✳✳.

Cultivation Grow the larger types in fertile, moist but well-drained soil in full sun or partial shade. Grow alpine species in well-drained soil in full sun and mulch (*see p.388*) with grit. **Sow** seed in a container in a cold frame as soon as it is ripe (*see pp.391–392*). Seed of alpine species may take two years to germinate. Columbines do self-seed freely if seed is allowed to ripen on the plants, so do not be hasty in cutting back stems in autumn.

Aquilegia **McKana Group**
↕75cm (30in) ↔ 60cm (24in), flowers from late spring to midsummer, vigorous but short-lived

Aquilegia fragrans
↕15–40cm (6–16in) ↔ 15–20cm (6–8in), fragrant flowers may be tinged blue in early summer, needs rich soil, tolerates light shade

Aquilegia vulgaris 'Nivea' ♥
↕90cm (36in) ↔ 45cm (18in), grey-green foliage, flowers in late spring and early summer

Aquilegia vulgaris 'Nora Barlow' ♥
↕90cm (36in) ↔ 45cm (18in), vigorous, with uncharacteristic spurless, double pompon flowers, good in a cottage garden

Aquilegia alpina (Alpine aquilegia)
↕45cm (18in) sometimes more ↔ to 30cm (12in), flowers in late spring, prefers rich soil in sun or partial shade

FLOWERING PLANTS

ARABIS

Rock cress — *late spring to early summer*

THESE SMALL, MAT-FORMING, evergreen or semi-evergreen perennials can bring colour to poor or dry sites where many other plants would not survive. Loose clusters of cross-shaped flowers are borne on slender stems during late spring and early summer. The leaves are often hairy, and on some cultivars are variegated white or yellow. Rock cress is very easy to grow and *Arabis alpina* subsp. *caucasica* is a good ground-cover option for dry soils. It is often used as a spreading plant in a rock garden, at the edge of a border, or in crevices in a wall.

Hardiness Fully hardy ✴✴✴.

Cultivation Grow rock cress in any well-drained soil in full sun. It will tolerate poor, infertile soils, even in very hot or dry conditions. **Protect** *A. blepharophylla* 'Frühlingszauber' from winter wet (*see p.372*). **Site** vigorous species, such as *A. alpina* subsp. *caucasica*, with care as they may swamp small neighbours. **Trim** with shears, after flowering, to keep plants dense and neat. **Sow** seed (*see pp.391–392*) in a container in autumn and give seedlings the protection of a cold frame. Alternatively, take softwood cuttings (*see p.394*) in summer.

Arabis procurrens 'Variegata' ♥
↕ 5–8cm (2–3in) ↔ 30–40cm (12–16in), evergreen or semi-evergreen, remove any stems with non-variegated leaves

ARCTOTIS

African daisy — *midsummer to autumn*

SILVERY LEAVES AND A SOUTH AFRICAN origin mark out these annuals and perennials as heat-loving plants. Long, sturdy stems support the daisies from midsummer until autumn. They are brightly coloured orange, white, or creamy yellow; the petals are often marked near the base with a contrasting shade. The flowers have a tendency to close on dull days or in mid-afternoon, although modern varieties have been bred to stay open longer. African daisies are often used in summer bedding displays, and are wonderful in gravel gardens or in containers. In cool climates, the perennials are often grown as annuals, or dug up and kept in frost-free conditions over winter.

Hardiness Frost-tender ❀.

Cultivation Grow in sharply drained, but preferably moist soil in full sun. **Sow** seed (*see pp.391–393*) at 16–18°C (61–64°F) in early spring or autumn. After gemination, prick seedlings out into individual 10cm (4in) pots to minimize root disturbance before planting out. **Root** stem cuttings (*see p.394*) at any time – it is the best method for propagating plants with especially fine flowers, because seed may not come true.

Arabis alpina subsp. *caucasica* 'Variegata'
↕ 15cm (6in) ↔ 50cm (20in) or more, when the fragrant flowers have finished, the cream-margined evergreen leaves attract attention

Arabis blepharophylla 'Frühlingszauber' ♥
↕ 10cm (4in) ↔ 20cm (8in), mat- or cushion-forming evergreen that may be short-lived, especially if subjected to winter wet

Arctotis fastuosa (Monarch of the veldt)
↕ 30–60cm (12–24in) ↔ 30cm (12in), treated as a half-hardy bedding plant in cool climates, with flowers 10cm (4in) across

Arctotis fastuosa 'Zulu Prince'
‡30–60cm (12–24in) ↔ 30cm (12in), silver foliage combines with brightly marked white flowers to make an eye-catching plant

ARENARIA
Sandwort *late spring to early summer*

MOST OF THE SANDWORTS are low-growing or spreading perennials; some of them are evergreen, although there are a few annual species. All have narrow, greyish-green leaves, borne on wiry stems that can form loose mats or dense cushions. From late spring until early summer, they bear a profusion of small, cup-shaped, usually white flowers. Sandworts, which come from mountainous regions, thrive in a rock garden or the crevices of dry stone walls. They are excellent, too, for planting between paving slabs to soften the hard edges and will transform a bare patio if grown in this way with other mat-forming plants such as aubrietas (*see p.195*) and arabis (*see p.186*).

Hardiness Fully hardy ❄❄❄.

Cultivation Grow in moist, but well-drained, sandy or poor soil, in full sun. *Arenaria balearica* grows well in partial shade; *A. tetraquetra* needs very well-drained soil. **Divide** plants (*see p.395*) in early spring. **Sow** seed (*see pp.391–392*) in a cold frame in autumn, or take new shoots from the base and treat as softwood cuttings (*see p.394*) in early summer.

ARGEMONE
Prickly poppy *summer to autumn*

‡1–1.5m (3–5ft)
↔ to 40cm (16in)

AS YOU MIGHT EXPECT from its common name, an argemone rather resembles a cross between a thistle and a poppy. This group of annuals and short-lived perennials form clumps of grey-green, often very spiky leaves. The main attraction, though, is their paper-thin, white, yellow, or mauve flowers that are borne from summer right through until autumn, and are followed by very spiny seedpods. Complement their colouring by planting them with other silver-leaved plants such as artemisias (*see p.25*) or mulleins (*see Verbascum, p.336*) in a hot, sunny border or gravel garden. Perennial argemones are often grown as annuals. All species self-seed freely.

Hardiness Half-hardy ❄.

Cultivation Argemones like very poor, gritty or stony soil in full sun. **Deadhead** regularly (*see p.390*) to prolong the flowering period. **Sow** seed (*see pp.391–392*) at 18°C (64°F) in early spring, and prick out seedlings into 10cm (5in) pots. **Plant out** as soon as possible after the last frost because older plants resent disturbance.

① *balearica* (Corsican sandwort) ‡1cm (½in) ↔ 30cm (12in) or more ② *montana* ♀ ‡2–5cm (1–2in) ↔ 30cm (12in), flowers only in early summer

Argemone mexicana (Devil's fig, Prickly poppy)
‡1m (3ft) ↔ 30–40cm (12–16in), the slightly scented flowers, up to 8cm (3in) across, appear in late summer and early autumn

FLOWERING PLANTS

ARMERIA

Sea pink, Thrift **late spring to summer**

THRIFTS ARE A DELIGHTFUL group of clump-forming perennials, familiar to some as seaside plants. They are loved for their small and fluffy, rounded flowerheads in late spring to summer, borne at the tips of slender stems above the rather grassy foliage. Flower colours range from white to pale and dark pink. Whether you garden inland or by the coast, these are ideal plants for growing in a rock garden or at the front of a mixed border. They also make a decorative edging plant alongside a path, and thrive between cracks in paving. Try growing them in a trough with other small rock-garden plants like haberleas (*see p.254*) and rhodiolas (*see p.316*).

Hardiness Fully hardy ✻✻✻.

Cultivation Grow in well-drained, poor to reasonably fertile soil in an open spot in full sun. **Sow** seed in a pot or tray (*see pp.391–393*) in a cold frame in spring or autumn. **Divide** plants in early spring (*see p.395*).

ARNEBIA PULCHRA

Prophet flower **summer**

THE FUZZY-HAIRY FOLIAGE of this arnebia has a certain similarity to that of the lungworts (*see Pulmonaria, p.314*), but it is the small clusters of trumpet-shaped, summer flowers for which this plant is grown. These are golden yellow, with purple-black spots at the base of the petals which fade as the petals age. *Arnebia pulchra* is a short-lived, clump-forming perennial and is easy to grow. It suits a range of sites, from rock gardens to the front of a mixed border. Try combining it with other herbaceous perennials such as evening primroses (*see Oenothera, p.294*), arenarias (*see p.187*), and armerias (*see left*).

Hardiness Fully hardy ✻✻✻.

Cultivation Grow *A. pulchra* in partial shade in moist but well-drained soil. It will tolerate full sun so long as the soil is reliably moist. **Sow** seed in a container in a cold frame as soon as it is ripe (*see pp.391–392*). **Take** root cuttings in winter or divide plants in spring (*see pp.394–395*) to increase stock.

ARTEMISIA

see also p.25

Mugwort, Sagebrush, Wormwood **year-round**

GARDENERS ARE ATTRACTED by artemisias' silvery and aromatic, ferny foliage, which is shown to advantage when set beside plants with bold or plain leaves. Most artemisias have a bushy habit, but there are some creeping or spreading forms, such as *Artemisia stelleriana* 'Boughton Silver', which make good ground-cover plants. The majority are perennial, and a few are classed as shrubs (*see p.25*). If the small and insignificant flowers spoil the overall appearance, snip these off as they appear in summer. Artemisias make splendid partners for many plants, including silver-leaved shrubs such as lavenders (*see p.80*), and plants with purple, pink, or red flowers. They also look good at the base of roses (*see pp.110–113 and 150–151*).

Hardiness Fully hardy ✻✻✻ to frost-hardy ✻✻.

Cultivation Grow in well-drained, fertile soil in full sun. Improve heavy soils before planting by digging in plenty of coarse grit. **Cut back** in spring to maintain a compact habit. **Divide** plants in spring or autumn (*see p.395*). **Sow** seed in containers in a cold frame in spring (*see pp.391–392*). **Take** greenwood or heel cuttings in summer, slightly later than softwood cuttings when the stem is a little firmer (*see p.394*).

① *maritima* 'Splendens' (Sea thrift) ‡ to 20cm (8in) ↔ to 30cm (12in) ② *pseudarmeria* ‡ to 50cm (20in) ↔ 30cm (12in)

Arnebia pulchra
‡↔ to 30cm (12in)

Artemisia schmidtiana 'Nana' ♀
‡ 8cm (3in) ↔ 30cm (12in), low, compact plant with silky, silvery foliage that is ideal for rock gardens and troughs ✻✻✻

midsummer

THE GRASSY, BLUE- OR GREY-GREEN leaves and small, starry flowers in midsummer are the main points of interest of this little-known group of evergreen and deciduous perennials. Relatives of the lily, arthropodiums grow from short rhizomes, producing leaves that are up to 25cm (10in) long. The pendulous, white, pale violet, or blue flowers are borne in loose clusters, and have a wiry delicacy. *Arthropodium candidum* and *A. milleflorum* are the two most commonly grown plants in this group, suiting sunny rock gardens or sheltered herbaceous and mixed borders, where they mix well with foliage plants such as tradescantias (*see p.331*).

Hardiness Frost-hardy ✳✳; will withstand temperatures down to -10°C (14°F) if given good drainage.

Cultivation Grow in fertile, well-drained, gritty soil in full sun. In frosty areas, grow at the base of a warm, sheltered wall, or in a cold or cool greenhouse or conservatory. **Sow** seed in containers in a cold frame in autumn or early spring (*see pp.391–392*). **Divide** plants in early spring (*see p.395*). Young plants are best overwintered in frost-free conditions. New growth is vulnerable to slugs (*see p.398*).

Artemisia pontica
↕40–80cm (16–32in) ↔ 90cm (36in), forms dense, all-year ground cover, but it can be too vigorous for small areas ✳✳✳

Artemisia 'Powis Castle' ♀
↕ 60cm (24in) ↔ 90cm (36in), this silvery artemisia forms a fine, billowing clump of foliage but may not survive severe winters ✳✳

Artemisia stelleriana 'Boughton Silver'
↕ to 15cm (6in) ↔ 30–45cm (12–36in), good for ground cover in well-drained sites, and an attractive plant for large pots ✳✳✳

Arthropodium milleflorum
↕ to 50cm (20in) ↔ to 20cm (8in), the bluish- or greyish-green foliage is spangled with flowers in midsummer

ARUM

Lords and ladies

late spring, summer, and autumn

‡15–50cm (6–20in)
↔ 15cm (6in)

WITH THEIR ARROW-SHAPED LEAVES emerging in late autumn and winter, these tuberous perennials make good foliage plants at a time of year when fresh growth is particularly welcomed. Reaching 35cm (14in) long, the leaves can be glossy green and have pale green or cream marbling. Between late spring and summer, leaf-like flowers are produced in pale green, white, or yellow. Enclosed within is a prominent spike, which bears persistent, bright orange-red berries later in the year. The best and largest leaves are produced in light shade, but a sunny, open site is needed for the plant to flower well. All parts of the plant are toxic.

Hardiness Fully hardy ✳✳✳ to half-hardy ✳.

Cultivation Grow in a sheltered site in well-drained soil enriched with organic matter. **Plant** tubers up to 15cm (6in) deep in autumn or spring. **Divide** after flowering to make new plants (*see p.395*).

ARUNCUS

Goatsbeard

early to midsummer

‡to 2m (6ft)
↔ to 1.2m (4ft)

FEATHERY PLUMES OF FLOWERS are borne above mounds of handsome, heavily veined leaves from early to midsummer. Goatsbeards belong to a small genus, related to filipendulas (*see p.244*) and spiraeas (*see p.118*), containing just a few species, all perennial. The tiny cream or white flowers that form the plumes may be either male or female, with the females subsequently producing small, green seedpods that will scatter seed freely if they are not deadheaded. Both seedheads and flowerheads are popular for indoor arrangements. In the garden, this clump-forming plant thrives in moist soil and suits being grown at the edge of a pond or in damp woodland. *Aruncus aethusifolius* is a small, very compact form.

Hardiness Fully hardy ✳✳✳.

Cultivation Grow in moist, fertile soil, in partial shade. **Plant out** in autumn or early spring. **Sow** seed in containers (*see pp.391–393*) placed in a cold frame. **Lift and divide** in spring or autumn every two or three years to make new plants and maintain vigour (*see p.395*).

ASARINA PROCUMBENS

Creeping snapdragon

early summer to autumn

‡5cm (2in) ↔ to 60cm (24in)

THE DELICATE, PALE YELLOW flowers of this trailing, evergreen perennial closely resemble those of the snapdragon (*see Antirrhinum, p.184*), giving rise to its common name. Appearing from early summer until early autumn, the flowers have deep yellow throats with light purple veining and reach 3.5cm (1½in) long. They are borne above grey-green leaves that are soft, hairy, and slightly sticky. Asarina's trailing habit makes it a favourite for growing as a ground cover over the edge of a shady wall, a raised bed, or the stony slopes of a rock garden. The plant tends to be short-lived, but does seed itself freely about the garden.

Hardiness Hardy to -10°C (14°F) ✳✳✳.

Cultivation Grow in well-drained soil enriched with well-rotted organic matter. **Plant** in partial shade for best results. **Sow** seed in early spring (*see pp.391–392*) at a temperature of 16°C (61°F).

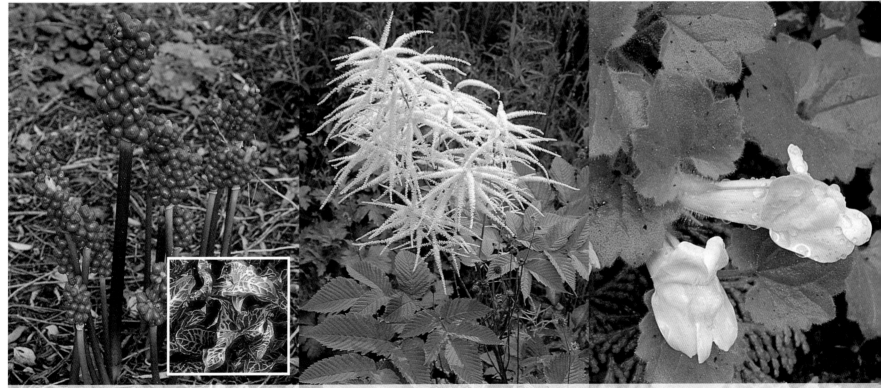

Arum italicum 'Marmoratum' ♡
‡30cm (12in) ↔ 15cm (6in), marbled leaves are striking from winter to late spring, flowers in early summer, berries last to autumn ✳✳✳

Aruncus dioicus ♡
‡2m (6ft) ↔ 1.2m (4ft), will tolerate drier conditions than other types, but much prefers a fairly damp site

Asarina procumbens

ASCLEPIAS
Silkweed, Milkweed   *midsummer to autumn*

COLOURFUL CLUSTERS OF FLOWERS are produced by this large group of perennials (and a few shrubs) in such abundance that they attract great numbers of butterflies and bees, especially the butterfly weed, *Asclepias tuberosa*. The flowers range in colour from purple-pink, deep pink, and orange-red to yellow and appear from midsummer until autumn. They are followed by fruits which split when ripe to reveal rows of seeds with long, silky hairs, hence the common name of silkweed. The leaves and tips of the stems contain a milky sap, which can irritate skin. Silkweeds like a variety of sites from sunny borders to pondsides; many are suited to wildflower plantings.

Hardiness Fully hardy ✳✳✳ to frost-tender ❀.

Cultivation Most grow well in fertile, well-drained soil in full sun, although *A. incarnata* prefers fairly moist conditions. In frost-prone areas, grow frost-tender types in a cool greenhouse or conservatory. **Sow** seed in spring in containers in a cold frame (*see pp.391–392*). **Divide** in spring to make new plants (*see p.395*) and, if necessary, keep clumps under control. Some, especially *A. hallii* and *A. syriaca*, spread quickly by underground suckers and can be invasive.

ASPHODELINE
Jacob's rod   *spring and summer*

‡1–1.5m (3–5ft)
↔30cm (12in)

STRIKING SPIRES OF YELLOW OR WHITE starry flowers emerge in spring and summer, rising above the clumps of blue-green, grassy leaves. These herbaceous biennial and perennial plants, natives of the Mediterranean, grow from swollen, fleshy roots (rhizomes), which allow them to withstand dry conditions. They thrive in dry, sunny sites such as banks and well-drained beds and borders. Good companions include many annuals, such as the corn marigold (*Xanthophthalum segetum*), eryngiums (*see p.238*), and other Mediterranean plants like rosemary (*p.114*) and phlomis (*p.306*).

Hardiness Fully hardy ✳✳✳.

Cultivation Grow in reasonably fertile, well-drained soil in full sun. **Mulch** for winter protection in very cold areas by spreading a thick layer of straw, bark chippings, or other organic matter over clumps in late autumn. **Sow** seed in a container (*see pp.391–393*) in a cold frame in spring. **Divide** plants (*see p.395*) in late summer or early autumn, taking care not to damage the roots.

ASPHODELUS
Asphodel   *late spring and early summer*

GROWN FOR THEIR SLENDER SPIKES of delicate flowers in shades of white or pink, asphodels, like their close cousins asphodelines (*see left*), are excellent plants for a dry, sunny border. Those grown in gardens are mostly perennial, but there are also some annuals. The flowers open in late spring and early summer and often have attractive, contrasting markings on the petals. The tall flower stems rise up from dense tufts of grassy foliage. Natives of warm, well-drained, sometimes quite barren places, asphodels need a sheltered site and free-draining soil in cool climates where winters tend to be wet. A beautifully bold plant for naturalistic plantings.

Hardiness Fully hardy ✳✳✳.

Cultivation Grow in well-drained soil in full sun. **Sow** seed in a container (*see pp.391–393*) in a cold frame in spring. *Asphodelus fistulosis* is generally grown as an annual and needs to be raised from seed each year. **Divide** plants (*see p.395*) in late summer or early autumn, taking care not to damage the roots.

Asclepias incarnata (Swamp milkweed)
‡1.2m (4ft) ↔ 60cm (24in), likes a moist site and grows well near streams and pools ✳✳✳

Asphodeline lutea (Yellow asphodel, King's spear)
‡1.5m (5ft) ↔ 30cm 12in), fragrant flowers in late spring, the spires of seedpods are also attractive

Asphodelus albus
‡90cm (36in) ↔ 30cm (12in), clumping perennial, flowers in mid- or late spring

ASTER

late summer to autumn

ASTERS BRING CHEER TO THE LATE-SUMMER and autumn garden with masses of daisy flowers, which give *Aster novi-belgii* types the name Michaelmas daisy. Varying in hue from sky blue to white, scarlet, pink, and lavender, all with bright golden centres, flowers are carried at the tips of the stems, either singly or in clusters. Asters are mostly perennial, but also include a few annuals, biennials, and shrubby types; they range from tiny alpines no more than 15cm (6in) tall to upright, clumps of 1.2m (4ft) or more. There are asters for most positions in a garden, since they grow naturally in both moist woodland and mountainous areas. Try smaller asters at the front of borders or in rock gardens; taller ones look best in a mixed border. Flowering times vary slightly. Some such as *A. × frikartii* and *A. thomsonii* put on a particularly long display.

Hardiness Perennials are mostly hardy ✳✳✳, shrubby types are frost-tender ✿.

Cultivation Asters grow in a variety of sites from open sun to partial shade. Plant them according to which of the three cultivation groups they fall into. **Group 1** needs moist, fertile, well-cultivated soil in sun or partial shade. **Group 2** needs open, well-drained, moderately fertile soil, and a position in full sun. **Group 3** needs moist, moderately fertile soil in partial shade. **Support** taller asters to prevent them from keeling over (*see below*); this is best done in early spring. **Cut down** old stems in autumn, making it easier to give plants a winter mulch, or if preferred leave and cut down in winter or early spring. **Divide** clumps (*see p.395*) every three to four years, both to give more plants and to maintain vigorous growth, especially for *A. novae-angliae* and *A. novi-belgii* cultivars. **Sow** seed (*see pp.391–393*) in spring or autumn in a cold frame. Grey mould (botrytis) and powdery mildew can affect plants, particularly in cultivars of *A. novi-belgii*; remove infected parts and spray with fungicide. *Aster amellus* and *A. × frikartii* types are generally trouble-free.

How to stake asters

Canes and twine *This is the most inexpensive method of staking. Space the canes evenly around the plants and among clumps and weave the twine around them, keeping it taut, to provide support. This may look unsightly at first, but both canes and twine will soon be completely hidden by the foliage and flowers. Put a cap on all canes to prevent accidental damage to your eyes. L-shaped linking stakes are a proprietary alternative, adaptable to any size of clump and easy to store.*

Peasticks *These branching, twiggy sticks are the most versatile method of staking. The garden may look a little like a forest immediately after they are put in, but they are soon hidden once the plants grow and cover them. The tops of peasticks can be bent over, providing additional support for the plants to grow through. The sticks should last for several seasons. If you cannot find peasticks, try stems from tall shrubs like buddleja (see p.29) that are pruned in early spring, just when staking is needed.*

Grow-through supports *These consist of a mesh or grid of rigid plastic across a hoop supported by four legs. The support is simply pushed into place over the plant, which grows through the mesh. Grow-through supports can gradually be raised as plants become taller. It is essential to get this type of support in place over the aster early in the season, when the plant has made about 30cm (12in) of growth. Grow-through supports are easily removed when the old stems are cut back in autumn.*

① *Aster alpinus* ♀ ‡25cm (10in) ↔ 45cm (18in), Gp 2 ② *amellus* 'King George' ♀ ‡↔ 45cm (18in), Gp 2 ③ *cordifolius* 'Silver Spray' ‡1.2m (4ft) ↔ 45cm (18in), Gp 3 ④ × *frikartii* 'Mönch' ♀ ‡70cm (28in) ↔ 35–40cm (14–16in), Gp 2 ⑤ × *frikartii* 'Wunder von Stäfa' ♀ ‡70cm (28in) ↔ 35–40cm (14–16in), Gp 2 ⑥ *lateriflorus* var. *horizontalis* ♀ ‡60cm (2ft) ↔ 30cm (1ft), Gp 3 ⑦ *novae-angliae* 'Harrington's Pink' ♀ ‡1.2m (4ft) ↔ 60cm (2ft), Gp 1 ⑧ *novi-belgii* 'Carnival'

‡60cm (2ft) ↔ 90cm (3ft), Gp 1 ⑨ *novi-belgii* 'Chequers' ‡60cm (2ft) ↔ 90cm (3ft), Gp 1 ⑩ *novi-belgii* 'Jenny' ‡30cm (1ft) ↔ 45cm (18in), Gp 1 ⑪ *novi-belgii* 'Kristina' ‡30cm (1ft) ↔ 45cm (18in), Gp 1 ⑫ *novi-belgii* 'Lady in Blue' ‡30cm (1ft) ↔ 50cm (20in), Gp 1 ⑬ *novi-belgii* 'Little Pink Lady' ‡40cm (15in) ↔ 50cm (20in), Gp 1 ⑭ *novi-belgii* 'Marie Ballard' ‡90cm (3ft) ↔ 60cm (2ft), Gp 1 ⑮ *novi-belgii* 'Patricia Ballard' ‡90cm (3ft) ↔ 60cm (2ft), Gp 1 ⑯ *novi-belgii* 'Schöne von Dietlikon' ‡to 1m (3ft) ↔ 45cm (18in), Gp 1 ⑰ *novi-belgii* 'Snowsprite' ‡25–30cm (10–12in) ↔ 45cm (18in), Gp 3 ⑱ *pilosus* var. *demotus* ♀ ‡1.2m (4ft) ↔ 45cm (18in), Gp 3 ⑲ *pilosus* 'Monte Cassino' ♀ ‡1m (3ft) ↔ 30cm (1ft), Gp 1 or 3 ⑳ *pyrenaeus* 'Lutetia' ‡60cm (2ft) ↔ to 1m (3ft), Gp 2 ㉑ *sedifolius* ‡1.2m (4ft) ↔ 60cm (2ft), Gp 2 ㉒ *thomsonii* 'Nanus' ‡45cm (18in) ↔ 25cm (10in), Gp 3 ㉓ *turbinellus* ‡1.2m (4ft) ↔ 60cm (2ft), Gp 2

FLOWERING PLANTS

ASTILBE

early to late summer

WITH THEIR PLUMES OF TINY, STARRY flowers, astilbes bring both elegance and texture to the garden. The flowerheads, in shades of white, cream, pink, and red, are produced in summer and, if left on the plant to fade, turn a rich russet brown, extending the period of interest from autumn into winter. The cut flowers also last well in water in arrangements. Handsome, mid- to dark green, divided leaves add to the attractions of these clump-forming perennials. They particularly suit damp sites close to ponds and streams, or in bog gardens, and combine well with daylilies (*see Hemerocallis, p.258*), ferns (*see pp.356–365*), and grasses (*see pp.340–355*).

Hardiness Fully hardy ✳✳✳.

Cultivation Grow in moist soil enriched with plenty of well-rotted organic matter in sun or partial shade. Astilbes will not thrive in soils that dry out in summer. **Divide** plants in late winter or early spring every three or four years to maintain vigour (*see p.395*). The flowers and young leaves can, occasionally, be damaged by late frosts. Foliage may also be marred by a greyish-white coating of powdery mildew, mainly if plants are in too dry a site.

Astilbe 'Straussenfeder' ♛
↕90cm (36in) ↔ 60cm (24in), flowers in late summer and early autumn, young foliage has a bronze tint, needs ample moisture

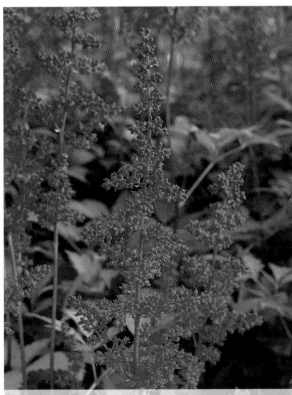

Astilbe 'Fanal' ♛
↕60cm (24in) ↔ 45cm (18in), the crimson flower plumes appear in early summer

Astilbe chinensis 'Purpurlanze'
↕1.2m (4ft) ↔ 90cm (36in), vigorous, flowers in late summer and early autumn, tolerates drier conditions than most

Astilbe 'Irrlicht'
↕↔ 50cm (18in), flowers in late spring and early summer, somewhat smaller than many astilbes

ASTRANTIA

Hattie's pincushion, Masterwort

early and midsummer

THE DELICATE AND DISTINCTIVE FLOWERHEADS that grace these clump-forming perennials are in fact composed of an outer circle of papery bracts (modified leaves) and a central cluster of pinhead-like true flowers. In early and midsummer, strong stems hold the blooms of white, pink, or red well above the foliage. *Astrantia major* 'Sunningdale Variegated' has leaves with creamy yellow margins, at their most striking early in the season. The flowers look attractive in dried flower arrangements. Astrantias make good companions for many other herbaceous perennials, including asters (*see pp.192–193*), astilbes (*see left*), and rudbeckias (*see p.317*).

Hardiness Fully hardy ✲✲✲.

Cultivation Grow in moist, fertile soil, enriched with well-rotted organic matter, in sun or partial shade. 'Sunningdale Variegated' needs full sun for the best foliage colour. **Remove** faded flowers if you do not want plants to self-seed. **Divide** plants in spring (*see p.395*) to maintain vigour and make new plants. **Sow** seed in a container in a cold frame as soon as it is ripe (*see pp.391–392*). **Powdery mildew** may spoil the leaves in dry or overcrowded sites (*see p.399*).

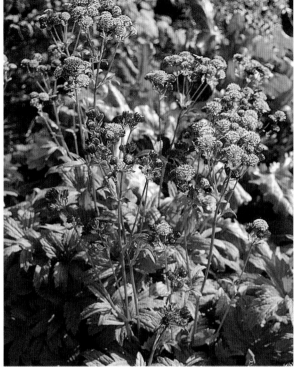

Astrantia major 'Rubra'
‡60cm (24in) ↔ 45cm (18in), will tolerate slightly drier conditions

AUBRIETA

Aubretia

spring

‡5cm (2in)
↔60cm (24in)

MATS OR LOW HUMMOCKS of pink, magenta, mauve, and purple flowers, make aubretia a mainstay of the spring rock garden and border edge. It is a useful plant, too, for growing in crevices in walls. When in bloom, the small, cross-shaped flowers, which may be single or double, obscure the evergreen foliage, although in silver- or gold-variegated aubretias such as 'Argenteovariegata' and 'Aureovariegata' this also makes a good show after the flowers have faded. This spreading perennial is most popularly combined with rock-garden plants of a similar habit, such as soapworts (*see Saponaria, p.319*) or saxifrages (*see pp.320–321*).

Hardiness Fully hardy ✲✲✲.

Cultivation Grow in reasonably fertile, well-drained soil, preferably neutral to alkaline (limy), in full sun. **Cut back** hard after flowering to maintain a compact habit and prevent the centre from becoming straggly and bare. **Sow** seed (*see pp.391–393*) in a cold frame in spring or autumn; named cultivars rarely come true to type. **Take** softwood cuttings in early summer (*see p.394*).

Astrantia 'Hadspen Blood'
‡60cm (24in) ↔ 45cm (18in), one of the darkest of all astrantias and useful for adding depth of colour to planting schemes

Astrantia major alba
‡60cm (24in) ↔ 45cm (18in), the delicate white flowers will enliven a shady corner

Aubrieta 'Joy'
‡5cm (2in) ↔ 60cm (24in), mat-forming variety with double flowers in spring

BAPTISIA

False indigo, Wild indigo — *early summer*

FALSE INDIGO IS A VIGOROUS, clump-forming perennial that sends up tall, lupin-like spires of royal blue, purple, or white, pea-like flowers in early summer, followed by large, puffy seedpods that last into the autumn months. Informal in form, it can be used to add height to a wildflower garden, but also thrives when grown among other clump-forming plants of medium height, benefiting from their support. Grow it towards the centre of a traditional border with other robust perennials such as lupins (*see p.280*), eryngiums (*p.238*) and Oriental poppies (*see Papaver, p.299*), or mix with tall grasses such as calamagrostis (*see p.344*), *Stipa gigantea* (*p.355*), and miscanthus (*p.350*) for a prairie-like effect.

Hardiness Fully hardy ✳✳✳.

Cultivation Grow in full sun in a well-drained soil. Take care to choose the right site, because the plants resent root disturbance once established. Plants grown in open or windy sites usually benefit from staking. **Sow** seed (*see pp.391–392*) in pots in a cold frame as soon as it is ripe. **Divide** (*see p.395*) in early spring, keeping the sections of rootball as intact and large as possible.

BEGONIA

summer and year-round

MOST BEGONIAS USED IN THE GARDEN produce spectacular flowers – great either in individual size or their sheer number – in whites, yellows, apricots and pinks, through to bright orange, cerise, and rich reds. There are also types grown chiefly for their heavily patterned foliage. The most familiar are the small, fibrous-rooted *Begonia semperflorens* plants, so widely used for bedding and containers. Larger types make useful dot plants for summer accents in borders and in patio containers; use trailing begonias for hanging baskets. Overwinter in frost-free conditions.

Hardiness Half-hardy ✳ to frost-tender ❀.

Cultivation Grow in fertile, well-drained soil in full sun or partial shade. In pots, use a multipurpose compost; keep well watered, and feed weekly with tomato feed. **Deadhead** to prolong the flowering period. **Cut back** semperflorens kinds in autumn; lift and pot them up if necessary; and bring them into a conservatory or cool room; place in good light and water moderately until spring. **Lift tubers** before first frosts, and store them, clean and dry, over winter; in spring, pot them up, and start into growth by watering. **Sow** seed (*see pp.391–392*) in late winter or early spring at 21°C (70°F). **Take** stem-tip cuttings (*see p.394*) in spring or summer.

Begonia 'Illumination Orange' ❦
↕ 60cm (24in) ↔ 30cm (12in), tuberous, trailing habit, huge flowers in summer ❀ (min. 10°C/50°F)

Baptisia australis ❦ (False indigo)
↕ 1.5m (5ft) ↔ 60cm (24in), erect to spreading, flowers in early summer followed by pods, at both stages good for cutting

Begonia sutherlandii ❦
↕ 45cm (18in), tuberous-rooted, trailing, small but many-flowered, tubers must be lifted and stored each winter ✳

Begonia 'Can-can'
↕ 90cm (36in) ↔ 45cm (18in), tuberous, upright habit, flowers to 18cm (7in) across in summer, ❀ (min. 10°C/50°F)

BELLIS

Daisy, Double daisy

late winter to late summer

ALTHOUGH BELLIS ARE IN FACT PERENNIALS, they are very often grown as biennials; with wallflowers (*see Erysimum, p.239*) and forget-me-nots (*see Myosotis, p.287*), they form a classic triumvirate of spring bedding. Their small, perky flowerheads, to 8cm (3in) across, in white tinged with maroon, pink, or red, are borne from late winter until late summer. These highly bred varieties of the lawn-type daisy make great cottage-garden plants, and are also good for containers. Those with tight, pompon flowerheads can also have a formal, old-fashioned charm; use them in blocks to fill beds in a potager, herb, or knot garden, before summer salads, herbs, or bedding plants go in.

Hardiness Fully hardy ✳✳✳.

Cultivation Grow in well-drained soil, in full sun or partial shade. **Deadhead** to prolong the flowering display of bedding plants, or to prevent plants grown as perennials from self-seeding. **Sow** seed (*see pp.391–393*) in containers in early spring, or outdoors in early summer where the plants are to grow – or, if raising bedding for the next year, in a nursery bed. **Divide** plants grown as perennials just after flowering (*see p.395*).

Begonia 'Apricot Delight'
↕ 60cm (24in) ↔ 45cm (18in), tuberous, upright with pendent flowers from early summer to mid-autumn ❁ (min. 10°C/50°F)

Begonia 'Crystal Brook'
↕ 15cm (6in) ↔ 1m (3ft), fibrous-rooted perennial, small and spreading, overwinter under cover in pots ❁

Begonia 'Président Carnot'
↕ 1.5–2m (5–6ft) ↔ 60cm (2ft), pink flowers in summer, good light vital for good leaf colour, cut back in spring, overwinter in pots ❁

Bellis perennis Tasso Series
↕↔ 5–20cm (2–8in), flowers to 6cm (2½in) across, raise plants in early summer or buy in late summer to flower early the next spring

BERGENIA

Elephant-eared saxifrage, Elephant's ears

spring and early summer

AS THEIR COMMON NAME so aptly describes, bergenias have large, glossy or leathery, tough leaves, and the plant spreads to make excellent ground cover. Bergenias are evergreen perennials that produce clusters of creamy-pink to purple-pink flowers on sturdy stems in spring and early summer. The rounded leaves are usually mid- to dark green but in some such as 'Ballawley', they turn bronze-red in winter. Bergenias can be grown at the front of a border, but may need cutting back if they spread too far. They are, however, particularly useful for covering dry and shady areas in the shadows of walls or shrubs and trees.

Hardiness Fully hardy ✳✳✳ to frost-hardy ✳✳.

Cultivation Grow in well-drained soil enriched with well-rotted organic matter, in full sun or partial shade. Poorer soils enhance the winter leaf colour. **Slice down** with a spade to remove growth exceeding the allotted space. **Divide** old, leggy-looking clumps every three to five years after flowering or in autumn (*see p.395*), replanting healthy sections of rhizome with roots and one or more leaves. Pick off any foliage that develops dark leaf spots (*see p.399*).

BIDENS FERULIFOLIA

midsummer to autumn

THE MOST POPULAR GARDEN BIDENS is *Bidens ferulifolia*, which has fresh, finely divided leaves and a succession of flowers from midsummer to autumn. Although perennial, it is usually treated as an annual since it grows quickly. Yellow-flowered, it has orange or orange-red forms too. Its sprawling habit makes it a good choice for growing in hanging baskets or wall pots where the stems will tumble over the edge of the container. Bidens look cheerful with other summer bedding plants that enjoy similarly warm, well-drained conditions, such as felicias (*see p.244*) and marigolds (*see Tagetes, p.329*), or sit well in a gravel garden with rock roses (*see Cistus, p.40*).

Hardiness Frost-hardy ✳✳.

Cultivation Grow in reasonably fertile, moist but well-drained soil, in full sun. If growing them in hanging baskets or other containers, water regularly during summer and feed weekly with a balanced fertilizer. **Sow** seed at 13–18°C (55–64°F) in spring (*see pp.391–393*). **Take** stem-tip cuttings after flowering in autumn (*see p.394*). **Cut back** plants in autumn and overwinter in a frost-free greenhouse, keeping the plants on the dry side until spring.

BLETILLA

spring to early summer

‡30–60cm (12–24in)
↔60cm (24in)

THESE ORCHIDS ARE NATIVE to temperate regions of China and Japan. They have delicate, bell-shaped, magenta flowers that are arranged in upright clusters, with up to 12 flowers on each cluster. The narrow, mid-green leaves that spring up from the bulbous, fleshy rootstock die back in winter. Bletillas look charming in a sheltered woodland setting with other small, spring-flowering plants, such as *Anemone blanda* (*see p.181*). They can also be grown in a raised bed, bringing their exquisite flowers nearer the eye. In frost-prone areas they need winter protection, either in situ with a thick mulch or cold frame, or potted up under cover.

Hardiness Half-hardy ✳ to frost-tender ❀.

Cultivation Grow in in partial shade, in moist but well-drained soil enriched with well-rotted organic matter, or in soil-based compost with added leafmould. **Mulch** in autumn with a layer of organic matter at least 5cm (2in) thick to protect from frost. Alternatively, lift and overwinter in a frost-free place. **Divide** in early spring (*see p.395*).

① 'Ballawley' ♈ ‡60cm (24in), winter foliage shown
② 'Silberlicht' ♈ ‡30–45cm (12–18in) ③ *stracheyi*
‡15–30cm (6–12in) ④ 'Sunningdale' ‡30–45cm (12–18in)

Bidens ferulifolia ♈
‡to 30m (12in) ↔ to 90cm (30in), slender, spreading stems

Bletilla striata
‡↔ 30–60cm (12–24in), fleshy underground storage organs known as pseudobulbs, flowers from spring to early summer ✳

BOLTONIA

late summer to autumn

‡ to 2m (6ft)
↔ 60cm (24in)

THERE ARE AROUND EIGHT SPECIES of these perennials, all of which thrive in moist, sunny sites. They have masses of daisy flowers in shades of white, lilac, or pinkish-purple with canary-yellow centres. The flowers are set off by blue-green or mid-green, sometimes finely toothed foliage. Their loose, relaxed appearance is ideal for a wild garden, or they can add a light, airy feel to a border. The flowers are also good for cutting. Boltonias are tolerant of most garden soils and will put up with partly shaded conditions. Plant alongside other tall perennial daisies, such as Michaelmas daisies (*see Aster, pp.192–193*) and rudbeckias (*p.317*). Stonecrops (*see Sedum, p.324*) are also good companions.

Hardiness Fully hardy ✳✳✳.

Cultivation Grow in any reasonably fertile, moist, well-drained soil, in full sun or partial shade. **Divide** plants in spring every two or three years to maintain their vigour (*see p.395*). **Sow** seed in containers in a cold frame in autumn (*see pp.391–392*). Can be susceptible to powdery mildew (*see pp.398–399*) in dry conditions.

BORAGO

Borage   *summer to autumn*

BORAGE GROWS WILD IN ROCKY PLACES in western and southern Europe. They are robust plants with hairy stems and leaves, and flower for long periods over summer, producing nodding heads of intensely blue, or occasionally white, starry flowers. *Borago pygmaea* is a shade-loving perennial, suitable for a rock or gravel garden, growing to about 60cm (24in) tall and wide. The annual, common borage, *B. officinalis,* needs sun and tolerates dry places. It has cucumber-flavoured leaves that are often added to fruit cups, alcoholic drinks, and salads, and the flowers make a pretty garnish. It looks attractive growing with mint, sage, and feverfew, but may be too thuggish for a small, neat herb garden; if so, it looks fine in a border. All species self-seed freely.

Hardiness Fully hardy ✳✳✳ to frost-hardy ✳✳.

Cultivation Grow in any reasonably well-drained soil, in full sun or partial shade. **Sow** seed of *B. officinalis* where you want it to grow in spring (*see pp.391–393*). **Take** cuttings of young sideshoots of *B. pygmaea* in summer (*see p.394*) and overwinter the young plants in a cold frame.

BOYKINIA

spring and summer

ORIGINATING IN MOIST WOODLAND and mountain regions, boykinias are clump-forming perennials with dark green foliage that is occasionally tinted bronze when young. The mounds of round to kidney-shaped leaves that develop around the base of the plants make good ground cover. In spring or summer, lax clusters of crimson or white, bell-shaped flowers rise above the leaves on long stalks. Boykinias thrive in cool, moist soil in partial shade. In the garden, they are best suited to a shady border or rock garden, or woodland edge. Pair them with violas (*see p.338*), or grow in clumps among other low, informal perennials that are not too vigorous and enjoy similar conditions, such as heucheras (*see p.259*) and dicentras (*p.228*). Small species also grow well in troughs and sinks.

Hardiness Fully hardy ✳✳✳.

Cultivation Grow in lime-free (acid) soil, or ericaceous compost with added grit, in partial shade. **Divide** in spring (*see p.395*). **Sow** seed in containers in a cold frame as soon as it is ripe (*see pp.391–392*).

Boltonia asteroides
‡2m (6ft) ↔ 1m (3ft), glaucous, blue-green leaves become greener with age, flowers in late summer to mid-autumn

Borago officinalis (Borage)
‡60cm (24in) ↔ 45cm (18in), freely branching annual, will flower until the first frosts, attractive to bees ✳✳✳

Boykinia jamesii
‡↔ 15cm (6in), flowering in mid- and late spring, the frilled flowers have green centres

BRACHYSCOME IBERIDIFOLIA

Swan river daisy   *summer*

THESE DROUGHT-TOLERANT PLANTS, often also called brachycome, without the "s", are grown for their cheerful, scented daisies. Borne in summer, these may be white, pinkish-purple, or blue, with bright golden-yellow or, in the Splendour Series, rather jazzy black centres. The soft foliage is green or downy-grey, often very finely divided and feathery. Grow these bushy or spreading annuals in a summer bedding scheme, or let them spill over the edges of containers such as windowboxes and large pots.

Hardiness Half-hardy ❉.

Cultivation Grow in fertile, well-drained soil and position in a sheltered spot in full sun. Use a loam-based compost if growing them in containers, watering freely during summer and feeding weekly with a balanced fertilizer. **Pinch out** the tips of young plants to encourage a bushy habit and plenty of flowers. **Sow** seed (*see pp.391–393*) at 18°C (64°F) in spring and plant out in early summer when any threat of frost has passed.

BRODIAEA

early summer

THESE PLANTS ARE PERENNIALS, growing from corms, that in early summer produce funnel-shaped flowers in shades of violet, lilac, deep purple, or pink. The flowers are carried in large, open clusters, with each flower on its own short stalk, at the top of tall stems, and are excellent for cutting. Strappy, blue-green or mid-green leaves grow from the base of the plant, often dying back before the flowers emerge. Altogether they look similar to agapanthus (*see p.171*), but smaller. Grow brodiaeas at the front of a border, or in a rock garden or raised bed, in mild areas, or in shallow pots and bowls where they need to be stored under cover over winter.

Hardiness *Frost-hardy* ❉❉.

Cultivation Grow in light, well-drained soil in full sun or partial shade. **Plant** corms 8cm (3in) deep in autumn. **Water** freely when plants are in full growth, but keep warm and dry after they die down in summer. **Protect** with a winter mulch of well-rotted organic matter (*see p.388*) in frost-prone areas, or bring container-grown plants under cover. **Sow** seed (*see pp.391–392*) at 13–16°C (55–61°F) as soon as ripe. Remove offsets (*see p.395*) when the corms are dormant.

BROWALLIA

Amethyst violet,   *summer*
Bush violet

GROWN FOR THEIR MASS of deep blue and pure white flowers, these are woody-based perennials that flower profusely in their first year, and are more often grown as annuals. Each flower is a tube opening to a flat face, up to 8cm (3in) across in some selections. They are produced during summer either singly or in small clusters where the leaves join the stems. The leaves are narrow and pointed, and feel slightly sticky. Outdoors, these plants combine well with other summer bedding plants such as heliotropes (*see p.70*), pelargoniums (*see pp.300–303*) or marigolds (*see Tagetes, p.329*). They make fine container plants, and are also popular as winter pot plants indoors.

Hardiness Frost-tender ❋.

Cultivation Grow in fertile, well-drained soil, in full sun or partial shade. Use a loam-based potting compost if growing them in containers; water freely during summer; feed with a balanced fertilizer at weekly intervals. **Sow** seed (*see pp.391–393*) at 18°C (64°F) in early spring for summer flowering or in late summer for winter-flowering pot plants. Aphids and whiteflies may be a problem under cover (*see pp.398–399*).

Brachyscome iberidifolia
↕ to 45cm (18in) ↔ 35cm (14in), the flowers are usually purplish-blue, but may be white or violet-pink

Brodiaea californica
↕ 50cm (20in) ↔ 8cm (3in), the flowers may be violet, lilac, pink or white in this species

Browallia speciosa 'White Troll'
↕ to 25cm (10in) ↔ 25cm (10in), this is half the height of *B. speciosa*

BRUNNERA MACROPHYLLA

mid- to late spring

‡45cm (18in)
↔60cm (24in)

THIS CLUMP-FORMING perennial and its cultivars have both delicate flowers and attractive foliage. In mid- and late spring, they produce clusters of small, usually bright blue flowers similar to those of forget-me-nots (*see Myosotis, p.287*). The softly hairy leaves on the stems are broadly lance-shaped, those at the base larger and more heart-shaped. Excellent for woodland areas beneath deciduous trees and shrubs, brunneras also make good ground cover in borders – especially those with patterned foliage that remain attractive once flowering is over. Grow them with other spring-flowering perennials such as leopard's bane (*see Doronicum, p.231*).

Hardiness Fully hardy ✳✳✳.

Cultivation Grow in reasonably fertile soil that is moist but well-drained, preferably in a cool site in part shade. Dig in well-rotted organic matter when planting. **Divide** established plants (*see p.395*) in spring. **Sow** seeds (*see pp.391–392*) in a container in a cold frame in early spring. Take root cuttings in winter (*see p.394*).

***Brunnera macrophylla* 'Langtrees'**
This spotted form is easy to grow, tolerating moderate variation in soil moisture and some morning sun

BUGLOSSOIDES

early summer

THESE ARE FINE, FAST-GROWING GROUND-COVER plants – they are fairly vigorous, and the tips of the spreading shoots root easily when they come into contact with the soil, extending the plant ever farther. In spring or early summer, erect stems bear clusters of flat-faced flowers. These are purple when they first open, later maturing to clear blue. There are about 15 species, including annuals, perennials, and subshrubs. The leaves are mid- to dark green, variably shaped, and generally rough or hairy. These plants are at home in a woodland or wild garden, or in a border with other spreading, spring-flowering plants such as aubrietas (*see p.195*) or with bulbs.

Hardiness Fully hardy ✳✳✳.

Cultivation Grow in a fertile, well-drained soil that is neutral to alkaline (limy). Position in full sun, but preferably with some shade around midday. **Sow** seed (*see pp.391–392*) in containers in a cold frame in autumn or spring. **Divide** perennials (*see p.395*) in early spring. **Take** stem-tip cuttings (*see p.394*) of subshrubs in summer.

***Brunnera macrophylla* 'Dawson's White'**
The wide creamy edges of the leaves help to brighten the light shade that this plant needs to thrive, but this plant needs richer soil than other forms and is slightly less easy to grow

Buglossides purpurocaerulea
‡ to 60cm (24in) ↔ variable, perennial species, with underground stems, or rhizomes, flowers in late spring and early summer

BULBOCODIUM VERNUM

Spring meadow saffron *spring*

THIS PLANT RESEMBLES THE autumn crocus (*see Colchicum, p.215*) but with flowers that appear in spring or even in late winter in mild areas. These are pinkish-purple and turn from funnel- to star-shaped as the petals open. The leaves follow soon after, but do not reach their full height, 15cm (6in), until after the flowers are finished. Although the spring meadow saffron is fully hardy, it has the reputation of being rather fussy, resenting excessive winter wet, but it should thrive in sunny rock gardens, raised beds, and well-drained borders. It also grows well in pots. Pair it with other spring-flowering bulbs such as crocuses (*see p.220*) and small daffodils (*see Narcissus, pp.288–289*).

Hardiness Fully hardy ✳✳✳, but protect from excessive winter wet.
Cultivation Plant corms 8cm (3in) deep in autumn, in full sun or partial shade, in soil enriched with well-rotted organic matter. **Sow** seed in a pot in a cold frame in autumn or spring (*see pp.391–392*). Offsets from corms can be removed in summer (*see p.395*).

BUPHTHALMUM SALICIFOLIUM

Yellow oxeye *early summer to autumn*

WITH FLOWERS LIKE CHRYSANTHEMUMS, *Buphthalmum salicifolium* is an easy-to-grow perennial suitable for most garden soils, including those on chalk. It produces masses of bright yellow daisies from early summer and into autumn, when they almost completely hide the dark green, willowy leaves. The flowers last well when cut, making them useful for indoor arrangements. The plant forms spreading clumps. Well suited to a wildflower planting, this is also a good plant for the front of an informal herbaceous border with other perennials like achilleas (*see p.166*), phloxes (*see p.306*), and monardas (*see p.286*), or try growing it among hostas (*see pp.260–261*) to brighten dappled shade.

Hardiness Fully hardy ✳✳✳.
Cultivation Grow in poor soil in full sun or partial shade; tall plants may need to be supported. **Divide** mature plants in early spring (*see p.395*). **Sow** seed in a container in a cold frame in spring (*see pp.391–392*).

CALANDRINIA

summer

THESE FLESHY-LEAVED PERENNIALS form mats of evergreen foliage topped with long-lasting displays of vivid, purple-red, pale pink, or purple flowers in summer. *Calandrinia umbellata* is most often grown; it tends to be short-lived and is usually treated as an annual or as a biennial – where the seeds are sown one year to flower the following year, just like wallflowers (*see Erysimum, p.239*). Each flower lasts for just two days, but there are always plenty to continue the display into late summer. Rock purslanes are drought-tolerant plants for the rock garden, associating well with small pinks (*see Dianthus, pp.226–227*) and other plants with grey or silvery foliage.

Hardiness Frost-hardy ✳✳; dislikes cold wet conditions.
Cultivation Grow in slightly acid (lime-free) soil that is sharply drained and in full sun. **Sow** seed at 16–18°C (61–64°F) in early spring (*see pp.391–393*), or in autumn, planting out the following spring. **Take** stem-tip cuttings in spring (*see p.394*). If growing the plant as a perennial, take cuttings regularly, as it can be short-lived. Young plants may need protection from slugs and snails (*see p.398*).

Bulbocodium vernum
↕ 4–8cm (1½–3in) ↔ 5cm (2in)

Buphthalmum salicifolium
↕ 60cm (24in) ↔ 45cm (18in)

Calandrinia umbellata (Rock purslane)
↕↔ 15–20cm (6–8in), blue or grey-green leaves, flowers to 2cm (¾in) across in summer

CALCEOLARIA

Pouch flower, Slipper flower, Slipperwort

spring and summer

THE CURIOUS FLOWERS of calceolarias always arouse interest, with their vivid colours and strange balloon or pouch shapes. They are a group of annuals and perennials that generally flower throughout spring and summer, depending on when the seeds are sown. On flowering, they form massed or loose clusters of red, orange to yellow, even rich brown blooms, which are often spotted. The bedding forms like 'Bright Bikinis' are short-lived and can be prone to frost damage, but they make striking spring and summer container plants. The hardier perennial and alpine species are ideal for a rock garden or trough.

Hardiness Fully hardy ✳✳✳ to frost-tender ❀.

Cultivation Grow in light, reasonably fertile soil in sun or partial shade. They require cool, moist conditions to flower freely. Grow alpine species like *C. arachnoidea* in moist, gritty soil and protect from winter wet. **Sow** seed of hardy and alpine species, which must be exposed to cold, in containers outdoors in a cold frame in autumn (*see pp.391–393*). Cover alpine seeds with grit rather than compost. Sow seed of 'Bright Bikinis' and other bedding types at 18°C (64°F) in late summer or spring. Do not cover these tiny seeds with compost; cover the pots instead (*see below right*) to prevent them drying out.

Calceolaria tenella
↕ 5cm (2in) ↔ to 30cm (12in), perennial, forms creeping mats of pale, evergreen foliage, flowers in summer, rock-garden plant ✳✳✳

Calceolaria arachnoidea
↕ 20–25cm (8–10in) ↔ to 15cm (6in), evergreen alpine perennial, white-hairy leaves, flowers from summer to autumn ✳✳

KEEPING SEED MOIST
Surface-sow seed of non-alpine species, then cover with clingfilm. Remove as soon as the seed germinates.

Calceolaria 'Bright Bikinis'
↕ 20–45cm (8–18in) ↔ 15–30cm (6–12in), bedding biennial with compact growth and dense flower clusters in summer, perfect for a patio pot or windowbox ✳

Calceolaria 'Walter Shrimpton'
↕ 10cm (4in) ↔ 23cm (9in), evergreen perennial, glossy, dark green, leafy rosettes, flowers in summer ✳✳✳

CALENDULA OFFICINALIS

English marigold,
Marigold, Pot marigold

summer

THIS ANNUAL CALENDULA is the one most widely
grown in gardens: they are exceptionally easy, fast-
growing plants that bear a succession of vibrant
orange, yellow, soft cream, or apricot, daisy-like
flowers from summer to autumn. The wide range
of cultivars includes many with double or "pompon"
flowers, varying from compact, dwarf plants to taller
forms. All make good cut flowers. Pot marigolds
continue flowering into winter if unchecked by frost
and, although annual, can survive into the following
year. They make excellent, robust plants for hardy
annual borders, and are equally useful in bedding
schemes or in containers. Plants self-seed prolifically
so they can be enjoyed year after year.

Hardiness Fully hardy ✽✽✽.

Cultivation **Sow** seed outdoors in spring or autumn where
plants are to grow (*see pp.391–393*), in sun or partial shade. Thin
out seedlings to 15cm (6in) apart. Autumn-sown seedlings will benefit
from cloche protection to keep off the worst of the winter weather.
Deadhead flowers regularly to prolong flowering (*see p.390*).

Calendula officinalis
‡30–75cm (12–18in) ↔ 30–45cm (12–30in), softly hairy,
aromatic leaves, flowers 10cm (4in) across

CALLA PALUSTRIS

Bog arum

midsummer

‡20–25cm (8–10in)
↔15–50cm (6–20in)

THIS EASY-TO-GROW PERENNIAL is
an excellent marginal aquatic plant
and looks particularly attractive
growing along slow-moving stream
edges. It spreads through shallow
water – no more than 25cm (10in)
deep – by means of creeping underground stems
(rhizomes) below the soil. In midsummer, large white
"hoods" appear that surround the cone-like flower
clusters, which in autumn develop into spikes of scarlet
berries. The leaves remain on the plant during mild
winters. Contact with the foliage may cause skin
allergies, so wear gloves when handling the plant.

Hardiness Fully hardy ✽✽✽.

Cultivation Grow bog arums in very moist soil at the edge of a
stream or pond. **Plant** in aquatic planting baskets using garden soil or
aquatic compost, or directly into mud in shallow water, which should
be still or slow-moving. Position the plants in full sun to encourage
more flowers. **Divide** (*see p.395*) in spring, severing the underground
stems carefully. **Sow** seed (*see pp.391–392*) in late summer in
containers submerged in shallow water.

Calendula officinalis 'Fiesta Gitana' ♀
‡30cm (12in) ↔ 30–45cm (12–18in), dwarf annual, double flowers in a variety of warm shades,
sometimes bicoloured

Calla palustris

CALOCHORTUS

Cat's ears, Fairy lantern,
Mariposa tulip

spring and summer

‡to 70m (28ft)

SHYLY NODDING, BUT EYE-CATCHING, cup-shaped flowers, produced in spring and summer, are the key attraction of these bulbous perennials. The flower colours range from shades of white to pale pink or yellow, all bearing distinctive, contrasting markings on the insides of the petals. The leaves are long and strappy and mid- to grey-green in colour. Calochortus look good in herbaceous or mixed borders with other bulbs such as late-flowering tulips (*see pp.334–335*).

Hardiness Frost-hardy ✷✷.

Cultivation Plant bulbs 10–15cm (4–6in) deep in autumn, in full sun, in free-draining soil. In areas of heavy rainfall or on heavy soils, it is better to grow them in pots and place them in a cold frame to keep dry because the bulbs may rot in winter wet. In pots, use a loam-based potting compost with added grit for good drainage. **Water** bulbs in pots freely when growing, but keep dry when the bulbs are dormant in winter. **Sow** seed in a cold frame as soon as it is ripe (*see pp.391–392*). Some species produce bulbils in the joints between stems and leaves, as lilies do (*see p.274*), and these can be grown on in late spring or early summer.

CALTHA PALUSTRIS

Kingcup,
Marsh marigold

spring to early summer

THIS MOISTURE-LOVING PERENNIAL and its cultivars display striking yellow or white flowers in spring and early summer, which are followed by architectural, heart-shaped leaves up to 15cm (6in) in diameter. The plants spread by means of underground stems (rhizomes), and prefer a moist soil at the edge of water, although they will thrive in non-aquatic garden sites provided that the soil remains reliably moist. *Caltha palustris* will tolerate being grown in water up to 23cm (9in) deep, but prefers more shallow water or a boggy soil. Grow them with other moisture-loving plants such as mimulus (*see p.286*), or with bright pink waterside primulas (*see pp.312–313*).

Hardiness Fully hardy ✷✷✷.

Cultivation Marsh marigolds prefer an open site with constantly moist soil in full sun. When planting in water, use an aquatic planting basket and top with gravel. **Divide** plants (*see p.395*) in late summer or early spring. Marsh marigolds are prone to powdery mildew (*see pp.398–399*) when conditions are hot and dry, especially when they are growing in soil rather than water.

CAMASSIA

Quamash

late spring to early summer

THESE BULBOUS PERENNIALS are grown for their tall spikes of large flowers, in sky-blue or creamy white. These are borne in late spring and early summer amid clumps of strappy, prominently veined, grey-green leaves. There are many types to choose from, but all are very similar. Grow them near the front or in the middle of a border, in a wildflower or meadow planting, or in containers. The frilly flower spikes would contrast well with the drumstick flowers of alliums such as 'Globemaster' (*see p.174*), perhaps underplanted with soft yellow cowslips (*see Primula veris, p.313*). The flowers are ideal for cutting, lasting well in indoor arrangements.

Hardiness Fully hardy ✷✷✷ to frost-hardy ✷✷.

Cultivation Plant bulbs 10cm (4in) deep in autumn, in moist but well-drained soil enriched with well-rotted organic matter, in full sun or partial shade. In heavy clay soils, fork in grit before planting to improve drainage. **Protect** with a winter mulch in cold areas (*see p.388*). **Sow** seed (*see pp.391–392*) in a container in a cold frame as soon as it is ripe, or remove bulb offsets (*see p.395*) in summer when the bulbs are dormant.

① *amabilis* ‡20–50cm (8–20in), flowers spring to early summer
② *umpquaensis* ‡20–30cm (8–12in), flowers in late spring

① *palustris* ♈ ‡10–40cm (4–16in) ↔ 45cm (18in)
② *palustris* 'Flore Pleno' ♈ ‡↔25cm (10in)

Camassia leichtlinii ♈
‡60–130cm (2–4½ft), flowers in late spring ✷✷

CAMPANULA

Bellflower   *early summer to autumn*

CAMPANULAS ARE OLD FAVOURITES in cottage gardens for their pretty tubular, bell- or star-shaped flowers. They are borne in clusters, or occasionally singly, in a range of shades from white to lavender, sky-blue, and soft lilac-pink. Campanulas form a large group of perennial, biennial, or annual plants and vary greatly in habit from spreading mats no more than 5cm (2in) tall, and clump-forming or trailing plants, to upright giants 1.5m (5ft) tall. Smaller species are best for rock gardens or raised beds. Tall campanulas can punctuate mixed borders or be naturalized in wildflower beds.

Hardiness Fully hardy ✳✳✳ to frost-tender ✲.

Cultivation To make cultivation easy, campanulas are divided into groups. **Group 1** need fertile, well-drained, slightly alkaline soil, in sun or partial shade. Taller species require staking. Cut back after flowering to encourage more flowers later. **Group 2** are rock-garden species that need well-drained soil in sun or partial shade. **Groups 3 and 4** are specialist alpine or tender plants that are not often grown in temperate gardens. **Rust**, a fungal disease that causes orange or brown patches to develop on leaves or stems, may afflict some campanulas. Remove affected foliage and thin out congested growth of affected plants. Use an appropriate fungicide if necessary.

Campanula alliariifolia (Ivory bells)
↕ 30–60cm (12–24in) ↔ 45cm (18in), clump-forming perennial, flowers from midsummer to early autumn, cultivation group 1 ✳✳✳

SOWING SEED To ensure that you sow the fine seed evenly, mix it first with some horticultural silver sand. Don't use builder's sand; it may contain chemicals that inhibit seed germination.

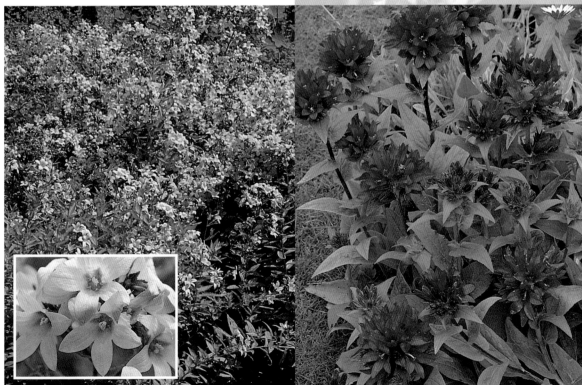

Campanula lactiflora 'Loddon Anna' ♥
↕ 1.2–1.5m (4–5ft) ↔ 60cm (24in), upright perennial, flowers from early summer to early autumn, cultivation group 1 ✳✳✳

Campanula glomerata 'Superba' ♥ (Clustered bellflower)
↕ 60cm (24in) ↔ indefinite, perennial, spreading clumps of upright stems, flowers throughout summer, cultivation group 1 ✳✳✳

Campanula persicifolia 'Telham Beauty'
↕↔ 90cm (36in), rosette-forming perennial with upright stems, flowers in early and midsummer, cultivation group 1 ✳✳✳

CANNA

Indian shot plant *midsummer to autumn*

‡ to 2.2m (7ft)
↔ to 50m (20ft)

THESE STRIKING PERENNIALS bring a touch of the exotic to any garden and height to otherwise low borders. They have dramatic foliage, with large leaves in shades of purple-brown to mid-green, sometimes with attractive veining, as well as showy, gladioli-like flowers. The flowers appear in pairs from midsummer to early autumn, in bright shades of scarlet to golden yellow. Cannas have underground stems (rhizomes) which can suffer frost damage in colder areas; lift and store the plants overwinter or grow them as annuals.

Hardiness Half-hardy ✳ to frost-tender ❅.

Cultivation Grow cannas in sheltered borders in fertile soil and full sun. In temperate areas, plant outside after all threat of frost is past, in early summer. **Water** well during summer and feed monthly with a high-potash fertilizer to encourage flowers. Deadhead regularly to prolong flowering. **Lift** the plants in autumn, cut them down, and store the rhizomes in peat-free compost in frost-free conditions. **Sow** seed (*see pp.391–393*) in spring or autumn at 21°C (70°F). **Divide** the rhizomes (*see p.395*) in early spring, making sure that each piece has a healthy bud before replanting it.

Canna 'Durban'
‡ 1.2m (4ft) ↔ 50cm (20in), bears burnt orange flowers in late summer ✳

Campanula 'G.F. Wilson'
‡ to 10cm (4in) ↔ to 20cm (8in), mound-forming perennial, flowers in mid- and late summer, cultivation group 2 ✳✳✳

Campanula carpatica 'Weisse Clips' (syn. 'White Clips')
‡ 20cm (8in) ↔ 30–60cm (12–24in), clump-forming perennial, flowers throughout summer, cultivation group 2 ✳✳✳

Canna 'Assaut'
‡ 2m (6ft) ↔ 50cm (20in), purple-brown leaves, flowers from midsummer to autumn ✳

Canna 'Rosemond Coles'
‡ 1.5m (5ft) ↔ 50cm (20in), flowers from midsummer to early autumn ✳

CARDAMINE

Bittercress *late spring to early summer*

A LARGE GROUP, the bittercresses include both dainty garden plants, mostly perennial, and invasive weeds, mostly annual. Ornamental types are grown for the four-petalled flowers that they bear in late spring and early summer. The flowers are in shades of pale purple, lilac, white, and occasionally pink. The leaves are variable, sometimes made up of smaller leaflets, and may be lance-shaped and toothed in some species, rounded or kidney-shaped in others. The small, compact types are ideal for growing in a rock garden or at the front of a border with other plants that flower in late spring, such as camassias (*see p.205*). Other, larger species suit woodland gardens.

Hardiness Fully hardy ❋❋❋.

Cultivation Grow in moist soil that has been enriched with plenty of well-rotted organic matter. Position in full sun or partial shade. **Divide** plants (*see p.395*) in spring or after flowering. **Sow** seed in containers in a cold frame in autumn or spring (*see pp.391–392*).

CARDIOCRINUM

Giant lily *summer*

THESE COVETABLE, STATELY PLANTS grow to around 4m (12ft) in ideal conditions, so need careful siting. Grow a small group as a specimen planting in woodland or in a shady border. They are bulbous perennials, related to lilies (*see Lilium, pp.274–277*). Trumpet-shaped, scented white flowers, occasionally tinged with maroon-purple or green at the base, are borne in clusters in summer. The stems are strong and stout, and the leaves glossy green and heart-shaped. The bulbs die after flowering, but leave many offsets that will flower in four or five years: the spectacular show is well worth the wait.

Hardiness Fully hardy ❋❋❋; new growth may be damaged by frost.

Cultivation Plant bulbs just below the soil surface in autumn, in a moist but well-drained, deep, fertile soil. Site in a sheltered spot in partial shade; they will not do well in hot, dry places. **Feed** with a balanced fertilizer two or three times during the growing season to encourage the development of offsets. Top-dress annually with well-rotted organic matter. **Divide** and grow on the bulb offsets (*see p.395*) or sow seed in a deep tray (*see pp.391–392*) in a cool shady place as soon as ripe; seed-raised plants may take seven years to flower.

CATANANCHE

Blue cupidone, Cupid's dart *midsummer to autumn*

GROWN FOR THEIR BRIGHT summer flowers, this is a small group of annuals and perennials. Their flowerheads, up to 5cm (2in) across, are similar to those of cornflowers (*see Centaurea, facing page*) and are good for cutting and drying. Produced from midsummer until autumn, they may be lilac-blue, yellow, or white with purple centres. Grass-like, hairy leaves grow from the base. Grow *Catananche caerulea* as an annual with other summer bedding plants like asters (*see pp.192–193*), annual rudbeckias (*see p.317*), and impatiens (*p.263*); *C. caespitosa* is a plant of high, dry meadows, and is best grown in pots and over-wintered under glass to protect it from winter wet.

Hardiness Fully hardy ❋❋❋.

Cultivation Grow in any well-drained soil: *C. caespitosa* can be short-lived, particularly if grown in heavy soil. Position in full sun. **Sow** seed (*see pp.391–393*) in a container in a cold frame in early spring or in drills outside in mid-spring. **Divide** plants grown as perennials in spring (*see p.395*). **Take** root cuttings in winter (*see p.394*) of plants grown as perennials. If powdery mildew is a problem (*see pp.398–399*), avoid wetting the leaves.

Cardamine pratensis 'Flore Pleno'
↕20cm (8in) ↔ 30cm (12in), flowers in late spring and has glossy dark green leaves; produces many plantlets at the base

Cardiocrinum giganteum
↕1.5–4m (5–12ft) ↔ 45cm (18in), has up to 20 strongly scented flowers in each cluster, on tall stout stems (*see inset*)

Catananche caerulea 'Bicolor'
↕50–90cm (20–36in) ↔ 30cm (12in), this perennial is treated as an annual or biennial because it flowers best when young

CELMISIA

New Zealand daisy
spring and summer

IDEAL FOR A ROCK GARDEN, New Zealand daisies are a large group of perennials grown for their attractive evergreen foliage and cheerful daisies. They flower freely in spring and summer, but also have long, thin, leathery leaves, which are silvery green and make them worthwhile for the rest of the year. The flowerheads are around 5cm (2in) across and and are borne on dense, whitish, woolly stems in early summer. They are white, sometimes tinged pink or purple, with yellow centres. Grow them among small shrubs such as lavenders (*see Lavandula, p.80*) and cotton lavenders (*see Santolina, p.116*).

Hardiness Fully hardy ✿✿✿.

Cultivation Grow in moist but well-drained, slightly acid (lime-free) soil, in sun or partial shade. Grow smaller types in pots of gritty compost and shelter under glass in winter. **Divide** plants (*see p.395*) in spring or take individual rosettes of leaves with roots and treat as cuttings in spring (*see p.394*). **Sow** seed (*see pp.391–392*) in a container in a cold frame as soon as it is ripe: New Zealand daisies hybridize freely in the garden, but produce few viable seeds.

CENTAUREA

Hardheads, Knapweed
summer

STRIKING, THISTLE-LIKE FLOWERHEADS, which last for many weeks over summer, are the main attraction of this group of plants, which includes annuals, biennials, and perennials. Characteristically rounded, the flowerheads may be purple, pink, blue, or yellow, and are often deeply and sometimes darkly fringed; they attract bees and butterflies. The leaves, which are not particularly attractive, are sometimes toothed, and occasionally grey-green beneath. Try centaureas in a wild planting, or among other bright herbaceous perennials such as achilleas (*see pp.166–167*), daylilies (*see Hemerocallis, p.258*), phloxes (*see p.306*), or loosestrifes (*see Lythrum, p.283*).

Hardiness Fully hardy ✿✿✿ to frost-hardy ✿✿.

Cultivation Most will tolerate some drought and can be grown in well-drained soil in full sun. Taller varieties may need support in the border. **Grow** selections of *C. macrocephala* and *C. montana* in moist but well-drained soil; they tolerate some shade. **Divide** perennials (*see p.395*) in spring or autumn. **Sow** seed in containers in a cold frame (*see pp.391–392*) in spring. Powdery mildew may be a problem (*see pp.398–399*) in dry summers; avoid wetting the leaves.

SUPPORTING PLANTS
Once plants are growing, place a ring of short canes around each and tie string securely around these. The foliage will soon hide them completely.

Centaurea 'John Coutts'
↕ 60cm (24in) ↔ 45cm (18in), clump-forming perennial, flowers are long-lasting and fragrant in summer ✿✿✿

Celmisia spectabilis
↕↔ to 30cm (12in), tufted, clump-forming New Zealand daisy that flowers in early summer

Centaurea dealbata 'Steenbergii'
↕↔ 60cm (24in), easy-to-grow, clump-forming perennial, needs support, flowers in midsummer, excellent for cutting ✿✿✿

Centaurea cyanus (Cornflower)
↕ 20–80cm (8–32in) ↔ 15cm (6in) upright annual, flowers from late spring to midsummer, white and pink forms exist ✿✿✿

CERASTIUM

late spring to summer

MAINLY CARPET-FORMING, this is a large group of annuals and vigorous perennials; a few are grown in gardens, while many others are regarded as invasive weeds. They produce masses of small, starry flowers, singly or in clusters, and have usually simple and hairy leaves. The species grown in gardens, of which the best-known is *Cerastium tomentosum*, make excellent ground-cover plants. They will spread to cover a large area and can become invasive, but are fairly easily to control by simply chopping down with a spade around the edges and uprooting the surplus. These should not be grown among other small plants, however, which they tend to grow into and smother; they are best used to cover an area such as a dry bank where little else will grow.

Hardiness Fully hardy ✳✳✳.

Cultivation Grow these plants in any well-drained soil, in full sun; *C. tomentosum* tolerates even poor soils. **Divide** established plants (*see p.395*) in early spring. **Sow** seed in a container in a cold frame in autumn (*see pp.391–392*). **Take** stem-tip cuttings (*see p.394*) in early summer.

CERINTHE

Honeywort,
Wax flower

late spring to summer

EXOTIC-LOOKING BUT EASY-TO-GROW, these flower from late spring until summer and attract bees. At the tips of the stems, petal-like bracts (modified leaves) that are often sea-blue are packed around small clusters of tubular, nodding flowers, which may be rich purple-blue, dark red, yellow, or white, often combining two colours. The leaves are fleshy and blue-green, and there is often white mottling on the foliage and stems. This small group includes annuals, biennials, and short-lived perennials, but all are usually grown as annuals. Use them in borders or with other summer bedding plants such as China asters (*see pp.192–193*), begonias (*see pp.196–197*), impatiens (*see p.263*), and marigolds (*Tagetes, see p.329*).

Hardiness Frost-tender ✿.

Cultivation Grow in any well-drained soil, in full sun. Provide a winter mulch or some other winter protection if grown as perennials; they can also be taken indoors as pot plants. **Sow** seed (*see pp.391–392*) in spring at 20–30°C (65–86°F), and plant out the young plants in early summer when any threat of frost has passed.

Cerinthe 'Golden Bouquet'
↕ 35cm (14in) ↔ 40cm (16in), spotted leaves, evergreen in frost-free gardens, flowers midsummer to first frosts

Cerastium tomentosum (Snow-in-summer)
↕ 5–8cm (2–3in) ↔ indefinite, rampant perennial, usually smothered with flowers during late spring and summer

Cerinthe major 'Purpurascens'
↕ to 60cm (24in) ↔ 45cm (18in), bracts change from blue-green to purple and then deep blue, from spring to early summer; *C. major* itself has yellow flowers marked with purple

CHAMAEMELUM

Chamomile   *summer*

THESE AROMATIC, MAT-FORMING, hairy perennials and annuals have feathery or thread-like, fresh green leaves and bear daisy-like white flowerheads with yellow centres in summer. The lawn or Roman chamomile, *Chamaemelum nobile,* is the best known and is attractive in a herb border, as edging or for growing in crevices in paving. The scent from the foliage, which is reminiscent of apples, is released when it is crushed. The non-flowering form 'Treneague' is often used for making a scented lawn; although it does not need mowing, it is not hard-wearing, and so is not suitable for areas that are frequently walked over.

Hardiness Fully hardy ✳✳✳.

Cultivation Grow in well-drained soil, in full sun, in an open site. **Cut back** plants regularly to maintain a compact habit. **Sow** seed where it is to grow (*see p.393*), or divide plants in spring (*see p.395*). 'Treneague' is always grown from divisions. **Plant** divided sections 13–15cm (5–6in) apart to make a lawn, and weed and water regularly until established. Roll lawns occasionally to help keep them level.

CHELONE

Turtlehead   *late summer to autumn*

‡ to 1.2m (4ft)
↔ to 60cm (24in)

THE CURIOUSLY SHAPED, white, purple, or pink flowers of these perennials give them the common name of turtlehead. These showy flowers are carried in short clusters at the tops of the stems from late summer until mid-autumn, and are valuable when many other plants are past their best. Although they are upright in habit, they spread by underground runners so need a bit of space to grow; a clump of them makes good ground cover and suppresses weeds. The flowers stand up well to autumn weather, and make a vivid colour contrast to other late-flowering perennials such as coreopsis (*see p.217*), crocosmias (*see p.219*), and rudbeckias (*see p.317*).

Hardiness Fully hardy ✳✳✳.

Cultivation Grow in deep, fertile, moist soil; turtleheads will grow in a bog garden and tolerate heavy clay soils. Position in an open site or in partial shade. **Mulch** with well-rotted organic matter (*see p.388*) in mid-spring. **Sow** seed (*see pp.391–392*) in containers in a cold frame in early spring. **Take** soft-tip cuttings (*see p.394*) in late spring or early summer.

CHIONODOXA

Glory of the snow   *early spring*

‡ 10–20cm (4–8in)
↔ 3cm (1¼in)

IN EARLY SPRING, these easy, bulbous perennials produce starry, clear blue or pink flowers with white eyes. The glossy green leaves usually curve outwards, showing off the flowers.
This is a small group of plants, related to the later-flowering scillas (*see p.323*). Grow them in a rock garden or raised bed, or naturalized in grass, where they will self-seed freely. Like cyclamens (*see p.221*), they make a pool of colour if planted around the base of deciduous shrubs, so can be useful in drawing the eye to an interesting winter silhouette such as that of *Corylus avellana* 'Contorta' (*see p.44*).

Hardiness Fully hardy ✳✳✳.

Cultivation Grow in any well-drained soil in full sun; only *C. nana* needs protection from winter wet, all others are undemanding plants. **Plant** bulbs 8cm (3in) deep in autumn. **Sow** seed (*see pp.391–392*) in containers in a cold frame as soon as it is ripe, or remove offsets from bulbs (*see p.395*) in summer; either of these methods should produce bulbs of flowering size after about three years.

Chamaemelum nobile 'Flore Pleno'
‡ 15cm (6in) ↔ 45cm (18in), double flowers, shorter than the single-flowered form, ideal for edging

Chelone obliqua
‡ 40–60cm (16–24in) ↔ 30cm (12in), has spikes of dark pink or purple flowers up to 2cm (¾in) long

① *luciliae* ♀ the species names are sometimes confused on labels, so it may be best to buy it in flower ② '**Pink Giant**' is named for the size of its flowers, rather than its height

CHRYSANTHEMUM

late summer to autumn

POPULAR FOR THEIR BRIGHT, SHOWY FLOWERS, these upright, bushy annuals and herbaceous perennials are the stars of late summer and autumn. They are grown primarily for border displays, for cutting, and for exhibition (specialist mail-order suppliers offer hundreds of cultivars suitable for showing). Chrysanthemums come in a range of glowing colours from ivory to pink, crimson, and gold, with blooms that vary vastly in shape, size, and form. Petals may, for instance, be reflexed, incurved, or spoon-shaped. There are ten chrysanthemum flowerhead categories all together. Some, especially the huge exhibition varieties, can be demanding since rain may damage the flowers and many are not hardy. Those classed as Rubellum Group chrysanthemums, such as 'Clara Curtis', are among the easiest to grow and are ideal for beds and borders, as are the many hardy pompon and spray types, which include the 'Pennine' cultivars. Annual *Chrysanthemum* (syn. *Xanthophthalum*) *segetum* (corn marigold) and *X. carinatum* put on a long, colourful display.

Hardiness Fully hardy ✳✳✳ to frost tender ❁.

Cultivation Check the plant label or supplier's catalogue for growing requirements and hardiness when buying. **Plant** from late spring in a sheltered site in full sun, in fertile, moist, but well-drained soil. **Support** tall varieties with canes and tie in regularly. Pinch out (*see below*) to improve plant shape and flowering. **Water** freely during dry spells and feed with a balanced fertilizer every 7–10 days from midsummer until the buds begin to show some colour. **Lift** non-hardy types after the first frost and store in a frost-free place for winter. Hardy chrysanthemums can remain in the ground.

Pinch pruning chrysanthemums

Pinch pruning a plant – taking out the growing tip or tips – encourages it to produce plenty of sideshoots from the buds in the leaf axils (where leaf stalk joins stem) lower down the stem. This results not only in a bushier, more attractive shape, but also in extra flowers on plants such as chrysanthemums and fuchsias. The more frequently a plant is pinch pruned, the greater the number of sideshoots and flowers it will produce. This is a technique much used by show exhibitors, but it can also be worthwhile in the garden, especially in containers, where you may want to maintain a more compact style of growth. For the greatest success, plants need to be growing strongly, so if necessary feed them with a balanced fertilizer.

Next generation of shoots have all their tips taken out

Stems branch after pinch pinching

Shoot tip only is removed

❶ *When the plant is 15–20cm (6–8in) high, pinch out the tip of the shoot just above a leaf joint, using your finger and thumb. Remove only the small tip to encourage the maximum number of flower-bearing sideshoots (known as breaks).*

❷ *Side buds grow and develop into shoots. When these shoots have developed four leaves, repeat the pinching (called the second stop). Pinch pruning stimulates shoots from the tip and lower down the stem, creating a much bushier plant.*

❸ *Keep pinching out the tips of the shoots until the plant is furnished with plenty of bushy growth. Stop pinching in early autumn to let flowering shoots develop. Here, several plants have been pinch pruned into a spectacular, colourful display.*

① *Chrysanthemum* 'Alison Kirk' ↕ 1.2m (4ft) ↔ 40cm (16in) ❁ ② 'Autumn Days' ↕ 1.2m (4ft) ↔ 75cm (30in) ❁ ③ 'Brietner's Supreme' ↕ 1.2m (4ft) ↔ 75cm (30in) ✳✳ ④ 'Bronze Fairie' ♀ ↕↔ 60cm (30in) ✳✳✳ ⑤ 'Bronze Hedgerow' ↕ 1.5m (5ft) ↔ 75–100cm (30–39in) ❁ ⑥ 'Bronze Yvonne Arnaud' ↕ 1.2m (4ft) ↔ 60–75cm (24–30in) ✳✳ ⑦ 'Buff Margaret' ↕ 1.2m (4ft) ↔ 60–75cm (24–30in) ✳✳✳ ⑧ *carinatum* (syn. *Xanthophthalum carinatum*) 'Court Jesters' ↕ 60cm (2ft)

↔ 30cm (1ft), annual ✷ ⑨ 'Clara Curtis' ‡75cm (30in) ↔ 60cm (2ft), Rubellum Group ✷✷✷
⑩ 'George Griffiths' ♀ ‡1.5m (5ft) ↔ 1m (3ft), ✷✷ ⑪ 'Madeleine' ♀ ‡1.2m (4ft) ↔ 75cm (30in)
✷✷✷ ⑫ 'Maria' ‡45cm (18in) ↔ 30–60cm (12–24in) ✷✷✷ ⑬ 'Marion' ‡1.2m (4ft) ↔ 75cm (30in)
✷✷✷ ⑭ 'Marlene Jones' ‡1m (3ft) ↔ 60cm (24in) ✷✷ ⑮ 'Pavilion' ‡1.3m (4½ft) ↔ 60–75cm
(24–30in) ✷ ⑯ 'Pennine Alfie' ♀ ‡1.2m (4ft) ↔ 75cm (30in) ✷✷✷ ⑰ 'Pennine Flute' ♀ ‡1.2m

(4ft) ↔ 75cm (30in) ✷✷✷ ⑱ 'Pennine Oriel' ♀ ‡1.2m (4ft) ↔ 60–75cm (24–30in) ✷✷✷
⑲ 'Purple Pennine Wine' ♀ ‡1.2m (4ft) ↔ 75cm (30in) ✷✷✷ ⑳ 'Roy Coopland' ♀ ‡1.4m
(4½ft) ↔ 60cm (24in) ❀ ㉑ 'Salmon Fairie' ♀ ‡30–60cm (12–24in) ↔ 60cm (24in) ✷✷✷
㉒ 'Satin Pink Gin' ♀ ‡1.2m (4ft) ↔ 75–100cm (30–39in), ❀ ㉓ 'Wendy' ♀ ‡1.2m (4ft)
↔ 60–75cm (24–30in) ✷✷✷ ㉔ 'Yvonne Arnaud' ♀ ‡1.2m (4ft) ↔ 60–75cm (24–30in) ✷✷

CIRSIUM

Plumed thistle,
Creeping thistle

summer to autumn

THE OPULENT, JEWEL-LIKE SHADES sported by the flowers of the cirsium deserve a place in every garden. The hues range from deep crimson-purple to rich reds, yellows, and sometimes white. The flowers, up to 3cm (1¼in) across, are carried singly or in small clusters over dark green, prickly leaves in summer and autumn. Cirsiums belong to a large group of perennials and biennials; some form clumps, others spread by means of underground stems (rhizomes) and can be invasive. Cirsiums look dramatic grown among fine grasses (*see pp.340–355*) or with other summer-flowering perennials such as coreopsis (*see p.217*), phloxes (*see p.306*), and cranesbills (*see Geranium, pp.250–251*). They also blend in well in naturalistic borders or wildflower gardens.

Hardiness Fully hardy ✽✽✽.

Cultivation Cirsiums need moist but well-drained soil, in full sun. **Deadhead** to avoid self-seeding if growing cirsiums in a formal garden. **Sow** seed (*see pp.391–393*) in a cold frame in spring or divide plants (*see p.395*) in autumn or spring.

CLARKIA

Godetia

summer

THESE HARDY ANNUALS are widely grown for their satiny, paper-thin flowers borne in abundance over many weeks in summer. There are many species and an ever-increasing number of cultivars, offering both single or double flowers. These come in soft pastel hues and brighter shades of red, purple, and salmon-pink. Easy-to-grow, the bushy plants have a maximum height of 50cm (20in) and spread of 30cm (12in), and have green to grey-green leaves. Clarkias make ideal cut flowers. They look good in annual borders with other annuals like corn cockles (*see Agrostemma, p.172*), California poppies (*see Eschscholtzia, p.241*), and pot marigolds (*see Calendula officinalis, p.204*).

Hardiness Fully hardy ✽✽✽.

Cultivation Well-drained, slightly acid and moderately fertile soil, in sun or partial shade, suits clarkias. They dislike hot, humid spots. Avoid fertilizing all but poor soils before sowing to avoid leaf growth at the expense of flowers. **Sow** seed (*see pp.391–393*) in autumn or spring in shallow drills where they are to grow; clarkias do not like being transplanted. **Thin** seedlings to 15cm (6in) apart. Protect autumn-sown seedlings with a cloche over winter.

CLEMATIS

see also pp.136–139

Old man's beard,
Virgin's bower

summer to late autumn

THERE ARE A FEW CLEMATIS that are herbaceous perennials, forming open, sometimes woody-based plants smothered in delicate, often scented flowers. These appear in summer to late autumn. All the herbaceous clematis have very attractive, dark, mid- or grey-green leaves that vary in shape. Their soft stems require some support to stop them flopping over with the weight of the flowers. Plant these clematis in large containers or towards the centres of herbaceous or mixed borders among other summer-flowering perennials such as achilleas (*see p.166*) and cranesbills (*see Geranium, pp.250–251*).

Hardiness Fully hardy ✽✽✽ to frost-hardy ✽✽.

Cultivation These clematis require full sun in fertile soil that has been enriched with well-rotted organic matter. **Prune** (*see pp.382–383*) the previous year's growth back to two or three buds, about 15–20cm (6–8in) from the base of the plant, before new growth starts in early spring. **Support** the stems with twiggy peasticks. **Mulch** with a layer of garden compost or well-rotted manure in late winter. **Divide** in spring (*see p.395*) or take semi-ripe cuttings (*see p.394*) in summer.

Cirsium rivulare 'Atropurpureum'
↕1.2m (4ft) ↔ 60cm (24in), clump-forming perennial, flowers in early and midsummer

Clarkia 'Sundowner'
↕75cm (30in) ↔ 45cm (18in), good for cutting, grow in full sun

Clematis integrifolia
↕↔ 60cm (24in), flowers in summer, followed by silvery brown, silky seedheads ✽✽✽

Clematis tubulosa (syn. *C. heracleifolia*) 'Wyevale' ♀
‡75cm (30in) ↔ 1m (3ft), open bush, scented, light to mid-blue
flowers that are 4cm (1¼ in) long in summer ✿✿✿

CLEOME
Spider flower

early summer to early autumn

THE CURIOUSLY SPIKY FLOWERS and sharply spined
stems of the flowers reveal how this plant gained its
common name. Of the many species, only the bushy
annuals are widely grown. These produce upright
stems to 1.5m (5ft) tall, with hairy leaves. They bear
dense clusters of white, pink, red, or violet-purple,
scented flowers from early summer to early autumn.
Cleomes make good gap-fillers in beds and borders
where they are useful for extending colour into late
summer and autumn. Alternatively, grow in large
containers or with other annuals such as clarkias
(*see facing page*) and rudbeckias (*see p.317*). The
long stems of cleomes make them ideal for cutting.

Hardiness Frost-tender ✲.

Cultivation Grow cleomes in full sun, in light, fertile, free-draining –
preferably sandy – soil. **Water** freely in dry weather. In containers, use
a loam-based compost; water the plants regularly; and feed them
with a balanced fertilizer at weekly intervals. **Deadhead** fading flowers
regularly to prolong flowering. **Sow** seed at 18°C (64°F) in spring (*see
pp.391–393*); harden off and plant out seedlings after the last frosts.

COLCHICUM
Autumn crocus, Naked ~~~~

AUTUMN CROCUSES ARE A LATE-SEASO~~
their flowers emerging seemingly from now~~
in autumn before the leaves appear. A few appea~~
spring. The flowers are sometimes fragrant and come~~
in delicate shades of lilac-pink or white. The strappy
leaves of these bulbous perennials last from winter to
spring. Sizes vary from large cultivars such as 'The
Giant' which has a height of 20cm (8in) and spread
of 10cm (4in) to the tiny *Colchicum kesselringii*
which, with a height and spread of 2.5cm (1in), is
best grown as an alpine. Large-leaved colchicums such
as 'Autumn Queen' sprawl untidily after the wind or
rain and should be grown in the shelter of deciduous
shrubs. Naturalize others such as *C. speciosum* and
C. autumnale in grass. All are highly toxic.

Hardiness Fully hardy ✿✿✿ to half-hardy ✿✿.

Cultivation Plant the corms 10cm (4in) deep, in deep, fertile, well-
drained, moisture-retentive soil, in summer or early autumn. Choose
an open, sunny site. Small alpine species need gritty, sharply draining
soil. **Feed** with a low-nitrogen fertilizer before growth starts. **Divide** large
clumps (*see p.395*) in summer.

Clematis recta
‡1–2m (3–6ft) ↔ 75cm (30in), clump-forming, heavily scented
flowers from midsummer to autumn, decorative seedheads ✿✿✿

Cleome hassleriana 'Colour Fountain'
‡1.2m (4ft) ↔ 45cm (18in), hairy annual, with scented flowers in
violet-pink, rose-red, or white to 10cm (4in) across in summer

① *autumnale* 'Album' ‡10–15cm (4–6in) ✿✿✿
② *byzantinum* ♀ ‡13cm (5in) ✿✿✿ ③ *speciosum* 'Album'
♀ ‡18cm (7in) ✿✿✿ ④ 'Waterlily' ♀ ‡13cm (5in) ✿✿✿

summer |

...NIUMS, these ...produce daintier ...r spikes over a ...during summer. ...n shades of blue, lilac-...e. They are good for ...onger-stemmed types, and ...age is feathery and downy, usua... ...- to dark green in colour. They are ... s for growing with other hardy annuals, such a... ...golds (*see Calendula officinalis, p.204*), coneflowers (*see Rudbeckia, p.317*), and clarkias (*see p.214*). Larkspurs make charming additions to a cottage garden or annual border.

Hardiness Fully hardy ✽✽✽.

Cultivation Larkspurs grow best in full sun and with their roots in light, fertile, well-drained soil. **Support** may be necessary with canes or twiggy peasticks. Pay attention to watering in dry weather, because the soil must not dry out. **Remove** fading flowers to prolong flowering. **Sow** seed (*see pp.391–393*) directly in the garden in spring or autumn, when seedlings benefit from cloche protection over winter.

CONVALLARIA MAJALIS

Lily-of-the-valley

late spring to early summer |

FAMED FOR THEIR STRONG FRAGRANCE, the dainty white flowers of this small, creeping perennial are borne on arching stems in late spring to early summer. Lily-of-the-valley has mid- to dark green leaves, and makes an excellent ground cover in a woodland garden or moist, shady border. It spreads by means of underground stems (rhizomes) and rapidly forms new colonies in favourable conditions. To show off these plants at their best, grow them under deciduous shrubs so that their bell-shaped flowers stand out against a background of newly opening spring leaves. Forms with pink flowers or variegated leaves are available.

Hardiness Fully hardy ✽✽✽.

Cultivation A shady position in moist, fertile soil that has been enriched with well-rotted organic matter is best for lily-of-the-valley. **Lift** some of the rhizomes and pot them up in autumn for a display of fragrant flowers indoors. Replant them outdoors after flowering in the spring. **Sow** seed (*see pp.391–393*) in containers in a cold frame as soon as it is ripe.

CONVOLVULUS

Bindweed

summer to autumn |

DO NOT CONFUSE these annuals and perennials with the pernicious, choking weed that shares their common name. These plants produce flowers in several shades, from white, blue, and creamy white, often with a contrasting coloured centre, and are suitable for mixed borders, rock gardens, and sunny banks. The more compact forms grow to only around 30cm (12in) tall. *Convolvulus sabatius* is good in containers, including hanging baskets. The perennials are short-lived and are often treated as annuals. Grow convolvulus with annuals such as marigolds (*see Calendula officinalis, p.204*) and larkspurs (*see p.216*).

Hardiness Fully hardy ✽✽✽ to frost-hardy ✽✽.

Cultivation These trouble-free plants require poor to moderately fertile, well-drained soil and a sunny, sheltered site. **Deadhead** flowers to prolong the flowering period into autumn. **Container-grown** plants require loam-based compost, frequent watering in dry weather, and a weekly feed with a balanced fertilizer. **Sow** seed (*see pp.391–393*) of annuals directly in the garden in mid-spring, or in autumn with cloche protection over winter. **Divide** (*see p.395*) perennials in spring.

Consolida 'Frosted Skies'
‡30–45cm (12–18in) ↔ 15–23cm (6–9in), semi-double flowers in summer, prefers heavy soil, needs staking

Convallaria majalis ♀
‡23cm (9in) ↔ 30cm (12in), waxy flowers are held in graceful sprays, good for cutting

Convolvulus tricolor 'Royal Ensign'
‡30cm (12in) ↔ 23–30cm (9–12in), bushy, short-lived perennial or annual, flowers throughout summer ✽✽✽

Convolvulus sabatius ♀
‡15cm (6in) ↔ 50cm (20in), trailing, slender-stemmed perennial,
pale to deep lavender flowers from summer to early autumn ✲✲

COREOPSIS

Tickseed   *late spring to late summer*

‡to 75cm (30in)
↔ to 60cm (24in)

BOTH THE PERENNIALS and annuals
are grown for their bright, daisy-like,
summer-long flowers. Masses of single
or double flowers, all in shades of gold,
are produced on stems rising above
fine foliage. The flowers not only
attract bees into the garden, they also make successful
cut flowers. Many of the perennials are short-lived,
however, and are grown as annuals – usually flowering
freely in their first year from seed sown in spring.
Grow them in a sunny border with perennials such
as achilleas (*see p.166*) and phloxes (*see p.306*).

Hardiness Fully hardy ✲✲✲ to frost-tender ❀.

Cultivation Fertile, well-drained soil and a position in full sun or
partial shade are required for this plant. **Remove** fading flowers to
prolong flowering. **Stake** taller-growing plants to support the flower
stems. **Sow** seed (*see pp.391–393*) in a seedbed outdoors in spring
or indoors at 13–16°C (55–61°F) in late winter or early spring; sow
in small batches from early spring to early summer for a longer
succession of flowers. **Divide** (*see p.395*) perennials in early spring.

CORYDALIS

spring to autumn

LOW-GROWING AND CLUMP-FORMING, the numerous
perennials, annuals, and biennials are favoured by
gardeners for their distinctive flowers. These occur
in shades of blue, white, and red, and are borne in
clusters above the foliage in the spring, summer, or
autumn. The ferny leaves are usually mid- to light
green and in a few species, such as *Corydalis lutea*
and *C. ochroleuca*, are evergreen. The perennials have
tuberous ('George Baker') or rhizomatous roots. Some
species will self-seed freely. They are best grown in a
border or rock garden, but often survive in soil-filled
cracks in walls and paving. Some corydalis require
a dry, dormant summer period and protection from
winter wet, and are best grown in shallow pots in
an unheated greenhouse or cold frame.

Hardiness Fully hardy ✲✲✲ to frost-hardy ✲✲.

Cultivation All need free-draining, moderately fertile soil enriched
with well-rotted organic matter. Some corydalis prefer sun, others like
partial shade. **Sow** seed (*see pp.391–393*) in pots in an open frame as
soon as it is ripe; germination can be erratic. **Divide** spring-flowering
species in autumn, and summer-flowering ones in spring (*see p.395*).

① 'Schnittgold' ‡80cm (32in) ↔ 60cm (24in), flowers in early to
midsummer ✲✲✲ ② 'Sunray' ‡45–90cm (18–36in) ↔ 45cm
(18in), flowers late spring to late summer ✲✲✲

① *flexuosa* ♀ ‡30cm (12in) ↔ 20cm (8in) ② *lutea* ‡40cm
(16in) ↔ 30cm (12in) ③ *ochroleuca* ‡↔ 30cm (12in) ④ *solida*
'George Baker' ♀ ‡25cm (10in) ↔ 20cm (8in) – all ✲✲✲

COSMOS

midsummer to autumn

COSMOS ARE INVALUABLE plants for informal gardens. They include easy-to-grow tuberous perennials and annuals favoured for their attractive crimson-red, pink, or white, bowl- or saucer-shaped flowers, produced on long, graceful stems in summer. The perennial chocolate cosmos (*Cosmos atrosanguineus*), with reddish-brown stems and spoon-shaped, dark green leaves, has velvety, chocolate-scented flowers from midsummer until autumn. Slightly tender, it needs winter protection once the foliage dies back. Grow them with other border plants such as phloxes (*see p.306*) and grey-leaved plants like santolinas (*see p.116*) to contrast with the dark flowers. Sow the annual *C. bipinnatus* in a drift, or plant to fill mid- and late-summer gaps in a border.

Hardiness Frost-hardy ✳✳ to frost-tender ✿.

Cultivation Grow in reasonably fertile soil that is moist but well-drained, in full sun. Deadhead to prolong flowering. **Lift** and store tubers in autumn and keep in frost-free conditions. **Sow** annuals where they are to grow in spring or autumn in milder gardens, or in pots (*see pp.391–393*). Thin seedlings to 15cm (6in).

CRAMBE

late spring to midsummer

TALL, BUT WITH AN AIRY PRESENCE, these woody-based annuals or perennials are grown for their handsome, wavy-edged leaves and sprays of tiny, often white, sometimes fragrant flowers which attract bees. The flowers appear from late spring to midsummer, carried on strong stems above undulating, dark green or blue-grey foliage. The large leaves are decorative when young, but tend to die down in mid- to late summer. While crambes are magnificent in a mixed border, taller species, such as *Crambe cordifolia*, need lots of space. They are a good choice for coastal sites because the tough foliage withstands sea spray and salt-laden winds. Grow them with old garden roses (*see pp.110–113*) and philadelphus (*see p.93*).

Hardiness Fully hardy ✳✳✳.

Cultivation Grow crambes in deep, fertile, well-drained soil in full sun, although they also tolerate poor soil and partial shade. Shelter from strong winds. **Sow** seed (*see pp.391–393*) in a pot in a cold frame in spring or autumn. **Divide** plants (*see p.395*) in early spring. **Clubroot**, a persistent, soil-borne disease that can affect crambes, wallflowers, and other members of the cabbage family, causes deformed roots and stunted plants. Dig out and burn affected plants.

CRINUM

spring to autumn

‡50cm–1.5m (20in–5ft)
↔ 15–30cm (6–12in)

REMINISCENT OF LILIES, crinums belong to a large group of stately, deciduous and evergreen bulbous perennials. They are grown for their showy, white and pink flowers that are often scented; these are borne on long, leafless stalks from spring to autumn, depending on the species. The long, strappy leaves are a glossy, light to mid-green. Crinums are best grown outside in a warm, sheltered border with other perennials like *Anemone hupehensis* and forms of *A. × hybrida* (*see p.180*), border phloxes (*see p.306*) and daylilies (*see Hemerocallis, p.258*).

Hardiness Fully hardy ✳✳✳ (borderline) to frost-tender ✿.

Cultivation Plant in spring with the neck of each bulb just above soil level, in deep, fertile soil that is moist but very well-drained, and enriched with well-rotted organic matter. Choose a position in full sun, preferably by a wall. **Water** generously when crinums are in growth and keep moist after flowering. **Divide** large clumps of the huge bulbs in spring (*see below and p.395*) to increase your stock.

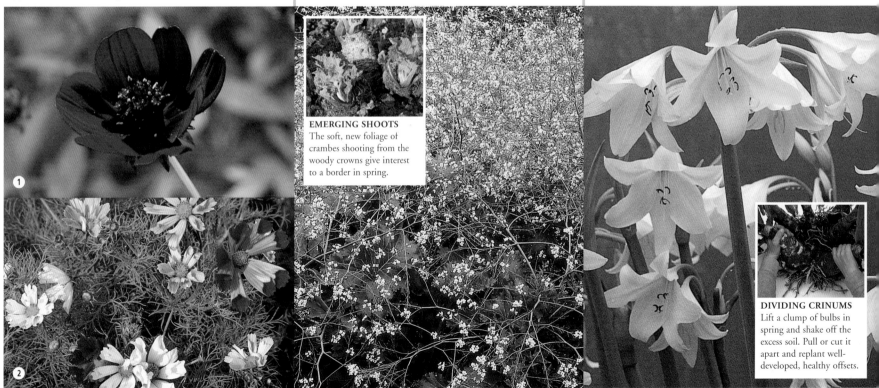

EMERGING SHOOTS
The soft, new foliage of crambes shooting from the woody crowns give interest to a border in spring.

DIVIDING CRINUMS
Lift a clump of bulbs in spring and shake off the excess soil. Pull or cut it apart and replant well-developed, healthy offsets.

① *atrosanguineus* ‡75cm (30in) ↔ 45cm (18in) ✳✳
② *bipinnatus* 'Sea Shells' ‡to 90cm (3ft) ↔ 45cm (18in), with ferny foliage, good for cutting ✳

Crambe cordifolia ♡
‡to 2.5m (8ft) ↔ 1.5m (5ft), perennial, bristly leaves to 35cm (14in) across, flowers from late spring to midsummer ✳✳✳

Crinum × powellii 'Album' ♡
‡1.5m (5ft) ↔ 30cm (12in), deciduous, up to ten fragrant flowers per stem from late summer to autumn ✳✳✳ (borderline)

CROCOSMIA

Montbretia

mid- to late summer

PERFECT FOR HOT-COLOURED BORDERS, these eye-catching perennials produce arching sprays of flowers in vivid shades of scarlet, orange, and yellow, as well as bicolors in red and orange. From mid- to late summer, long-lasting flowers are held on wiry stems that may be branched or unbranched – they are good for cutting. Crocosmias are robust, forming clumps of flat, sword-like, often ribbed leaves that stand erect but fan out slightly, making a strong accent in a bed or border. Established clumps spread to around 60cm (2ft). Plant crocosmia corms in a shrub border or with other late-summer perennials, such as Michaelmas daisies (*see Aster, pp.192–193*), rudbeckias (*see p.317*), and sedums (*see p.324*).

Hardiness Fully hardy ✳✳✳ to frost-hardy ✳✳.

Cultivation Plant corms in spring, 8–10cm (3–4in) deep, in soil enriched with well-rotted organic matter, in sun or partial shade. In frost-prone gardens, plant the corms close to a sheltered wall.
Divide congested clumps in spring or autumn every three or four years to maintain the vigour of the plants (*see right and p.395*).

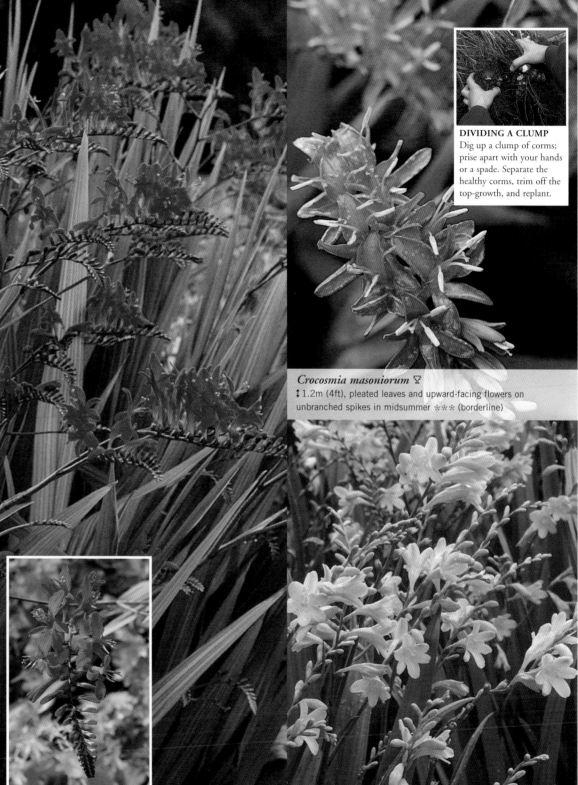

DIVIDING A CLUMP
Dig up a clump of corms; prise apart with your hands or a spade. Separate the healthy corms, trim off the top-growth, and replant.

Crocosmia masoniorum ♛
↕ 1.2m (4ft), pleated leaves and upward-facing flowers on unbranched spikes in midsummer ✳✳✳ (borderline)

Crocosmia × crocosmiiflora 'Star of the East' ♛
↕ 70cm (28in), flowers from late summer to early autumn on branched stems ✳✳

Crocosmia 'Lucifer' ♛
↕ 1–1.2m (3–4ft), flowers 5cm (2in) long in midsummer on sparsely branched spikes ✳✳✳ (borderline)

Crocosmia × crocosmiiflora 'Gerbe d'Or'
↕ 60–75cm (24–30in), also called 'Golden Fleece', flowers on arching stems from mid- to late summer ✳✳✳

CROCUS

spring and autumn

NOT JUST WELCOME SIGN OF SPRING, some crocuses also extend the season well into autumn. This is a large group of dwarf perennials that grow from corms, producing flowers at the same time as, or just before, the narrow, grassy foliage. The flowers come in vivid or pastel shades from yellow to lilac, purple, and white and are sometimes striped or shaded. The leaves are mid-green with a central, silver-green stripe. Crocuses are easy to grow and look best planted in drifts at the front of a border or naturalized in short grass for carpets of colour. Grow them with spring-flowering bulbs like dwarf narcissi (*see pp.288–289*) or autumn-flowering hardy cyclamens (*see p.221*).

Hardiness Fully hardy ✳✳✳ to frost-hardy ✳✳.

Cultivation Most prefer gritty, not too rich, well-drained soil in full sun or partial shade. **Plant** in situ; spring-flowering types 8–10cm (3–4in) deep in autumn, autumn-flowering ones in late summer. Autumn crocuses can be planted densely in containers and brought indoors to flower. **Divide** cormlets (*see p.395*) while the plants are dormant and replant them, or leave to self-seed freely. **Rodents** may feed on the corms; deter them by covering groups of corms at planting with a layer of chicken wire before replacing the soil.

Crocus chrysanthus 'Snow Bunting' ♀
‡8cm (3in) ↔ 5cm (2in), scented flowers in early spring, up to four per plant ✳✳✳

Crocus speciosus ♀
‡10–15cm (4–6in) ↔ 5cm (2in), autumn-flowering crocus which increases rapidly; flowers produced before the leaves ✳✳✳

Crocus chrysanthus 'Gipsy Girl'
‡8cm (3in) ↔ 5cm (2in), flowers in early spring ✳✳✳

Crocus sieberi 'Hubert Edelsten' ♀
‡5–8cm (2–3in) ↔ 2.5cm (1in), flowers in late winter to early spring ✳✳✳

Crocus sieberi 'Albus' ♀
‡5–8cm (2–3in) ↔ 2.5cm (1in), flowers 3–4.5cm (¾–1¼in) long with deep yellow throats, in early spring ✳✳✳

CYCLAMEN

Sowbread

autumn to late winter

HARDY CYCLAMEN BRING WINTER CHEER to gardens and windowboxes. The elegant flowers of these tuberous perennials are held aloft on leafless flower stalks. They are produced, depending on the species, from autumn until late winter and vary in hue from white to pink to carmine-red. The leaves are heart-shaped to rounded, attractively marked with silver zones or patterns; they last through winter to spring. Grow these hardy cyclamens under trees, or at the front of a shrub border with early bulbs such as snowdrops (*see Galanthus, p.247*) and spring-flowering crocuses (*see facing page*); they also do well in a rock garden, raised bed, or container. Do not confuse them with winter-flowering cyclamens sold as houseplants, which are not hardy.

Hardiness Fully hardy ✳✳✳ to frost-hardy ✳✳.

Cultivation Plant the corms 2.5–5cm (1–2in) deep in well-drained, humus-rich, fertile soil. They prefer dryish conditions in summer. **Mulch** (*see p.388*) with leafmould every year after the leaves die down. **Rodents** can be deterred by placing a layer of chicken wire over the tubers at planting time before replacing the soil.

Cyclamen cilicium ♀
↕ 5cm (2in) ↔ 8cm (3in), pink or white flowers in autumn, stained carmine-red at the mouth, strongly patterned leaves ✳✳

PLANTING CYCLAMEN
To ensure flowers in the first year, plant tubers in root growth, with the tops just visible at soil level. Fill in with soil and firm gently.

Cyclamen hederifolium ♀
↕ 10–13cm (4–5in) ↔ 15cm (6in), sometimes scented flowers in mid- and late autumn, before the variously patterned leaves ✳✳✳

Cyclamen coum ♀
↕ 5–8cm (2–3in) ↔ 10cm (4in), compact white, pink, or carmine-red flowers in winter or early spring, plain or marbled leaves ✳✳✳

CYNARA

summer to autumn

↕ 1.5–2m (5–6ft)
↔ 1.2m (4ft)

THESE IMPOSING, ARCHITECTURAL plants have great presence in a border. The clump-forming perennials produce tall, thistle-like flowerheads in shades of blue and violet from summer until autumn. The unopened buds of the globe artichoke (*Cynara scolymus*) are edible, and the flowers can be dried and used in indoor arrangements. The boldly cut, silver or greyish-green leaves arch elegantly in the manner of a fountain, making this an impressive foliage plant for the back of a mixed or herbaceous border with other perennials such as veronicas (*see p.337*), salvias (*see p.318*), or daylilies (*see Hemerocallis, p.258*). Cynaras also attract bees and other pollinating insects into the garden.

Hardiness Fully hardy ✳✳✳ to frost-hardy ✳✳.

Cultivation Grow in any reasonably fertile soil that is well-drained and in full sun. Where winters are very cold, protect with a mulch of organic matter (*see p.388*). **Sow** seed (*see pp.391–393*) in a container in a cold frame or divide plants (*see p.395*) in spring. New shoots are vulnerable to slugs and snails.

Cynara cardunculus ♀ (Cardoon)
↕ 1.5m (5ft) ↔ 1.2m (4ft), spiny leaves, woolly grey stems, flowers early to late summer, blanched leaf-stalks and midribs edible ✳✳✳

DAHLIA

midsummer to autumn

DAHLIAS ARE DESERVEDLY POPULAR GARDEN PLANTS, putting on a bravura performance from midsummer until the first frosts of autumn, in shades from white to vivid yellow, orange, scarlet, pink, and purple. In addition to bringing welcome colour as summer plants fade, the blooms are good for cutting, and a few cultivars have rich, chocolate-coloured foliage. Dahlias, which grow from tubers, are generally tender perennials. In permanent plantings, reserve spaces for them because tubers cannot be set out until late spring or early summer, except in mild, frost-free areas. The smaller bedding types are often treated as annuals and grown from seed each year; they are superb for edging borders or growing in containers. Dahlia flowers come in a striking range of shapes, sizes, and forms, which as well as brightening gardens and cut-flower arrangements, have great appeal for show exhibitors. There are several categories including singles and fully doubles, with collarettes and waterlilies somewhere in between. Cactus types have spiky, quill-shaped petals, while pompons and balls have a pleasing geometry. The giant decoratives may have flowers the size of a tea plate. Dahlias readily mutate and therefore also appeal to plant breeders, who have produced an extraordinary number of cultivars to choose from.

Hardiness Frost-hardy ✽✽.

Cultivation Grow in full sun in deep, fertile soil enriched with plenty of well-rotted farmyard manure or garden compost. Bedding dahlias tolerate less rich conditions. In milder areas, tubers can be left in the ground, covered with a dry mulch over winter. **Plant out** young plants in leaf when the threat of frost has passed in early summer – dormant tubers a little earlier – and lift in mid-autumn (*see below*). **Support** with stout stakes or three canes inserted at planting and tie in new growth regularly. Bedding dahlias do not need staking. **Water** well in dry periods, and feed regularly during the growing season with nitrogenous fertilizer; from midsummer switch to a high-potash fertilizer to encourage flowering. **Cut** flowers regularly to ensure a succession of blooms; for large flowers restrict the plants to two or three shoots. **Propagate** by starting tubers into growth in spring in a greenhouse or cold frame. Divide the tuber into sections, each with a growing shoot, and pot up each as a new plant. Slugs (*see p.398*) and earwigs (*see p.397*) may eat the leaves and flowers.

Storing dahlias over winter

❶ In mid-autumn, ideally after the foliage has been blackened by the first frost, cut the old stems back, taking care to leave about 15cm (6in) of stem attached to each tuber. Loosen the soil and lift the tubers out gently. Clean off any excess soil from the tubers and attach a label to each around one of the stems.

❷ Store the tubers upside-down for about three weeks in a frost-free place, to allow moisture to drain from the stems, which are hollow. When the stems have dried out, put the tubers in a cool, frost-free place and cover with a layer of bark chippings. Keep them dry until spring, but inspect them occasionally for disease.

❸ In spring, about six weeks before the last frosts are expected, plant out dormant tubers. Before planting tall types, insert a stout 1m (3ft) stake in the planting hole. Add soil around the tuber so that the crown, where the stem and tubers are joined, is 2.5–5cm (1–2in) below soil level. Shoots will show in about six weeks.

① *Dahlia* 'Bishop of Llandaff' ♀ ‡1.1m (3½ft) ↔ 45cm (18in), chocolate-coloured foliage ② 'Candy Cane' ‡1–1.2m (3–4ft) ↔ 60cm (2ft), miniature waterlily ③ 'Clair de Lune' ♀ ‡1.1m (3½ft) ↔ 60cm (2ft), collerette ④ 'Conway' ‡1.1m (3½ft) ↔ 60cm (2ft), small semi-cactus ⑤ 'Corton Olympic' ‡1.2m (4ft) ↔ 60cm (2ft), giant decorative ⑥ 'Davenport Sunlight' ‡1.2m (4ft) ↔ 60cm (2ft), medium semi-cactus ⑦ 'David Howard' ♀ ‡↔ 90cm (3ft), miniature decorative ⑧ 'Fascination' ♀

‡60cm (2ft) ↔ 45cm (18in), annual bedding ⑨ 'Hamari Accord' ♀ ‡1.2m (4ft) ↔ 60cm (2ft), large semi-cactus ⑩ 'Hamari Gold' ♀ ‡1.2m (4ft) ↔ 60cm (2ft), giant decorative ⑪ 'Hillcrest Royal' ♀ ‡1.1m (3½ft) ↔ 60cm (24in), medium cactus ⑫ 'Nina Chester' ‡1.1m (3½ft) ↔ 60cm (2ft), small decorative ⑬ 'Noreen' ‡1m (3ft) ↔ 45cm (18in), pompon ⑭ 'Pontiac' ‡1.2m (4ft) ↔ 60cm (2ft), semi-cactus ⑮ 'Preston Park' ♀ ‡↔45cm (18in), annual bedding ⑯ 'Rhonda' ‡1.1m (3½ft) ↔ 60cm (2ft), pompon ⑰ 'Rokesly Mini' ‡1m (3ft) ↔ 45cm (18in), semi-cactus ⑱ 'Small World' ♀ ‡1.1m (3½ft) ↔ 60cm (2ft), pompon ⑲ 'So Dainty' ♀ ‡1.1m (3½ft) ↔ 60cm (2ft), miniature semi-cactus ⑳ 'White Alva's' ♀ ‡1.2m (4ft) ↔ 60cm (2ft), giant decorative ㉑ 'Wootton Cupid' ♀ ‡1.1m (3½ft) ↔ 60cm (2ft), miniature ball ㉒ 'Wootton Impact' ♀ ‡1.2m (4ft) ↔ 60cm (2ft), semi-cactus ㉓ 'Zorro' ♀ ‡1.2m (4ft) ↔ 60cm (2ft), giant decorative

FLOWERING PLANTS

DARMERA PELTATA

late spring

HANDSOME AND UNUSUAL, this spreading perennial enjoys moisture. In late spring, pink or white flowers are borne in clusters at the tips of sturdy, hairy stems that can grow to 2m (6ft) in height. It is only when the flowers begin to fade that the rounded, long-stemmed leaves, which are up to 60cm (24in) across, begin to unfurl. This impressive foliage turns scarlet in autumn, before dying down over winter. *Darmera peltata* is a large plant that needs plenty of space, and although it will grow in a shady border, darmeras prefer sites in bog gardens or by water. Try it with other moisture-loving plants like astilbes (*see p.194*) or primulas (*see pp.312–313*), or plant a group of them together to emphasise their striking forms.

Hardiness Fully hardy ✳✳✳, although flowers may be damaged by late frosts.

Cultivation This plant prefers moist or boggy soil in sun or shade, but it will tolerate drier soil in shade. **Sow** seed (*see pp.391–392*) in containers in a cold frame in spring or autumn, or divide plants (*see p.395*) in spring.

DELPHINIUM

early to midsummer

WITH THEIR TOWERING SPIKES of flowers, delphiniums are perfect for adding height and form to a border. The blooms are borne in early and midsummer, in a wide range of colours from creamy whites through to lilac-pinks, sky-blues, and deepest, darkest indigo. The mid-green leaves form clumps around the bases of the flower stems. The garden delphiniums are usually herbaceous perennials. Their flower spikes make the stems top-heavy and prone to snapping in winds, so they need support and a sheltered position. This can often be provided by placing them at the back of a border by a wall or fence. Small species and dwarf varieties are suited to more exposed areas. Belladonna types are easier to grow.

Hardiness Fully hardy ✳✳✳.

Cultivation Delphiniums like fertile, moist but well-drained soil in full sun. Provide support with sturdy bamboo canes (*see below, facing page*). **Deadhead** regularly (*see p.390*) and you may be rewarded with another flush of flowers later in the summer, but do not expect them to be as spectacular as the first. **Sow** seed (*see pp.391–393*) at 13°C (55°F) in early spring. **Slugs** and snails (*see p.398*), and powdery mildew (caused by damp leaves and dry soil) can be troublesome.

Delphinium 'Bruce' ♀
↕2m (6ft) ↔ 60–90cm (24–36in), clump-forming perennial

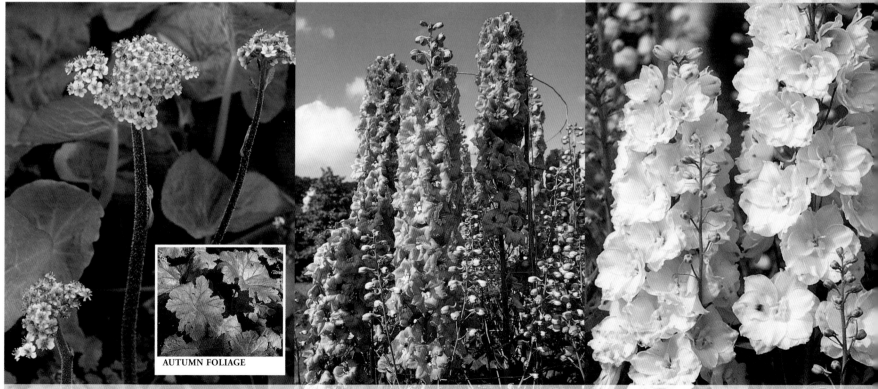

AUTUMN FOLIAGE

Darmera peltata ♀
↕2m (6ft) ↔ 1m (3ft) or more

Delphinium 'Fanfare'
↕2.2m (7ft) ↔ 60–90cm (24–36in), clump-forming perennial

Delphinium 'Sungleam' ♀
↕1.5m (5ft) ↔ 60–90cm (24–36in), clump-forming perennial

hinium nudicaule
90cm (24–36in) ↔ 20cm (8in), short perennial grown as an
l, flowers in midsummer only

Delphinium 'Emily Hawkins' ♀
‡ 1.7m (5½ft) ↔ 60–90cm (24–36in), clump-forming perennial

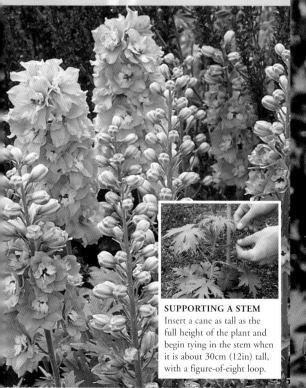

SUPPORTING A STEM
Insert a cane as tall as the
full height of the plant and
begin tying in the stem when
it is about 30cm (12in) tall,
with a figure-of-eight loop.

Delphinium **Blue Fountains Group**
‡ 60–90cm (2–3ft) ↔ 60–90cm (24–36in), clump-forming
perennial, good for small or windy gardens

Delphinium 'Blue Nile' ♀
‡ 1.7m (5½ft) ↔ 60–90cm (24–36in), clump-forming perennial

Delphinium 'Mighty Atom'
‡ 1.5m (5ft) ↔ 60–90cm (24–36in), clump-forming perennial,
flowers and stems may be deformed if too many flowers are pollinated

DIANTHUS

Carnation, Pink

summer

‡8–90cm (3–36in)
↔ 20–40cm (8–16in)

THE MAIN GARDEN PLANTS IN THIS GROUP of evergreen perennials and annuals are pinks and border carnations. In summer, both bear a profusion of bright flowers, which last well when cut, above narrow, silvery leaves. The flowers are single or double in many shades of pink, white, carmine, salmon, and mauve, often with darker, contrasting markings on the petals. Some are fragrant, particularly the rich, spicy "clove-scented" cultivars. Pinks are smaller than carnations and have fewer petals, but other than this their flowers and growth habits are similar. Smaller pinks, including the alpine types like *Dianthus* 'Little Jock', are excellent in rock gardens and troughs. The perpetual carnations, grown under glass for cut flowers, are by far the tallest in the group. Sweet William (*D. barbatus*) is a short-lived perennial usually grown as a biennial from seed sown in summer; plants flower in the following year.

Hardiness Fully hardy ✳✳✳; perpetual carnations half-hardy ✳.

Cultivation All dianthus require a well-drained, neutral to alkaline soil enriched with well-rotted manure or garden compost. Position plants in full sun. Alpine cultivars, especially, benefit from sharp drainage in alpine troughs and raised beds. **Plant out** young plants in spring and early summer and feed with a balanced fertilizer in spring. **Support** tall cultivars in spring using thin canes and string. **Deadhead** (remove fading flowers) to encourage plants to produce more flowers and maintain a compact growth habit (*see p.390*). Annuals and biennials are discarded after flowering.

Increasing pinks

Taking pipings is an easy way to propagate all kinds of Dianthus, but especially pinks. Choose non-flowering shoots. Hold a shoot near the base and sharply pull out the tip. The shoot should break easily at a leaf joint, giving a cutting or piping about 8–10cm (3–4in) long with three or four pairs of leaves. Remove the lowest pair of leaves and insert the pipings in pots containing equal parts cuttings compost and sharp sand. Place in a shady spot, keep moist, and when they have rooted, after three or four weeks, pot up the young plants separately.

Layering border carnations

❶ *Loosen the soil around the plant and mix in equal parts sharp sand and peat-free compost. Select non-flowering sideshoots and remove all but the top four or five leaves on each shoot. Below a bud, cut into the stem along its length to form a tongue (see inset). Wounding the stem in this way encourages roots to form. Dust the cut surface with hormone rooting powder.*

❷ *Push the tongue of each shoot into the prepared soil and pin down with a piece of bent wire. Tie the leafy part of the shoot to a cane so it is held upright and the cut is held open. Water lightly, cover the shoot with soil, and put a stone over it to retain moisture. Check if roots have formed after five or six weeks. Separate and lift the layers from the parent plant and plant out.*

① *Dianthus alpinus* 'Joan's Blood' ♥ ‡8cm (3in) ↔ 10cm (4in), alpine pink ② 'Becky Robinson' ♥ ‡45cm (18in) ↔ 40cm (16in), scented pink ③ 'Bovey Belle' ♥ ‡45cm (18in) ↔ 40cm (16in), scented pink ④ 'Brympton Red' ‡45cm (18in) ↔ 30cm (1ft), pink ⑤ 'Christine Hough' ‡1.5m (5ft) ↔ 30cm (1ft), carnation ⑥ 'Christopher' ‡38cm (15in) ↔ 30cm (1ft), pink ⑦ 'Dad's Favourite' ‡45cm (18in) ↔ 30cm (1ft), pink ⑧ 'Dainty Dame' ♥ ‡10cm (4in) ↔ 20cm (8in), alpine pink ⑨ *deltoides* 'Leuchtfunk' ‡20cm (8in), ↔30cm (1ft), pink ⑩ 'Doris' ♀ ‡45cm (18in) ↔40cm (16in), scented pink ⑪ 'Forest Treasure' ‡60cm (2ft) ↔40cm (16in), carnation ⑫ 'Golden Cross' ♀ ‡60cm (2ft) ↔40cm (16in), carnation ⑬ 'Gran's Favourite' ♀ ‡45cm (18in) ↔40cm (16in), scented pink ⑭ 'Haytor White' ♀ ‡45cm (18in) ↔40cm (16in), scented pink ⑮ 'Houndspool Ruby' ♀ ‡45cm (18in) ↔40cm (16in), pink ⑯ 'La Bourboule' ♀ ‡20cm (8in), ↔30cm (1ft), scented alpine

pink ⑰ 'Little Jock' ‡20cm (8in), ↔30cm (1ft), scented alpine pink ⑱ 'London Brocade' ‡↔45cm (18in), scented pink ⑲ 'Mrs Sinkins' ‡45cm (18in) ↔30cm (1ft), scented pink ⑳ 'Musgrave's Pink' ‡45cm (18in) ↔30cm (1ft), pink ㉑ PIERROT ('Kobusa') ‡to 1.5m (5ft) ↔30cm (1ft), perpetual carnation ㉒ 'Valda Wyatt' ♀ ‡45cm (18in) ↔40cm (16in), scented pink ㉓ 'Warden Hybrid' ‡10cm (4in) ↔20cm (8in), alpine pink

DIASCIA

early summer to autumn

FOR THEIR LENGTH OF FLOWERING ALONE, these annuals and semi-evergreen perennials are worthy of any garden. Loose, densely packed flowerheads bloom from early summer to mid-autumn above heart-shaped, mid-green leaves. The main flush of flowers is in early summer, but if you trim back plants after this, they produce another flush later in summer. The colour range includes shades of apricot, deep pink, rose-pink, purplish-pink, or salmon-pink. Try growing diascias at the front of a herbaceous border, under roses, or in a rock garden. Most are creeping or mat-forming, but some diascias have a trailing habit which makes them excellent in containers. Diascias are not reliably hardy, so take cuttings to ensure that you keep them for next year.

Hardiness Most are hardy to -8°C (18°F) ✳✳.

Cultivation Diascias prefer moist but well-drained, fertile soil, in full sun. Water in dry periods. **Sow** seed (*see pp.391–393*) at 16°C (61°F) as soon as it is ripe, or in spring. Take semi-ripe cuttings in late summer (*see p.394*). Overwinter young plants in frost-free conditions.

DICENTRA

see also p.140

spring to early summer

‡ to 1.2m (4ft)
↔ 45cm (18in)

THIS COTTAGE-GARDEN FAVOURITE is grown both for its finely cut foliage and heart-shaped flowers. Most are perennials and form compact clumps with ferny, often greyish leaves and arching stems from which the flowers are suspended. Flowers are produced from spring to early summer in a range of shades from red, purple, and deep pink to white or yellow. Dicentras are also at home in a mixed border, cottage-garden planting, or in woodland garden. They may die down early in dry summers. Their delicate flowers and foliage contrasts nicely with the broad young foliage of hostas (*see pp.260–261*).

Hardiness Fully hardy ✳✳✳, but frost can damage early growth.

Cultivation Most decentras thrive in partial shade and moist, fertile, slightly alkaline (limy) soil enriched with well-rotted organic matter. *D. chrysantha* needs a dry, sunny site; *D. spectabilis* tolerates sun if in moist soil. **Sow** seed (*see pages 391–393*) in a container in a cold frame as soon as it is ripe, or in spring. **Divide** the fleshy-rooted plants (*see p.395*) carefully in spring or after the leaves die down.

Dicentra formosa (Wild bleeding heart)
‡ 45cm (18in) ↔ 60–90cm (24–36in), spreading perennial, leaves glaucous below, late spring and early summer flowers fade to white

PINK-FLOWERED FORM

① *barberae* 'Blackthorn Apricot' ♀ ② *barberae* 'Fisher's Flora' ♀ ③ *fetcaniensis* – all these ‡ 25cm (10in) ↔ 50cm (20in) ④ *rigescens* ♀ ‡ 30cm (12in) ↔ 50cm (20in)

Dicentra spectabilis ♀ (Bleeding heart, Lyre flower)
‡ to 1.2m (4ft) ↔ 45cm (18in), clumping perennial, light green leaves, flowers in late spring and early summer

Dicentra cucullaria (Dutchman's breeches)
‡ to 20cm (8in) ↔ 25cm (10in), tuberous perennial, compact clumps, white or pink flowers in early spring, needs gritty soil

Dicentra spectabilis 'Alba' �
‡ to 1.2m (4ft) ↔ 45cm (18in), robust, clump-forming perennial,
light green leaves, flowers from late spring until midsummer

DICTAMNUS ALBUS

Burning bush, Dittany   *early summer*

‡40–90cm
(16–36in)
↔60cm (24in)

THIS TALL, WOODY-BASED perennial is
grown for its dense spikes of fragrant
flowers, produced above lemon-scented
foliage in summer. The leathery leaves are
composed of light green leaflets. Volatile,
aromatic oils produced by the flowers and
ripening seedpods can be ignited in hot
weather, giving rise to the common name of burning
bush. This clumping plant mixes well in a herbaceous
or mixed border with other tall perennials such as
achilleas (*see p.166*), phloxes (*see p.306*), daylilies
(*see Hemerocallis, p.258*) and loosestrifes (*see Lythrum,
p.283*). Contact with the foliage may cause skin
irritation aggravated by sunlight (photodermatitis).

Hardiness Fully hardy ✳✳✳.

Cultivation Grow this plant in any well-drained, reasonably fertile
soil, in full sun or partial shade. **Sow** seed (*see pp.391–393*) in
containers in a cold frame as soon as it is ripe. **Divide** plants (*see
p.395*) in autumn or spring; bear in mind that the woody rootstocks
may take some time to get established again.

DIERAMA

Angel's fishing rod,   *summer*
Wandflower

ONE OF THE MOST DELICATE-LOOKING and mobile
plants in the garden, dieramas carry their flowers on
long, gently arching stems, so slender that they move
in every breeze. The funnel- or bell-shaped flowers in
shades of coral-pink to red, bright pink, or purple-
pink, are borne in succession and hang from the
stems on individual flower spikes. The fine, grassy,
green to grey-green leaves of these evergreen
perennials grow from tufts at the base and can be
up to 90cm (30in) long. Grow dieramas with other
summer-flowering perennials such as acanthus (*see
p.166*), penstemons (*see p.304*), phloxes (*see p.306*),
and salvias (*see p.318*).

Hardiness Frost-hardy ✳✳ to half-hardy ✳; established clumps
tolerate temperatures down to -10°C (14°F).

Cultivation Plant the corms 5–8cm (2–3in) deep in spring; site
them in well-drained soil enriched with rotted organic matter, in a
sheltered site in full sun. Do not let plants dry out in summer. In frost-
prone areas, cover them with a protective dry mulch over winter.
Young plants take some time to settle, but once established grow
freely. **Sow** seed (*see pp.391–393*) in a seedbed or in containers in a
cold frame as soon as it is ripe. **Divide** clumps (*see p.395*) in spring.

① *albus* white or pinkish-white flowers
② *albus* var. *purpureus* ♀ purplish-pink flowers

Dierama pulcherrimum
‡ 1–1.5m (3–5ft) ↔ 60cm (24in), flowers pale to deep magenta-
pink, occasionally white or purple-red, in summer ✳✳

DIGITALIS

Foxglove

spring to midsummer

CLASSIC COTTAGE-GARDEN PLANTS, foxgloves form a large group of biennials and short-lived perennials. Their imposing flower spikes come in a variety of shades, from the classic purple of *Digitalis purpurea* to pink, white, and yellow, and appear from spring through to midsummer in the second year. They are striking plants, with one or more leafy rosettes at the base, and flower stems often reaching 1.5m (5ft) or more. Use them to give height to a mixed or an herbaceous border with other early-flowering perennials such as dicentras (*see p.228*) and doronicums (*see facing page*) or in a woodland planting. They self-seed prolifically, adding a natural charm to the garden. All foxgloves are toxic.

Hardiness Fully hardy ✳✳✳ to frost-hardy ✳✳.

Cultivation Grow in almost any soil and situation, except extremely wet or dry conditions. Most prefer soil enriched with well-rotted organic matter in partial shade. **Deadhead** after flowering if you do not want the seedlings springing up everywhere. **Collect** the seed and sow in containers in a cold frame in late spring (*see pp.391–393*). The leaves might be disfigured (*see p.399*) by leaf spot and powdery mildew: avoid splashing the foliage when watering and pick off affected leaves.

Digitalis grandiflora ♡
↕ to 90cm (3ft) ↔ 45cm (18in), clumping biennial or perennial, veined leaves up to 25cm (10in), flowers in early and midsummer ✳✳✳

SELF-SOWN SEEDLINGS
Check for seedlings at the foot of each plant in early autumn. Lift them with a trowel so each retains a ball of soil around its roots and replant them 30cm (12in) apart.

Digitalis davisiana
↕ to 70cm (28in) ↔ 45cm (18in), perennial with underground stems (rhizomes), flowers in early summer ✳✳

Digitalis* × *mertonensis ♡
↕ to 90cm (3ft) ↔ 30cm (12in), clump-forming perennial, flowers in late spring and early summer, comes true from seed ✳✳✳

***Digitalis purpurea* Excelsior Group**
↕ 90cm–2m (3–6ft) ↔ to 60cm (24in), biennial or perennial, at their best when grown annually from seed, good for cut flowers ✳✳✳

DODECATHEON

American cowslip,
Shooting stars

late spring to early summer

‡ to 40cm (16in)
↔ 25cm (10in)

THESE PERENNIALS MAKE an impressive display in spring and summer. They thrive alongside ponds and at the edge of bog gardens, as well as in rock gardens and mixed and herbaceous borders. Their cyclamen-like flowers, in shades of purple-pink, reddish-purple, magenta-pink, lavender, or white, are borne in clusters on long, arching stems. They have basal rosettes of lance or spoon-shaped leaves. After flowering in summer, the plants become dormant. Grow with other spring and early summer-flowering perennials like doronicums (*see right*), lupins (*see p.280*), and poppies (*see Papaver, p.299*).

Hardiness Fully hardy ✳✳✳.

Cultivation Grow these in well-drained, moist but not waterlogged, soil enriched with well-rotted organic matter in sun or partial shade. Keep them well watered during the growing season. **Sow** seed (*see pp.391–393*) as soon as it is ripe in a container and place in an open cold frame, although it will need exposure to cold before germination can take place. **Divide** plants in spring (*see p.395*). **Protect** the young leaves from slugs and snails (*see p.260*).

DORONICUM

Leopard's bane

spring

LEOPARD'S BANE ARE GROWN FOR their delightful yellow flowers, which can be single or double. They are held, on their own or in small clusters, on slender stems high above the leaves. These perennials flower for several weeks over spring, but may come into bloom in mid- or late winter if the weather is mild. Some species are bulbous and have tubers or rhizomes. Leopard's bane look quite at home in a woodland garden; alternatively, plant them in a herbaceous border with daffodils (*see Narcissus, pp.288–289*), pulmonarias (*see p.314*) and primulas (*see pp.312–313*). They are also good for cutting.

Hardiness Fully hardy ✳✳✳.

Cultivation Grow in moist soil enriched with well-rotted organic matter, in part or dappled shade. *D. orientale* and its cultivars are vulnerable to root rot, especially on heavy clay soils that are wet in winter: dig in plenty of coarse grit to improve drainage on heavy soils. Raising the soil level by 5–8cm (2–3in) can also help. **Water** well in the growing season and deadhead to prolong flowering. **Sow** seed in containers in a cold frame in spring (*see pp.391–393*). **Divide** plants in early autumn (*see p.395*). Powdery mildew may affect the leaves if the soil is dry but the air is damp; avoid splashing leaves when watering.

DRABA

Whitlow grass

spring to early summer

THESE DELICATE ALPINES ARE usually found in mountainous areas. The garden plants in this group are mat- or cushion-forming perennials that produce a mass of yellow or white flowers in spring or early summer. The tiny, green to grey-green leaves form tight, evergreen or semi-evergreen rosettes. They are best grown in a rock garden or raised bed, although some need protection from winter wet in temperate climates. In the autumn, place a sheet of glass or clear plastic over each plant, supported by short pieces of cane, then put a stone on top to hold it in place. Alternatively, grow the plant in a shallow pot, or pan, and move it over winter into a well-ventilated cold frame or unheated greenhouse.

Hardiness Fully hardy ✳✳✳, but protect from winter wet.

Cultivation Grow drabas in gritty, sharply drained soil in full sun, with a gravel mulch. If growing them in pots, use loam-based compost with added grit. Avoid wetting the foliage. **Sow** seed in an open frame in autumn; they need a cold winter to germinate (*see pp.391–393*). **Take rosettes** of larger species as cuttings in late spring (*see p.394*).

① *dentatum* ♀ ‡↔ to 20cm (8in), 2–5 white flowers on each stem in late spring ② *pulchellum* 'Red Wings' ‡35cm (14in) ↔ 20cm (8in), 20 flowers per stem in late spring and early summer

Doronicum 'Miss Mason' ♀
‡13–60cm (5–24in) ↔ 60cm (24in), clumps spread by underground stems (rhizomes), flowers in mid- and late spring

Draba mollissima
‡8cm (3in) ↔ 20cm (8in), hummock-forming evergreen, grey-green, hairy leaves, flowers in late spring

DRACOCEPHALUM

Dragon's head *early to midsummer*

THE ANNUALS AND PERENNIALS in this group are grown for their sage-like, tubular flowers in shades of white and blue. The flowers are produced from early to midsummer in spikes up to 30cm (12in) or more long. Their leaves are often aromatic. Originating in rocky, grassy regions and dry woodland areas, they make a bright and colourful addition to free-draining, mixed or herbaceous borders, and rock gardens. They associate well with such plants as poppies (*see Papaver, p.299*) or cranesbills (*see Geranium, pp.250–251*). Annuals combine well with grasses and are useful gap-fillers in borders. Some will naturalize in partial shade.

Hardiness Fully hardy ✳✳✳.

Cultivation Well-drained, moderately fertile soil and full sun are the requirements for these plants, although some shade from the midday sun is also needed. *Dracocephalum forrestii* requires sharply drained soil and protection from excessive winter wet. *D. ruyschiana* tolerates dry soil. **Sow** seed (*see pp.391–393*) of annuals in mid-spring directly in the soil. Thin seedlings to around 15cm (6in) apart. **Divide** mature clumps (*see p.395*) or sow seed of perennials in autumn or spring in containers in a cold frame. **Take** new shoots from the base and treat as softwood cuttings (*see p.394*) in mid- or late spring.

DRYAS

Mountain avens *spring to early summer*

MATS OF PLEASING, EVERGREEN FOLIAGE distinguish these prostrate, low-growing, woody-based perennials. The oak-like, leathery leaves have a whitish down on their undersides. The plants are also valued for their large, white or yellowish flowers produced from spring to early summer. Upright or nodding, they have a central boss of golden stamens and are borne singly at the tips of slender stems. Pinkish, feathery seedheads follow. An open, sunny site at the front of a border suits these easy-to-grow, carpeting plants. They will also happily scramble over rocks in a rock garden or even colonize dry-stone walls. There are small types suitable for growing in troughs with other, dwarf alpines, such as drabas (*see p.231*).

Hardiness Fully hardy ✳✳✳.

Cultivation Grow these plants in well-drained soil enriched with well-rotted organic matter. They will grow in full sun or partial shade. **Add** plenty of grit to maintain good drainage. **Sow** seed (*see pp.391–393*) in a container in a cold frame as soon as they are ripe, or take softwood cuttings (*see p.394*) in early summer. **Lift**, detach, and transplant rooted stems in spring.

ECHINACEA

Coneflower *midsummer to autumn*

WITH THEIR LARGE DAISIES in shades of purple, rose-pink, or white, these tall perennials from dry prairies, open woodland, and gravelly hillsides make an eye-catching display in a late-summer border. The large central cone standing proud of its petals gives rise to the plant's common name and may be brownish-yellow to ochre. Each daisy is up to 15cm (6in) across and is held on stout, upright stems. The flowers persist for about two months and they also make a long-lasting cut flowers. The leaves reach up to 20cm (8in) in length. Grow these undemanding plants in a border with other late-flowering perennials, such as sedums (*see p.324*) and rudbeckias (*see p.317*). The seedheads continue looking good into winter.

Hardiness Fully hardy ✳✳✳.

Cultivation Coneflowers need deep, fertile, well-drained soil enriched with well-rotted organic matter and full sun, although they tolerate some shade. **Cut back** the stems as the flowers fade for more blooms. **Sow** seed (*see pp.391–393*) in spring. **Divide** in spring or autumn (*see p.395*). **Take** root cuttings (*see p.394*) in late autumn.

Dracocephalum argunense
↕ 45cm (18in) ↔ 30cm (12in), clump-forming perennial, hairy leaves 5–8cm (2–3in) long, flowers in midsummer

Dryas octopetala ♀ (Mountain avens)
↕ 10cm (4in) ↔ 1m (36in), mat-forming, flowers in late spring or early summer, suitable for the rock garden

Echinacea purpurea 'Green Edge'
↕ 1.5m (5ft) ↔ 45cm (18in), flowerheads 13cm (5in) across from midsummer to early autumn

FROSTED SEEDHEADS

inacea purpurea
m (5ft) ↔ 45cm (18in), stems sometimes red-tinted, flowers
3cm (5in) across and borne from midsummer to early autumn

Echinacea purpurea 'White Lustre'
↕ 80cm (32in) ↔ 45cm (18in), flowers from midsummer to early
autumn

Echinacea purpurea 'Magnus' ♈
↕ 1.5m (5ft) ↔ 45cm (18in), extra-large flowers are 18cm (7in)
across and borne from midsummer to early autumn

Echinacea purpurea 'Kim's Knee High'
↕ 45–60cm (18–24in) ↔ 30–60cm (12–24in), unusually compact, dwarf habit, flowers from
midsummer to early autumn, drought-tolerant, can be grown in containers

Echinacea purpurea 'Robert Bloom'
↕ 1.2m (4ft) ↔ 50cm (20in), flowers from midsummer to
early autumn

ECHINOPS

Globe thistle

midsummer to autumn

GROWN FOR THEIR THISTLE-LIKE FLOWERS that appear from midsummer until autumn, these perennials, biennials, and annuals are very undemanding plants. The flowers can be up to 4cm (1½in) across, often have bristly bracts (modified leaves), and are usually blue or white and carried on stout stems. Globe thistles usually form clumps and often have dissected foliage that is spiny and greyish-white. The flowers are also good for cutting and drying. Plant them in a wild garden, or grow them with other perennials such as echinaceas (*see p.232*), monardas (*see p.286*), and phloxes (*see p.306*).

Hardiness Fully hardy ✳✳✳ to frost-hardy ✳✳.

Cultivation Globe thistles are best grown in poor, well-drained soil in full sun, but they will tolerate almost any situation. **Remove** fading flowers to prevent self-seeding. **Sow** seed in a seedbed in mid-spring (*see pp.391–393*). **Divide** established plants from autumn to spring or take root cuttings in winter (*see pp.394–395*).

Echinops ritro 'Veitch's Blue'
↕ to 90cm (3ft) ↔ 45cm (18in), compact perennial, leaves have white, downy undersides, flowers in late summer ✳✳✳

ECHIUM

summer

THIS IS A LARGE GROUP OF ANNUALS, biennials, and evergreen perennials, with charming flowers that appear from early to late summer in shades of deep blue, pink, purple, or white. They are carried either on large, impressive spikes, or in dense clusters close to the stems. The bristly, hairy leaves are usually borne in basal rosettes and on the stems. Grow echiums in borders with echinaceas (*see p.232*), chrysanthemums (*see pp.212–213*), and phloxes (*see p.306*). Wear gloves when handling echiums because contact with the bristly foliage may irritate your skin.

Hardiness Fully hardy ✳✳✳ to frost-tender ❅.

Cultivation Grow these plants in reasonably fertile, well-drained soil, in full sun. **Protect** the perennials in winter in frost-prone areas by covering them with horticultural fleece. As a precaution, it is also wise to take cuttings of perennials in summer (*see p.394*). **Sow** seed at 13–16°C (55–61°F) in summer and overwinter the seedlings in a frost-free greenhouse or cold frame; annuals can be sown in spring where they are to grow (*see pp.391–393*).

Echium vulgare 'Blue Bedder'
↕ 45cm (18in) ↔ 30cm (12in), evergreen biennial with upright, bushy habit, light blue flowers in early summer age to bluish-pink ✳✳✳

EPILOBIUM

Willow herb

summer to autumn

THE COTTAGE GARDEN FAVOURITES from this large group of annuals, biennials, and perennials produce clusters of white or pink flowers from the bases of the leaves over several weeks from summer through to autumn. They can be invasive if allowed to self-seed, like their wildflower cousin the rosebay willow herb, but are easy to control by regular deadheading. There are great variations in height and spread: some grow to around 1.5m (5ft), spreading to 90cm (3ft), and are best in a mixed or herbaceous border. The smaller ones, suitable for a rock garden, have a height and spread of around 30cm (12in).

Hardiness Fully hardy ✳✳✳.

Cultivation Grow in soil enriched with well-rotted organic matter in sun or partial shade. The smaller, alpine species benefit from some shade around midday. **Remove** fading flowers to encourage more blooms and prevent self-seeding. **Sow** seed in containers in a cold frame as soon as they are ripe or in spring (*see pp.391–393*). **Divide** established plants in autumn or spring or take softwood cuttings in spring (*see pp.394–395*). Willow herb is prone to damage from slugs and snails (*see p.398*) and to powdery mildew on the leaves.

① *angustifolium* var. *album* (syn. *Chamerion angustifolium* 'Album') ↕ 1.5m (5ft) ↔ 90cm (3ft), spreading perennial ② *wilsonii* Petrie ↕↔ 20cm (8in), semi-evergreen, mat-forming, likes damp shade

EPIMEDIUM

Barrenwort,
Bishop's mitre

spring to early summer

THE FOLIAGE IS PRIZED AS MUCH AS THE FLOWERS
with these perennials. The mid- to light-green leaves
are lost in autumn in some species or after new leaves
have formed in others. They often develop attractive
tones in autumn and occasionally bronze tips on the
new leaves in spring. From spring until early summer,
loose clusters of saucer- to cup-shaped flowers,
often with spurs, are produced in a range of colours
including gold, beige, white, pink, crimson, and
purple. They make excellent ground-cover plants,
especially under trees where little else will grow.

Hardiness Fully hardy ✽✽✽, although sharp frosts may damage
young foliage and flowers.

Cultivation Grow epimediums in fertile soil, enriched with well-
rotted organic matter, in partial shade. Provide shelter from strong,
cold winds. **Sow** seed in a container in a cold frame as soon as it is
ripe (*see pp.391–393*). **Divide** established plants in autumn or just
after flowering (*see p.395*). Good hygiene in the garden is important
(*see pp.396–399*) because epimediums can be at risk from vine
weevils eating the leaves and mosaic virus, which causes stunted,
mottled growth. Destroy any plants afflicted with virus.

SPRING PRUNING Use shears
to clip old leaves to the ground in
late winter or early spring, before
the new flower spikes appear, to
encourage new growth, except
for *E. perralderianum*.

Epimedium × youngianum 'Niveum' ♀
‡20–30cm (8–12in) ↔ 30cm (12in), deciduous clump, red-tinted
leaf stalks, coloured foliage when young, flowers mid- to late spring

Epimedium acuminatum
‡30cm (12in) ↔ 45cm (18in), clumping evergreen, leaf undersides
have waxy or powdery bloom, flowers in mid-spring to early summer

Epimedium pinnatum subsp. *colchicum* ♀
‡30–40cm (12–16in) ↔ 25cm (10in), slow-growing, clump-forming
evergreen, new leaves have white or red hairs, flowers in spring

Epimedium 'Versicolor'
‡↔ 30cm (12in), clump-forming evergreen, young leaves copper-red
and brown (inset) turning mid-green, flowers in mid- and late spring

EPIPACTIS

Helleborine — *late spring to summer*

These hardy orchids come mainly from temperate regions of the northern hemisphere, where they favour marshes, meadows, woodland and even dunes. They are therefore one of the few orchids that can be grown in temperate gardens – in a damp, shady border or a woodland setting. They have fleshy underground stems, or rhizomes, which produce twisted stalks bearing loose or dense clusters of flowers from spring to early summer. Some of the blooms are greenish-white while others are brown-tinted and streaked with violet, white, or pink. Epipactis usually have ribbed, mid-green leaves that are to 20cm (8in) in length.

Hardiness Fully hardy ✳✳✳.

Cultivation Epipactis require soil enriched with well-rotted organic matter; it must be moist but well-drained, and in partial or deep shade. Given favourable conditions, they will spread freely by sending out creeping rhizomes. **Divide** clumps (*see p.395*) in early spring, ensuring that each piece of rhizome has at least one healthy growing point before replanting. **Slugs** and snails (*see p.398*) may be attracted to the fleshy flowers and shoots.

ERANTHIS HYEMALIS

Winter aconite — *late winter*

WINTER ACONITES PROVIDE A SPLASH OF GOLD to signal the end of winter. Their buttercup-like flowers bloom from late winter to early spring; each appears to sit on an elegant ruff of finely dissected leaves. The leaves at the bases are broader and deeply lobed. These clump-forming perennials grow from knobbly tubers just below soil level in damp, shady places. They look best under deciduous shrubs or trees where, once established, they rapidly spread to form a carpet of colour, especially on alkaline (limy) soils. Winter aconites also naturalize well in grass and combine well with other winter- and early-spring bulbs, such as snowdrops (*see Galanthus, p.247*). Contact with the sap may aggravate skin allergies.

Hardiness Fully hardy ✳✳✳ to frost-hardy ✳✳.

Cultivation Fertile soil that does not dry out in summer and a position in full sun or light, dappled shade are required here. **Plant** the tubers 5cm (2in) deep in autumn. Dried-out tubers will not thrive. *E.pinnatifida* needs acid soil in a raised bed. **Sow** seed (*see pp.391–393*) in containers in a cold frame in late spring. Lift and divide large clumps (*see p.395*) in spring after flowering.

EREMURUS

Desert candle, Foxtail lily — *spring to early summer*

‡1–3m (3–10ft)
↔ to 1.2m (4ft)

MAJESTIC FLOWER SPIKES densely covered in pink, white, or golden, starry flowers soar skywards in spring and early summer. Usually, these clump-forming perennials produce only one flowering stem from each crown. Their long, fleshy, strappy leaves deteriorate quickly, however, so foxtail lilies are best positioned toward the middle or back of a border among shrubs or herbaceous perennials, where the dying foliage will be hidden from view. The flowers are long-lasting when cut. Since grasslands and semi-desserts are the natural home of foxtail lilies, their large, starfish-shaped, fleshy rootstocks are prone to rot in damp conditions.

Hardiness Fully hardy ✳✳✳; although young growth is often damaged by frosts.

Cultivation Plant in well-drained, fertile soil, in full sun with shelter from winds. To improve drainage on heavy clay soils, dig in plenty of coarse grit around the planting area; fork extra into the bottom of the planting hole. **Support** in exposed sites. **Sow** seed (*see pp.391–393*) in containers in a cold frame in autumn or late winter. **Divide** plants after flowering (*see p.395*); handle the brittle rootstocks gently.

Epipactis gigantea (Giant helleborine)
‡30–40cm (12–16in) ↔ to 1.5m (5ft), loose terminal spikes of up to 15 flowers from late spring to early summer

Eranthis hyemalis ♀ (Winter aconite)
‡5–8cm (2–3in) ↔ 5cm (2in), rapid colonizer especially in alkaline (limy) soils, flowers 2–3cm (¾–1¼in) across ✳✳✳

① *himalaicus* ‡1.2–2m (4–6ft) ↔ 60cm (24in), green leaves, flowers in late spring to early summer ② *robustus* ♀ ‡ 3m (10ft) ↔ 1.2m (4ft), blue-green leaves, flowers in early and midsummer

ERIGERON
Fleabane

summer

LONG-LASTING, SINGLE OR DOUBLE DAISIES are borne over many weeks in summer by the annuals, biennials, and perennials in this group. The flowers are available in a wide range of shades, from white, pink, purple, or blue to yellow or orange. All have a bright yellow eye and are borne singly or in small clusters. The leaves are found mostly at the bases of the plants, are sometimes spoon-shaped, and mid- or light green. Erigerons range from low-growing alpines to medium-sized clumps, so need a position at the front of a border. They also stand up well to salt-laden winds, making them invaluable in coastal gardens. The flowers last well if they are cut when fully open.

Hardiness Fully hardy ❋❋❋.

Cultivation Erigerons prefer fertile, well-drained soil that does not dry out in summer in sun, preferably with some shade around midday. **Alpine** species need sharply drained soil and protection from winter wet. **Stake** taller species. **Remove** fading flowers regularly for more flowers; cut down old growth in autumn. **Divide** plants every 2–3 years in late spring (*see p.395*). **Take** root cuttings (*see p.394*) in spring or detach new shoots near the base and treat as softwood cuttings.

Erigeron karvinskianus ♀
‡ 15–30cm (6–12in) ↔ 1m (3ft) or more, vigorous carpeting species suitable for cracks in walls or paving, white flowers fade to pink

Erigeron 'Dunkelste Aller' ♀
‡ 60cm (24in) ↔ 45cm (18in), also called 'Darkest of All', clump-forming border perennial, flowers in early and midsummer

Erigeron 'Quakeress'
‡ 60cm (24in) ↔ 45cm (18in), vigorous, clump-forming border perennial, clusters of single flowers in early and midsummer

Erigeron aureus 'Canary Bird' ♀
‡ to 10cm (4in) ↔ to 15cm (6in), hairy-leaved perennial, flowers in summer, needs protection from winter wet

ERINUS

Fairy foxglove   *late spring to summer*

DAINTY, OPEN FLOWERS in shades of pink, purple, or white are borne in clusters by these trouble-free plants. There are only two species, which are semi-evergreen, short-lived perennials. The leaves are lance- to wedge-shaped, softly textured, and produced in rosettes. Fairy foxgloves are ideal for alpine or rock gardens, or for growing in crevices in old walls or between gaps in paving. If you let them, they will self-seed themselves around the garden.

Hardiness Fully hardy ✳✳✳.

Cultivation Grow these plants in light, reasonably fertile soil that is well-drained, in full sun or partial shade. **Sow** seed in the ground where they are to grow or in containers in a cold frame in autumn (*see pp.391–393*). **Take rosettes** as cuttings in spring (*see p.394*).

ERODIUM

Heron's bill, Stork's bill   *summer to autumn*

THE FOLIAGE AND LONG FLOWERING PERIOD of the annual and perennial erodiums make them valuable plants for the garden. The flowers resemble those of cranesbills (*see Geranium, pp.250–251*) and are produced singly from the joints of leaves and stems or in clusters at the ends of the stems. Flower hues range from pink to purple, and occasionally yellow or white. The curious, pointed seed pods give the plant its common name. Grow the smaller species in a rock garden and the taller ones in a mixed or herbaceous border with other summer-flowering perennials such as achilleas (*see p.166*), cranesbills, phloxes (*see p.306*), or among shrub roses (*see pp.110–113*).

Hardiness Fully hardy ✳✳✳ to frost-hardy ✳✳.

Cultivation Grow the plants in well-drained soil that is neutral to alkaline (limy), in full sun. **Protect** the smaller species from excessive winter wet to avoid them rotting off by covering them with an open-sided cloche. **Sow** seed as soon as it is ripe in containers in a cold frame (*see pp.391–393*). **Divide** plants in spring or take stem cuttings in late spring or early summer (*see pp.394–395*).

ERYNGIUM

Eryngo, Sea holly   *midsummer to autumn*

SEA HOLLIES ARE STRIKING, ARCHITECTURAL plants that lift any border, while some can be naturalized in a wildflower meadow. Most form basal rosettes of leaves that are often spiny, with attractive silvery white veins. From midsummer to autumn, they bear thistle-like flowers on branched stems. These consist of round to cone-shaped heads of tiny flowers, that are surrounded by conspicuous ruffs, also usually silvery white. Grow smaller sea hollies in a rock garden and taller ones in a herbaceous border, where their skeletal forms can be enjoyed through winter. The flowers can be dried, but cut them before they are fully open for best effect. Eryngiums are a large group of annuals, biennials, and deciduous and evergreen perennials.

Hardiness Fully hardy ✳✳✳ to frost-hardy ✳✳.

Cultivation All sea hollies prefer well-drained soil in full sun, but some like poor to moderately fertile soil and protection from excessive winter wet whereas others need moist, rich soil. **Sow** seed as soon as they are ripe in containers in a cold frame (*see pp.391–393*). **Divide** plants in spring – they can be slow to re-establish; take root cuttings of perennials in winter (*see pp.394–395*). Despite their spines, sea hollies are prey to slugs and snails.

Erinus alpinus ♀
‡8cm (3in) ↔ 10cm (4in), sticky leaves, pink, purple, or white flowers from late spring to summer

① *glandulosum* ♀ ‡10–20cm (4–8in) ↔ 20cm (8in), perennial, flowers in summer ✳✳✳ ② *manescavii* ‡20–45cm (8–18in) ↔ 20cm (8in), clumping perennial, flowers summer to autumn ✳✳✳

Eryngium × *oliverianum* ♀
‡90cm (3ft) ↔ 45cm (18in), clumping perennial, dark green spiny leaf rosettes, blue stems, flowers midsummer to early autumn ✳✳✳

Eryngium alpinum ♀
‡70cm (28in) ↔ 45cm (18in), rosette-forming perennial, mid-green, spiny leaves are toothed, flowers are
steel-blue or white in midsummer to early autumn, keep soil moist, protect from winter rains ❋❋❋

ERYSIMUM
Wallflower **spring to early summer**

THE MOST COMMONLY GROWN wallflowers are those
used as spring bedding plants. They are usually grown
as biennials from seed sown in summer or plants
bought bare-rooted in autumn. The fragrant flowers
are produced in pastel and brilliant hues of scarlet,
orange, and gold, with some purples. Wallflowers
spread only 20–60cm (8–24in), so are ideal for
containers, a rock garden, or the front of a mixed
border. Use with spring-flowering plants such as
forget-me-nots (*see Myosotis, p.287*), primulas
(*see pp.312–313*), and tulips (*see pp.334–335*).

Hardiness Fully hardy ❋❋❋ to frost-hardy ❋❋.
Cultivation Grow in poor to reasonably fertile, well-drained, slightly
alkaline (limy) soil, or loam-based compost with added grit, in full
sun. **Trim** perennials lightly after flowering to keep them compact.
Soak bare-root plants in a bucket of water for an hour before planting.
Sow seed of perennials in containers in a cold frame in spring; and
of biennials in early summer. Transplant to flowering positions in
autumn (*see pp.391–393*). **Take** softwood cuttings from woody-based
perennials in summer (*see p.394*). Wallflowers are susceptible to club
root disease so plant them in a different spot each year and maintain
good garden hygiene (*see pp.396–399*).

Eryngium × tripartitum ♀
‡60–90cm (2–3ft) ↔ 50cm (20in), clump-forming perennial, dark
green toothed leaves, flowers midsummer to early autumn ❋❋❋

Eryngium variifolium
‡30–40cm (12–16in) ↔ 25cm (10in), clump-forming evergreen,
flowers in mid- and late summer, protect from winter wet ❋❋❋

① 'Bowles' Mauve' ♀ ‡75cm (30in) ❋❋❋ ② 'Bredon' ♀
‡30cm (12in) ❋❋❋ ③ 'John Codrington' ‡25cm (10in)
❋❋❋ ④ linifolium 'Variegatum' ‡45cm (18in) ❋❋❋

ERYTHRONIUM

Dog's-tooth violet,
Trout lily

spring to early summer

THE ELEGANT, DROOPING FLOWERS of these perennials are produced from spring until early summer, singly or in clusters on slender, upright stems. They have distinctive, swept-back petals, in shades of purple, violet, pink, yellow, or white, and conspicuously long stamens. The broad leaves grow from the base and may be glossy or glaucous; some have a strong bronze marbling, as in *Erythronium dens-canis*, or are veined with white. The common name derives from the long-pointed, tooth-like bulbs from which these clump-forming perennials grow. Natives of meadows and woodlands, they thrive in a rock garden or beneath deciduous trees, and also if naturalized with other bulbs such as dwarf narcissi (*see pp.288–289*) and crocuses (*see p.220*).

Hardiness Fully hardy ❁❁❁.

Cultivation These plants like deep, fertile soil that does not dry out, in partial or light, dappled shade. Plant the bulbs at least 10cm (4in) deep in autumn; keep them slightly damp if stored before planting.
Divide established clumps (*see right and p.395*) after flowering.

DIVIDING CLUMPS
After the leaves wither, lift the bulbs carefully with a fork; separate the offsets, and replant them.

Erythronium 'Pagoda' ❤
‡15–35cm (6–14in) ↔ 10cm (4in), very vigorous, leaves are glossy green and marbled bronze, clusters of up to ten flowers in spring

Erythronium californicum 'White Beauty' ❤
‡15–35cm (6–14in) ↔ 10cm (4in), vigorous, soon forms a large clump, bears clusters of up to three flowers in spring

Erythronium revolutum ❤ (American trout lily)
‡20–30cm (8–12in) ↔ 10cm (4in), clusters of up to four flowers in mid-spring, sometimes slow to establish, but self-seeds freely once it is settled, leaves heavily marbled bronze

Erythronium dens-canis ❤ (European dog's-tooth violet)
‡10–15cm (4–6in) ↔ 10cm (4in), pink, white, or lilac flowers with blue or purple-blue anthers singly in spring, naturalizes well in grass

ESCHSCHOLZIA

California poppy *summer*

IN FIERY SHADES OF ORANGE, gold, and scarlet, and sometimes cream, white, pink, or purple, the tissue-thin, satiny flowers of California poppies are carried singly on slender stems. They may be simple and cup-shaped, double, or even ruffled. Although they open fully only in sun, the flowers are still colourful when closed and are good for cutting. The ferny foliage is light to blue-green. The most commonly grown are the summer-flowering hardy annuals – often in a border with other annuals such as clarkias (*see p.214*) and annual phloxes (*see p.306*) or in a gravel garden. *Eschscholzia californica* types also do well in containers and hanging baskets. These poppies' fragile appearance belies their robust nature; they self-seed freely, even into cracks in paving or concrete.

Hardiness Fully hardy ✳✳✳.

Cultivation These poppies thrive in a poor, well-drained soil, in full sun. **Sow** seed (*see pp.391–393*) of annuals where they are to grow in spring or early autumn. Repeat sowings at two or three week intervals to provide a succession of flowers. Thin to around 15cm (6in) apart.

WIRE SUPPORT
California poppies tend to sprawl. A chicken wire cage over young plants provides support and will soon be entirely hidden by the foliage.

Eschscholzia caespitosa ♀
‡↔ to 15cm (6in), diminutive tufted annual, thread-like leaves, scented flowers in summer, useful edging plant

Eschscholzia californica ♀ (California poppy)
‡ to 30cm (12in) ↔ to 15cm (6in), very variable habit, often sprawling, flowers orange, red, white, and gold in summer

EUCOMIS

Pineapple flower,
Pineapple lily *late summer to autumn*

‡ 15–75cm (6–30in)
↔ 15–20cm (6–8in)

THESE STRIKING PLANTS are grown for their unusual clusters of flowers in late summer and early autumn. The starry flowers are usually pale greenish-white or white, but what sets them apart is the tuft of green bracts leaves, similar to that on a pineapple, that tops each tight cluster. The flowers are followed by long-lasting seed pods. In mild or sheltered places, grow these bulbous perennials at the base of a warm wall or in a sunny border, where the upright stems and strappy leaves contrast well with bold foliage plants such as hostas (*see pp.260–261*). Elsewhere grow them in containers so they can be overwintered under cover.

Hardiness Fully hardy ✳✳✳ (borderline) to frost-tender ❁.

Cultivation Plant the bulbs 15cm (6in) deep in fertile, well-drained soil in full sun. **Mulch** in winter (*see p.388*) with a layer of organic matter. In pots, use a loam-based compost with added coarse grit for drainage, and water freely in summer and sparingly in winter. **Sow** seed (*see pp.391–393*) at 16°C (61°F) in autumn or spring or remove bulb offsets (*see p.395*) in spring.

Eucomis bicolor ♀
‡ 30–60cm (12–24in) ↔ 20cm (8in), maroon-spotted, light green stems and leaves ✳✳✳ (borderline)

EUPATORIUM

Hemp agrimony **_summer to autumn_**

ADORED BY BEES AND BUTTERFLIES, the clusters of tiny flowers on upright, leafy stems are the attraction of the hardy eupatoriums. The flowers come in shades of white, pink, violet, or purple and are mostly borne from summer until early autumn. There are many, varied annuals and perennial eupatoriums that are worthy of the garden, with leaves that differ in shape and shade. The large, hardy, herbaceous perennials such as *Eupatorium cannabinum* look lush in large borders, with grasses (*see pp.340–355*) or in a wild or woodland garden. *E. purpureum* is even taller and has similarly strong stems that need no support.

Hardiness Fully hardy ✳✳✳ to frost-tender ❅.

Cultivation Eupatoriums thrive in any soil, providing it remains moist, in full sun or partial shade. **Deadhead** fading flowers. **Divide** hardy species (*see p.395*) and take softwood cuttings of tender species (*see p.394*) in spring. Sow seed in spring (*see pp.391–393*).

EUPHORBIA

Milkweed, Spurge **_spring to autumn_** see also *p.57*

THE FLAMBOYANT, ACID-YELLOW BRACTS characteristic of many garden spurges contrast dramatically with other plants, and ensure that they always catch the eye. The bracts, which are really modified leaves, surround tiny flowers, borne in clusters at the stem tips. As well as acid-yellow, plants with bracts in warm shades of red, orange, purple, or brown are available. The leaves are usually green to blue-green. This huge and incredibly varied group that includes annuals, biennials, evergreen and semi-evergreen perennials, and succulents, and you can find a euphorbia to suit almost any garden situation. Spurges can be short-lived, particularly in wet soils; luckily, many such as *Euphorbia polychroma* self-seed freely about.

Hardiness Fully hardy ✳✳✳ to frost-tender ❅.

Cultivation Most herbaceous euphorbias like either well-drained, light soils in full sun or moist, humus-rich soils in light, dappled shade. **Sow** seed (*see pp.391–393*) in containers in a cold frame. **Divide** plants in early spring (*see p.395*). Tender and succulent species should be overwintered in a cool greenhouse or conservatory.

Euphorbia schillingii ♆
‡1m (3ft) ↔ 30cm (12in), clump-forming perennial for moisture and light shade, flowers from midsummer to mid-autumn ✳✳✳

Eupatorium purpureum (Joe Pye weed)
‡2.2m (7ft) ↔ 1m (3ft), clump-forming perennial, flowers from midsummer to early autumn, prefers alkaline soil ✳✳✳

Euphorbia polychroma ♆
‡40cm (16in) ↔ 60cm (24in), perennial, likes sun, flowers mid-spring to midsummer, good ground cover, can be invasive ✳✳✳

BEWARE THE SAP
All euphorbias exude a milky sap which irritates the skin, so wear gloves when handling the plants.

Euphorbia griffithii 'Fireglow'
‡75cm (30in) ↔ 1m (3ft), perennial, for moist, light shade, autumn leaves red and gold, flowers in early summer, can be invasive ✳✳✳

EXACUM AFFINE

Persian violet *summer*

FRAGRANT, SUMMER FLOWERS in shades of lavender-blue or, less frequently, rose-pink or white are borne by this annual, or short-lived perennial. The blooms are set off against glossy leaves in a small, bushy, evergreen plant which achieves a maximum height and spread of 30cm (12in). Persian violets, often grown as house or conservatory plants, are best grown outdoors in containers for a summer display and overwintered in a greenhouse or conservatory. In milder areas, they can also be grown as summer bedding, or to fill in mixed beds and borders. Try them with plants such as asters (*see pp.192–193*), begonias (*see pp.196–197*), and petunias (*see p.306*).

Hardiness Frost-tender ❀.

Cultivation Position Persian violets in full sun, in moderately fertile, well-drained soil. For plants in containers, mix sharp sand with a preferably loam-based compost to improve the drainage. **Water** well and feed with a balanced fertilizer at weekly intervals in summer. **Sow** seed (*see pp.391–393*) at 18°C (64°F) in early spring.

Euphorbia dulcis 'Chameleon'
↕↔ 30cm, spreading perennial, tolerates dry shade, dark green or bronze leaves colour well in autumn, flowers in summer ✽✽✽

Euphorbia palustris ♀
↕↔ 90cm (36in), vigorous perennial, prefers moist situations, leaves turn yellow and orange in autumn, flowers in late spring ✽✽✽

Euphorbia myrsinites ♀
↕ 10cm (4in) ↔ 30cm (12in), evergreen succulent, trailing stems, flowers in spring, needs good drainage and sun ✽✽✽

Exacum affine ♀ (Persian violet)
↕↔ 23–30cm (9–12in), flowers 2cm (¾in) across

FELICIA

Blue daisy *summer*

MASSES OF DAISIES OF PURE BLUE, or occasionally white, mauve, or lilac, smother felicias throughout summer, making the plant a popular choice for bedding and containers including hanging baskets. Felicias are not entirely hardy, so are generally treated as annuals or tender perennials. In mild, dry winters, they should survive to form substantial, bushy plants with a maximum height and spread of 30–50cm (12–20in). The plentiful, tiny leaves are grey- or mid-green in colour; those of *Felicia amoena* 'Variegata' have bright creamy-white edges.

Hardiness Frost-hardy ✳ to half-hardy ✳.

Cultivation Grow felicias in poor to moderately fertile, well-drained soil, in full sun. They do not thrive in damp conditions. For plants in containers, use a loam-based compost; then water them well in summer; and feed at weekly intervals with a balanced fertilizer. **Pinch back** young shoots regularly to encourage a bushy habit. **Sow** seed (*see p.391–393*) at 10–18°C (50–64°F) in spring. Take softwood cuttings (*see p.394*) in late summer and overwinter the young plants in frost-free conditions under glass.

FILIPENDULA

spring to summer

FROM A DISTANCE, THE FLOWERS of filipendulas look like a cloud of foam floating above a sea of bright green leaves. At closer quarters, their unusual, musky fragrance can be detected. These perennials bear large heads of fluffy white, cream, pink, or red flowers on branching stems in late spring and summer. They thrive in damp soil, so are most at home in woodland plantings in soil that stays moist through summer. Try them with other moisture-loving perennials such as eupatoriums (*see p.242*) or hostas (*see pp.260–261*). *Filipendula vulgaris* tolerates drier conditions, and prefers alkaline (limy) soils in full sun; it has dark green, ferny leaves, which look good with lupins (*see p.280*) and poppies (*see Papaver, p.299*).

Hardiness Fully hardy ✳✳✳.

Cultivation Grow filipendulas in moderately fertile, moist but well-drained soil, in sun or partial shade. Planting gold-leaved cultivars in shade results in a stronger colour. **Sow** seed (*see pp.391–393*) in autumn in pots and place them in a cold frame, or sow in spring at 10–13°C (50–55°F). **Divide** plants (*see p.395*) in autumn or spring. Take root cuttings (*see p.394*) from late winter until early spring.

Filipendula rubra 'Venusta' ♀
↕2–2.5m (6–8ft) ↔ 1.2m (4ft), spreading to large clumps, flowers in early and midsummer, becoming paler as they age

Felicia amelloides 'Santa Anita' ♀
↕↔ 30–60cm (12–24in), subshrub, often grown as annual, deep green leaves, 5cm (2in) flowers from summer to autumn ✳✳

Filipendula palmata
↕1.2m (4ft) ↔ 60cm (24in), clump-forming, variable leaves to 30cm (12in) long with densely woolly, white undersides, pale to deep pink flowers 20cm (8in) across borne in midsummer

FOENICULUM VULGARE

Fennel *summer*

THE LARGE, BILLOWING CLUMPS of green or purple filigree foliage make fennel a star in bed and borders, where the finely cut leaves contrast well with broad-leaved plants or blowsy flowers. Try purple fennel with the huge, dusky pink blooms of the oriental poppy, 'Patty's Plum'. Fennel is perhaps best known as an aromatic herb with a strong anise flavour used for flavouring foods, and all parts have the strong aroma of anise. This perennial reaches a height of 2m (6ft) and spread of 45cm (18in) from large, deep roots. During mid- and late summer, flat clusters of tiny, yellow flowers appear, followed by large, aromatic seeds. Herb fennel and ornamental fennels both work well in borders or in a herb garden.

Hardiness Fully hardy ✳✳✳, although new shoots may be damaged by frosts.
Cultivation Fennels prefer fertile, moist but well-drained soil, in full sun. **Deadhead** flowerheads before the seeds form to prevent prolific self-seeding. **Sow** seed (*see pp.391–393*) in spring at 13–18°C (55–64°F) or outdoors where the plants are to grow.

FRAGARIA

Strawberry *spring to autumn*

IN THE RUSH FOR THE DELICIOUS, early-summer fruits, the ornamental cultivars of the perennial strawberry plants should not be overlooked. These bear clusters of up to ten pink or white flowers from late spring until mid-autumn. *Fragaria vesca* 'Variegata' has attractively variegated, cream and grey-green leaves. Strawberries increase by means of stems that creep along the ground, producing young plantlets at their tips. They spread rapidly, but without becoming invasive, which makes them very useful as a weed-suppressing ground cover. Strawberries are quite vigorous plants and evergreen, except through harsh winters. Use them to edge beds and borders, in cracks and crevices of paving, containers, or hanging baskets.

Hardiness Fully hardy ✳✳✳.
Cultivation Fertile, moist but well-drained soil, in full sun or partial shade is required. Strawberries prefer neutral to alkaline soils, but will tolerate acid soil. **Sow** seed (*see pp.391–393*) in spring at 13–18°C (55–64°F). **Remove** and transplant rooted runners in late summer.

FRANCOA

Bridal wreath *summer and autumn*

WIDELY GROWN AS A FLOWER FOR CUTTING, bridal wreath has graceful, dainty flower spikes of pink or white that give an airy feel to a border. The main flowering period of these few evergreen perennials is summer, but often the plants produce a second flush of flowers in autumn. They are 60–90cm (24–36in) tall, and have attractive rosettes of softly hairy leaves with wavy edges that spread to about 45cm (18in). Bridal wreaths happily seed themselves about without becoming invasive. Place them in mixed borders with plants such as persicarias (*see p.305*), phloxes (*see p.306*), and daylilies (*see Hemerocallis, p.258*), or use them in containers or as edging plants.

Hardiness Frost-hardy ✳✳, although may survive to -10°C (14°F).
Cultivation Undemanding, these plants like moist but well-drained soil, that has been enriched with well-rotted organic matter, in full sun or partial shade. **Water** freely in summer and apply a balanced feed every four weeks. **Divide** plants (*see p.395*) in spring. **Sow** seed (*see pp.391–393*) at 15–24°C (59–75°F) in spring.

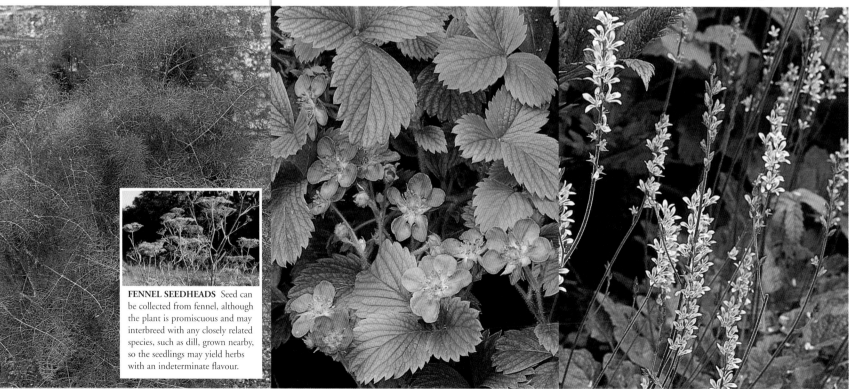

FENNEL SEEDHEADS Seed can be collected from fennel, although the plant is promiscuous and may interbreed with any closely related species, such as dill, grown nearby, so the seedlings may yield herbs with an indeterminate flavour.

Foeniculum vulgare 'Purpureum'
↕ 2m (6ft) ↔ 45cm (18in), bronze-purple foliage when young, turning glaucous green with age

Fragaria PINK PANDA ('Frel')
↕ 10–15cm (4–6in) ↔ indefinite, flowers to 2.5cm (1in) across, borne from late spring to mid-autumn, rarely bears fruit

Francoa sonchifolia
↕ 60–90cm (24–36in) ↔ 45cm (18in)

FRITILLARIA

Fritillary   *spring to early summer*

ELEGANT, NODDING BELLS are the common feature
of this diverse group of perennial bulbs. The flowers
come in muted shades such as soft green, tawny reds,
and purples, often with strikingly patterned petals,
and are borne in spring and early summer, singly or
in clusters. Fritillaries vary from diminutive, delicate
types only 8cm (3in) tall to more robust species with
stout stems up to 1.5m (5ft). Crown imperials thrive
in mixed borders. The more demure snake's head
fritillary (*F. meleagris*) can be naturalized in moist
meadows or in the dappled shade under trees and
shrubs. Alpine species can be tricky to grow and need
sharp drainage and usually alpine-house conditions.

Hardiness Fully hardy ✳✳✳ to frost-hardy ✳✳.

Cultivation Plant the bulbs at four times their depth. Fritillarias
differ in their needs, but most garden plants need fertile, well-drained,
moisture-retentive soil in full sun, or moist, humus-rich soil in light
shade. **Divide** large clumps (*see p.395*) in late summer. Smaller
species such as *F. acmopetala*, produce numerous but tiny bulblets
(called "rice"); treat them like seeds and grow on in a seed tray
(*see pp.391–393*).

Fritillaria imperialis (Crown imperial)
↕ 1.5m (5ft) ↔ 25–30cm (10–12in), orange, red, or yellow flowers
in early summer, needs fertile, well-drained soil in full sun ✳✳✳

GAILLARDIA

Blanket flower   *summer to autumn*

THESE PLANTS HAVE CHEERFUL, LARGE DAISIES that
appear for a long period throughout summer and into
autumn. The flowers, which are up to 14cm (5½in)
across, are yellow, crimson, or orange with contrasting
bosses in purple, brown, red, or yellow. These are held
on long stems up to 90cm (36in) tall above bushy
plants with soft, hairy, long leaves. Cultivars of the
short-lived perennial *Gaillardia × grandiflora* are most
commonly grown of the group, which also includes
annuals and biennials. They brighten up containers
or mixed or annual borders; try them with pinks (*see
Dianthus, p.226–227*), pot marigolds (*see Calendula
officinalis, p.204*), and rudbeckias (*see p.317*).
Gaillardias are also good for cutting.

Hardiness Fully hardy ✳✳✳ to frost-hardy ✳✳.

Cultivation Gaillardias prefer fertile, well-drained soil in full sun;
they will also tolerate poor soils. **Deadhead** regularly to encourage more
flowers. **Cut back** perennials to around 15cm (6in) in late summer to
encourage fresh growth at the base. **Sow** seed (*see pp.391–393*) at
13–18°C (55–64°F) in early spring. Seed of annuals can also be sown
in situ in late spring or early summer. **Divide** perennials (*see p.395*) in
spring or take root cuttings (*see p.394*) in winter.

Fritillaria meleagris (Snake's head fritillary)
↕ 30cm (12in) ↔ 5–8cm (2–3in), purple or white flowers in spring,
needs moist, enriched soil in full sun or light shade ✳✳✳

Fritillaria acmopetala ♥
↕ 40cm (16in) ↔ 5–8cm (2–3in), robust, flowers in late spring,
needs fertile, well-drained soil in full sun ✳✳✳

***Gaillardia* 'Dazzler'** ♥
↕ 60–85cm (24–34in) ↔ 45cm (18in), short-lived perennial, mid-
to grey-green leaves, flowers from early summer to early autumn ✳✳✳

GALANTHUS
Snowdrop

winter to early spring

SNOWDROPS NEED LITTLE INTRODUCTION: this hugely popular flower is a welcome sight in late winter and early spring, appearing when little else is in flower. There are hundreds of different kinds with subtly different petal shapes and green markings; snowdrop fanciers, called galanthophiles, will travel miles to see new forms. Each snowdrop bulb usually produces a single, white, pendent flower on an arching flower stalk. Some have scented flowers. Most snowdrops are vigorous and easily grown, often forming large clumps, and spread by self-seeding. They look particularly good if naturalized in grass. *Galanthus reginae-olgae* flowers in autumn. Contact with the bulbs may cause a rash.

Hardiness Fully hardy ❀❀❀ to frost-hardy ❀❀.

Cultivation Soil enriched with well-rotted organic matter, that does not dry out in summer, in sun or partial shade, suits snowdrops. **Divide** clumps of bulbs every 3–4 years to stop the plants becoming congested and losing vigour; this is done in spring after flowering while the bulbs are "in the green" (*see below*). Snowdrops cross-pollinate freely so may not come true to type from seed.

Galanthus 'Atkinsii' ♀
↕20cm (8in) ↔ 8cm (3in), flowers 3cm (1¼in) long appear in late winter ❀❀❀

DIVIDING SNOWDROPS
Snowdrops should be divided "in the green" while they still have leaves and shortly after the flowers have faded. Carefully dig up the clumps with a fork, pull apart the bulbs, and replant individually or in small groups where required.

GALAX URCEOLATA
Wandflower

late spring and summer

THIS EVERGREEN PERENNIAL IS GROWN for its elegant wands of small, white flowers produced in late spring and summer, followed by rich, red-bronze foliage in autumn. The flower spikes are up to 25cm (10in) tall and the leaves up to 8cm (3in) across. It spreads by creeping roots and makes a useful ground cover under shrubs in a shady bed or border or in a woodland garden. It is also happy in a large rock garden. Try it with other shade-loving, early summer-flowering perennials, such as cranesbills (*see Geranium, pp.250–251*), lupins (*see p.280*), and poppies (*see Papaver, p.299*).

Hardiness Fully hardy ❀❀❀.

Cultivation This plants thrives in moist, acid (lime-free) soil in partial shade; make sure that the roots will not dry out. **Mulch** annually in spring with pine needles or leafmould. **Sow** seed (*see pp.391–393*) in containers of lime-free (ericaceous) compost in an open frame outdoors in autumn. **Separate** rooted runners in early spring: carefully dig up the rooted stem; trim back the stub; and transplant the divided pieces where required.

Galanthus 'S. Arnott' ♀
↕20cm (8in) ↔ 8cm (3in), strongly honey-scented flowers, 2.5–3.5cm (1–1½in) long, in late winter and early spring ❀❀❀

Galanthus nivalis 'Flore Pleno' ♀
↕↔ 10cm (4in), robust, double-flowered, spreads rapidly from offsets, honey-scented, irregular flowers in winter ❀❀❀

Galax urceolata
↕30cm (12in) ↔ 1m (3ft)

GALEGA

Goat's rue, French lilac

summer to autumn

‡30cm–1.5m (1–5ft)
↔ 60–90cm (2–3ft)

THE TALL, FLOPPY stems of these bushy, spreading perennials are very graceful, but tend to fall over other plants unless staked. The many clusters of pea-like flowers come in shades or bicolours of white, blue, and mauve. Viewed from a distance, the mass of small flowers creates a vivid wash of colour over the bright green foliage. Flowering usually in summer, but also in spring or autumn, galegas are best in borders with summer-flowering plants like lychnis (*see p.282*), lythrums (*see p.283*), monardas (*see p.286*), and sunflowers (*see p.256*). They also naturalize well and are good for cutting. *Galega officinalis* is most often seen in gardens.

Hardiness Fully hardy ✳✳✳.

Cultivation Galegas thrive in any moist soil in full sun or partial shade. **Deadhead** to prevent self-seeding; cut back to ground level after flowering. **Sow** seed, soaked overnight, of species (*see pp.391–393*) in containers in a cold frame in spring. **Divide** cultivars (*see p.395*) between late autumn and spring.

GALTONIA

late summer

‡to 1.2m (4ft)
↔ 10cm (4in)

LIKE A LATE-SUMMER HYACINTH, *Galtonia candicans* has tall, elegant spikes of pure white, slightly fragrant flowers. The only commonly grown species, it is particularly useful in the garden, and deserves wider recognition, because few bulbs of this beauty flower at this time of year. The grey-green, strappy leaves are quite fleshy. This trouble-free, bulbous perennial mixes well with grasses and other perennials like dicentras (*see p.228*), lythrums (*see p.283*), monardas (*see p.286*), poppies (*see Papaver, p.299*), rudbeckias (*see p.317*), and sedums (*see p.324*). *G. viridiflora* has pale green, nodding flowers, but is less hardy to frost.

Hardiness Fully hardy ✳✳✳ to frost-hardy ✳✳.

Cultivation Fertile, well-drained soil that is reliably moist in summer, in full sun, suits galtonias. **Lift** the bulbs in late autumn in areas with severe winters, and overwinter in pots in a frost-free greenhouse or conservatory. Alternatively, leave the bulbs in the soil and cover with a deep winter mulch (*see p.388*). **Sow** seed in a container (*see pp.391–393*) in a cold frame as soon as it is ripe. **Divide** large clumps (*see p.395*) and replant in early spring.

GAURA LINDHEIMERI

summer to autumn

THE SUMMER AND AUTUMN FLOWERS of this gracious perennial would soften any border with their light, airy growth. Each bloom nestles inside the leaves and is short-lived, but is soon replaced by another, keeping up a continuous display for several weeks. This trouble-free plant forms a bushy clump. *Gaura lindheimeri* has several pretty cultivars – 'Corrie's Gold' has gold-edged leaves and 'Siskiyou Pink' has pinkish flowers. 'Whirling Butterflies' is named after the shape of its reddish flowers; it forms a smaller clump, and is very free-flowering. Gauras contrast well with late-flowering perennials that have large, fleshy blooms, like chrysanthemums (*see pp.212–213*), rudbeckias (*see p.317*), and sedums (*see p.324*).

Hardiness Fully hardy ✳✳✳.

Cultivation Any fertile, moist but well-drained soil, in full sun will do; drought and partial shade are tolerated. **Sow** seed (*see pp.391–393*) in containers in a cold frame from spring until early summer. **Divide** clumps (*see p.395*) in spring to increase stock. Take softwood cuttings in spring or heel cuttings in summer (*see p.394*).

Galega 'His Majesty'
‡to 1.5m (5ft) ↔ 90cm (36in), flowers from early summer to early autumn; 'Lady Wilson' ♔ has similar flowers, 'Alba' ♔ is a white form

Galtonia candicans ♔
‡1–1.2m (3–4ft) ↔ 10cm (4in), tubular flowers open from the base of the flower spike in late midsummer ✳✳✳

Gaura lindheimeri ♔
‡to 1.5m (5ft) ↔ 90cm (36in), pinkish buds open at dawn to white flowers that fade to pink, from late spring to early autumn

GAZANIA

summer

THE BRIGHT AND CHEERY, sunflower-like blooms of these small annuals or evergreen perennials are most often seen in summer bedding displays, windowboxes, and patio containers in climates with frosty winters. Hybrids are usually grown and are treated as annuals with other bedding plants like marigolds (*see p.204 and p.329*) and pelargoniums (*see pp.300–303*). The summer flowers come in a wide range of bold colours, often with darker centres and markings on the petals. They need a sunny site because they close up on dull days. The dark green, hairy foliage is a good foil to the flowers. Gazanias grow well in coastal areas.

Hardiness Half-hardy ✳ to frost-tender ❉, but most can survive short periods at 0°C (32°F).

Cultivation Grow gazanias in light, sandy, well-drained soil, in full sun. **Remove** dead blooms to prolong flowering. **Sow** seed at 18–20°C (64–68°F) in late winter or early spring (*see pp.391–393*). **Take** new shoots from the base and treat as softwood cuttings (*see p.394*) in late summer or early autumn. Overwinter the new plants in frost-free conditions; these may suffer from grey mould (botrytis) if poorly ventilated, and aphids may be a problem – remove any plants that are severely infested.

Gazania 'Talent Yellow'
‡↔ to 25cm (10in), vigorous evergreen perennial, grey felty leaves, flowers in summer ✳

GENTIANA

Gentian

late spring to autumn

IT IS THE INTENSE BLUE, trumpet- or bell-shaped flowers that draw gardeners to gentians, but there are also white-, yellow- and rarely, red-flowered forms. Flowering times vary, from late spring (*G. acaulis*), summer (*G. saxosa*), late summer (*G. septemfida*), and autumn (*G. sino-ornata*). Gentians are a large and varied group, but perennials are usually grown; they may be deciduous, evergreen, or semi-evergreen, and range from low mats and trailing types to clumping or upright forms. Many are alpines, needing rock-garden conditions; a few suit herbaceous borders, such as the relatively tall, shade-loving *G. asclepiadea* with late-summer flowers. Some gentians have very specific soil needs, so you may have to grow them in containers. Autumn-flowering gentians have rosettes of leaves.

Hardiness Fully hardy ✳✳✳.

Cultivation Most need light but rich, well-drained but moist soil, in full sun only where summers are cool. Provide partial shade in warmer areas. Autumn-flowering gentians need neutral to acid soil. **Sow** seed (*see pp.391–393*) of species as soon as it is ripe in a cold frame. **Divide** rooted offshoots (*see p.395*) carefully in spring.

Gazania Mini Star Series
‡to 20cm (8in) ↔ to 25cm (10in), compact, tuft-forming, evergreen perennial, white silky hairs beneath leaves, summer flowers may be bright yellow, orange, copper, bronze, white, pink, and beige ✳

① *acaulis* ♀ ‡8cm (3in) ↔ 30cm (12in) ② *saxosa* ‡8cm (3in) ↔ 10cm (4in) ③ *septemfida* ♀ ‡15–20cm (6–8in) ↔ 30cm (12in) ④ *sino-ornata* ♀ ‡to 8cm (3in) ↔ 15–30cm (6–12in)

FLOWERING PLANTS

Cranesbill

early summer to autumn

EASY-TO-GROW, VERSATILE, AND LONG-FLOWERING, few plants are as useful in the garden as hardy geraniums. The genus contains about 300 annuals, biennials, and herbaceous perennials, some of them semi-evergreen or evergreen. The flowers are delicate and abundant, with colours ranging from white, shades of pink and purple, to blue, often with contrasting veins. Leaves are usually rounded or palm-like (palmate) and are frequently aromatic. Some types have colourful autumn foliage. They are often confused with the non-hardy bedding and container plant, *Pelargonium* (*see pp.300–303*), which is popularly called geranium. Cranesbills are found in many habitats, except in very wet areas, and can be grown almost anywhere in the garden, and in pots. There are compact varieties to 15cm (6in) tall, suitable for a rock garden, and plants of 1.4m (4ft) or more for mixed and herbaceous borders. Mat-forming species like *Geranium macrorrhizum* are useful as ground cover, including on slopes, where the dense root system helps to prevent soil erosion.

Hardiness Fully hardy ✷✷✷ to half-hardy ✷.

Cultivation Grow the larger species and hybrids in fertile soil in full sun or partial shade. Small species need a well-drained site in full sun. Avoid soils that are excessively wet in winter. **Water** plants well during dry spells and feed with a liquid fertilizer monthly. **Trim off** the faded blooms and foliage after the first flush of flowers in early or midsummer, to encourage fresh leaves and another show of flowers. **Sow** seed (*see pp.391–393*) of hardy species outdoors in containers as soon as it is ripe or in spring. Seed of half-hardy species is sown at 13–18°C (55–64°F) in spring. **Divide** overgrown clumps in spring (*see p.395*). **Take** basal cuttings (the base of the stem and a small piece of the crown) in spring. Treat them in the same way as soft-tip cuttings (*see p.394*).

Using geraniums in the garden

◁ **Woodland planting** *Loose, spreading shapes and plentiful flowers, even in dappled shade, make geraniums an appropriate choice for the woodland garden. Here, the airy foliage and dainty pink flowers of* G. endressii *make an effective contrast to the solid forms of the tree trunks. This species, together with* G. himalayense *and* G. macrorrhizum *and their cultivars, and* G. nodosum, *all make good cover in any shady site.*

▷ **Ground cover** *Geranium ×* magnificum *is used here as ground cover under climbing roses. Roses and geraniums are a classic garden combination. A geranium's vigorous, spreading habit camouflages bare soil and hides dull rose stems – and its small, saucer-shaped flowers are good foils to the showier rose blooms. Their characteristic blue, mauve, and pink hues harmonize with many rose colours. Here, a profusion of rich violet blooms makes an eye-catching contrast to the bright scarlet roses.*

① *Geranium* 'Ann Folkard' ♀ ↕60cm (24in) ↔ 1m (3ft) ② *asphodeloides* ↕30–45cm (12–18in), ↔ 30cm (12in), evergreen ③ × *cantabrigiense* ↕30cm (12in) ↔ 60cm (24in), evergreen, aromatic ④ × *cantabrigiense* 'Biokovo' ↕30cm (12in) ↔ 75–90cm (30–36in), evergreen ⑤ *cinereum* 'Ballerina' ♀ ↕15cm (6in) ↔ 30cm (12in), evergreen, needs good drainage ⑥ *cinereum* var. *subcaulescens* ♀ ↕15cm (6in) ↔ 30cm (12in), evergreen, needs good drainage ⑦ *clarkei* 'Kashmir White' ♀ ↕45cm

(18in) ↔ indefinite ⑧ *dalmaticum* ♀ ‡15cm (6in) ↔ 50cm (20in), evergreen ⑨ *endressii* ♀ ‡45cm (18in) ↔ 60cm (24in), evergreen ⑩ *erianthum* ‡45–60cm (18–24in) ↔ 30cm (12in), good autumn leaf colour ⑪ *himalayense* ‡30–45cm (12–18in) ↔ 60cm (24in) ⑫ *himalayense* 'Gravetye' ♀ ‡30cm (12in) ↔ 60cm (24in) ⑬ *ibericum* ‡50cm (20in) ↔ 60cm (24in) ⑭ *macrorrhizum* ‡50cm (20in) ↔ 60cm (24in), aromatic ⑮ *macrorrhizum* 'Ingwersen's Variety' ♀ ‡50cm (20in) ↔ 60cm (24in), semi-evergreen ⑯ *maculatum* ‡60–75cm (24–30in) ↔ 45cm (18in) ⑰ *maderense* ♀ ‡↔ 1.2–1.5m (4–5ft), evergreen ✳ ⑱ × *magnificum* ♀ ‡↔ 60cm (24in) ⑲ *nodosum* ‡30–50cm (12–20in), ↔ 50cm (20in) ⑳ *orientalitibeticum* ‡30cm (12in) ↔ 1m (3ft) ㉑ × *oxonianum* ‡80cm (32in) ↔ 60cm (24in), evergreen ㉒ × *oxonianum* 'Southcombe Star' ‡80cm (32in) ↔ 60cm (24in), evergreen ㉓ × *oxonianum* 'Winscombe' ‡↔ 45cm (18in), evergreen

GEUM

Avens

spring to summer

LOOKING RATHER LIKE BUTTERCUPS or small roses, the bold flowers of geums come in attractive shades of red, orange, and yellow. They appear from late spring into summer and are held above clumps of deep green, wrinkled and divided leaves. The smaller geums are suitable for growing in a rock garden, while the larger ones are almost tailor-made for the front of a sunny border. Combine them with other herbaceous perennials such as the closely related potentillas (*see p.311*), which have a similar style of flower, and cranesbills (*see Geranium, pp.250–251*).

Hardiness Fully hardy ✳✳✳.

Cultivation Grow most geums in fertile, well-drained soil in full sun. *Geum rivale* and its cultivars, need more moisture and plenty of organic matter, but avoid soil that becomes waterlogged in winter. **Sow** seed in containers in a cold frame in spring or autumn (*see pp.391–393*). 'Lady Stratheden' and 'Mrs J. Bradshaw' generally come true from seed, but the majority of the larger geums cross-pollinate freely and produce unpredictable offspring. **Divide** other named varieties (*see p.395*) to be sure that new plants are true to type.

Geum montanum ♀
‡15cm (6in) ↔ to 30cm (12in), one of the smaller geums that is ideally suited to a rock garden; it flowers in spring and early summer

GLADIOLUS

summer

WITH THEIR TALL, STRONGLY UPRIGHT spikes of summer flowers, gladioli can look especially striking in cut-flower displays as well as in the garden. The funnel-shaped flowers open from the bottom of the stem upwards and come in shades of white, red, pink, yellow, orange, and some bicolours, sometimes with dainty splotches on the lower petals. Gladioli grow from corms, with long, sword-like leaves arranged in fans. Many are not hardy and need a warm, sheltered border. Partner them with other herbaceous perennials such as daylilies (*see Hemerocallis, p.258*) and grasses. They are sometimes grown in rows in the vegetable garden specifically for cutting.

Hardiness Fully hardy ✳✳✳ to frost-tender ❄.

Cultivation Grow in fertile, well-drained soil in full sun. **Plant** corms 10–15cm (4–6in) deep in spring. In heavy soil, fork coarse grit into the planting area. Large-flowered kinds need staking. **Lift** corms in frost-prone areas once leaves begin to yellow, dry them for a fortnight or so, then remove all leafy remains. **Separate** the corms, discarding the old, dried-up, dark brown ones, and store over winter in a cool, frost-free place. Check occasionally and remove any that show signs of mould.

***Geum* 'Lady Stratheden'** ♀
‡40–60cm (16–24in) ↔ 60cm (24in), a popular geum for a sunny border, where its large flowers will be produced all summer

***Geum* 'Red Wings'**
‡to 60cm (24in) ↔ to 40cm (16in), the semi-double, bright red or scarlet flowers appear very freely throughout summer

***Gladiolus* 'Elvira'**
‡80cm (32in) ↔ 8–10cm (3–4in), each corm produces two or three slender flower spikes in early summer that are ideal for cutting ✳

Gladiolus tristis
‡45–150cm (1½–5ft) ↔ 5cm (2in), pale yellow or creamy white flowers in spring, strong evening scent ✳

Gladiolus communis subsp. *byzantinus* ♈
‡to 1m (3ft) ↔ 8cm (3in), vigorous, spreading, flowers in early summer, mulch over winter in cold areas ✳✳✳ (borderline)

Gladiolus 'Anna Leorah'
‡1.6m (5½ft) ↔ 15cm (6in), each towering flower spike is densely packed with pink-edged blooms from early to late summer ✳

GLECHOMA
Ground ivy   *spring to summer*

THE CREEPING NATURE of these perennials makes them useful ground-cover plants, especially in partially shaded areas. The small, toothed leaves appear on long, slender stems, which readily root into the soil. Some forms can be quite invasive and their spread needs to be checked from time to time. The small, violet-blue flowers are borne from spring through summer. Good companions include bugles (*see Ajuga, p.172*), corydalis (*see p.217*), lamiums (*see p.269*), violets (*see p.338*), and snowdrops (*see Galanthus, p.247*). The white-marbled leaves of *Glechoma hederacea* 'Variegata', the most commonly grown type, make a good foil for summer bedding plants such as pelargoniums (*see pp.300–303*) and fuchsias (*see pp.60–63*) in container displays, and mixes well with silver-leaved helichrysums.

Hardiness Fully hardy ✳✳✳.
Cultivation Grow in reasonably fertile, well-drained soil in full sun or partial shade. **Divide** plants in spring or autumn (*see p.395*), or take softwood cuttings in late spring (*see p.394*).

Glechoma hederacea 'Variegata'
‡to 15cm (6in) ↔ to 2m (6ft) or more, the trailing foliage makes an all-year display in hanging baskets and windowboxes

GUNNERA

spring to autumn

THE FOLIAGE OF GUNNERAS is one of gardening's sensations. Although there are diminutive mat-forming gunneras like *Gunnera magellanica*, which is no more than 15cm (6in) tall, it is the giant rhubarb, *G. manicata*, for which this group of perennials is famed. This plant reaches a majestic 2.5m (8ft) or more within a season. The undersides of the rhubarb-like leaves and their thick stalks are coarsely spined. The flower spikes are also attractive in some species. Large-leaved specimens make excellent architectural plants for stream- or pondsides, but in large gardens only. They combine well with other moisture-loving plants, such as astilbes (*see p.194*). The small gunneras are best in a rock garden.

Hardiness Fully hardy ✳✳✳ to frost-hardy ✳✳.

Cultivation Grow in deep, permanently moist soil in sun or partial shade in a sheltered position. In frosty areas, protect their crowns in winter with a covering of the old leaves. **Increase** large species by taking cuttings of leafy, basal buds, with a section of root attached, in spring. **Divide** small species in spring (*see p.395*). **Sow** seed (*see pp.391–393*) in containers in a cold frame as soon as it is ripe.

GYPSOPHILA

summer

THE DIFFUSE, STARRY SPRAYS of small, white or pink summer flowers of gypsophilas will be familiar to anyone who buys cut flowers. They make a pretty and airy filler for indoor arrangements and the same principle applies to gypsophilas in the garden. Small types are ideal for rock gardens or for tumbling over retaining walls; the annual and larger perennial gypsophilas such as *G. paniculata* suit borders. The clouds of flowers look good with many herbaceous perennials, for example coreopsis (*see p.217*), cranesbills (*see Geranium, pp.250–251*), and geums (*see p.252*). Popular cultivars include 'Bristol Fairy' and 'Perfekta', with double white flowers, and 'Flamingo', with lilac-pink double flowers. All are good for cutting.

Hardiness Fully hardy ✳✳✳ to frost-hardy ✳✳.

Cultivation Grow in deep, light, preferably alkaline (limy) soil that is sharply drained and in full sun. **Sow** seed of annuals where they are to flower in spring (*see p.393*), and thin out seedlings to around 15cm (6in) apart. Seed of perennials should be sown at 13–18°C (55–64°F) in spring (*see pp.391–392*). **Take** root cuttings of perennials in winter (*see p.394*) as an alternative way of making new plants.

HABERLEA

spring to early summer

SUITED TO A SHADY ROCK GARDEN, these stemless, evergreen perennials can gradually colonize an area with their rosettes of dark green leaves, which are brightened in spring and early summer by loose clusters of nodding, trumpet-shaped flowers. These appear in shades of lavender-blue or pale violet-blue. Haberleas, which grow only to about 15cm (6in), are ideal for growing in the pockets of a dry-stone wall, in rock crevices, or in an alpine house (a well-ventilated, cold greenhouse). They combine well with a wide range of other rock plants.

Hardiness Fully hardy ✳✳✳.

Cultivation Grow in moist, but well-drained, preferably alkaline (limy) soil in full or partial shade. In an alpine house, grow them in free-draining, loam-based compost. Once planted, they resent root disturbance. **Protect** from excessive winter wet; haberleas prefer to be planted on their sides to prevent water from accumulating in the crowns of the plants. **Sow** seed at 13–18°C (55–64°F) in spring (*see pp.391–392*). **Divide** clumps of rosettes in early summer (*see p.395*). Slugs and snails may attack the foliage (*see p.398*) of plants outside.

Gunnera tinctoria
↕ 1.5m (5ft) ↔ 2m (6ft), the enormous leaves and rusty flowerheads are slightly smaller than those of the hardier *G. manicata* ✳✳

Gypsophila 'Rosenschleier' ♥
↕ 40–50cm (16–20in) ↔ 1m (3ft), also known as 'Rosy Veil' for its billowing clusters of pale pink, semi-double flowers ✳✳✳

Haberlea rhodopensis 'Virginalis'
↕ 15cm (6in) ↔ to 15cm (10in), leaves are softly hairy

HACQUETIA EPIPACTIS

early spring

THE BRIGHT, EARLY FLOWERS of this species are composed of a central boss of tiny, yellow true flowers surrounded by bright green bracts (modified leaves). They are borne in dense clusters from late winter to mid-spring. The plant has glossy, green leaves that only fully develop once the flowers are finished. This is a small clump-forming perennial for a moist, shady site. An ideal position would be a damp rock garden in shade or a woodland border with plants such as snowdrops (*see Galanthus, p.247*), dwarf daffodils (*see Narcissus, pp.288–289*), anemones (*see p.180*), winter aconites (*Eranthis hyemalis, see p.236*), and corydalis (*see p.217*). Other natural companions include hellebores (*see p.256*) and epimediums (*see p.235*).

Hardiness Fully hardy ✳✳✳.

Cultivation This plant will thrive in any reliably moist but not waterlogged, neutral to acid (lime-free) soil, that has been enriched with well-rotted organic matter. **Sow** seed in a container in a cold frame as soon as it is ripe or in autumn (*see pp.391–392*). **Divide** plants in spring (*see p.395*) to increase stock and to maintain vigour, or take root cuttings in winter (*see p.394*).

HELENIUM

Helen's flower   *late summer to autumn*

A TOP CHOICE FOR THE AUTUMN BORDER, heleniums make a superb late-flowering contribution to the garden. Their daisy flowers, in wonderfully hot colours, appear over a long period from summer to autumn. These relatively tall, clump-forming perennials slowly spread over the years to create bold expanses of colour in shades of yellow, bronze, orange, and red. The flowers are good for cutting and also attract bees and other beneficial insects into the garden. Grow in a herbaceous border with such late-flowering perennials such as sedums (*see p.324*), rudbeckias (*see p.317*), and asters (*see pp.192–193*). Contact with foliage may aggravate skin allergies.

Hardiness Fully hardy ✳✳✳ to frost-hardy ✳✳.

Cultivation Grow in any fertile, moist but well-drained soil in full sun. **Provide** support for tall varieties. **Divide** clumps every few years in autumn or spring (*see p.395*) to increase stock or maintain vigour. **Sow** seed (*see pp.391–392*) of species in containers in a cold frame in spring. **Propagate** cultivars by taking new shoots from the base of the plant in spring and treating them as softwood cuttings (*see p.394*).

Helenium 'Moerheim Beauty' ♥
‡90cm (36in) ↔ 60cm (24in), flowers from early to late summer ✳✳✳

Hacquetia epipactis ♥
‡5cm (2in) ↔ to 15cm (6in), a fascinating colour combination that will help to light up damp areas in shade

Helenium 'Crimson Beauty'
‡90cm (36in) ↔ 60cm (24in), the shaggy, red flowers take on a brownish tinge with age ✳✳✳

Helenium autumnale (Sneezeweed)
‡to 1.5m (5ft) ↔ 45cm (18in), flowers from late summer to mid-autumn; use twiggy sticks to support stems ✳✳✳

HELIANTHUS

Sunflower
summer

↕ to 5m (15ft)
↔ to 1.2m (4ft)

A FAVOURITE FOR CHILDREN'S gardens, these annuals and perennials are grown for their dramatic height and often huge, bright, daisy flowerheads. These appear in summer and autumn in shades of yellow, red, bronze, and mahogany, and are borne singly or in loose clusters. The flowers of some annuals may measure up to 30cm (12in) across. Despite their coarse foliage, they make showy plants for the border; some of the dwarfer annuals also do well in containers. Sunflowers are good for cutting; they attract pollinating insects into the garden, and the seedheads may provide food for birds. Tall types make a good, fast-growing summer screen.

Hardiness Fully hardy ✳✳✳ to frost-hardy ✳✳.

Cultivation Grow in reasonably fertile soil that is well-drained, neutral to alkaline (limy) and in full sun. Tall types, especially those with large, heavy heads, will need support. **Sow** seed (*see pp.391–393*) of perennials in containers in a cold frame in spring. Sow annuals at 16°C (61°F) in spring. **Divide** (*see p.395*) and replant perennials every two to four years in spring or autumn to maintain vigour.

HELIOPSIS

Ox eye
midsummer to autumn

ORIGINATING IN THE DRY PRAIRIES of North America, these clump-forming perennials are valuable for their long flowering period and for being relatively trouble-free. Their cheerful, golden yellow, daisies, up to 8cm (3in) in diameter, are produced from midsummer through to early autumn. Ox eyes have stiff, branching stems to 1m (3ft) tall, clothed with mid- or dark green foliage. The flowers may be single or double. These are useful plants in a mixed or an herbaceous border; grow them with other colourful perennials such as achilleas (*see p.166*), rudbeckias (*see p.317*), cranesbills (*see Geranium, pp.250–251*), and campanulas (*see p.206*).

Hardiness Fully hardy ✳✳✳.

Cultivation Grow in reasonably fertile, well-drained soil enriched with well-rotted organic matter, in full sun. The taller types may need supporting with twiggy sticks or canes. **Divide** plants (*see p.395*) every two to three years to maintain vigour. **Sow** seed (*see pp.391–392*) in a container in a cold frame in spring. **Take** cuttings of new shoots at the base of the plant in spring and treat as softwood cuttings (*see p.394*). Young shoots are prone to slug damage (*see p.398*).

HELLEBORUS

Hellebore
winter to spring

HELLEBORES ARE STARS OF THE WINTER garden. All species in this group of mainly evergreen perennials are grown for their handsome, glossy foliage which sets off the exquisite flowers in subtle shades of purple, pink, green, white, and cream, many with contrasting spots. The flowers are extremely long-lasting; some face outwards, others look gracefully to the ground, and a few are scented. Hellebores are most effective when grown in groups in a mixed or shrub border or in a natural woodland setting. Grow them with winter-flowering shrubs like witch hazels (*see Hamamelis, p.68*), Christmas box (*see Sarcococca, p.116*), and viburnums (*see pp.126–127*).

Hardiness Fully hardy ✳✳✳ to frost-hardy ✳✳.

Cultivation Hellebores tolerate a fairly wide range of soil types and conditions. Most prefer neutral to alkaline (slightly limy) soil in sun or shade. Avoid dry or waterlogged soils. **Dig in** plenty of well-rotted organic matter before planting and mulch with a layer of organic matter in autumn. **Sow** seed (*see p.391–392*) in containers in a cold frame as soon as it is ripe; named forms will not come true. Hellebores self-seed freely. **Divide** (*see p.395*) in early spring or late summer.

① ② ③ ④

SEEDLINGS
Lift and transplant self-sown seedlings found at the base of a plant in spring, when each has at least one true leaf.

① **'Lemon Queen'** ♛ ↕ 1.7m (5½ft) ✳✳✳ ② **'Monarch'** ♛ ↕ to-2m (6ft) ✳✳ ③ **'Soleil d'Or'** ↕ to 2m (6ft) ✳✳✳ ④ **'Velvet Queen'** ↕ 1.5m (5ft) ✳✳✳

Heliopsis helianthoides **'Sommersonne'** ↕ 90cm (36in) ↔ 60cm (24in), deep gold flowers sometimes flushed orange-yellow, good source of cut flowers for the house

Helleborus foetidus ♛ (Stinking hellebore) ↕ to 80cm (32in) ↔ 45cm (18in), deeply cut foliage, which smells only when crushed, flowers from midwinter to mid-spring ✳✳✳

Helleborus × *hybridus* (Lenten rose)
↕↔ to 45cm (18in), flowers, in white, purple, yellow, green, or pink, from midwinter to mid-spring, remove old, tattered leaves before the flowerbuds open ✱✱✱

Helleborus argutifolius ♀ (Corsican hellebore)
↕ to 1.2m (4ft) ↔ 90cm (3ft), overwintering leaves, shallow pale green flowers in late winter and early spring ✱✱✱

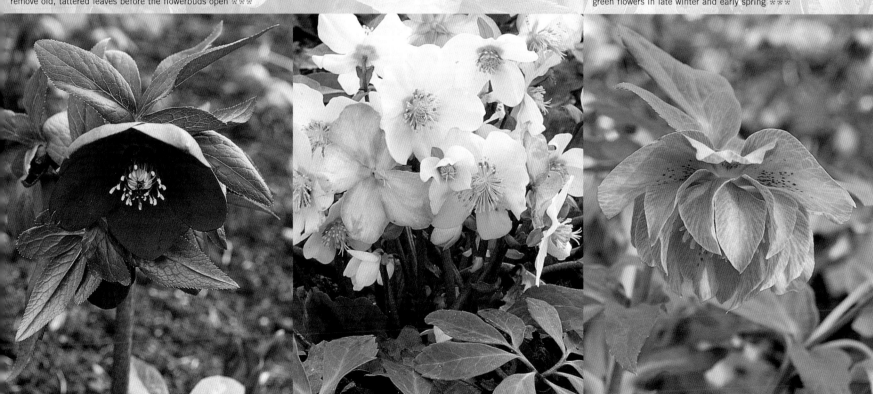

Helleborus × *hybridus* Slaty blue
↕↔ 45cm (18in), usually grown from seed, flowers from midwinter to mid-spring ✱✱✱

Helleborus niger 'Potter's Wheel' (Christmas rose)
↕ to 30cm (12in) ↔ 45cm (18in), overwintering leaves, particularly large flowers from early winter to early spring ✱✱✱

Helleborus × *hybridus* Ashwood Garden hybrids
↕↔ 45cm (18in), variously spotted and speckled, some double flowers in midwinter to mid-spring ✱✱✱

HEMEROCALLIS

Daylily

summer

‡25cm–1.2m (10in–4ft)
↔30cm–1.2m (12in–4ft)

THE EXOTIC BLOOMS of daylilies last for only one day – hence the name – but more buds open to take their place. Thousands of cultivars are available, with blooms in dazzling hues from near-white, gold, and apricot to orange, red, and blue, that vary in shape from spidery or flat to very full doubles. Deciduous, evergreen, or semi-evergreen, these easy-to-grow, clump-forming perennials flower from spring to late summer, adding height and long-lasting colour to a border. Many flower repeatedly through the season (remontant). They are especially successful in drifts in a wild garden. Dwarf daylilies are good in containers.

Hardiness Fully hardy ✳✳✳; some evergreens are frost-hardy ✳✳.

Cultivation Daylilies like fertile, moist but well-drained soil; most need full sun for best colour but also grow in partial shade. **Divide** plants (*see p.395*) every 2–3 years to maintain vigour; divide or plant evergreens only in spring. Maggots of hemerocallis gall midges may infest and kill early buds; destroy abnormally swollen buds at once.

HEPATICA

late winter to early spring

THIS SMALL GROUP OF EARLY-FLOWERING perennials is related to anemones (*see p.180*). Their solitary, bowl- or star-shaped flowers are unusual in that they open from late winter until early spring, before the leaves have fully developed. The flowers come in shades of white, pale pink to crimson, pale blue to mauve, and purple, and are often mottled or marbled. The leaves are often purple underneath and sometimes marbled in silver or white. They form basal rosettes to 13cm (5in) across and last all summer after the flowers fade. Hepaticas do well in moist soil in partial shade, such as in a woodland planting or shady corner of a rock garden. They combine well with small spring bulbs.

Hardiness Fully hardy ✳✳✳.

Cultivation Hepaticas grow well in partial shade, in heavy, neutral to alkaline (slightly limy) soils, but will also thrive in well-drained soils that have been enriched with well-rotted organic matter. **Top-dress** with a layer of leafmould or garden compost around the plants in spring or autumn. Hepaticas do not transplant well since they resent root disturbance. **Sow** seed (*see pp.391–393*) in a cold frame as soon as it is ripe. Divide plants in spring (*see p.395*); divisions are slow to re-establish.

① **Gentle Shepherd'** ‡65cm (26in) ✳✳✳ ② **'Golden Chimes'** ♀ ‡90cm (36in) ✳✳✳ ③ **'Lemon Bells'** ♀ ‡1.2m (4ft) ✳✳✳ ④ **'Marion Vaughn'** ♀ ‡85cm (34in) ✳✳✳

Hepatica nobilis ♀
‡10cm (4in) ↔ 15cm (6in), slow-growing, domed, semi-evergreen, white, pink, blue, or purple flowers in early spring

Hepatica nobilis var. *japonica*
‡to 8cm (3in) ↔ 15cm (6in), slow-growing, domed, semi-evergreen, flowers in white, pink, or blue in early spring, suits alpine trough

HESPERIS MATRONALIS

Sweet rocket, Dame's violet *late spring*

‡ to 90cm (36in)
↔ 45cm (18in)

THE SWEET-SCENTED FLOWERS of hesperis are borne on tall, swaying stems above rosettes of hairy, dark green leaves. Only the biennial or the short-lived perennial, *Hesperis matronalis*, and its cultivars are usually grown. The blooms are usually lilac or purple, appear in late spring to early summer, and have an intensely spicy fragrance at evening. Some cultivars have double flowers and they are all good for cutting. Hesperis is usually grown as a biennial and freely self-seeds. It works well in a cottage garden, herbaceous border, or wild garden, with other early flowerers, such as poppies (*see Papaver, p.299*).

Hardiness Fully hardy ✲✲✲.

Cultivation Grow this plant in fertile, moist but well-drained soil that is neutral to alkaline (limy), in sun or partial shade. **Sow** seed (*see pp.391–393*) in spring or early summer, in spare ground, or where the plants are to grow, and plant out in autumn.

HEUCHERA

Coral flower *early to midsummer*

RICHLY COLOURED FOLIAGE is the chief feature of heucheras. Evergreen and semi-evergreen, the lobed, rounded, or scalloped leaves are often tinted bronze or purple, are mottled or marbled, and have bold veins. They form neat mounds, above which rise airy spikes of dainty flowers in shades of pink to almost pure white from early to midsummer. They are good for cutting and drying, and attract bees into the garden. Commonly used as ground cover in borders and as edging for pathways, heucheras also look good in borders, and woodland and rock gardens. Contrast the foliage with that of plants like *Stachys byzantina* (*see p.328*) or *Choisya ternata* SUNDANCE (*see p.40*).

Hardiness Fully hardy ✲✲✲ to frost-hardy ✲✲.

Cultivation Heucheras prefer a neutral, fertile soil that is moist but well-drained, in sun or partial shade. They tolerate deep shade if the soil is moist. **Sow** seed of species in containers (*see pp.391–393*) in a cold frame in spring. **Divide** all types each autumn (*see below and p.395*) to stop the woody rootstock pushing up from the soil. Vine weevil larvae may eat the roots, causing the plant to wilt; destroy affected plants immediately.

Heuchera cylindrica 'Greenfinch'
‡ to 90cm (36in) ↔ 60cm (24in), mound-forming, often hairy leaves, flowers from mid-spring to midsummer ✲✲✲

Hesperis matronalis var. *albiflora*
Flowers 3–4cm (1¼–1½in) across, attractive to insects, seedlings are white if no other hesperis are grown nearby

DIVIDE CLUMPS of heucheras each year to prevent them from becoming too woody and sparse at the centre.

Heuchera micrantha 'Palace Purple'
‡ ↔ 45–60m (18–24in), mound- or clump-forming, leaves to 15cm (6in) long, free-flowering in early summer, pink seed heads ✲✲✲

Heuchera 'Red Spangles'
‡ 50cm (20in) ↔ 25cm (10in), clumping, round- to kidney-shaped, dark green leaves are marbled pale green, flowers all summer ✲✲✲

HOSTA

Plantain lily

spring to summer

HOSTAS ARE AMONG THE MOST IMPRESSIVE OF FOLIAGE PLANTS, their ribbed, sometimes huge, leaves appearing in shades of green, yellow, blue-green, and blue-grey. In many cultivars, they are edged or banded with white or cream. In summer, spires of trumpet-shaped flowers are held well above the foliage. These herbaceous perennials grow naturally along rocky streamsides, and in woodland and alpine meadows. Most form clumps, but a few spread by underground stems. All make excellent ground-cover plants because the dense, overlapping leaves block out light from the soil surface, preventing weed seeds from germinating. They are ideal, too, for shady sites, but if planted under trees will need plenty of well-rotted organic matter adding to the soil to retain moisture. Hostas also look effective in pots, where they are easier to protect against slug damage. Their lush, rounded foliage looks especially pleasing by ponds or streams, or when contrasted with tall, spiky plants, such as grasses. The neat, small-leaved cultivars are good for growing in rock gardens.

Hardiness Fully hardy ✳✳✳.

Cultivation Grow hostas in fertile, moist but well-drained soil, sheltering them from cold, drying winds. Never let the soil dry out and water plants thoroughly during dry spells. Most hostas prefer a site in full or partial shade, although yellow-leaved and variegated cultivars have better leaf colour in sun. Too strong sunshine, however, may cause scorch. **Mulch** (*see p.388*) between plants in spring to help conserve soil moisture. **Propagate** by division in spring (*see p.395*). Hostas are very prone to damage from slugs and snails and protective measures generally need to be taken (*see below*). The roots of container-grown plants may be eaten by vine weevil larvae (*see p.398*).

Preventing slug and snail damage

The leaves of hostas are stunning, but they also often prove irresistible to slugs and snails, which leave irregular holes and silvery slime trails. It is not uncommon to find some leaves completely shredded after slugs have been feasting at night. There are several ways to control them without resorting to the use of slug pellets, which may harm beneficial wildlife such as birds and hedgehogs (*see p.397*). Slug traps can be purchased, or you can construct a "slug pub"

(*see below*) by sinking a container in the ground and filling it with beer to attract slugs and snails. Coarse grit, gravel, crushed eggshells, or cocoa shells spread around the plants may act as a deterrent as they dislike crossing rough surfaces (put the material in place before the leaves emerge in spring and renew when necessary). Collect slugs and snails at nightfall with the aid of a torch, especially in damp weather.

Band of copper Containers can offer hostas a degree of protection. As a further barrier, stick adhesive copper tape, available at good garden centres, around the pot rim. The copper produces a natural electric charge to which molluscs are sensitive and they will not cross.

Old plastic carton is ideal

Fill container half to three-quarters full

Dead slugs can be composted

Slug pub A slug pub is an organic way to catch slugs and snails. Attracted by the smell of the beer, they fall into the container and drown. Sink the container in the ground with the rim about 2.5cm (1in) above soil level to prevent beneficial creatures such as ground beetles tumbling in.

① *Hosta* 'Aureomarginata' ‡50cm (20in) ↔ 1m (3ft), tolerates sun or partial shade ② 'Blue Blush' ‡20cm (8in) ↔ 35–40cm (14–16in), lavender blue flowers ③ 'Emerald Tiara' ‡35cm (14in) ↔ 65cm (26in), violet flowers ④ *fortunei* var. *albopicta* ♀ ‡55cm (22in) ↔ 1m (3ft) ⑤ *fortunei* var. *aureomarginata* ♀ ‡55cm (22in) ↔ 1m (3ft), tolerates sun or partial shade ⑥ 'Francee' ♀ ‡55cm (22in) ↔ 1m (3ft) ⑦ 'Frances Williams' ♀ ‡60cm (24in) ↔ 1m (3ft), greyish-white flowers

⑧ **'Golden Prayers'** ‡35cm (14in) ↔ 60cm (24in) ⑨ **'Halcyon'** ♀ ‡35–40cm (14–16in) ↔ 70cm (28in), lavender-grey flowers ⑩ **'Honeybells'** ♀ ‡75cm (30in) ↔ 1.2m (4ft), fragrant, white or lavender-blue-striped flowers ⑪ *lancifolia* ♀ ‡45cm (18in) ↔ 75cm (30in), purple flowers, red-dotted stems ⑫ **'Love Pat'** ♀ ‡45cm (18in) ↔ 1m (3ft), off-white flowers ⑬ **'Regal Splendor'** ‡75cm (30in) ↔ 1m (3ft) ⑭ **'Royal Standard'** ♀ ‡60cm (24in) ↔ 1.2m (4ft), fragrant ⑮ **'September Sun'** ‡65cm (26in) ↔ 1m (3ft) ⑯ **'Shade Fanfare'** ♀ ‡45cm (18in) ↔ 60cm (24in) ⑰ *sieboldiana* var. *elegans* ♀ ‡1m (3ft) ↔ 1.2m (4ft) ⑱ **'Sum and Substance'** ♀ ‡75cm (30in) ↔ 1.2m (4ft), pale lilac flowers ⑲ *undulata* ‡1m (3ft) ↔ 45cm (18in), mauve flowers ⑳ *undulata* var. *univittata* ♀ ‡45cm (18in) ↔ 70cm (28in) ㉑ *ventricosa* ♀ ‡50cm (20in) ↔ 1m (3ft) ㉒ *venusta* ♀ ‡5cm (2in) ↔ 25cm (10in) ㉓ **'Wide Brim'** ♀ ‡45cm (18in) ↔ 1m (3ft)

HYACINTHOIDES

Bluebell   *late spring*

BLUEBELLS ARE FAMILIAR TO US as a shimmering blue carpet of blooms in woodland in late spring. They can become invasive, but are easy to control by digging up unwanted bulbs. The small flowers, usually violet-blue but occasionally white or pink, are held on sturdy stems above strappy, mid-green foliage. Plant the English bluebell (*Hyacinthoides non-scripta*) in dappled shade *en masse* beneath deciduous trees; the flower colour will seem all the more intense. Assure yourself when buying that the bulbs have not been collected from the wild, an illegal practice. The larger, more robust Spanish bluebell (*H. hispanica*) tolerates sun and drier conditions. Bluebells may be naturalized in grass or in a wild garden, but in a border *H. hispanica* is likely to become a nuisance.

Hardiness Fully hardy ✳✳✳.

Cultivation Plant bulbs 8cm (3in) deep in autumn, in reasonably fertile soil that is well-drained, in partial shade. Remove flowers as they fade to prevent self-seeding, except where planted in woodland. **Sow** seed (*see pp.391–393*) in a container in a cold frame as soon as it is ripe or divide clumps in summer (*see p.395*).

HYACINTHUS

Hyacinth   *early to late spring*

POSSIBLY THE MOST SWEETLY SCENTED of all spring-flowering bulbs, hyacinths are grown for their densely packed flowerheads in white, pink, red, yellow, and shades of purple. Each sturdy flower stem rises up above the deep green, strappy leaves. All cultivated forms derive from *H. orientalis*, growing 20–30cm (8–12in) tall. Make a virtue of their slightly unnatural appearance by using them in formalized spring bedding displays, with polyanthus (*see Primula, pp.312–313*), winter-flowering pansies (*see Viola, p.338*) and tulips (*see pp.334–335*). Hyacinths can be forced to flower earlier in pots than outdoors.

Hardiness Fully hardy ✳✳✳ in the ground, but may be damaged by frost if grown in containers outdoors.

Cultivation **Plant** bulbs 10cm (4in) deep and 8cm (3in) apart in autumn. Grow in well-drained, reasonably fertile soil in sun or partial shade. Protect container-grown bulbs from excessive winter wet. **For forcing,** plant specially prepared bulbs in containers in autumn; use bulb fibre in bowls with no drainage holes. Keep in a cool, dark place for 6 weeks and bring into light and warmth when shoots are 2.5cm (1in) tall. After flowering, plant forced bulbs outside in a secluded spot; they go on to produce smaller, less showy flower clusters.

IBERIS

Candytuft   *late spring to early summer*

CLUSTERS OF SMALL, OFTEN SCENTED FLOWERS almost conceal candytuft's low mounds of spoon-shaped, dark green leaves. This group of spreading perennials and bushy annuals flower in shades of white, purple, red, or pink from late spring until early summer. Evergreen *Iberis sempervirens*, 30cm (12in) tall, produces round heads of densely packed, white flowers, while compact *I. umbellata* has flowerheads in pinks and purples. Perennial forms are good plants for rock gardens and walls, where their growth can spread and tumble, hiding hard edges. Grow the annuals as bedding, at the front of borders or in containers; good companions include other hardy annuals such as clarkias (*see p.214*) and nigellas (*p.291*).

Hardiness Fully hardy ✳✳✳ to frost-hardy ✳✳.

Cultivation **Grow** in poor to reasonably fertile soil that is moist but well-drained, in sun. After flowering, trim perennials back to tidy. **Sow** seed of annuals where they are to grow (*see p.393*), in spring or autumn. Sow seed of perennials in containers in a cold frame in autumn (*see pp.391–392*). **Take** softwood cuttings in late spring, or semi-ripe cuttings in summer (*see p.394*).

① *hispanica* (Spanish bluebell) ↕40cm (16in) ② *hispanica* 'Excelsior' ↕50–55cm (20–22in)

① *orientalis* 'Blue Jacket' ♈ flowers in early spring
② *orientalis* 'City of Haarlem' ♈ flowers in late spring

Iberis umbellata **Fairy Series**
↕15–30cm (6–12in) ↔ to 23cm (9in), annual, with a mixture of pink, lilac-purple, and white, scented flowers ✳✳✳

IMPATIENS

Busy Lizzie

summer to autumn

FREE-FLOWERING EVEN IN SHADE, busy Lizzies are among the most useful plants for long-lived summer colour. They produce a profusion of flowers, in reds, purples, pinks, and white, and many bicolours, from early summer until well into autumn. Most grown in gardens are either annuals, or tender perennials grown as annuals – used as summer bedding plants and discarded at the end of the season. All have brittle, almost succulent stems with fleshy leaves. The New Guinea hybrids (*Impatiens schlechteri*) and *I. walleriana* varieties are invaluable both in borders and containers in shady spots; try some of the more unusual types in a windowbox or in pots on a patio to bring their flowers nearer the eye.

Hardiness Fully hardy ✲✲✲ to frost-tender ✲.

Cultivation Grow in soil enriched with well-rotted organic matter in partial shade, with shelter from cold winds. In pots, use loam-based compost and keep well watered; feed with a balanced fertilizer every week. **Sow** seed (*see pp.391–393*) at 16–18°C (61–64°F) in early spring. **Take** softwood cuttings (*see p.394*) in spring and summer to overwinter. Moulds (*see pp.398–399*) may affect flower buds in damp conditions; pick them off promptly and healthy ones should follow.

INULA

summer

THESE ROBUST, HERBACEOUS PERENNIALS produce a mass of yellow, daisies with prominent, yellow centres and narrow, dainty petals. The flowers are borne either singly or in flat-topped clusters throughout summer. The leaves are large at the base, becoming progressively smaller up the stem. Heights vary tremendously, from *Inula ensifolia* 'Compacta', only 15cm (6in) tall and suitable for a rock garden, to towering species such as *I. magnifica*, growing to 2m (6ft) tall, which with their rather coarse foliage suits the back of a border or a wild garden. Those of medium height can be grown in an informal border, with other cheerful, summer-flowering perennials. Some species can become invasive, but are quite easy to control by digging out unwanted clumps.

Hardiness Fully hardy ✲✲✲ to frost-hardy ✲✲.

Cultivation Grow all but rock-garden species in deep, fertile soil that is well-drained, in full sun or partial shade. **Divide** perennials (*see p.395*) in spring or autumn. **Sow** seed (*see pp.391–393*) in containers in a cold frame in spring or autumn. The taller species may need support. **Powdery mildew** can be a problem in dry conditions.

IPHEION

spring

THE STARRY FLOWERS OF THESE PLANTS sit like jewels among their grassy leaves in spring. This is a small group of bulbous perennials whose blue, violet, or white flowers are often strongly honey-scented. Most other parts of the plant, especially the leaves, smell of onions when crushed. The most commonly grown species, *Ipheion uniflorum*, may be small, but is sturdy and quickly clump-forming. These are beautiful plants for a rock garden, or can be used in a border to underplant herbaceous perennials such as hostas (*see pp.260–261*) and peonies (*see p.298*). They need winter protection in colder areas; if grown in pots and bowls, they can be brought under cover in winter.

Hardiness Frost-hardy ✲✲ to frost-tender ✲.

Cultivation Grow in reasonably fertile, well-drained soil enriched with well-rotted organic matter, or in loam-based compost, in full sun. Plant the bulbs 8cm (3in) deep, 5cm (2in) apart in autumn. **Provide** a protective mulch (a thick layer of organic matter) where temperatures regularly fall below -10°C (14°F). **Divide** (*see p.395*) in summer, when the plants are dormant. **Sow** seed (*see pp.391–393*) in containers in a cold frame as soon as it is ripe, or in spring.

① *balsamina* **Tom Thumb Series** ‡ to 30cm (12in), double-flowered annual ✲ ② *niamniamensis* **'Congo Cockatoo'** ‡ 90cm (36in), erect, short-lived perennial ✲

Inula hookeri
‡ 60–75cm (24–30in) ↔ 60cm (24in), softly hairy stems and leaves, flowers from late summer to mid-autumn ✲✲✲

Ipheion uniflorum **'Wisley Blue'** ♥
‡ 15–20cm (6–8in), leaves produced in late autumn, scented solitary flowers in spring ✲✲

midwinter to midsummer

IRISES PRODUCE THEIR DISTINCTIVE, HANDSOME FLOWERS mainly from midwinter to midsummer on plants that vary greatly in height. Diminutive types such as *Iris danfordiae* and *I. histrioides* unfold their petals when snow may be on the ground. These are bulbous irises, one of the many types included in this wide-ranging genus. Other irises grow from rhizomes, fleshy stems that creep on or below the soil surface. Those with this kind of rootstock include the widely-grown bearded irises, with stiff, sword-like leaves shooting from fat surface rhizomes. They are at their peak in early summer. Beardless irises lack the decorative tuft on the lower petals of the bearded types, but their flowers are often beautifully marked. They include early summer-flowering Siberian irises (which grow from below-soil rhizomes), and moisture-loving water, or flag, irises. Those classed as crested irises also spread by rhizomes and produce showy but flatter-shaped flowers. There are many more garden-worthy irises besides. All are perennial, and on a few the strappy leaves are evergreen. Taller irises often make typical cottage-garden plants and have a stately presence in mixed or herbaceous borders. Smaller varieties tend to be best suited to a rock garden, raised bed, or container.

Hardiness Fully hardy ✳✳✳ to frost-tender ❋.

Cultivation Different types of iris require different growing conditions, so check the label carefully when you buy. **Plant** bearded irises in well-drained soil in sun (*see below*). Moisture-loving species need the soil to be damp at all times and suit bog gardens or pond margins. Most types grow well in slightly neutral to slightly acid soil, but a few have special requirements: I. *laevigata* and Pacific Coast irises, for instance, need acid soil, and winter-flowering I. *unguicularis* needs alkaline soil as well as a sheltered site. **Remove** faded flowers and spent flower stems if unsightly, for example on bearded irises, but leave them if you want the decorative seedheads, as with I. *foetidissima*. **Divide** rhizomes from midsummer until early autumn (*see below*). **Sow** seed in containers in spring or autumn (*see pp.391–393*). Bearded irises are susceptible to rot if the soil is not sufficiently well-drained.

How to divide iris rhizomes

❶ Lift the iris (here Iris pseudacorus) and wash the soil from the roots. Split the clump apart with your hands or an old knife. Make sure there is one good rhizome with roots and leaves for each new clump.

❷ Use a sharp knife to trim the rhizome carefully. Discard any pieces that do not have any new shoots. Trim the roots by up to one-third, then cut down the leaves to 15cm (6in) to prevent wind rock. The leaves can act like sails.

How to plant irises

Water irises should be replanted in a basket if destined for a pond, or in damp ground. In baskets, use aquatic compost and a top-dressing of gravel to prevent the compost from washing away.

Bearded irises need to be planted with the roots in the soil but the rhizomes set on the surface, 13cm (5in) apart. Firm in and water to settle the soil around the roots. Water regularly until established.

① *Iris* 'Alcazar' ‡60–90cm (24–36in), bearded ② 'Annabel Jane' ‡1.2m (4ft), bearded, late spring ③ 'Austrian Sky' ‡40–45cm (16–18in), bulbous, late winter or spring ④ 'Blue Denim' ‡40–45cm (16–18in), bulbous, late winter or spring ⑤ 'Braithwaite' ‡60–90cm (24–36in), bearded, early summer ⑥ *bulleyana* ‡35–45cm (14–18in), Siberian, early summer ⑦ 'Cantab' ‡10–15cm (4–6in), dwarf bulbous, late winter ⑧ *chrysographes* ♈ ‡40–50cm (16–20in), Siberian, early summer

⑨ *confusa* ♀ ‡1m (3ft), crested, mid-spring ⑩ *danfordiae* ‡8–15cm (3–6in), dwarf bulbous, late winter ⑪ *decora* ‡30cm (12in), beardless, best raised from seed, early summer ⑫ *delavayi* ♀ ‡1.5m (5ft), Siberian, summer ⑬ *douglasiana* ♀ ‡15–70cm (6–28in), beardless, late spring ⑭ 'Early Light' ♀ ‡1m (3ft), bearded, mid-spring ⑮ *ensata* ‡90cm (36in), bulbous water iris, midsummer ⑯ 'Eyebright' ♀ ‡30cm (12in), bearded, early spring ⑰ *foetidissima* ♀ ‡30–90cm (12–36in),

beardless, seedheads in autumn, purple flowers tinged yellow in early summer ⑱ *forrestii* ♀ ‡35–40cm (14–16in), Siberian, early summer ⑲ 'George' ♀ ‡13cm (5in), bulbous, early spring ⑳ *graminea* ♀ ‡20–40cm (8–16in), beardless, scented, late spring ㉑ 'Harmony' ‡10–15cm (4–6in), bulbous, late winter ㉒ *histrioides* 'Major' ‡10–15cm (4–6in), dwarf bulbous, early spring ㉓ *innominata* ‡15–25cm (6–10in), beardless, early summer

㉔ 'Jane Phillips' ♀ ‡60–90cm (24–36in), bearded, early summer ㉕ 'Joyce' ‡13cm (5in), dwarf bulbous, early spring ㉖ 'Katherine Hodgkin' ♀ ‡13cm (5in), dwarf bulbous, late winter ㉗ *kerneriana* ♀ ‡30–50cm (12–20in), beardless, early summer ㉘ *lacustris* ♀ ‡5cm (2in), crested, late spring ㉙ *laevigata* ♀ ‡80cm (32in), beardless water iris, early summer ㉚ *laevigata* 'Variegata' ♀ ‡80cm (32in), beardless water iris, early summer ㉛ 'Langport Flame' ‡30–45cm (12–18in), bearded, mid-spring ㉜ *magnifica* ♀ ‡30–60cm (12–24in), bulbous, mid-spring ㉝ *missouriensis* ♀ ‡20–50cm (8–20in), beardless, early summer ㉞ 'Natascha' ‡13cm (5in), bulbous, early spring ㉟ *orientalis* ♀ ‡90cm (36in), beardless, late spring ㊱ *pallida* 'Variegata' ♀ ‡1.2m (4ft), bearded, late spring ㊲ 'Red Revival' ‡60–90cm (24–36in), bearded, scented, late spring, later flushes ㊳ *prismatica* ‡40–80cm (16–32in), beardless, early summer ㊴ *pseudacorus* ♀

‡90cm–1.5m (3–5ft), beardless water iris, midsummer ④⓪ 'Queechee' ‡60–90cm (24–36in), bearded, early summer ④① *ruthenica* ‡20cm (8in), beardless, scented, late spring ④② 'Sable' ‡60–90cm (24–36in), bearded, early summer ④③ *setosa* ♀ ‡15–90cm (6–36in), beardless, late spring ④④ *sibirica* 'Anniversary' ‡75cm (30in), Siberian, mid-spring ④⑤ *sibirica* 'Butter and Sugar' ♀ ‡70cm (28in), Siberian, mid-spring ④⑥ *sibirica* 'Ruffled Velvet' ♀ ‡55cm (22in), Siberian, early summer

④⑦ *sibirica* 'Shirley Pope' ♀ ‡85cm (34in), Siberian, early summer ④⑧ *sibirica* 'Wisley White' ‡1m (3ft), Siberian, early summer ④⑨ *tectorum* ‡25–40cm (10–16in), crested, early summer ⑤⓪ *tenax* ‡20–35cm (8–14in), beardless, mid-spring ⑤① *unguicularis* ♀ ‡30cm (12in), beardless, fragrant, late winter ⑤② *unguicularis* 'Mary Barnard' ♀ ‡30cm (12in), beardless, midwinter ⑤③ *variegata* ♀ ‡20–45cm (8–20in), bearded, midsummer

KNAUTIA

summer to autumn

‡ 1.5m (5ft)
↔ 45cm (18in)

THESE CHARMING PLANTS are particularly suited to growing in a cottage garden, or a wildflower area, where their exuberant habit lends an air of informality to the planting. Garden knautias are perennials, but there are annual species. They have basal rosettes of simple, broad leaves that last through the winter and tall, slender stems. From summer to autumn, these bear numerous, long-lasting, bluish-lilac to purple flowers, similar to those of scabious (*see p.322*), that wave gracefully in the breeze and attract bees. If the plants flower profusely for 2–3 years, they may become exhausted and have to be replaced.

Hardiness Fully hardy ✳✳✳.

Cultivation Grow in any moderately fertile, well-drained soil, preferably alkaline (limy), and in full sun. Knautias can be prone to rot in wet soils during winter. **Dig in** plenty of coarse grit to improve drainage permanently on heavy clay soils. Raising the level of the soil by 5–8cm (2–3in) can also help to improve drainage. **Sow** seed (*see pp.391–393*) in containers or take cuttings (*see p.394*) from the base of the plant in spring.

KNIPHOFIA

Red hot poker, Torch lily   *summer to autumn*

THE SPIKY FLOWERHEADS IN BRAZEN HUES and erect habit of these striking perennials reveal how they became known as red hot pokers. Most form large clumps with arching, strappy, light green or blue-green leaves. During summer, strong stems soar up to 2m (6ft) and bear flower spikes composed of many small, tubular flowers. They may be in shades of scarlet, orange, gold, white, or greenish-white – some flower spikes are bicoloured. There are also dwarf kniphofias that are no more than 50cm (20in) tall. Use these plants in borders to provide a vertical contrast to plants with broad foliage such as hostas (*see pp.260–261*).

Hardiness Fully hardy ✳✳✳ to frost-tender ❀.

Cultivation Grow in fertile, well-drained, preferably sandy soil with plenty of well-rotted organic matter added to it before planting. Kniphofias prefer a sandy soil in full sun or partial shade. **Protect** the plants from severe frost in the first winter by putting a layer of straw or leaves over deciduous plants, or tying together the stems of evergreens. **Sow** seed (*see pp.391–393*) in containers in a cold frame in spring. **Divide** (*see p.395*) established clumps in late spring.

Knautia macedonica
‡ 60–80cm (24–32in) ↔ 45cm (18in), flowers 1.5–3cm (½–1¼in) across in mid- and late summer

Kniphofia 'Green Jade'
‡ to 1.5m (5ft) ↔ 60–75cm (24–30in), evergreen, flowers fade to cream and then white in late summer and early autumn ✳✳✳

Kniphofia 'Bees' Sunset' ♧
‡ 90m (3ft) ↔ 60m (2ft), deciduous, flowers early to late summer ✳✳✳

Kniphofia 'Ice Queen'
‡ to 1.5m (5ft) ↔ 75cm (30in), deciduous, green buds open to pale primrose, then to ivory, in late summer to early autumn ✳✳✳

LAMIUM
Dead nettle   *spring to summer*

THIS GROUP OF ANNUALS AND PERENNIALS are grown mainly for their very decorative foliage, and make good ground-cover plants among shrubs and larger, vigorous perennials. The leaves are roughly textured and, in some plants, are mottled or tinted. Lamiums have the distinctive square stems of plants belonging to the nettle family, but fortunately no stings. From late spring until summer, the two-lipped flowers are borne either singly or in tiers in dense clusters or spikes. Easily grown, the larger species can be invasive in very rich soils, but less so in poorer soils. Lamiums look particularly good at the front of a border or in a woodland setting with light, dappled shade.

Hardiness Fully hardy ✳✳✳.

Cultivation Grow vigorous species in moist but well-drained soil in shade. Dig out the spreading underground stems (rhizomes) if needed, to keep them away from less robust plants. Less vigorous lamiums prefer sharply drained soil in full sun or partial shade. **Trim** straggly plants with shears in early spring or in summer after flowering. **Sow** seed (*see pp.391–393*) in autumn or spring in pots in a cold frame; take stem-tip cuttings (*see p.394*) in early summer.

LATHYRUS VERNUS   see also p.145
Spring vetchling   *spring*

THIS DENSE, CLUMP-FORMING herbaceous perennial is related to the climbing sweet pea (*Lathyrus odorata*). However, despite the plant's pea-like appearance it does not climb.

↔ 45cm (18in)

In spring, it bears one-sided clusters of 3–6 flowers, poised above dark to mid-green pointed leaflets. The plant dies back in summer after flowering. Since the spring vetchling grows only 20–45cm (8–18in) tall and spreads to only 45cm (18in), it is suitable for rock gardens and woodland settings. It can also be grown in herbaceous and mixed borders, but the plants should be placed near the back of the border so that they are hidden when their foliage dies back. There is also a fine pink- and white-flowered form, *Lathyrus vernus* 'Alboroseus'.

Hardiness Fully hardy ✳✳✳.

Cultivation Spring vetchlings prefer well-drained soil in full sun or partial shade. They will tolerate poor soil, but resent being disturbed or transplanted. **Sow** seed (*see pp.391–393*) in pots in spring or directly into the soil where they are to grow.

Kniphofia 'Royal Standard' ♀
‡ 90–100cm (36–39in) ↔ 60cm (2ft), deciduous, scarlet buds, flowers in mid- and late summer ✳✳✳

① *galeobdolon* 'Hermann's Pride' ‡ 60cm (2ft) ↔ indefinite
② *maculatum* ‡ 20cm (8in) ↔ 1m (3ft) ③ *maculatum* 'Album'
④ *maculatum* 'Beacon Silver' both ‡ 15cm (6in) ↔ 60cm (2ft)

Lathyrus vernus ♀
Flowers are 2cm (¾in) across

LAVATERA

see also p.81

Mallow

summer to autumn

‡ most to 1.2m (4ft)
↔ 60cm (24in)

THE ANNUAL MALLOWS have very similar flowers to the shrubby types, and like them grow vigorously and flower very profusely in a single season, but once seed is set, they die. They produce masses of showy, open, funnel-shaped flowers in shades from white to pale pink to reddish- or purple-pink. The leaves are mid- to dark green with heart-shaped bases. The flowers are also good for cutting. Mallows grow wild in dry, rocky places and in the garden they thrive in sunny herbaceous borders or summer bedding displays. For a traditional cottage-garden look, grow them with other annuals such as calendulas (*see p.204*), clarkias (*see p.214*), and nasturtiums (*see Tropaeolum, p.333*).

Hardiness Fully hardy ✳✳✳ to frost-hardy ✳✳.

Cultivation Grow in ideally light to moderately fertile soil, in full sun. The plants can grow quite tall, and so may need supporting with twiggy sticks in exposed gardens. **Sow** seed in containers under glass in mid-spring, or slightly later outside where plants are to grow (*see pp.391–393*).

Lavatera trimestris 'Silver Cup' ♀
‡ 75cm (30in) ↔ 45cm (18in), one of the brightest coloured mallows, with large flowers in summer ✳✳✳

Lavatera trimestris 'Mont Blanc'
‡ 50cm (20in) ↔ 45cm (18in), compact plant that does not need staking, very dark green foliage, flowers in summer ✳✳✳

Lavatera cachemiriana
‡ 2.5m (8ft) ↔ 1.2m (4ft), short-lived, woody perennial grown as an annual, flowers in summer, good as temporary hedge ✳✳✳

Lavatera trimestris 'Pink Beauty' ♀
‡ to 60cm (24in) ↔ to 45cm (18in), soft, hairy leaves, flowers measure 8–10cm (3–4in) across, excellent for cutting, easily raised from seed to flower from early summer until early autumn ✳✳✳

LEUCANTHEMUM

summer to autumn

ROBUST AND CLUMP-FORMING, these perennials and annuals bloom for long periods in summer through to early autumn and the dense flowerheads are carried singly at the ends of long stems, well above the foliage. The flowers are excellent for cutting. The dark green leaves are long and toothed. *Leucanthemum vulgare* is the common marguerite or ox-eye daisy, a classic plant for meadows and wildlife gardens, while *L.* × *superbum* cultivars (shasta daisies) are what used to be called *Chrysanthemum maximum* – also white-flowered, but usually with fancy petal details. Grow them in a wild or informal area, or in mixed or herbaceous borders to lighten planting schemes in which richer colours predominate.

Hardiness Fully hardy ✳✳✳ to frost-hardy ✳✳.

Cultivation Grow in reasonably fertile soil that is well-drained, in full sun or partial shade. Taller plants may need support with twiggy sticks. **Divide** perennials in early spring or late summer (*see p.395*). **Sow** seed of annuals where plants are to grow, in spring. Sow seed of perennials in containers in a cold frame in spring or autumn (*see pp.391–393*).

Leucanthemum × *superbum* 'Phyllis Smith'
‡90cm (36in) ↔ 60cm (24in), sturdy perennial with single flowers 10–13cm (4–5in) across, excellent for cutting ✳✳✳

LEUCOJUM

Snowflake   *spring and autumn*

SIMILAR TO SNOWDROPS, although some are larger, these bulbous perennials flower at various times of year, giving more scope for pairing them with other plants. The flowers have attractive greenish spots on the tips of the petals. The slender, strappy leaves grow direct from the bulbs. The larger species are good in a border or near water, whilst the smaller species are ideal for a rock garden or alpine trough. *Leucojum vernum* and *L. aestivum*, both spring-flowering, associate well with other bulbs, such as crocuses (*see p.220*) and narcissus (*see pp.288–289*).

Hardiness Fully hardy ✳✳✳ to frost-hardy ✳✳.

Cultivation Plant bulbs 8–10cm (3–4in) deep in autumn, in moist but well-drained soil in full sun. Add plenty of organic matter for *L. aestivum* and *L. vernum*, which need soil that retains moisture reliably. **Sow** seed in a container in a cold frame in autumn (*see pp.391–392*), or remove well-rooted offsets (*see p.395*) once the leaves have died down.

Leucanthemum × *superbum* 'Wirral Supreme' ♛
‡90cm (36in) ↔ 75cm (30in), strong-stemmed perennial with glossy leaves and dense, double flowerheads ✳✳✳

Leucanthemum × *superbum* 'Cobham Gold'
‡60cm (24in) ↔ 75cm (30in), robust perennial, double flowerheads on short stems, dark green leaves ✳✳✳

Leucojum aestivum 'Gravetye Giant' ♛
‡90cm (36in) ↔ 8cm (3in), the largest of the snowflakes, spring flowers are faintly chocolate-scented, likes damp conditions

FLOWERING PLANTS

LEWISIA

spring to summer

THESE POPULAR, HARDY ALPINES are grown for the pretty, often bright colours of their flowers. There are both deciduous and evergreen kinds, forming either rosettes or tufts of fleshy leaves. The deciduous species are more commonly native to high meadows or to grassland, and will die down after flowering; the evergreens are found in shady crevices among rocks. Lewisias have many-petalled flowers in shades of pink, peach, magenta, purple, yellow or white – they are often striped. They bloom for many weeks in spring and summer. Grow them in a rock garden or in crevices in a dry-stone wall, with other rock plants and perhaps aubrietas (*see p.195*).

Hardiness Fully hardy ❋❋❋.

Cultivation Grow in reasonably fertile, sharply drained, neutral to acid (lime-free) soil, in full sun or partial shade. Protect all lewisias from winter wet. In containers, grow in equal parts loam, leafmould, and sharp sand. **Sow** seed in containers in a cold frame in autumn (*see pp.391–392*). Seed of *L. cotyledon* hybrids produces plants that may look different to their parents. Evergreens may produce plantlets around the main rosette of leaves, which can be removed and potted up in early summer. Prone to attack from slugs and snails (*see p.398*).

Lewisia brachycalyx ♀
‡↔ to 8cm (3in), deciduous perennial, flowers often tinged with pale pink on short leafless stems in late spring and early summer

LIATRIS

Blazing star, Gayfeather

late summer to autumn

THE TALL FLOWER SPIKES OF LIATRIS are unusual in that they open from the top of the spike downwards, instead of from the bottom upwards, giving them a distinctive bottle-brush shape that is emphasized by the thread-like appearance of the tightly packed flowers. These are produced on stiff stems in shades of purple, reddish-purple, blue-purple or white, and are highly attractive to bees. Liatris grow wild on prairies and in open woodland. In the garden, they provide late-summer colour in a border. The flowers are good for cutting, too. Try growing them with perennials with open-faced flowers, such as erigerons (*see p.237*), coreopsis (*see p.217*), and geums (*see p.252*), to accentuate their striking form.

Hardiness Fully hardy ❋❋❋.

Cultivation Grow in light, reasonably fertile, moist but well-drained soil in full sun. *L. spicata* needs soil that is reliably moist. In heavy soils, plant on a layer of coarse gravel to improve drainage, or plants may rot in wet winters. **Divide** in spring (*see p.395*). **Sow** seed in a container in a cold frame in autumn (*see pp.391–392*). Prone to attack by slugs and snails (*see p.398*), and mice.

Lewisia cotyledon hybrids
‡15–30cm (6–12in) ↔ 20–40cm (8–16in), evergreen perennial, yellow, orange, magenta, or pink flowers in late spring to summer

Lewisia 'George Henley'
‡10cm (4in) ↔ 10cm (4in), evergreen perennial, small rosettes but tall flower stems with many flowers from late spring to summer

Liatris spicata 'Kobold'
‡to 1.5m (5ft) ↔ 45cm (18in), broad, long-lasting flower spikes in late summer and early autumn

LIBERTIA

late spring to summer

VALUED FOR THEIR STRIKING FORMS, libertias have stiff, narrow, evergreen leaves that are a feature all year round. At the base, the leaves are leathery and long; those on the stem are smaller and more sparse. In late spring and summer, libertias produce slender spires of saucer-shaped, white, yellow-white or blue flowers. These are followed by shiny, light brown seedheads that are useful in flower arranging. The leaves and seeds of *Libertia ixioides* are tinted orange in late autumn and winter. These clump-forming perennials should be grown towards the front of a mixed or herbaceous border; they make perfect partners for the garden tradescantias (*see p.331*), and also look good with bronze-tinted grasses.

Hardiness Fully hardy ✳✳✳ (borderline) to frost-hardy ✳✳, but with protection, all can survive all but the coldest winters.

Cultivation Grow in reasonably fertile soil enriched with well-rotted organic matter, in full sun. In frost-prone areas, protect with a thick mulch of organic matter in winter. **Divide** in spring (*see p.395*). **Sow** seed in containers outdoors as soon as it is ripe (*see pp.391–392*).

LIGULARIA

midsummer to autumn

THESE ARCHITECTURAL PLANTS are large, robust, clump-forming perennials grown for their pyramid-shaped spikes of flowers, produced in shades of yellow and orange from midsummer until early autumn. Each individual flower is daisy-like, often with a contrasting centre. The large, usually rounded or kidney-shaped, mid-green leaves are equally bold. Ligularias look imposing grown in a mixed or herbaceous border, with other moisture-loving perennials such as astilbes (*see p.194*), daylilies (*see Hemerocallis, p.258*), and border phloxes (*see p.306*). Tall species, such as *Ligularia przewalskii,* need to be at the back of planting schemes. They also look very striking by a stream or pond, where they will enjoy the damp conditions.

Hardiness Fully hardy ✳✳✳.

Cultivation Grow in reasonably fertile, deep and reliably moist soil, in full sun or partial shade. Provide shelter from strong winds, otherwise taller plants may need staking with twiggy sticks. **Divide** in spring or after flowering (*see p.395*). **Sow** seed of species outdoors in autumn or spring (*see pp.391–393*).

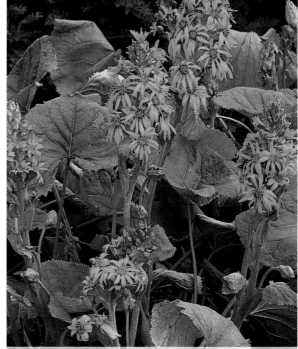

Ligularia 'Gregynog Gold' ♛
↕ to 2m (6ft) ↔ 1m (3ft), rounded to heart-shaped leaves, flowers with brown centres in late summer and early autumn

Libertia grandiflora ♛
↕ to 90cm (36in) ↔ 60cm (24in), forms dense clumps, flowers early spring to early summer ✳✳✳ (borderline)

Ligularia 'The Rocket' ♛
↕ 2m (6ft) ↔ 1m (3ft), sturdy black stems, large, boldly toothed leaves with purple veins, tall "candles" of flowers with orange-yellow centres, flowers in early and late summer

Lily

summer to autumn

LILIES HAVE LONG GRACED GARDENS, both in the West and in the East, where many originate. Their appeal lies in their extravagant, often fragrant, summer blooms, which can measure up to 8cm (3in) across and over 10cm (4in) long. There are about 100 species; all are perennial bulbs. Some of the earliest in cultivation are among the most demanding, for instance the Madonna lily, *Lilium candidum*, which can be disease-prone. Others have definite preferences for acid or alkaline soil. Modern hybrids, however, tend to be vigorous, disease-resistant, and less fussy about soil. Lilies are available in most colours except blue, and the flowers come in four distinct shapes: trumpet, funnel, bowl, and turkscap, with swept-back petals. One of the easiest ways to grow them is in a container on the patio where their perfume is readily appreciated. Most do well in sunny borders; some, such as *L. martagon*, prefer the dappled shade of a woodland garden. A few dwarf species are at home in the rock garden.

Hardiness Fully hardy ✳✳✳ to half-hardy ✳, but young shoots may be damaged by frost.

Cultivation Grow in any well-drained soil enriched with well-rotted organic matter or in containers in good potting compost. On heavy clay soils, improve drainage by digging in plenty of coarse grit in the area of the planting hole. Most lilies prefer full sun, but some tolerate partial shade. **Plant** bulbs in autumn or spring at a depth of 2–3 times their height; the distance between should be three times the diameter of the bulb. **Water** regularly during dry spells in summer and feed with a high-potash fertilizer in the growing season. **Stake** tall varieties in exposed sites. **Deadhead** fading flowers before seed sets to maintain the plant's vigour. **Sow** seed (*see pp.391–392*) as soon as it is ripe in pots in a cold frame. **Detach** stem bulbils and bulblets from those cultivars that produce them (*see below*). Plants, including the flowers, may be eaten by slugs and snails (*see p.398*), and lily beetles. Pick off and destroy the distinctive, bright orange beetles, or spray the plant with a proprietary insecticide.

① *Lilium* African Queen Group ♀ ↕1.5–2m (5–6ft), scented ✳✳ ② 'Angela North' ↕70–120cm (28–48in) ✳✳✳ ③ 'Ariadne' ↕80cm–1.4m (2½–4½ft), scented ✳✳✳ ④ *auratum* var. *platyphyllum* ↕1.5m (5ft), scented ✳✳✳ ⑤ Bellingham Group ↕2–2.2m (6–7ft), increases rapidly, acid soil, partial shade ✳✳✳ ⑥ 'Black Beauty' ↕1.4–2m (4½–6ft), scented ✳✳✳ ⑦ 'Bright Star' ↕1–1.5m (3–5ft), scented, lime-tolerant ✳✳✳ ⑧ *bulbiferum* var. *croceum*

Propagating from bulblets

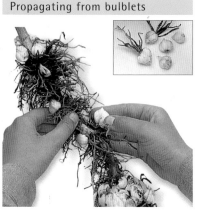

Lilies such as L. auratum, L. longiflorum, *and* L. speciosum *naturally produce bulblets (small rooted bulbs that will grow into flowering plants in 3–4 years). These form below ground at the base of the main stem. Lift the parent plant in autumn, remove the bulblets and replant the mature bulb. Prepare pots of moist, loam-based compost. Insert the bulblets to twice their own depth, and cover the compost with a layer of grit. Label and keep in a frost-free place before planting out the young lilies in the following autumn.*

Propagating from bulbils

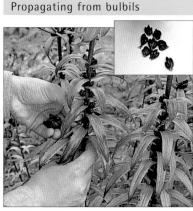

Bulbils are *tiny bulbs which form where the leaf stalks join stems of lilies such as* L. bulbiferum, L. chalcedonicum, L. lancifolium, *as well as* L. × testaceum, *and their hybrids. They ripen in summer, and will produce flowering plants in 3–4 years. Take them only from healthy plants as bulbils can transfer disease. Fill a pot with moist, loam-based compost and press the bulbils into the surface. Cover with a 1cm (½in) layer of coarse sand and label. Grow on in a frost-free place until planting out the following autumn.*

‡40–150cm (16–60in) ✳✳✳ ⑨ *canadense* ‡1–1.6m (3–5½ft) ✳✳✳ ⑩ *candidum* ♀ ‡1–2m (3–6ft), scented, neutral to alkaline soil ✳✳✳ ⑪ 'Casa Blanca' ♀ ‡1–1.2m (3–4ft), scented ✳✳✳ ⑫ *chalcedonicum* ‡60cm–1.5m (2–5ft), unpleasantly scented but thrives in any soil, sun or shade, ✳✳✳ ⑬ Citronella Group ‡1–1.5m (3–5ft) ✳✳✳ ⑭ 'Connecticut King' ‡1m (3ft) ✳✳✳ ⑮ × *dalhansonii* ‡1–1.5m (3–5ft), unpleasantly scented ✳✳✳ ⑯ *davidii* var. *willmottiae*

‡2m (6ft) ✳✳✳ ⑰ *duchartrei* ‡60–100cm (24–39in), scented ✳✳✳ ⑱ 'Enchantment' ‡60–100cm (24–39in), easy to grow, good for cutting ✳✳✳ ⑲ 'Fire King' ‡1–1.2m (3–4ft), good in containers ✳✳✳ ⑳ *formosanum* var. *pricei* ‡10–30cm (4–12in), scented, ✳✳ ㉑ Golden Splendor Group ♀ ‡1.2–2m (4–6ft), scented ✳✳✳ ㉒ 'Gran Paradiso' ‡90cm (36in) ✳✳✳ ㉓ *grayi* ‡1–1.7m (3–5½ft), scented, needs moist, acid soil ✳✳✳

24 *hansonii* ‡1–1.5m (3–5ft), scented, partial shade, early summer ✱✱✱ 25 *henryi* ♀ ‡1–3m (3–10ft), neutral to alkaline soil, partial shade, late summer ✱✱✱ 26 'Journey's End' ‡1–2m (3–6ft), late summer ✱✱✱ 27 'Lady Bowes Lyon' ‡1–1.2m (3–4ft) ✱✱✱ 28 *lancifolium* ‡60cm–1.5m (2–5ft), acid soil but tolerates some lime, late summer and early autumn ✱✱✱ 29 *longiflorum* ♀ ‡40–100cm (16–39in), lime-tolerant, partial shade ✱ 30 *mackliniae* ‡30–60cm (12–24in) ✱✱✱ 31 'Magic Pink' ‡1.2m (4ft) ✱✱✱ 32 *martagon* ♀ ‡90cm–2m (3–6ft), rank scent, well-drained soil, sun or partial shade ✱✱✱ 33 *martagon* var. *album* ♀ ‡90cm–2m (3–6ft), rank scent, well-drained soil, sun or partial shade ✱✱✱ 34 *medeoloides* ‡45–75cm (16–30in), acid soil, partial shade ✱✱✱ 35 *monadelphum* ‡1–1.5m (3–5ft), scented, early summer ✱✱✱ 36 'Mont Blanc' ‡60–70cm (24–28in) ✱✱✱ 37 *nanum* ‡6–30cm (2½–12in), scented, acid soil, partial shade ✱✱✱

38 *nepalense* ↕60–100cm (24–39in), acid soil, partial shade, early to midsummer ❄ 39 *pardalinum* ♋
↕1.5–2.5m (5–8ft) ❄❄❄ 40 'Peggy North' ↕1.2–1.5m (4–5ft) ❄❄❄ 41 Pink Perfection Group ♋
↕1.5–2m (5–6ft), scented ❄❄❄ 42 *pomponium* ↕1m (3ft), rank scent, alkaline soil ❄❄❄ 43 *pyrenaicum*
↕30–100cm (12–39in), rank scent, neutral to alkaline soil ❄❄❄ 44 'Red Night' ↕70–100cm (28–39in)
❄❄❄ 45 *regale* ♋ ↕60cm–2m (2–6ft), scented, full sun, midsummer ❄❄❄ 46 'Rosemary North'

↕90–100cm (36–39in) ❄❄❄ 47 *rubellum* ↕30–80cm (12–32in), acid soil, partial shade, early
summer ❄❄❄ 48 *speciosum* var. *rubrum* ↕1–1.7m (3–5½ft), scented, acid soil, partial shade,
late summer and early autumn ❄❄❄ 49 'Star Gazer' ↕1–1.5m (3–5ft) ❄❄❄ 50 'Sterling Star'
↕1–1.2m (3–4ft) ❄❄❄ 51 'Sun Ray' ↕1m (3ft) ❄❄❄ 52 *superbum* ↕1.5–3m (5–10ft), acid soil,
late summer and early autumn ❄❄❄ 53 *tsingtauense* ↕70–100cm (28–39in), acid soil ❄❄❄

LIMNANTHES DOUGLASII

Poached egg plant   *summer to autumn*

THIS IS A FAST-GROWING ANNUAL with sweetly scented flowers similar to those of buttercups from summer to autumn. It has yellow, glossy flowers with white tips to the petals. Although annual, it does self-seed prolifically – once you sow it, you will never be without it. The flowers are rich in nectar and so are attractive to bees and hoverflies. Hoverflies are good allies to have in the garden as they consume many aphids over the summer. The poached egg plant makes neat, bright splashes of colour at the front of a border – perhaps with other vividly coloured annuals, such as calendulas (*see p.204*) and nasturtiums (*see Tropaeolum, p.333*) – at a path edge, or scattered among paving. It makes an attractive rockery plant, although you will almost certainly find yourself weeding out surplus self-set seedlings.

Hardiness   Fully hardy ✳✳✳.

Cultivation   Grow in fertile, moist but well-drained soil, in full sun. **Sow** seed (*see p.393*) where plants are to grow in spring or autumn. Protect autumn sowings with cloches in frost-prone areas.

LINARIA

Toadflax   *spring to autumn*

THIS IS A LARGE GROUP of annuals, biennials, and herbaceous perennials. Their stems, which can be erect, trailing, or branched, are clothed with clusters of flowers that look like tiny snapdragons. They bloom abundantly from spring to autumn, in hues of white, pink, red, purple, orange, and yellow. The smaller species suit a rock garden, scree bed (a sharply drained area with a deep layer of chippings and a thin layer of loam), or wall crevice. Taller annuals and perennials, such as *Linaria vulgaris*, are a popular choice for the foreground of borders, forming soft masses of colour that act as foils to plants with bolder flowers; they also grow and look well in gravel beds.

Hardiness   Fully hardy ✳✳✳ to half-hardy ✳. All shown below are fully hardy ✳✳✳.

Cultivation   Grow in reasonably fertile, well-drained soil, in full sun. Divide perennials in early spring (*see p.395*). **Sow** seed of annuals where they are to flower in early spring (*see p.393*). Thin the seedlings to around 15cm (6in). Sow seed of perennials in containers in a cold frame in early spring (*see pp.391–392*). **Take** softwood cuttings of perennials in spring (*see p.394*).

LINUM

see also p.83

Flax   *early to late summer*

THESE ANNUALS, BIENNIALS, AND PERENNIALS produce clouds of brilliantly coloured, saucer-shaped flowers on graceful, wiry stems. The flowers appear for many weeks from early to late summer, and are mainly in pale primary colours – yellow, blue, or red – or white. The flowers of *Linum perenne* last for only one day, but are replaced by more the next day. The perennials tend to be short-lived, but are easy to raise from seed. The smaller flaxes are at home in a rock garden, while the larger ones make a stunning display *en masse* in borders; grow them in drifts among other herbaceous plants with soft outlines, such as cranesbills (*see Geranium, pp.250–251*) and monardas (*see p.286*).

Hardiness   Fully hardy ✳✳✳ to frost-hardy ✳✳.

Cultivation   Grow in light, reasonably fertile soil enriched with well-rotted organic matter in full sun. Smaller alpine species need sharply drained soil and protection from winter wet. **Sow** seed in spring or autumn. Annuals can be sown where they are to grow; sow perennials in containers in a cold frame (*see pp.391–392*). **Take** stem-tip cuttings of perennials in early summer (*see p.394*).

Limnanthes douglasii ♀
↕↔ 15cm (6in) or more, sprawling habit, ferny, yellow-green leaves

① *alpina* ↕ ↔ 15cm (6in) ② *dalmatica* ↕ 1m (3ft) ↔ 20cm (24in) ③ *purpurea* '**Canon Went**' ↕ to 90cm (36in) ↔ 30cm (12in) ④ *vulgaris* ↕ to 90cm (36in) ↔ 30cm (12in)

Linum perenne (Perennial flax)
↕ 10–60cm (4–24in) ↔ 30m (12in), relative of the flax used for linseed oil and linen, short-lived perennial, but seeds freely ✳✳✳

LOBELIA

summer

ANNUAL BEDDING LOBELIA IS HUGELY POPULAR, producing masses of flowers in the familier blues, but also pink, purple, and white. Use it in summer beds, as edging, or trailing from hanging baskets and windowboxes. Planted around the edges of containers, they are perfect partners for fuchsias (*see pp.60–63*) and other summer bedding. There are also hardier, perennial lobelias, from such diverse habitats as the meadow, riverbank, and woodland. They usually bear their flowers in erect spikes, in jewel-like shades of azure, violet, carmine-red, and scarlet. The perennials can be grown in borders or, as in the case of *Lobelia cardinalis,* in bog gardens or even shallow water.

Hardiness Fully hardy ✲✲✲ to frost-tender ✲.

Cultivation Grow in deep, fertile, reliably moist soil, in sun or partial shade. *L. cardinalis* can be grown in baskets (*see p.381*) in water 8–10cm (3–4in) deep. Bedding lobelia flowers for longer in shade. In containers, it needs weekly feeding with a balanced fertilizer. **Protect** perennials in frost-prone areas with a thick winter mulch (*see p.388*). **Divide** perennials in spring; aquatics in summer (*see p.395*). **Sow** seed of perennials as soon as ripe; annuals in late winter, at 13–18°C (55–64°F) (*see pp.391–393*). Prone to slug damage (*see p.398*).

LOBULARIA

Sweet alyssum,
Sweet Alison

summer to early autumn

FROM SUMMER UNTIL EARLY AUTUMN, sweet alyssum forms cushions of densely packed, 4-petalled flowers in shades of white, pink, rose-pink, mauve- and deep purple. In some cultivars, the flowers are honey-scented, too. There are both annuals and perennials in the group, and their long-flowering season and colourful blooms make them a popular choice in the garden. They originate from maritime areas and thus thrive in similar conditions – light soil and full sun – in gardens. Sweet alyssum is a useful edging plant for borders and in raised beds; white-flowered forms are often grown with blue trailing lobelia for a jaunty, nautical display. Gravels beds and cracks and crevices in paving also suit it well, and it will often self-seed into sunny niches such as this.

Hardiness Fully hardy ✲✲✲.

Cultivation Grow in light, reasonably fertile soil that is well-drained and in full sun. **Trim** the plants after the first flush of blooms has faded to encourage more flowers later on. **Sow** seed where plants are to grow (*see p.393*) in late spring.

Linum flavum 'Compactum' (Golden flax)
↕↔ 15cm (6in), upright perennial, dark green leaves, dense flowers that open in summer sun ✲✲✲

Lobelia 'Bees' Flame'
↕ 75cm (30in) ↔ 30cm (12in), clump-forming perennial, dark leaves, tall flower spikes in mid- and late summer ✲✲✲

Lobularia 'Royal Carpet'
↕ 10cm (4in) ↔ 30cm (12in), grow in pots or raised beds to appreciate the sweet scent of the flowers

LUNARIA

Honesty,
Satin flower

late spring to summer

FLOWERS, SEED PODS, AND LEAVES are all decorative in this small group of plants. They bear purple or white flowers in late spring and early summer, followed by flat, silvery or beige seed capsules, the sides of which fall to reveal a satiny inner membrane. The capsules last quite well into autumn, although for use in dried flower arrangements they are usually cut in late summer and dried indoors to avoid any damage from autumn weather. The leaves vary in shape and have toothed edges. Annual, biennial, or perennial, honesty self-seeds easily and naturalizes well in a wild garden. It can also be grown in a shrub border or with herbaceous perennials like aquilegias (*see p.185*), lupins (*see right*), and poppies (*see Papaver, p.299*).

Hardiness Fully hardy ✳✳✳.

Cultivation Grow in fertile, moist but well-drained soil, in full sun or partial shade. **Divide** *L. rediviva* (*see p.395*) in spring. **Sow** seed (*see pp.391–392*) in a seedbed: *L. rediviva* in spring, and *L. annua* in early summer. If plants are stunted, pull one up to see if the roots are knobbly and deformed; if so, burn all affected plants; they may have clubroot (*see Crambe, p.218*), a persistent soil-borne disease.

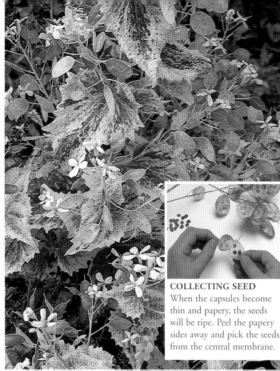

COLLECTING SEED
When the capsules become thin and papery, the seeds will be ripe. Peel the papery sides away and pick the seeds from the central membrane.

Lunaria annua 'Alba Variegata'
‡to 90cm (36in) ↔ to 30cm (12in), the white flowers will be followed by seed pods that are silvery outside and inside

LUPINUS

Lupin

early summer

THE ENDURINGLY POPULAR FLOWER SPIKES of lupins provide some of the brightest colours to be seen in the early-summer garden. There are plenty to choose from, in almost any colour and even bicolours; they last well when cut. The attractive foliage is mid-green with lance-shaped leaflets; a rain shower will leave it starred with small, silvery droplets. Most lupins grown in gardens are stately perennials, to be paired with other classic herbaceous plants such as delphiniums (*see p.224*) and Oriental poppies (*see Papaver orientale, p.299*). However, there are smaller-flowered, less formal low-growing annuals.

Hardiness Fully hardy ✳✳✳ to half-hardy ✳.

Cultivation Grow in reasonably fertile, well-drained soil in full sun or partial shade. **Deadhead** (*see p.390*) for a second flush of flowers. **Sow** seed, after soaking for 24 hours, in spring or autumn, outside or in containers in a cold frame (*see pp.391–393*). **Take** cuttings of new shoots of named varieties in mid-spring (*see p.394*). Lupins are likely to be attacked by slugs and snails (*see p.398*). It is worth taking precautions against these pests.

Lunaria rediviva (Perennial honesty)
‡60–90cm (24–36in) ↔ 30cm (12in), the flowers are fragrant; the seed pods of this species are more fawn-coloured than silvery

Lunaria annua 'Variegata'
‡to 90cm (36in) ↔ to 30cm (12in), as well as white-edged leaves, this has more deeply coloured flowers than *L. annua*

Lupinus 'The Chatelaine'
‡90cm (36in) ↔ 75cm (30in), this crisp combination is popular and among the brightest of the bicoloured forms

Lupinus 'Beryl, Viscountess Cowdray'
↕90cm (36in) ↔ 75cm (30in), this is something of a rarity but
worth seeking out for its rich red flowers

Lupinus 'Noble Maiden'
↕90cm (36in) ↔ 75cm (30in), the densely packed flower spikes
such as this make a strong impact in the border

Lupinus 'Chandelier'
↕90cm (36in) ↔ 75cm (30in), restrained creamy-yellow spikes like
church candles allow the form and foliage to shine

Lupinus Russell hybrids
↕90cm (36in) ↔ 75cm (30in), among the earliest and most reliable
hybrids, these have a wide colour range

Lupinus 'The Page'
↕90cm (36in) ↔ 75cm (30in), more open flower spikes such as
these allow some lupins to look at home in an informal scheme

LYCHNIS

Campion, Catchfly   *early to late summer*

CAMPIONS HAVE BRIGHT SUMMER FLOWERS in shades of vivid scarlet, purple, and pink as well as in white. The flowers are usually tubular or star-shaped and borne singly or in small clusters. The erect flower stems make them ideal for cutting. Butterflies find the flowers attractive, so they are a good choice for a wild garden. The leaves may be hairy. Campions are biennial or perennial. Smaller species are pretty in rock gardens, and the taller ones are best in informal borders with other perennials including aquilegias (*see p.185*), lupins (*see p.280*), and Oriental poppies (*see Papaver orientale, p.299*). Some campions, such as *Lychnis chalcedonica*, have brittle stems and need the support of twiggy pea sticks.

Hardiness Fully hardy ✳✳✳.

Cultivation Campions thrive in reasonably fertile soil that is well-drained, in full sun or partial shade. Grey-leaved species produce the best leaf colour in well-drained soil in full sun. **Remove** fading flowers regularly. **Sow** seed in containers (*see pp.391–392*) in a cold frame when it is ripe or in spring. **Divide** plants (*see p.395*) or take cuttings (*see p.394*) from new shoots at the base in spring.

LYSICHITON

Skunk cabbage   *early spring*

THESE STRIKINGLY SHAPED, COLOURFUL perennials flower in early spring. Dense spikes of tiny, greenish flowers are surrounded by elegantly sculptural, hooded bracts (modified leaves). These are followed by clusters of large, glossy, mid- to dark green leaves springing directly from the ground. The yellow skunk cabbage, *Lysichiton americanus*, is larger than the white-flowered *L. camtschatcensis*, which has 40cm (16in) hoods and leaves up to 100cm (39in) long; it has a height and spread of 75cm (30in). Both plants have a musky, some would say unpleasant, smell. Their native habitat is beside water, so grow them by a pond or stream along with *Caltha palustris* (*see p.205*) and other moisture-loving marginal plants.

Hardiness Fully hardy ✳✳✳.

Cultivation Fertile soil enriched with plenty of well-rotted organic matter, at the edge of a stream or pond, in full sun or partial shade will suit these aquatic marginals. Allow sufficient space for the leaves to develop without swamping other plants. **Remove** offsets (*see p.395*) at the bases of the main stems in spring or summer.

Lychnis chalcedonica ♥ (Jerusalem cross, Maltese cross)
‡90cm–1.2m (3–4ft) ↔ 30cm (12in), perennial, flowers in early and midsummer, self-seeds freely

Lychnis coronaria ♥ (Dusty miller, Rose campion)
‡80cm (32in) ↔ 45cm (18in), biennial or short-lived perennial, flowers in late summer, self-seeds freely

Lysichiton americanus ♥ (Yellow skunk cabbage)
‡1m (3ft) ↔ 1.2m (4ft), the hooded flowers are up to 40cm (16in) long, leaves up to 120cm (48in) long

LYSIMACHIA

Loosestrife *summer*

LOOSESTRIFES ARE A LARGE AND VARIED GROUP that includes many herbaceous perennials, and some evergreens. Flowers appear from mid- to late summer, and may be star-, saucer- or cup-shaped; they are usually white or yellow, but sometimes are pink or purple. Larger loosestrifes are suitable for planting in damp herbaceous and mixed borders along with other moisture-loving perennials such as astilbes (*see p.194*), daylilies (*see Hemerocallis, p.258*), and border phloxes (*see p.306*). They are happy in a bog garden or by pool margins and also look at home when naturalized in a woodland garden. Creeping Jenny (*Lysmachia nummularia*) makes a good ground-cover plant. Yellow-flowered *L. punctata* can spread and become a problem, but is less invasive on dryish soil.

Hardiness Fully hardy ✳✳✳ to frost-tender ❀.

Cultivation Grow these plants in soil that is well-drained but enriched with well-rotted organic matter, in full sun or partial shade, and in a site that does not dry out in summer. **Support** tall species with twiggy pea sticks. **Sow** seed in containers outdoors (*see pp.391–392*) in spring or divide plants in spring or autumn (*see p.395*).

Lysimachia nummularia (Creeping Jenny)
‡ to 5cm (2in) ↔ indefinite, mat-forming evergreen, rooting stems spread rapidly, cup-shaped, bright yellow flowers all summer ✳✳✳

LYTHRUM

Loosestrife *summer to autumn*

EVEN LONGER-FLOWERING THAN THEIR NAMESAKES (*see left*), these upright annuals and perennials are valued for their slender spikes of pretty flowers in shades of purplish-pink, or occasionally white. Individual flowers are up to 2cm (¾in) wide, with 4–8 petals, and are borne along the ends of tapering, square stems in summer to autumn. The leaves are up to 10cm (4in) long and sometimes add to autumnal displays by turning yellow. Some of these loosestrifes flourish at the margins of streams and ponds. For a colourful, natural display, combine them with other flowering plants such as astilbes (*see p.194*), bergamots (*see Monarda, p.286*), montbretias (*see Crocosmia, p.219*), and phloxes (*see p.306*).

Hardiness Fully hardy ✳✳✳.

Cultivation These loosestrifes thrive in any fertile, moist soil in full sun. **Remove** fading flowers to prevent self-seeding. **Sow** seed at 13–18°C (55–64°F) in spring (*see pp.391–393*) or divide plants in spring (*see p.395*). Take cuttings from new shoots at the base of the plant (*see p.394*) in spring or early summer.

Lysimachia clethroides ♈
‡ 90cm (36in) ↔ 60cm (24in), spreading, hairy leaves, flowerheads appear mid- to late summer becoming upright as they mature ✳✳✳

Lysimachia ciliata 'Firecracker' ♈
‡ 1.2m (4ft) ↔ 60cm (24in), flowers in midsummer ✳✳✳

Lythrum virgatum 'The Rocket'
‡ 80cm (32in) ↔ 45cm (18in), clump-forming perennial, leaves 10cm (4in) long, flowers from early to late summer

MACLEAYA

Plume poppy   *early to midsummer*

THESE MAJESTIC HERBACEOUS perennials are grown
for their handsome foliage and graceful plumes of
tiny, petalless flowers. The feathery flower plumes, in
buff-white, cream, or soft apricot to coral pink, are
carried on erect blue- or grey-green stems from early
to midsummer, and appear to almost float above the
foliage. The fine leaves, in grey-green to olive-green,
are deeply lobed and may be up to 25cm (10in)
across. Plume poppies can grow quite tall, up to 2.5m
(8ft), so are best planted at the back of a border,
where they have great presence; they can be invasive,
however. Grow them in a spacious border with other
summer-flowering perennials; they can also be used to
create superbly subtle effects with tall grasses.

Hardiness Fully hardy ✽✽✽, but the new growth may be damaged
by late frosts.
Cultivation Grow in any soil that is moist but well-drained, in full
sun or partial shade. Provide shelter from cold, drying winds. **Divide**
plants in spring or autumn. **Sow** seed (*see pp.391–392*) in containers
in a cold frame in spring. **Take** root cuttings in winter (*see p.394*) or
separate the rhizomes (*see p.395*).

MALVA

Mallow   *summer*

‡20cm–1.2m (8in–4ft)
↔ 23–60cm (9–24in)

MALLOWS ARE EASY AND REWARDING
plants to grow and flourish on the
poorest of soils. This colourful group
of annuals, biennials, and woody-
based perennials produce leafy spikes
of pink, purple, blue, or white flowers
throughout summer on upright plants. The flowers
are bowl- or saucer-shaped and last for many weeks,
making mallows useful plants for mixed, annual, and
herbaceous borders alike. Use them as gap-fillers
among other summer-flowering plants such as
campanulas (*see p.206*), phloxes (*see p.306*), and lilies
(*see pp.274–277*), or for a more informal look, with
flowering grasses such as *Lagarus ovatus* (*see p.349*).

Hardiness Fully hardy ✽✽✽.
Cultivation Grow in any moist but well-drained soil in full sun.
Provide some support especially if growing in very fertile soil. Perennial
cultivars and species are often short-lived, but they self-seed freely.
Sow seed of annuals where the plants are to grow, or in containers, in
spring or early summer (*see pp.391–393*). **Take** cuttings of new young
shoots from perennials in spring (*see p.394*).

MATTHIOLA

Gillyflower, Stock   *late spring to summer*

FOR SWEET FRAGRANCE, few plants can better stocks.
They include the dainty, annual, night-scented
stock (*Matthiola longipetala* subsp. *bicornis*) and the
chunkier gillyflowers (*M. incana*), widely sold as cut
flowers. Both are essentials for a cottage-style garden.
Gillyflowers, which include the popular Brompton
stocks, although perennial are grown as biennials or
annuals. There are tall and dwarf forms with single
or double flowers in bright or pastel shades of purple,
violet, pink, and white. Dwarf verieties make good
container plants. Night-scented stocks come in similar
colours and can be grown in pots, but must be direct-
sown. Grow them in a sunny spot, near a door, seat,
or window and enjoy their evening fragrance.

Hardiness Fully hardy ✽✽✽ to frost-hardy ✽✽.
Cultivation Grow in any moist but well-drained soil in full sun;
incana types tolerate partial shade. Tall forms may need some support.
Sow seed (*see pp.391–393*) of *incana* types for summer flowering in
early spring at 10–18°C (50–64°F) and for spring-flowering outdoors
in summer; overwinter in a cold frame to plant out the following spring.
Sow night-scented stocks in situ and thin to 10–15cm (4–6in) apart.

Macleaya microcarpa **'Kelway's Coral Plume'** ♀
‡2.5m (7ft) ↔ 1m (3ft), grey-green leaves are 5- to 7-lobed, buff
to coral-pink flowers in early and midsummer

① *moschata* ‡90cm (36in) ↔ 60cm (24in), erect perennial
② *sylvestris* **'Primley Blue'** ‡to 20cm (8in) ↔ 30–60cm
(12–24in), prostrate perennial

Matthiola incana **Cinderella Series** ♀
‡20–25cm (8–10in) ↔ to 25cm (10in), double flowers held in
dense spikes 15cm (6in) tall, in late spring to summer ✽✽

MECONOPSIS

early to midsummer

‡to 2.5m (8ft)
↔ to 1m (3ft)

THIS COSMOPOLITAN GROUP of plants includes both the cheerful yellow Welsh poppy (*Meconopsis cambrica*) and the sapphire-blue Himalayan poppy (*M. betonicifolia*); despite the must-have appeal of the latter, it must be said that the former is much easier to grow. However, if you have the ideal site – a cool, moist woodland garden, or a sheltered border that mimics these conditions, with soil rich in humus or leafmould – you can grow any meconopsis, in eye-catching shades of turquoise and faded denim, pomegranate-pink, and clear yellows. Their silky flowers, with yellow or cream stamens, appear from early to midsummer. The plants may be short-lived, but all are worth it; some self-seed.

Hardiness Fully hardy ✳✳✳, but frost may damage young growth.

Cultivation Grow in moist but well-drained, slightly acid (lime-free) soil, in partial shade, with shelter from cold winds. **Divide** established plants after flowering (*see p.395*). **Sow** seed (*see pp.391–392*) in containers in a cold frame as soon as ripe, overwintering seedlings in the frame, or in spring. Sow thinly, on the surface of the compost.

MELISSA OFFICINALIS

Lemon balm, Bee balm

spring to summer

‡to 1.2m (4ft)
↔ to 45cm (18in)

THE LEAVES OF THIS POPULAR HERB give off a clear, fresh lemon aroma when they are crushed or brushed in passing. Apart from their scent, these bushy, upright perennials are grown mainly for their attractive nettle-like foliage, which is hairy and light to bright green, or splashed with golden yellow in variegated forms. The young shoots are popular ingredients in pot-pourri and herb teas. In summer, the plants also produce spikes of small, tubular two-lipped, whitish flowers, which attract bees. Grow balms in a herbaceous or mixed border or with other herbs in a herb garden. While they enjoy full sun, these plants are also useful for dry shade.

Hardiness Fully hardy ✳✳✳.

Cultivation Grow in any poor soil in full sun, but provide protection from heavy winter rain. **Cut back** hard after flowering to encourage a fresh flush of foliage and to prevent self-seeding. Variegated forms are better trimmed back before flowering to encourage bright foliage (*see below*). **Divide** plants (*see p.395*) as growth starts in spring, or in autumn. **Sow** seed in containers in a cold frame in the spring (*see pp.391–392*) or transplant self-sown seedlings.

MELITTIS MELISSOPHYLLUM

Bastard balm

late spring to early summer

‡20–70cm (8–28in)
↔ 50cm (20in)

THIS HERBACEOUS PERENNIAL is grown for its tubular flowers produced in late spring and early summer. They occur in shades of pink and purple, or white with creamy white, marked with pink or purple, and they stud the stems, appearing in the leaf joints. The oval leaves are hairy and wrinkled; they have an aromatic or honeyed scent. Grow bastard balm in a cool border with other plants that are happy in light shade, such as bergenias (*see p.198*) and aquilegias (*see p.185*), or in a woodland garden. Its flowers will attract bees and other pollinating insects into the garden.

Hardiness Fully hardy ✳✳✳.

Cultivation Grow in reasonably fertile, moist but well-drained soil, in partial shade. **Divide** plants (*see p.395*) in spring as new growth begins. **Sow** seed in a container in a cold frame as soon as it is ripe, or in spring (*see pp.391–392*).

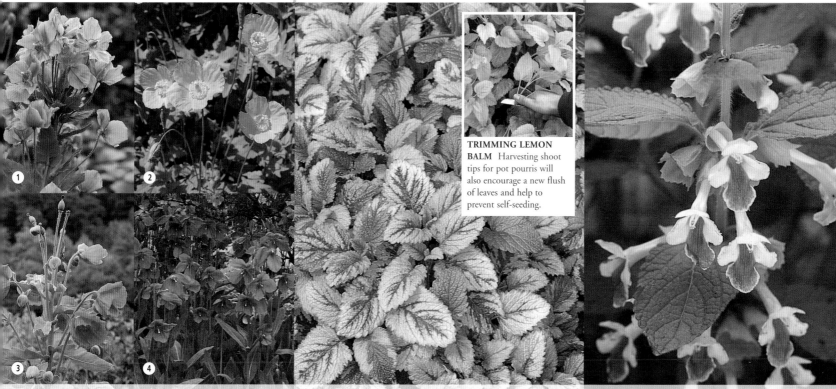

TRIMMING LEMON BALM Harvesting shoot tips for pot pourris will also encourage a new flush of leaves and help to prevent self-seeding.

① *betonicifolia* ♀ ‡1.2m (4ft) ② *cambrica* ‡45cm (18in), grows in all but very dry soils ③ *napaulensis* ‡2.5m (8ft), evergreen ④ × *sheldonii* ‡1.2–1.4m (4–5ft)

Melissa officinalis 'Aurea' (Golden lemon balm)
Hairy stems, off-white flowers in summer

Melittis melissophylum
Woodland plant found growing wild throughout most of Europe

MIMULUS

Monkey flower,
Musk

early summer to
autumn

THE NUMEROUS HYBRID MIMULUS are grown as annuals for their bright flowers that bring cheer to containers or borders from early summer right through to autumn. These resemble snapdragons and are trumpet-shaped or tubular, in a variety of colours and usually heavily freckled with a contrasting hue. The pale- to dark-green leaves often have silvery hairs. Mimulus often have a creeping habit, but may be upright and bushy; some are perennial. Most prefer moist or even boggy soil; *Mimulus luteus* and *M. ringens* thrive in shallow water at pond edges.

Hardiness Fully hardy ❋❋❋ to frost-tender ❋.

Cultivation These plants need very moist soil in sun or semi-shade, although *M. cardinalis* will tolerate drier soil; the bedding hybrids and *M. aurantiacus* require well-drained ground and sun. Mimulus is short-lived, so it is worth propagating regularly. **Sow** seed (*see pp.391–393*) of hardy species in containers in a cold frame in autumn or spring; sow tender bedding at 6–12°C (43–54°F) in spring. **Root** softwood cuttings in early summer (*see p.394*). **Divide** perennials (*see p.395*) in spring. **Slugs** (*see p.398*) can cause damage.

MOLUCCELLA LAEVIS

Bells of Ireland,
Shell flower

late
summer

❋90cm (36in)
↔23cm (9in)

THE EXTRAORDINARY, LEAFY FLOWERS and pale-green foliage are the attractions of this commonly cultivated annual – a favourite with flower arrangers. In late summer, it produces spikes up to 30cm (12in) tall that, near the tips, bear tiny, white or pink flowers cupped in large, green collars (called calyces). The calyces become white-veined and papery as the seeds develop and can be used in dried flower arrangements. The flowers are also fragrant. Moluccellas can be used to provide an eye-catching addition to a border of more common bedding plants such as French marigolds (*see Tagetes, p.329*) or heliotropes (*see p.70*).

Hardiness Half-hardy ❋.

Cultivation Moluccellas will grow in any moist, but well-drained soil in full sun. **Sow** seed (*see pp.391–393*) at 13–18°C (55–64°F) in early or mid-spring, or in situ in late spring.

MONARDA

Bergamot

midsummer to autumn

❋90cm (3ft)
↔45cm (18in)

WITH SPIDERY FLOWERHEADS and lush foliage, bergamots enhance any garden. Most widely grown are the clump-forming, herbaceous perennials, but there are a few annuals. From midsummer to early autumn, they produce clusters of tubular flowers, in shades of crimson, pink, white, or violet, at the tips of the stems. The leaves are mid- to dark green, with prominent, dark veins, and are often flushed purple. Bergamots are highly aromatic; both the leaves and flowers are used in the fragrance industry. Use these splendid plants in any border where they will attract bees and other pollinating insects to the garden.

Hardiness Fully hardy ❋❋❋.

Cultivation Any moist but well-drained soil, that does not dry out in summer, is suitable – in full sun or dappled shade. **Sow** seed (*see pp.391–392*) in a container in a cold frame, in spring or autumn. **Divide** plants (*see p.395*) in spring before new growth begins. **Slugs** may attack in spring. Powdery mildew may become a problem in dry weather (*see p.398*); mildew-resistant cultivars are available.

① *aurantiacus* ♈ ❋↔1m (3ft) ❋❋ ② *cardinalis* ♈ ❋1m (3ft)
↔60cm (2ft) ❋❋❋ ③ *lewisii* ♈ ❋60cm (2ft) ↔45cm (18in)
❋❋ ④ *luteus* ❋30cm (1ft) ↔60cm (2ft) ❋❋❋

Moluccella laevis

① '**Cambridge Scarlet**' ♈ ❋90cm (36in) ↔45cm (18in),
clump-forming perennial ② '**Croftway Pink**' ♈ ❋90cm (36in)
↔45cm (18in), clump-forming perennial

MUSCARI

Grape hyacinth   *spring*

THESE BULBOUS PLANTS, although rarely more than 20cm (8in) in height, are very versatile. In spring, and occasionally in autumn, they bear tight clusters of tiny flowers that are usually blue, but sometimes yellow, white, purple, or even black. Some species are very fragrant. The flowerheads are held above clumps of fleshy, mid-, blue- or grey-green leaves. Plant grape hyacinths in large groups in a border, or in carpets beneath deciduous shrubs and trees. They are often grown naturalized in grass with other colourful, spring-flowering bulbs such as daffodils (*Narcissus, see pp.288–289*) and tulips (*see pp.334–335*). Some species are invasive in favourable conditions; ensure they do not encroach on other plants.

Hardiness Fully hardy ✽✽✽ to frost-hardy ✽✽.

Cultivation Plant the bulbs 10cm (4in) deep in autumn, in any well-drained soil, in sun or dappled shade. **Lift and divide** (*see p.395*) clumps every five or six years, in summer, to maintain vigour and improve flowering. **Sow** seed in containers in a cold frame in autumn (*see pp.391–393*). **Viruses** may be a problem: destroy any plants that are stunted, distorted, or marked with yellow streaks or patches.

MYOSOTIS

Forget-me-not   *mid-spring to midsummer*

A LARGE GROUP OF ANNUALS, biennials, and short-lived perennials grown for their delightful flowers and hairy leaves. Most forget-me-nots have blooms in shades of blue, with white or golden eyes, but pink, yellow, or white varieties are available. The biennial *Myosotis sylvatica* and its cultivars, widely used in bedding schemes and containers, are also easy to grow in borders. The water forget-me-not (*M. scorpioides*) is happiest in mud or shallow water, and some of the small, mat-forming perennials, like the alpine forget-me-not (*M. alpestris*), prefer very sharply drained conditions. Nearly all self-seed freely, so can be left to create large drifts of colour in wildflower gardens.

Hardiness Fully hardy ✽✽✽.

Cultivation Forget-me-nots thrive in any moist but well-drained, not too fertile, soil, in sun or semi-shade. **Sow** seed (*see pp.391–393*) of all mysotis in situ in spring; seed of annuals and biennials can be sown in a cold frame in summer for earlier flowers in the following year. Seed of *M. scorpioides* should be sown in pondside mud. **Divide** plants (*see p.395*) when they are dormant. **Mildew** can create white patches on the foliage (*see p.398*) in damp conditions.

Muscari macrocarpum
↕ 10–15cm (4–6in) ↔ 8cm (3in), clumps spread much farther, spring flowers are strongly fragrant, prefers hot, dry summers ✽✽

Muscari armeniacum 'Blue Spike'
↕ 20cm (8in) ↔ 5cm (2in), may form large clumps and become invasive, mid-green leaves in autumn, flowers in spring ✽✽✽

Myosotis 'Indigo'
↕↔ 30cm (12in) ↔ 15cm (6in), biennial, one of the darkest blue cultivars, flowers from mid-spring to midsummer

FLOWERING PLANTS

Daffodil

winter to spring

DAFFODILS AND NARCISSI ARE THE HARBINGERS OF SPRING. The flowers, in cheerful yellows, creams, and white, occasionally tinged with pink or a hint of green, are a welcome sight after a long winter. The range of species and cultivars runs into thousands, varying enormously in height and flower shape, with flowers that may be borne singly or several per stem. All are bulbous perennials. The tall, showy varieties look splendid growing among shrubs in borders or used as spring bedding along with clumps of polyanthus primulas. The smaller types are to be preferred for more naturalistic plantings and are often at their most effective in drifts in grass or in a woodland setting, where they will gradually spread if left undisturbed. Dwarf types are suitable for rock gardens. Some, including many of the jonquil, tazetta, and poeticus narcissi, are fragrant. Grow these where you can catch their delicious scent, such as in a trough by the door, or in a windowbox. Some may also be "forced" (*see below*), grown indoors and made to flower early, usually for Christmas. Most daffodils also make excellent cut flowers.

Hardiness   Fully hardy ✳✳✳ to half-hardy ✳.

Cultivation   Daffodils and narcissi tolerate a wide range of soil types, but most grow best in fertile, well-drained soil that is moist during the growing season. Position them in full sun or partial shade. **Plant** the bulbs to twice their own depth in autumn, slightly deeper in light, sandy soils and when naturalizing them in grass. **Water** late-flowering daffodils during dry spring weather to encourage good blooms. **Deadhead** faded flowerheads before the seedheads form, but leave the foliage to die down naturally. This helps the bulb to build up food reserves for the following year, needed for the formation of flower buds. **Feed** foliage until it dies down with a high-potash fertilizer to encourage subsequent flowering. If daffodils are being grown in grass, delay mowing until the foliage has died down.
Lift and divide bulbs (*see p.395*) if flowering deteriorates, usually where bulbs become congested after four or five years. The tiny young bulbs can be grown on into new plants, which need three to four years to begin flowering. Poor flowering, or "blindness", may also be due to bulbs not having been planted deeply enough and replanting may be necessary. Stunted, mottled, or streaked foliage is a sign of virus attack and infected plants are best dug up and destroyed.

Forcing daffodil bulbs

❶ *Mix some washed gravel with a little charcoal. Fill the container to three-quarters full of gravel. Make a gentle dip in the surface with your finger and place a bulb (here Grand Soleil d'Or) in it, "nose" upwards. Plant the remaining bulbs, making sure they do not touch.*

❷ *When you have finished planting, add water until it is just below the bottom of the bulbs. Unless you have prepared bulbs, which can be left in the light, cover the container with a black plastic bag, secure it with string, and stand in a cool, dark place.*

❸ *Check the bulbs after about four weeks to see if they need more water. After 8–10 weeks, the bulbs should have grown 1–2cm and can be brought into the light. As the plants grow taller, support any weak leaves or stems by securing them to split canes with plant ties.*

① *Narcissus* 'Actaea' ♀ ‡45cm (18in), late spring, scented ② 'Baby Moon' ‡25–30cm (10–12in), late spring ③ *bulbocodium* ♀ ‡10–15cm (4–6in), mid-spring, can be naturalized in grass, suitable for growing in a rock garden ④ 'Cassata' ‡40cm (16in), mid-spring ⑤ 'Cheerfulness' ♀ ‡40cm (16in), mid-spring, scented ⑥ 'Dove Wings' ♀ ‡30cm (12in), early spring ⑦ 'February Gold' ♀ ‡30cm (12in), early spring, can be naturalized in grass, suitable for forcing ⑧ 'Fortune' ‡45cm

(18in), mid-spring ⑨ **'Golden Ducat'** ↕35cm (14in), mid-spring ⑩ **'Grand Soleil d'Or'** ↕45cm (18in), mid-spring, scented, suitable for forcing ❀❀ ⑪ **'Hawera'** ♀ ↕18cm (7in), late spring ❀❀ ⑫ **'Ice Follies'** ♀ ↕40cm (16in), mid-spring, prolific ⑬ **'Jack Snipe'** ♀ ↕20cm (8in), early and mid-spring, increases rapidly ⑭ **'Jenny'** ♀ ↕30cm (12in), early and mid-spring, can be naturalized in grass, suitable for forcing ⑮ **'Liberty Bells'** ↕30cm (12in), mid-spring ⑯ **'Little Beauty'** ♀ ↕15cm (6in),

dwarf, early spring ⑰ **'Mount Hood'** ♀ ↕45cm (18in), early spring ⑱ **'Pencrebar'** ↕18cm (7in), mid-spring, scented ⑲ *romieuxii* ♀ ↕8–10cm (3–4in), early spring ❀❀ ⑳ **'Salome'** ♀ ↕45cm (18in), mid-spring, produces consistently good-quality flowers ㉑ **'Sweetness'** ♀ ↕40cm (16in), mid-spring, vigorous, scented, long-lasting as a cut flower ㉒ **'Thalia'** ↕35cm (14in), mid-spring, scented ㉓ *triandrus* ♀ ↕10–25cm (4–10in), mid-spring

NEMESIA

summer

ANNUAL NEMESIAS ARE POPULARLY used as riotous summer bedding or container plants. They are easy to grow and produce abundant, brightly coloured flowers in an assortment of blues, reds, pinks, yellows, oranges, and whites. Many are bicoloured, too. The perennials are taller and less brash in appearance, flowering mainly in mauve and white; they may not survive cold winters unless grown in pots and brought under cover. Some of the newer named perennials are more reliably hardy, and will withstand being left in a sheltered position outside over winter, especially if given a protective mulch.

Hardiness Frost-hardy ✳✳ to half-hardy ✳.

Cultivation Grow in any moist but well-drained soil in full sun. Nemesias may suffer from root rot in wet soils. **Pinch out** the growing tips of annuals to promote a bushy habit and plenty of flowers. Ensure plants in pots are waterd regularly. **Sow** seed at 15°C (59°F) from early to late spring, or in autumn (*see pp.391–392*). **Take** softwood cuttings from perennials in late summer (*see p.394*) and overwinter young plants in frost-free conditions.

NEMOPHILA

early to midsummer

THE SLENDER, FLESHY STEMS OF NEMOPHILAS carry large, open flowers with distinctively marked petals. The flowers are saucer-shaped and usually blue or white, with veins, tints, patches, or centres in contrasting shades of blue, purple, white, or yellow. The showy blooms are set off by feathery, mid- or grey-green leaves. Nemophilas are low-growing annuals that bloom for several weeks in early to midsummer, with more flowers being produced in cool, moist conditions. They are useful for edging a path or filling gaps in the front of a border. Neat and compact, they also suit any type of container, or a rock garden that has moisture-retentive soil.

Hardiness Fully hardy ✳✳✳.

Cultivation Grow in any moist but well-drained soil, or in loam-based compost, in full sun or partial shade. **Water** well during dry spells, or plants may stop flowering. **Sow** seed where it is to grow outdoors in spring or autumn (*see p.393*), in shallow drills about 15cm (6in) apart. Thin the seedlings along the rows to about the same distance. Will also self-seed freely.

NEPETA

Catmint   *early summer to autumn*

THE CATMINT BEST KNOWN for its strongly aromatic leaves is catnip (*Nepeta cataria*) which cats find hypnotic, but there are other varieties widely grown in gardens that are less appealing to cats. They are perennials with soft, silvery grey foliage and small, erect flower spikes in white and shades of blue, purple, and sometimes yellow. Most have a loose, spreading habit and act as good ground-cover plants since the dense growth suppresses weeds. They can be used to line a broad, sunny path where their scent can be enjoyed whilst walking; some tiny species also suit a rock garden. Taller catmints are best sited in a mixed or herbaceous border.

Hardiness Fully hardy ✳✳✳ to half-hardy ✳.

Cultivation Grow in any well-drained soil in full sun or partial shade. The more loosely growing, taller nepetas may benefit from staking (*see p.390*). **Trim** the plants after flowering to maintain a compact habit and encourage more flowers. **Divide** plants in spring or autumn (*see p.395*). **Sow** seed in a container in a cold frame in autumn (*see pp.391–392*).

① *denticulata* ♀ ‡25cm (10in), perennial, ✳✳✳ but may need winter protection ② *strumosa* **Carnival Series** ‡17–23cm (7–9in), dwarf annual with large blooms ✳

Nemophila maculata (Five spot)
‡↔ 15–30cm (6–12in), named for the markings at the tips of its five petals, sometimes veined in mauve also

① *govaniana* ‡90cm (36in) ↔ 60cm (24in) ② *sibirica* ‡90cm (36in) ↔ 45cm (18in) ③ **'Six Hills Giant'** ‡90cm (36in) ↔ 60cm (24in) ④ *subsessilis* ‡ to 90cm (36in) ↔ 30cm (12in)

NERINE

autumn

THESE BULBOUS PERENNIALS have the most unlikely flowers for autumn – delicate, trumpet-shaped clusters in bright pink, or occasionally crimson or orange-red. They cannot help but lend an invigorating, airy feel to the garden at a time when most other plants are fading. Nerines enjoy well-drained, dry conditions, and usually flourish under a south- or west-facing wall or in a sheltered rock garden. In most, only once the flowers open or even die down do the strappy, mid-green leaves start to emerge, making the bare-stemmed flowers stand out even more dramatically; they are stunning seen in isolated groups against dark soil, pale stone, or painted masonry. Alternatively, plant them with other late-flowering bulbs, such as schizostylis and *Scilla scilloides* (*see p.323*).

Hardiness Fully hardy ✳✳✳ to half-hardy ✳.

Cultivation Plant in well-drained soil in full sun in early spring. Try to site them carefully, because they are best left undisturbed to form a large clump. In cold areas, provide a deep, dry mulch (a layer of straw or organic matter spread over the growing area) for protection. May need protection against slugs (*see p.398*).

NICOTIANA

Tobacco plant

summer to autumn

THE PERFUMED, TRUMPET-SHAPED FLOWERS are the main reason for growing this group of annuals, biennials, and perennials. The flowers, in shades of lime-green, red, pink, apple-green and white, last for many weeks over summer and autumn. They usually open fully only in the evening, when they release their heady scent, but some newer cultivars will open during the day if sited in part-shade. Most tobacco plants have sticky, mid-green leaves. Although some are herbaceous perennials, most are usually grown as annuals and are raised from seed every year. Plant in groups for the best effect and site them on a patio or near the house so that their rich evening fragrance can waft across and into doorways. Contact with the foliage can irritate the skin.

Hardiness Frost-hardy ✳✳ to half-hardy ✳.

Cultivation Grow in any moist but well-drained soil in full sun or partial shade. **Stake** tall plants in exposed positions. **Sow** seed at 18°C (64°F) in spring on the surface of the compost (*see pp.391–392*); they need light to germinate.

NIGELLA

Love-in-a-mist, Devil-in-a-bush

summer

NIGELLA HAS BEEN GROWN IN GARDENS for centuries, and today is available in several colours – white, mauve, rose-pink, deep pink, and yellow – as well as the original blue. Some seed mixtures, such as the popular Persian Jewels, produce flowers in several harmonizing shades. These bushy annuals flourish on rocky slopes and wastelands, and will grow almost anywhere. Their dainty summer flowers sit within a hazy ruff of feathery foliage (the "mist" of the common name), and are followed by inflated seed pods, equally good for cutting. Sky-blue 'Miss Jekyll' with yellow and orange eschscholzias (*see p.241*) makes a fine and fast-growing, summery contrast. Both of these easy plants fill your garden with colour at very little cost since they self-seed freely.

Hardiness Fully hardy ✳✳✳.

Cultivation Grow in any well-drained soil in full sun. **Sow** seed where it is to grow (*see p.393*) in shallow drills about 15cm (6in) apart and thin seedlings to about the same distance. Seed can be sown in spring or autumn, but autumn-sown seedlings benefit from protection, for example with a cloche, over winter.

Nerine bowdenii ♀
↕45cm (18in) ↔ 8cm (3in), robust plant, broad leaves to 30cm (12in) long, faintly scented flowers ✳✳✳

① **'Lime Green'** ♀ ↕60cm (24in) ↔ 25cm (10in), upright annual, flowers 13cm (5in) long ✳ ② *sylvestris* ♀ ↕ to 1.5m (5ft) ↔ to 60cm (24in), perennial in mild areas, strongly perfumed ✳

Nigella damascena 'Miss Jekyll' ♀
↕to 50cm (20in) ↔ to 23cm (9in), self-seeded offspring may flower in different shades, good for cutting

NYMPHAEA

Water lily

summer

WITH THEIR JEWEL-LIKE, OFTEN FRAGRANT, BLOOMS, water lilies bring an exotic touch to garden ponds and pools. These herbaceous, submerged, aquatic plants grow from tubers or rhizomes (underground stems) that run at or just below the soil surface. There are hardy and non-hardy water lilies, all of which flower in summer. Hardy varieties have mostly white, yellow, or crimson flowers that float on the surface and open during the day (unless overcast). Non-hardy tropical water lilies bloom either in the day or at night and the flowers, which include shades of blue, are held above the water. Water lilies look stunning in large ponds, and there are dwarf varieties to suit small pools, even pools in containers such as half-barrels. Their handsome leaves cover the water and provide shade for fish and also have the effect of reducing algal growth in the water by cutting out sunlight. Hardy water lilies survive even when water is frozen: the old foliage dies and new leaves grow in spring. Tropical water lilies grow as perennials in frost-free areas, but are often treated as annuals in cool climates. Regular attention is needed to keep water lilies flowering freely.

Hardiness Fully hardy ✷✷✷ to frost-tender ✸.

Cultivation Grow in still water in full sun at the correct depth for the variety; water lilies will not thrive in moving or rippling water. **Plant** hardy types in early summer in aquatic compost – or ordinary garden topsoil is usually suitable – in planting baskets lined in hessian. Insert the rhizomes just under the soil surface and top-dress with gravel to help keep soil in place. **Submerge** the basket so that it sits with 15–25cm (6–10in) of water above it. It can be placed on a stack of bricks if the pond is too deep. Once the plant is established, gradually lower the basket (removing bricks if necessary), allowing the leaves to grow to the surface between each move, until it sits at the right depth. Most water lilies grow at a depth of 30–45cm (12–18in), but a few prefer shallower or deeper planting (*see below*). In a natural pond lined with mud, you can plant directly into the mud. **Remove** fading flowers, if possible, to encourage further flowering. **Cut off** dead or dying foliage to prevent it rotting and giving off poisonous gases that can harm fish. **Divide** established plants after three or four years (*see below*).

How to divide and replant water lilies

Water lilies grow vigorously and will eventually become overcrowded and exhausted. A sure sign of this is when their leaves begin to stand out of the water instead of resting on the surface, and plants start to produce fewer flowers than normal.

If this is the case, they need dividing. This is best done in spring when plants are starting into growth, preferably in late spring, when the warmer water and longer daylight hours ensure that the plants will re-establish quickly.

❶ Lift a mature clump during spring, when the new leaves are beginning to show. Dip the plant in fresh water to remove any soil or algae from the roots.

❷ Using a sharp knife, cut the rhizome into several sections, with each having 2–3 buds. Trim off any coarse or damaged roots, and pot each section.

❸ Plant in a basket with the crown just below soil level. Top with a layer of gravel. Place the basket in shallow water until the plant is established.

① *Nymphaea alba* ↔ 1.7m (5½ft), water depth 30–90cm (1–3ft) ✷✷✷ ② **'American Star'** ↔ 1.2–1.5m (4–5ft), water depth 45cm–1.2m (1½–4ft) ✷✷✷ ③ **'Attraction'** ↔ 1.2–1.5m (4–5ft), water depth 45cm–1.2m (1½–4ft) ✷✷✷ ④ **'Aurora'** ↔ 90cm–1.5m (3–5ft) ✷✷✷ ⑤ **'Escarboucle'** ♀ ↔ 1.2–1.5m (4–5ft), flowers 15–18cm (6–7in) across, water depth 30–60cm (1–2ft) ✷✷✷ ⑥ **'Fabiola'** ↔ 1.5cm (5ft), water depth 15–30cm (6–12in) ✷✷✷ ⑦ **'Fire Crest'** ↔ 1.2m (4ft) ✷✷✷

OENOTHERA

Evening primrose,
Sundrops

**late spring to
late summer**

THE DELICATE, PAPERY FLOWERS of evening primrose grace the garden from late spring until summer's end. Although individually short-lived, they are borne in such profusion that new flowers constantly unfurl to replace their predecessors. This varied group includes annuals, biennials, and perennials that produce yellow, white, or pink flowers. Some have the additional attraction of decorative, red or coral flower buds that form subtle colour contrasts with the open flowers. Heights range from low-growing species suitable for rock gardens or raised beds, such as *Oenothera macrocarpa*, to border plants such as the tall, graceful wands of *O. biennis*, which attains a height of 1–1.5m (3–5ft) and spreads to 60cm (24in). Grow these larger plants in mixed or herbaceous borders, or in pots.

Hardiness Fully hardy ✳✳✳ to frost-hardy ✳✳.

Cultivation Grow in well-drained soil in full sun – rock plants in a site not prone to excessive winter wet. **Divide** perennials (*see p.395*) in early spring, or take softwood cuttings (*see p.394*) from late spring to midsummer. **Sow** seed in pots in a cold frame (*see pp.391–392*), of perennials in early spring and of biennials in early summer.

Oenothera macrocarpa ♀
‡ 15cm (6in) ↔ 50cm (20in), vigorous perennial with hairy, branching, red-tinted stems, flowers in late spring ✳✳✳

OMPHALODES

Navelwort

spring and summer

SPRAYS OF BLUE OR WHITE FLOWERS that are similar to those of forget-me-nots (*see Myosotis, p.287*) are produced in spring and summer. The flowers are held on long, wiry, upright stems, which gives them the look of fairylights, particularly when they shine out in shade. This small group of annuals, biennials, and perennials, some evergreen or semi-evergreen, have a spreading habit that makes good ground cover. Some are suitable for shady borders where the plant choice is limited; companions could include hostas (*see pp.260–261*), carexes (*p.345*), or *Arum italicum* 'Marmoratum' (*p.190*). *Omphalodes linifolia* and *O. luciliae* prefer sun: grow them in a raised gravel bed or rock garden to enjoy the dainty flowers close up.

Hardiness Fully hardy ✳✳✳.

Cultivation Grow *O. cappadocica* and *O. verna* in moist, fertile soil in partial shade. *O. linifolia* and *O. luciliae* require sun and well-drained soil or gritty compost, which must be alkaline for the latter. **Sow** seed (*see pp.391–393*) in spring; annuals where they are to grow, and perennials in pots in a cold frame. **Divide** perennials (*see p.395*) in early spring. Prone to damage by slugs and snails (*see p.398*).

Oenothera fruticosa 'Fyrverkeri' ♀
‡ 30–90cm (12–36in) ↔ 30cm (12in), perennial, purple-brown flushed leaves, flowers from late spring to late summer ✳✳✳

Oenothera speciosa 'Rosea'
‡↔ 30cm (12in), spreading perennial, a long flowering season from early summer to autumn, can be invasive, dislikes winter wet ✳✳✳

Omphalodes cappadocica 'Cherry Ingram' ♀
‡ 25cm (10in) ↔ 40cm (16in), evergreen perennial, flowers that are larger than those of the species, in early spring

OPHIOPOGON

Lilyturf   *summer*

THE GRASSY LEAVES OF THESE PLANTS range in colour
from an unusual shade of near-black to light green
with cream, yellow, or white margins. In summer,
they produce small clusters of bell-shaped, lilac, pink,
or white flowers, followed by glossy, round, blue or
black seed pods. Their unusual hues associate well
with many other plants, including small grasses
(*see pp.340–355*) such as *Lagarus ovatus*, brizas
and carexes. Blue fescue (*Festuca*) makes a striking
contrast to the dark 'Nigrescens'. Alternatively, use
as a ground-cover plant. Although all are evergreen
perennials, they can be raised from seed as summer
bedding each year – the dark-leaved forms, planted
en masse, form a stark contrast to brighter bedding,
such as flame-coloured begonias (*see p.196*).

Hardiness Fully hardy ✳✳✳ to half-hardy ✳.

Cultivation Grow in moist, but well-drained soil that is slightly
acid (lime-free), in full sun or partial shade. **Divide** plants in spring
(*see p.395*) as the new growth appears. **Sow** seed in containers
in a cold frame (*see pp.391–392*) as soon as it is ripe. Slugs
(*see p.398*) can damage young leaves.

ORIGANUM   *see also p.91*

Marjoram, Oregano   *summer*

BEST KNOWN AS CULINARY HERBS, marjorams have
eye-catching flowers, aromatic foliage, and varied
habits that make them useful and ornamental garden
plants. These perennials have tiny flowers that are
usually pink, surrounded by bracts (modified leaves)
which determine the dominant colour, in shades of
purple, pink, or green. The justly popular *Origanum
laevigatum* 'Herrenhausen' has branched stems to
45cm (18in) tall, clothed with leaves that are flushed
purple when young, and dense clusters of flowers
with red-purple bracts. *O. majorana*, *O. onites*, and
O. vulgare, which has a gold-leaved form, are the well-
known culinary herbs. Grow marjorams in a mixed or
herbaceous border or herb garden, and smaller species
in a rock garden, as edging, or in paving crevices.

Hardiness Fully hardy ✳✳✳ to frost-hardy ✳✳.

Cultivation Grow in full sun in well-drained and, preferably,
alkaline soil. **Cut back** flowered stems in spring. **Divide** (*see p.395*)
or take cuttings (*see p.394*) in spring. **Sow** seed (*see pp.391–392*)
in pots in autumn or at 10–13°C (50–55°F) in spring.

Ophiopogon planiscapus 'Nigrescens' ♥
‡20cm (8in) ↔ 15cm (12in), purplish-white flowers borne in
summer, followed by round, dark blue-black fruits ✳✳✳

Ophiopogon jaburan 'Vittatus'
‡60cm (24in) ↔ 30cm (12in), white, sometimes lilac-tinted flowers
in late summer and oblong, violet-blue fruits ✳✳

① *laevigatum* ♥ ‡50–60cm (20–24in) ↔ 45cm (18in)
woody-based perennial ✳✳✳ ② *vulgare* ‡↔ 30–90cm (12–36in),
woody-based perennial ✳✳✳

ORNITHOGALUM

Star-of-Bethlehem

spring and early summer

GLISTENING, SILVERY WHITE FLOWERS that shine through the dusk of evening are the key charm of these bulbous perennials. The flowers are cup-, star-, or funnel-shaped, occasionally scented, and borne on stout stems in spring and summer. Each thick, long leaf curls attractively to a point and some have a silver stripe down the centre. Plants vary in height from *Ornithogalum lanceolatum*, which is only 5–10cm (2–4in) tall, to *O. pyramidale* which can reach up to 120cm (48in). Smaller species are suitable for a rock garden. *O. nutans* and *O. umbellatum* can be invasive; they are best naturalized in short grass or at the base of shrubs. Tender species can be grown in containers and moved under cover in winter.

Hardiness Fully hardy ✳✳✳ to frost-tender ❀.

Cultivation Plant hardy and half-hardy bulbs in autumn, 10cm (4in) deep in reasonably fertile, well-drained soil in full sun; some tolerate partial shade. Tender bulbs are best planted in spring, for summer flowers, in cool climates. On heavy clay soils, plant bulbs on a layer of coarse grit to improve drainage. **Lift** and separate offsets (*see p.395*) when the bulbs are dormant in summer.

OSTEOSPERMUM

late spring to autumn

BEGUILING DAISIES WITH A SATIN SHEEN and soft evergreen foliage make these plants worthy of any border. Several new cultivars are brought out each year in an ever-increasing range of flower colours. The petals are sometimes spoon-shaped and either white washed with a delicate shade of violet, pink, lilac, or blue, or saturated with a single hue, from cream or magenta to purple. The central boss of each bloom has a contrasting tint. Osteospermums can flower from late spring until autumn. They include annuals and subshrubs, but perennials are most commonly grown in borders; half-hardy perennials are grown as annual bedding in cooler areas. Osteospermums can become a little straggly after a few years, but are easily increased from cuttings to replace old plants.

Hardiness Fully hardy ✳✳✳ to half-hardy ✳.

Cultivation Grow these in light, moderately fertile, well-drained soil, in a warm, sheltered site in full sun. **Remove** fading flowers regularly. **Take** softwood cuttings in late spring and semi-ripe cuttings in late summer (*see p.394*). **Sow** seed at 18°C (64°F) in spring (*see pp.391–393*).

Osteospermum 'Nairobi Purple'
‡15cm (6in) ↔ 90cm (36in), spreading subshrub, flowers flushed white beneath ✳

① *narbonense* ‡30–90cm (12–36in), long leaves are grey-green, flowers in late spring and early summer ✳✳✳ ② *nutans* ♀ ‡20–60cm (8–24in), flowers borne in spring ✳✳✳

Osteospermum 'Buttermilk' ♀
‡↔ 60cm (24in), upright subshrub, toothed mid-green leaves have pale yellow edges, flowers are bronze-yellow beneath ✳✳

Osteospermum jucundum ♀
‡10–50cm (4–20in) ↔ 50–40cm (20–36in), clumping perennial, flowers have bronze undersides ✳✳✳ (borderline)

OXALIS
Shamrock, Sorrel

spring and summer

LOW CLUMPS OF PRETTY, CLOVER-LIKE LEAVES provide a fine setting for these plants' small flowers. These appear in spring and summer, and may be funnel-, cup-, or bowl-shaped and tinted in shades of pink, yellow, and reddish-purple. In dull weather, the flowers close up. Some oxalis are spreading weeds, and some of the ornamental types can also be invasive, and are best planted in isolation. Bulbous perennials, these plants may spring from tubers, rhizomes, or true bulbs. Many oxalis thrive in the free-draining soil of a rock garden or in a container. Others, such as *Oxalis acetosella* and *O. oregana* are happy in woodland or shady sites where they have plenty of space to spread.

Hardiness Fully hardy ✳✳✳ to frost-tender ❅.

Cultivation Woodland species need moist, humus-rich, fertile soil in sun or partial shade; hardy species need moderately fertile, humus-rich, well-drained soils in full sun. For plants in containers, use a loam-based compost with extra grit for good drainage. **Sow** seed at 13–18°C (55–64°F) in late winter or early spring (*see pp.391–393*). **Divide** plants (*see p.395*) in spring.

PACHYSANDRA

spring to early summer

GOOD GROUND-COVER PLANTS, these low, bushy perennials quickly spread to create an evergreen, or semi-evergreen, carpet of dark or grey-green foliage. These leaves are sometimes toothed and cluster at the tips of upright, fleshy stems. *Pachysandra terminalis* 'Variegata' has pleasing white leaf margins. In spring to early summer, pachysandras produce small spikes of greenish-white female, and white male, flowers. These are easy plants to grow and look very much at home in shady areas or at the feet of flowering shrubs, for example rhododendrons (*see pp.104–107*) and camellias (*see pp.32–33*). Pachysandras spread particularly freely where the soil is moist and the conditions are humid.

Hardiness Fully hardy ✳✳✳.

Cultivation Any soil is suitable – except very dry soil – in full sun or partial shade. Soil enriched with plenty of organic matter is best. **Divide** established plants (*see p.395*) in spring or take softwood cuttings (*see p.394*) in early summer.

Osteospermum 'Whirlygig' ♥
↕↔ 60cm (24in), spreading subshrub, petals are slate- or powder-blue on reverse, flowers have slate-blue central boss ✳

Oxalis adenophylla ♥
↕ 10cm (4in) ↔ to 15cm (6in), true bulb, prefers sun and free-draining soil such as a raised bed or rock garden ✳✳✳

Pachysandra terminalis ♥
↕ 20cm (8in) ↔ indefinite, evergreen, leaves to 10cm (4in) long, male flowers in early summer

FLOWERING PLANTS

Peony

late spring to early summer

↕ 34–110cm
(14–40in)

WITH THEIR SPECTACULAR BLOOMS and bold, lush foliage, the many herbaceous perennial peonies remain a classic choice for any border. The flowers open from large buds, usually in early summer, and vary from single cups, some with golden stamens, to blowsy doubles. They range in size from 5cm (2in) to an impressive 20cm (8in) or more. The large leaves of these clump-forming plants are usually blue-, grey-, or dark-green, and deeply divided. Think carefully before you plant peonies – they are long-lived plants, and suffer if moved once they are established.

Hardiness Fully hardy ✸✸✸ to frost-hardy ✸✸, but early flowers and young foliage may be damaged in a late frost.

Cultivation Grow in fertile, moist but well-drained soil, and dig in well-rotted organic matter before you plant. Choose a position in full sun or partial shade. **Support** stems of peonies with very large flowers. **Take** root cuttings (*see p.394*) in winter or divide the tuberous roots in autumn or early spring (*see p.395*). **Peony wilt** may cause stems to blacken and flop: if a brown patch or grey, fuzzy fungal growth develops round the bases, cut affected stems back to healthy growth, beneath the soil if necessary.

Paeonia lactiflora 'Festiva Maxima' ♀
↕↔ 90–100cm (36–39in), abundant mid-green leaves, fragrant flowers on strong, erect stems are over 20cm (8in) across ✸✸✸

RING STAKES provide support for the huge flowers: simply let young stems grow up through the gaps.

Paeonia lactiflora 'Sarah Bernhardt' ♀
↕↔ 90–100cm (36–39in), vigorous, with mid-green leaves and erect stems, fragrant flowers are over 20cm (8in) across ✸✸✸

Paeonia cambessedesii ♀ (Majorcan peony)
↕↔ 45–55cm (18–22in), leaves are purple-red beneath with purple veins, flowers up to 10cm (4in) across in mid- and late spring ✸✸✸

Paeonia mlokosewitschii ♀ (Caucasian peony)
↕↔ 65–90m (26–36in), erect stems, leaves hairy beneath, flowers up to 13cm (5in) across in late spring and early summer ✸✸✸

PAPAVER
Poppy

late spring to summer

THESE COTTAGE-GARDEN FAVOURITES are beloved by gardeners for their bright, papery, summer blooms. As well as the classic blood-red, poppies come in glowing oranges, and more subtle pinks, yellows, and white; many are smudged black at the bases of their petals. Each flower is short-lived, but is followed by many more, and later by striking, pepper-pot seedheads. The light to mid-green, often hairy or bristly, ferny leaves are very distinctive, even as seedlings. The flowers of annuals and biennials are generally more delicate than the bold, brash blooms of the perennial oriental poppies, but they all have a place. Large poppies look good in any border; annuals thrive in a rock or gravel garden and self-seed freely.

Hardiness Fully hardy ✳✳✳ to frost-hardy ✳✳.

Cultivation Grow in fertile, well-drained soil in full sun. **Sow** seed (*see pp.391–393*) in spring: annuals and biennials in situ; perennials in a cold frame. **Avoid** high-nitrogen fertilizers because they may cause flowers to fall early. **Cut back** oriental poppies after flowering for a second flush later in summer. **Divide** perennials (*see p.395*) in spring, or raise them from root cuttings (*see p.394*) in autumn and winter. **Mildew** (*see p.398*) may be troublesome in damp summers.

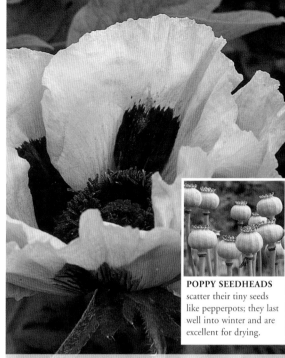

POPPY SEEDHEADS scatter their tiny seeds like pepperpots; they last well into winter and are excellent for drying.

Papaver orientale 'Cedric Morris' ♀
↕ 45–90cm (18–36in) ↔ 60–90cm (24–36in), clumping perennial, hairy, grey leaves, 16cm (6in) flowers late spring to midsummer ✳✳✳

Papaver rhoeas 'Mother of Pearl'
↕ 90cm (36in) ↔ 30cm (12in), annual, downy leaves, summer flowers in soft shades such as dove-grey, pink, and lilac-blue ✳✳✳

Papaver orientale 'Black and White' ♀
↕ 45–90cm (18–36in) ↔ 60–90cm (24–36in), clumping perennial, large bristly leaves, flowers in late spring to midsummer ✳✳✳

Papaver orientale 'Beauty of Livermere'
↕ 45–90cm (18–36in) ↔ 60–90cm (24–36in), clumping perennial, flowers to 20cm (8in) across in late spring to midsummer ✳✳✳

Papaver rhoeas Shirley Group
↕ 90cm (36in) ↔ 30cm (12in), annual, downy leaves, single to double flowers in yellow, pink, orange, and red in summer ✳✳✳

Pelargonium, Bedding geranium

spring to autumn

THESE POPULAR PLANTS ARE WIDELY, but incorrectly, called geraniums. They are related to the cranesbills (*see Geranium, pp.250–251*), but are quite different in many ways, not least in being almost universally frost-tender. Pelargoniums have deservedly been garden favourites for many years. There is a huge range to choose from, with not only beautiful flowers, but attractive, multicoloured, and often fragrant leaves as well. Pelargoniums are generally used as bedding plants, or in hanging baskets and other containers, producing dense clusters of bright flowers from summer until autumn. Flower forms vary from the double, heavily frilled 'Apple Blossom Rosebud' to the delicate 'Bird Dancer', and colours range from orange to pink, red or purple, in soft and restrained or bold and vivid shades. Most form upright, bushy plants with rounded or divided leaves, sometimes with darker zones, but there are also trailing forms (details of main types are given below).

Hardiness Almost all are frost-tender ❀.

Cultivation Grow in fertile, well-drained soil, or in a loam-based or soiless compost. Position most plants in full sun; zonal pelargoniums will tolerate some shade. **Deadhead** regularly. **Feed** with a high-potash fertilizer through the summer to encourage plenty of flowers. **Lift** the plants in autumn, and keep them almost dry in a frost-free place over winter. Cut back the top-growth by about one-third and repot the plants in late winter as growth begins. **Cuttings** can be taken in spring, summer, and autumn (*see p.394*), but these will need to be kept in a frost-free place over winter; alternatively young plants and plug plants (*see p.393*) are widely available in garden centres in early summer. **Sow** seed (*see pp.391–392*) with bottom heat in spring. Pelargoniums are generally trouble-free, but in pots they are susceptible to attack by vine weevils (*see p.398*). If plants suffer from grey mould (botrytis), cut out all affected parts and treat with a fungicide if necessary.

Ivy-leaved pelargoniums

These trailing perennials make a spectacular show in containers such as windowboxes and hanging baskets, or even as small climbers, if tied into suitable supports. They have clusters of single or double flowers in shades of red, pink, mauve, and purple or white. As their name suggests, they resemble ivy in both their habit and in the shape of their stiff, fleshy, evergreen leaves, 2.5–13cm (1–5in) long, which are lobed and occasionally pointed.

Regal pelargoniums

Bushy, evergreen, and usually grown under glass, these bear dense clusters of single or double flowers to 4cm (1½in) across, in red, pink, purple, orange, white, or reddish-black, often with more than one shade. The rounded leaves are up to 9cm (3½in) long. Some plants become quite large and should be cut back in spring. Those described as unique types have larger leaves, sometimes divided and often scented; angel types have smaller leaves and flowers.

Scented-leaved pelargoniums

Plant these in containers where you can touch them easily so that the leaves release their scent, or along a path where you will brush against them. Each cultivar has its own delicious perfume, from sweet to spicy or citrus. These pelargoniums are grown mainly for their leaves, which are usually mid-green, occasionally variegated, 1.5–13cm (½–5in) long, and varying in shape. The flowers, in shades of mauve, pink, purple, and white, are usually not very large.

Zonal pelargoniums

The most popular of all the types, zonal pelargoniums are long-established favourites for patio containers, summer bedding or conservatories. They are bushy, evergreen perennials with short-jointed stems. The round leaves are marked with zones of dark bronze-green or maroon; those of fancy-leaved cultivars may be tricoloured, with white or green, bronze, silver, and gold. The flowers are single to fully double, in white and many shades of orange, purple, pink, and scarlet.

① *Pelargonium* 'Alberta' ↕50cm (20in) ↔ 25cm (10in), zonal ② 'Amethyst' ↕30cm (12in) ↔ 25cm (10in), ivy-leaved ③ 'Ann Hoystead' ♀ ↕45cm (18in) ↔ 25cm (10in), regal ④ 'Apple Blossom Rosebud' ♀ ↕40cm (16in) ↔ 25cm (10in), zonal ⑤ 'Bird Dancer' ♀ ↕20cm (8in) ↔ 15cm (6in), zonal ⑥ 'Caligula' ↕13cm (5in) ↔ 10cm (4in), zonal ⑦ 'Clorinda' ↕50cm (20in) ↔ 25cm (10in), cedar-scented leaves ⑧ 'Coddenham' ↕13cm (5in) ↔ 10cm (4in), zonal ⑨ *crispum* 'Variegatum' ♀

‡35cm (18in) ↔ 15cm (6in), lemon-scented leaves ⑩ **'Crystal Palace Gem'** ‡45cm (18in) ↔ 30cm (12in), zonal ⑪ **'Dale Queen'** ‡40cm (16in) ↔ 20cm (8in), zonal ⑫ **'Dolly Varden'** ♀ ‡30cm (12in) ↔ 15cm (6in), zonal ⑬ **'Fair Ellen'** ‡40cm (16in) ↔ 20cm (8in), spicy-scented leaves ⑭ **'Flower of Spring'** ♀ ‡60cm (24in) ↔ 25cm (10in), zonal ⑮ **Fragrans Group** ‡25cm (10in) ↔ 20cm (8in), pine-scented leaves ⑯ **'Francis Parrett'** ♀ ‡13cm (5in) ↔ 10cm (4in), zonal ⑰ **'Freckles'** ‡↔ to 30cm (12in), zonal ⑱ **'Friesdorf'** ‡20cm (8in) ↔ 13cm (5in), zonal ⑲ **'Golden Wedding'** ‡↔ 60cm (24in), zonal ⑳ **'Graveolens'** ‡60cm (24in) ↔ 40cm (16in), lemon-rose-scented leaves ㉑ **'Happy Thought'** ♀ ‡45cm (18in) ↔ 25cm (10in), zonal ㉒ **'Irene'** ♀ ‡45cm (18in) ↔ 30cm (12in), zonal ㉓ **'Ivalo'** ‡30cm (12in) ↔ 25cm (10in), zonal ㉔ **'Lachskönigin'** ‡30cm (12in) ↔ 20cm (8in), ivy-leaved

㉕ *Pelargonium* 'Lady Plymouth' ♀ ‡40cm (16in) ↔ 20cm (8in), eucalyptus-scented leaves
㉖ 'Lavender Grand Slam' ♀ ‡40cm (16in) ↔ 20cm (8in), regal ㉗ 'L'Elégante' ♀ ‡25cm
(10in) ↔ 20cm (8in), ivy-leaved ㉘ 'Lemon Fancy' ‡40cm (16in) ↔ 20cm (8in), citrus-
scented leaves ㉙ 'Lesley Judd' ‡40cm (16in) ↔ 20cm (8in), regal ㉚ 'Mabel Grey' ♀
‡35cm (14in) ↔ 15cm (6in), lemon-scented leaves ㉛ 'Madame Fournier' ‡13cm (5in)

↔ 10cm (4in), zonal ㉜ 'Mr Everaarts' ‡20cm (8in) ↔ 13cm (5in), zonal ㉝ 'Mr Henry Cox' ♀
‡30cm (12in) ↔ 13cm (5in), zonal ㉞ 'Mrs Pollock' ‡ 30cm (12in) ↔ 15cm (6in), zonal ㉟ 'Mrs Quilter'
♀ ‡40cm (16in) ↔ 15cm (6in), zonal ㊱ Multibloom Series ♀ ‡↔ 30cm (12in), zonal ㊲ 'Old
Spice' ‡30cm (12in) ↔ 15cm (6in), spicy-scented leaves ㊳ 'Orsett' ♀ ‡70cm (28in) ↔ 50cm (20in),
spicy mint-scented leaves ㊴ 'Paton's Unique' ♀ ‡45cm (18in) ↔ 20cm (8in), unique

㊵ 'Paul Humphries' ‡30cm (12in) ↔ 20cm (8in), zonal ㊶ 'Pixie Rose' ‡30cm (12in) ↔ 20cm (8in), zonal ㊷ 'Polka' ‡50cm (20in) ↔ 25cm (10in), unique ㊸ 'Purple Emperor' ‡40cm (16in) ↔ 20cm (8in), regal ㊹ 'Robe' ‡45cm (18in) ↔ 20cm (8in), zonal ㊺ 'Rollisson's Unique' ‡45cm (18in) ↔ 20cm (8in), unique ㊻ 'Rouletta' ‡60cm (24in) ↔ 20cm (8in), ivy-leaved ㊼ 'Royal Oak' ♀ ‡40cm (16in) ↔ 30cm (12in), spicy-scented leaves ㊽ 'Schöne Helena' ‡40cm (16in) ↔ 25cm (10in), zonal

㊾ 'Sefton' ♀ ‡40cm (16in) ↔ 20cm (8in), regal ㊿ 'Strawberry Sundae' ‡60cm (24in) ↔ 30cm (12in), regal �51 'The Boar' ♀ ‡60cm (24in) ↔ 25cm (10in), trailing �52 'Timothy Clifford' ‡13cm (5in) ↔ 10cm (4in), zonal �53 'Tip Top Duet' ♀ ‡40cm (16in) ↔ 20cm (8in), angel �54 *tomentosum* ♀ ‡90cm (36in) ↔ 75cm (30in), peppermint-scented leaves �55 Tornado Series ‡25cm (10in) ↔ 20cm (8in), ivy-leaved

midsummer to autumn

THESE FLAMBOYANT PLANTS bring colour to the garden from midsummer, often lasting until the first frosts. Upright spires produce a continuous succession of tubular flowers, similar to foxgloves, in rich hues of purple, scarlet, pink, yellow, and white; many are bicoloured. This is a large group of mostly evergreen, bushy but neat perennials. They range from dwarf kinds around 15cm (6in) tall, that are suitable for rock gardens, to taller border plants of 60cm (24in) or more; these may need staking (*see below and p.390*). The leaves may be narrow and up to 8cm (3in) long or oval, from 13cm (5in) long.

Hardiness Fully hardy ✳✳✳ to half-hardy ✳.

Cultivation Border penstemons like fertile, well-drained soil in full sun or partial shade; dwarf and shrubby species need gritty, sharply drained, poor to moderate soil. **Protect** plants with a dry mulch in winter in frost-prone areas. **Deadhead** unless seed is needed. **Sow** seed (*see pp.391–393*) in late winter or spring at 131–18°C (55–64°F). **Take** softwood cuttings in early summer or semi-ripe cuttings in midsummer (*see p.394*). **Divide** plants (*see p.395*) in spring.

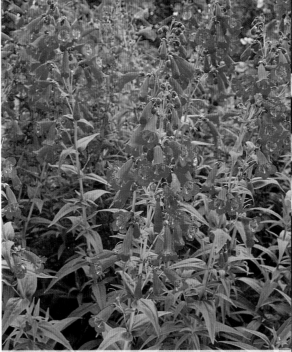

Penstemon 'Chester Scarlet' ♀
‡ 60cm (24in) ↔ 45cm (18in), large leaves and flowers 5–8cm (2–3in) long from midsummer to mid-autumn ✳

SUPPORTING CLUMPS
Put cane and twine or metal supports in place before penstemons grow too tall so that they can develop a natural habit.

Penstemon 'Apple Blossom' ♀
‡↔ 45–60cm (18–24in), narrow leaves, white-throated flowers from midsummer to early or mid-autumn ✳✳✳ (borderline)

Penstemon 'Evelyn' ♀
‡ 45–60cm (18–24in) ↔ 30cm (12in), bushy, narrow leaves, flowers 2.5–3cm (1–1¼in), paler inside, midsummer to mid-autumn ✳✳✳

Penstemon 'Stapleford Gem' ♀
‡ to 60cm (24in) ↔ 45cm (18in), large leaves, flowers 5–8cm (2–3in) long from midsummer to early autumn ✳✳✳

Penstemon 'Pennington Gem' ♥
↕ to 75cm (30in) ↔ 45cm (18in), narrow leaves, flowers 5–8cm
(2–3in) long from midsummer to early or mid-autumn ✲✲

PERSICARIA

summer to autumn

SHORT, BOTTLEBRUSH BLOOMS – made of tiny pink,
white, or red, funnel- or bell-shaped flowers that
cluster tightly on wiry stems appear from summer to
autumn. Persicarias also have pleasing foliage: with
broad, long-stalked leaves at the base and smaller
leaves clothing the fleshy stems. Many of these clump-
forming perennials and annuals spread by means of
creeping stems and can become invasive, but are easily
kept under control if necessary. Ranging in height
from 5cm (2in) to 1.2m (4ft), most are medium-sized
and make an undemanding, weed-suppressing ground
cover. Grow persicarias with phygelius (*see p.95*), and
perennials like cranesbills (*see Geranium, pp.250–251*)
and monardas (*see p.286*).

Hardiness Fully hardy ✲✲✲ to frost-hardy ✲.
Cultivation Any moist soil in full sun or partial shade suits this
plant; the best flower colour is obtained in full sun. *Persicaria bistorta*
tolerates dry soil. **Sow** seed (*see pp.391–392*) in a container in a cold
frame in spring. **Divide** perennials in spring or autumn (*see p.395*).

PETRORHAGIA

summer

CLOSELY RELATED TO GYPSOPHILA (*see p.254*) and
dianthus (*see pp.226–227*), these perennials and
annuals are grown for their clusters of white, or
occasionally pink or yellow, flowers that are borne all
through summer. The delicate flowers are held on the
tips of wiry stems above grassy leaves. Petrorhagias are
best grown in a sunny position at the front of a mixed
or herbaceous border, on a sunny bank, or against a
wall. You could also grow them in a rock garden with
other low alpines, such as dianthus and saxifrages
(*see pp.320–321*). Try planting petrorhagias in an
alpine trough where the stems and flowers can be
allowed to spill out and soften the trough's hard edges.

Hardiness Fully hardy ✲✲✲ if soil is well-drained.
Cultivation Petrorhagias thrive in any poor to reasonably fertile,
well-drained soil in full sun. **Sow** seed (*see pp.391–392*) in a container
in a cold frame in autumn. **Take** stem-tip cuttings (*see p.394*) in early
summer. Slugs and snails (*see p.398*) can be a problem.

Penstemon 'White Bedder' ♥
↕ 60cm (24in) ↔ 45cm (18in), large leaves, flowers become tinged
pink as they age, from midsummer to mid-autumn ✲✲

Persicaria bistorta 'Superba' ♥ (Bistort)
↕ to 90cm (36in) ↔ 45cm (18in), semi-evergreen, mat-forming
perennial, autumn leaves rich brown, flowers over long period ✲✲✲

Petrorhagia saxifraga ♥ (Tunic flower)
↕ 10cm (4in) ↔ 20cm (8in), mat-forming perennial, long-lasting
white or pink flowers – 1cm (½in) across – in summer ✲✲✲

FLOWERING PLANTS

PETUNIA

late spring to autumn

STAPLE BEDDING AND CONTAINER PLANTS, petunias are prized for their showy, velvety flowers borne from late spring to late autumn. They may be single or double, and often brightly veined or striped with a contrasting colour; the choice of forms increases every year. There are two groups: Grandiflora types have large flowers up to 10cm (4in) across and include the Surfinias and others that are less weather-resistant. The bushier, and often more resilient, Multifloras bear masses of smaller blooms, to 5cm (2in) across. Trailing petunias are perfect for hanging baskets. Use Multifloras to carpet large beds or borders. Petunia leaves and stems are sticky and hairy. Many petunias are perennial, but most are grown as annuals.

Hardiness Half-hardy ✳.

Cultivation Petunias enjoy light, well-drained soil or compost in full sun. Feed plants in containers with a tomato fertilizer every 10–14 days. **Deadhead** regularly (*see p.390*) to keep them in bloom. **Sow** seed (*see pp.391–393*) at 13–18°C (55–64°F) in autumn or mid-spring, or root softwood cuttings (*see p.394*) in summer. Overwinter seedlings under cover; plant out when all danger of frost has passed.

PHLOMIS

see also p.94

summer

THE HERBACEOUS PERENNIAL phlomis are good year-round plants. Although the silvery or grey-green, sage-like leaves die down in winter, the attractive seedheads remain to provide interest through the barest months. In spring, white-woolly young shoots emerge, to form an erect or spreading clump of foliage. Clusters of hooded flowers, somewhat like the dead nettle (*see Lamium, p.269*), are borne on tall stems in summer, and are usually white, dusty pink, or soft yellow. Phlomis is a very good choice of plant for hot, dry areas – for example, beside a patio or in a gravel garden – because their hairy leaves help them to retain moisture. They are also lovely planted in groups to form softly-coloured mounds in a warm, sunny border. There are also shrubby types of phlomis.

Hardiness Fully hardy ✳✳✳ to frost-hardy ✳✳.

Cultivation Grow in any fertile, well-drained soil in full sun, although *Phlomis russeliana* and *P. samia* will tolerate some shade. **Sow** seed (*see pp.391–393*) at 13–18°C (55–64°F) in spring. **Divide** (*see p.395*) large clumps, ideally in spring, but also in autumn.

PHLOX

spring to autumn

PHLOXES ARE TREASURED for their flat, blue, milky-to bright pink, or red flowers, which are borne in fat clusters at the tips of tall stems. They are a diverse group that include spreading to erect, evergreen and herbaceous perennials, and some annuals. Spring-flowering, dwarf varieties, such as Phlox subulata, are perfect in a rock garden; early summer-flowering plants, such as 'Chattahoochee', prefer a woodland area, where their pale flowers seem to glow in the shade. Tall, midsummer-flowering phloxes, such as perennial *P. maculata* or *P. paniculata*, make a colourful addition to a sunny border. Annual bedding phloxes (forms of *P. drummondii*) flower from late spring to autumn.

Hardiness Fully hardy ✳✳✳ to half-hardy ✳.

Cultivation Perennial border phloxes prefer well-drained soil in sun or partial shade; annuals and rock garden types need well-drained soil in full sun. Woodland phloxes such as *P. divaricata* require moist soil and shade. **Deadhead** (*see p.390*) *P. maculata* and *P. paniculata* regularly. **Sow** seed (*see pp.391–393*) of annuals at 13–18°C (55–64°F) in spring; that of perennials in containers in a cold frame when ripe, or in spring. **Divide** (*see p.395*) tall plants in spring or in autumn, or take root cuttings (*see p.394*) in autumn or winter.

① **SURFINIA PURPLE** ♀ ↕23–40cm (9–16in) ↔ 30–90cm (12–36in) ② **SURFINIA WHITE** ↕23–40cm (9–16in) ↔ 30–90cm (12–36in), both ✳, tolerate wet weather without damage

Phlomis russeliana ♀
↕90cm (36in) ↔ 75cm (30in), upright, hairy leaves up to 20cm (8in) long, flowers from late spring to early autumn ✳✳✳

Phlox divaricata 'Chattahoochee' ♀
↕15cm (6in) ↔ 30cm (12in), short-lived, semi-evergreen perennial, prostrate, purplish leaves, flowers summer and early autumn ✳✳✳

Phlox 'Kelly's Eye' ♀
‡10cm (4in) ↔ 30cm (12in), evergreen, mounding perennial, long narrow leaves, flowers in late spring to early summer ✳✳✳

Phlox maculata 'Omega' ♀
‡90cm (36in) ↔ 45cm (18in), herbaceous perennial, fragrant flowers in early and midsummer ✳✳✳

Phlox paniculata 'Graf Zeppelin'
‡1.2m (4ft) ↔ 60–100cm (24–39in), herbaceous perennial, ideal for a border, scented flowers from summer to mid-autumn ✳✳✳

THINNING SHOOTS
Pinch out one-third of the shoots at the base to reduce congestion and the chance of powdery mildew, and ensure strong, healthy growth.

Phlox paniculata 'Harlequin'
‡1.2m (4ft) ↔ 60–100cm (24–39in), herbaceous perennial, ideal for a border, fragrant flowers from summer to mid-autumn ✳✳✳

Phlox paniculata 'Windsor' ♀
‡1.2m (4ft) ↔ 60–100cm (24–39in), herbaceous perennial, ideal for a border, flowers from summer to mid-autumn ✳✳✳

Phlox subulata 'Lilacina'
‡5–15cm (2–6in) ↔ 50cm (20in), dense, mat-forming, evergreen perennial, flowers in late spring and early summer ✳✳✳

PHUOPSIS STYLOSA

summer

THIS IS A MAT-FORMING PERENNIAL with slender, branching stems bearing clusters of up to eight narrow, pointed leaves that have a musky fragrance. Over many months in summer, it produces a profusion of round heads of tiny, pink flowers at the tips of the stems. These are delicately scented. Phuopsis spreads by rooting stems and makes a good ground-cover plant at the front of a border or on a sunny bank. You could also try it in a rock garden with other alpines such as phloxes (*see p.306*) and saponarias (*see p.319*).

Hardiness Fully hardy ✵✵✵.

Cultivation This plant needs reasonably fertile, moist but well-drained soil, in full sun or partial shade. **Cut back** the top-growth after flowering to maintain a compact habit. **Sow** seed (*see pp.391–392*) in a container in an open cold frame in autumn. **Divide** established plants (*see p.395*) or take stem-tip cuttings (*see p.394*) from spring until early summer.

PHYSALIS

Ground cherry

autumn

‡60–75cm (24–30in)
↔90cm (36in)

WITH THEIR STRIKING SEEDHEADS, this group of upright, bushy annuals and perennials bring welcome colour to the garden in autumn. Clusters of tiny, white or cream flowers appear in the summer, but it is the seedheads that give these plants their impact. Vivid orange or scarlet, papery lanterns, or calyces, enclose bright red, gold, or purple berries. These lanterns retain their colour well when dried for decorative use or they may be left on the plant through winter to decay into skeletons, revealing the berries inside. The leaves often have silvery hairs. Physalis can be invasive in rich soils.

Hardiness Fully hardy ✵✵✵ to frost-hardy ✵✵.

Cultivation Any well-drained soil in full sun or partial shade will suit these plants. **Cut** stems for drying as the calyces begin to colour. **Sow** seed (*see pp.391–393*) of perennials in containers in a cold frame in spring; sow seed of annuals where they are to grow in mid-spring. **Divide** perennials (*see p.395*) in spring.

PHYSOSTEGIA

Obedient plant

mid- to late summer

VALUABLE IN THE LATE-SUMMER BORDER, the upright, herbaceous perennials in this group form dense clumps. Their flower spikes rise up in midsummer, crowded with almost stalkless blooms in shades of pink, lilac-pink, magenta-pink, or white. The flowers usually face in one of two directions; if they are moved on the stalks, the flowers remain in their new position, earning them the name of obedient plant. Like dead nettles (*see Lamium, p.269*), to which they are related, physostegias have square stems. The variably shaped leaves often have toothed edges. Physostegias spread by underground stems (rhizomes) and can be invasive in rich soils, but are well-behaved in poor soils. Combine them with perennials such as phlomis (*see p.306*) and persicarias (*see p.305*). They are also good for cutting.

Hardiness Fully hardy ✵✵✵ to frost-hardy ✵✵.

Cultivation Moderately fertile soil that is reliably moist, in full sun or partial shade, suits these plants. **Sow** seed (*see pp.391–392*) in a container in a cold frame in autumn. **Divide** plants (*see p.395*) in winter or early spring before growth starts.

Phuopsis stylosa
‡15cm (6in) ↔ 50cm (20in) or more, individual flowers are 1.5–2cm (½–¾in) long

Physalis alkekengi ♈ (Chinese lantern, Japanese lantern)
‡60–75cm (24–30in) ↔ 90cm (36in) or more, vigorous perennial, spreads by underground stems, lanterns are 5cm (2in) across ✵✵✵

Physostegia virginiana 'Vivid' ♈
‡30–60cm (12–24in) ↔ 30cm (12in), toothed leaves to 13cm (5in) long, flowers from midsummer to early autumn ✵✵✵

PLATYCODON GRANDIFLORUS

Balloon flower   *late summer*

LARGE BUDS LIKE MINIATURE BALLOONS give this plant its common name. The several cultivated forms of this perennial are grown for the pretty flowers borne in late summer, in blue, lilac purple, pale pink, or white. The balloon flower varies in habit, but most form neat, compact clumps with toothed, blue-green leaves. These are lovely plants for a large rock garden or a border, and are also good for cutting. Try them with other herbaceous perennials, such as achilleas (*see p.166*), physostegias (*see left*), and lythrums (*see p.283*). Once they are well-established, the plants should not be moved because they do not recover well if their roots are disturbed.

Hardiness Fully hardy ✳✳✳.

Cultivation The balloon flower prefers deep, fertile, well-drained but reliably moist soil, in full sun or partial shade. **Support** the stems if necessary in exposed positions (*see p.390*). **Sow** seed (*see pp.391–392*) in pots in a cold frame in spring. **Divide** plants (*see p.395*) in summer. You can also try removing shoots that have rooted at the base in early summer and using them as cuttings (*see p.394*).

POLEMONIUM

Jacob's ladder   *late spring to late summer*

NAMED FOR THEIR DISTINCTIVE LEAVES, these mostly clump-forming annuals and perennials are favourites in cottage gardens. The leaves are composed of many paired leaflets that resemble the rungs of a ladder, and are produced in rosettes, from which spring erect stems. The cup-, bell-, or saucer-shaped flowers are borne in spring and summer and are either solitary or held in small clusters at the stem tips. Usually blue or white, they can be purple, pink, or yellow. Taller species look good in a mixed or herbaceous border, with other spring- or summer-flowering perennials such as aquilegias (*see p.185*) or tradescantias (*see p.331*) while small ones look best in a rock garden. *Polemonium caeruleum* can be naturalized in grass in a wildflower garden.

Hardiness Fully hardy ✳✳✳.

Cultivation Taller species thrive in any well-drained but moist soil in full sun or partial shade. Small species prefer very gritty, sharply drained soil in full sun. **Deadhead** regularly to prolong flowering. **Sow** seed (*see pp.391–392*) in a container in a cold frame in autumn or spring. **Divide** plants (*see p.395*) in spring.

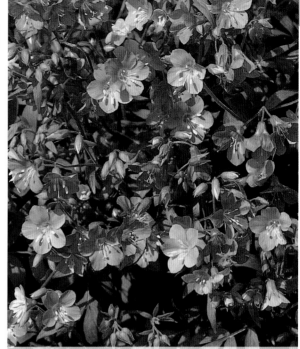

Polemonium 'Lambrook Mauve' ♥
↕↔ 45cm (18in), also called 'Lambrook Manor', rounded mounds of neat leaves, free-flowering in late spring and early summer

Platycodon grandiflorus ♥
↕ to 60cm (24in) ↔ 30cm (12in), compact clump, flowers to 5cm (2in) across

Polemonium caeruleum (Greek valerian, Jacob's ladder)
↕ 30–90cm (12–36in) ↔ 30cm (12in), leaves 40cm (16in) long, flowers, rarely white, on ends of branching stems in early summer

Polemonium pauciflorum
↕↔ to 50cm (20in), short-lived, leaves to 15cm (6in) long, red-tinted flowers single or in sparse clusters from early to late summer

POLYGALA

late spring to summer

BY FAR THE MOST WIDELY GROWN in gardens are the tiny rock polygalas, with their rich flower colours. *Polygala calcarea* and its varieties flower in particularly distinctive marine blues; use them to create pools of colour over pale stone chippings or, for a more unusual effect, dark slate or coloured glass pebbles. Commonly known as milkwort, this species was once used in herbal tonics for nursing mothers. *P. chamaebuxus* flowers in a mix of yellows; it also has white and bicoloured forms. Both these polygalas are evergreen, with small, leathery leaves, and flower in late spring and early summer. Grow them in a rock garden, or in an alpine trough or sink garden.

Hardiness Fully hardy ✱✱✱ to frost-tender ✿.

Cultivation Grow in moist but well-drained soil in full sun or dappled shade. In containers, use a soilless multipurpose compost, and top-dress with a layer of grit. **Sow** seed in containers in a cold frame in autumn (*see pp.391–392*). **Take** softwood cuttings in early summer or semi-ripe cuttings in mid- to late summer (*see p.394*).

POLYGONATUM

Solomon's seal · *spring to early summer*

ARCHING, LEAFY STEMS dripping with pendent flowers are the defining characteristic of most Solomon's seal – vigorous, clump-forming perennials with creeping, fleshy roots that thrive in shade. With their drooping habit, even the tallest ones have a shy look that is perfect for a woodland garden. The bell-shaped, subtly fragrant flowers that hang from the stems in spring and early summer are creamy-white or sometimes pink, with green markings, and are followed by red or black berries. Plant Solomon's seal amongst shrubs or beneath trees, or use them in pots on a shady patio to create a lush, textural display together with hostas (*see pp.260–261*) and ferns (*see pp.356–365*).

Hardiness Fully hardy ✱✱✱ to frost-hardy ✱✱.

Cultivation Grow in moist soil or soil-based compost enriched with well-rotted organic matter, in deep or partial shade. **Divide** large species (*see p.395*) as growth begins in spring, but take care not to damage brittle young shoots. **Sow** seed in containers in a cold frame in autumn (*see pp.391–392*).

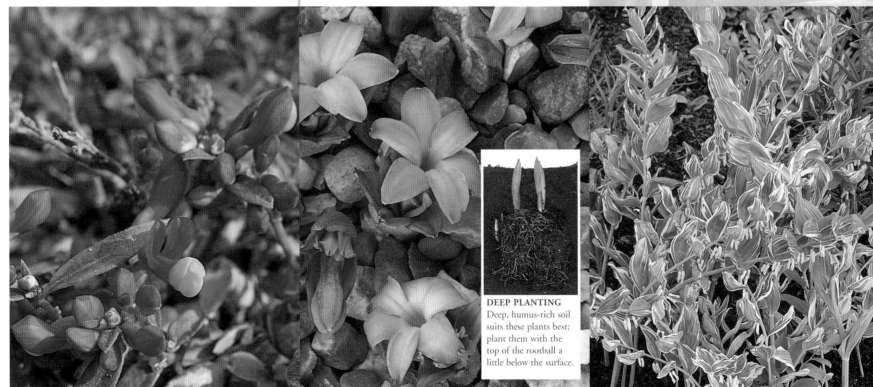

Polygonatum hirtum
↕ 1.2m (4ft) ↔ 60cm (24in), erect zigzag stems, flowers from late spring to midsummer, blue-black berries ✱✱✱

DEEP PLANTING
Deep, humus-rich soil suits these plants best; plant them with the top of the rootball a little below the surface.

Polygala chamaebuxus var. *grandiflora* ♀
↕ 5–15cm (2–6in) ↔ 30cm (12in), spreading evergreen, purple "wings" are plain yellow in the species ✱✱✱

Polygonatum hookeri
↕ 10cm (4in) ↔ 30cm (12in), small, creeping perennial, flowers in late spring and early summer, needs rich soil ✱✱✱

Polygonatum × hybridum 'Striatum'
↕ 90cm (36in) ↔ 25cm (10in), brightens dark areas, flowers in late spring, the berries that follow are black ✱✱✱

POTENTILLA

see also p.99

Cinquefoil   *summer to autumn*

CINQUEFOIL IS A REFERENCE to the five-petalled flowers. The heavily veined foliage of these herbaceous perennials is very reminiscent of the foliage of strawberry plants. These plants are valued both for their brightly coloured flowers and mid- to dark green foliage. Their saucer-shaped, single or double blooms are borne throughout summer and into early autumn. The smaller types suit a rock garden, while the taller, clump-forming potentillas are popular choices for beds, borders, and cottage gardens, where together with other late-flowering favourites such as asters (*see pp.192–193*) and chrysanthemums (*see pp.212–213*), they continue to warm up the fading garden into autumn with fiery shades of blood-red, burnt orange, and golden-yellow.

Hardiness Fully hardy ❊❊❊.

Cultivation Grow in full sun and well-drained soil; flowering is better on poorer soils. **Divide** (*see p.395*) in autumn or spring. **Sow** seed in containers in a cold frame in autumn or spring (*see pp.391–392*).

Potentilla 'Monsieur Rouillard'
↕45cm (18in) ↔ 60cm (24in), bears semi-double, satin-petalled flowers from early to late summer

Polygonatum stewartianum
↕20–90cm (8–36in) ↔ 25cm (10in), flowers from late spring to midsummer, followed by red berries with white spots ❊❊❊

Potentilla 'Gibson's Scarlet' ♈
↕45cm (18in) ↔ 60cm (24in), extremely popular, flowers to 3cm (1¼in) across from early to late summer

Potentilla megalantha ♈
↕15–30cm (6–12in) ↔ 15cm (6in), widely available, hairy leaves, flowers from mid- to late summer

PRIMULA

Primrose

early spring to early summer

THERE IS A PRIMULA FOR ALMOST EVERY SITUATION in the garden, and the majority are long-flowering and easy to grow. This diverse group of herbaceous perennials grows naturally in a wide range of habitats from boggy marshes to woodland and alpine areas. Most bloom in early spring and early summer, although a few flower from winter onwards. Their delicate clusters of flowers come in an appealing range of colours from deep purple and maroon through to pink, scarlet, and several shades of yellow, cream, and white. Occasionally the flowers, stems, and foliage are covered with a white or yellow meal, or "farina". Garden primulas are divided into three groups: candelabra, auricula and polyanthus (*see below*), although these groups do not include all species. Polyanthus types are easiest to grow. Compact varieties make a bright display in containers, while more robust ones are suitable for the herbaceous border or cottage garden, or can be naturalized in lawns. Many primulas enjoy the dappled shade of the woodland edge, and work well planted with other woodland plants, such as lilies (*see pp.274–277*) and trilliums (*see p.332*). Water-loving candelabras thrive in bog gardens or on the banks of streams and ponds. Grow tender species in a cool greenhouse or conservatory.

Hardiness   Fully hardy ✳✳✳ to frost-tender ❀.

Cultivation   Grow primulas in full sun or partial shade, for the most part in moisture-retentive soil. **Dig in** plenty of well-rotted organic matter (such as leafmould, manure, or garden compost) before planting. Mix coarse grit into the soil or compost before planting alpine species, since these require excellent drainage. **Water** plants well in dry weather. **Deadhead** the flowers as they fade to prevent unwanted self-seeding, or allow seedheads to develop to collect your own seed. **Sow** seed as soon as it is ripe (*see pp.391–392*). Scatter those of hardy species on the compost's surface in pots or trays and place in a cold frame. **Divide** hybrids and cultivars, which will not come true from seed, between autumn and spring (*see p.395*). Vine weevil grubs (*see p.398*) may eat roots, especially in pots.

Candelabra primulas

These grow best in moist soil in a shady glade or at the edge of a pond. Robust perennials, they produce their rings of flowers, in many different colours, all the way up their sturdy stems. Candelabra primulas are deciduous and die back in autumn. Once established, plants will freely scatter their seed, which germinates quite easily and eventually make a large and colourful colony. Unwanted seedlings are easy to control by weeding, or can be transplanted in spring to other parts of the garden.

Auricula primulas

The beautiful markings and colourings of many auriculas are a result of several hundred years of selection by enthusiasts. Developed originally for showing, these evergreen primulas, with rather leathery leaves, have been highly bred. Show types need the protection of an alpine house, as do many alpine auriculas, although these will also thrive in rock gardens. Those classed as border auriculas are the ones to choose for general garden cultivation. They particularly suit cottage-style plantings and can look good in troughs.

Polyanthus group

This group includes many of the most familiar primulas, including our native primroses and cowslips and the bright- and bold-flowered polyanthus that are used as biennials in spring bedding. Primroses and polyanthus bear their flowers in two, quite different ways. Primroses produce lots of flower stems, each with a single flower. Polyanthus (see left) have one central, sturdy stem topped by a cluster of flowers. When grown together in the garden, the two types will freely hybridize and may produce unique seedlings.

① *Primula* 'Adrian Jones' ‡30cm (1ft) ↔ 25cm (10in), alpine auricula ② *allionii* ♀ ‡10cm (4in) ↔ 20cm (8in), evergreen, flowers late winter ③ *auricula* var. *albocincta* ‡20cm (8in) ↔ 25cm (10in), evergreen ④ *auricula* 'Blairside Yellow' ‡50cm (20in) ↔ 30cm (1ft), border auricula ⑤ *auricula* 'Orb' ‡15cm (6in) ↔ 25cm (10in), show auricula ⑥ *beesiana* ‡↔ 60cm (2ft), candelabra ⑦ 'Buckland Wine' ‡10cm (4in) ↔ 25cm (10in), polyanthus ⑧ *bulleyana* ♀ ‡↔ 60cm (2ft), candelabra ⑨ **Crescendo Series,** ↕↔15cm (6in), polyanthus ⑩ *denticulata* var. *alba* ↕↔45cm (18in), drumstick ⑪ *elatior* ♀ ↕30cm (1ft) ↔25cm (10in), evergreen, suits woodland ⑫ *flaccida* ↕50cm (20in) ↔30cm (1ft) ⑬ *florindae* ♀ ↕1.2m (4ft) ↔90cm (3ft), fragrant cowslip, for bogs and streams ⑭ *frondosa* ♀ ↕15cm (6in) ↔25cm (10in) ⑮ **Gold-laced Group** ↕25cm (10in) ↔30cm (1ft), polyanthus ⑯ **'Guinevere'** ♀ ↕13cm (5in) ↔25cm (10in), polyanthus ⑰ **'Inverewe'** ♀ ↕60cm

(2ft), semi-evergreen, candelabra ⑱ *marginata* 'Linda Pope' ♀ ↕15cm (6in) ↔30cm (1ft), evergreen ⑲ *prolifera* ♀ ↕↔60cm (2ft), candelabra, moist shade ⑳ *rosea* ♀ ↕↔20cm (8in) ㉑ *veris* ♀ ↕25cm (10in), evergreen, fragrant cowslip ㉒ *vialii* ♀ ↕60cm (2ft) ↔30cm (1ft), moist shade ㉓ *vulgaris* subsp. *sibthorpii* ♀ ↕20cm (8in) ↔35cm (14in), suits woodland ㉔ **'Wanda'** ♀ ↕15cm (6in) ↔40cm (16in), evergreen, likes sun or shade

PULMONARIA

Lungwort

late winter to early summer

‡ 15–45cm (6–18in)
↔ 45–90cm (18–36in)

OFTEN HANDSOMELY SPOTTED in silver or white, the deciduous or evergreen leaves were said in medieval times to resemble lung tissue and were used in remedies for chest complaints. Today, they make pulmonarias invaluable as ground cover that spreads slowly by underground stems (rhizomes). Pulmonaria flowers are a welcome sight in the late-winter garden, and the display continues until late spring or even early summer. The delicate blooms may be blue, pink, red, or white and are held above the foliage in small clusters; they attract bees into the garden. Show off the flowers beneath deciduous trees and shrubs or with bulbs for a jewelled carpet in spring.

Hardiness Fully hardy ✻✻✻.

Cultivation Grow in moist, but not wet, humus-rich soil in full or dappled shade; *Pulmonaria officinalis* tolerates sun. **Cut back** after flowering to promote new foliage. **Divide** (*see p.395*) every three to five years to keep plants healthy. **Sow** seed (*see pp.391–393*) when ripe; seedlings will vary. **Powdery mildew** may spoil leaves in dry weather.

PULSATILLA

spring to early summer

AMONG THE MOST BEAUTIFUL of perennial alpine plants, pulsatillas have fine, ferny foliage, large, silky flowers, and round, fluffy seedheads. The leaves, buds, and petals are often covered with soft, silvery down. In spring and early summer, blooms appear in white or shades of yellow, pink, and purple – usually with a large, central boss of golden stamens. As the seedheads develop, the flower stems grow even taller. Pulsatillas form clumps in a rock garden or at the front of a border, if you have well-drained soil, with other spring-flowering plants such as aubrietas (*see p.195*) or scillas (*see p.323*). In areas with heavy soil, it is best to grow pulsatillas in containers so they can enjoy free-draining soil and be moved easily to a position sheltered from the worst of the winter rain.

Hardiness Fully hardy ✻✻✻.

Cultivation Pulsatillas prefer fertile, very well-drained, gritty soil in full sun. They resent being disturbed; plant them out while they are young and site them carefully so they do not have to be moved. **Sow** seed (*see pp.391–393*) as soon as it is ripe in a cold frame. **Take** root cuttings (*see p.394*) in winter.

Pulsatilla halleri ♀
‡ 20cm (8in) ↔ 15cm (6in), violet-purple to lavender-blue flowers that are 9cm (3½in) across in late spring

① 'Lewis Palmer' ♀ ‡↔ 40cm (16in) ② *rubra* 'Redstart' ‡ 40cm (16in) ↔ 90cm (36in) ③ *saccharata* ‡ 30cm (12in) ↔ 60cm (24in) ④ 'Sissinghurst White' ♀ ‡↔ 40cm (16in)

Pulsatilla vernalis ♀
‡↔ 10cm (4in), semi-evergreen, flowers to 6cm (2½in) across in spring, requires sharp drainage and protection from winter wet

Pulsatilla vulgaris ♀ (Pasque flower)
‡ 10–20cm (4–8in) ↔ 20cm (8in), young leaves very hairy, pale to deep purple flowers 4–9cm (2½–4½in) across, rarely white, in spring

PUSCHKINIA SCILLOIDES

spring

THIS LITTLE BULB HAS a snowdrop-like flower, with each delicate white, or very pale blue, petal marked with a thin, dark blue stripe. The blooms are borne in thick spikes on arching stems in spring. Each bulb has two leaves. *Puschkinia scilloides* var. *libanotica* has smaller, pure white flowers. Puschkinias spread freely in a rock garden, or can be used for a pretty display beneath deciduous trees and shrubs before the leaf cover becomes too dense. They are easily naturalized in short grass with other bulbs for a colourful carpet in spring. In common with other rock-garden or alpine plants, puschkinias can be successfully grown in containers; they enjoy the well-drained conditions, especially while they are dormant.

Hardiness Fully hardy ✳✳✳.

Cultivation This plant likes any well-drained soil in full sun or dappled shade. **Sow** seed (*see pp.391–392*) in a container in a cold frame in spring or autumn; seedlings may take 2–3 years to reach flowering size. **Divide** clumps of bulbs (*see p.395*) as leaves die down in summer.

RANUNCULUS

Buttercup, Crowfoot

spring to autumn

THERE ARE HUNDREDS OF TYPES of buttercup – some are annuals and biennials – but herbaceous perennials are by far the most common; some are evergreen. They are very variable in habit, with widely ranging needs, so there should be one suited to any spot in the garden. Buttercups all bear cupped flowers, with bold central stamens, in spring, summer, or occasionally in autumn. They are mainly golden yellow, but white, pink, orange, or scarlet varieties are available.

Hardiness Fully hardy ✳✳✳; *Ranunculus asiaticus* is half-hardy ✳.
Cultivation Buttercups have a range of cultivation requirements. **Most species** are fine in fertile, moist but well-drained soil, in sun or semi-shade. **Woodland** buttercups, which often have bronze-tinted leaves, need rich, moist soil in shade. **Alpine** plants are small, with relatively large flowers, and require full sun and gritty, sharply drained soil, as do many of the tuberous buttercups. **Aquatic** or bog plants are often tall and have lots of lush, bright green leaves. They need wet soil at the edge of a stream or pond. **Sow** seed (*see pp.391–392*) of most buttercups in a container in a cold frame as soon as it is ripe. Alpine seed is best sown while it is unripe and its germination can be erratic and may take several years. **Divide** (*see p.395*) all but alpines, in spring or autumn.

Ranunculus ficaria **var. *albus*** (Lesser celandine)
↕5cm (2in) ↔ 20cm (8in), woodland type, early-spring flowers fade from pale yellow to white, may spread rapidly

Puschkinia scilloides
↕ 20cm (8in) ↔ 5cm (2in), although larger clumps will quickly form

Ranunculus aconitifolius 'Flore Pleno' ♀ (Fair maids of France, Fair maids of Kent, White bachelor's buttons)
↕60cm (24in) ↔ 45cm (18in), flowers late spring and early summer

Ranunculus ficaria 'Brazen Hussy' (Lesser celandine)
↕5cm (2in) ↔ 30cm (12in), woodland type, flowers are bronzed underneath and borne in early spring, may spread rapidly

RHEUM

Rhubarb

spring to autumn

‡1.2–2.5m (4–8ft)
↔60cm–2m (2–6ft)

THESE IMPRESSIVE, clump-forming perennials have bold, handsome foliage and feathery flower plumes. The huge, rounded leaves, which are up to 90cm (36in) across, often emerge crimson-purple from bright red buds in spring. They mature to a glossy, dark green, but often retain a scarlet flush, especially on the undersides. In summer, large plumes of tiny pink, pale green, or cream flowers are held above the foliage on thick, hollow stems. Rheums revel in moist conditions: use them to create a lush display by a stream or pond, in damp borders or in woodland gardens. Although this group includes edible rhubarb, the ornamental varieties can cause severe discomfort if eaten.

Hardiness Fully hardy ✳✳✳.

Cultivation Rheums need deep, damp soil that has been enriched with organic matter, in sun or shade. **Mulch** (*see p.388*) in spring to retain moisture. **Sow** seed (*see pp.391–392*) in pots in a cold frame in autumn. **Divide** the large, woody rhizomes (*see p.395*) in early spring.

RHODIOLA

late spring to summer

AS LONG AS THEY ARE GROWN in full sun, these perennials will thrive, and are useful for bringing subtle colour and texture into a rock- or gravel garden, or to the front of a bed or border. They form clumps of straight stems clothed in fleshy, grey-green leaves that complement plants with white flowers or silver foliage, such as artemisias (*see p.25 and p.188*). Each stem is topped by a fluffy flowerhead of many tiny, starry, yellow, green, orange, or crimson flowers. As well as flowers in late spring or summer, both the buds and seedheads provide ornamental displays.

Hardiness Fully hardy ✳✳✳.

Cultivation Grow rhodiolas in any reasonably fertile soil in full sun. **Sow** seed (*see pp.391–392*) in containers in a cold frame in spring or autumn. **Divide** the rhizomes (*see p.395*) in spring or early summer.

RODGERSIA

spring to autumn

‡90cm–2m (3–6ft)
↔75cm–2m (30in–6ft)

A SUPERB CHOICE FOR MOIST SOIL, these vigorous, clump-forming perennials are valued for their fabulous foliage and tall flower spikes. The giant leaves are up to 90cm (36in) across, and are dark green and glossy. They are often boldly veined or wrinkled, especially when young, and occasionally tinged purple or bronze. Some varieties also display rich, reddish-brown autumn tints. The flower stems are often dark purple, and bear fluffy clusters of tiny, sometimes scented, blooms in summer, in shades of pink or white. Grow rodgersias by the edge of a pond or stream, or in a damp border.

Hardiness Fully hardy ✳✳✳, although late frosts may damage young leaves.

Cultivation Reliably moist soil, enriched with well-rotted organic matter, in full sun or partial shade, with shelter from cold, drying winds is required. Drier soil is tolerated in shadier areas. **Mulch** (*see p.388*) with a thick layer of organic matter in spring to help retain soil moisture. **Sow** seed (*see pp.391–392*) in containers in a cold frame in spring. **Divide** (*see p.395*) plants in early spring.

***Rheum palmatum* 'Atrosanguineum'** ♥
‡2.5m (8ft) ↔ 2m (6ft), plumes of flowers up to 2m (6ft) tall in early summer

***Rhodiola rosea* (Roseroot)**
‡5–30cm (1½–12in) ↔ 20cm (8in), variable habit, leaves to 4cm (1½in) long with reddish-green tips, flowers in summer

***Rodgersia pinnata* 'Superba'** ♥
‡1.2m (4ft) ↔ 75cm (30in), new purple foliage (*as shown*) matures to dark green, stalks reddish-green, flowers in mid- and late summer

ROSCOEA

summer to autumn

DESPITE THEIR EXOTIC, ORCHID-LIKE flowers, these tuberous perennials thrive in cool climates. They are invaluable in damp, shady borders where they are used to add a long season of bright colour to areas that are usually the preserve of shade-loving foliage plants, such as ferns (*see pp.356–365*), hostas (*see pp.260–261*), and Solomon's seal (*see Polygonatum, p.310*). Most roscoeas bear flowers all summer and into autumn, in shades of white, gold, or purple, occasionally with contrasting marks on their petals. They often start to bloom before the arching leaves, which reach up to 40cm (16in) long, are fully grown.

Hardiness Fully hardy ✳✳✳ to frost-hardy ✳✳.

Cultivation Roscoeas prefer a cool, sheltered, shaded site, in moist but well-drained, moderately fertile soil. Dig in plenty of well-rotted organic matter. **Plant** tubers 15cm (6in) deep in winter or early spring. In very cold areas, plant tubers even deeper: the extra insulation of the soil helps them survive temperatures down to -20°C (-4°F). **Mulch** thickly (*see p.388*) with organic matter in winter in frost-prone areas. **Sow** seed as soon as it is ripe (*see pp.391–392*) in containers. **Divide** established plants (*see p.395*) in spring.

RUDBECKIA

Coneflower   *late summer to autumn*

THIS LARGE GROUP OF ANNUALS, biennials, and perennials are grown for their large, brightly coloured daisies in late summer and autumn. They bloom in many shades from burnt orange to vivid yellow and last for many weeks – seeming to glow in the golden autumn light. The prominent, conical centres may be black, brown, or green and give the plant its common name. Rudbeckias form leafy clumps with the flowers at the tips of sturdy, upright stems. The perennial *Rudbeckia hirta* and its cultivars are often used as annual bedding. Very easy to grow, rudbeckias provide a wonderful late burst of colour, try them with sedums (*see p.324*) and Michaelmas daisies (*see Aster, pp.192–193*). They are also good for cutting.

Hardiness Fully hardy ✳✳✳ to half-hardy ✳.

Cultivation Reliably moist, heavy but well-drained, moderately fertile soil, in full sun or partial shade, is needed. **Sow** seed (*see pp.391–392*) of perennials in containers in a cold frame in early spring. Sow seed of annuals at 16–18°C (61–64°F) in spring and plant out young plants when all threat of frost has passed. **Divide** established plants (*p.395*) in spring or autumn.

Rudbeckia laciniata
↕ 1.5m–3m (5–10ft) ↔ 1m (3ft), loosely clumping perennial, flowers 8–15cm (3–6in) across in midsummer to early autumn ✳✳✳

Roscoea cautleyoides ♀
↕ 55cm (22in) ↔ 15cm (6in), leaves 15cm (6in) tall at flowering, midsummer flowers are yellow, white, or purple ✳✳✳ (borderline)

Rudbeckia laciniata 'Herbstsonne' ♀
↕ 2m (6ft) ↔ 90cm (36in), rhizomatous perennial, flowers 10–13cm (4–5in) across in midsummer to early autumn ✳✳✳

Rudbeckia maxima
↕ 1.5m (5ft) ↔ 45–60cm (18–24in), perennial, large, waxy, grey-green leaves, flowers from midsummer to autumn ✳✳✳

SALPIGLOSSIS

summer to autumn

‡to 60cm (24in)
↔ to 30cm (12in)

SELECTED FOR THEIR CHEERFUL, funnel-shaped flowers, this small group of annuals brings bold colour to summer beds and containers. The flowers, with heavily veined and strikingly marked petals, come in a variety of bright shades, from rich red to yellow, bronze, violet-blue, and purple. They are produced in the leaf joints of the slender, branching stems and last from summer through to autumn. Grow with other bright summer bedding, such as pelargoniums (*see pp.300–303*) or salvias (*see right*), or use them to fill gaps in herbaceous and mixed borders. Salpiglossis are excellent plants for containers.

Hardiness Half-hardy ✳.

Cultivation Grow in reasonably fertile, moist, but well-drained soil in full sun. In containers, use a loam-based compost; water freely during summer and feed fortnightly with a balanced fertilizer. **Remove** fading flowers to prevent seed forming and prolong the flowering period. Provide thin, twiggy sticks for support in open sites. **Sow** seed at 18–24°C (64–75°F) in spring or autumn (*see pp.391–392*). In very mild areas, sow seed outdoors where plants are to grow (*see p.393*).

SALVIA

Sage

summer to autumn

THE HARDY CULINARY SAGE (*Salvia officinalis*), grown for its pungent leaves, is attractive enough for borders. Few of the herbaceous perennials are hardy, but will grace a sheltered spot or container with elegant flower spires in clear blues and reds. Salvias grown as annuals and biennials fall into two broad groups: the half-hardy, brightly coloured bedding plants typified by scarlet salvias, and hardy, more bushy plants in subtler colours, such as the clary sages, that look good in an informal or a herb garden. Hairy, woolly, or even white-mealy leaved salvias are more demanding, best grown in rock gardens or raised beds.

Hardiness Fully hardy ✳✳✳ to frost-tender ✿.

Cultivation Grow in reasonably fertile, well-drained soil, in sun or partial shade. Small species with hairy leaves need sharply drained soil in full sun and protection from winter wet. **Divide** perennials (*see p.395*) in spring. **Take** cuttings from new shoots in spring or early summer (*see p.394*). **Sow** seed (*see pp.391–393*) of half-hardy annuals at 16–18°C (61–64°F) in spring. Sow hardy annuals in situ in spring.

Salvia argentea ⚥
‡90cm (36in) ↔ 60cm (24in), rosette-forming biennial or perennial, woolly-leaved, protect from winter wet ✳✳✳ (borderline)

Salpiglossis Casino Series
‡to 60cm (24in) ↔ to 30cm (12in), compact and branching, with flowers to 5cm (2in) across

Salvia coccinea 'Lady in Red' ⚥
‡40cm (16in) ↔ to 30cm (12in), erect, bushy annual with flowers 2cm (¾in) long from summer to autumn ✳

Salvia patens 'Cambridge Blue' ⚥
‡45–60cm (18–24in) ↔ 45cm (18in), erect perennial with true blue flowers from midsummer to mid-autumn ✳✳

Salvia discolor ♀
‡ 45cm (18in) ↔ 30cm (12in), erect perennial bearing spires of very
dark indigo flowers in late summer and early autumn ☀

SANGUISORBA
Burnet   *midsummer to autumn*

FOR AN UNUSUAL SUMMER HIGHLIGHT in a moist
border or corner of a garden, this small group of tall,
clump-forming perennials is ideal. The wiry stems
clothed with attractive leaves produce bottlebrush-like
spires of small, fluffy flowers in red, pink, white, or
greenish-white, with prominent stamens. The leaves
are composed of toothed leaflets that are heavily
veined and sometimes greyish. Burnets are suitable
for mixed and herbaceous borders or particularly for
naturalizing in a damp meadow or wildflower garden
as they form spreading clumps. The flowers and foliage
are good for cutting. Grow them with other perennials
and with tall ornamental grasses (*see pp.340–355*).

Hardiness Fully hardy ☀☀☀.

Cultivation Grow in any reasonably fertile soil that is moist but
well-drained, in sun or partial shade. Taller species may need some
support. In ideal conditions, plants may become invasive, but can be
controlled by regular division (*see p.395*) in spring or autumn. **Sow** seed
in a container in a cold frame in spring or autumn (*see pp.391–392*).

SAPONARIA
Soapwort   *summer to autumn*

THE SAP OF SOAPWORT was once used for laundering
clothes as well as medicinally, for skin complaints.
This group of sprawling and upright perennials is now
grown for its profusion of tiny, pink to deep pink
flowers in summer and autumn, as well as its ground-
covering ability and for keeping down weeds. The
plants thrive in sunny, dry sites. The low-growing,
mat-forming species are excellent for the front of a
border, perhaps spilling over paving, or in a rock
garden. Grow taller ones with old-fashioned, pastel
perennials such as pinks (*see Dianthus, pp.226–227*).

Hardiness Fully hardy ☀☀☀.

Cultivation Grow border perennials in reasonably fertile soil that
is well drained and neutral to alkaline (limy), in full sun. Compact
species such as *S. caespitosa* require sharply drained soil in a rock
garden or between paving. Cut *S. ocymoides* hard back after flowering
to maintain a compact habit. **Divide** border perennials (*see p.395*) in
autumn or spring. **Sow** seed in containers in a cold frame in spring or
autumn (*see pp.391–392*). **Take** softwood cuttings in early summer
(*see p.394*). Saponarias may be damaged by slugs and snails; lay
traps or pick them off by hand (*see p.398*).

Salvia fulgens ♀
‡ 50–100cm (20–39in) ↔ 40–90cm (16–36in), woody-based
perennial with downy leaves and flowers in summer ☀☀

Sanguisorba canadensis
‡ to 2m (6ft) ↔ 1m (3ft), hairy leaves, flower spikes, to 20cm (8in)
long, from midsummer to mid-autumn

Saponaria ocymoides ♀ (Tumbling Ted)
‡ 8cm (3in) ↔ 45cm (18in), mat-forming perennial, flowers in
summer, can swamp small plants

FLOWERING PLANTS

SAXIFRAGA

Saxifrage

spring to autumn

A STAPLE OF THE ROCK GARDEN, saxifrages are mostly low-growing plants that make dense mounds or mats of foliage, carpeting the ground or cascading down walls. There are more than 400 species, including evergreen, semi-evergreen, or deciduous perennials, biennials, and a few annuals, many of which come from cool, mountain regions. Arising from the foliage are masses of delicate, star- or saucer-shaped flowers in shades from white to lemon, bright yellow to rose, and indigo. In some, the tiny rosettes of leaves are attractive in themselves. Apart from rock gardens, saxifrages are grown in raised beds and alpine troughs and in alpine houses (unheated, well ventilated greenhouses). They are also often used to soften walls and paving (*see below*). A few larger and more vigorous types, such as London pride (*Saxifraga × urbium*) and *S. fortunei*, make good path edgings or ground cover in borders and woodland gardens. The botanical categories applied to saxifrages are many and various but, for growing in the garden, plants can be divided into four main groups (*see below*).

Hardiness Fully hardy ✳✳✳; *S. stolonifera* and its cultivars are frost-hardy ✳✳.

Cultivation Saxifrages fall into four broad groups for cultivation. **Group 1** need moist, well-drained soil in deep or partial shade. Suitable for borders and rock gardens. **Group 2** prefer humus-rich soil (with plenty of organic matter added), but with sharp drainage. Neutral to alkaline soil in light shade is best. Suitable for rock gardens, crevices, scree beds (sloping areas where soil is mixed, and usually covered, with gravel or stone chippings), or alpine houses. **Group 3** like fertile, well-drained, neutral to alkaline soil, with their roots moist. They tolerate full sun in cool areas. Suitable for rock gardens or alpine troughs. **Group 4** require fertile but sharply drained, alkaline soil in full sun. Suitable for rock gardens, troughs and alpine houses. Some will not tolerate winter wet. **Sow** seed (*see pp.391–392*) in autumn in containers and put in a cold frame. **Divide** herbaceous types in spring (*see p.395*). Single rosettes can be detached and rooted as cuttings (*see p.394*) in late spring and early summer.

Planting saxifrages in paving

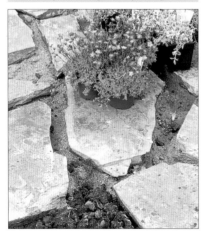

When laying paving, leave a few gaps for robust saxifrages. They will spread over the edges of the slabs, giving the paving a soft, naturalistic look. Before planting, incorporate gritty compost into the soil in the planting gaps. This helps the roots to penetrate easily and also improves drainage. Water well until the plants are established.

Planting in wall crevices

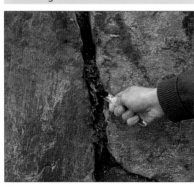

❶ *Mix equal parts of soil, grit, and leafmould. Scrape out space in a crevice, put a stone in the bottom, and add a 2.5cm (1in) layer of mixture. Ease in the roots of the plant. Sprinkle another 2.5cm (1in) layer of compost mix over the roots.*

❷ *To hold the plant in place, cap the compost with a small stone that slopes down into the rock-face. Add more plants, around 10cm (4in) apart. Cover the roots of the last plant with compost and trickle in water to settle the soil around the roots.*

① *Saxifraga* **'Apple Blossom'** ‡15cm (6in) ↔ indefinite, suitable for crevices and borders, group 4
② **'Aureopunctata'** ‡30cm (12in) ↔ indefinite, good for hanging baskets, group 3 or 4
③ *burseriana* ‡5cm (2in) ↔ 15cm (6in), group 3 or 4 ④ **'Cloth of Gold'** ‡10cm (4in) ↔ 30cm (12in), group 2, best in shade ⑤ *fortunei* ♀ ‡↔ 30cm (12in), group 1 ⑥ × *geum* ‡↔ 20cm (8in), group 1 ⑦ *granulata* ‡20–35cm (8–14in) ↔ 15cm (6in), group 1, tolerates full sun in moist soil

⑧ 'Gregor Mendel' ♀ ‡10cm (4in) ↔ 30cm (12in), group 3, can be grown in crevices ⑨ 'Hindhead Seedling' ‡5cm (2in) ↔ 15cm (6in), group 3 or 4 ⑩ 'Jenkinsiae' ♀ ‡5cm (2in) ↔ 20cm (8in), group 3 ⑪ 'Kathleen Pinsent' ♀ ‡↔ 20cm (8in), group 1 ⑫ 'Mount Nachi' ‡15cm (6in) ↔ indefinite, group 3 or 4 ⑬ *oppositifolia* ‡2.5cm (1in) ↔ 20cm (8in), group 3 ⑭ *paniculata* ‡15cm (6in) ↔ 25cm (10in), group 4 ⑮ *sancta* ‡5cm (2in) ↔ 20cm (8in), group 3 ⑯ *sempervivum* ‡10cm (4in) ↔ 20cm (8in), cushion-forming, group 4 ⑰ 'Southside Seedling' ♀ ‡30cm (12in) ↔ 20cm (8in), group 3 or 4 ⑱ *spathularis* ‡50cm (20in) ↔ indefinite, group 3 or 4 ⑲ 'Stansfieldii' ‡10cm (4in) ↔ 20–23cm (8–9in), group 3 or 4 ⑳ 'Tricolor' ♀ ‡↔ 30cm (12in), group 1, good for hanging baskets ❁❁ ㉑ 'Tumbling Waters' ♀ ‡10cm (4in) ↔ 30cm (12in), group 3 ㉒ 'Variegata' ‡30cm (12in) ↔ indefinite, group 3 or 4 ㉓ 'Wisley' ♀ ‡10cm (4in) ↔ 15cm (6in), group 4

FLOWERING PLANTS

SCABIOSA

Pincushion flower,
Scabious

midsummer to autumn

AS THE COMMON NAME SUGGESTS, the centres of these plants' flowers look like pincushions. Whether you choose to grow the annuals, biennials, or perennials, each bears masses of delicate, solitary, sometimes fragrant flowers in summer to autumn. Shades range from lilac, purple, or white to deep crimson. Most of the leaves cluster at the bases of the stems. All attract bees and other beneficial insects into the garden. The tall-stemmed species, such as *Scabiosa caucasica* which has a height and spread of 60cm (24in), are good for cutting. Scabious blend in well in informal or cottage-garden plantings, in mixed borders, or in containers.

Hardiness Fully hardy ✳✳✳ to frost-hardy ✳✳.

Cultivation Scabious prefer well-drained, moderately fertile soil that is neutral to slightly alkaline (limy), in full sun and with protection from excessive winter wet. **Sow** seed (*see pp.391–393*) of annuals at 6–12°C (43–54°F) in early spring or where they are to flower in mid-spring. Sow seed of perennials in containers in a cold frame as soon as it is ripe, or in spring. **Deadhead** regularly to encourage more flowers (*see p.390*). **Divide** established plants (*see p.395*) or take stem-tip cuttings (*see p.394*) of perennials in spring.

Scabiosa caucasica 'Miss Willmott' ♀
↕90cm (36in) ↔ 60cm (24in), clump-forming perennial, flowers from mid- to late summer ✳✳✳

SCAEVOLA

spring to autumn

UNUSUAL, FAN-SHAPED FLOWERS in shades of purple-blue, lilac, or blue are produced by scaevolas in large numbers between spring and autumn. The flowers are borne singly or in clusters on slender stems, above spoon-shaped, mid-green leaves. Most are short-lived, mainly evergreen perennials. The perennial *Scaevola aemula* and its cultivars are most commonly grown in gardens. It is the only species that can be grown in temperate parts outdoors in summer and is generally treated as an annual. Grow scaevolas in mixed borders, in hanging baskets, or in large containers, where they make attractive specimen plants that can be moved under cover for winter.

Hardiness Frost-tender ❋, but survives to -3°C (27°F) on sharply drained soil.

Cultivation Scaevolas require a well-drained, reasonably fertile soil, in full sun or partial shade. Use a loam-based compost for plants grown in containers; water freely in summer; and feed with a balanced fertilizer at monthly intervals. **Sow** seed (*see pp.391–392*) at 19–24°C (66–75°F) in spring, or take softwood cuttings (*see p.394*) in late spring or summer.

Scabiosa 'Butterfly Blue'
↕↔ 40cm (16in), hairy, herbaceous perennial with branched stems, flowers to 4cm (1½in) across in mid- and late summer ✳✳✳

Scaevola aemula (Fairy fan flower)
↕↔ to 50cm (20in), erect or prostrate, hairy stems, purple-blue or blue flowers to 2.5cm (1in) across in summer

SCHIZANTHUS

Butterfly flower,   *summer*
Poor man's orchid

EXOTIC-LOOKING, ORCHID-LIKE FLOWERS that almost smother the entire plant and last for many weeks over summer make this an excellent summer bedding plant. There is a wide range of flower colours to choose from including yellows, purples, pinks, reds, and white. The flowers also last well when cut. The spreading, bushy foliage is attractively fern-like, with leaves made up of deeply lobed leaflets. This group of mostly annuals and some biennials thrive with other summer bedding plants such as pot marigolds (*see Calendula officinalis, p.204*), salvias (*see p.318*), or fuchsias (*see pp.60–63*), in mixed borders or containers. It is a good, long-flowering pot plant in a conservatory.

Hardiness Frost-tender ❀.

Cultivation Full sun and reasonably fertile soil is needed to grow schizanthus. For plants in containers, use a loam-based compost; water them well in summer; and feed with a balanced fertilizer at weekly intervals. **Support** flowering stems with twiggy pea sticks if necessary. **Pinch back** the young shoots to encourage a bushy habit. **Sow** seed (*see pp.391–392*) at 16°C (61°F) in spring for summer flowers; for spring flowers in containers indoors, sow in late summer and overwinter the seedlings in frost-free conditions.

SCHIZOSTYLIS COCCINEA

Kaffir lily   *late summer to autumn*

TALL SPIKES OF DELICATE, SHIMMERING flowers in hot shades of red, pink, or scarlet make the kaffir lily a welcome addition to any garden. They resemble the gladiolus and are borne on stems up to 60cm (24in) in height, in late summer, autumn, or early winter, when there is little else in flower. A native of southern Africa, this vigorous, clump-forming perennial and its cultivars spread by means of underground stems (rhizomes). Try placing it in mixed borders with other late-flowering plants – for example Michaelmas daisies (*see Aster, pp.192–193*) or coneflowers (*see Rudbeckia, p.317*) – in containers, in waterside plantings, or by a sunny wall. The flowers are excellent for cutting.

Hardiness Frost-hardy to -10°C (14°F); flower spikes can be damaged by frost ✳✳.

Cutivation Grow in moist but well-drained, fertile soil in full sun. **Support** the flower stems if necessary with twiggy sticks in exposed gardens. **Protect** the plants with a mulch of organic matter in winter when the flowers are finished. **Divide** clumps (*see p.395*) in spring to maintain their vigour. **Sow** seed (*see pp.391–392*) at 13–16°C (55–61°F) in spring.

SCILLA

Squill   *spring, summer, and autumn*

‡8–120cm (3–48in)
↔5–10cm (2–4in)

THE DAINTY, DIMINUTIVE FLOWERS of scillas are extremely eye-catching, often with attractive, contrasting markings to the petals. They may be star- or bell-shaped, mostly in shades of blue but sometimes in purple or white, and are borne in loose or tight clusters amid strappy leaves in spring, summer, and autumn. Scillas are bulbous plants that will grow in a wide range of conditions and if left to their own devices, will self-seed freely. Naturalize the bulbs in grass, in rock or gravel gardens, or grow them in mixed borders, beneath deciduous shrubs and trees where they will receive plenty of light before the woody plants put on leaves. Scillas are also suitable for coastal gardens.

Hardiness Fully hardy ✳✳✳ to frost-hardy ✳✳.

Cultivation Plant bulbs 8–10cm (3–4in) deep in late summer or early autumn, in well-drained, humus-rich, fertile soil that is in full sun or partial shade. **Sow** seed (*see pp.391–392*) in pots and place in a cold frame. **Divide** and pot up offsets (*see p.395*) when the bulbs are dormant in summer.

Schizanthus × *wisetonensis* 'Hit Parade'
‡↔ 23–30cm (9–12in), annual with white, pink, gold, purple, or scarlet flowers to 8cm (3in) across from spring to autumn

Schizostylis coccinea 'Major' ♀
‡60cm (24in) ↔ 30cm (12in), flowers 5–6cm (2–2½in) across are borne on stiff stems in late summer

① *bifolia* ♀ ‡8–15cm (3–6in) ✳✳✳ ② *peruviana* 'Alba'
‡15–30cm (6–12in) ✳✳ ③ *scilloides* ‡15–20cm (6–8in) ✳✳✳
④ *siberica* 'Spring Beauty' ‡20cm (8in) ✳✳✳

SEDUM

Stonecrop

*summer to autumn,
and year-round*

SEDUMS BRING A RANGE OF TEXTURES and shapes to a garden; there are hundreds of annuals and perennials, many of which are succulent. There are low, creeping plants with tiny flowers that hug the ground, such as the common stonecrop (*Sedum acre*). This thrives in a rock or gravel garden, or in the crevices of paving or stone walls. The tall herbaceous perennials usually form architectural clumps, with large, flat heads of pink or white flowers. These provide late-season colour in summer and autumn, attract butterflies, and their tawny seedheads persist through winter. Sedums are often vigorous and very easy to grow.

Hardiness Fully hardy ✳✳✳ to frost-tender ✿.

Cultivation Sedums like moderately fertile, neutral to alkaline (limy), well-drained soil in full sun, although vigorous plants tolerate light shade. **Trim** spreading species after flowering to keep them neat. Support sedums with heavy flowerheads early on to stop the stems collapsing outwards. **Divide** (*see p.395 and right*) large herbaceous plants every 3–4 years in spring to improve flowering. **Sow** seed in containers in a cold frame in autumn (*see pp.391–392*). **Take** softwood cuttings of perennials (*see p.394*) in early summer. **Rots** may occur in wet conditions or heavy soils.

LIFT LARGE SEDUMS with care as the fleshy growth is very brittle. Pull a clump into pieces the size of a large hand; discard old, woody growth. Replant.

Sedum 'Ruby Glow' ♛
‡25cm (10in) ↔ 45cm (18in), low, spreading, deciduous perennial, flowers from midsummer to early autumn ✳✳✳

Sedum spathulifolium 'Cape Blanco' ♛
‡10cm (4in) ↔ 60cm (24in), mat-forming, evergreen perennial, powdery bloom on leaves, summer flowers, stands light shade ✳✳✳

Sedum populifolium
‡20–30cm (8–12in) ↔ 45cm (18in), deciduous perennial with lax stems, fragrant flowers in late summer and early autumn ✳✳✳

Sedum spathulifolium 'Purpureum' ♛
‡10cm (4in) ↔ 60cm (24in), vigorous, mat-forming, evergreen perennial, golden flowers in summer, tolerates light shade ✳✳✳

Sedum spectabile 'Brilliant' ♛ (Ice plant)
‡↔ 45cm (18in), clumping, deciduous perennial, flowerheads 15cm (6in) across in late summer, seedheads persist, needs support ✳✳✳

SEMPERVIVUM

Houseleek

summer, and year-round

THESE EVERGREEN SUCCULENTS are grown for their fleshy rosettes of leaves, which are often flushed red or purple, and sometimes thickly covered in hairs. There are numerous varieties with leaves of differing colours, sizes, and shapes. Although each plant is small, they spread across the soil by rooting stems, or runners, that produce new plantlets to form large mats of densely packed rosettes. In summer, starry, white, yellow, red, or purple flowers cluster on sturdy, fleshy stems. After a rosette flowers, it dies, but the gap is quickly filled by a new offset. Houseleeks need only shallow soil, so thrive in rock or gravel gardens or containers, with other alpines such as saxifrages (*see pp.320–321*) or pinks (*see Dianthus, pp.226–227*). They are even used to clothe tops of walls or roofs.

Hardiness Fully hardy ✳✳✳.

Cultivation Houseleeks grow in full sun, in poor, sharply drained soil and add plenty of grit or gritty compost. Shield hairy houseleeks from winter rain to avoid rots. **Sow** seed (*see pp.391–392*) in pots in a cold frame in spring. **Detach** rooted offsets in spring or early summer; they establish more quickly if kept out of direct sun.

SENECIO

see also p.116

summer to autumn

THERE ARE HUNDREDS OF SENECIOS, including annuals and biennials, shrubs, trees, and climbers. Whereas the shrubs are often grown in the garden for their foliage, the clump-forming annuals and perennials are mostly valued for their daisies. They bloom from early summer until late autumn in shades of white, yellow, blue, crimson, and purple; usually with a golden yellow centre. Since senecios are so varied, check the plant label or with the nursery about each plant's specific needs before you buy. Generally, annuals are used as summer bedding or in containers; small perennials in rock or gravel gardens, and larger varieties in borders or areas devoted to wild flowers. Some senecios are quite tender, but can be grown in containers and moved under cover in winter.

Hardiness Fully hardy ✳✳✳ to frost-tender ✳.

Cultivation Senecios may need gritty or moist, poor or moderately fertile, well-drained soil, in full sun or partial shade. **Sow** seed (*see pp.391–392*) in spring at 19–24°C (66–75°F); seed of bog plants and alpines can be sown in a cold frame. **Take** softwood cuttings (*see p.394*) of perennials in early summer.

SIDALCEA

False mallow,
Prairie mallow

early to midsummer

FROM EARLY TO MIDSUMMER, these annuals and perennials produce tall spires of long-lasting flowers, rather like those of hollyhocks. The petals are thin and silky, sometimes fringed round the edges, and in clear shades of pink, purple-pink, or white. They are good value because they often produce a second flush of blooms in autumn if the fading flowers are cut back before seeds develop. Another bonus is that the dense clumps of attractive, lobed or serrated, round leaves cover the soil and suppress weeds. Use sidalceas to add some height to a bed or border; they also are excellent for cutting.

Hardiness Fully hardy ✳✳✳.

Cultivation A site in full sun, with moderately fertile, neutral to acid, moist but well-drained soil, enriched with well-rotted organic matter, is best. Sidalceas tolerate a range of soils, but do not like to be too wet, especially in winter. **Mulch** (*see p.388*) with straw or bracken where winters are cold. **Cut back** stems hard after the first flowering. **Sow** seed (*see pp.391–392*) in a container in a cold frame in spring or autumn. **Divide** (*see p.395*) in spring or autumn. **Remove** leaves affected by rust (orange-brown pustules); thin the foliage to improve air circulation and help prevent a recurrence.

① *arachnoideum* ✲ (Cobweb houseleek) ↕8cm (3in) ↔30cm (12in), pink flowers ② *tectorum* ✲ (Common houseleek) ↕15cm (6in) ↔50cm (20in), red-purple flowers

Senecio pulcher
↕45–60cm (18–24in) ↔50cm (20in), perennial, flowers in mid- to late autumn, survives winters outside in mild areas ✳✳

Sidalcea 'Oberon'
↕1.2m (4ft) ↔45cm (18in), rounded or kidney-shaped leaves, flowers in early and midsummer

SILENE

Campion, Catchfly
summer to autumn

THERE ARE HUNDREDS of these annuals, biennials, and deciduous and evergreen perennials. They are grown for their pretty flowers which have delicately notched or split petals. In summer, erect stems bear blooms, singly or in clusters, in shades from dark pink to pure white. Most campions are easy to grow; many are prolific self-seeders. This makes them an excellent choice for a wild flower garden. If they are regularly deadheaded, smaller perennials can be used in a rock or gravel garden; place taller varieties in beds and borders. Annuals are often used as summer bedding. Some catchflies have sticky hairs on their leaves that trap insects – hence the common name.

Hardiness Fully hardy ✳✳✳ to half-hardy ✳.

Cultivation Grow these plants in moderately fertile, neutral to alkaline (limy), well-drained soil, in full sun or dappled shade. Smaller alpine species need gritty, sharply drained soil. *Silene hookeri* prefers acid (lime-free) soil. **Sow** seed (*see pp.391–393*) of perennials in a cold frame in autumn. Sow hardy annuals in situ in autumn or spring; half-hardy varieties at 16–19°C (61–66°F) in spring. Harden them off and plant out when the threat of frost has passed. **Take** new shoots from the base in spring and treat as softwood cuttings (*see p.394*).

SILYBUM MARIANUM

Blessed Mary's thistle
summer to autumn

‡1.5m (5ft)
↔60–90cm (24–36in)

THIS TALL, PRICKLY BIENNIAL forms an impressive rosette of glossy, dark green, spiny leaves up to 50cm (20in) long in its first year, that are spectacularly veined and marbled with white. In the second year, large, slightly scented flowerheads appear throughout the summer and autumn. If you wish to keep the leaf variegation at its best and prolong the life of the plant, pinch out the flowers as they form. Silybums are excellent in groups in borders, where their architectural foliage contrasts with softer, round-leaved plants. Plant it singly in a gravel garden, so its handsome form can be appreciated.

Hardiness Fully hardy ✳✳✳.

Cultivation Silybums prefer well-drained, neutral or slightly alkaline (limy) soil, in full sun. They dislike wet winters, so provide shelter if possible to avoid rots. **Sow** seed (*see pp.391–393*) in situ, in spring or early summer, then thin seedlings to 60cm (24in) apart. If grown for foliage, sow seed under cover in late winter or early spring; pot up into 9cm (3½in) pots; harden off and plant out in spring.

SISYRINCHIUM

spring to summer

PRETTY, STAR- OR CUP-SHAPED FLOWERS are produced by these annuals and perennials in profusion over many weeks in spring or summer. They bloom in rich blues and mauves, or subtle yellows and whites, singly at the tips of stems or in tall flower spikes. The long leaves, sometimes variegated with creamy white stripes, form grassy clumps or large, iris-like fans. The spiky foliage complements that of ornamental grasses (*see pp.340–355*) or provides a textural contrast to plants with feathery or broad leaves. Smaller varieties are best in a rock or gravel garden where they can be left to self-seed, for a pleasing natural effect, and will not get swamped by large, vigorous plants; the tall sisyrinchiums are able to hold their own in a border.

Hardiness Fully hardy ✳✳✳ to half-hardy ✳.

Cultivation Poor to moderately fertile, neutral to alkaline (limy), well-drained soil in full sun, is required, with protection from extreme winter wet which encourages root rot. Some small or half-hardy plants are best grown in pots and moved under cover in damp winters. **Sow** seed (*see pp.391–392*) in a container in a cold frame in spring or autumn. **Divide** clumps (*see p.395*) in spring.

PLANT SISYRINCHIUMS
with their crowns slightly above soil level. This allows water to drain away quickly in wet weather and reduce the risk of rot in the crowns.

Silene schafta ♀
‡25cm (10in) ↔ 30cm (12in), clumping, semi-evergreen perennial, flowers in late summer and autumn, good for rock gardens ✳✳✳

Silybum marianum

Sisyrinchium striatum 'Aunt May'
‡50cm (20in) ↔ 25cm (10in), clumping perennial, flowers 2.5cm (1in) across borne in early and midsummer ✳✳✳

SMILACINA

False Solomon's seal

mid-spring to midsummer

THE LUSH FOLIAGE OF THESE VIGOROUS perennials is much like that of Solomon's seal (*see Polygonatum, p.310*) – hence the common name. The resemblance ends when they burst into bloom from mid-spring to midsummer, producing dense clusters of tiny, starry flowers at the tips of arching stems. The flowers are creamy white and have a delicate scent that hangs in the still, damp air of a woodland garden. Green berries follow that ripen to red in autumn, at the same time as the leaves of many smilacinas turn a rich yellow. In favourable conditions, these trouble-free plants can be invasive, but are easily dug up if they spread too far. Use smilacinas with other shade-loving plants, for example ferns (*see pp.356–365*).

Hardiness Fully hardy ✳✳✳.

Cultivation Smilacinas thrive in moderately fertile, preferably slightly acid (lime-free) soil that has been enriched with well-rotted organic matter. Choose a position in full or dappled shade that is sheltered from cold winds. **Sow** seed (*see pp.391–392*) in containers in a cold frame in autumn. **Divide** the rhizomes of established plants (*see p.395*) in spring.

SOLIDAGO

Golden rod, Aaron's rod

late summer to autumn

THE WARM YELLOW FLOWERS of these vigorous, woody-based perennials glow in the golden light of late summer and autumn. They are borne in spikes or clusters, densely packed with tiny blooms, on stiff, upright stems. The leaves are usually mid-green. Species golden rods can be invasive, and although they can be controlled by digging them out, they are best reserved for wildflower gardens. Happily, many less unruly hybrids, with larger flowerheads, are available. They add late colour to the garden, and to the house because they are excellent for cutting. Use them with other autumn flowers such as rudbeckias (*see p.317*) and asters (*see pp.192–193*) among earlier-flowering plants for a prolonged seasonal display.

Hardiness Fully hardy ✳✳✳.

Cultivation Golden rods thrive in poor to moderately fertile, preferably sandy, well-drained soil, in full sun. **Deadhead** regularly to prevent self-seeding. **Divide** (*see p.395*) plants every three or four years in autumn or spring to keep them healthy: discard the old, woody centres. **Powdery mildew** may be disfiguring in dry summers.

x SOLIDASTER LUTEUS

midsummer to autumn

‡90cm (36in)
↔80cm (32in)

THIS HYBRID IS A CROSS between a solidago and an aster: as you might expect, it combines elements of both plants. Much like golden rod (*see left*), it bears a profusion of tiny blooms in dense clusters from midsummer through to autumn. The flowers themselves are daisy-like, and similar to those of an aster (*see pp.192–193*). They open a pale, creamy yellow with a darker centre, then fade as they age. The plant forms a clump with erect stems. Like both its parents, this perennial is a splendid choice for adding late-summer colour to a border, and makes an excellent cut flower.

Hardiness Fully hardy ✳✳✳.

Cultivation Moderately fertile, well-drained soil, in full sun or dappled shade, suits this plant. Take care not to over-fertilize the soil, because this encourages foliage at the expense of flowers. **Divide** clumps in autumn or spring (*see p.395*) every three or four years to maintain vigour and discard the congested, woody centres. Take new shoots from the base in spring and treat as softwood cuttings (*see p.394*). **Powdery mildew** may be disfiguring in dry summers.

AUTUMN FOLIAGE

Smilacina racemosa ♀ (syn. *Maianthemum racemosum*) (False spikenard)
‡90cm (36in) ↔ 60cm (24in), clump-forming, leaves downy beneath

Solidago 'Goldenmosa' ♀
‡75cm (30in) ↔ 45cm (18in), compact bush, wrinkled foliage, 30cm (12in) long flower spikes in late summer and early autumn

× *Solidaster luteus* 'Lemore' ♀
‡↔ 80cm (32in), more spreading habit and a paler yellow than the species

STACHYS

Betony, Hedge nettle, Woundwort

early summer to autumn

CARPETS OF LARGE, FELTED OR VELVETY LEAVES are the main attraction of these plants. Held on square stems, the leaves are usually covered in fine hairs; in some species, they are aromatic. Stachys include many spreading perennials that make excellent ground-cover plants, for example *Stachys byzantina* of which 'Silver Carpet' is a non-flowering form ideal for edging. Their silvery foliage will complement many border plants: try crocosmias (*see p.219*), penstemons (*see p.304*), and shrub roses (*see pp.110–113*). The flower spikes, in white or shades of pink, purple, or gold, appear in summer and attract bees, butterflies, and other beneficial insects into the garden. Low-growing species, like *Stachys candida*, are good for dry banks or gravel gardens.

Hardiness Fully hardy ✳✳✳ to frost-hardy ✳✳.

Cultivation Grow in well-drained, reasonably fertile soil in full sun. Smaller rock garden species need very sharply drained soil. **Sow** seed (*see pp.391–392*) in a container in a cold frame in autumn or spring. **Lift and divide** entire plants (*see p.395*) in spring, as growth starts, or cut off and replant rooted sections from the outside of large clumps.

Stachys byzantina (Lambs' ears, Lambs' tongues)
‡45cm (18in) ↔ 60cm (24in), mat-forming perennial, woolly pink-purple flowers from early summer to early autumn ✳✳✳

SYMPHYTUM

Comfrey

late spring to late summer

‡↔ 30cm–2m (1–6ft) or more

PRIZED FOR THEIR SHADE tolerance, these hairy, clump-forming perennials make useful ground cover in a shady border or woodland garden. Although essentially coarse plants, they have decorative, crinkly foliage and pretty, long-lasting flowers. These are tubular or bell-shaped, in shades of bright blue, pale blue, cream, pale yellow, purple-violet, or white, and are borne in clusters amid the foliage from late spring to late summer. The leaves may be plain green, cream- or gold-variegated. Pick a site carefully because all but the variegated species can be invasive. They thrive under trees or in borders, where little else will grow.

Hardiness Fully hardy ✳✳✳.

Cultivation Grow in moist soil in sun or shade, or in dry shade. **Remove** flowers from variegated species for the best foliage colour. **Divide** plants (*see p.395*) in spring; comfrey spreads by underground stems (rhizomes) and will reshoot from a tiny bit of stem left in the soil. Comfrey leaves make a rich, if smelly, liquid feed: one-third fill a bucket with leaves and top up with water. Cover and leave for 2–3 weeks, then use diluted one part comfrey liquid with two parts water.

Stachys candida
‡15cm (6in) ↔ 30cm (12in), spreading, flowers in summer, needs excellent drainage and protection from winter rains ✳✳✳

Stachys macrantha 'Superba'
‡60cm (24in) ↔ 30cm (12in), erect, hairy perennial, rosettes of dark green leaves, flowers from early summer to early autumn ✳✳✳

Symphytum 'Hidcote Blue'
‡↔ 45cm (18in), hairy, erect then lax stems, red buds, flowers to 1.5cm (½in) long in mid- and late spring that fade with age

Symphytum caucasicum ♥
‡↔ 60cm (24in) then spreads, clump-forming hairy perennial, erect then lax stems, rosettes of leaves, flowers from early to late summer

TAGETES
Marigold   *early summer to autumn*

FOR LENGTH OF FLOWERING AND SHOW of colour, marigolds have few rivals, and make excellent subjects for a formal bedding display. The many annuals and perennials are usually treated as half-hardy annuals and sown in spring. Germination is swift and they start flowering just a few weeks after sowing. The flowers, in a range of shades from deep orange to bright yellow, are produced from early summer until the first frosts of autumn. In some forms, they are single, often with contrasting darker markings on the petals; in others they are like carnations. The ferny foliage is usually strongly aromatic. Taller African marigolds, with pompon flowers, are best grown in a border, but others, including French marigolds, are equally at home in containers or borders.

Hardiness Half-hardy ✳.

Cultivation Any reasonably well-drained soil in full sun will suit marigolds. **Deadhead** regularly to prolong the flowering period and water freely in dry weather. If growing marigolds in containers, water them well, and feed with a balanced fertilizer at weekly intervals. **Sow** seed (*see pp.391–392*) at 21°C (70°F) in spring.

TANACETUM
Pyrethrum   *early to midsummer*

MOST SPECIES IN THIS LARGE, DIVERSE group of annuals and perennials have finely cut, pungently aromatic leaves and daisy flowers in early and midsummer. Some flowerheads have a prominent central disc and others have small, double pompons. The ferny leaves are very decorative. *Tanacetum balsamita* smells minty and is an ingredient of pot pourri. Some species, such as *Tanacetum haradjanii*, are suitable for a rock garden, while others, such as forms of *T. parthenium*, can be grown in a herb garden or as an edging to mixed or herbaceous borders. Pyrethrums also make interesting plants for raised beds and containers.

Hardiness Fully hardy ✳✳✳ to half-hardy ✳.

Cultivation Grow these plants in any well-drained soil in full sun. Dwarf and silver-leaved species prefer sharply drained soil. **Cut back** the flowers of *T. coccineum* after flowering to encourage a further flush of blooms. Feverfew self-seeds prolifically. **Sow** seed at 10–13°C (50–55°F) in early spring (*see pp.391–392*). **Divide** perennials (*see p.395*) or take new shoots from the base and treat as cuttings (*see p.394*) in spring. **Chrysanthemum** eelworm in the roots may cause leaves to turn brown and die from the base; destroy affected plants.

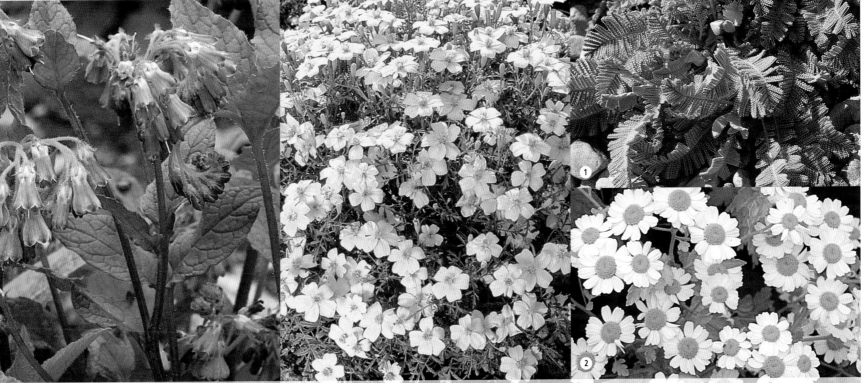

Tagetes 'Lemon Gem'
‡23cm (9in) ↔ to 40cm (16in), Signet marigold, flowers to 2.5cm (1in) across from late spring to early autumn

① *haradjanii* ‡to 15cm (6in), mat-forming evergreen, tiny yellow daisies in late summer ✳✳✳ ② *parthenium* (Feverfew) ‡45–60cm (18–24in), bushy perennial, flowers in summer ✳✳✳

THALICTRUM

Meadow rue

early to late summer

‡2.5m (8ft)
↔60cm (24in)

THALICTRUMS ARE A LARGE GROUP of moisture-loving perennials with delicate, grey-green foliage and airy clouds of tiny flowers from early to late summer. The numerous flowers may be coloured white, pink, and purple to yellow, often with showy central stamens, which create a fluffy effect from a distance. The leaves are composed of many fine-textured leaflets. They are mostly upright plants, although some, such as *Thalictrum kiusianum*, are mat-forming. Taller species are excellent in mixed and herbaceous borders with perennials like achilleas (*see p.166*), sidalceas (*see p.325*), and golden rod (*see Solidago, p.327*), or in a woodland planting. Small ones add grace to a shady rock garden.

Hardiness Fully hardy ✳✳✳ to frost–tender ✿.

Cultivation Grow in partial shade, in moist soil enriched with well-rotted organic matter. Small species like well-drained soil in cool, partial shade. **Stake** taller plants. **Sow** seed (*see pp.391–392*) in a container when ripe or in early spring. **Divide** plants (*see p.395*) as growth begins in spring. Powdery mildew can be a problem in dry soil.

Thalictrum delavayi 'Album'
‡1.2m (4ft) or more ↔ 60cm (24in), erect clumps, leaves up to 35cm (14in) long, flowers from midsummer to early autumn ✳✳✳

TIARELLA

Foam flower

late spring to midsummer

FROTHY SPIRES OF TINY FLOWERS appear to float above the foliage of these herbaceous perennials. The white or pinkish-white flowers are borne over a long period from late spring to midsummer. The foliage is also a valuable feature of these plants, being oval to heart-shaped and pale to mid-green with bristly hairs. In autumn, the leaves turn reddish-copper. Since the foliage is so dense, and some species have a spreading habit, foam flowers make attractive and effective ground-cover plants, particularly in a shady border or a woodland garden. They combine well with other shade- or moisture-loving perennials such as coral flowers (*see Heuchera, p.259*), hostas (*see pp.260–261*), and speedwells (*see Veronica, p.337*).

Hardiness Fully hardy ✳✳✳.

Cultivation Foam flowers thrive in any moist soil that has been enriched with well-rotted organic matter, in deep or partial shade. **Protect** the crowns from winter wet if necessary. **Sow** seed in a container (*see pp.391–392*) in a cold frame as soon as they are ripe. **Divide** plants (*see p.395*) in spring.

Thalictrum aquilegiifolium
‡to 1m (3ft) ↔ 45cm (18in), erect clumps, leaves up to 30cm (12in) long, flowers in early summer ✳✳✳

Thalictrum delavayi 'Hewitt's Double' ♀
‡1.2m (4ft) or more ↔ 60cm (24in), leaves up to 35cm (14in) long, long-lasting flowers from midsummer to early summer ✳✳✳

Tiarella cordifolia ♀ (Foam flower)
‡10–30cm (4–12in) ↔ to 30cm (12in), hairy leaves bronze-red in autumn, flower spikes 10–30cm (4–12in) long in summer

---

TOLMIEA MENZIESII

Pick-a-back plant, Youth-on-age

late spring to summer

‡30–60cm (12–24in)
↔1–2m (3–6ft)

THE APPEAL OF THIS FAST-GROWING, clump-forming perennial lies in its foliage. Its softly hairy, usually light green, pretty leaves produce new plantlets at the points where the leaf stalks and leaf blades meet, hence the name of pick-a-back plant. From late spring to early summer, it bears long clusters of up to 50 slightly scented flowers with purple-brown petals. *Tolmiea menziesii* and its cultivars spread by means of creeping stems. Use it as ground cover in a woodland setting with perennials such as coral flowers (*see Heuchera, p.259*) and foam flowers (*see facing page*).

Hardiness Fully hardy ✳✳✳.

Cultivation Plant this perennial in moist soil in partial or deep shade. Full sun can scorch the leaves. For a container-grown plant, use a loam-based compost; water freely during the growing season; and feed with a balanced fertilizer weekly. **Sow** seed (*see pp.391–392*) in a container in a cold frame in autumn, or divide (*see p.395*) in spring. You could also try removing plantlets and rooting them in the same way as a cutting (*see below and p.394*).

TRADESCANTIA

summer to autumn

THE HARDY TRADESCANTIAS are very useful, clump-forming perennials, and although each flower is short-lived, they are produced in profusion in summer and much of autumn. The blue, purple, rose-pink, rose-red, or white blooms stud the mounds of matt-green, or occasionally purple-tinged, grassy foliage. Grow these easy-going plants in a mixed border, perhaps married with ornamental grasses such as hakonechloas (*see p.348*), or with other herbaceous perennials. The tender tradescantias are familiar as house plants with trailing stems and evergreen, often stripy or purple leaves. These also have a place outside in summer schemes, for example with fuchsias or busy Lizzies, or tumbling over the edges of hanging baskets, windowboxes, or pots.

Hardiness Fully hardy ✳✳✳ to frost-tender ❅.

Cultivation Hardy species prefer moist, fertile soil, in full sun or partial shade. **Cut back** hard after flowering to prevent seed setting and for a further flush of flower. **Divide** hardy tradescantias in spring or autumn (*see p.395*).

TRICYRTIS

Toad lily

summer and autumn

TOAD LILIES HAVE SPECTACULAR FLOWERS, produced in white, shades of pinkish-white, or green flushed white or yellow, and frequently spotted with contrasting markings in pink or purple. They are star- or funnel-shaped and borne singly or in small clusters during summer and autumn. The leaves are often glossy, dark green to pale green, and usually clasp erect or arching stems. Some foliage is spotted or has prominent veins. Toad lilies are herbaceous perennials and particularly suitable for woodland gardens and shady borders. Try combining them with other perennials that enjoy moist, shady situations such as Solomon's seal (*see Polygonatum, p.310*).

Hardiness Fully hardy ✳✳✳.

Cultivation Toad lilies prefer moist but well-drained soil, that is humus-rich, in partial shade. In colder areas, grow late-flowering species in a warm, sheltered shrub border, protected from wind and frost, which could damage late flowers. **Mulch** thickly with organic matter over the growing area in winter to protect the plants from severe frosts. **Sow** seed as soon as it is ripe in a cold frame and overwinter seedling plants in frost-free conditions (*see pp.391–392*). **Divide** plants (*see p.395*) in early spring while they are still dormant.

ROOTING PLANTLETS In mid- to late summer, cut off a plantlet below the leaf; fold the leaf as shown. Pot in cuttings compost so the leaf is just covered.

Tolmiea menziesii 'Taff's Gold' ♀
Leaves up to 13cm (5in) long, particularly prone to sun scorch

① 'J.C. Weguelin' ♀ ‡40–60cm (16–24in) ↔ 45–60cm (18–24in) ✳✳✳ ② 'Purewell Giant' ‡↔ 45cm (18in) ✳✳✳ – both flower from early summer to early autumn

① *formosana* ♀ ‡to 80cm (32in) ② *hirta* 'Alba' ‡to 80cm (32in) ③ *macrantha* subsp. *macranthopsis* ‡40–80cm (16–32in) ④ *ohsumiensis* ‡to 50cm (20in)

TRILLIUM

Wood lily, Trinity flower,
Wake robin

spring

THESE SPRING-FLOWERING PLANTS of the woodland floor are prized for their curious three-petalled flowers held above the foliage, also grouped in threes. A small group of deciduous perennials, they are clump-forming and vigorous once established. The flowers, in white and shades of pink, dark red, and yellow, are held at the tips of slender stems in spring and summer. The rich or dark green leaves are sometimes mottled or marbled with silver or purple. Trilliums can be slow to get going, but once established resent being disturbed, so site them carefully. They are suitable for moist, shady borders or woodland gardens, in the company of plants such as hostas (*see pp.260–261*).

Hardiness Fully hardy ✳✳✳.

Cultivation Grow in moist soil, preferably slightly acid (lime-free), in deep or partial shade. **Divide** plants (*see p.395*) after flowering, preferably by lifting small, rooted sections; try to keep the central clump undisturbed. **Sow** seed as soon as it is ripe in containers in a cold frame (*see pp.391–392*). Plants may take up to seven years to reach flowering size from seed. Young leaves can be damaged by slugs and snails, so lay traps or pick off by hand (*see p.398*).

Trillium cernuum
↕ to 60cm (24in) ↔ to 25cm (10in), pendent flowers with prominent centres, flowers in spring

Trillium chloropetalum
↕ to 40cm (16in) ↔ to 20cm (8in), with thick red-green stems and fragrant flowers in spring

Trillium luteum ♀
↕ to 40cm (16in) ↔ to 30cm (12in), leaves palely mottled, stalkless sweet-scented flowers in spring

Trillium grandiflorum ♀ (Wake robin)
↕ to 40cm (16in) ↔ to 30cm (12in), vigorous, with the largest flowers to 8cm (3in) long, in spring and summer

Trillium rivale ♀
↕ to 13cm (5in) ↔ to 15cm (6in), dwarf species with leaves only 3cm (1¼in) long, flowers in spring

TROLLIUS
Globeflower
late spring to early summer

‡to 90m (36in)
↔ 60cm (24in)

RELATED TO BUTTERCUPS, these moisture-loving perennials take their common name from their bowl-shaped flowers. Flower colour ranges from pale cream to deep orange, with all shades in-between. The flowers may be single, semi-double, or double, and appear from late spring to early summer, borne on tall stems; single flowers often have prominent central stamens. The rosettes of mid-green leaves are much divided and often deeply cut, and may be glossy. Grow in a moist border, bog garden, or beside a pond or stream, with plants that enjoy similar conditions, like *Caltha palustris* (*see p.205*) or lysichitons (*see p.282*).

Hardiness Fully hardy ✳✳✳.

Cultivation Grow in very moist soil, in full sun or partial shade. Cut back stems after the first flush of flowers to encourage more later in the season. **Divide** plants (*see p.395*) as new growth begins or after flowering. **Sow** seed (*see pp.391–392*) in a container in a cold frame as soon as it is ripe, or in spring; it can take two years to germinate.

TROPAEOLUM
see also p.154

summer to autumn

NASTURTIUMS ARE THE MOST FAMILIAR of these vigorous, scrambling annuals and half-hardy perennials, grown for their cheerful, spurred flowers from summer until the first frosts of autumn. The trumpet-shaped flowers are borne in a variety of warm colours from red to orange and yellow, many bicoloured or with contrasting markings on the petals. The round or lobed, light to mid-green leaves are held on long stalks. The bushy plants are best with other annuals or as border gap-fillers. Those with trailing stems scramble over the ground or climb; use them to clothe new structures quickly over the summer. Semi-trailing types are ideal for hanging baskets. Tender perennials grown in pots may be overwintered under glass.

Hardiness Frost-hardy ✳✳ to frost-tender ❆.

Cultivation Grow in moist but well-drained soil, in sun or partial shade. Water plants in pots freely in summer; feed weekly with a balanced fertilizer. **Sow** seed (*see pp.391–393*) of annuals where they are to grow, in mid-spring; sow seed of perennials in a container in a cold frame as soon as ripe. Watch out for blackfly (*see Aphids, p.398*).

Trillium sessile (Toad shade)
‡ to 30cm (12in) ↔ to 20cm (8in), patterned leaves and dark, stalkless flowers in late spring

Trollius × *cultorum* 'Orange Princess' ♀
‡ to 90cm (36in) ↔ 45cm (18in), with glossy leaves, large at the base of the plant, and flowers in late spring and early summer

① *majus* Alaska Series ♀ (Nasturtium) ‡ to 30cm (12in), annual, variegated leaves ✳ ② *polyphyllum* ‡ 5–8cm (2–3in), trailing perennial, blue-green leaves, flowers all summer ✳✳

Tulip

late winter to late spring

‡min. 10cm (4in)
‡max. 75cm (30in)

TULIPS HAVE BEEN PRIZED FOR CENTURIES for their brilliantly coloured spring blooms. They were one of the first of the many bulbous perennials to be introduced into western gardens from the eastern Mediterranean. Here, in the parched summer earth of their native lands, the sun "ripens" the bulbs, helping the buds to form that produce the following season's flowers. Single or double, these come in a dazzling array of colours, often fascinatingly flushed or streaked with other shades. Petals may be frilled, fringed, pointed, waisted, or tinged with green, as in the viridiflora types such as 'Spring Green'. The species tulips, for instance *Tulipa sprengeri*, *T. tarda*, and the Greigii types, are often the smallest and among the easiest to grow. They suit borders, rock gardens, and areas of naturalistic planting. The taller, more highly bred hybrids put on an eye-catching display, but flowers can diminish over the years and are best lifted (*see below*) or treated as annuals. All are excellent in pots.

Hardiness Fully hardy ✳✳✳.

Cultivation Grow in well-drained, fertile soil in full sun. All tulips dislike heavy damp soil. Plant at twice the bulb's own depth in late autumn. **Deadhead** to prevent seedheads forming, thereby concentrating the plant's energy into developing the bulb and next year's flower bud within. **Apply** a balanced liquid fertilizer once a fortnight after flowering until the foliage withers, to build up the bulb. **Lift** bulbs (except for small species tulips) once the foliage has died down (*see below*), and discard or separate small offsets. **Plant** large bulbs in late autumn. If you want, grow on offsets in a spare corner until they reach flowering size (up to seven years). **Aphids** may spread an untreatable virus that causes petal streaking, which, although sometimes attractive, usually triggers a plant's decline.

Planting tulip bulbs for easy lifting

Most tall, hybrid tulip bulbs are best lifted once the foliage withers, then dried (if possible in a greenhouse or cold frame), and stored until autumn. This, to some extent, mimics their natural ripening process in the wild and helps bulbs perform well for years, especially on heavy soils. Species tulips, including the Greigii and Kaufmanniana types, need not be lifted.

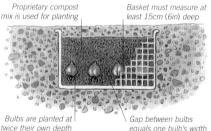

Proprietary compost mix is used for planting

Basket must measure at least 15cm (6in) deep

Bulbs are planted at twice their own depth

Gap between bulbs equals one bulb's width

◁ ❶ *Planting tulips in a basket means that they can be easily lifted after flowering and stored when not in season. Use a container with plenty of drainage holes in the bottom – a lattice basket for pond plants is ideal. Lift carefully, so as not to damage roots that have grown through the basket. Bury the basket in a resting place in the garden so the top of it is just below the soil surface. Remember to label the basket and water it in well.*

▷ ❷ *Tulips planted directly in the soil can be gently lifted with a fork. Shake off any soil and leave them in a dry place, such as a garden shed, to dry off. Once dry, remove any old soil, withered leaves and flaking skin. Any bulbs showing signs of disease with soft spots on them should be thrown away. Keep the bulbs in a cool, dark and dry place. Check them at intervals to prevent disease spreading. Replant in autumn for flowering the following spring.*

① *Tulipa acuminata* ‡50cm (20in), early and mid-spring ② 'Ancilla' ♀ ‡15cm (6in), mid-spring, good for rock gardens ③ 'Angélique' ♀ ‡30cm (12in), mid-spring, suitable for bedding or borders ④ 'Apeldoorn' ‡60cm (24in), mid-spring ⑤ *biflora* ‡10cm (4in), late winter to spring, fragrant ⑥ 'Carnaval de Nice' ♀ ‡40cm (16in), late spring ⑦ 'China Pink' ♀ ‡50cm (20in), late spring ⑧ *clusiana* var. *chrysantha* ♀ ‡30cm (12in), early and mid-spring ⑨ 'Douglas Bader' ‡45cm

(18in), late spring ⑩ *linifolia* ♀ ↕20cm (8in), early and mid-spring ⑪ *linifolia* Batalinii Group ♀ ↕35cm (14in), late winter to late spring ⑫ 'Madame Lefeber' ↕35cm (14in), early spring, large blooms, may need staking ⑬ 'Mount Tacoma' ↕40cm (16in), late spring ⑭ 'Oriental Splendour' ♀ ↕30cm (12in), early spring, leaves marked bluish-purple ⑮ *praestans* 'Van Tubergen's Variety' ↕50cm (20in), early and mid-spring, easy to grow ⑯ 'Prinses Irene' ♀ ↕35cm (14in), mid-spring, good for cut flowers ⑰ 'Purissima' ♀ ↕35cm (14in), mid-spring ⑱ 'Queen of Night' ↕60cm (24in), late spring ⑲ *sprengeri* ♀ ↕50cm (20in), early summer, will self-seed in sun or partial shade ⑳ 'Spring Green' ♀ ↕40cm (16in), late spring ㉑ *tarda* ♀ ↕15cm (6in), early and mid-spring ㉒ *turkestanica* ♀ ↕30cm (12in), early and mid-spring, unpleasant fragrance ㉓ 'West Point' ♀ ↕50cm (20in), late spring ㉔ 'White Parrot' ↕55cm (22in), late spring

VERBASCUM

Mullein *summer to autumn*

THESE STATELY PLANTS are grown for their tall flower spikes, densely set with saucer-shaped blooms from summer to autumn. The short-stemmed flowers occur usually in shades of yellow, but are occasionally purple, scarlet, brownish-red, or white. While the individual flowers are short-lived, there are always more opening to sustain the display. Most garden mulleins are vigorous, rosette-forming plants that are useful in any border, particularly in gravel and cottage gardens. The often woolly, silvery rosettes of leaves remain attractive into winter. They generally are not long-lived, being biennials, short-lived perennials, and some annuals. Mulleins self-seed prolifically if allowed to do so, although the seedlings may not come true.

Hardiness Fully hardy ✳✳✳ to frost-hardy ✳✳.

Cultivation Grow in well-drained, alkaline (limy) soil in full sun. Tall plants may require support, especially in rich soil. **Sow** seed (*see pp.391–392*) of perennials in containers in a cold frame in late spring or early summer. Sow seed of biennials in early summer to flower the following year. **Divide** perennials (*see p.395*) in spring. **Take** root cuttings (*see p.394*) in winter.

***Verbascum* 'Cotswold Queen'**
‡1.2m (4ft) ↔ 30cm (12in), semi-evergreen, upright perennial with grey-green leaves, flowers from early to late summer ✳✳✳

***Verbascum* 'Gainsborough'** ♀
‡to 1.2m (4ft) ↔ to 30cm (12in), semi-evergreen perennial, grey-green rosettes, tall flower spikes from early to late summer ✳✳✳

***Verbascum chaixii* 'Album'** ♀
‡90cm (36in) ↔ 45cm (18in), rosette-forming, semi-evergreen perennial, flower spikes to 40cm (16in) mid- to late summer ✳✳✳

***Verbascum* 'Letitia'** ♀
‡to 25cm (10in) ↔ to 30cm (12in), dense, bushy evergreen, flower spikes to 10cm (4in) long all summer, needs sharp drainage ✳✳✳

Verbascum nigrum (Dark mullein)
‡90cm (36in) ↔ 60cm (24in), rosette-forming, semi-evergreen or evergreen perennial, flowers midsummer to early autumn ✳✳✳

VERBENA

summer to autumn

THIS LARGE GROUP OF ANNUALS AND PERENNIALS are invaluable in a summer garden, with dense clusters of small flowers in shades of red, blue, pink, lilac, and violet borne on stiff, square stems. All are long-flowering, but only a few are reliably hardy. Verbenas fall into two main groups: the hardy perennials, such as *Verbena bonariensis*, will grow quite tall and bring height and an airy feel to a border, while the many shorter-growing, half-hardy perennials tend to sprawl. Grown as annual bedding they will add colour to containers and hanging baskets as well as the edges of borders. Grow perennials with tall plants like *Cynara cardunculus* (*see p.221*) and annuals with bedding plants such as pelargoniums (*see pp.300–303*).

Hardiness Fully hardy ✽✽✽ to frost-tender ❀.

Cultivation Moist but well-drained soil in full sun is best for verbenas. In containers, use a loam-based or soilless compost – water well in summer, and feed with a balanced fertilizer at weekly intervals. **Sow** seed (*see pp.391–392*) at 18–21°C (64–70°F) in early spring. **Divide** perennials (*see p.395*) in spring and take stem-tip cuttings (*see p.394*) in late summer. Powdery mildew can be a problem.

VERONICA

Speedwell   *spring to autumn*

THE SLENDER, GRACEFUL SPIRES of veronica carry small, outward-facing flowers in intense or pastel shades of blue, pink, purple, or white. The numerous annuals and perennials in this group are mostly mat- or cushion-forming, but sometimes upright and branching. Their long or rounded leaves have toothed edges and are mid- to dark green, sometimes felted. Speedwells flower over a long period, from spring to autumn, and are excellent garden plants, especially for the front of a sunny border. They make good partners for shrubby or perennial plants such as lavenders (*see p.80*) and cranesbills (*see Geranium, pp.250–251*). The smaller types are best grown in a rock garden.

Hardiness Fully hardy ✽✽✽ to frost-hardy ✽✽.

Cultivation Alpine speedwells require sharply drained, poor to moderate soil, in full sun and protection from winter wet for those with felted leaves. Others like any fertile soil in full sun or partial shade. **Sow** seed (*see pp.391–392*) in a container in a cold frame in autumn. **Divide** perennials (*see p.395*) in spring or autumn. Veronicas may suffer from powdery mildew in dry weather; remove affected parts.

Veronica austriaca 'Kapitän'
↕ to 30cm (12in) ↔ to 40cm (16in), mat-forming perennial with flower spires 10–15cm (4–6in) long all summer ✽✽✽

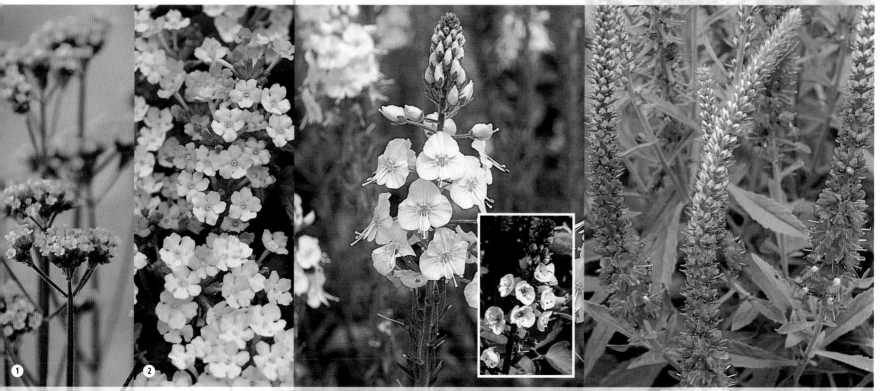

① *bonariensis* ♥ ↕ to 2m (6ft), perennial, flowers late summer to autumn, apply a winter mulch ✽✽ ② '**Peaches and Cream**' ♥ ↕ to 45cm (18in), sprawling perennial grown as annual ✽

Veronica gentianoides ♥
↕↔ to 45cm (18in), mat-forming perennial, dark green leaves, pale blue (*see inset*) or, more rarely, white flowers in early summer ✽✽✽

Veronica spicata '**Rotfuchs**' (syn. 'Red Fox')
↕↔ to 30cm (12in), mat-forming perennial, spreads by rooting stems, flowers from early to late summer ✽✽✽

VIOLA
Pansy, Violet

year-round

THE RICHLY-COLOURED AND OPEN "FACES" of these well-loved flowers bring cheer to the garden all year around. Hundreds of forms are available, with flowers in hues of gold, orange, crimson, purple, black, blue, lilac, and white; many are bicoloured and or even tricoloured. Traditional violas are compact, tufted perennials, with dainty, often scented flowers, such as the classic English violet, *Viola odorata*. This is an evergreen perennial with a strong, sweet scent and is a good ground cover for a shady spot. Garden pansies include the brasher, large-flowered hybrids, mostly unscented; they are grown as bedding, and include winter-flowering forms. There are also annual violas. Violas look pretty as border edging or in hanging baskets and other containers.

Hardiness Fully hardy ✳✳✳ to half-hardy ✳.

Cultivation Violas like fertile, humus-rich, moist but well-drained soil, in full sun or partial shade. Violas can be short-lived, so it is best to raise new plants regularly. **Sow** seed (*see pp.391–392*) in late winter for summer flowers, or in summer for winter or spring flowers. **Take** softwood cuttings of perennials (*see p.394*) in spring or late summer.

Viola 'Nellie Britton' ♀
‡15cm (30cm) ↔ 30cm (12in), clump-forming, evergreen perennial, abundant flowers, 2.5cm (1in) across, all summer ✳✳✳

Viola 'Jeannie Bellew'
‡20–23cm (8–9in) ↔ 25–30cm (10–12in), bushy, spreading perennial, flowers from mid-spring to mid-autumn ✳✳✳

Viola 'Jackanapes' ♀
‡13cm (5in) ↔ 30cm (12in), clump-forming, short-lived, evergreen perennial, 2cm (¾in) flowers in late spring and summer ✳✳✳

DEADHEAD regularly to prolong flowering. Cut out faded flowers near the base of the stalks to encourage new shoots to grow.

Viola 'Rebecca'
‡10cm (4in) ↔ 25cm (10in), spreading perennial, heavily scented flowers – tinged blue in cold conditions – borne in summer ✳✳✳

Viola tricolor (Heartsease, Love-in-idleness, Wild pansy)
‡8–13cm (3–5in) ↔ 10–15cm (4–6in), annual, biennial, or short-lived evergreen perennial, flowers from spring to autumn ✳✳✳

WALDSTEINIA

Barren strawberry

late spring to early summer

EXCELLENT AS GROUND COVER for a shady spot, waldsteinias quickly carpet the earth with small tufts of lush, green foliage, which resembles that of the strawberry plant (*see Frageria, p.245*). The foliage is in turn smothered in bright yellow flowers, either singly or in small, loose clusters, from late spring to early summer. These trouble-free, herbaceous or semi-evergreen perennials cover the ground by means of creeping stems (rhizomes) that spread underground and produce a weed-suppressing mat. They can be invasive in favourable conditions, so choose a site carefully. Waldsteinias are happy in a woodland garden, at the front of shady mixed beds, borders, or banks, or in herbaceous borders.

Hardiness Fully hardy ✳✳✳.

Cultivation Any moderately fertile soil in full or partial shade suits this undemanding plant. **Divide** mature plants (*see p.395*) in early spring. **Sow** seed (*see pp.391–392*) in containers in spring or autumn and place in a cold frame overwinter.

ZANTEDESCHIA

Arum lily

spring and summer

THESE IMPOSING, ARCHITECTURAL PERENNIALS have lush foliage and elegant, funnel-shaped blooms. The flowers are borne in spring and summer on stems up to 90cm (36in) tall and are usually clear yellow, although white, pink, lilac, or dark purple forms are available. The large, mid- to dark green leaves are arrow-shaped and sometimes spotted. *Zantesdeschia aethiopica* can be grown in moist borders, where it can form large clumps, or as a marginal aquatic in water up to 30cm (12in) deep, in a 25–30cm (10–12in) aquatic basket filled with heavy loam.

Hardiness Fully hardy ✳✳✳ to frost-tender ❅.

Cultivation *Z. aethiopica* needs moist soil, enriched with organic matter, in full sun. In frost-prone areas, protect the crowns with a deep winter mulch. *Z. elliottiana* is best raised in pots under frost-free glass and stood outside for summer display. Use a soil-based compost and feed weekly at flowering time with a balanced fertilizer. **Divide** (*see p.395*) in spring. **Sow** seed (*see pp.391–392*) at 21–27°C (70–81°F).

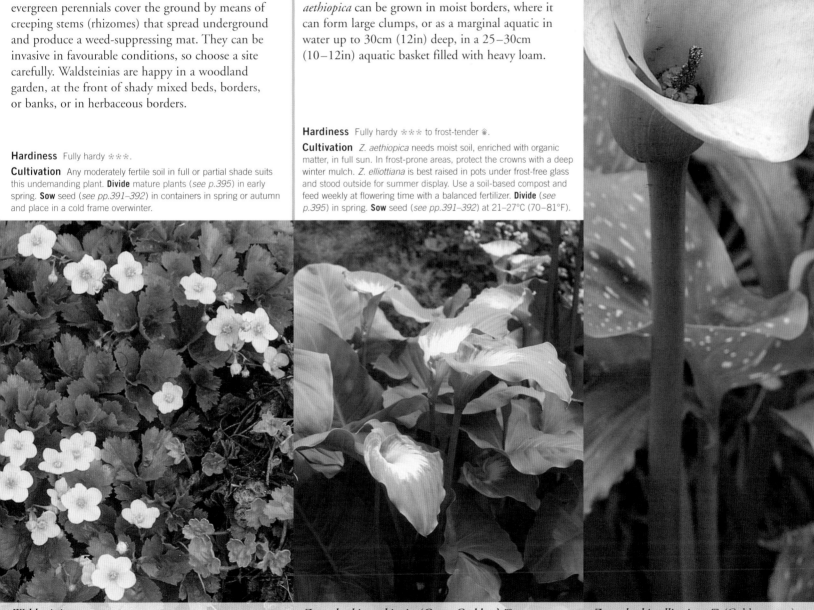

Waldsteinia ternata
‡ 10cm (4in) ↔ 60cm (24in), vigorous semi-evergreen, leaves to 6cm (2½in) long, flowers up to 1.5cm (½in) across

Zantedeschia aethiopica 'Green Goddess' ♀
‡ 90cm (36in) ↔ 60cm (24in), clumping, evergreen in mild areas, 15–20cm (6–8in) flowers from late spring to midsummer ✳✳

Zantedeschia elliottiana ♀ (Golden arum)
‡ 60–90cm (24–36in) ↔ 20cm (8in), erect habit, leaves to 45cm (8in) long, flowers 15cm (6in) long in summer ❅

Bamboos and Grasses

choosing grassy plants

Ornamental grasses include several groups of grass-like plants. True grasses include lawn grasses; they may be annual or perennial and most have flowerheads formed of many tiny flowers in clusters or spikes. Bamboos are very large, handsome, evergreen grasses with segmented woody stems, or canes, and delicate, divided leaves. Many are vigorous, and once established can spread over a large area. Rushes have tightly packed, upright leaves arising straight out of the soil. They prefer moist or wet conditions, and thrive in pond margins. Sedges are low-growing, usually perennial and evergreen, and – like rushes – are valued for their foliage. Their stems feel distinctly ridged.

BENEFITS OF GRASSES

Grasses are an autumn blessing: silhouetted against clear skies, their long-lasting, late fluffy or feathery flowerheads help extend the season of interest and look just as graceful when they go to seed. Some also have colour to contribute as their architectural foliage turns brown or bronze – and they hold these russet tones right through the winter, providing structure during the bleakest months of the year.

Another good reason for leaving your grasses uncut during winter is so that birds can enjoy their seeds. Beneficial insects such as beetles also like to shelter in the bases of the plants until spring.

PLANTING IDEAS

Many grassy plants thrive in most situations. True grasses may tolerate very dry conditions, but rushes and sedges prefer moister soils. Before planting, however, it is a good idea to incorporate plenty of well-rotted organic matter into dry soils to ensure moisture retention. Heavier clay soils need coarse grit dug in to improve drainage. Grasses require little further attention, apart from cutting down old foliage in spring.

There are plenty of ways to use ornamental grasses, bamboos, and sedges. Large grasses like pampas grass (*Cortaderia*) and *Stipa gigantea* make excellent specimens in sunny gravel gardens. Alternatively take advantage of the wonderful contrasts of foliage colour, shape, and height by planting them in drifts, creating a dedicated border that shimmers and changes with every passing breeze. Vary the pace by placing tall, bold grasses next to fine-leaved ones.

Grasses and sedges are equally at home in mixed or herbaceous borders. They provide the perfect foil to broad-leaved hostas or bright flowering annuals and perennials. Their slender stems allow you to glimpse other flowering plants through them, giving a light, airy feel to the planting. Tall grasses can be planted in clumps at intervals to act as focal points, or grown as a screen – bamboos with coloured stems are a handsome choice.

Pampas grass (*Cortaderia*) is a dramatic plant; here it adds height to the border without overwhelming it, and the plumes will last throughout the winter months.

Pennisetum villosum p.351   *Festuca glauca p.347*   *Milium effusum* 'Aureum' *p.350*   *Deschampsia cespitosa* 'Goldtau' *p.347*

Sasa veitchii p.353   *Briza maxima p.344*   *Pennisetum alopecuroides p.351*   *Carex pendula p.345*

Cortaderia selloana 'Pumila' *p.346*   *Semiarundinaria fastuosa p.354*   *Helictotrichon sempervirens p.348*   *Cortaderia selloana p.346*

Schoenoplectus lacustris 'Zebrinus' *p.354*   *Pleioblastus variegatus p.353*   *Lagurus ovatus p.349*   *Phyllostachys nigra p.352*

ALOPECURUS

Foxtail grass

mid-spring to autumn

FOXTAIL GRASSES MAKE LOW, loose, spreading clumps of flat leaves, and in spring and summer bear dense, narrow, hairy spikes of flowers that resemble a fox's brush. Although spreading, they are not invasive, so are suitable for borders and for rock gardens. The tall flowering stems, rising above the basal tufts of leaves, make them interesting plants for growing in containers on the patio. The blue-green perennial *Alopecurus lanatus*, with its leaves covered in fine hairs, hates winter wet and is a plant for alpine-style rock gardens. The fine, striped foliage of the perennial *A. pratensis* 'Aureovariegatus' acts as a perfect contrast to plants with large, flat leaves, such as hostas (*see pp.260–261*). There are also annual foxtail grasses.

Hardiness Fully hardy ✽✽✽.

Cultivation Grow in gritty, well-drained soil in sun or partial shade. On heavier soils, dig coarse grit into the planting area to improve the drainage. **Cut back** the old foliage in spring to get the best foliage effect from new growth. **Sow** seed (*see pp.391–392*) in containers in a cold frame as soon as it is ripe, or in spring. **Lift** and divide the plants (*see p.395*) carefully in spring or early summer.

BRIZA

Quaking grass

late spring to autumn

‡ to 90cm (3ft)
↔ 30cm (12in)

THE DELICATE SHIMMERING effect created by the drooping heads of these grasses in the smallest summer breeze adds movement and interest to any border or rock garden, and gives the plants their common name. The flowers, almost hop-like, are tinged red-brown or purple when young, and turn straw-coloured in autumn. They are popular for dried flower displays, either in their natural state or dyed. The loose tufts of narrow leaves vary in colour from light green to blue-green. There are three commonly grown quaking grasses: the largest, *Briza media*, at 60–90cm (2–3ft), is a perennial, while *B. maxima* (*see below*) and *B. minor*, the smallest at 45cm (18in), are annuals.

Hardiness Fully hardy ✽✽✽.

Cultivation All types require a well-drained soil. Grow the annual species in any such soil with a site in full sun; perennial species will tolerate a range of soils and a position in sun or partial shade. **Sow** seed of annuals where they are grown in spring (*see pp.391–393*). **Divide** perennials (*see p.395*) from mid-spring to midsummer.

CALAMAGROSTIS

Reed grass

spring to autumn

THE MOST WIDELY GROWN REED GRASSES are cultivars of *Calamagrostis × acutiflora*. These are perennial grasses, generally slow-spreading and clump-forming, with particularly soft and elegant plumes of flowers in subtle shades. Their upright, architectural forms add height to herbaceous or mixed borders, while their open habits allow you to see other plants growing behind them. They give excellent value through the year, coming into growth early and bearing open clusters of summer flowers which slowly compress to become narrow seedheads that are retained through the autumn. 'Karl Foerster' has pink-bronze flowers fading to buff; 'Stricta' has red-brown flowers; and 'Overdam' has purplish summer flowers that fade to greyish-pink.

Hardiness Fully hardy ✽✽✽.

Cultivation Grow in moist soil, ideally enriched with plenty of well-rotted organic matter, but all but the poorest soils are tolerated. Position in sun or partial shade. **Leave** the season's growth uncut for winter effect, then cut down in early spring, before new growth starts. **Divide** overgrown clumps in spring (*see p.395*).

Alopecurus pratensis 'Aureovariegatus'
‡ to 1.2m (4ft) ↔ 40cm (16in), produces pale green to purple spikes of flowers from mid-spring to midsummer

Briza maxima (Greater quaking grass)
‡ 45–60m (18–24in) ↔ 25cm (10in), flowerheads from late spring to late summer

Calamagrostis × acutiflora 'Overdam'
‡ to 1.2m (4ft) ↔ 60cm (24in), pale yellow edges and stripes on the leaves, which fade to pink-flushed white as they age

Sedge   *summer to autumn*

THESE GRASSY, TUFTED perennials are grown mainly for their form, and the colours or markings on their long, narrow leaves. There are many sedges in shades of copper or russet, and others striped with gold or silvery white. Mixed groups – for example, rich yellow *Carex elata* 'Aurea' next to the red-brown *C. flagellifera* – create unusual colour contrasts. Some also have attractive clusters of flowers, drooping in *C. pendula*, or spiky seedheads, like *C. grayi*. Most are evergreen, some deciduous, and while some prefer a damp spot, others are very unfussy.

Hardiness All sedges described here are fully hardy ✳✳✳. Others from New Zealand, such as *C. conica*, *C. morrowii*, and *C. comans* 'Frosted Curls' are frost-hardy ✳✳, and benefit from a winter mulch.

Cultivation Sedges can be grouped by their differing cultivation requirements. **Group 1** will thrive in any soil in sun or partial shade. **Group 2** needs a moist, fertile, but well-drained alkaline soil and a position in sun or partial shade. **Group 3** includes *C. flagellifera* and *C. siderosticha* 'Variegata' and requires fertile, moist or wet soil in sun or partial shade. **Cut back** deciduous species in spring. Trim out any dead leaves on evergreen species in summer. **Divide** plants (*see p.395*) between mid-spring and early summer. Aphids (*see p.398*) occasionally attack the bases of the stems.

Carex oshimensis 'Evergold' ♔
↕ 30cm (12in) ↔ 35cm (14in), group 2, evergreen

MULCHING CAREX with gravel or bark gives a decorative finish and will help protect frost-hardy varieties in winter. Spread the mulch over the root area during mild, moist autumn weather.

Carex elata 'Aurea' ♔ (Bowles' golden sedge)
↕ to 70cm (28in) ↔ 45cm (18in), group 3, deciduous

Carex testacea
↕ to 1.5m (5ft) ↔ 60cm (24in), group 1, evergreen

Carex pendula (Weeping sedge)
↕ to 1.4m (4½ft) ↔ 1.5m (5ft), group 3, evergreen, self-seeds freely

CHUSQUEA

spring to autumn

THIS LARGE GROUP OF BAMBOOS form dense clumps of glossy, solid canes. They make distinctive evergreen specimens in a lawn or in a woodland garden, or can be grown with large ferns, such as *Woodwardia radicans* (*see p.365*), for dramatic, contrasting foliage effects. They are a good choice for a coastal garden. The hardy types, the most popular being *Chusquea culeou*, typically reach 6m (20ft). The stems are yellowish, with long, tapering, papery white leaf sheaths. These stay on the plant for the first year, giving an attractive striped appearance to the young canes. Clusters of sideshoots grow from the leaf joints, bearing many thin, mid-green leaves. When leaves fall from the lower part of older canes, the branching growth and leaf stalks remain at the tips, giving them a "whiskery" look.

Hardiness Fully hardy ✳✳✳ to frost-tender ❀.

Cultivation Grow in well-drained soil, enriched with plenty of well-rotted organic matter. Position in sun or partial shade, with shelter from cold, drying winds. **Divide** clumps (*see p.395*) in spring.

CORTADERIA

Pampas grass, Tussock grass *late summer*

LARGE AND STATELY EVERGREEN GRASSES, these are grown for their arching, ornamental foliage and large, feathery plumes of flowers in shades of white and silver. They form dense clumps of stiff, narrow, leaves with sharp edges (take care when siting it in family gardens), with flowers held on strong, upright stems above the foliage. The plumes can be used fresh or dried in flower arrangements. Pampas grass has a "retro" image, and still looks rather kitsch in a lawn or front garden, but it makes a fine full stop to a border, perhaps in front of a dark green hedge that will highlight its silvery plumes, or can be used to add often needed height and drama to a modern planting scheme of perennials and grasses.

Hardiness Fully hardy ✳✳✳ to frost-hardy ✳✳.

Cultivation Grow in fertile, well-drained soil in full sun with plenty of space to develop. **Protect** the crowns of young plants in their first winter, and plants of all ages in cold areas, with a winter mulch. **Cut back** the old and dead growth in late winter or early spring; take care because the leaf edges are sharp. **Sow** seed (*see pp.391–392*) with bottom heat in spring. **Divide** (*see p.395*) in spring.

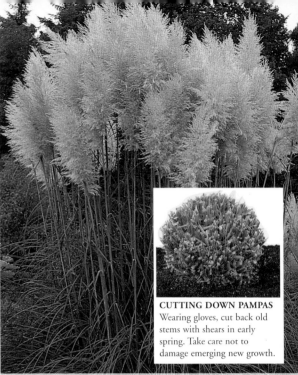

CUTTING DOWN PAMPAS
Wearing gloves, cut back old stems with shears in early spring. Take care not to damage emerging new growth.

Cortaderia selloana 'Sunningdale Silver' ♀
↕ 3m (10ft) or more ↔ to 2.5m (8ft), weather-resistant plumes from late summer ✳✳✳

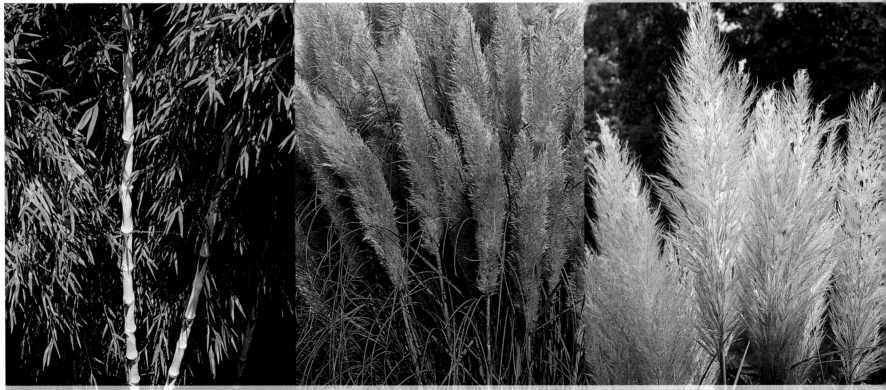

Chusquea culeou ♀
↕ to 6m (20ft) ↔ 2.5m (8ft), canes become very chunky, up to 3cm (1¼in) across ✳✳✳

Cortaderia selloana 'Pumila' ♀
↕ to 1.5m (5ft) ↔ to 1.2m (4ft), flowerheads open in late summer ✳✳✳

Cortaderia selloana
↕ 2.5–3m (8–10ft) ↔ 1.5m (5ft), flower spikes, often flushed pink or purple, from late summer ✳✳✳

DESCHAMPSIA

Hair grass   *summer to autumn*

CLOUD-LIKE, AIRY FLOWERHEADS and graceful habits
make these perennial grasses worth including in any
garden. The tussocks of thread-like leaves may be
evergreen or deciduous. Many of the hair grasses
grown in gardens are cultivars of *Deschampsia
cespitosa*, with flowers from silvery reddish-brown
to gold, changing colour as they age in autumn.
This species grows up to 2m (6ft) tall, although it
has several more compact varieties; *D. flexuosa*, at
60cm (24in), also suits smaller gardens. All are
effective alongside plants with open clusters of
flowers, such as *Campanula lactiflora* (*see p.206*);
the soft lilac-pink flowers of *C. lactiflora* 'Loddon
Anna', for example, make a perfect contrast to the
golden flowers of *D. cespitosa* 'Goldtau'.

Hardiness Fully hardy ✷✷✷.

Cultivation Best in neutral to acid soil. Dig in plenty of well-rotted
organic matter if your soil is light and sandy, to help retain moisture.
Position in sun or part shade. **Prune** old flowerheads in spring before
new growth begins. **Sow** seed in spring or autumn where plants are
to grow (*see p.393*). **Divide** (*see p.395*) in spring or early summer.

FARGESIA

                              year-round

THESE CLUMP-FORMING BAMBOOS have slender,
arching stems and lance-shaped leaves growing from
purplish sheaths. The large, striking *Fargesia murielae*
makes a fine focal point or a hardy hedging or
screening plant. The stems are white-powdery when
young, maturing to yellow-green and then yellow.
They arch under the weight of the leaves, which are
up to 15cm (6in) long, with drawn-out tips. The leaf
sheaths age to pale brown. For wonderful foliage
contrast, grow it next to the bold gunnera (*see p.254*),
although you will need a fair amount of space to
accommodate both plants. The similarly large
F. nitida has very slender, purplish canes and long,
narrow leaves, which give it a more airy, delicate
appearance, despite its hardiness.

Hardiness Fully hardy ✷✷✷ to half-hardy ✷.

Cultivation Grow in fertile, moisture-retentive soil. Position *F. nitida*
in dappled shade with shelter; *F. murielae* will tolerate full sun and
windy sites. **Divide** established clumps (*see p.395*). Take root cuttings
(*see p.394*) of lengths of underground stem (rhizomes) in spring.

FESTUCA

Fescue   *early summer to autumn*

FESCUES ARE A LARGE, VARIED GROUP, deciduous and
evergreen, mostly suited to sunny positions. They are
grown mainly for the narrow, arching, smooth leaves,
but also bear flowerheads that fade to golden shades.
The densely tufted evergreen perennial *Festuca glauca*
and its many new cultivars are very popular; the larger
F. amethystina, which turns purplish after flowering,
is also attractive. Grow fescues as edging or to provide
a contrast to other smallish plants with bolder leaves:
most are too small to make specimen plants. Blue
flowers, like those of felicias (*see p.244*), complement
the steely blue of *F. glauca*, while silver foliage
plants, such as *Stachys byzantina* (*see p.328*), make
a wonderful contrast. A mulch of dark, chipped
slate would complete a striking, urban look.

Hardiness Fully hardy ✷✷✷.

Cultivation Grow fescues in poor to moderately fertile, well-drained
soil, in full sun. **Sow** seed (*see pp.391–392*) from autumn until spring
in containers in a cold frame. **Divide** and replant (*see p.395*) in spring
every two to three years to maintain good foliage colour and keep
plants vigorous.

Deschampsia cespitosa 'Goldtau'
↕↔ to 75cm (30in), reddish-silver young flowerheads mature from
early to late summer to golden yellow

Fargesia murielae ♀ (Umbrella bamboo)
↕ to 4m (12ft) ↔ to 1.5m (5ft) ✷✷✷

Festuca glauca (Blue fescue)
↕ to 30cm (12in) ↔ 25cm (10in) evergreen, violet to blue-green
flowerheads in early and midsummer

GLYCERIA MAXIMA

Sweet grass,
Manna grass

spring to late summer

THIS IS A DENSE, VIGOROUS, spreading perennial. Unusually for grasses, it grows naturally not just along the damp edges of ponds or streams, but also in shallow water, to a depth of 75cm (30in). There are many forms, but the only one widely grown is *Glyceria maxima* var. *variegata*. This has narrow, strappy leaves; tinged with pink when they emerge in spring, they later become deep green striped with white. Plume-like clusters of green to purplish-green flowers appear in mid- and late summer on reed-like stems. It is useful for shading and softening the edges of a large pool, or in problem sites with wet soil, but with its invasive, spreading habit it may best be grown in a container or planting basket if the conditions in your garden suit it too well.

Hardiness Fully hardy ✴✴✴.

Cultivation Grow *G. maxima* var. *variegata* in any moisture-retentive soil, or in water to 15cm (6in) deep, planted in an aquatic basket to restrict the spread of the roots. It also needs full sun. **Divide** plants in spring (*see p.395*).

HAKONECHLOA MACRA

Hakone grass

spring to autumn

THIS BRIGHTLY COLOURED GRASS brings warmth and light to low-level plantings or the front of a border, forming a dense mound of narrow, arching, pale green leaves and producing reddish-brown flower spikes in summer. It is a deciduous perennial, flushed with orange and rust in autumn and slowly spreading to form mats. The leaves remain on the plant well into winter and often keep their colour, forming a bright splash in winter. This is one of the most attractive ornamental grasses to grow in containers on a patio, forming a neat, bushy mop of gently arching foliage that will almost completely cover its pot. There are several cultivars with differing variegation.

Hardiness Fully hardy ✴✴✴.

Cultivation Grow in fertile soil enriched with well-rotted organic matter, or loam-based potting compost, in full sun or partial shade. **Cut off** the old foliage in autumn if its winter show is not wanted, or in spring. **Divide** plants (*see p.395*) in spring.

HELICTOTRICHON

summer to autumn

FORMING TUSSOCKS OF LEAVES in shades of blue-grey or mid- to light green, these grasses come from open sites, often with poor soils. They are particularly suited to the conditions offered by rock gardens or gravel plantings, but are happy in borders with well-drained soil. There are many species, both deciduous and evergreen, and all perennial. In summer, upright or nodding clusters of flowers glisten in the light; these age to a straw colour. *Helictotrichon sempervirens*, is especially popular, forming a dense, fine clump of tightly rolled leaves. Its flattened spikes of flowers, tinged with purple, have a graceful, nodding habit. These grasses make good specimens and associate well with purple or silver foliage plants.

Hardiness Fully hardy ✴✴✴.

Cultivation Grow in well-drained, poor to moderately fertile soil, preferably alkaline (limy), in full sun. **Cut back** dead foliage and flowers in spring. **Sow** seed (*see pp.391–392*) in spring in containers in a cold frame or on a windowsill. **Divide** (*see p.395*) in spring. Rust (*see p.399*) can be a problem, particularly in damp summers, but can be treated with a suitable fungicide.

Glyceria maxima var. *variegata*
↕ 80cm (32in) ↔ indefinite, can become invasive both in ponds and in damp soil

Hakonechloa macra 'Aureola' ♥
↕ 35cm (14in) ↔ 40cm (16in), leaves flushed red in autumn, is best grown in partial shade

Helictotrichon sempervirens ♥ (Blue oat grass)
↕ to 1.4m (4ft) ↔ 60cm (24in), evergreen, grey-blue leaves fade in autumn (*see above*), flower spikes in early and midsummer

HORDEUM
Barley · *early to midsummer*

THIS GROUP OF ORNAMENTAL GRASSES contains about 20 annual and perennial species and includes the cereal crop, barley. The narrow leaves may be flat or rolled, and range from light to mid-green or blue-green. Flowers are produced in dense, cylindrical, or flattened spikes with distinctive long bristles. The type most often grown in gardens is *Hordeum jubatum*, which has spikes up to 13cm (5in) long of silky, bristled flowers. Squirrel tail grass is often grown as an annual with hardy annual "wild flowers" such as cornflowers (*Centaurea, see p.209*); a pretty look for a garden bordering open countryside. Many species are good to use in dried flower arrangements. They also look good in a wild garden or meadow planting, or among blue campanulas (*see pp.206–207*).

Hardiness Fully hardy ✳✳✳.
Cultivation Grow in moderately fertile, well-drained soil, in full sun. **Sow** seed where it is to grow (*see pp.391–393*) in spring or autumn. **Cut** flowerheads for drying before they are fully mature.

LAGURUS OVATUS
Hare's tail · *late summer to autumn*

‡ to 50cm (20in)
↔ 30cm (12in)

THIS ANNUAL GRASS grows naturally in open spaces in the Mediterranean region. It is valued for the appealing, softly hairy flowerheads that give it its name. These are pale green, tinged with purple, and mature to a pale, creamy buff colour in late summer and autumn. The flat, narrow leaves are pale green. A small and unassuming plant, hare's tail has most impact when planted in groups. It is best grown in drifts or among other hardy annuals such as calendulas (*see p.204*), cosmos (*see p.218*), and annual chrysanthemums (*see pp.212–213*). It also makes a useful gap-filler in herbaceous borders. The flowerheads can be used in fresh or dried flower arrangements.

Hardiness Fully hardy ✳✳✳.
Cultivation Prefers light, sandy soil that is well-drained and moderately fertile. Position in full sun. **Sow** seed (*see pp.391–393*) in spring where the plants are to grow, or in containers in a cold frame in autumn. **Pick** flowerheads for drying before they are fully mature.

LUZULA
Woodrush · *spring to summer*

VALUED FOR THEIR TOLERANCE of shade, these rushes provide good ground cover in woodland or mixed borders. Woodrushes are mostly evergreen perennials from heaths, moors, and scrubby woodland, forming tussocks of grassy leaves with white hairs on them, particularly along the edges. Clusters of tiny flowers are produced in spring or summer. The greater woodrush, *Luzula sylvatica*, will grow in dry shade and makes an excellent, weed-suppressing ground cover. Its leaves are glossy, dark green, and in mid-spring and early summer it bears chestnut-brown flowers in open clusters. Snowy woodrush, *L. nivea*, has pure white flowers, in early and midsummer.

Hardiness Fully hardy ✳✳✳.
Cultivation Grow in poor to reasonably fertile, well-drained soil. Position in partial or deep shade; woodrushes can be grown in full sun where the soil is always moist. **Sow** seed (*see pp.391–392*) in containers in spring or autumn. **Divide** plants (*see p.395*) between spring and early summer.

Hordeum jubatum (Squirrel tail grass)
‡ 50cm (20in) ↔ 30cm (12in), annual or perennial, red- or purple-flushed flowers from early to midsummer that fade to beige

Lagurus ovatus ♀

Luzula sylvatica 'Aurea'
‡ to 70–80cm (28–32in) ↔ 45cm (18in), yellow-green leaves become bright, shiny yellow in winter, needs light, dappled shade

MILIUM

Wood millet · *spring to midsummer*

MAINLY WOODLAND GRASSES, these are a small group of annuals and perennials. The leaves are sometimes quite broad, and yellow-green to light green. Open, delicate flower clusters appear from spring to midsummer. Milium adds a bright splash of colour to herbaceous borders or the dappled shade at the edge of a woodland. Plants with dark green leaves, such as astilbes (*see p.194*) or some hostas (*see pp.260–261*), will highlight the leaf colour. *Milium effusum* 'Aureum', is named for E.A. Bowles – a famous gardener and writer – with smooth, flat, arching, golden leaves, at their best in early spring, fading slightly as summer goes on. Miliums associate well with other grasses such as pennisetums (*see facing page*) or woodrushes (*Luzula, see p.349*).

Hardiness Fully hardy ❋❋❋.

Cultivation Grow in fertile, moist but well-drained soil with plenty of organic matter. Position in partial shade; may be grown in sun if the soil remains moist at all times. **Sow** seed (*see pp.391–393*) outdoors in spring. **Divide** plants (*see p.395*) in early spring and early summer.

MISCANTHUS

summer and autumn

GRACEFUL SPECIMEN PLANTS in a lawn or in borders, these wonderful grasses add height without over-powering other plants. They bring movement and a rustling sound in the lightest breeze, and although they look delicate, the flowering stems stand up well to wind; this and their often fine autumn colour gives them added value late in the season. Miscanthus form large clumps of arching, narrow, light green foliage. Many cultivars of eulalia grass (*Miscanthus sinensis*) are widely grown. During late summer and autumn, they produce large, distinctive tassels of silky, hairy flowers, some red-tinted, others silvery. These grasses are deciduous, but the dying foliage of many develops russet or golden tints in autumn.

Hardiness Fully hardy ❋❋❋ to frost-hardy ❋❋.

Cultivation Tolerant of most conditions, but they grow best in fertile, moist but well-drained soil in full sun. May be slow to settle in. **Protect** from excessive winter rains. **Cut** old foliage to the ground in early spring before growth starts. **Sow** seed (*see pp.391–392*) in spring in a cold frame or on the windowsill. **Divide** plants (*see p.395*) as new growth emerges in spring.

Miscanthus sinensis 'Zebrinus' ❦ (Zebra grass)
↕ to 1.2m (4ft) ↔ 1.2m (4ft), the most spreading of several striped cultivars, lighter bands on leaves in summer ❋❋❋

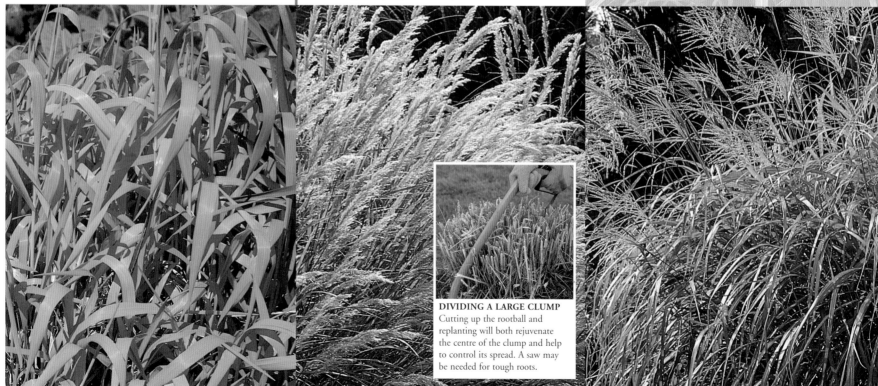

DIVIDING A LARGE CLUMP
Cutting up the rootball and replanting will both rejuvenate the centre of the clump and help to control its spread. A saw may be needed for tough roots.

Milium effusum 'Aureum' ❦ (Bowles' golden grass)
↕ to 60cm (24in) ↔ 30cm (12in), perennial with slender, nodding, golden flower spikes from late spring to midsummer

Miscanthus sinensis 'Gracillimus' (Maiden grass)
↕ 1.3m (4½ft) ↔ 1.2m (4ft), dense, fine leaves with good bronze tints in autumn, may not flower in cooler summers ❋❋❋

Miscanthus sinensis 'Silberfeder' ❦
↕ to 2.5m (8ft) ↔ 1.2m (4ft), abundant flowerheads that age to silver and are retained into winter, particularly dislikes wet soil ❋❋❋

MOLINIA CAERULEA

Purple moor grass

spring to autumn

ONLY THIS SPECIES is grown in gardens, but there are a number of different varieties. These are tall and slender grasses, making excellent structural plants for mixed and herbaceous borders, or for the far edges of informal ponds. They are grown for their attractive habits, forming clumps of narrow, dark green leaves, and for dense, purple flower spikes, which are held on graceful, arching, golden stems over a long period from spring to autumn. The flowerheads and leaves in some cultivars turn glorious shades of golden yellow in autumn, but the flowering stems do not usually last into winter. A beautiful way to highlight the purple flowers and yellow-tinted stems is by growing tall, pale blue delphiniums (*see pp.224–225*) behind it.

Hardiness Fully hardy ✳✳✳.

Cultivation Grow in any moist but well-drained soil, preferably acid to neutral (lime-free), in full sun or partial shade. **Sow** seed (*see pp.391–393*) in spring in containers in a cold frame or on the windowsill. **Divide** plants (*see p.395*) in spring and pot up until they become established and then replant in the garden.

PENNISETUM

summer and autumn

THESE ORNAMENTAL GRASSES are grown for their feathery clusters of flowers or over-arching stems, produced in summer and autumn and popular in fresh and dried flower arrangements. Several types of these clump-forming perennials and annuals are grown. The evergreen fountain grass, *Pennisetum alopecuroides*, up to 1.5m (5ft) tall, has flat, dark green leaves, with bottlebrush-shaped, bristly flowerheads in yellowish-green to dark purple. The smaller, deciduous fountain grass, *P. orientale*, has distinctive, pink flowerheads and combines well with Mediterranean plants such as lavenders (*Lavandula, see pp.80–81*). Feathertop, *P. villosum*, although a deciduous perennial, is often grown as an annual in cool climates.

Hardiness Fully hardy ✳✳✳ to frost-tender ❋.

Cultivation Grow in light, reasonably fertile soil in full sun. **Cut back** dead growth in spring. **Sow** seed (*see p.391–392*) in heat in early spring. **Divide** plants (*see p.395*) in late spring or early summer.

Molinia caerulea subsp. *arundinacea*

↕ to 1.5m (5ft) ↔ 40cm (16in), this subspecies and its cultivars are particularly noted for their autumn colour

Pennisetum alopecuroides 'Hameln'

↕↔ 50cm (20in), compact and early flowering, dark-green leaves turn golden yellow in autumn, may not survive cold, wet winters ✳✳

Pennisetum villosum ♀ (Feathertop)

↕↔ 60cm (24in), flat leaves, soft flowerheads in late summer and early autumn, maturing to purple ✳✳

PHALARIS ARUNDINACEA

Reed canary grass,
Ribbon grass

*early to
late summer*

THIS SPREADING PERENNIAL and its cultivars are widely grown. It is an erect, evergreen grass with flat leaves. From early to midsummer, it bears narrow clusters of silky, pale green flowers that age to buff. It makes highly effective ground cover, crowding out weeds, and looks at home by a pond or stream. This grass can be invasive, so needs plenty of space or firm control: it requires lifting and dividing regularly when grown in small gardens, or in mixed borders. There are several variegated cultivars. *Platycodon grandiflorus* (*see p.309*) is a striking plant to grow alongside these grasses – its blue flowers will be highlighted by the bright white stripes on the foliage.

Hardiness Fully hardy ✵✵✵.

Cultivation Tolerates any soil in full sun or partial shade. Contain its spread if necessary by planting it in a sunken, bottomless half-barrel. **Cut back** the dead foliage in spring. Variegated types may revert to plain green foliage in midsummer; cut down all but young shoots in early summer to encourage new, variegated foliage. **Divide** plants (*see p.395*) from mid-spring to midsummer.

PHYLLOSTACHYS

Black, Golden, or Zigzag bamboo

year-round

VALUED FOR THEIR GRACEFUL forms, fine stems, and rustling foliage, these medium to large, evergreen bamboos can be included in almost any garden. They spread by underground stems (rhizomes) to form slowly expanding clumps, but can become invasive in mild gardens. Phyllostachys can be grown in shrub borders or in containers outdoors. They also thrive in woodland gardens and have become popular as an elegant alternative to traditional hedging plants. These bamboos are particularly noted for their grooved, beautifully coloured stems: brilliant yellow in *Phyllostachys aureosulcata* f. *aureocaulis* or purple in *P. violascens*. They often grow in a zig-zag fashion and have a branching habit, bearing fairly small leaves.

Hardiness Fully hardy ✵✵✵.

Cultivation Grow in well-drained soil enriched with well-rotted organic matter. Position in full sun or dappled shade. In containers, use a soil-based compost such as John Innes No.3 and feed with a liquid fertilizer monthly. **Shelter** from cold, drying winds that can scorch leaf edges. **Cut out** some of the old canes each year. **Divide** clumps (*see p.395*) in spring.

Phalaris arundinacea* var. *picta (Gardener's garters)
↕ to 1m (3ft) ↔ indefinite, variable, white-striped leaves, classic pond- and stream-side plant where space is not a problem

Phyllostachys aurea ♀ (Golden, or Fishpole bamboo)
↕ 2–10m (6–30ft) ↔ indefinite, stiffly upright young canes are bright to mid-green, maturing to brownish-yellow

Phyllostachys nigra ♀ (Black bamboo)
↕ 3–5m (10–15ft) ↔ 2–3m (6–10ft), arching, slender young canes are green, turning to shiny black over two years

PLEIOBLASTUS

year-round

MOST PLEIOBLASTUS ARE DWARF only in relation to other bamboos, most being 1–1.5m (3–5ft) in height, although the pygmy bamboo, *Pleioblastus pygmaeus*, grows to only 40cm (16in) tall. This generally reduced stature, however, makes them ideal bamboos for containers, as they will not appear top-heavy. Growing them in large pots also has the advantage of restraining their vigorously spreading habit, the pygmy bamboo being a particular offender in this respect. *P. auricomis* (syn. *P. viridistriatus*) and *P. variegatus* are naturally more restrained, especially in cooler climates. They make dense thickets of erect, leafy canes, and while they will thrive in open woodland glades, enjoying the shelter, they should be used cautiously in borders.

Hardiness Fully hardy ✳✳✳.

Cultivation Grow in moist, well-drained soil enriched with well-rotted organic matter. Position in full sun or partial shade, sheltered from cold, drying winds that may scorch leaf edges. **Restrain** their spread by confining the roots if necessary. **Take** root cuttings in spring and plant out widely spaced, keeping the soil reliably moist until plants are established.

PSEUDOSASA

year-round

GROWN FOR THEIR ERECT, WOODY CANES, this small group of robust, thicket-forming bamboos require quite a bit of space, such as in a woodland or wild garden. They do have features that strongly recommend them in spite of this, making excellent screening plants to hide ugly structures, such as sheds or compost heaps. Cooler climates help to keep them clump-forming rather than invasive, but *Pseudosasa amabilis* may look ragged if not sheltered. The leaf sheaths tend to remain on the stems for some time, giving a striped appearance. The leaves are generally large, lance-shaped, and mid- or dark green. Rarely, lax clusters of small spike-like green flowers are produced. Unlike many bamboos, these often survive flowering, although they are weakened.

Hardiness Fully hardy ✳✳✳.

Cultivation Grow in moist but well-drained, fertile soil; *P. japonica* tolerates poor, dry, or wet soils. Position in sun or partial shade. **Divide** the clumps (*see p.395*) in spring and keep the divisions moist until they are well established. **Cut back** plants if they flower, and apply fertilizer and a deep organic mulch.

SASA

year-round

‡ to 2m (6ft)
↔ indefinite

THESE THICKET-FORMING bamboos are small to medium in height, and grown as much for their handsome foliage as for their canes. The leaves are large and turn white and dry around the edges from autumn onwards, giving a variegated appearance. Sasas are useful for ground cover, or as a hedge if you have the space. The moderately spreading *Sasa veitchii* is invaluable under trees, tolerating deep shade: its natural habitat is in damp hollows in woodland. More rampant is the broad-leaved *S. palmata*; the purple-streaked canes of *S. palmata* f. *nebulosa* are attractive, but this is a bamboo to plant only where there is plenty of space.

Hardiness Fully hardy ✳✳✳.

Cultivation Tolerant of most sites and soils, except for dry soils in full sun. Dig in well-rotted organic matter before planting. Contain its spread by growing in a large tub sunk in the soil. **Divide** plants (*see p.395*) in spring, or cut off pieces of rhizomes (underground stems).

① *auricomus* (syn. *viridistriatus*) ♀ ‡ to 1.5m (5ft) ↔ 1.5m (5ft), leaves edged with fine bristles ② *variegatus* ♀ ‡ 75cm (30in) ↔ 1.2m (4ft), leaves hairy, pale green canes

Pseudosasa japonica ♀ (Arrow bamboo)
‡ 6m (20ft) ↔ indeterminate, canes are olive green when young and mature to pale beige, stands up well to winds

Sasa veitchii
‡ 1.2–2m (4–6ft) ↔ indefinite, slender, purple canes are smooth and round with a fine bloom, bristly sheaths protect new leaves

SCHOENOPLECTUS

Bullrush, Club-rush   *early to late summer*

THIS GROUP OF SEDGES includes both annuals and evergreen perennials, suitable for a bog garden or as aquatic plants in still or gently moving water. They are valued mainly for their stems and for their grassy leaves. Growing in planting baskets around the edges of a pond, the narrow foliage makes an interesting textural contrast to the broader leaves of water irises (*see pp.264–267*). The brown flowers, which are borne from early to late summer in clusters, are a fairly low-key display. Among the most widely grown is the variegated club-rush *Schoenoplectus lacustris* 'Zebrinus': striking stems are reminiscent of tiny tide-marker poles rising from the water.

Hardiness Fully hardy ✳✳✳.

Cultivation Grow in fertile, wet soil or in water to a depth of up to 30cm (12in), in a position in full sun. **Restrict** growth in small ponds by cutting back the roots every year. **Cut out** any plain green stems to the ground on variegated rushes. **Propagate** by uprooting and planting out sections of underground stem (rhizome) from mid-spring to midsummer.

SEMIARUNDINARIA

year-round

↕ 7m (22ft)
↔ 2m (6ft)

THESE ARE TALL, UPRIGHT bamboos, forming thickets in warmer climates, but clumps in cooler climates. These bamboos are at home in a woodland garden, making elegant companions to slender, small-leaved trees such as birches (*Betula, see p.28*). Their strongly vertical forms also make fine informal screens if you have the space. The leaf sheaths often hang onto the canes by the bases for some time before falling. *Semiarundinaria fastuosa* is widely grown. The lower levels of its canes are bare of leaves, making it ideal to position among lower plants in a shrub border. The glossy, mid-green canes have purple-brown stripes that are most prominent when the leaves are young.

Hardiness Fully hardy ✳✳✳ to frost-hardy ✳✳.

Cultivation Grow in well-drained, reasonably fertile soil, adding plenty of well-rotted organic matter. Position in full sun or light shade. **Divide** clumps (*see p.395*), or uproot and plant out sections of underground stem (rhizome) in spring. Young shoots may be damaged by slugs (*see p.398*).

SPARTINA

Cord grass, Marsh grass   *summer to autumn*

ADAPTABLE AND HARDY, these herbaceous perennial grasses are found in swamps, marshes, and wet prairies. They are grown for their arching leaves and make excellent ground cover at the margins of ponds. In damp soil, they spread quickly by underground stems (rhizomes); they tolerate all but the driest soils, however, and the drier the soil, the easier they are to contain. Cord grasses tolerate salty conditions well, making them useful in coastal gardens. Grow prairie cord grass, *S. pectinata*, alongside late-flowering perennials that come from similar habitats, such as heleniums (*see p.255*) and rudbeckias (*see p.317*); the bright golden yellow to brown, autumn colour of the grass is a perfect foil for the yellows, oranges, and rich reds of these flowers.

Hardiness Fully hardy ✳✳✳.

Cultivation Grow in reasonably fertile, damp to well-drained soil with plenty of well-rotted organic matter added to it. They prefer full sun but tolerate light, dappled shade. **Cut down** the old foliage in early spring. **Divide** clumps (*see p.395*) in spring. Young shoots may be damaged by slugs (*see p.398*).

Schoenoplectus lacustris 'Zebrinus'
↕ 1m (3ft) ↔ 60cm (24in), perennial, almost leafless stems arise at intervals from rhizomes

Semiarundinaria fastuosa ♛ (Narihira bamboo)
↕ to 7m (22ft) ↔ 2m (6ft) or more, glossy, mid-green leaves, sheaths reveal a polished, deep-red interior when they open ✳✳✳

Spartina pectinata 'Aureomarginata'
↕ to 2m (6ft) ↔ indefinite, retains its yellow autumn leaves and elegant silhouette during winter

STIPA

Feather grass, Needle grass, Spear grass

summer to autumn

THIS LARGE GROUP OF PERENNIAL grasses includes evergreen and deciduous types that form lax tufts of narrow foliage, above which tall flower stems rustle and wave. The growth habit alone is appealing; the flowering display in summer and early autumn is spectacular, ranging from the ethereal, drooping flowers of *Stipa arundinacea* (syn. *Anemanthele lessoniana*) to the feathery, upright *S. tenuissima* and the towering stems of *S. gigantea*. Elegant in dried flower arrangements, many age to rich golden yellow and russet, keeping their colours into winter. There is a range of shapes and sizes suitable for use in most situations. Plant *S. gigantea* in a border with the tall, open *Verbena bonariensis* (*see p.337*) to lend an airy feel to the planting scheme.

Hardiness Fully hardy ✳✳✳ to frost-hardy ✳✳.

Cultivation Grow in any reasonably fertile soil that is well-drained, in full sun. Dig in some coarse grit on heavier soils to improve drainage. **Cut back** deciduous species in early winter or spring. **Sow** seed in containers in spring (*see pp.391–392*). **Divide** plants (*see p.395*) from mid-spring to early summer.

Stipa gigantea ♀ (Giant feather grass, Golden oats)
‡ to 2.5m (8ft) ↔ 1.2m (4ft), evergeen or semi-evergreen, purple-green flowers are gold when ripe in summer ✳✳✳

UNCINIA

Hook sedge

summer to autumn

GENERALLY GROWN FOR THEIR shiny, richly coloured, grassy leaves, these evergreen sedges are small perennials with a loosely tufted habit, at home in damp places. Upright, triangular to cylindrical stems bear flowers in narrow spikes, with male flowers at the top and female flowers beneath them, followed by the hooked, nut-like fruits that give the plants their common name. The most widely grown hook sedges are the russet-leaved *Uncinia rubra* and the smaller *U. unciniata,* both of which resemble the New Zealand species of carex (*see p.345*) in many ways. Uncinias look very attractive surrounded by a gravel mulch, although the soil below must be moisture-retentive.

Hardiness Frost-hardy ✳✳.

Cultivation Grow in reasonably fertile, but well-drained soil, containing plenty of well-rotted organic matter. Position in full sun or dappled shade. **Sow** seed (*see pp.391–392*) in heat in spring. **Divide** well-grown plants (*see p.395*) between spring and midsummer.

Stipa calamagrostis
‡ 1m (3ft) ↔ 1.2m (4ft), deciduous, blue-green leaves, summer flowerheads are silvery and buff to purplish-tinted ✳✳✳

Uncinia rubra
‡ 30cm (12in) ↔ 35cm (14in), greenish-red or reddish brown foliage, russet, then dark brown to black flowers in mid- to late summer

Ferns

choosing ferns

Ferns are perennial foliage plants: some are evergreen and others are deciduous. Unlike other plants, which flower and then set seed, ferns reproduce by means of tiny spores. Spore cases form on the undersides of the fronds; these fall from the plant when ripe, as part of the plant's reproductive process.

SHAPE, COLOUR, AND TEXTURE

With astonishingly varied shapes and habits, ferns often appear to defy attempts at generalization. They may be stiff and upright, or gracefully arching. Some ferns have tough, leathery, and glossy fronds; others are more dainty and fragile. And when it comes to colour, there's more choice than you might expect: ferns come in a vast range of different greens, often with subtle hues of silver and bronze.

Many ferns are very attractive in spring as new fronds unfurl; they often have a brown, furry coating which glows in low spring sun, and makes them excellent companions for bulbs. The new fronds of the sensitive fern (*Onoclea sensibilis*) have a pinkish-bronze tint, and emerging foliage of Wallich's wood fern (*Dryopteris wallichiana*) is yellowish-green. Combine clumps of several types to create stunning textural contrasts.

WHERE TO PLANT FERNS

Hardy ferns are generally easy to grow in moist, shady areas. As they are quite tough, their needs are minimal and they need very little maintenance once they are established. Most ferns need a site in dappled, partial, or full shade – strong sunlight can scorch the thin fronds. The cold winds that blow over exposed sites can also cause scorching, so choose a sheltered spot. The few exceptions to this include lip ferns (*Cheilanthes*) and some polypodiums, which tolerate drier conditions and sun.

Good garden soil that is rich in organic matter is best for most ferns. Before planting, dig in as much well-rotted organic matter as you can to help the soil retain moisture. Most ferns require neutral to alkaline soils but there are some, such as the hard ferns (*Blechnum*) and cryptogrammas that prefer acid conditions.

Humidity is important for ferns to thrive, so damp corners, bog gardens, and pond-side areas, with sheltered, still air, provide ideal conditions for lush foliage growth.

MAKING MORE FERNS

The easiest way to propagate ferns is to lift and divide their clumps (see p.395). Some ferns, such as *Asplenium bulbiferum* and some polystichums, form bulbils on the fronds. Detach a frond of bulbils and peg it on to a tray of compost. Keep it watered, warm and well lit until plantlets form and root. Detach and pot up plantlets when they are big enough to handle.

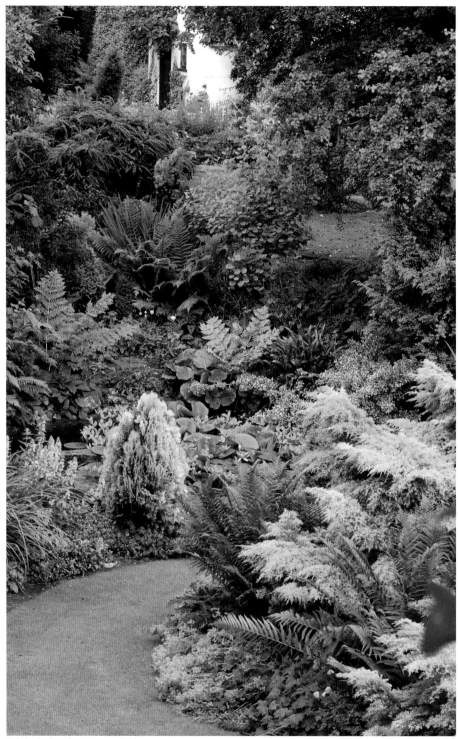

Subtle shades of green provided by ferns and other contrasting foliage plants gives this garden a relaxing and calming atmosphere in the cool of the shade.

Athyrium filix-femina 'Frizelliae' *p.361*   *Matteuccia struthiopteris p.363*   *Adiantum venustum p.360*   *Polypodium vulgare p.364*

Onoclea sensibilis p.363   *Asplenium ceterach p.360*   *Osmunda regalis p.364*   *Cryptogramma crispa p.362*

Blechnum penna-marina p.361   *Dryopteris wallichiana p.363*   *Asplenium scolopendrium p.360*   *Woodwardia radicans p.365*

Blechnum gibbum p.361   *Asplenium trichomanes p.360*   *Thelypteris palustris p.365*   *Polypodium glycyrrhiza p.364*

ADIANTUM

Maidenhair fern

spring to autumn

GRACEFUL, OFTEN FINELY DIVIDED FOLIAGE is the most desirable characteristic of this large group of evergreen, semi-evergreen, and deciduous ferns often grown as house plants. The fronds are usually mid-green, but may be paler green or even bronze-pink when young. They have black or brown-black stems which stand out well against the foliage. These ferns can spread widely by underground stems (rhizomes). They require shady areas, such as under trees or large shrubs, and also flourish beside water. Show off the delicate foliage by contrasting it with the bold foliage of plants such as hostas (*see pp.260–261*).

Hardiness Fully hardy ✳✳✳ to frost-tender ❀.

Cultivation Grow hardy ferns in moist but well-drained, reasonably fertile soil in partial or deep shade. *A. capillus-veneris* likes moist, alkaline soil. **Cut** old foliage from deciduous species in late winter or early spring. **Divide** rhizomes in early spring every three or four years. Pull apart the rhizomes to obtain about three new ferns and replant, or grow them on in a pot of loam-based compost (*see also p.395*).

ASPLENIUM

Spleenwort

spring to autumn

THIS HUGE AND VARIED GROUP OF FERNS includes evergreens and semi-evergreens. The green fronds range in shape and texture from fine and feathery to long, pointed, and glossy. The hen-and-chicken fern (*Asplenium bulbiferum*) is one of many with fronds composed of tiny leaflets. Spleenworts grow from erect, sometimes creeping, rhizomes. Plant small species in wall crevices, or in a rock garden or alpine trough. Grow larger species in woodland or among shrubs in a shady border.

Hardiness Fully hardy ✳✳✳ to frost-tender ❀.

Cultivation These ferns need partial shade and moist but well-drained soil, enriched with plenty of well-rotted organic matter. Most need an acid (lime-free) soil, but *A. ceterach, A. scolopendrium,* and *A. trichomanes* prefer alkaline (limy) soils. **Divide** hardy species (*see p.395*) in spring every four or five years to obtain new plants with at least two leaves; replant them or pot up in loam-based compost.

In wet winters, *A. scolopendrium* is prone to rust disease; if you see orange or brown patches, remove the affected fronds.

Asplenium ceterach (Rusty-back fern)
↕15cm (6in) ↔ 20cm (8in), evergreen fronds up to 20cm (8in) long, rusty-brown scales on undersides ✳✳✳

Adiantum venustum ♀ (Himalayan maidenhair fern)
↕15cm (6in) ↔ indefinite, evergreen fronds 15–30cm (6–12in) long, bright bronze-pink in late winter and early spring ✳✳✳

Asplenium scolopendrium ♀ (Hart's tongue fern)
↕45–70cm (18–28in) ↔ 60cm (24in), evergreen, fronds 40cm (16in) or more long, prefers alkaline (limy) soils ✳✳✳

Asplenium trichomanes ♀ (Maidenhair spleenwort)
↕15cm (6in) ↔ 20cm (8in), evergreen or semi-evergreen, fronds 10–20cm (4–8in) long, rusty-red spores on undersides ✳✳✳

ATHYRIUM
Lady fern   *spring to autumn*

THE LACY-LEAVED FRONDS of *Athyrium filix-femina* and its cultivars, and the silvery green, deeply divided fronds of *A. niponicum* mean that these deciduous lady ferns are decorative plants for shady areas. The midribs are reddish in colour, contrasting sharply with the foliage. The ferns are found growing wild in moist woodlands or forests, and they also look best grown in a woodland setting in the garden. You can create a natural-looking habitat for them by placing old logs in a shady border and planting the lady ferns among them as if they were growing among fallen trees.

Hardiness Fully hardy ✳✳✳ to frost-tender ❀; *A. filix-femina* is hardy to -30°C (-22°F).

Cultivation Grow lady ferns in moist, fertile soil that is neutral to acid and enriched with plenty of well-rotted organic matter. Choose a site that is both shaded and sheltered. Lady ferns will tolerate all but the driest sites. **Divide** hardy species in spring every four or five years. Use a spade to cut up larger clumps, obtaining several new plants with two or three leaves each. Replant the new pieces in prepared ground.

BLECHNUM
Hard fern   *year-round*

SOME SPECIES OF HARD FERNS have spectacular foliage, which bursts upwards and outwards in a fountain shape, sometimes from a small "trunk". This trunk is in fact an upright rhizome, up to 90cm (36in) tall, and covered in black scales; the fronds grow out from the top. Other species, such as *Blechnum penna-marina* have creeping rhizomes and are more suitable as ground-cover plants. Hard ferns are generally evergreen, with tough fronds standing through the winter. They flourish in moist soil under trees or in shady borders. The smaller species are also suitable for a shady corner in a rock garden.

Hardiness Fully hardy ✳✳✳ to frost-tender ❀.

Cultivation Hard ferns like moist soil, preferably acid, enriched with well-rotted organic matter to retain moisture. **Grow** hard ferns in pots of bark-based compost or ericaceous (lime-free) compost mixed with plenty of sharp sand or grit. Hard ferns need partial to deep shade. **Grow** tender species in large pots and keep them in frost-free conditions over winter; in mild areas, they may survive winter outdoors if protected with straw held in place with netting. **Divide** *B. penna-marina* and *B. spicant* in spring (*see p.395*); other species can be divided, but take longer to re-establish.

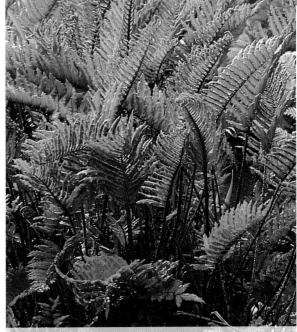

Blechnum chilense ♟
↕90cm–2m (3–6ft) ↔ indefinite, trunk-like rhizomes, fronds up to 1m (3ft) long with scaly stalks ✳✳✳

Athyrium filix-femina 'Frizelliae' ♟ (Mrs. Frizell's lady fern, Tatting fern)
↕20cm (8in) ↔ 30cm (12in), fronds 10–20cm (4–8in) long ✳✳✳

Blechnum penna-marina ♟
↕10–20cm (4–8in) ↔ indefinite, creeping, fronds are 10–20cm (4–8in) long and glossy or matt, depending on the form ✳✳✳

Blechnum gibbum
↕↔ to 90cm (36in), trunk-like rhizomes, fronds 90cm (36in) or more long, spectacular conservatory plant ❀ (minimum 18°C/64°F)

CRYPTOGRAMMA CRISPA

Parsley fern

summer to autumn

‡ 15–23cm (6–9in)
↔ 15–30cm (6–12in)

THIS DELIGHTFUL SMALL FERN is grown for its delicate foliage. The only cryptogramma commonly grown in gardens, it has deciduous fronds that turn an attractive, bright rust-brown during autumn. The old fronds usually persist all through winter. Since it is a fairly low-growing fern, the parsley fern is suitable for growing in a shaded crevice of a rock garden or at the front of a shady border. The lacy, pale green fronds make a good contrast to darker and bolder foliage on plants such as astilbes (*see p.194*) and rodgersias (*see p.316*).

Hardiness Fully hardy ✳✳✳.

Cultivation This fern prefers partial or full shade in fertile soil that has been enriched with well-rotted organic matter to help retain moisture. The soil should be acid or neutral (lime-free), so if your soil is alkaline (limy) grow the fern in a container or a raised bed that contains ericaceous (lime-free) compost mixed with plenty of grit or sharp sand, or a bark-based compost. **Remove** the faded fronds in spring before new ones grow. The parsley fern is deep-rooted and difficult to propagate by division.

CYSTOPTERIS

Bladder fern

spring to autumn

THE FINELY DIVIDED FRONDS of the bladder ferns make them a valuable asset in the garden. Bladder ferns are deciduous and their fronds grow in clumps or rosettes from fleshy stems (rhizomes), which may creep or grow upright above ground. The fronds tend to be pale or grey-green. These ferns will be happy in shady areas of a rock garden or in a shady border under shrubs or trees. They also blend in well in a border or woodland area that is dedicated to ferns; such a planting will highlight their differing textures, forms, and shades of green, and make a restful feature.

Hardiness Fully hardy ✳✳✳.

Cultivation Grow in fertile, moist soil, incorporating well-rotted organic matter to help retain moisture in partial or full shade. Provide shelter from cold, drying winds. **Divide** rhizomes in spring (*see p.395*), planting them in the ground. **Alternatively**, increase them by using the bulbils that ripen on the undersides of the fronds in late summer or early autumn; one frond should produce many plants. Peg each frond into a tray of compost. Once the bulbils have rooted, transfer the plants to 8cm (3in) pots of soil-less compost; keep them in frost-free conditions over the winter; and plant them out in spring.

DICKSONIA

year-round

SPECTACULAR, TREE-LIKE FORMS and dramatic foliage distinguish these very large, semi-evergreen or evergreen ferns. They have thick, furry "trunks" formed from a mass of old stems and leaf bases. Each stem can be up to 60cm (24in) in diameter and has only a few roots – most of its nutrients are derived in the wild from decaying matter that collects in the fronds. The large, leathery fronds grow to 3m (10ft) and sprout from the top of the stem. The new fronds have a furry protective coating as they unfurl in spring (*see inset, below*). Dicksonias grow to their full height only in favourable conditions; they are very slow-growing and so are quite expensive. If you invest in one, take good care of it. Show it to its best advantage as a specimen or with other ferns in a shady border.

Hardiness Frost-hardy ✳✳ to frost-tender ✾.

Cultivation Dicksonias need fertile soil in partial or full shade. In spells of hot, dry weather, hose the trunk with water daily. **Protect** the trunk and leaves in winter by attaching wire netting loosely around the trunk and over the crown and stuffing the gap with straw. **Cut off** old fronds in early spring. These ferns are difficult to propagate.

Cryptogramma crispa
Fronds are up to 23cm (9in) long

Cystopteris fragilis (Brittle bladder fern)
‡↔ 20cm (8in), clump-forming with upright rhizomes, fronds are 15–45cm (6–18in) long

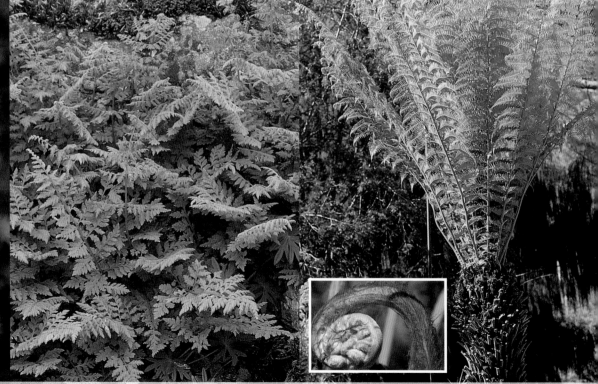

Dicksonia antarctica ♀ (Man fern, Soft tree fern)
‡ to 6m (20ft), usually much less ↔ 4m (12ft), flourishes in a mild, damp climate sheltered from wind and sun ✳✳

DRYOPTERIS
Buckler fern   *spring to autumn*

THIS LARGE GROUP OF FERNS, popular in cultivation, produces long, elegant fronds, often in a shuttlecock shape. Many retain their leaves over winter in mild, sheltered conditions, although they die down in less favourable climates. The evergreen fronds of the golden male fern (*Dryopteris affinis*) are pale green when young, contrasting with golden brown midribs. *D. erythrosora* has copper foliage in spring, turning dark green, with green midribs. The midribs of *D. wallichiana* are covered with dark brown or black scales, and are particularly striking in spring against the new yellow-green fronds; these age to dark green. With their distinctive shapes, they add height to a mixed fern border or look good as foliage plants in a shady, herbaceous border.

Hardiness Most fully hardy ✳✳✳; a few are frost-hardy ✳✳ and frost-tender ✿.

Cultivation Grow these ferns in partial shade in soil with plenty of well-rotted organic matter to retain moisture. **Shelter** from cold, drying winds. **Divide** mature plants (*see p.395*) in spring or autumn every five or six years; use a spade for older clumps.

MATTEUCCIA
                           spring to autumn

SHUTTLECOCK-SHAPED ROSETTES of upright, gently arching fronds are characteristic of the three or four species in this group of deciduous ferns. During mid- to late summer, smaller, dark brown fronds appear in the centre of each rosette; these are fertile fronds, while the green ones around the edge are sterile. The ferns spread by creeping stems (rhizomes) from which more fronds sprout. They are striking foliage plants for a damp, shady border in woodland or by water, and work well with other shade-loving plants such as rhododendrons (*see pp.104–107*).

Hardiness Fully hardy ✳✳✳.

Cultivation Grow these ferns in moist but well-drained soil, incorporating well-rotted organic matter to help retain moisture. Matteuccias prefer neutral to acid soil in partial shade. If your soil is alkaline (limy), grow them in containers or raised beds containing ericaceous (lime-free) compost mixed with plenty of grit or sharp sand, or a bark-based compost. **Divide** established clumps (*see p.395*) in early spring to obtain four or five new plants, each with at least two or three vigorous fronds.

ONOCLEA SENSIBILIS
Sensitive fern   *spring to autumn*

‡to 1m (3ft)
↔ indefinite

UPRIGHT AND ARCHING FRONDS up to 1m (3ft) long are produced by this single, deciduous fern. Its name derives from the fact that all its top-growth dies down at the first frost. In spring, its new, sterile fronds are sometimes pinkish-bronze; these turn pale green. They are very deeply divided, giving them a feathery appearance. In late summer, a number of fertile fronds with a contrasting, stiffly upright habit grow to 60cm (2ft). The sensitive fern thrives by the edge of water or in shady borders in damp soil. Try it with other shade- and damp-loving plants such as candelabra primulas (*see pp.312–313*).

Hardiness Fully hardy ✳✳✳.

Cultivation Plant this fern in a sheltered site away from cold, drying winds. The sensitive fern prefers moist, fertile, acid (lime-free) soil in light, dappled shade; the fronds will be scorched if they are exposed to strong sun. **Divide** established clumps (*see p.395*) in spring; ensure each new clump has at least two or three fronds.

Dryopteris wallichiana ♀ (Wallich's wood fern)
‡90cm (36in), sometimes to 2m (6ft) ↔ 75cm (30in), upright rhizome, deciduous fronds 90cm (36in) or more long ✳✳✳

Matteuccia struthiopteris ♀ (Ostrich fern, Shuttlecock fern)
‡1.7m (5½ft) ↔ to 1m (3ft), sterile green fronds 1.2m (4ft) long

Onoclea sensibilis ♀
Sterile fronds

OSMUNDA

spring to autumn

OSMUNDAS ARE IMPOSING, DECIDUOUS FERNS, with upright, blue-green or bright green fronds, which fade to yellow or brown in autumn. In the centre of these sterile fronds are erect, fertile fronds that contrast pleasingly with the surrounding green foliage. In the royal fern (*Osmunda regalis*), they are brown or rust-coloured; the cinnamon fern (*O. cinnamomea*) is named after the rich colour of its fertile fronds. Use these large, architectural ferns as specimen plants in a mixed border or by a pond or stream. The royal fern also makes an excellent container plant provided that it is watered regularly, especially in warm weather. Its roots are fibrous, absorbing lots of water and, as osmunda fibre, they were used as orchid compost – although this practice is now banned.

Hardiness Fully hardy ✳✳✳.

Cultivation Osmundas like moist, fertile, preferably acid (lime-free) soil in light, dappled shade. The royal fern does require a wet soil, but will do well in sun as long as the soil is moist. **Divide** established clumps (*see p.395*) in autumn or early spring using a spade.

POLYPODIUM

year-round

THESE ADAPTABLE FERNS make excellent ground cover with their spreading habit and beautiful, sculptural fronds. Many produce relatively long, arching fronds randomly from the creeping stems, or rhizomes. The fronds reach 60cm (24in) in the case of the southern polypody (*Polypodium cambricum*). Some have spores on the undersides of the fronds in contrasting colours. Unlike most ferns, polypodiums are also drought-tolerant and are happy in full sun. The mostly evergreen ferns in this group look particularly good growing in mixed borders or on a bank where ground cover is required. Their spreading habit helps to suppress weeds.

Hardiness Fully hardy ✳✳✳ to frost-tender ❀.

Cultivation Grow polypodiums in well-drained, moderately fertile soil, with plenty of well-rotted organic matter added. On heavy clay soils, dig in coarse grit to improve drainage. *P. cambricum* prefers a neutral to alkaline soil. **Site** in full sun or partial shade and provide shelter from cold, drying winds. **Divide** in spring or early summer (*see p.395*) when the plants are four or five years old.

Osmunda regalis ♀ (Flowering fern, Royal fern)
↕ 2m (6ft) ↔ 4m (12ft), sterile fronds are 1m (3ft) or more long

Polypodium vulgare (Common polypody)
↕ 30cm (12in) ↔ indefinite, thin to leathery fronds are 40cm (16in) long ✳✳✳

Polypodium glycyrrhiza (Licorice fern)
↕ 30cm (12in) ↔ indefinite, mid- to dark green fronds up to 35cm (14in) long, rhizomes have a sweet licorice taste ✳✳✳

POLYSTICHUM
Holly fern, Shield fern   *year-round*

THE FINE FOLIAGE OF THESE FERNS is usually arranged in shapely "shuttlecocks", forming exuberant bursts of often dark green fronds. The fronds tend to be highly intricate, especially in the soft shield fern (*Polystichum setiferum*) and its cultivars, and the leaflets may end in a sharp bristle, hence the common name of holly fern. This large group of mostly evergreen ferns includes plants that are 40cm–1.2m (16in–4ft) tall. These all combine well with other ferns, or with other woodland plants such as hydrangeas (*see pp.72–73*) in a well-drained woodland planting. The smaller shield ferns are best displayed in a shady rock garden.

Hardiness Fully hardy ✻✻✻ to frost-tender ❋.

Cultivation Holly ferns prefer fertile soil enriched with well-rotted organic matter, in deep or partial shade. **Protect** the crowns from excessive winter wet with a mulch of organic matter. In early spring, remove any dead fronds. **Divide** the rhizomes in spring. In late summer or early autumn, detach fronds with bulbils and peg each frond into a tray of compost. Once they have rooted, transfer to 8cm (3in) pots of soilless compost with added grit; keep frost-free; and plant out in spring.

THELYPTERIS PALUSTRIS
Marsh fern   *spring to autumn*

↕60cm (24in)
↔ to 1m (3ft)

THIS IS A DECIDUOUS FERN of swamps and bogs. In summer, if there is good light, fertile fronds, that are longer than the sterile ones, are produced. Spores are borne in abundance on the undersides of the leaflets, creating a brown haze over the ferns in late summer. Try growing this fern with other moisture-loving plants such as hostas (*see pp.260–261*), primulas (*see pp.312–313*), and marsh marigolds (*Caltha, see p.205*) at the edge of a pond. The marsh fern can be invasive, spreading by long, creeping underground stems (rhizomes), so allow it plenty of space, but it is also easy to keep under control by digging out unwanted pieces.

Hardiness Fully hardy ✻✻✻.

Cultivation Grow the fern in any reliably moist, moderately fertile soil. **Dig in** well-rotted organic matter to increase moisture retention, in sun or partial shade. **Divide** in spring or summer (*see p.395*), replant and keep well watered, especially in summer.

WOODWARDIA
Chain fern   *spring to summer*

LARGE, SPREADING, AND ARCHING plants, the chain ferns are so-called because the spores are arranged on the undersides of the fronds in a chain-like formation. This small group of ferns includes evergreen and deciduous species. The intricate fronds are particularly attractive as they unfurl in spring. On their upper surfaces, small bulbils may be produced over the summer near the tips. The chain fern is ideal for covering a shady bank that has moist soil. It looks particularly natural near water, and it combines well with bold foliage plants, such as gunneras (*see p.254*), that also like moist soil.

Hardiness Fully hardy ✻✻✻ to frost-hardy ✻✻.

Cultivation Chain ferns like neutral, reasonably fertile, damp soil in partial shade. In cold areas, shelter the ferns from cold, drying winds. **Protect** chain ferns over winter in frost-prone areas with a mulch of straw held in place with netting. **Divide** the plants in spring using a spade (*see p.395*) or sharp knife; replant the pieces in a similar site. Alternatively, propagate from bulbils in late summer or early autumn; detach fronds with bulbils and peg each frond into a tray of compost. Once they have rooted, pot into 8cm (3in) pots of soilless compost; keep them frost-free over winter; and plant out in spring.

Polystichum setiferum 'Pulcherrimum Bevis' ♀
↕↔ 60–80cm (24–32in), very rarely fertile ✻✻✻

Thelypteris palustris
Fronds up to 90cm (36in) long

Woodwardia radicans ♀ (European chain fern)
↕2m (6ft) ↔ 3m (10ft), evergreen, each leaflet to 30cm (12in) long ✻✻

CARING FOR PLANTS

If you choose plants for your garden wisely, you can reduce the amount of work you have to do to maintain them, but they will perform at their peak only if you give them a certain amount of attention, particularly in the growing season. In this chapter, you are guided through the basic principles of caring for garden plants, from assessing where to plant them and what to look for when you buy them, to all aspects of caring for them once they are in the ground. There are also guidelines on easy ways to increase stocks of your favourite plants.

planning your garden

Whether adapting an existing garden or designing one from scratch, there are many things to consider before rushing out and buying lots of plants. Taking time at the planning stage will help you to avoid making costly mistakes and ensure that you end up with your ideal garden.

First, make a rough sketch of your garden, preferably to scale on squared paper. Then list the things you want to include, how you want it to look, how you intend using it (*see box, right*). With this information in mind, take another look at your sketch and see what changes need to be made.

Moving into a new house and then creating a garden completely from scratch can seem daunting. It does however have the great advantage of giving you complete freedom to develop your own design. Unlike an established garden that may be full of plants, a bare plot of freshly laid turf gives few clues as to what plants can be grown successfully. So it is essential to take into account the garden's location, effect of the local climate (*see p.371*), and soil type (*see pp.376–377*) before buying any plants.

If you are redesigning an existing garden, don't be too hasty in your initial assessment of the site, as you may inadvertently remove some useful plants and features. Make changes gradually, over a full year if possible, adapting existing features to your plan.

Flowers and foliage come in an infinite palette of shades, providing the opportunity to experiment with colour schemes and moods in the borders. Do your homework before buying trees, shrubs, climbers, and perennials since these can be expensive and will form the permanent structure of the garden. By comparison, annuals and biennials – including bedding plants – last for one growing season and are much cheaper, so you can ring the changes from year to year, if you wish.

When organizing the layout of your borders, try to show each plant to its best advantage. It is important not to place new plants too close together: allow room for them to reach their full size, even if it leaves a few gaps at first.

Good planning ensures a long season of colour.

Assessing your priorities in the garden

- How will you use your garden?
- Do you enjoy gardening or just want a place in which to relax?
- Do you want to maximize your planting space or increase the amount of hard landscaping for a low-maintenance option?
- Is an outdoor entertaining or dining area required?
- Informal or formal? Which garden style do you prefer?
- What should the mood of the garden be – restful or vibrant?
- If children use the garden, do they need their own play area?
- Are new paths or steps needed?
- Are you happy to grow fruit and vegetables among other plants, or do you want a kitchen garden?
- Is there space for a utility area for a shed and compost bins? (Hide them behind hedges or trellis.)
- Do you want a pond or some sort of water feature ?

◁ **Night lights** Carefully positioned lighting allows you to continue using and enjoying the garden during the evening. Here, gentle spotlights create a pool of light that picks out the colours and textures of the plants and rocks in this naturalistic pond.

Fruit and vegetables can be combined with ornamental plants to create some stunning planting effects. Also, by growing the plants together in borders, they will be less susceptible to attack from pests and diseases.

Quiet corners After a busy day, enjoy the peace and quiet of a secluded corner filled with scented plants. An old railway sleeper resting on a stone boulder and a brick pillar makes a simple but comfortable bench.

Choosing a style of planting

The plants are the most important element in a garden. No matter how many ornamental features you may include, the space will still look bare until the plants are in place, bringing movement and life into the garden.

There are many styles of planting to choose from and thousands of plants with which to plan a scheme. If you are looking for inspiration, one of the best ways to discover what style or theme would suit your plot is to visit gardens that are open to the public. Wandering around your neighbourhood and looking at other people's gardens will give you a good idea of different layouts and of which plants would be most happy growing in the local soil and climate.

Extending the interest over several seasons is the key to getting the most out of a small garden. Ideally, each plant you choose should remain attractive over many months, for example displaying spring blossom or autumn leaf colour as well as flowers.

△ **Formality and order** Large areas of hard landscaping are often a feature of formal gardens, but although it allows for easy maintenance it can look clinical. A balance can be struck with planting. Here, bricks have been set into a sweep of stone slabs to warm up the colour and to add texture, while the hard edges of the paving are softened by the large drifts of restrained planting that spill over onto the stone.

▷ **Informal charm** The free-flowing charms of the cottage garden call for an unforced naturalness and spontaneity, created by intermingling plants so that they appear to jostle for space. The plants take centre stage and are allowed to self-seed where they will. Given a free rein, they will grow together to create borders of great charm.

Ponds and water features

Informal pond Unlike formal ponds which are regular in shape, an informal pond is designed to look as natural as possible. To help it blend into the rest of the garden, the edges may be lined with rocks, cobbles, slate, or wood. Plants that grow in the shallow water around the edge (called "marginals") conceal the outline of the pond completely, creating a lush appearance.

A water feature always adds an extra dimension to a garden, whether it is a formal or natural pond, or a half-barrel of water. It is also a magnet for wildlife – birds will bathe in the shallows, while frogs and toads, which help to control slugs and snails, will become regular visitors.

Consider the style of pond you prefer and how it relates to the overall plan of your garden. Ponds are not easy to move once installed. To help visualize it in detail, mark the outline on the ground using rope or a length of hose. Avoid siting the pond under a tree because falling leaves will foul the water.

If you want to keep fish, ask your aquatic supplier to recommend numbers for your size of pond.

A bubble fountain is a safe option if you have young children. A pump circulates water from a shallow tank to splash over a tray of cobbles so you can enjoy the tranquil sound of water without any danger.

Using containers

Bring colour right up to the windows of your house by planting containers with an ever-changing selection of plants, from spring bulbs and summer bedding, to shrubs and even small trees. Choose planters, pots, and windowboxes in materials that enhance, not compete with, the planting. Roots will quickly become restricted within the confines of a container, so replenish the nutrients in the compost and water regularly.

Bulbs in containers Most bulbs can be grown successfully in containers. These pink tulips, top-dressed with moss, should be planted out in the garden after flowering.

Using colour in the garden

Garden flowers come in an infinitely varied and dazzling array of colours and shades. However, foliage, bark, stems, berries, and seedheads can be colourful, too, and foliage and bark often have a longer season of interest than flowers. How you combine colour is a matter of personal preference, but there are a few ways to ensure successful planting schemes. Many designers use a colour wheel for inspiration. This is simply a circle divided into six wedges, coloured in this order: yellow, green, blue, purple, red, and orange. Colours adjacent to each other on the wheel create harmonious effects, while colours opposing each other on the wheel make for lively contrasts. Yellows through to reds are warm and stimulating; while greens to purples are restful and cool.

Restricting the colour palette can produce a more pleasing effect than using very many colours, which often looks rather fussy. Strong colours attract the eye and could be used for specimen plants. Colour can be used to set a mood – reds, golds, and oranges, typical of a hot scheme, are exciting and dominant; while blues, soft pinks, and whites are soothing and subtle.

Hot reds and yellows *Kniphofia caulescens*

Cool blues *Delphinium* Blue Fountains Group

Foliage and form

Contrasting leaves With so many colours, shapes, and textures available, it is possible to make dramatic planting schemes with foliage alone. Here, luxuriant hostas and feathery ferns combine to great effect with colourful shrubs.

Growing beautiful flowers is one of gardening's obvious pleasures, but you can have great fun designing with plants grown specifically for their attractive growth habits and strikingly shaped or coloured foliage. Unlike a brief burst of flower colour, a foliage plant will offer a long season of interest. Plants with different types of foliage can be used to build up three-dimensional layers of texture, giving even a narrow border a feeling of depth and movement.

Create a collage of leaf shapes and sizes by planting spiky specimens, such as grasses and yuccas, next to round-leaved cultivars, such as hostas (*see pp.260–261*) and bergenias (*see p.198*). Look for subtle contrasts in leaf texture, such as glossy or hairy leaves, as well as striking variegation and complementary colours, from silver and cream to purple and gold.

Seasonal interest

The huge choice of herbaceous and bedding plants available makes planning a beautiful summer garden relatively easy. Colourful borders need not be a transient pleasure – there are many plants that provide interest over a longer period, such as the peony (*see below*). As well as creating a permanent framework, trees and shrubs are often blessed with attractive spring blossom, followed in autumn by good leaf colour or berries and hips. There may also be attractive stems or bark to enjoy in winter. Keep the colour coming with spring bulbs, commencing in late winter with snowdrops (*Galanthus, see p.247*).

Spring The emerging shoots of *Paeonia mlokosewitschii* glow in the spring sun.

Late spring Over the next couple of months, the elegant leaves turn blue-green.

Early summer Lemon flowers appear, each one measuring up to 13cm (5in) across.

Autumn Seed pods split open to reveal brilliant-red fruits and black seeds.

climate and location

Not only does the weather dictate when certain jobs can be tackled in the garden, but the local climate will determine the types of plants that will thrive in your plot. Although many plants are adaptable, choosing ones that are most suited to your locality and particular aspects in the garden is fundamental to success. Providing suitable conditions for all the plants and matching as closely as possible their natural habitats, is both challenging and satisfying.

The weather – temperature, frost, snow, rain, humidity, sun, and wind – affects how plants grow and will dictate the length of the growing season. Only when the weather turns milder can we plant out tender bedding or start sowing seed outdoors. Colder areas tend to have later springs, sometimes weeks later than warmer areas farther south, as well as shorter growing seasons. Inland regions are often drier than areas by the coast. Although plants have to contend with salt spray and strong winds, coastal areas are also generally much milder.

You don't have to travel far, however, to discover significant variations in climate. There is a huge difference between the growing conditions on a sheltered valley floor compared to the exposed slopes of the surrounding hills. In the same way, while most of your garden may be warm and sunny, it may contain a range of different microclimates, where the growing conditions are modified by factors such as the shelter of a warm wall or the heavy shade cast by an evergreen tree. Such areas in the garden will need to be treated and planted differently.

Since the local climate will dictate which kinds of plants you can grow successfully, it is worth taking some time to find out what weather patterns you can expect over the course of the year. Consider joining a gardening club – gardeners are always willing to share their experiences with like-minded people and they will be a valuable source of information.

Assessing your garden

Before making any changes it is worth assessing your garden to give yourself an idea of the plants you can grow.

- How high above sea level are you? The higher you are, the colder it is because of exposure to strong winds.
- Does the garden face north or south? This will have a bearing on how much sun the garden gets.
- How shady is the garden? Is there heavy shade cast by established trees and shrubs or by the house?
- Is the garden on a slope? Cold air will gather at the bottom of a slope to cause a frost pocket (*see p.372*).
- Does it get very cold in the winter or very hot in summer? Temperature extremes can stress plants and you may have to take extra care of them.

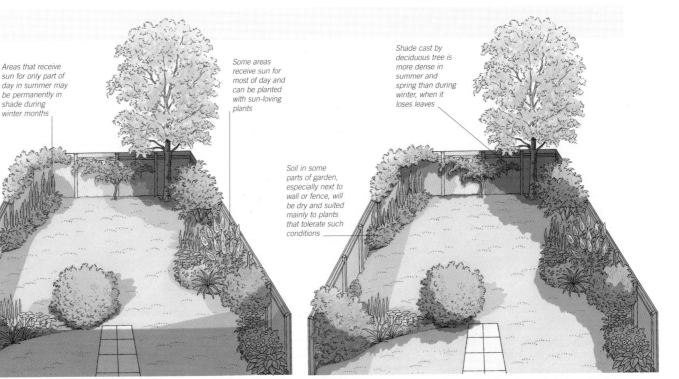

Areas that receive sun for only part of day in summer may be permanently in shade during winter months

Some areas receive sun for most of day and can be planted with sun-loving plants

Shade cast by deciduous tree is more dense in summer and spring than during winter, when it loses leaves

Soil in some parts of garden, especially next to wall or fence, will be dry and suited mainly to plants that tolerate such conditions

North-facing garden The shade cast by the house keeps the air cool and the soil moist.

South-facing garden is warm and sunny, but the soil may dry out in summer.

The dangers of frost

One of the greatest hazards that a gardener has to contend with is frost, especially in spring and autumn. An unexpected spring frost can destroy flower buds, ruining the display for the year. Tender, new shoots are also susceptible. Still, clear nights often signal that a frost is on the way, and quick action can protect vulnerable plants. If you cannot bring them under cover, loosely wrap them in some horticultural fleece, newspapers or a similar insulating material.

The incidence of late spring frosts in your area will determine the time at which it is safe to plant out tender plants, such as summer bedding. The onset of autumnal frosts determines the end of their growing season.

Where there are low points in the garden, frost pockets (see below) may form. If there is a frosty hollow in the garden, avoid growing fruit there and choose plants that are fully hardy (see right) and will not suffer in low temperatures.

Cold air is heavier than warm air and sinks to lowest possible point

Cold air is trapped behind solid barrier, such as dense hedge

Frost pocket Cold air is denser than warm air; it always flows downhill and becomes trapped in any slight dip or hollow. Frost also collects at the bases of fences, walls, and closely planted, thick hedges, or even large objects such as a statue or solid seat.

Hardiness of plants

The hardiness of a plant refers to its ability to withstand year-round climatic conditions, including frost, without any protection. Fully hardy plants withstand temperatures down to -15°C (5°F). Frost-hardy plants are happy in temperatures down to -5°C (23°F), whereas half-hardy ones prefer temperatures above 0°C (32°F) and are damaged by frost. Frost-tender plants need shelter in conditions cooler than 5°C (41°F).

Hardier plants need less nurturing because they survive without harm in the garden all winter. The more tender plants, on the other hand, have to be brought under cover before the first frost in autumn and can be planted out only when all danger of frost has passed, in spring. This varies from one area to another, but is generally around late spring to early summer.

Snowy shrub Although it looks pretty, heavy snow can weigh down branches, causing them to break. After a fall of snow, go out with a broom and knock it off the plant. If more falls are forecast, tie vulnerable branches into the main stem – this works well with conifers.

Helping plants to survive the winter

Young or slightly tender plants need protection to help them survive a severe winter. Protect top-growth by covering plants with horticultural fleece, hessian sacking, bubble plastic, or some layers of newspaper.

Wrapping plants, such as tree ferns, in dry bracken or straw will trap any warm air escaping from the soil and provide valuable insulation on a cold night. When temperatures are above freezing, unwrap the plants to give them a chance to breathe and prevent the build-up of moulds and pests. A thick mulch of garden compost spread over the crowns of plants, such as herbaceous perennials

that have died down over winter, will give protection from several degrees of frost. A mound of dried leaves, held in place over the plant with chicken wire, works well too.

Cloches, usually made of glass or rigid or film plastic, are excellent for keeping a few degrees of frost off plants. On exposed sites, protect the plants from cold winds with proprietary windbreaks or fine-mesh netting supported on stout stakes.

Frost-tender plants (see above, right) must be taken over winter into a greenhouse or a conservatory where gentle heating keeps the temperature a few degrees above freezing.

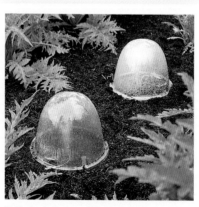

Bell cloches As well as making an attractive feature in the border, these bell cloches offer effective winter protection for less hardy plants. Glass cloches are beautiful, but very expensive and vulnerable to breakage – plastic ones, like these, do the job just as well.

Winter coat Wrapping containers with hessian (see above) or with bubble plastic protects the roots from freezing. This is a useful technique where the container is too large to take indoors. A double or triple layer of wrapping offers good protection from severe frosts.

Wind and its effect on your garden

Strong winds can have positive benefits, helping to disperse pollen and seeds. However, they can be a destructive force causing damage to plants, especially young ones that have yet to become established. They can also discourage beneficial insects that help to control pests. Although they have a cooling effect on plants, strong winds increase the rate at which water vapour is lost from plants' leaves (called desiccation), causing browning and leaf drop.

When woody plants are exposed to strong winds, their top-growth becomes unbalanced, making the plants appear one-sided. The tips of shoots and leaves are also at risk of being damaged, or scorched. The higher the wind speed, the more

Stream of air passing over barrier whips up turbulence beneath it

Air remains disturbed for distance of twice height of barrier

Effects may extend over entire garden

As wind hits fence, air is forced up, causing turbulence

damage is done, with stems being broken and, in severe cases, entire plants being uprooted.

Protect vulnerable plants with a windbreak. Choose a material that will allow about 50 per cent of the wind to pass through, because a solid

structure will create problems of its own (*see above*). Hedging plants are ideal, or choose open-weave fencing or special windbreak netting. For best protection, a windbreak should be 4m (12ft) tall, but a lower one would work well for smaller plants.

Action of wind In the same way that your washing dries more quickly on a blustery day, wind rushing over your plants causes rapid water loss from the leaves. Strong winds will rock any tall, unstaked plants until their roots become loosened in the soil, while greenhouses and other garden structures may be damaged. On light, sandy soil, there is a risk of the topsoil being blown away.

The effects of shade

Shady areas of the garden generally have dryish soil and plants have to cope with very low light levels. The ground under trees poses a real challenge to gardeners, because some types of tree and hedging plant, such as conifers and other evergreens, cast deep shadow and take lots of water and nutrients from the soil. The soil at the base of walls and fences can also be shady and dry. However, if the soil is enriched by digging in plenty of well-rotted manure or garden compost (*see p.377*), and any overhanging plants are judiciously pruned, a number of beautiful plants can be grown, for example *Cyclamen hederifolium* (*see p.221*). You may also have areas of cool,

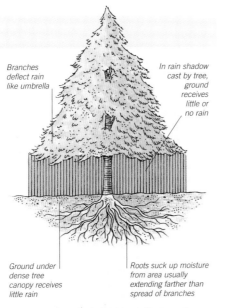

Branches deflect rain like umbrella

In rain shadow cast by tree, ground receives little or no rain

Ground under dense tree canopy receives little rain

Roots suck up moisture from area usually extending farther than spread of branches

moist, dappled shade – often under deciduous trees. In such conditions, there are plenty of woodland plants that will thrive.

Providing shelter

If you are planting on an exposed site, most young plants, especially evergreen shrubs and perennials, will require protection from strong winds and fierce sun until their root systems become established. If the garden does not enjoy the natural shelter of trees and hedging plants (*see above*), there are several temporary measures you can take.

Open-weave fencing or hurdles provide a suitable solution, as does planting fast-growing climbers to cover trellis panels. For an instant and economical fix, make a small windbreak using mesh and canes (*see right*). For best results, erect the shelter on the windward side of the plant or, if fierce sun is the problem, on the sunny side.

Temporary shelter Staple a length of fine mesh (available from garden centres) or hessian sacking to two long canes. Push the canes firmly into the ground around the plant. If the site is very windy, you may need to insert extra canes to stabilize the structure. Remove the shade or windbreak as soon as the plant becomes established.

buying plants

The old saying, "You get what you pay for", is never truer than when buying plants. Young plants do not have the resources to survive too many shocks and so it is essential they get a good start in life. Buying quality plants from a reputable nursery is always money well spent. You may be tempted by trays of knock-down bedding but they may have been on the shelf for ages, starved of food and water and so they will never grow as vigorously as good-quality stock.

When selecting a plant, look for one that is well-balanced, with plenty of healthy growth and, where appropriate, lots of flower buds. If the plant shows any signs of pests or disease, choose another one. Yellowing leaves may signify a lack of nutrients, a sign that the plant has not been looked after very well. Wilting leaves are caused by a lack of water; if the compost dries out too often the plant becomes stressed and vulnerable to pests and diseases. Gently knock the plant out of its pot and take a look at the root system. Do not buy it if the roots are tangled and crammed tight – it has become pot-bound (*see facing page*) and probably will not grow properly.

Bare-root plants

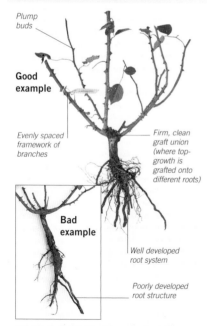

Plump buds

Good example

Evenly spaced framework of branches

Firm, clean graft union (where top-growth is grafted onto different roots)

Bad example

Well developed root system

Poorly developed root structure

Bareroot plants, like this rose, should have a good root system to support the plant. To encourage fibrous, feeding roots to form, trim the longest of the thick roots back hard.

Woody plants, including deciduous trees, shrubs, and roses, are often sold as bare-root plants. Grown in the ground rather than in pots, they are cheaper to produce in bulk and the nurseries can pass on their savings to their customers. The plants also tend to be bigger and stronger than similarly priced container plants. Bare-root plants are available in nurseries, but they are generally sold by mail order.

The plants are dug up in their dormant season, cleaned of soil, wrapped for posting and dispatched in time for planting in early winter. Unwrap them as soon as they arrive and plant without delay to prevent the roots drying out – they should then be well established before the spring. If the soil is frozen, store them for a few days wrapped in damp newspaper in a cool shed.

Container-grown plants

Most plants are now available in containers, from summer bedding in plastic strips to large shrubs and trees in pots. The big advantage to buying plants grown in this way is that the root system remains undisturbed during planting so that there is no check on growth. These advantages, however, come at a premium price.

Most hardy container-grown plants can be planted out at any time of year. The exception is tender summer bedding, which often goes on sale in early spring. If you cannot resist buying, grow the plants on under cover, and move them outdoors after the last frost, usually in late spring or early summer.

When choosing a container-grown plant beware of neglect – signs include algal growth on the compost, pests and disease, a stunted appearance, dry compost, and yellowing leaves. If you can, gently knock the plant out of its container and inspect the root system. If it looks pot-bound (*see facing page*), don't buy it.

Leaves look fresh with no signs of wilting

Sickly pot plant

Unbalanced growth

This busy Lizzie has yellowing leaves

Healthy, blemish-free, lush foliage (here, of pansies) with no long roots growing out of drainage holes

Healthy root system will ensure this holly gets off to good start

Healthy shrub Look for strong, bushy growth.

Healthy bedding has lots of flower buds.

Pot-bound plants

Pot-bound roots may be visible on surface of compost

Pot-bound root ball The tangled mass of roots indicates this plant has been in its pot for too long. Such severe constriction may inhibit the plant's ability to take up water and nutrients.

Before buying a plant, do not be shy about gently knocking it out of its pot to check the root system. If lots of roots are growing through the drainage holes, or you find a solid mass of roots growing round the outside of the root ball, then the plant is pot-bound. In this state, the plant's growth will have been severely stunted and it may never fully recover and thrive.

If you find you have purchased a pot-bound plant, then tease out the roots carefully and cut off some of the thicker sections. This will encourage new roots to venture out into the surrounding soil. Before planting it, soak the root ball in a bucket of water for a couple of hours and water the planting hole.

Water-garden plants

Always take care to introduce only healthy plants into a pond, otherwise the delicate ecosystem may be disturbed by pests or diseases carried in on the plants. Choose those with clean, green leaves and a good crown (the point where the leaves and roots meet) with several buds. If leaves are slimy or yellow, or if the water the plants are growing in is murky, then select another plant.

The best time to buy water-garden, or aquatic, plants is in late spring and early summer so that they have a chance to become established before winter sets in. Most aquatic plants tolerate being out of the water for only a short time. Take them home in a plastic bag and put them into the pond as soon as possible.

Leaves of this water hawthorn are lush, green, and float well

Stems are sturdy

New shoots

Basket is top-dressed with gravel to prevent loss of compost

Aquatic plants help to keep the pond healthy.

Root-balled plants

Netting stops roots drying out

Evergreens, like this conifer, are often sold root-balled

Root-balled plants are grown in open ground rather than in pots. They are lifted with a ball of roots and soil which is wrapped in net or hessian. Many shrubs and trees are sold in this way in spring and autumn by specialist nurseries, often by mail order. Check that the root ball feels firm and that the net is intact or the roots may dry out. Soak the netted root ball in water for an hour, then unwrap and plant it immediately.

Bulbous plants

Spring-flowering bulbs, corms, and tubers are sold in autumn, whereas summer-flowering cultivars will be available in spring. Always buy bulbs as soon as they go on sale, when they will be in prime condition (firm, plump, and blemish- and rot-free). The longer you delay, the more dried out they will become, and the plants will not perform as well. Inspect the bulbs and reject any that show signs of disease, such as soft patches.

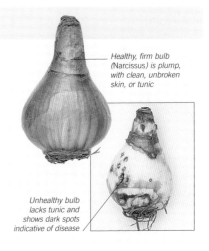

Healthy, firm bulb (Narcissus) is plump, with clean, unbroken skin, or tunic

Unhealthy bulb lacks tunic and shows dark spots indicative of disease

Mail-order plants

If buying plants by mail order, always deal with a reputable supplier, placing your order early to get the ones you want. The plants will be despatched in special packs, such as moulded, snap-shut containers, designed to keep them moist. As soon as the plants arrive, open the package and check the plants, making sure that they are healthy and the ones you ordered. Pot up the plants in potting compost and grow on for planting.

Plants are kept moist in sealed plastic bag

Healthy plants with no sign of pests and diseases, ready to grow on

soils and compost

Soils are made from minute particles of rock and organic matter that has been weathered and broken down over time. Fertile soil is essential for healthy plant growth and success in the garden. The soil supports the plant, supplying it with water, air, and nutrients. Not every type of soil is suitable for the widest range of plants, but almost any soil can be improved over the years, especially if good garden compost is worked into it on a regular basis.

Treat the soil well and you should be able to grow a wide range of plants successfully.

It is important to know what type of soil you have in your garden so that you can grow plants that thrive in it. It is relatively easy to determine your soil type (*see right*) and its pH (*see facing page*). The soil within the garden, however, can vary so you may have to choose different plants to suit each site.

To ensure that your plants get off to a good start, it is always a worthwhile investment to condition the soil (*see facing page*) before planting with plenty of well-rotted organic matter, such as home-made garden compost (*see p.378*) or commercial soil conditioners.

Types of garden soil

The soil type you have largely dictates the plants you can grow. Soils in different sites, or even in different parts of a garden, vary in terms of their fertility, ease of cultivation, and how easy it is for plant roots to penetrate. There are several basic kinds of garden soil.

Loam has an ideal balance of clay and sand particles. It is the perfect growing medium – rich in nutrients and with a friable, crumbly texture that allows good drainage and water-retention. Chalk soil is very free-draining and quick to lose moisture. It is reasonably fertile and contains a lot of lime so is very alkaline.

Clay soil is often very fertile, but slow-draining. Heavy clay soil can be difficult to work. If you open up its structure by digging in grit and organic matter, clay soil can support vigorous plant growth. Peat soil is acid and in winter can become waterlogged. It is high in organic matter and, if well-drained, provides good growing conditions. Add lime to grow more types of plants on it.

Sandy soil feels gritty and light, is easy to work, and warms up quickly in spring. Very free-draining, it dries out fast; nutrients can be washed out easily by rain and by watering, so it needs regular additions of organic matter and fertilizer.

Silty soil is neither gritty nor sticky, but silky to the touch. It can be badly drained, and when it is wet, packs down and becomes quite waterlogged. Improve it by adding plenty of well-rotted organic matter. Silty soil is also reasonably fertile.

Chalk soil is very pale, loose-textured (*see inset*), and full of chalk stones and flints. The topsoil is usually very shallow and has solid chalk rock beneath it.

Clay soil is heavy, cold, and sticky when wet. In dry conditions, it sets like concrete and then cracks. Clay has a very fine texture (*inset*) and rolls into a soft ball that is shiny if smoothed.

Peat soil is spongy and holds a lot of water. Its very dark colour shows it is rich in decomposed organic matter, parts of which are still visible (*see inset*).

What is soil pH?

Before buying any plants, check the pH of your soil to ensure that they will thrive in it. The pH reflects the level of lime in the soil. Soils lying over limestone or chalk are rich in lime and known as alkaline, but soils over sands become acid. Soil pH is measured on a scale of 1–14. Neutral soil, in which most plants thrive, has a pH of 7; soils of more than pH7 are alkaline (limy) while those of less than pH7 are acid (lime-free). Soil testing kits, which indicate pH by reacting with soil and changing colour (*see right*), are available from garden centres.

Soil pH affects the solubility of vital nutrients in the soil and their availability to plants. Acid and alkaline soils vary in the amounts of nutrients they contain. Plants like or tolerate different levels of lime, so some, such as azaleas and many ericas, thrive only on acid (called lime-free) soils and others, such as clematis and pinks, are happy in limy soils. The optimum soil pH for plant growth is within pH5.5–7.5.

pH scale and soil testing kits

Strongly alkaline soil: unsuitable for some ornamental plants, especially acid-lovers such as camellias and rhododendrons

Neutral pH

Slightly acidic soil: best for many ornamental plants

Strongly acid soil: unsuitable for most plants

8

7

6

5

4

Conditioning the soil

There are many soil-conditioning materials available from garden centres. The best are bulky organic materials, like manures, composted bark, or garden compost, which improve the soil structure so that it drains freely but retains moisture in dry weather. Manures and compost also replace some of the nutrients taken up by plants or washed out of the soil. Organic matter must be well-rotted; if not, it will deplete the soil of nutrients as it rots.

The more organic matter you add to the soil, the more organisms such as bacteria and worms will populate the soil, help to work it, and improve its structure.

Well-rotted horse manure is one of the best soil conditioners, but can be hard to obtain. Making garden compost is easy and costs nothing (*see p.378*). Spent mushroom compost contains rotted manure and peat. It also has some lime, so do not use it where acid-loving plants are grown. Seaweed is an excellent conditioner because it makes the soil more friable and is rich in trace elements. Composted straw and leafmould use otherwise wasted resources, but they take two years to rot. Pelleted chicken manure adds vital nutrients, but has no conditioning value since the pellets have little bulk.

Incorporating manure or other well-rotted organic matter into the soil is most effectively done by digging it in during autumn. Scatter a thick layer all over the bed and fork it in (*see right*). Alternatively, leave it as a surface mulch. This will help to protect the roots of vulnerable plants over winter, and in the course of the year, the material will be incorporated into the soil by worms and other beneficial soil organisms.

The importance of good soil drainage

The amount of water available to plants through their roots depends on the type of soil (*see facing page*) and how free-draining it is. In well-structured soils, like loam, sufficient water and air is held in the spaces, or pores, between the soil particles to supply most plants adequately. A soil with poor structure may dry out very quickly or become waterlogged.

For example, finely textured clay soils hold most moisture, but it is

bound up in such a way that it is unavailable to plants. The large pores of sandy soils make water easily available to plant roots, but it drains away quickly. Peat soils can become waterlogged and compacted silt and clay soils often are poorly drained.

Digging in well-rotted organic matter (*see above, right*) will improve the structure of both clay and sandy soils. Drainage can also be improved by adding gravel (*see right*).

Improving soil drainage with gravel
You can greatly improve the drainage of heavy clay and silty soils by incorporating coarse grit or gravel into the soil. Digging in the gravel will open up the structure and facilitate the flow of water through the soil. Spread a good 5–8cm (2–3in) layer over the area and dig it in with a fork. Any smaller amount will be ineffective. The gravel should make an instant and permanent improvement to the soil aeration and drainage, making it easier for plant roots to penetrate and extract the moisture and nutrients that they need.

Making garden compost

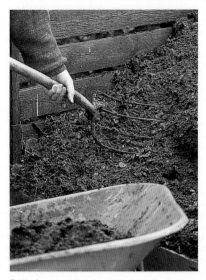

Rotted compost is dark, friable, and odourless.

Even in the smallest garden, it is worth making your own compost – it enables you to recycle waste and return it to the garden in a form which is unsurpassed for improving soil structure and fertility. It also saves you the expense of buying proprietory soil conditioners.

To make good garden compost, you first need a suitable container.

There are many compost bins on the market, but you can make one easily at home, for example from builders' pallets or old wood. The main thing to bear in mind is that the bin should be 1–1.5m (3–5ft) square, with fairly solid sides to retain heat and moisture. It should also have a cover; a piece of old carpet will do.

The best compost is made from mixing fast-rotting, succulent material, such as grass clippings and vegetable trimmings, with drier material, such as straw and shredded newspaper, which is slower to decompose. Try to add materials in well-mixed layers.

Compost takes about a year to rot down, but the process can be speeded up if the heap is turned at least once to mix the contents thoroughly. The easiest way to do this, if space allows, is to have two bins, so you can turn the contents of one bin into the other. If the compost is slimy and smelly, mix in more "dry" material; if it is dry and not rotting, add sappy stuff.

Garden compost ingredients

Almost any materials of organic origin can be recycled into compost. You can add any plant waste from the garden into the heap, except perennial weeds. Seedheads must be removed because seeds will survive and cause problems in future; any diseased material should be burned or binned. Shred woody prunings, thick, fibrous stems, newspapers, cardboard, and old clothing. Vegetable kitchen waste can also be used, but meat, fish, and cooked foods will attract vermin. Litter from small pets such as rabbits, guinea pigs, or birds is suitable, but not from cats and dogs. You can also add manure and autumn leaves.

Grass clippings need to be mixed with coarser material like straw or paper.

Woody prunings are slow to rot and must first be shredded into small pieces.

Annual weeds with the seedheads removed are usable, as well as dandelion leaves.

Kitchen waste of vegetable material only – to avoid attracting vermin.

Natural fibres, such as 100 per cent wool or cotton, rot quickly if cut into small pieces.

Woollen carpet must be cut into pieces and mixed with green stuff to break it down.

Feathers rot better if they are taken out of the pillow and mixed with other waste.

Newspapers, torn into strips, are good for mixing with soft grass clippings.

How to make leafmould

Autumn leaves rot slowly and if you have large quantities, you can compost them separately in an open bin made from a timber frame and wire netting (*see right*) or in sealed plastic sacks with a few holes punched in them. The resulting leafmould takes about two years to form. It is very crumbly and makes an excellent mulch (*see p.388*) and soil conditioner.

Leafmould bin is open to the elements.

Using a worm bin

Worms feed on organic matter and eject the waste in the form of worm casts. This process can create a fine, crumbly, nutrient-rich compost that can be used in potting mixes and as a top-dressing or plant feed.

You can buy a kit complete with worms, or make your own wormery from a dustbin. Drill drainage holes in the base and stand the bin on some bricks. Put a 15cm (6in) layer of garden soil in the bottom and add a large potful of worms; brandlings – thin, red worms – are best. Top with a small layer of garden or kitchen waste, allowing the worms to digest each layer before adding more. Worms don't like citrus fruits or onions, but do like lime, such as crushed egg shells. When the bin is full, sieve out the worms and start again.

planting basics

Give your plants a good start in life and there is every chance that they will grow strong and healthy. The first and most important step is to create a welcoming environment for their roots, encouraging them to spread out into the surrounding soil where they will take up water and nutrients.

Good planting practice results in healthy plants.

All plants appreciate being planted in a suitable and well-prepared site. Generally, the better the soil, the quicker they will become established. It is best to choose plants that are suited to the conditions you can offer. For example, if the soil in your garden is very light and dries out quickly, you can do much to improve its condition by enriching it with well-rotted organic matter, such as farmyard manure or garden compost (*see p.377*). However, if you then opt for plants that require rich, moist soil, they will struggle and flower indifferently. You will have far better results with plants that need free-drainage and tolerate dry conditions.

Before starting to plant, clear the plot of any weeds that could compete with your plants for water and nutrients.

Take care to ensure that each plant has room to grow to its full size. Check the mature height and spread on the care label and mark it out around each planting hole. You can fill the gaps with bedding plants until they mature. If a plant outgrows its space, transplant it in autumn or spring: dig it up, saving as much of the root mass as possible, and replant it in a previously prepared site.

Plants always look more natural in a border when grouped in odd numbers because the brain automatically sorts even numbers into pairs.

Many trees and shrubs are planted in the same way as those grown in containers (*see right*), but bare-root and root-balled plants (*see pp.374–375*) require slightly different treatment.

Plant bare-root plants in early winter so they can establish before summer. Even with careful handling, they may suffer some root damage. To encourage new growth, cut damaged or dry roots back hard; to compensate for the loss of roots, trim the top-growth back hard.

Root-balled plants are best planted in autumn or spring. After soaking the root ball, remove the netting and tease out the roots. Both root-balled and bare-root plants should be planted with the old soil mark level with the surface.

Planting container-grown trees and shrubs

Container-grown plants can be planted (*see below*) at any time, so long as the soil is not waterlogged or frozen, but the best results are from autumn or spring planting. If you plant in summer you must keep the roots watered while the plant establishes itself. Before planting, prune out any dead or diseased growth and awkwardly placed shoots. Scrape away the top layer of compost from the pot to remove any weed seeds, then stand it in its pot in a bucket of water for two hours to soak the root ball thoroughly.

Dig a good-sized planting hole. Fill the hole with water and allow it to seep away. Next, fork a thick layer of well-rotted farmyard manure or garden compost into the bottom of the hole to give the plant a good start. Shrubs also appreciate some slow-release fertilizer. If the soil gets very wet in winter, improve the drainage by forking in coarse grit. Gently knock off the pot and place the plant in the prepared hole.

Planting at the correct depth is crucial to avoid a check in growth. With a few exceptions – such as some clematis (*see pp.136–139*) which like to be planted deep – you should keep the plant at the same depth as it was in its container.

It also helps to enrich the removed soil by mixing it with well-rotted organic matter. If the plant needs support, insert canes or stakes, taking care not to damage the root ball, and tie in the main stem. ,

How to plant a container-grown tree or shrub
❶ *Soak the plant's root ball in a bucket of water for 1–2 hours before planting. Dig a hole that is at least twice as wide and one-and-a-half times deeper than the root ball. Fork in plenty of well-rotted organic matter and, if it is needed for improved drainage, some coarse grit.*
❷ *Set the plant at the same depth as it was in its original pot. Use a cane to check that the root ball is level with the soil surface.*
❸ *Fill in the hole with soil. Use your heel to firm the soil around the plant to remove air pockets.*
❹ *Water the plant well to settle the soil, even if it is raining. Apply a 5cm (2in) layer of well-rotted compost or bark as a mulch over the root area to help retain moisture and suppress weeds.*

Planting non-woody plants

The principles of planting are much the same for perennials, annuals, and other bedding plants as for shrubs (*see p.379*). However, these plants are more prone to drying out, so should be planted without delay. Some plants are sold in pots (*see below*), but bedding plants are usually sold in modular trays, with one seedling per module to stop the roots being disturbed during planting. As soon as you buy bedding plants, give them a good soaking and plant them or, if there is still a risk of frost, pot them up separately to grow on under cover until it is safe to plant them out.

Planting a perennial
❶ *Dig a planting hole and loosen the soil around the edges. Mix some well-rotted organic matter or general fertilizer into the removed soil. Gently knock out the plant while holding the crown in one hand.*
❷ *Tease out the roots and hold the root ball level with the surface. Fill in the hole, and firm with your fingers. Water well and mulch; keep watered until plant is established.*

Planting climbers

The soil at the base of a wall or fence can be extremely dry because it is in a rain shadow, where rain rarely reaches the soil. When planting a climber, you should first improve the soil's moisture-retention by digging in plenty of well-rotted organic matter (such as garden compost). Follow the technique for planting a container-grown shrub (*see p.379*), but make sure that the planting hole is at least 30–45cm (12–18in) away from the wall. Also don't forget to angle the top of the root ball towards the wall, while keeping the crown of the plant level with the soil surface.

Before planting, fix up a support. The easiest system is horizontal wires threaded through galvanized vine eyes in the wall, or trellis panels (*see p.390*) attached to battens.

Training a climber Once the climber has been planted, separate out the shoots and tie them into the supports, using garden twine. Canes pushed into the ground and angled towards the wall will encourage the shoots to grow towards it.

Planting bulbs

There are a couple of important points to remember when planting bulbs. Firstly, most should be planted at a depth equivalent to three times their size. For example, if a bulb stands 5cm (2in) tall, then there should be 10cm (4in) of soil on top of it, and the planting hole should therefore be 15cm (6in) deep. Check the care label because some bulbs, such as nerines and some lilies, prefer to have their tops level with the soil surface.

If bulbs are planted at the wrong depth, they may fail to flower (a condition referred to as "blindness"). Blindness can also occur when the bulbs become crowded; lifting and replanting bulbs every three to four years should prevent this problem.

The second point to bear in mind is to check that the bulb is the right way up. This is easily done with true bulbs, like narcissi, but on corms and tubers the buds are not always very distinct.

The most natural way to grow bulbs is in large drifts in grass. There are two ways to do this – but first, cut the grass as short as possible, leaving it uncut until the bulb foliage dies down in early summer.

Using a bulb planter This tool takes out a neat plug of soil just big enough for one bulb. Push it vertically into the ground, giving it a firm twist before lifting out the plug of soil. If the planter doesn't have depth markings on its side, use a ruler to measure the hole. If it is too deep, top up the level with soil, compost or grit.

With large bulbs, such as daffodils, scatter them over the chosen area. Check they are all at least 10cm (4in) apart, then plant each bulb where it fell. Use a bulb planter (*see above*) or trowel to dig a hole, insert the bulb, and replace the soil.

To plant a large number of small bulbs, such as crocuses, make an "H"-shaped cut in the lawn using a half-moon edger or spade. Turn back the turf flaps. Take out the soil to the correct depth if necessary; plant the bulbs about 2.5cm (1in) apart; then fold back and firm the turf.

Planting depths The correct planting depth for each type of bulb depends on its size. As a rough guide, plant each bulb at a depth equal to three times the bulb's height. In light soils, bulbs should be planted slightly deeper.

Bulb is planted at three times its height

Wet conditions In soil with poor drainage, it is a good idea to fork grit into the surrounding soil and also to sit each bulb on a thick bed of grit. This will help to prevent the bulb from rotting.

Dry conditions Light soils dry out very quickly, especially in hot conditions. To stop the roots of bulbs drying out, sit each one on a layer of well-rotted organic matter such as garden compost.

Preparing containers

Most plants grow happily in containers but they will demand more attention than if they had been planted in the garden.

Terracotta pots are very attractive but, once planted up, they can be heavy to move around. They are also porous and dry out more quickly than metal or plastic ones. You will need to line the base with broken crocks to stop the drainage hole becoming blocked up with compost. Plastic containers may not look as elegant, but they are cheap, light, and good at retaining moisture. They also don't need crocks because they usually have several drainage holes.

Choose a loam-based compost, which holds water better than a soilless one, for containers. Mix water-retaining granules and slow-release fertilizer into it to cut down on watering and feeding later.

Break polystyrene plant trays into pieces and use to line pot

Large containers can be heavy. If they are to be planted with shallow-rooted plants, fill the excess depth with polystyrene pieces, then top up with compost. Take care the pot does not become top-heavy and unstable. Pots planted with deep-rooted plants are most easily and safely moved using a specially designed trolley.

Planting a hanging basket

A hanging basket packed full with colourful plants is a spectacular sight, yet it is not that difficult to achieve. There are many types of basket but the most popular ones are made of wire mesh. These need lining to hold the compost in place. Sphagnum moss should be conserved, so is no longer recommended, but there are now plenty of modern alternatives, including liners made from coconut fibre, plastic, or wool.

The number of plants you will need to plant up a basket depends on its size, but you can pack them in quite tightly. The plants and compost will be very heavy, especially when watered, so it is best to use a lighter, soilless compost. Don't forget to add a slow-release fertilizer to avoid

Planting a basket
❶ *Steady the basket by standing it on an upturned pot. Insert the liner and place a saucer or piece of plastic in the base. Cover with compost. Cut slits in the sides and push through trailing plants from the outside, holding them by their roots. Fill with compost.*
❷ *Plant tall plants in the centre and more trailing plants around the edge. Fill any gaps with compost. Firm and water.*

having to feed the basket. You can also improve moisture retention by mixing in water-retaining granules.

The baskets should be planted thickly so that the plants will grow to conceal the sides. Work from the base of the basket upwards, cutting slit holes in the liner and feeding the plant roots through. Protect the foliage of the plants by rolling them in a tube of paper first.

Plant baskets of summer bedding in mid-spring, and keep under cover until after the last frost. Baskets of hardier perennials, planted in spring or autumn, can go straight outdoors.

Planting water-garden plants

Late spring or early summer are the best planting times. The majority of aquatic plants benefit from being planted in a basket. There are many different planting baskets to choose from – the most common ones are made of plastic mesh and require lining with a piece of hessian to contain the soil. The mesh allows water to penetrate to the roots, while helping to contain the growth of more rampant plants.

Aquatic plants are generally easy to grow. There is available special low-nitrogen aquatic compost (too much nitrogen in water causes green algae to grow), but ordinary garden soil works just as well if no fertilizer has been added to it.

Correct planting depth is vital: marginal plants need shallow water, while deep-water aquatics, such as water lilies, need deep water to thrive. Always check the care label.

Marginal plants, like this iris, need shallow water

Deep-water aquatics, like this water lily, sit on pond floor

Correct planting depth is vital to plant survival.

Planting in an aquatic basket
Line the basket with hessian so the soil does not escape. Partly fill the basket with soil. Sit the plant (here a water lily) so its crown is level with the top of the basket. Fill in soil around the roots and firm. Top-dress with a thin layer of gravel, so the growing points are exposed, to hold the soil in place. Soak the compost well before setting the basket in shallow water. Move into deeper water as the stems grow.

pruning

If you grow woody plants, sooner or later you will have to prune them to keep them looking good. Pruning is often regarded with dread by gardeners, but it really is just a matter of common sense and learning a few fundamental rules. Also, good-quality tools make the job easier.

Pruning encourages new, strong growth and increases the number of flowers, maintains a well-balanced shape, and keeps a plant to the desired size. The methods vary depending on the type of plant. It is most important in a plant's early years because early pruning affects the shape of the established plant. However, renovation pruning (*see p.384*) can also breathe new life into an old plant. By pruning out dead and diseased growth, you can also improve the health of an ailing plant.

It may seem contrary, but by cutting back a plant you encourage it to grow bigger and stronger, because it reacts by sending out new shoots from below the cuts. You can also persuade a plant

to grow in a particular direction and regulate the quantity and vigour of that growth. Conifers do not need much pruning, except when grown as hedging (*see p.384*) or topiary.

When pruning, make a clean cut just above a bud or leaf joint (*see below*). The cut should not be too close or you may cause the bud to die, but if you cut too wide, the stub will die back and may become diseased.

Before you start pruning, take a good look at the plant. Give some thought to the cuts you are about to make. If you rush in with the secateurs, you could end up with a badly shaped plant or lose a season of flowering because you have cut out the wrong stems.

Basic tools for pruning

If you invest in a few good-quality pruning tools, it will make your job much easier. Using good cutting tools will also ensure that the pruning cuts are clean and heal quickly without becoming vulnerable to disease. For most pruning tasks, you need only a pair of secateurs, a pruning saw, and

perhaps some loppers. Use a tool suited to the stem size – if you try to cut a large stem with secateurs, you will damage it and make a blunt cut. Keep blades clean and sharp: blunt blades tear rather than cut, allowing disease to take hold.

Loppers, like long-handled secateurs, give extra leverage and cut branches up to 2.5cm (1in) in diameter. They also enable you to reach high-up branches.

Secateurs are the most commonly used pruning tool. They will cut all shoots up to 1cm (½in) in diameter. Always cut with the thin blade towards the bud or joint to enable you to cut closer: the cut will be cleaner and will heal more quickly.

Folding pruning saws are single-toothed. They cut quite large branches, are easy to use in awkward spaces, and fold up for safe storage.

Basic principles of pruning

Single bud Make your cut at a 45° angle, 5mm (¼in) above the bud so any moisture runs off.

Remove dead wood to stop disease spreading. Cut back to a strong bud or healthy, new shoot.

Cut straight across stem with thin blade towards buds

Take care not to cut into tips of buds

Opposite buds Cut straight across the stem as close as possible to the tips of the buds.

Prune above outward-facing bud for new growth away from heart of plant

No matter what type of plant you are pruning, certain basic principles apply. Fast-growing plants that put on more than 30cm (12in) growth in a year respond well to hard pruning. Slow-growing plants usually do not respond well to being pruned back hard, so avoid it unless absolutely necessary.

When pruning dead or diseased wood, wipe the blades between cuts with a proprietory disinfectant to avoid spreading spores or infection to the next plant that you prune.

Crossing stems rub together causing chafing damage to bark, creating a wound where disease can enter. Overcrowded stems are weak, block out light, and trap damp air which encourages disease. Thinning out such stems restores a plant's vigour.

After hard pruning, always give the plant a good feed and mulch, and water it if necessary. Inspect your plants regularly and take out any broken or damaged stems without delay to minimize the risk of disease.

Pruning a spring-flowering plant

Spring- or early flowering plants are best pruned after they flower and before they start to put on new growth. This is because their flowers develop from buds growing on the previous year's stems. If pruning is left too late in the season, you might remove next year's flowering shoots.

Start by thinning out any old, damaged, and diseased wood. Then cut some older stems right back to the ground. Next, cut shoots with buds back to five or six buds, even if they have started to put on new growth at the tips. The following year's flowering shoots will develop from these buds.

Many spring-flowering shrubs can be trained flat against a wall. On planting, tie in all the main stems and sideshoots into a support. Cut back any shoots that cannot be tied in to one or two buds and pinch out the tips of forward-facing shoots so that they branch sideways. Shorten the longest sideshoots, especially where growth is sparse. In later years, after flowering, tie in new growth and

cut back badly placed or overly long shoots. Take out any diseased or dead wood; check ties are not too tight. Cut back the flowered shoots to 5–6 buds; some shrubs, such as flowering quinces (*Chaenomeles, see p.38*) and pyracanthas (*see p.102*), are pruned to 2–3 buds for prolific flowering.

Unpruned sideshoots flower sparsely

Sideshoots pruned to 2–3 buds produce more flowers

Results of pruning Unpruned stems (*see left*) of flowering quince produce few flowers; pruning stimulates profuse flowering (*see right*).

Pruning a late-summer flowering plant

In the first spring, aim to form a base of strong, woody stems from which spring-flowering shoots will grow each year. Cut out any weak or diseased stems and shorten the remainder to 15–45cm (6–18in), or if a large plant is required to 1.2m (4ft). Prune in subsequent early springs before growth starts. Restore the original framework by pruning all the old flowering stems to leave two or three pairs of fat, healthy buds from the previous year's growth. At the same time, if it is necessary, thin out dense congested stems.

Previous year's shoots (here of Buddleja davidii)

Thin out old, congested stems and badly positioned growth by cutting them to base

Cut back remaining stems to within 2–3 pairs of healthy buds

Late-summer flowering plants produce flowers on growth made in the current growing season. Early spring is the best time to prune them, because it diverts each plant's energy to existing buds rather than to developing more, and gives it sufficient time to produce new flowering shoots from the buds.

Hard annual pruning suits many deciduous shrubs and climbers, such as caryopteris, ceanothus, *Hydrangea*

paniculata, and phygelius – as well as many grey-leaved evergreens, for example lavenders. It produces the best-quality flowers and prevents the plant from becoming too big. Old or neglected late-summer flowering shrubs respond well to hard pruning.

On windy sites, shorten tall growth by about one half in autumn to prevent the winds from rocking the plant and loosening the roots.

Pruning an early summer-flowering plant

Early summer-flowering shrubs, for example philadelphus (*see p.93*) and weigelas (*see p.128*), and climbing plants are generally pruned in late summer, immediately after flowering has finished. You should aim to open up the plant to allow light and air to reach the centre while retaining an uncluttered, balanced shape.

In the first year after planting, remove all weak and crossing shoots by cutting each out just above an

outward-facing bud or at the base. Trim back any overlong shoots to within the overall outline, again cutting each to an outward-facing bud.

In subsequent years, thin out the plant by removing about one in four of the oldest stems, cutting them back to the ground. This makes room for new stems to grow from the base. Shorten younger stems to encourage flowering sideshoots. Wayward stems should be pruned back to maintain a good shape.

Pruning a mature shrub after flowering
Using loppers, cut out one in four of the old stems (here of philadelphus) just above the base. Take care to leave a few strong buds on each. Shorten any younger shoots by a quarter to one-third. This will open up the shrub and encourage new, vigorous growth to flower next year. Any dead, damaged, diseased, or crossing shoots on the remaining stems should be pruned out at the same time.

Renovation pruning

When trees, shrubs, and climbers become overgrown or neglected, their growth weakens and flowering declines. Provided that the plants are basically healthy, renovation pruning can give them a new lease of life, spurring strong growth and flower production. Many deciduous plants, like willows (*Salix*), lilacs (*Syringa*), and buddlejas, respond well to renovation pruning.

The best time is in late winter or spring because the plants have a chance to put on new growth before the next winter. Many plants, though, tolerate drastic pruning at their usual pruning time, for example early summer-flowering philadelphus can be tackled in late summer after flowering.

The stems of some shrubs, like berberis, become so tangled that they need cutting right back to ground level. Less vigorous woody plants, particularly evergreens such as rhododendrons, must be cut back in stages over 2–3 years, to give them a chance to recover.

Unfortunately, not all old shrubs survive such drastic pruning, so be prepared for some losses.

Lilac (Syringa)

Pull any suckers away from plant below soil level

Remove heavy top-growth before pruning main stems to prevent tearing

Prune all main stems to 30–60cm (12–24in)

Drastic renovation involves pruning all growth.

Rhododendron

Each year, prune half of remaining old stems that have not yet been pruned, cutting them to ground level

Thin out new growth arising from last year's cuts to 2–3 strong stems

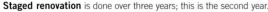

Staged renovation is done over three years; this is the second year.

Pruning hedges

Regular trimming not only keeps a hedge looking neat, it also promotes strong, dense growth and longevity. Trim established evergreen hedges, for example privet and fast-growing conifers, in late spring or early summer and again in late summer or in early autumn, while they are in growth. Deciduous hedges, such as beech and hawthorn, are best trimmed in summer. A second tidy up can be given in autumn. Time pruning of flowering hedges to suit their flowering periods (*see p.383*).

It is especially important to prune evergreen and coniferous hedges regularly, because very few will reshoot from old wood. When training an evergreen or conifer hedge, keep the sides trimmed, but allow the main stem to reach the desired height before pruning it.

Aim to create a hedge that is wider at the base than at the top. It is less vulnerable to damage from snow and strong winds, and light can reach the lower branches.

As with shears, keep the blade parallel to the hedge for an even cut. Always wear eye and ear protectors and gloves. Sweep the blade away from your body and the cable.

Keeping a climbing plant within bounds

Many climbers, such as *Clematis montana* and rambling roses, make a lot of growth in one season. Prune spring-flowering climbers after flowering; summer-flowering plants in spring. Remove overlong shoots and unhealthy growth. However, do not over-prune them because it will encourage leafy growth rather than flowering shoots. You can thin out congested climbers (*see below*), but only once every three years or so.

Prune crowded shoots by cutting back to pair of healthy buds or to base of stems

Trim overlong stems to healthy buds

Cut damaged or weak stems to 2 buds or to base

Pruning a congested climber

routine tasks

A little time spent regularly on maintenance, such as feeding, watering, weeding, mulching, and deadheading, will keep your plants in top condition so that they perform at their best. Enjoy the chance these simple tasks give you to enjoy your garden, and take in all its scents and colours.

Mulching a raised bed keeps down the weeds and keeps the soil moist for the plants (here azaleas).

Any job in the garden is easier if you use the correct tools. Essentials include a spade, a fork, a hand trowel and hand fork, and a hoe and short-tined rake for soil cultivation and weeding. Secateurs are needed to deadhead and prune plants and if you have trees, shrubs, or woody climbers, loppers and a pruning saw are useful. If you have a lawn, a good lawnmower and a long-tined lawn rake will help you to keep it looking good. Add to those a watering can and a wheelbarrow and you can undertake most routine tasks in the garden. Always buy the best-quality tools you can afford since cheap ones may last only one or two seasons.

Routine tasks can be minimized by making sure that plants are growing in a position with a soil and conditions that suit them (*see Climate and location, pp.371–373, and Soils and compost, pp.376–378*). If you grow a plant in an unsuitable site, it is unlikely to flourish and will need much more attention. It is also essential that plants have space to grow to maturity; you may be tempted to cram them in for immediate effect, but this will make them weak and more prone to attack from pests and diseases.

Above all, it is more effective and easier to care for your plants by doing a little quite often, rather than leaving tasks until the garden becomes neglected.

What to do when

Spring
- Cut back any old growth left over winter and clear away insulation
- Begin mowing lawns, with cutting blade set at maximum height, as grass begins to grow; tidy up edges
- Feed and mulch all woody and herbaceous perennial plants as soon as soil starts to warm up
- Repot or top-dress plants grown in containers
- After they flower, prune spring-flowering deciduous shrubs and climbers; also prune late-flowering shrubs and climbers, all bush roses (*see p.110*), and groups 2 and 3 clematis (*see p.136*)
- Prune or trim evergreens if needed
- Divide clump-forming perennials, bamboos, and grasses
- Plant new plants and autumn-flowering bulbs, and sow seed
- Provide support now for perennials and biennials that will need it when fully grown
- In late spring, start to bring container-grown plants that have been overwintered under cover out into the garden
- Keep young and newly planted varieties watered regularly
- Keep on top of routine tasks such as deadheading, and weeding; start to feed plants in containers
- Layer shrubs and climbers
- Plant, thin, and divide oxygenating plants in ponds

Summer
- Mow lawns regularly
- Clip hedges

- After they flower, finish pruning spring-flowering deciduous shrubs and climbers and group 1 clematis (*see p.136*)
- Continue routine tasks such as feeding, deadheading, and weeding
- Prune *Prunus* trees and shrubs in midsummer to avoid infection by silver leaf and other diseases
- Take soft and semi-ripe cuttings
- In late summer, prune early summer-flowering deciduous shrubs and climbers

Autumn
- Keep up with routine tasks such as weeding and deadheading; stop feeding plants
- Prune flowering hedges and rambling roses after flowering
- Clear dying growth of perennials and grasses, but leave it in cold regions to act as winter insulation
- Lift tender rootstocks, such as dahlias, and store over winter
- Mow lawns at maximum height
- Move tender plants under cover
- Plant hardy trees, shrubs, climbers, perennials, and spring-flowering bulbs; sow seed of hardy plants
- Take hardwood cuttings
- Clear out any leaves and dead material from ponds

Winter
- Plant hardy trees, shrubs, hedges, climbers, and perennials
- Brush snow from conifers
- Plan what seeds and plants you wish to order for next year
- Take root cuttings

feeding

Using fertilizers

Plants need nutrients to encourage strong, healthy growth and plentiful flowers. Whether you use organic or non-organic fertilizers is down to personal choice. Organic feeds tend to release nutrients over a longer period; chemicals give a fast, but short-lived, boost to growth. Both are available as granules, powders, or liquids. Powdered or granular feeds, such as poultry pellets, can be scattered over the entire planting area or around individual plants. Dry fertilizers, such as bonemeal, have to be watered into the soil, because plants can absorb nutrients only once they are dissolved in water. Liquid feeds are quick-acting and easy to apply, using a special hose-end applicator or watering can.

Apply fertilizers from mid-spring to midsummer, when the plants are growing rapidly and will benefit from extra nutrients. Take care when applying a concentrated fertilizer because it may scorch the stems and foliage. Always take heed of the manufacturer's instructions, and avoid the temptation to overfeed the plants; it is wasteful and results in weak, sappy growth and fewer flowers.

Fertilizer pellets
These slow-release pellets are useful for containers.

Forking in fertilizer
Fertilizer granules should be worked into the soil surface around the plant, taking care not to fork too deeply and damage the roots. Unless heavy rain is expected, water the area well to release the nutrients into the soil.

Foliar feeding
Liquid feed can be sprayed onto plants as a fast, effective pick-me-up if they are not doing well. Most is absorbed through the leaves, and any excess is taken up by the roots. To avoid scorch, apply in the evening or on dull days.

Applying a top-dressing

Compost in containers becomes less fertile over time as its nutrients are taken up and used by the plant, and leached out by rain and watering. If the plant has not outgrown the pot and become root-bound, you can apply an annual top-dressing at the beginning of the growing season to replenish the nutrients. Remove the top layer of old soil, and replace it with fresh compost (*see right*).

Alternatively, for shrubs and trees, you could use garden compost or composted bark. A mulch (*see p.388*) of bark chips or gravel will conserve moisture and give a decorative finish.

Rock-garden plants, especially alpine species, like very well-drained soil; a top-dressing of gravel, pebbles, pea shingle, or even glass chips, avoids water puddling around the plants and causing rot. Top-dressing will mix in with the soil or get washed away, so in spring, scrape it off, fertilize the soil, and top with a fresh layer of grit.

Top-dressing a container
Carefully remove the top 5–8cm (2–3in) of old soil, taking care not to go too deep and damage the roots (*see inset*). Then fill the container back up to the original level, using fresh compost of the same type mixed with slow-release fertilizer. Finally, water it in well.

Gently scrape soil away using trowel

watering

Why water?

Watering is essential for healthy, growing plants. Moisture is taken up from the soil and used by the plant to make and transport vital nutrients for survival. Water keeps every plant cell turgid, so the first visible sign of thirst is the wilting of leaves and stems.

Dry conditions can cause a check in growth and leave plants more vulnerable to attack by diseases or pests. Although you should expect some watering to be necessary after planting and during very hot spells, it can be reduced by choosing plants that tolerate such conditions.

Drought-tolerant plants, such as lavender and stachys, naturally prefer a well-drained, or sunny area. Their leaves are often small and silvery or are protected by a hairy or waxy layer. Thirsty plants usually have large, thin leaves, for example trollius or primulas, and thrive in damp, sheltered spots.

To reduce water loss from the soil surface, apply a mulch (*see p.388*); avoid leaving large areas unplanted; and if needed provide a windbreak. Wind draws moisture from leaves in the same way as it dries your washing.

Although drought is damaging, waterlogging is also harmful. The soil becomes saturated so plant roots cannot breathe and begin to rot. It occurs after very wet periods, or on heavy soils with poor drainage. Plant moisture-loving plants in these situations.

When to water

How often you need to water will depend on the local conditions. Frequent rain should supply enough moisture, but in dry spells you may have to water beds, lawns, and containers daily. Some plants require moist soil and will quickly die if the ground starts to dry out, but others will be able to cope once they become established. New plantings are also at risk from drought until they form a strong root system.

Try basin watering (*see right*) to direct water to the roots. Another option is pot watering: sink a deep pot into the soil next to a plant; fill it with water and allow it to drain into the soil. Seedlings especially need constant attention – too much water and they will rot off, too little and they will quickly die.

In summer, water in the evening or early morning. The heat of the day increases evaporation so your efforts will be wasted and water droplets act like lenses to scorch the foliage.

Basin watering Plant slightly lower than the soil surface to create a hollow, or surround the plant with a raised dam of soil. Water into this basin so that all the water is directed straight to the roots, saving time and conserving water.

Watering cans

Every gardener needs a watering can for small areas of the garden and for containers. When buying one, go for the best you can afford because you will find yourself using it often.

Choose a watering can that is well balanced, and not too heavy for you to lift when it is full. Other useful features include an opening large enough to make it easy to fill by a tap or hose, and a strainer at the bottom of the spout so that it does not become clogged by debris. A long spout is useful for reaching to the back of the border.

Most watering cans are fitted with a removable rose. A fine rose is perfect for delicate plants (*see left*). A coarse rose will give a spray that is better for watering larger, more established plantings quickly. Keep a separate watering can for pesticides or weedkillers to avoid cross-contamination; buy a plastic one because some chemicals can corrode metal.

Watering seedlings Seedlings require only a gentle shower since their tiny roots are easily dislodged. Attach a fine, metal rose to your can so that it points upwards. Start watering to the side of the tray to establish an even spray, then pass it smoothly over the seedlings.

Hoses and sprinklers

Watering can be a time-consuming task, so consider investing in a hose that will carry water to where it is needed, without having to fill and refill a watering can. Reinforced hoses are less likely to kink than the cheaper, flat ones. Hoses that neatly wind onto their own reels are easy to store. All should be fitted with a nozzle that can adjust the flow of water from a stream to a fine spray, so you can water appropriately (*see right*). Other useful attachments, such as fertilizer applicators, are available.

Some types of hose are laid around the garden as a permanent irrigation system controlled by a tap or a timer. Seep hoses let water ooze out along their entire length; drip hoses deliver water through holes to individual plants in beds or containers. Both types are good for newly planted areas but are unsightly, so it is best to disguise them (*see below*). Sprinklers can be used for large areas. Their fine sprays soak the soil evenly, but they are wasteful, and have to be moved often to stop puddles forming.

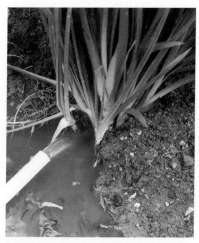

Using a hose Watering plants with a hose requires some care. A strong stream of water can erode soil from around the plant roots, leaving them exposed and prone to dry out (*see above*). Alternatively, if the ground is hard, it may not penetrate the soil at all and run over the surface away from where it is needed. Always use a spray nozzle on the hose, unless you are watering into a pot placed as a reservoir by the plant.

Installing a seep hose
❶ To lay a seep hose, wind it in loops around the plants in your border, allowing for it to moisten the soil for a distance of about 20cm (17in) on each side of the hose. If you find the hose will not lie flat, peg it down at intervals with hoops of strong, galvanized wire.

❷ With the hose in place, rake at least an 8cm (3in) thick layer of mulch, such as bark chips or gravel, between the plants. Cover the bare soil and the hose. The mulch gives a neat, decorative finish, suppresses weeds, and will help prevent moisture from evaporating from the soil. The finished bed is low-maintenance, especially if the seep hose is controlled by a timer.

mulching

Why do you need to mulch?

A mulch is a layer of material applied as a skin over the soil, and has many advantages over leaving the surface bare. Loose mulches maintain a more even soil temperature, that is warmer in winter and cooler in summer than naked ground. The need for watering is reduced, because moisture cannot evaporate from the soil so readily.

Gravel mulch *provides a good foil for grasses.*

Mulches also help to suppress weeds, especially the sheet mulches such as landscape fabric and black plastic. The weeds are prevented from germinating by the lack of light, although some persistent perennial weeds such as dandelions may grow through a loose mulch unless the soil has been throughly weeded beforehand (*see p.389*). Any weeds that appear after the mulch is laid will be easier to spot and remove. As well as being useful, mulches can also be very ornamental, especially if you use materials such as chipped bark, pebbles, or glass chips.

There are many types of organic and synthetic mulch available, but to be effective it should be long-lasting

and not easily dislodged by rain or blown away. Organic mulches such as compost will, in time, be carried down into the soil by worms, improving the soil structure and replenishing nutrients, filling the role of mulch and fertilizer in one. If you are using an organic material, make sure it has a loose texture that will allow moisture to pass through easily. If using black plastic, punch some holes in it so air and water can reach the soil.

Types of mulch

Organic mulches, such as well-rotted manure, improve soil structure, but do not use mushroom compost with acid-loving plants. Grass cuttings are free, but may turn slimy or spread weed seeds. Bark chips look good and use an otherwise wasted resource, as do sweet-smelling cocoa shells. Sheet mulches are effective, but need disguising (*see below*). Gravel is expensive, but makes a handsome mulch.

Applying and using mulches

A mulch will have the effect of stabilizing and maintaining soil conditions, so the best time to apply one is in autumn or spring. At these times of year, the soil should be reasonably warm, not too wet or too dry, and free from weeds – in other words, perfect for plant growth.

A loose mulch, such as gravel, well-rotted manure, and chipped bark, can be applied by spreading it liberally around plants with a shovel and raking it level (*see right*).

Sheet mulches of landscape fabric or plastic are easy to use if laid over a bed before planting. Cut the sheet

so that it is at least 15cm (6in) larger on all sides than the area to be covered. Secure the sheet at the edges with pegs, or push the edges into the ground with the edge of a spade, making sure that it is taut. The plants can then be inserted through planting holes (*see below*).

Using a sheet mulch
❶ *Rake the soil level and, if needed, water it well. Lay a sheet mulch (here of landscape fabric) over the bed. To plant, make two cuts, 15cm (6–8in) long and at right angles, in the sheet. Fold the flaps back and dig a planting hole.*

❷ *Insert the plant, firm, water, and replace the flaps. Add a 5cm (2in) layer of organic or mineral mulch to hide as well as hold down the sheet mulch.*

Applying organic mulch Spread loose mulches directly onto the soil to a depth of 5–8cm (2–3in) to control weeds or 10–15cm (4–6in) to provide winter insulation. Tuck the mulch under each plant but, if using an organic mulch, leave a 10cm (4in) gap to avoid rot setting in. Top up the mulch as needed.

weeding

Types of weed

Any plant growing where it is not wanted can be called a weed, although they are often thought of as wild plants. In favourable conditions, some ornamentals can be invasive. Weeds are a nuisance because they grow very fast, taking water, nutrients, and light from less vigorous, cultivated plants.

There are two types of weed: annual and perennial. Annual weeds, such as annual meadow grass, have thin, shallow roots and complete their life cycle within one year. Left to grow

they will self-seed prolifically and grow rapidly, producing up to three generations in a season. If you don't allow them to seed, they are fairly easy to control.

Perennial weeds usually have deep, fleshy, or spreading roots, such as the common dandelion, or creeping underground stems, for example ground elder. They are difficult to remove completely, and return year after year even if only a small piece of root is left in the soil after weeding.

Annual weeds

Common chickweed

Fat hen

Groundsel

Perennial weeds

Underground stems

Couch grass

Stinging nettle

Oxalis

Controlling weeds

The method of control you choose for your garden will depend on the types of weed, the scale of the invasion, and whether you are prepared to use chemicals.

If you want to avoid weedkillers, then mulching (*see facing page*) as well as using ground-cover plants will prevent weeds taking hold. If a few annual weeds do appear, they are simple to deal with. Cut them down with a hoe, or pull them up by hand, before they set seed.

Small patches of perennial weeds can be dug out with a fork, but may reappear unless you remove every last bit of root. If there is a very bad infestation, then a drastic solution may be needed. A sheet mulch (*see facing page*), will kill most weeds if it is left in place over two seasons.

Inevitably, chemical weedkillers save a lot of time and effort. Many are effective only in early summer and should be used on a dull, dry day. Some weedkillers are selective and will kill only certain types of plants, so first identify the problem weed. Several applications may be necessary to clear persistent perennial weeds. Always follow carefully the manufacturer's instructions when using chemicals.

Individual weeds can be targeted, but if an area has more weeds than desirable plants, consider digging up the ornamental plants and treating the entire area. Before replanting the ornamentals, wash the soil off the root balls, check, and remove any perennial weed fragments.

Using a hoe Walk backwards, pushing and pulling the blade along the surface as you go, aiming to slice off the tops of annual weeds without digging into the soil. This will be easiest to achieve when the soil is fairly dry. Either leave the hoed weeds to wither if it is hot, or if it is damp remove them and add them to the compost bin.

Chemical weedkiller Ready-mixed weedkillers are less hazardous than concentrates that need dilution. A small hand-sprayer like this is the safest method of application, but it is wise to shield nearby ornamental plants with plastic. Wash your hands throughly after use.

Weeding rows by hand Sowing seed in rows makes it easier to distinguish weed seedlings from the ornamental seedlings. Anything out of line can be pulled out by hand. Hand weeding is easiest to do when the soil is slightly moist.

supporting plants

Providing temporary supports

Many herbaceous plants need some support as they grow to prevent them from being snapped by wind or being flattened by heavy rain, so they look their best throughout the season. Push supports into the soil when the plant

Slot stakes together

Link stakes These come in varying heights and slot together easily (*see inset*). You can position them around any shape of clump. Insert to a depth of 10cm (4in) to keep them steady.

is no more than 30cm (12in) tall, so that it has time to grow through and disguise the support. If you delay staking the plant until it begins to flop, the supports will look obvious and unnatural.

Traditionally, bamboo canes are used – either singly, for tall plants such as gladioli, or in a circle with twine for clumping plants. A more natural alternative is peasticks – twiggy branches usually discarded from coppiced shrubs. You could use large plastic or wire mesh stretched between canes; the plant stems grow through the mesh and obscure it. There are also many metal and plastic staking systems available which are re-usable and versatile. Small climbers, like sweet peas (*Lathyrus, see p.145*), can be grown over a wigwam of canes, tied at the top with raffia, or over a wooden or metal obelisk.

Using trellis

Train climbers and wall shrubs on trellis used as a freestanding screen, fixed to battens on a wall, or to extend the height of a fence. Make sure that the wood has been treated with preservative before it is covered by the plant. Most plants grown on trellis need to be tied regularly into the support; a loose figure-of-eight loop of twine will allow for stems to grow. Once plants are established, check the ties at least once a year and loosen any that are too tight.

Fixing a trellis kit to a drainpipe This is a good way to conceal an unsightly feature. Use two or three narrow, 2m (6ft) trellis panels and place them around the drainpipe. Secure at 45cm (18in) intervals with plastic ties or wire.

keeping plants neat

Deadheading and pinch pruning

Deadheading woody plants Using secateurs, regularly remove withered flowers, cutting back to a strong, outward-facing bud to encourage open growth.

Deadheading by hand Grasp each fading flower of a herbaceous plant between thumb and forefinger, and bend it over so it snaps off.

Pinching out leafy shoots The tips of soft shoots (here of purple sage) are nipped out just above healthy buds or sideshoots to encourage denser growth.

During the growing season, you can prolong each plant's flowering period by deadheading. This directs energy that would have gone into producing seed into forming more flowers. Try to get into the habit of deadheading whenever you go into the garden, and you will be rewarded with a constant and tidy display of flowers.

Removing the spent flowers of most herbaceous plants can be done by hand. Some perennials, for example delphiniums, lupins, and oriental poppies, can be cut down to the base once the first flush of flower has ended to induce fresh foliage and a second display later in the season. Other plants, such as catmint, cranesbills, and pulmonarias can simply be sheared over.

To deadhead shrubs and woody climbers, use secateurs and cut back the flowered shoot to a healthy, outward-facing bud. The new shoot should grow in a direction that will

enhance the shape of the plant. Remember that many plants, including some roses, achilleas, and grasses, should not be deadheaded if you wish to enjoy their decorative seedheads in late autumn and winter.

If you want to save the seed of any annuals or biennials, you can still remove most of the spent flowers because each seedhead produces a large quantity of seeds.

You can also keep the foliage of plants, for example herbs, looking neat by pinch pruning. This is a similar process to deadheading, but involves removing the growing tips of shoots before flowering to encourage lots of new sideshoots and a dense, bushy habit. It is a technique often used with fuchsias and summer bedding plants early in the season; if you stop pinch pruning in midsummer, the plants will burst into bloom, producing a continuous mass of flowers.

raising your own

One of the great joys of gardening is propagating your own plants by taking cuttings, dividing, layering, and sowing seed. Not only are these techniques fun to learn, they will also save you a great deal of money – when compared with nursery plants the price of a packet of seed is negligible.

A potting tray stops compost spilling everywhere when sowing seed or potting up cuttings.

It is not necessary to purchase much equipment to raise your own plants, nor do you need a great deal of space – a sunny windowsill will do – but you do need clean containers, good-quality, fresh compost (not salvaged from other pots) and, if taking cuttings, a clean, sharp knife. Poor hygiene is the prime enemy of young seedlings and cuttings, because it allows diseases such as rots to attack the vulnerable young plants.

New seedlings and cuttings need the correct balance of nutrients, a good supply of oxygen and moisture, and appropriate light and temperature levels. All you have to do is provide suitable growing conditions and nature will do the rest for you. Seed and all cuttings, except hardwood ones, succeed in the protected environment of a propagator. Create a similar conditions by covering a pot with a clear plastic bag. Warming the compost gently will also help.

Division and layering are even easier ways of raising new plants, because they are undertaken outdoors, but these methods produce only one or a few new plants at a time.

growing plants from seed

Sowing seed in containers

Most plants are easy to raise from seed, including annuals, perennials, and even trees. If you have never sown seed before, it is best to buy packeted seed because it is quality controlled and comes with full instructions for each type of seed.

The most natural way to grow seed is, of course, outdoors but by sowing indoors you have more control over the environment and each seed has a better chance of survival. Indoor sowings can also be made earlier than outdoor ones, getting the plants off to a good start.

Sow seed thinly to avoid problems with overcrowding. Fine seed will be easier to sow if mixed with sand.

Whether you use a full- or half-sized seed tray will depend on the amount of seed that you are sowing. Many gardeners use modular trays or coir or peat seed blocks – if sown one per module or block, each seedling can grow to a good size before being disturbed. Biodegradable pots also avoid root disturbance because each seedling is planted out together with its pot. Seedlings that develop long roots, such as sweet peas, are best grown in tall tube pots.

You can use recycled containers: yoghurt pots and foil trays work well (just make drainage holes), while cardboard egg boxes and toilet roll tubes make biodegradable modules.

How to sow seed in a tray

❶ Fill the tray with good-quality, fresh seed compost. Tap the tray firmly on the bench two or three times to settle the compost and scrape off the excess with a ruler. Press another tray on the surface to firm the compost to 1cm (½in) below the rim. Stand the tray in a reservoir of water until the surface is just moist.

❷ Sprinkle seed thinly on the surface of the compost, then cover with a fine layer of sieved compost. Press large seeds into the compost, at a depth of twice their diameter; fill in the holes.

❸ Water the surface with a fine spray. Cover the tray to prevent moisture loss and maintain an even temperature – use a sheet of glass, clear kitchen film, or a purpose-made plastic lid. If it is very sunny, shade the tray with paper to prevent it overheating.

Germinating seed successfully

A seed contains a plant in embryo and to kickstart it into life, it needs the correct balance of warmth, air, and moisture. In most cases, you can achieve these conditions by placing pots or trays of seed in a propagator (*see right*). Electric propagators and heated trays provide what is called "bottom heat", gently warming the soil to encourage germination. Alternatively, cover the container with kitchen film or a sheet of glass.

Some seed needs special treatment to trigger it into germination, for example, low light levels. A period of

cold, to mimic winter, can be created by placing the seed container in the refrigerator or outdoors for a time. Some thick seed coatings need to be soaked before sowing. These details will be listed on the seed packet.

As soon as the seedlings emerge, increase ventilation or remove any film, but keep them out of the sun. If left covered, they may fall prey to damping off, a fungal disease that spreads fast in damp, still air. Seeing the affected seedlings blacken and die is disheartening, but you can protect them by observing good hygiene.

Propagator The cover of the propagator allows light through, while keeping the air moist. Open the vent to get rid of heavy condensation, but don't let the air dry out completely.

Caring for seedlings

Seedlings should never be allowed to dry out, nor should they sit in wet compost, which is a breeding ground for diseases such as damping off (*see above*). Watering from overhead can wash seedlings out of the compost. Instead, stand pots and trays in clean tap water and lift them out as soon as the surface of the compost starts to moisten. Allow any excess water to drain away.

Seedlings sown indoors tend to be taller and weaker than those sown outside. Gently stroking their tops 10–20 times a day with your fingers, or a piece of thin card, encourages shorter, sturdier growth.

Overcrowded seedlings compete for light, water, and space. They may grow leggy and more vulnerable to disease. They should therefore be transplanted, or pricked out, as soon as they have formed two true leaves above the first pair of seed leaves, to give them space.

Select the healthiest, strongest seedlings to grow on and discard the rest. You can thin them out, by pulling out unwanted seedlings with tweezers, or transplant them into new containers of fresh compost (*see below*). Insert them about 5cm (2in) apart with the seed leaves just above the compost. Pop them back in a ventilated propagator and shade from bright sun until they get established.

Etiolated seedlings are weak and spindly as a result of growing in poor light and may never thrive. Bright, diffuse light is best for seedlings – strong sun can burn tender shoots.

Pricking out Use a dibber to ease the seedlings out of the old compost. Try not to damage any roots. Make a hole for each seedling, lower its roots into the hole, and firm gently by pushing in the compost from the sides.

Chopstick makes good dibber

Hold seedlings by the leaves.

Hardening off

Hardening off acclimatizes young plants that have been indoors to the dryer and cooler conditions of the open garden. If this is not done, the young plants will be knocked back and suffer a check to their growth. It is best not to rush this final stage, so allow a week or two for the process.

Wait until all danger of frost has passed before moving young plants outdoors. Choose a warm, dry, but dull day to commence hardening off. In the early stages, cover the plants with a layer of horticultural fleece to protect them from windchill, and keep them out of heavy rain or strong sun. Bring them back under cover at night for the first few days.

If the weather stays mild, leave them out overnight under a double, and then a single, layer of fleece. If the plants look healthy, finally remove it altogether. Your plants will be fully hardened off and ready for planting out.

A cold frame is the ideal halfway house for hardening off. For the first few days, open the lid for 2–3 hours, but keep it shut at night. Increase the time the lid is left open during the day, and eventually, leave it open at night.

Making use of plug plants

Raising plants from seed is very satisfying and it is still the only way you can obtain some of the more unusual plant cultivars. There is no denying, however, that it can be time- and space-consuming.

Plug plants are a speedy alternative. These are young plants that have been grown in modules so that they have a well-developed root system that forms an easy-to-handle plug. You can still enjoy potting up the plants, growing them on to maturity, and hardening them off.

Plug plants and pots of seedlings are widely available, especially of

bedding annuals and perennials. They can be bought from nurseries and garden centres and are also dispatched by mail-order companies from early spring. Nurseries sell them in trays or strips, whereas mail-order plug plants are usually supplied in snap-shut plastic containers, which keep plants moist during transit. Pot up or plant out plug plants (*see p.380*) as soon as possible, and water them well.

Hippo plugs are more expensive than standard plugs; however, because they are larger plants, they should establish and flower more quickly.

Plug plant in compost

Plug plant in rockwool

Plugs may be joined at tops of root balls but are easily parted

Plug plants are usually grown in compost, but may also be supplied grown in rockwool plugs. Rockwool is made from spun molten rock, is sterile and has a good air- and water-holding capacity.

Plugs in strips Never pull plug plants out of their strips or module trays. Push them out of the container from the base – polystyrene strips have specially weakened drainage points for this purpose.

Sowing an annual border

You can create a colourful border full of hardy annuals by sowing seed directly outdoors. The sheer volume of seed sown (packets are still fairly cheap) will more than compensate for any seedlings you lose to pests and harsh conditions. Also, you do not have to worry about pricking out, growing on, and hardening off the seedlings. Start sowing outdoors as soon as the soil has started to warm up in early spring.

Give plants a good start in life by preparing the area thoroughly. Remove any weeds (which could compete for water, light, and nutrients) and large stones, then roughly level the surface. Do this in autumn, or several weeks prior to sowing, so the soil has time to settle and any germinating weeds can be removed. Before sowing, rake the soil until it resembles fine breadcrumbs (known as a "fine tilth") and the

surface is level. Water the plot well if it is dry, otherwise the freshly sown seed might dry out and die.

Fill a bottle with sand and use it to trickle out a line delineating the shape of each sowing area; make these plots irregularly shaped so that the different plants will form drifts.

You can either sow seed in rows, or drills, within each area (*see below*) or broadcast sow. The latter is done simply by scattering seed as evenly as possible

to fill each sowing area, then lightly raking over the plot to mix the seed into the soil. Rake the soil in two directions to ensure that the seed is evenly distributed. Broadcast sowing is quicker, but it is more difficult to spot weeds among the seedlings later.

Once they have appeared, cover the seedlings with horticultural fleece to protect them from frost or heavy rain and from pests such as mice, birds, and cats.

Sowing seed in drifts

❶ Mark out the sowing areas for each plant. Within each area, use a stick or a hoe to draw out drills (shallow trenches) for sowing the seed. Check the seed packets for the correct spacings of drills for each plant.

❷ Water the drills if the soil is dry, then sprinkle fine seed thinly along each row. Space sow large seed in twos and threes. Pull a thin layer of soil gently over the seed with a rake.

❸ When seedlings appear, thin them to leave the strongest ones at the correct spacings. Place your fingers around the base of each chosen seedling's stem to keep its roots firm as you pull out unwanted seedlings around it.

cuttings

Softwood, semi-ripe, and heel cuttings

A stem-tip cutting is the quickest and most successful way of propagating many perennials, shrubs, biennials, and alpines. It may be of soft or semi-ripe wood. A softwood, or slightly more mature greenwood, cutting is taken from the actively growing tip of a shoot in early summer. Look for strong, young growth. It will be a lighter green than older growth or wood. Later in the summer when the shoots begin to ripen or become woody and stiff, semi-ripe cuttings can be taken. Test stems by bending them – if they split they are still soft, if they spring back they are semi-ripe.

When taking a stem-tip cutting (*see below*), cut off a shoot about 10cm (4in) long. Handle it carefully: the tissues are soft and easily damaged. Cuttings wilt swiftly – keep them moist and prepare them as soon as possible so they have the best chance of rooting. You can dip the cuttings in fungicide to protect against rot and the ends in a hormone rooting compound to encourage rooting. You can also take cuttings of woody plants with a heel (*see below, right*).

Cover a pot of cuttings with a clear bag to retain moisture, or put it in a propagator, in a warm, light place.

Taking stem-tip cuttings
❶ *Cut just above a leaf joint using a clean, sharp knife, and place cuttings in a bucket of water or plastic bag to stop them wilting.*
❷ *Trim all but the top 2–4 leaves off each cutting and cut the end just below a leaf joint. Insert the cuttings in pots of moist, gritty cuttings compost, so that their leaves are not touching.*

Cuttings inserted so that leaves are just above surface

Heel cuttings Select a new sideshoot that is about 10cm (4in) long and semi-ripe. Gently pull it from the main stem (*see inset*) so that it retains a small sliver of bark. Trim the bark, using a clean, sharp knife, to leave a small "heel" on the cutting. The heel contains high levels of growth hormone that promotes rooting. Useful for rooting evergreens.

Heel

Hardwood cuttings

Hardwood cuttings are normally taken from the mature wood of deciduous and evergreen trees and shrubs at the end of the growing season (from late autumn until winter). Hardwood in this context, does not mean woody and old, it refers to shoots of the current season that have started to toughen up.

Look for stems that are the same thickness as a pencil. Cut them off just above a bud or leaf joint on the parent plant. Trim the cuttings to length and insert in a trench (*see below*) in a cool, sheltered spot in the garden. Hardwood cuttings tend not to dry out as quickly as other types of cuttings, but you should still keep them watered in dry spells. Instead of planting the cuttings in a trench, you could root them in deep pots of cuttings compost in a cold frame.

Leave the cuttings undisturbed for a year, watering and weeding them during the growing season. By the following autumn, they should have rooted and be ready to transplant.

Taking hardwood cuttings
❶ *Trim the cuttings to 20–23cm (8–9in) long. Use a clean, sharp knife to cut the bottom off just below a leaf joint. Trim off any soft wood at the top to just above a leaf joint.*
❷ *Use a spade to sink a shallow (slit) trench about 15cm (6in) deep. Line it with coarse sand. Dip the bases of the cuttings in hormone-rooting compound (see inset). Stand them in the trench, 10cm (4in) apart, firm and water.*

Root cuttings

Fleshy-rooted perennials, such as eryngiums, can be grown from root cuttings. Dig round a plant in autumn or winter to expose some roots. Cut off a few healthy, medium-thickness roots close to the crown. Wash off the soil and cut the roots in 5–10cm (2–4in) pieces. Dust with fungicide. Lay the pieces flat in a tray of cuttings compost and cover over.

Root cuttings root faster with bottom heat.

division

Methods of dividing plants

This is the easiest and quickest way of propagating herbaceous (but not woody) perennials, grasses, ferns, and many alpine and aquatic plants. Most of these plants form mats or clumps, and as they grow the centre of the plant becomes congested and begins to die. Lifting and dividing a plant every three or four years, in autumn or early spring when it is dormant, restores its vigour and gives the plant a new lease of life. Plants that are borderline hardy or that have large rhizomes are best divided in early spring or after flowering has finished.

When dividing a clump, always look for the natural divisions between the shoots; some plants will have distinct crowns or offsets. Replant only the young, fresh growth from the outside of a clump, or in the case of fleshy crowns, sections with healthy buds or roots. The old, exhausted centre will never regain its vigour.

There are various ways to divide a plant and which one you follow depends on the plant and the type of root system it has (*see below*). First shake or wash off as much soil as possible so that you can see the roots. Pull apart large clumps using forks; small plants with your hands. Cut fleshy crowns into sections.

Dividing with forks Large clumps are best divided with two forks. Push the forks back to back into the root mass and pull the handles apart to split the clump. Alternatively, cut the roots with a sharp kitchen knife or pruning saw.

Dividing by hand Small fibrous-rooted plants are easy to pull apart by hand; cut tough or tangled roots with a knife or secateurs.

Dividing rhizomes Use a clean, sharp knife to cut off young pieces with healthy buds, shoots, and roots from old, woody rhizomes. Replant the divided pieces (here of bearded iris), making sure that they sit on the surface so the sun can ripen them. To avoid wind rock, trim the leaves to 15cm (6in). Discard the old rhizomes.

Dividing bulbous plants

Many bulbs, corms, and tubers, of plants such as alliums, crocosmias, crocuses, daffodils (*Narcissus*), and gladioli, increase by producing offsets around the parent bulb or corm. These types of bulbous plant can quickly form congested clumps. Unless they are lifted every three or four years and divided, the plants will lose vigour and stop flowering.

After lifting, remove the offsets by pulling them away from the parent bulb. Many offsets will be small and may take three or four years to mature and reach flowering size, so grow them on in pots of gritty compost in a sheltered spot – a cold frame is ideal.

Replant large bulbs immediately, or if still in leaf temporarily plant them in a corner of a border until they are needed. Insert a label so you don't forget where they are. Alternatively, clean off any soil and store the bulbs in a cool, dark place for replanting at the appropriate time.

Pull offsets from the main parent bulb.

layering

Rooted stems

Some climbers, such as ivies, and woody plants, like heathers, spread by rooting from their stems wherever they touch the soil. Layering takes advantage of this natural tendency. It is a useful technique particularly for evergreens – their cuttings tend to dehydrate before they root.

Select a low-growing stem, and wound it, preferably near a bud, by scratching or twisting it. Bury the wounded part of the stem in soil leavened with grit and cuttings compost. Support the exposed shoot, which will receive nourishment from the parent plant while it develops roots.

After six months to two years, once there are signs of new growth, dig up the layered shoot, detach it and plant it out.

Layering a stem Strip the middle stem (here of rosemary) of leaves. Dig a hole beneath the stem, bend and wound it, then peg it to hold it in place. Fill in with soil and grit and keep watered. After 4–6 weeks, dig up the rooted shoot, cut off and plant out.

avoiding problems

If plants are given the best possible growing conditions so that they are healthy and strong, they will be able to survive most pests and diseases. Some problems in the garden are almost inevitable, but the majority are easily kept under control, or cured and prevented from returning.

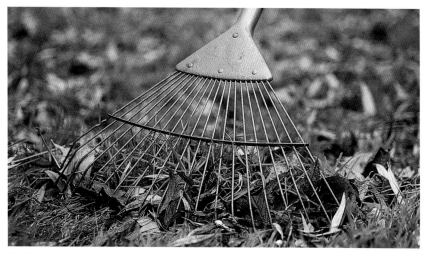

Raking up leaves makes the garden neat and deprives pests and diseases of a place to overwinter.

If you notice symptoms such as discoloured or distorted growth, or holes in leaves and flowers, they are usually caused by pests, diseases, or nutrient deficiencies. The best way to deal with these problems is to use an integrated approach, where cultural and organic methods are used to keep plants healthy, and chemicals are used only as a last line of defence.

Prevention is always better than cure; if given good growing conditions, plants will be strong enough to survive attacks without any lasting damage. Check plants thoroughly before you buy them for any sign of damage or disease, to avoid bringing problems into the garden. Keep cutting tools

clean so they do not spread infection. Promptly remove yellowing leaves and faded flowers, and clear plant debris that could harbour insects and spores.

Be vigilant, squashing pests and cutting out diseased parts as soon as you notice them. Some pests and diseases are persistent on certain plants, such as blackspot on roses. If you find the same problem is returning year after year, it is worth obtaining a resistant cultivar. For example, *Rosa* 'The Fairy' withstands many common rose problems. If you have to resort to chemicals, use a specific remedy if possible, and spray the entire plant thoroughly. If all else fails, remove the plant before the problem spreads.

Keeping a healthy garden

Thriving plants are better able to resist problems, so it is important to maintain a healthy garden. There are several ways in which you can ensure your plants remain in top condition.

Plants that are growing in sites or conditions that do not meet their needs become stressed and more prone to problems. To avoid this, take care to choose plants that are suited to each aspect in your garden and to the local conditions (*see Climate and location, pp.371–373*). It is rare to find perfect soil; before planting, prepare it well (*see Soils and compost, pp.376–378*).

Pay attention also to watering and feeding your plants appropriately so they do not suffer from insufficient or excessive water or nutrients (*see pp.386–387*). It is essential to weed regularly so that your plants do not have to compete with fast-growing

invaders for vital light, water, and nutrients (*see p.389*).

Diseases such as bacteria, fungi, and viruses are opportunists, and some infect a weak plant through an existing wound. Avoid giving them easy access by cutting cleanly when pruning (*see p.382*) and removing crossing branches that might chafe as they rub together.

Plants that are overgrown or are planted too closely often become weak and sickly, with elongated shoots as they fight for light. Fresh air cannot circulate freely around the stems and leaves, and the still, stagnant air encourages rots, moulds, and mildews. To avoid this, prune out congested growth (*see p.382*), divide herbaceous perennials (*see p.395*), and allow room for growth when planting any type of plant (*see p.379*).

Nutrient deficiency symptoms are usually first seen on leaves. A lack of magnesium, shown here, can be identified by yellowing between leaf veins because magnesium is used by the plant to make green chlorophyll. Boron, iron, nitrogen, and phosphates are also commonly deficient.

Waterlogged soils often develop blue mottling on the surface and a bad smell. Plant roots will "drown" through lack of air, rot, and die. The solution is to improve the soil drainage, or to grow bog plants that are adapted to cope in such wet conditions.

Encouraging beneficial wildlife

The only good aspect of insect pests is that they attract lots of wildlife in search of a meal. If you encourage a range of beneficial wildlife into the garden, the pests will be kept down to acceptable levels. Do not be alarmed if you see a few pests about, but allow their natural predators to take action before you think about resorting to chemical means.

Water attracts lots of animals, including frogs and toads, which eat many pests that crawl on the ground. The hedgehog is also a valuable friend, and a pile of logs or leaves, or a thick hedge, can provide a home so it stays to eat your slugs. Ladybird larvae and adults feed eagerly on the scourge of almost every garden: aphids (*see p.398*).

Birds can damage some seedlings or edible crops, but this is more than made up for by the number of insect pests they eat. Attract birds by planting trees and shrubs that give cover or bear berries, for example rowans and cotoneasters.

Toad

A song thrush is a useful ally because it will eat snails, which are a problem for many gardeners, especially on alkaline (limy) soils. Encourage a thrush to visit your garden by providing a large, flat stone that it can use as an anvil to smash the snail shells.

Smashed snail shells by a stone are a sure sign that a thrush has lent you a helping hand.

Ladybird larvae have voracious appetites for aphids. The adults hibernate in odd corners over winter to emerge in spring as aphid numbers rise.

How to control problems

By keeping a close watch on plants you can stop problems getting out of hand. If you see any pests, pick them off immediately. If you do spot symptoms of disease, remove the affected parts and burn or throw them in the rubbish bin.

Some plants are irresistible to aphids – if you notice that a plant is particularly affected, consider planting French marigolds (*Tagetes, see p.329*) nearby; they will attract hoverflies, the larvae of which feed on aphids. Aromatic plants such as catmint (*Nepeta, see p.290*), and garlic may repel or confuse pests.

Predators or parasites of some pests can be introduced into the garden as a biological control. Nematodes (microscopic worms) can be watered onto the soil or compost to kill slugs or vine weevil larvae, but they often need high temperatures and may be more effective in a greenhouse or conservatory than in the open garden.

If you do use chemicals, follow the manufacturer's instructions. Fertilizers cure deficiency diseases – if you can identify the missing nutrient, it is better to use a specific cure than an all-purpose feed. Organic pesticides, such as pyrethrum, made from plant extracts, and insecticidal soap, are available. Use them with the same care as any other chemical. A few inorganic pesticides are toxic to some ornamental plants. There is usually a list on the packaging; if in doubt, test the chemical on a plant before general use. Spray pesticides in the evening, when bees are not around, and in still weather so the wind does not carry spray where it is not wanted. Any chemicals past their use-by date should be disposed of safely; contact the local authority for advice.

Small mites (Amblyseius) are sold mixed in bran. Hang pack up in your greenhouse to control thrips, at minimum of 18°C (64°F)

Biological control for thrips

Encarsia parasites in tube ready for release into greenhouse

Biological control for greenhouse whitefly

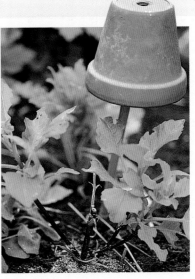

Earwig traps can be constructed by placing upside-down flower pots on top of canes among susceptible plants. Loosely fill the pots with hay or straw and the earwigs will crawl in overnight. In the morning, empty the pots and destroy the earwigs. These pests affect many plants including chrysanthemums, clematis, and dahlias, appearing after dark to feed and leaving large holes in petals or young leaves.

Number one pests

The most common garden pests crop up regularly from year to year. Slugs and snails attack a wide range of plants. They prefer seedlings and young or fleshy plants, and will eat large holes in leaves or stems or even the entire plant. Vine weevil larvae cause considerable damage to container-grown plants by eating all the roots. The adults graze on foliage, leaving large holes.

Aphids attack the soft shoots and buds of most plants, and introduce diseases through their piercing mouthparts. Red lily beetles eat entire flowers and leaves. Deal with these pests by either picking them off or using a specific biological or chemical control.

Slugs can be very destructive, grazing through stems at soil level and returning to the same plant night after night. They will even strip the soft bark off shrubs. You can hunt and destroy them under cover of darkness, make traps, or lay barriers (*see p.260*).

Vine weevil larvae are up to 10mm (½in) long, creamy white, and devour pot-plant roots. The first symptom of these pests is sudden wilting. Biological control is available.

Whole-plant problems

Occasionally you may notice that a plant is looking sick. The usual causes are incorrect watering, pests, disease, or nutrient deficiencies.

Newly planted and container-grown plants often wilt because of drought or overwatering (*see p.386*). Check the soil or the compost and either give it a good soak or allow it to dry out, as appropriate. Wilting can also be caused by disease, for example clematis wilt (*see p.136*), or pests such as vine weevils (*see left*). Lack of nutrients can make a plant sickly and yellow, but it should perk up after a liquid feed (*see p.386*). Clumping plants lose vigour (*see below*) unless they are divided regularly.

Wilted leaves due to poor watering

Old, woody, congested growth

Neglected plants are vulnerable to a range of problems. This heuchera has produced ugly, woody growth at its base and sparse foliage because it has not been regularly divided.

Stem problems

The stems of a plant support the leaves and flowers and contain veins that transport water and food to and from the deepest roots and the tallest shoots. Because they are so important, damage to them may result in the loss of an affected plant. Pests that attack plant stems may eat the skin or bark, suck sap by piercing the veins, or in some cases tunnel right through, or live in, the stem. The wounds that they leave then provide doorways for diseases that can spread through the plant and quickly kill it. Bad pruning and extremely cold, hot, or windy weather can also damage stems. Look out for dead, diseased, or damaged parts and quickly cut out and dispose of them so problems cannot spread to other plants.

Cuckoo spit is the foamy, protective coating made by froghoppers (small, jumping insects); it does little harm other than looking unsightly

Frost damage can kill, but if only new shoots are affected they often grow back. If frost is forecast, move tender plants under cover and drape early blossom and new shoots of hardy plants with horticultural fleece

Mildew is a white, powdery, fungal infection; it attacks if plants are already weak or congested so air cannot move around stems freely

Dieback can occur if pruning cuts are made too far from buds

Aphids such as greenfly and blackfly are very common; they suck sap from veins, leaving sticky honeydew behind on which sooty mould can develop

Canker first appears as zone of flattened, discoloured bark which later splits, forming ring of flaky bark that kills shoot. Canker affects many plants at any time of the year, and should be cut out

Possible stem problems These pests, disorders, and diseases are very common and you will certainly see them at some point. Although they can be severe enough to kill, most will cause little long-term damage – especially if they are dealt with quickly – and some can be easily prevented.

Leaf problems

Leaf problems can take the form of discoloured, distorted, or damaged growth, or premature leaf fall. This spoils the plant's appearance and reduces its ability to thrive.

Fungi can cause moulds, mildews, rusts, or spots. They attack weak plants and are unsightly, but rarely deadly, although some, for example silver leaf on ornamental cherries, are fatal. Bacteria can cause black spots on leaves; they are not raised or patchy like fungal spots, but appear more like dark shadows. Foliage with pale flecks, streaks, or mottling often has a viral infection.

Some pests, such as caterpillars, eat leaves and others, like leaf miners, burrow into them. Most plants can withstand an attack, but may become weak, providing an easy target for disease. Nutrient deficiencies – the usual cause of yellowing, or chlorosis – also compromise plant defences. With all leaf problems, the first thing

to do is to try and identify the cause, then take appropriate action. Pest control or removal of affected foliage is often required. Never put diseased material on the compost heap because that will often spread infection.

Lack of water, nutrients, light, and space all favour disease; and often pampering a plant by thinning stems, watering, and feeding, will make it strong enough to fight off infection. If all else fails, chemical controls are often effective. Use one specific to the problem if possible, following the manufacturer's instructions carefully.

Possible leaf problems
Some common disorders are shown here. Many of them occur on the undersides of the leaves. Be vigilant and occasionally check under leaves to make sure that there is no problem developing. If you use a contact fungicide or pesticide, spray the whole plant and make sure you include the undersides of the leaves where disease or infestation is usually concentrated.

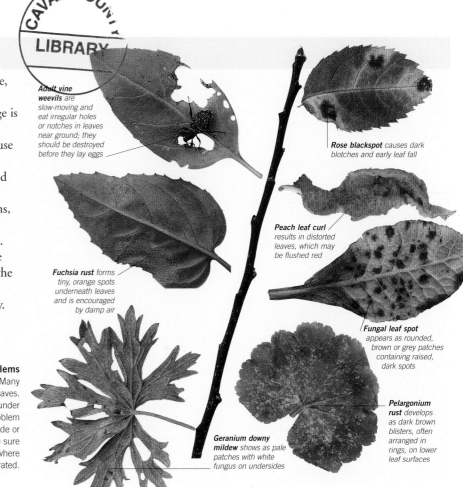

Adult vine weevils are slow-moving and eat irregular holes or notches in leaves near ground; they should be destroyed before they lay eggs

Rose blackspot causes dark blotches and early leaf fall

Peach leaf curl results in distorted leaves, which may be flushed red

Fuchsia rust forms tiny, orange spots underneath leaves and is encouraged by damp air

Fungal leaf spot appears as rounded, brown or grey patches containing raised, dark spots

Pelargonium rust develops as dark brown blisters, often arranged in rings, on lower leaf surfaces

Geranium downy mildew shows as pale patches with white fungus on undersides

Flower problems

Discoloured flowerheads may be a sign of pests such as thrips – tiny insects that suck sap from flower buds in hot, dry summers, causing petals with white flecks.

Most plants in the garden are grown for their flowers, but a few problems, including pests, diseases, and the weather, can affect them and spoil the show. If the first blooms are ruined, all is not lost; if you can cure the problem you may be able to encourage another, second flush of healthy flowers by regular deadheading and feeding.

Sap-sucking insects, such as aphids and thrips can distort or discolour blooms (*see left*); keep a watch for them and squash or spray them off. Other insects, for example earwigs, and birds may eat petals or buds

before they open. Diseases can also be a problem, and those affecting flowers are particularly bad if the weather is cool and damp. Symptoms to look out for include white spots, often edged with a darker ring, on the petals; these indicate the presence of grey mould (botrytis). Streaks or flecks, or deformed flowers, usually indicate a viral infection.

Weather damage is also a common problem for delicate blooms. The flowers of roses and other plants often fail to open if wet spells are followed by hot sun because of a condition

known as balling. The damp bud is scorched by the sun and cannot open, causing the inner petals to rot. Flowers that open in early spring are often prone to frost damage, made worse by the morning sun. Cold, drying winds can scorch petals, turning them brown, so position early-flowering plants with care.

Remain observant so any problems can be overcome before they get a firm hold. If you fail to cure a disease, then it is best to admit defeat and throw away the affected plant before it contaminates others.

plant selections

Every garden presents you with a different challenge. Some have heavy, seemingly unworkable soil; others excessive amounts of shade. The lists in this section are intended to help you identify plants for particular uses, such as herb and bog gardens, and for some of the most common problem areas, such as shaded and dry sites.

Exposed sites

Gardens on hillsides or in flat, open areas regularly experience high winds. Create a shelterbelt using hedges and trees to filter the worst of the wind, and choose hardy plants that are able to withstand a battering.

Acer pseudoplatanus and cultivars
Achillea
Ajuga reptans and cultivars
Alnus glutinosa 'Imperialis' ✿
Anaphalis triplinervis ✿
Anchusa azurea 'Loddon Royalist' ✿
Anemone × hybrida and cultivars
Antirrhinum majus and cultivars
Arbutus unedo ✿
Arctostaphylos
Artemisia abrotanum ✿
Artemisia 'Powis Castle' ✿
Berberis
Bergenia
Bupleurum fruticosum
Calendula officinalis and cultivars
Calluna vulgaris and cultivars
Caragana arborescens
Carpinus betulus 'Fastigiata' ✿
Chaenomeles
Chamaecyparis obtusa 'Nana Aurea' ✿
Chamaecyparis pisifera 'Filifera Aurea' ✿
Clethra arborea
Colutea arborescens
Coreopsis 'Schnittgold'
Coreopsis 'Sunray'
Cornus
Corylus avellana 'Contorta' ✿
Cotoneaster horizontalis ✿

Crataegus laevigata 'Paul's Scarlet' ✿
Cryptomeria japonica 'Elegans Compacta' ✿
× Cupressocyparis leylandii ✿
Cupressus macrocarpa 'Goldcrest' ✿
Deutzia
Dryas octopetala ✿
Echinacea purpurea 'Kim's Knee High'
Echinops ritro 'Veitch's Blue'
Elaeagnus
Erica carnea and cultivars
Erigeron aureus 'Canary Bird' ✿
Erigeron 'Dunkelste Aller' ✿
Erigeron karvinskianus ✿
Eryngium alpinum ✿
Eryngium × oliverianum ✿
Eryngium × tripartitum ✿
Escallonia 'Apple Blossom' ✿
Eschscholzia caespitosa ✿
Eschscholzia californica ✿
Eucalyptus
Euonymus alatus ✿
Euonymus fortunei and cultivars
Euphorbia characias 'John Tomlinson' ✿
Fagus sylvatica 'Dawyck Purple' ✿
Felicia amelloides 'Santa Anita' ✿
Ficus carica
Forsythia × intermedia and cultivars
Fraxinus excelsior
Fuchsia magellanica
Gaultheria
Genista aetnensis ✿
Ginkgo biloba ✿
Gleditsia triacanthos 'Sunburst' ✿
Griselinia littoralis ✿
Hamamelis

Helleborus niger ✿ and cultivars
Hippophae rhamnoides ✿
Hydrangea paniculata 'Grandiflora' ✿
Hypericum calycinum
Ilex aquifolium ✿
Iris sibirica ✿ and cultivars
Jasminum nudiflorum ✿
Juniperus
Kalmia angustifolia ✿
Kerria japonica and cultivars
Kerria japonica 'Picta'
Laburnum
Laurus nobilis ✿
Lavatera
Leucothoe fontanesiana 'Rainbow'
Limnanthes douglasii ✿
Miscanthus
Nepeta sintenisii
Nepeta 'Six Hills Giant'
Osmunda regalis ✿
Phalaris arundinacea var. picta
Phlox subulata 'Lilacina'
Picea abies
Pieris
Pinus nigra ✿
Populus × canadensis and cultivars
Potentilla
Primula
Prunus spinosa
Pulmonaria saccharata
Pyracantha
Quercus
Rubus cockburnianus
Salix alba
Sempervivum arachnoideum ✿
Sempervivum tectorum ✿
Senecio cineraria 'Silver Dust' ✿

Senecio cineraria 'White Diamond'
Sorbus aria
Sorbus aucuparia and cultivars
Spiraea
Symphoricarpos × doorenbosii 'White Hedge'
Tamarix
Tanacetum parthenium and cultivars
Taxus
Thuja plicata
Tiarella cordifolia ✿
Tilia
Tsuga canadensis and cultivars
Ulex
Viburnum × bodnantense 'Dawn' ✿
Viburnum × burkwoodii
Viburnum opulus 'Compactum' ✿
Viburnum rhytidophyllum
Viburnum tinus 'Eve Price' ✿

Seaside gardens

Coastal areas suffer from winter gales and the scorching salt spray that they bring. Create shelterbelts by planting trees around the perimeter, and go for tough plants that conserve moisture.

Achillea
Allium
Alstroemeria
Anaphalis triplinervis ✿
Anchusa azurea 'Loddon Royalist' ✿
Anthemis
Anthericum liliago
Antirrhinum majus and cultivars
Arbutus unedo ✿
Armeria

Artemisia abrotanum 🏆
Artemisia 'Powis Castle' 🏆
Aster
Aucuba
Bergenia
Buddleja davidii and cultivars
Bupleurum fruticosum
Campanula
Centaurea 'John Coutts'
Choisya ternata SUNDANCE 🏆 ('Lich')
Cistus
Cordyline australis 'Torbay Red' 🏆
Cotoneaster
Crataegus
Crocosmia
Cupressus macrocarpa
Cytisus
Dahlia
Dianthus
Dierama pulcherrimum
Echinacea purpurea 'White Lustre'
Echinops ritro 'Veitch's Blue' 🏆
Elaeagnus × ebbingei 'Gilt Edge' 🏆
Erica arborea var. alpina 🏆
Erica carnea and cultivars
Erigeron karvinskianus 🏆
Erigeron 'Quakeress'
Erodium glandulosum 🏆
Erodium manescavii
Eryngium alpinum 🏆
Escallonia 'Apple Blossom' 🏆
Eschscholzia caespitosa 🏆
Eucalyptus
Euonymous fortunei and cultivars
Euphorbia
Felicia amelloides 'Santa Anita' 🏆
Ficus carica
Filipendula rubra 'Venusta' 🏆
Forsythia × intermedia and cultivars
Fuchsia magellanica
Garrya elliptica
Gaultheria
Genista aetnensis 🏆
Geranium
Gleditsia triacanthos 'Sunburst' 🏆
Griselinia littoralis 🏆
Gypsophila 'Rosenschleier' 🏆
Halimium 'Susan' 🏆

Hebe
Hemerocallis
Heuchera
Hibiscus syriacus 'Oiseau Bleu' 🏆
Hippophae rhamnoides 🏆
Hydrangea macrophylla and cultivars
Ilex × altaclerensis and cultivars
Impatiens
Iris
Juniperus
Laburnum
Laurus nobilis 🏆
Lavandula
Lavatera
Leycesteria formosa 🏆
Lonicera nitida
Lonicera × purpusii 'Winter Beauty' 🏆
Lychnis coronaria 🏆
Melissa officinalis 'Aurea'
Monarda
Oenothera
Olearia
Origanum
Osmanthus delavayi 🏆
Pachysandra terminalis
Penstemon
Phormium tenax 🏆
Phygelius
Pinus nigra 🏆
Pittosporum
Populus tremula 🏆
Potentilla
Prunus spinosa
Pulsatilla
Pyracantha
Quercus ilex 🏆
Rosa (some)
Rosmarinus officinalis
Rubus cockburnianus
Salvia
Sambucus racemosa 'Plumosa Aurea'
Santolina
Sisyrinchium
Spartium junceum 🏆
Stachys
Tamarix
Ulex
Viburnum

Dry sun

Situations prone to drought include steeply sloping sunny banks with rapid drainage; the base of a warm south- or west-facing wall; and shallow, sandy, or stony soils in full sun.

Abelia
Acacia baileyana 🏆
Acaena saccaticupula 'Blue Haze'
Achillea
Agapanthus
Allium
Alstroemeria
Anaphalis triplinervis 🏆
Anchusa azurea 'Loddon Royalist' 🏆
Anthemis
Arabis
Arctotis
Armeria pseudarmeria
Artemisia
Asphodeline lutea
Betula
Brachyglottis 'Sunshine' 🏆
Brachyscome iberidifolia
Buddleja
Bupleurum fruticosum
Buxus
Caryopteris × clandonensis 'Kew Blue'
Catananche caerulea 'Bicolor'
Ceanothus 'Blue Mound' 🏆
Centaurea
Cerastium tomentosum
Ceratostigma willmottianum 🏆
Chamaemelum nobile 'Flore Pleno'
Chrysanthemum segetum
Cirsium rivulare 'Atropurpureum'
Cistus
Cleome hassleriana
Clerodendrum trichotomum var. fargesii 🏆
Cotoneaster
Crambe cordifolia 🏆
Crocosmia
× Cupressocyparis leylandii 🏆
Cynara cardunculus 🏆
Cytisus
Dianthus

Diascia
Dictamnus albus
Draba mollissima
Echinops ritro 'Veitch's Blue'
Epilobium
Erica arborea var. alpina 🏆
Erica cinerea and cultivars
Erodium glandulosum 🏆
Erodium manescavii
Eryngium alpinum 🏆
Erysimum
Escallonia
Eucalyptus
Euonymus
Euphorbia
Foeniculum vulgare 'Purpureum'
Fuchsia magellanica
Gaillardia 'Dazzler' 🏆
Gaultheria mucronata 'Mulberry Wine' 🏆
Gaura lindheimeri 🏆
Gazania Mini Star Series
Genista aetnensis 🏆
Genista lydia 🏆
Geranium
Gleditsia triacanthos
Gypsophila 'Rosenschleier' 🏆
Hebe
Helianthemum
Hippophae rhamnoides 🏆
Hypericum
Impatiens
Ipheion uniflorum 'Wisley Blue' 🏆
Iris foetidissima 🏆
Iris pallida 'Variegata' 🏆
Juniperus
Kniphofia
Kolkwitzia amabilis 'Pink Cloud' 🏆
Lavandula
Liatris spicata 'Kobold'
Limnanthes douglasii 🏆
Linaria alpina
Linum flavum 'Compactum'
Linum perenne
Lobularia 'Royal Carpet'
Lychnis coronaria 🏆
Melissa officinalis 'Aurea'
Nepeta

Nerine bowdenii 🏆
Oenothera
Olearia
Origanum laevigatum 🏆
Osteospermum
Papaver orientale and cultivars
Pelargonium
Penstemon
Perovskia 'Blue Spire' 🏆
Phlomis fruticosa 🏆
Phlox subulata 'Lilacina'
Phormium
Phygelius aequalis 'Yellow Trumpet' 🏆
Pinus mugo 'Mops' 🏆
Potentilla
Pulsatilla vulgaris 🏆
Quercus ilex 🏆
Ribes
Rosmarinus officinalis and cultivars
Salvia patens 'Cambridge Blue' 🏆
Sambucus racemosa 'Plumosa Aurea'
Santolina
Saponaria ocymoides 🏆
Schizanthus × wisetonensis 'Hit Parade'
Sedum
Sempervivum arachnoideum 🏆
Sempervivum tectorum 🏆
Solanum crispum 'Glasnevin' 🏆
Spartium junceum 🏆
Spiraea
Stachys byzantina
Stachys candida
Stachys macrantha 'Superba'
Stipa
Symphoricarpos × doorenbosii 'White Hedge'
Tagetes
Tamarix
Teucrium polium
Thymus
Tulipa
Ulex europaeus 'Flore Pleno' 🏆
Verbascum
Verbena bonariensis 🏆
Yucca gloriosa 🏆

Damp shade

A cool, humid woodland environment where the soil is reliably moist all year.

Acer cappadocicum
Acer griseum 🏆
Acer negundo 'Variegatum'
Acer palmatum f. atropurpureum
Acer saccharinum
Alchemilla mollis 🏆
Alnus
Aruncus dioicus 🏆
Asplenium scolopendrium 🏆
Astilbe
Athyrium filix-femina 'Frizelliae' 🏆
Aucuba japonica
Betula pendula 'Youngii'
Buxus sempervirens 🏆
Caltha palustris 🏆
Caltha palustris 'Flore Pleno' 🏆
Camellia japonica and cultivars
Cercidiphyllum japonicum 🏆
Clethra arborea
Convallaria majalis 🏆
Cornus canadensis 🏆
Crataegus
Daphne
Darmera peltata 🏆
Dicentra
Dryopteris wallichiana 🏆
Elaeagnus
Erythronium
Euonymus fortunei
Fatsia japonica 🏆
Fothergilla major 🏆
Gaultheria
Haberlea rhodopensis 'Virginalis'
Hamamelis
Helleborus
Hosta
Hydrangea
Hypericum calycinum
Ilex aquifolium 🏆
Iris sibirica 🏆 and cultivars
Ligularia 'The Rocket' 🏆
Lilium martagon 🏆
Lythrum virgatum 'The Rocket'
Mahonia aquifolium

Matteuccia struthiopteris 🏆
Metasequoia glyptostroboides 🏆
Monarda
Osmanthus × burkwoodii 🏆
Osmanthus delavayi 🏆
Pachysandra terminalis
Picea
Pieris
Polystichum setiferum 🏆
Populus
Primula (candelabra types)
Prunus laurocerasus 🏆
Prunus padus 'Watereri' 🏆
Quercus
Rhododendron
Rodgersia pinnata 'Superba' 🏆
Rubus
Salix
Sambucus racemosa 'Plumosa Aurea'
Sarcococca
Sasa veitchii
Saxifraga fortunei 🏆
Skimmia
Smilacina racemosa 🏆
Sorbus
Spiraea
Stachyurus praecox 🏆
Symphoricarpos
Symphytum
Taxus baccata 🏆 and cultivars
Viburnum davidii 🏆
Viburnum opulus
Viburnum rhytidophyllum

Dry shade

The combined problems of shade and drought are often found by walls, and beneath thirsty, shallow-rooting trees.

Acanthus spinosus 🏆
Ajuga reptans and cultivars
Alchemilla mollis 🏆
Amelanchier lamarckii 🏆
Aquilegia
Arum italicum 'Marmoratum' 🏆
Astrantia
Aucuba
Berberis

Bergenia
Betula
Buxus sempervirens 🏆
Cornus canadensis 🏆
Cortaderia
Cotoneaster
Daphne
Dicentra formosa
Digitalis
Epimedium
Euonymus fortunei
Fatsia japonica 🏆
Garrya elliptica
Geranium himalayense
Geranium macrorrhizum
Geranium nodosum
Hedera
Heuchera
Hippophae rhamnoides 🏆
Ilex aquifolium 🏆
Iris foetidissima 🏆
Juniperus × pfitzeriana
Lamium
Lunaria annua and cultivars
Mahonia
Meconopsis cambrica
Melissa officinalis 'Aurea'
Milium effusum 'Aureum' 🏆
Pachysandra terminalis
Pittosporum tenuifolium 🏆
Polygonatum
Polypodium vulgare
Prunus laurocerasus 🏆
Pulmonaria
Santolina
Skimmia
Symphoricarpos
Taxus baccata 🏆 and cultivars
Teucrium polium
Thalictrum
Tiarella
Tolmiea menziesii 'Taff's Gold' 🏆
Waldsteinia ternata

Deep shade

Permanently shaded positions may be beneath evergreen trees, by high walls, and between tall buildings. Use plants and structures in light colours to help brighten these areas.

Acer cappadocicum
Acer griseum ♀
Adiantum venustum ♀
Ajuga reptans and cultivars
Alchemilla mollis ♀
Aruncus dioicus ♀
Asplenium scolopendrium ♀
Astilbe
Athyrium filix-femina 'Frizelliae' ♀
Aucuba japonica
Betula nigra
Blechnum
Camellia
Cercidiphyllum japonicum ♀
Cotoneaster
Cryptogramma crispa
Daphne
Dicentra
Dicksonia antarctica ♀
Digitalis
Dryopteris wallichiana ♀
Epimedium
Erythronium
Fatsia japonica ♀
Fothergilla major ♀
Gaultheria
Helleborus
Hosta
Hydrangea
Ilex
Iris foetidissima ♀
Iris sibirica ♀
Mahonia
Matteuccia struthiopteris ♀
Osmanthus × *burkwoodii* ♀
Pachysandra terminalis
Pieris
Polypodium vulgare
Polystichum setiferum ♀
Primula (candelabra types)
Prunus laurocerasus ♀
Prunus lusitanica subsp. *azorica*
Pulmonaria
Rhododendron
Rodgersia pinnata 'Superba' ♀
Rubus cockburnianus
Salix
Skimmia
Symphoricarpos
Symphytum
Taxus baccata ♀ and cultivars
Viburnum davidii ♀
Viburnum rhytidophyllum
Woodwardia radicans ♀

Heavy soils

Heavy clay soils can be hard to work, but are often rich in nutrients. Select hardy plants, avoid alpines, and persist in digging in organic matter and grit to improve fertility and drainage.

Abelia
Acer
Aconitum
Aesculus
Ajuga reptans and cultivars
Alnus
Anemone × *hybrida* and cultivars
Aster
Aucuba japonica
Berberis
Betula
Campanula
Carpinus betulus 'Fastigiata' ♀
Chaenomeles
Choisya ternata SUNDANCE ♀ ('Lich')
Colutea arborescens
Cornus
Corylus avellana 'Contorta'
Cotinus 'Grace'
Cotoneaster
Crataegus
Crocosmia
Cytisus
Darmera peltata ♀
Digitalis
Echinops
Eranthis hyemalis ♀

Erigeron
Escallonia
Eucalyptus
Forsythia × *intermedia* and cultivars
Fraxinus excelsior 'Jaspidea' ♀
Geranium
Hamamelis
Hedera helix and cultivars
Helenium
Helleborus
Hemerocallis
Hibiscus syriacus
Hosta
Hypericum
Ilex
Kerria japonica and cultivars
Laburnum × *watereri* 'Vossii' ♀
Lysimachia clethroides ♀
Magnolia
Mahonia
Malus
Monarda
Osmanthus × *burkwoodii* ♀
Persicaria bistorta 'Superba' ♀
Physalis alkekengi ♀
Philadelphus
Pieris japonica 'Flamingo'
Populus
Potentilla
Prunus
Pyracantha
Pyrus salicifolia 'Pendula' ♀
Quercus
Ranunculus
Rheum palmatum 'Atrosanguineum' ♀
Rhododendron
Rodgersia
Rosa
Rudbeckia
Salix
Sasa veitchii
Sidalcea 'Oberon'
Solidago 'Goldenmosa' ♀
Sorbus
Symphoricarpos × *doorenbosii* 'White Hedge'
Symphytum caucasicum ♀
Syringa

Tilia
Tradescantia
Waldsteinia ternata
Weigela florida

Acid (lime-free) soils

Acid soils are typically very fertile, nutrient-rich, and moist with good drainage. You can create the right conditions for some acid-loving plants in containers of ericaceous compost.

Acer rubrum 'October Glory' ♀
Betula
Calluna vulgaris
Camellia
Cassiope 'Edinburgh' ♀
Cercidiphyllum japonicum ♀
Corylopsis glabrescens
Cryptomeria japonica 'Elegans Compacta' ♀
Daboecia cantabrica and cultivars
Erica
Gaultheria
Ilex aquifolium ♀
Kalmia angustifolia ♀
Leucothoe fontanesiana 'Rainbow'
Liquidambar styraciflua 'Golden Treasure'
Meconopsis betonicifolia ♀
Osmunda regalis ♀
Pinus nigra ♀
Populus tremula ♀
Rhododendron
Skimmia
Trillium grandiflorum ♀

Chalky, alkaline soils

Soil over chalk and limestone is almost invariably alkaline (limy). It is usually fairly fertile, but can be shallow and consequently dries out quickly. In such cases, use drought-tolerant plants.

Acanthus spinosus ♀
Acer cappadocicum
Acer griseum ♀
Amelanchier lamarckii ♀

Anthemis
Arbutus unedo ♧
Berberis
Buddleja davidii
Carpinus betulus ♧
Catalpa bignonioides ♧
Ceanothus 'Blue Mound' ♧
Clematis
Corylus avellana 'Contorta'
Daphne mezereum
Dianthus
Eremurus robustus ♧
Fagus sylvatica 'Dawyck Purple' ♧
Fraxinus excelsior 'Jaspidea' ♧
Gleditsia triacanthos 'Sunburst' ♧
Hebe
Kolkwitzia amabilis
Laburnum × watereri 'Vossii' ♧
Laurus nobilis ♧
Liriodendron tulipifera ♧
Malus
Paeonia
Papaver orientale and cultivars
Prunus (all Japanese cherries)
Pulsatilla vulgaris ♧
Pyrus salicifolia 'Pendula' ♧
Robinia pseudoacacia 'Frisia' ♧
Saponaria ocymoides ♧
Sedum spectabile ♧ and cultivars
Spartium junceum ♧
Syringa
Tradescantia
Verbascum

Ornamental herbs

Good-looking culinary plants that are equally at home in the herb garden or the shrub border.
Anethum graveolens
Angelica archangelica
Artemisia abrotanum ♧
Borago officinalis
Calendula officinalis
Chamaemelum nobile 'Flore Pleno'
Foeniculum vulgare 'Purpureum'
Hesperis matronalis var. albiflora
Laurus nobilis ♧

Lavandula angustifolia 'Hidcote' ♧
Melissa officinalis and cultivars
Rosmarinus officinalis
Salvia officinalis
Thymus

Rock-garden plants

Rock gardens and raised beds provide good drainage and make an ideal showcase for small plants and alpines.
Ajuga reptans and cultivars
Anchusa cespitosa
Arenaria balearica
Arenaria montana ♧
Armeria pseudarmeria
Aubrieta
Calluna
Campanula carpatica 'Weisse Clips'
Cassiope 'Edinburgh' ♧
Daboecia cantabrica and cultivars
Daphne cneorum
Dianthus
Erica
Erigeron karvinskianus ♧
Erinus alpinus ♧
Eryngium alpinum ♧
Euphorbia myrsinites ♧
Hebe pinguifolia 'Pagei' ♧
Helianthemum
Juniperus communis 'Compressa' ♧
Lamium maculatum
Linaria alpina
Lithodora diffusa 'Heavenly Blue' ♧
Phlox subulata 'Lilacina'
Saponaria ocymoides ♧
Saxifraga
Sedum spathulifolium 'Cape Blanco' ♧
Sempervivum tectorum ♧
Thymus
Veronica spicata 'Rotfuchs'
Waldsteinia ternata

Fragrant plants

To maximize your enjoyment of the wonderful aromas of scented plants, grow them near the house, or by paths.

Akebia quinata
Asphodeline lutea
Azara microphylla 'Variegata'
Buddleja
Chimonanthus praecox 'Grandiflorus' ♧
Choisya ternata SUNDANCE ♧ ('Lich')
Clematis armandii
Clematis flammula
Clematis rehderiana ♧
Convallaria majalis ♧
Corylopsis glabrescens
Cosmos atrosanguineus
Cytisus battandieri ♧
Daphne
Dianthus
Genista aetnensis ♧
Hamamelis
Iris unguicularis ♧
Laburnum × watereri 'Vossii' ♧
Lavandula
Lonicera fragrantissima
Lunaria rediviva
Mahonia
Malus floribunda ♧
Malus hupehensis ♧
Monarda
Osmanthus × burkwoodii ♧
Phlox paniculata and cultivars
Rosa
Sarcococca
Syringa
Tilia platyphyllos
Wisteria floribunda

Bog-garden plants

All these plants like permanently moist soil. Some will even grow in very shallow water at the edge of a pond.
Alnus incana
Aruncus dioicus ♧
Astilbe
Caltha palustris ♧
Cardamine pratensis 'Flore Pleno'
Cornus alba and cultivars
Darmera peltata ♧
Eupatorium purpureum
Euphorbia palustris ♧

Filipendula rubra 'Venusta' ♧
Gunnera tinctoria
Hemerocallis
Iris ensata ♧
Iris sibirica ♧ and cultivars
Ligularia
Lobelia 'Bees' Flame'
Osmunda regalis ♧
Primula bulleyana ♧
Primula denticulata ♧ and cultivars
Primula florindae ♧
Primula rosea ♧
Rheum palmatum 'Atrosanguineum' ♧
Rodgersia pinnata 'Superba' ♧
Salix alba and cultivars
Trollius × cultorum 'Orange Princess' ♧

Sloping sites

Ground-cover plants are ideal for slopes because they help to bind the soil, preventing erosion.
Ajuga reptans and cultivars
Bergenia
Cistus
Calluna
Clematis tubulosa 'Wyevale' ♧
Cotoneaster horizontalis ♧
Epimedium
Erica carnea and cultivars
Euonymus fortunei 'Emerald 'n' Gold' ♧
Gaultheria
Hedera
Hosta
Hypericum calycinum
Juniperus × pfitzeriana and cultivars
Juniperus squamata 'Blue Star' ♧
Lamium
Lavandula
Lysimachia nummularia
Potentilla
Prunus laurocerasus 'Otto Luyken' ♧
Rosmarinus officinalis and cultivars
Santolina pinnata 'Sulphurea'
Symphytum caucasicum ♧
Tiarella
Thymus

index

acknowledgements

Picture credits

The publisher would like to thank the following for their kind permission to reproduce their photographs; (Abbreviations key; t=top, b=below, r=right, l=left, c=centre, f=far, a=above)

6: Photographer: Steven Wooster; The Stonemarket Patio Garden by Geoffrey Whiten for Chelsea Flower Show 2002 (bl); **8-9**: Photographer: Steven Wooster; "The West Midlands-Shizoka Goodwill" garden for Chelsea Flower Show 2002 (10-11): Roger Smith/DK; **11**: Roger Smith/DK (tr, cra, br, cfra); **14**: Garden Picture Library/Jerry Pavia (bc); **16**: Bob Rundle (bc); **17**: Roger Smith/DK (tl); **18**: Roger Smith/DK (tl, bcl); **19**: Andrew Butler (tr), Roger Smith/DK (bcr, cbr); **20**: Roger Smith/DK (cra); **21**: Andrew Butler (br); **21**: Roger Smith/DK (bl); **23**: Roger Smith/DK (bcr); **24**: Bob Rundle (bc), Dave Watts (bl); **25**: Roger Smith/DK (crb); **26**: Garden Picture Library/Neil Holmes (bl), Roger Smith/DK (bc, bcl); **27**: Andrew Butler (br), Juliette Wade (bc), Roger Smith/DK (tr); **28**: Roger Smith/DK (clb, bc); **29**: C. Andrew Henley (cbr), Roger Smith/DK (bcl); **30**: Roger Smith/DK (bc); **32**: Roger Smith/DK (br); **33**: Roger Smith/DK (cla, crb, br, car, cbl); **35**: Roger Smith/DK (cra, bc); **37**: Roger Smith/DK (crb, bc); **38**: Juliette Wade (br, cra), Roger Smith/DK (tr, cb, bl); **39**: Juliette Wade (cbl), Roger Smith/DK (clb); **40**: Juliette Wade (bl), Andrew Lawson (bcr), Jo Whitworth (br); **41**: Dave Watts (bl), Roger Smith/DK (br); **42**: Andrew Butler (crb), Bob Rundle (car), Roger Smith/DK (cbr); **43**: Andrew Butler (clb, cal), Garden World Images (br), Roger Smith/DK (tcl); **44**: Roger Smith/DK (crb); **45**: Roger Smith/DK (cra, bcr); **47**: Roger Smith/DK (bl); **48**: Juliette Wade (bcr), Roger Smith/DK (bc); **49**: Juliette Wade (tl, bcr); **50**: Andrew Butler (bc), Juliette Wade (br), Sunniva Harte (bl); **51**: Roger Smith/DK (tl); **52**: Garden Picture Library/Neil Holmes (cfl); **53**: Dave Watts (bcl); **54**: Garden Picture Library/Brian Carter (bl), Garden World Images (clb); **55**: Roger Smith/DK (bcl, car); **56**: Jo Whitworth (bc); **57**: Andrew Butler (br, bcr), Roger Smith/DK (bl); **59**: Roger Smith/DK (bc); **60**: Sunniva Harte (tr, cra, bl), Garden World Images (bcr); **61**: Juliette Wade (cra); Sunniva Harte (cla, bcl, cal), Photos Horticultural (crb, cbr), Roger Smith/DK (cbl); **62**: Sunniva Harte (cla, clb, cbr), Garden and Wildlife Matters (car), Roger Smith/DK (cra); **63**: Sunniva Harte (tl, cal, car), Garden Picture Library/Brian Carter (cra), Photos Horticultural (cbr), Roger Smith/DK (cla, clb); **64**: Andrew Lawson (bl), Roger Smith/DK (bl); **65**: Andrew Butler (bl), Roger Smith/DK (br); **66**: Garden World Images (bc), Roger Smith/DK (br); **68**: Roger Smith/DK (bc, br); **69**: Roger Smith/DK (tl); **70**: Roger Smith/DK (tc); **71**: Roger Smith/DK (tc); **74**: Garden World Images (bc), Roger Smith/DK (tc); **75**: Andrew Lawson (br), Roger Smith/DK (tl, tc); **76**: Christine M. Douglas (bcl); **79**: Holt Studios International/Rosemary Mayer (br); **80**: Andrew Butler (tc, tr, bc); **81**: C. Andrew Henley (br), John Fielding (bcr), John Glover (bcl); **82**: Roger Smith/DK (bc); **83**: Andrew Butler (cb); **84**: Roger Smith/DK (bl); **85**: Roger Smith/DK (bl); **86**: Garden Picture Library/Howard Rice (bl), Photos Horticultural (clb); **87**: Andrew Butler (tl), Roger Smith/DK (tr, bl, br, bcl), Jo Whitworth (bc); **88**: Roger Smith/DK (tc, br, bcr); **89**: Roger Smith/DK (bl); **90**: Andrew Butler (br), Roger Smith/DK (bl); **91**: John Fielding (bcl), Roger Smith/DK (crb, bc); **92**: Juliette Wade (tr), Roger Smith/DK (bc, bcr); **93**: Andrew Butler (bcr), Annelise Evans (bl), Roger Smith/DK (cbr); **95**: Roger Smith/DK (cbr); **96**: Roger Smith/DK (bcr, cbl); **97**: Roger Smith/DK (bc); **98**: John Fielding (bcl), Juliette Wade (br), Garden World Images (cbr), Roger Smith/DK (cbl); **99**: Andrew Butler (bl, br, bcr), Hopley's Plants, Much Hadham (tl); **100**: Andrew Butler (cbl), Andrew Lawson/Bosvigo House, Cornwall (cbl), Garden World Images (clb); **101**: Andrew Butler (bl), Andrew Lawson (clb), Photos

Horticultural (bcr); **103**: Andrew Butler (tr, tcr), Roger Smith/DK (bc); **105**: Roger Smith/DK (cra, clb, cal); **106**: Roger Smith/DK (cra); **107**: John Fielding (cbr), Roger Smith/DK (cbl); **108**: Garden World Images (bc), Roger Smith/DK (br); **109**: Roger Smith/DK (cbr); **111**: Roger Smith/DK (bcr); **112**: R.N.R.S. St Albans (br); **113**: C. Andrew Henley (clb); **114**: Garden World Images (bcl), Roger Smith/DK (bc, cbl); **115**: Juliette Wade (tc), Roger Smith/DK (cfr); **116**: Roger Smith/DK (br); **117**: Roger Smith/DK (bl); **118**: Andrew Butler (bcl), Roger Smith/DK (bl, cbl); **119**: Garden World Images (crb, br), Roger Smith/DK (bl); **121**: Garden World Images (bl), Roger Smith/DK (tc, tr); **122**: Juliette Wade (cra), Roger Smith/DK (tr, bc); **123**: Juliette Wade (bcl, bcr); **124**: Andrew Butler (tc); **125**: Juliette Wade (bl), Garden World Images (bc); **126**: Roger Smith/DK (tr, car); **127**: Andrew Butler (bcl), Dave Watts (cbl), Photos Horticultural (bc), Roger Smith/DK (tcl); **128**: Andrew Butler (tc); **129**: Eric Crichton Photos (bc), Cambridge Botanic Gardens (br); **130-131**: Roger Smith/DK; **131**: Bob Rundle (cfra), Roger Smith/DK (cfrb); **134**: Roger Smith/DK (bcl); **136**: Raymond Evison (cbr); **137**: Roger Smith/DK (tl, cra); **138**: Raymond Evison (tr, bl), Roseland House Garden & Nursery, Truro, Cornwall (cla, car), Roger Smith/DK (cbl); **139**: Jill Cowley (car); **140**: Roger Smith/DK (br), Suttons Seeds (bc); **142**: National Trust (r), Roger Smith/DK (br); **143**: Roger Smith/DK (tl, bc); **144**: Mr Fothergill's Seeds (bcl); **145**: Garden World Images (tl, tr, br, bl); **147**: Roger Smith/DK (bc); **148**: Roger Smith/DK (cra, clb, cbl), John Vanderplank/National Collection of Passiflora (bc); **149**: John Vanderplank/National Collection of Passiflora (tl); **151**: Roger Smith/DK (bc); **152**: Garden World Images (bc); **155**: Roger Smith/DK (bl); **157**: Roger Smith/DK (tr, cra, br); **160**: Marianne Majerus/Cherry Tree Lodge Nursery, Lancs.; **162**: GAP Photos/S&O; **164**: GAP Photos/John Glover, Windy Ridge, Yorks; **166**: Photos Horticultural (bl), Roger Smith/DK (br, cbl); **168**: Photos Horticultural (c), Roger Smith/DK (bl, br); **169**: Photos Horticultural (bc), Garden World Images (bl), Roger Smith/DK (tc); **170**: Roger Smith/DK (cb, bl); **171**: Photos Horticultural (tc, bc); **172**: Roger Smith/DK (br); **174**: Garden World Images (bc), Roger Smith/DK (tc, bl); **175**: Roger Smith/DK (tl, br); **177**: Garden World Images (l), Roger Smith/DK (br); **178**: Thompson & Morgan (tr); **179**: Roger Smith/DK (bl, bc), Suttons Seeds (tr); **180**: Roger Smith/DK (bc, br); **182**: Photos Horticultural (bc), Roger Smith/DK (bl, br); **183**: Andrew Lawson (tr); **184**: Roger Smith/DK (bl), Thompson & Morgan (c, br); **185**: Eric Crichton Photos (br); **186**: Roger Smith/DK (bc, cal); **188**: Photos Horticultural (bc), Garden World Images (bl), Roger Smith/DK (clb); **189**: Photos Horticultural (bc), Garden World Images (br), Roger Smith/DK (tc); **190**: Roger Smith/DK (bl, bc, br, bcl); **191**: Roger Smith/DK (bc); **192**: Roger Smith/DK (crb, bcr, cbr); **193**: Beth Chatto (bcr), Roger Smith/DK (tr, crb, bl, cbr); **194**: Juliette Wade (c); **195**: Roger Smith/DK (tc, bc); **197**: Roger Smith/DK (bl, bc); **198**: Roger Smith/DK (bl, br); **199**: John Fielding (br), Roger Smith/DK (bl, bc); **200**: Garden World Images (bc), Roger Smith/DK (bl); **201**: Roger Smith/DK (tc, bl); **202**: C. Andrew Henley (br); **203**: Garden World Images (bl); **204**: Mr Fothergill's Seeds (tc, tc), Garden World Images (br); **205**: Roger Smith/DK (clb, cb, bl); **207**: Bob Rundle (br), Andrew Lawson (tr), Roger Smith/DK (bl); **208**: Roger Smith/DK (bcr); **209**: Garden World Images (bl); **210**: Roger Smith/DK (br), Thompson & Morgan (tr); **211**: Andrew Lawson (bl), Roger Smith/DK (bc); **214**: Marshalls Seeds (bc); **215**: Roger Smith/DK (crb, br, cbr); **216**: Marshalls Seeds (bl), Roger Smith/DK (br, cbl); **217**: Roger Smith/DK (bc); **218**: Roger Smith/DK (clb, cbl); **219**: Roger Smith/DK (tr, bl, bc); **220**: Photos Horticultural (br), Roger Smith/DK (tr, bl); **221**: Roger Smith/DK (bl, bc); **222**: Roger Smith/DK (car); **224**: Garden

World Images (br), Roger Smith/DK (bcl); **225**: Photos Horticultural (br), Garden World Images (c), Roger Smith/DK (bl); **226**: Roger Smith/DK (cra); **227**: Roger Smith/DK (cla, br, tcl); **228**: Roger Smith/DK (bl, bcl, bcl); **230**: Eric Crichton Photos (br), Roger Smith/DK (c); **231**: Eric Crichton Photos (bc), Roger Smith/DK (clb); **232**: Garden World Images (bl), Roger Smith/DK (bc, br); **233**: Roger Smith/DK (tl, tc, tr, cla, bl, br); **234**: Roger Smith/DK (bcr); **236**: Photos Horticultural (bl), Roger Smith/DK (bc); **237**: Roger Smith/DK (tl); **238**: Roger Smith/DK (bc); **239**: Roger Smith/DK (tl, crb, bl, bc, br, bcr); **240**: Roger Smith/DK (br); **241**: Roger Smith/DK (br); **242**: Roger Smith/DK (bl); **243**: Roger Smith/DK (l); **244**: Garden World Images (br); **245**: Garden and Wildlife Matters (bl), Roger Smith/DK (bcl); **246**: Roger Smith/DK (tc, bl); **247**: Roger Smith/DK (bc); **250**: Eric Crichton Photos (clb), Andrew Lawson (bcl), Garden World Images (clb), Roger Smith/DK (tr, cla, bcr); **251**: Hidcote Manor (car), Juliette Wade (cal), Andrew Lawson (crb), Photos Horticultural (tcl), Roger Smith/DK (cra); **252**: John Fielding (bc), Roger Smith/DK (br); **253**: Roger Smith/DK (bl); **254**: Roger Smith/DK (c, bl); **255**: Roger Smith/DK (c, br); **256**: Roger Smith/DK (clb), Thompson & Morgan (bcl); **257**: Roger Smith/DK (cl, bl, br); **258**: Roger Smith/DK (clb, bl, bcl); **259**: Roger Smith/DK (bl); **260**: Andrew Lawson (br); **262**: Roger Smith/DK (bl); **263**: Roger Smith/DK (bc); **264**: Eric Crichton (tr, crb), Garden Picture Library/Howard Rice (bcr), Roger Smith/DK (tcr); **265**: Eric Crichton (bl, br, bcl, car, cbl), Garden and Wildlife Matters (crb), Andrew Lawson (bcr), Roger Smith/DK (tl, tcr, tcr); **266**: Eric Crichton (cal, tcr); RHS Garden Wisley (tcl), Garden Picture Library/Densey Clyne (clb), John Glover (cra), Roger Smith/DK (tl, bcl, cbl, cfr); **267**: Andrew Butler (br), Eric Crichton (bl, cbl), John Fielding (tl), Garden Picture Library/JS Sira (cal), John Glover (tcl), Roger Smith/DK (tr, bcl, cfl); **270**: Roger Smith/DK(tr, bl); **271**: Roger Smith/DK (tc, br); **272**: Roger Smith/DK (bc, br); **273**: Peter Anderson (br); **274**: John Glover (br), Clive Nichols (crb), Roger Smith/DK (tcr); **275**: Garden and Wildlife Matters (cbl), Roger Smith/DK (cra, bcr); **276**: Andrew Lawson (cbr), Garden World Images (br), Roger Smith/DK (cla, bcr); **277**: Andrew Lawson (clb), Photos Horticultural (car), Garden World Images (cra, cbr), Roger Smith/DK (cal); **278**: Roger Smith/DK (bl, br); **279**: Mr Fothergill's Seeds (br); **280**: Roger Smith/DK (tc); **281**: Roger Smith/DK (tr, c, br); **282**: Beth Chatto (br), Roger Smith/DK (c, bl); **283**: Roger Smith/DK (bc); **284**: Roger Smith/DK (br); **285**: Roger Smith/DK (c, bl, bcl, cbl); **286**: Roger Smith/DK (bcl, bcr, cbl); **287**: Mr Fothergill's Seeds (br); **289**: Roger Smith/DK (cl); **290**: Roger Smith/DK (br, bcl, bcr); **291**: Roger Smith/DK (bl); **292**: Merebrook Online (www.pondplants.co.uk)/Roger Kings (crb); **293**: C. Andrew Henley (bcr, cal, tcl), Merebrook Online (www.pondplants.co.uk)/Roger Kings (tl, tr, clb); **294**: C. Andrew Henley (bc), Juliette Wade (br), Roger Smith/DK (tc, bl); **295**: Dave Watts (br); **296**: Andrew Lawson (bcl); **297**: Roger Smith/DK (bc); **298**: Roger Smith/DK (tr, c, bl); **299**: Roger Smith/DK (tc, car); **300**: Roger Smith/DK (bl); **301**: Garden World Images (br), Roger Smith/DK (crb, cal); **302**: Garden and Wildlife Matters (tl), Roger Smith/DK (tr, bcr); **303**: Roger Smith/DK (crb, cal); **304**: Roger Smith/DK (bl); **305**: Garden World Images (tl), Roger Smith/DK (bl, br); **306**: Roger Smith/DK (bl, bcl); **307**: Roger Smith/DK (bl); **309**: C. Andrew Henley (br), Roger Smith/DK (bc); **310**: John Fielding (tr), Roger Smith/DK (bl); **311**: Roger Smith/DK (tr); **312**: Country Park Nurseries, Hornchurch (crb); Eric Crichton (bcr), Juliette Wade (bcr), Roger Smith/DK (tcr); **313**: Barnsley House, Nr Cirencester (clb), Juliette Wade (bcl), Roger Smith/DK (cal, tcr); **314**: Roger Smith/DK (cra, br); **315**: Roger Smith/DK (bc, br); **316**: Roger Smith/DK (bl, br); **317**: Roger Smith/DK (tr, bl, bc, br); **318**: Roger Smith/DK (tr); **319**: Roger Smith/DK (tl, bl); **320**: Roger Smith/DK (tr, br, cbr, tcr); **321**: John Fielding (tcr), Roger Smith/DK (clb, bcr, cbr); **322**: C. Andrew Henley (bl), Garden World Images (br); **323**: Garden World Images (bcr), Roger Smith/DK (bc); **324**: Roger Smith/DK (tr, br); **325**: Roger Smith/DK (bl); **327**: Roger Smith/DK (br, bcl); **328**: Photos Horticultural (br), Roger Smith/DK (tc); **329**: Mr Fothergill's Seeds (bc), Roger Smith/DK (crb, br); **330**: John Fielding (tc), Roger Smith/DK (bc); **331**: Photos Horticultural (bcr), Roger Smith/DK (bl); **332**: Juliette Wade (tc), Roger Smith/DK (tr, bc); **333**: Roger Smith/DK (br, l); **334**: Roger Smith/DK (car, cbr); **335**: Photos Horticultural (car), Roger Smith/DK (tl, tr, cla, cal, tcl); **336**: Roger Smith/DK (br); **337**: Juliette Wade (br), Roger Smith/DK (bcr); **338**: Roger Smith/DK (tr, bc); **339**: Roger Smith/DK (r); **341**: Roger Smith/DK (tr, br); **344**: John Fielding (c), Roger Smith/DK (bl); **345**: Roger Smith/DK (bc); **346**: Roger Smith/DK (tr, bl, bc, br); **347**: Roger Smith/DK (bc); **349**: Roger Smith/DK (c); **350**: Roger Smith/DK (tr, bl, bc, br); **351**: Roger Smith/DK (c); **352**: Roger Smith/DK (bl, bc, bcr, r); **353**: Roger Smith/DK (r); **354**: Roger Smith/DK (bc, br); **356-357**: Roger Smith/DK; **358**: Garden Picture Library/Brigitte Thomas; **360**: Roger Smith/DK (tr); **361**: Peter Anderson (tr); John Fielding (br); **363**: Roger Smith/DK (bl, bc, br); **364**: Christine M. Douglas (r), Roger Smith/DK (c, bl); **365**: Christine M. Douglas (br), Roger Smith/DK (bl); **368**: Steve Wooster (br); **369**: Trish Gant (cl), Roger Smith/DK (bc); **370**: Roger Smith/DK (tc, tr, bl, bc, bc, br, bfr); **376**: Roger Smith/DK (cl); **377**: Gary Ombler (cr);

385: Trish Gant; **398**: Peter Anderson (tc); **400**: Photographer: Steven Wooster; "Flow Glow" garden for Chelsea Flower Show 2002 by Rebecca Phillips, Maria Ornberg and Rebecca Heard.

All other images © Dorling Kindersley.
For further information, see: www.dkimages.com

Author's acknowledgements
Although my name sits on the cover of this book, writing a book is very much a team effort, and I wish to express my heartfelt thanks to all of the people involved. Firstly, I must thank David Lamb, Annelise Evans, Anna Kruger, Lee Griffiths, Alison Donovan, Letitia Luff, Louise Abbott and Pamela Brown. I thank all of them for their professionalism and patience, and for keeping me on the right track.

I also wish to thank the editorial team of Joanna Chisholm, Helen Fewster, Candida Frith-Macdonald, Diana Galligan, Gail Griffiths, Jonathan Hilton, Andrea Loom, Carole McGlynn, Simon Maughan, Christine Morley, Jane Simmonds, Victoria Willan. Also special thanks to the RHS editorial team.

May I also thank the botanists at the RHS Garden, Wisley, for their generous help in providing information on some plants. I am sure they got tired of my incessant phone calls. And my thanks also to all the nurseries which I contacted for information on plants.

Finally, to anyone not mentioned, my apologies and sincere thanks.

Publishers' acknowledgements
Dorling Kindersley would like to thank Susanne Mitchell, Barbara Haynes, and Simon Maughan at the Royal Horticultural Society, Vincent Square for their time and assistance.

Editor for the RHS: Barbara Haynes

Illustrations: Karin Gavin and Gill Tomblin
Editorial assistance: Joanna Chisholm, Helen Fewster, Diana Galligan, Gail Griffiths, Jonathan Hilton, Andrea Loom, Carole McGlynn, Simon Maughan, Christine Morley, Jane Simmonds, Victoria Willan
Additional picture research: Neale Chamberlain, Archie Clapton, Romaine Werblow
Index: Hilary Bird

Second edition
Dorling Kindersley would like to thank Susannah Charlton and Simon Maughan of the Royal Horticultural Society for their help and advice on this revised edition.

Editorial assistance: Caroline Reed, Katie Dock
Design assistance: Elly King, Claire-Marie King, Heather McCarry
DTP assistance: Pete Quinlan